# HOW TO
# BUY
# SOFTWARE

# HOW TO BUY SOFTWARE

## THE MASTER GUIDE TO PICKING THE RIGHT PROGRAM

**Alfred Glossbrenner**

· · · · · · · · · · · · · · · · · · · · · · · · · · · · · · · · · · · · ·
· · · · · · · · · · · · · · · · · · · · · · · · · · · · · · · · · · · · ·
· · · · · · · · · · · · · · · · · · · · · · · · · · · · · · · · · · · · ·
· · · · · · · · · · · · · · · · · · · · · · · · · · · · · · · · · · · · ·

ST. MARTIN'S PRESS · NEW YORK

The author has made every effort to check information such as prices, addresses, telephone numbers and availability of updated products, but cautions the reader that these are subject to change. Readers should verify prices and product descriptions with the manufacturer before ordering.

Library of Congress Cataloging in Publication Data
Glossbrenner, Alfred.
How to buy software.

Includes bibliographical references and index.
1. Computer programs—Purchasing.   I. Title.
QA76.6.G58   1984      001.64'25      83-21175
ISBN 0-312-39551-5 (pbk.)

Copies of this book are available in quantity for promotional or premium use.
Please see page 648 for details.

# Contents

## Part I: Foundation

# Part II: Technique

# INTRODUCTION

So here you are. You've read the cover stories about personal computers in *Time, Newsweek, Forbes, Fortune, Business Week,* and the other major magazines, and you've noticed that these days there's hardly an issue of the *Wall Street Journal* that doesn't carry a personal-computer-related report. You've watched the stories on the evening news, and you've found that Dick Cavett, Bill Cosby, and William Shatner all want you to buy a system. Maybe you've even attended P.T.A. and school board meetings where the issue of acquiring machines for the schools was heatedly discussed.

Your friends have personal computers. Your friends' kids have them. Your competitors have them. Even your fellow managers have their own machines. And now you do too. You may have cleverly buried the cost in your research budget to keep the data processing department from putting the kibosh on your plans. You may have shouted the great American battle cry: "Charge it!" You may even have paid cash. But one way or another you've got yourself a system—or got yourself to the point where you're ready to buy one. Now what?

Well, now the fun *really* begins. If you thought selecting your computer and its peripherals was an experience to try the patience of God Himself—wait. Wait until you try to choose the software you need to transform your machine from a high-tech dust collector into a useful tool capable of saving you time, effort, and money, while expanding your horizons *and* generally making life easier and more rewarding. The best description of the experience can be found in another battle cry of sorts: *Atari!* For thousands of years, the Japanese have been playing a deceptively simple board and pebble game called *go.* In the game, the word *atari* is more or less equivalent to a chess player saying "checkmate" and is uttered in similar situations. Its rough English translation: "You are about to be overwhelmed."

*Catch-22 and Albert Camus*

There may be only a hundred or so computer manufacturers, and far fewer major firms. But there are as many as 40,000 separate software packages, and they're multiplying like coat hangers in a darkened closet. To enter the software marketplace today in search of a program is immediately to be stricken with a case of "overchoice" of almost crippling proportions. But it gets even better—if you like the Theater of the Absurd.

There is plenty of material to help you make up your mind. There are magazine articles, product brochures, direct mail solicitations, and catalogues—lots of catalogues. The software producers have generously supplied huge quantities of ads—both sharpening and broadening the point of an old joke:

> *First Computerist:* Say, did you see that article in *Byte* last month?
> *Second Computerist:* What? You mean *Byte* has *articles*?

Today, any number of magazines could be substituted for *Byte* in this exchange. Yet the quantity of available information and the "information overload" that it induces is not the best part. No, the best part is this:

> All of the literature, ads, and articles—all of the tools you are given to decide whether to spend $700 on this package or $250 on that one—are written in a *foreign language*. (Albert Camus, eat your heart out!)

If there is ever to be a "Catch-*23*," this situation ranks with the American federal tax code as a contender for top honors.

*"A Word from Our Sponsor . . . "*

That's right, friends. Step right up. Open any computer magazine or software catalogue and just look at all you get:

- "FASTER—8088 Code"
- "Works with any computer with an RS-232 I/O port"
- "MS-DOS File Structures . . . 8087 Support"
- BIOS, BDOS, and ROM
- "Specify 8080, Z80, 8086 . . . "

Sound incredible? Not at all. In fact, if you act now, we'll throw in these amazing items as well:

- CP/M-86, "C," UCSD Pascal and the p-System (run time)
- "Written in assembler with compiled BASIC overlays"
- "SS/SD, SS/DD, DS/SD, DS/DD disks (hard- or soft-sectored)"
- "Machine language programs . . . Apple Binary and Text files . . . DIF files too!"
- UNIX, XENIX, Logo, and Turtle Graphics
- "A 480 × 640 bit-mapped display and keyboard-addressable cursor. Full-screen editing. Completely interactive, of course!"

Isn't that amazing? But there's more. If you order today, you'll also get:

- Winchester hard-disk support, RAM drives, and S-100 systems
- Word-wrap, mail merge, VisiCalc templates, X-ON/X-OFF support
- Utilities, DBMS, ISAM file structures, and user-friendly front ends
- Plus . . . the ever-popular "Single and double precision floating point arithmetic!"

Sound hard to believe? Well, maybe. But if we receive your system call before midnight tonight, we'll also give you a People's Pocket Print Spooler, plus a year's supply of object code, absolutely free. Just send your parity checks or money orders to the memory address on your screen, or write to disk station. All major plug-in cards accepted. (Please add 3% for overhead and error handling.)

*They Can't Be Serious!*

You don't have to open a magazine or software catalogue to experience the frustrations of this foreign language. Just open the "documentation"—that densely printed, densely written text masquerading as an instruction manual—for that $300 word processing program you just bought, and see if you can figure out how to type and print a simple letter. Whether reading catalogues, ads, product literature, or instruction manuals, your reaction is likely to be: "They *can't* be serious!"

But they are. And if you're going to play in this game—if you are ever to tap the power and genuine life-improving potential of your computer—you have to be too. It would be one thing if it were a simple matter of holding up your end of the conversation at a cocktail party or a matter of heading off feelings of inadequacy when confronted with the computer-wise teenager (or ten-year-old!) at the computer store. But we're talking serious dollars here. These people want you to give them real money for products that you may only vaguely understand—because they're so poorly explained. Products that may ultimately prove unsuitable to the job you have in mind.

According to *Newsweek*'s market research department, if you're like 83% of all computer buyers, you made at least two or three trips to the dealer before buying a system. And when it came time to lay out the long green, you spent an average of $1,800 if you were buying a computer for home use, $3,750 if you bought it for business purposes. You also spent, according to the market research firm Frost & Sullivan, an average of $608 on software at the time you bought your system. And although you may not know it yet, you will spend statistically an additional $439 for software during the first year that you own your machine.

At least if you spent $1,000 on a motorcycle or a color television you'd have a pretty good idea of what you were getting. You could take the bike out on the road and see what it'll do in the straightaway. You could verify how closely the television manufacturer's definition of "cable-ready" matches your own. But $1,000 worth of computer programming is another story. Like cats, all floppy disks look alike when you're in the dark. And, if you don't know what to look *for*, you could easily end up like the businessman who bought a mailing-list program to do his company's bulk mailings each month—only to find that his expensive, non-returnable piece of software could not sort addresses by ZIP code.

### Tales from the Cryptic

Similar horror stories abound. The *Wall Street Journal*, for example, tells of a 33-year-old electrical engineer and company president who had what seems like a simple problem: He wanted his Apple II Plus to send out itemized bills for his firm. After spending a month trying to learn how to write his own billing program, the man concluded: "As an engineer, it was fascinating, but as a businessman, it was useless."

Over the next three months, the man pored over the magazines, visited computer stores, and sat through many a two-hour demonstration of various billing packages. Finally, he spent $1,000 on software that looked as though it might produce the itemized bills he wanted to send his customers.

Only after he began to use it did he discover that the program provided only *twenty-three characters* for a description of each charge. That's the space occupied by the italicized words in the previous sentence, and it wasn't nearly enough.

The story has a bittersweet ending. After several tries, the man found a programmer who was able to design and write a completely new billing program for $450. But altogether, the engineer/president estimates that for the $15,000 he spent on hardware, software, and labor, he could have hired a bookkeeper and saved himself a lot of aggravation.

Ah, but you're not buying software for business, you say. You just want a word processing program that will let you bat out bread-and-butter thank-you notes and simple letters at home. You feel that if the program has some built-in limitations, they aren't likely to make much difference to you. And that may be. But the price you pay will make a difference. A big difference.

That's something David Gabel, a senior editor at *Personal Computing*, discovered shortly after joining the magazine's staff. Mr. Gabel and a friend went shopping for a word processing package to run on their Apple II computers. "We want a word processing program," they told the computer store salesman. "No, you don't," came the reply. "If you want to do word processing, then you don't want Apples."

Mr. Gabel and friend patiently explained that they already *had* Apples. "Okay," the salesman said, "then you want WordStar."

"Why?"

"Because it's the best."

"Well, *why* is it the best?"

"Er, that is, because everyone says that it's the best."

Mr. Gabel then asked for a demonstration. "Sorry," the salesman said, "I can get it, but I don't have it in stock."

Even if the salesman had had a copy of the program to demonstrate, accepting his everyone-says-it's-the-best response could have had unsatisfactory and expensive consequences. In the first place, WordStar ($375 for the Apple II version) is a powerful word processing program that includes many features an average person may never use. PIE Writer for $150 or any of the newer word processing programs that sell for between $50 and $100 might have filled the bill—and reduced its size—quite nicely.

The salesman also neglected to point out that WordStar is a CP/M-based program and that in order to run it on an Apple II, the user must purchase a Z80 plug-in board like Microsoft's Softcard. That could add $260 or more to the cost of running WordStar on an Apple II. If one were to follow the salesman's recommendation in this instance, the total bill would come to $635 for the Z80 board and WordStar, versus perhaps $150 for a program like PIE Writer, a difference of $485.

If you don't know a Z80 board from a diving board, if you thought CP/M might mean "cost per thousand," if you want to know why everyone's so excited about UNIX, or the *real* reason why the new 16-bit computers are better than the eight-bit machines of the past, you will find the answer in Chapters 1 and 2. Indeed, you'll not only discover *what* these terms mean, you'll learn why they're important to you as a software buyer and where they fit in the overall scheme of things.

## The Lay of the Land

This book is designed to give you everything you need to become a knowledgeable software buyer. We'll show you what to look for, what to avoid, what questions to ask, and how to keep from spending more than you should. We'll help you decide when it's safe to buy at a discount through the mail—and how to get everything that's coming to you if you don't. And we'll show you how to "break" a program, or at least try to, during an in-store demonstration and thus avoid buying something that's likely to give you problems once you get it home. Most important of all, in this book you'll find everything you need to be able to buy software with *confidence*. You'll not only discover what features to look for when shopping for a program, you'll understand *why* they're important and what they can mean to you as a software buyer.

### Part I: Foundation

The first chapter looks at computers on a very mechanistic level. It will show you why an electronic computer is conceptually not all that different from an automatic potato peeler—both are literally *machines* for manipulating things. In one case it's potatoes, in the other it's electricity. You can forget about Boolean algebra, computer programming, and all the other debris that clutters most computer manuals. You don't need to know any of that stuff. Yet that is where most books start. Chapter 1 digs deeper. If you know how software works at the lowest physical level, you'll have a sound understanding of what to look for at the highest or consumer level. All of the layers in between are irrelevant and can safely be left to programmers.

The second chapter builds on the first to explain what may be one of the most mysterious and misunderstood aspects of all computerdom: operating systems. You'll see where the operating system fits in the scheme of things, what it does, and how the same computer can be given a completely different "personality" by loading in a different operating system. You'll also understand what CP/M and MS-DOS are all about and why they are important in your purchase decisions. Chapter 3 looks at BASIC, UCSD Pascal, and other computer languages, again from the standpoint of how they can affect your purchase decision.

The fourth chapter contains explanations of the terms you are most likely to encounter when reading a software ad: what they mean, where they fit, why they're important. The goal here is to put a large chunk of computerdom's "common body of knowledge" into your hands to help you understand the significance of the terms you'll find in many software ads, regardless of the type of program. As an experiment, you might select and read four or five ads. Then read Chapter 4 and see if the same ads make more sense when you look at them again.

If you've ever wondered about "single-sided, double-density, soft-sectored," and other cryptic messages found on floppy disk boxes, you'll find the answer in Chapter 5. We'll also look at hard disk drives or "Winchesters" and electronic RAM-based "disks"—what they are, how they can make your software easier to use, and why it's important to make sure that a program isn't "copy protected" if you want to take advantage of these conveniences.

Chapter 6 will help you decide what to look for when considering operating system software other than what was supplied with your computer. It will also help you understand the UNIX operating system and its relatives and why the computer industry is moving in its direction. Chapter 7 looks at another important software trend: multiple on-screen windows, "multi-tasking," and mice. Using Apple's Lisa, VisiCorp's VisiON, and a program called DesQ from Quarterdeck Office Systems as representative examples, we'll look at the three major approaches the industry is taking and what they can mean to you.

*Part II: Technique*

Part II presents the hands-on, how-to information every computer owner needs to locate, test, and buy software. Chapter 8, for example, will show you how to deal with the deluge of software available for your machine by surveying the field and developing a list of "possibles." It will show you how to locate, obtain, and make the most of those all-important software reviews. Chapter 8 will also explain why most people should buy only four main programs. The chapter concludes by showing you how to use your computer itself to tap the vast software information sources available "online" from CompuServe and The Source, and how to search electronically through a list of over 10,000 personal computer programs and over 15,000 software reviews and articles via a database called The Knowledge Index.

Chapter 9 will show you how to locate knowledgeable dealers and salespeople and how to arrange for a software demonstration. It will give you a step-by-step checklist for evaluating documentation. And it will show you how to put a program through its paces—before you buy. When you have made your choice, Chapter 10 is the place to turn when you're trying to decide whether to buy through the mail or from your local dealer. We'll look at both the risks and the potential savings, and show you what to look for when picking a mail-order house. We'll also look at "teledelivery," and see how software can be sold and delivered over the telephone.

Chapter 11 presents 12 rules for software success that can make your sojourn through the microworld less hazardous and more rewarding. And Chapter 12 will show you how to obtain thousands of CP/M, Apple, Commodore, IBM/PC, Atari, TRS-80, and other programs for FREE! If your computer is equipped for telephone communications, it's a simple matter of dialing the phone, connecting with a computer bulletin board system, and "downloading" the software directly into your machine.

*Part III: Toolchest*

In this section, you'll find chapters on how-to-buy every major type of personal computer software. Each chapter begins by explaining the basic idea of the program, what it does, how it works, and how you might use it in your personal or business life. The chapters explain what features are likely to be most important to you—and *why*—and help you identify the ones that are mere window dressing and not worth paying for. These chapters will also tell you what to watch out for, where the pitfalls are likely to be, and how to avoid unpleasant surprises. Each chapter ends with a Software Buyer's Quick-Reference Checklist to keep you on top of the situation when you're in the store and to help you make sure that you cover all the bases.

You'll learn why it's important to have a "dialing directory" in a communications program; why you might not want to buy certain word processing programs if you plan to write long pieces (some can only handle 15 pages at a time); why it may not be a good idea to buy *any* personal finance program; and how to use a word processing program to issue your checks each month and where to get personalized, continuous-form checks to feed your printer. And, of course, much more.

Whether it's an educational program, an accounting package, a spelling checker, or software for running a professional's office, the chapters and checklists in this section are designed to give you the tools you need to pick the program that's right for you.

*Appendices and the Jargon Interpreter*

In the appendices you'll find information that can help you locate and obtain many of the major software guides, as well as the names and addresses for many helpful magazines and newsletters that often aren't available on the newsstands. There is also a summary of the commercial databases offering online software reviews (what they cost, whom to call, how to get a subscription, etc.).

Finally, Appendix D presents the phone numbers for over 300 computer bulletin board systems throughout the continent. Privately owned and operated, these "BBS's" contain huge collections of free, public domain software, as well as reams of high-quality advice, sources of hardware and software, tips and tricks for using your particular brand of computer, "patches" to "enhance" the software you already own, and much, much more. Compiled by Jim Cambron, editor and publisher of "The On-Line Computer Telephone Directory," the list in Appendix D is one of the most accurate summaries of BBS numbers anywhere.

The Computerese and Jargon Interpreter is designed for quick reference when you are reading a software review, product literature, or an ad. Though not intended to be as comprehensive as a computer dictionary, it includes both terms explained elsewhere in the book and many of the sometimes vital, usually puzzling words that you are likely to encounter when reading about or searching for software.

## How to Use This Book

This book is designed to give you everything you need to know to be a successful software buyer. The "Foundation" section can be read as a unit, though if you are a new computer owner, you should probably read Chapters 1 through 5 and then move on to the "Technique" section and appropriate "Toolchest" chapters. If you are an experienced user, you may find Chapter 1 interesting, but already know enough about standard operating systems and the material covered in Chapters 3 through 5. You might want to start with the secondary OS's and UNIX in Chapter 6 and see if there's a window in your future in Chapter 7. If you're someplace in between, just "plug in" wherever it seems appropriate.

The Software Buyer's Quick Reference Checklists at the end of each "Toolchest" chapter are there for you to use. You may find it most convenient to photocopy them, possibly making one copy for each specific program you are considering, and take them to the computer store with you—or have them beside you as you peruse the latest batch of software reviews and ads.

---

**SoftTip:** Last, but not least, throughout the book you will find numerous boxes like this one. Some of them contain suggestions and ideas or nonvital elaborations on the subject at hand. Many contain the addresses and phone numbers of places and people you may want to contact. And some are addressed to the more knowledgeable software buyer. If you're not a knowledgeable software buyer, you soon will be with the help of this book.

# Part I

# —FOUNDATION—

# ...1...

# Hardware and Software:
## *Everything Your Manuals Never Tell You*

F orget about bits and bytes. Forget about floppy disks, cassette tapes, and "firmware" cartridges. Forget about word processors, VisiCalc and Visi-clone spreadsheets, graphics programs, and games. Software is all of these things—and none of them. To really understand software, you've got to start at the beginning. If you reduce personal computer software to its bare essentials, you'll find that it consists of just one thing: switch settings.

Software *is* switch settings.

This is a simple, easily understood fact. Yet it's something that all too often gets lost in the shuffle as people rush to tell you more than you ever want or need to know about binary arithmetic, Boolean algebra, and programming flow charts. A second fact that's virtually always overlooked is like unto it: A computer, for all of its marvelous capabilities and often uncannily humanlike behavior, is a collection of switches.

It's a vast collection, to be sure. The "64K" of memory you hear spoken of, for example, refers to an area of a computer containing 524,288 individual switches—a formidable number by any standards—but switches, plain old switches, nonetheless. There is thus nothing magical about computers or the programs that control them. What's "magical" is the collective technology and human creativity that have made it possible to construct such extraordinary machines out of such ordinary devices.

*The Missing Concept*

Fortunately, when deciding what software to buy for your personal computer, you don't have to know how its millions of switches are interconnected or exactly how they work. When you want to evaluate a particular software package, you can read the literature supplied by the manufacturer and look at the reviews and ads published in the various computer magazines. You can also ask your computer salesperson to demonstrate the program if it happens to be in stock.

Yet, for millions of people, it's difficult to avoid the feeling that something's missing. There are terms that aren't quite understood, ideas that aren't fully explained, and no one ever tells you *why* things are the way they are. You can be as thorough and methodical as is humanly possible, and still end up with the uneasy feeling that, for all of your work, you're still flying blind when it comes to making your decision.

What's often missing is a basic conceptual understanding of what a computer does on a *physical* level and how software makes it do it. You don't have to know about accumulators and registers, clock signals, and the instruction set of the Z80 microprocessor. *You do not have to know anything about computer programming.* But when deciding which software package is best for you, you do need to know more about a computer than how to slip a disk into a slot and press a key to get the program to load.

To see this more clearly, it might be helpful to compare computers and their software to your stereo and record albums. In fact, it's probably fair to say that you should know as much about the one as you do about the other. You may not be an electronics whiz, but if you stop to think about it, you'll be surprised at how much you really do know about your stereo and how it actually works.

For example, if you pull out your old Led Zeppelin or Moody Blues records and the sound is scratchy, you immediately know what the problem is: The albums have been through too many party weekends and the record grooves are pitted and dirty. If one of your speakers doesn't work, you automatically check to see if one of its wires has come loose. Your equipment and the general concepts behind it are so familiar to you that you don't even have to think about such things.

Would that it were so with a personal computer. If you knew as much about your computer as you do about your stereo, it would not only make selecting software a lot easier, but also your knowledge would probably qualify you for a high-paying job with most computer stores, since even there computer understanding can be a rare commodity. The trouble is that computers represent a foreign body right now to most people. They're distinctly unfamiliar, and they have characteristics that make it difficult to think of them as ordinary machines or appliances.

For all their complexity, though, personal computers can be understood on a level approximately equal to your understanding of your stereo system. You really don't have to know much *more* than that, but you do need a foundation for making informed choices, regardless of the specific type of software you're considering.

*"Machine What?"*

For example, in some ads and reviews you'll see the phrase, "Written in machine language." To which you have every right to respond with a heartfelt, "Huh?" If you ask the salespeople at a computer store what this means, they may be able to tell you that it makes the program run faster. Then again, they may not:

> "Well, what other language *could* it be written in? And *why* does it run faster? And is the speed difference important? And am I going to have to pay extra for this?"

> "I, uh . . . " the salesperson may respond. "That is . . . Look, fella, I'm real busy right now. Do you want the program or not? We take Visa, MasterCard, American Express, and cash. I've got customers waiting."

Clearly it would be helpful to have some idea of *why* any word processing, communications, or other program written in machine language runs faster than one written in, say, BASIC.

---

**SoftTip:** The short answer is that programs written in BASIC and some other languages must go through an elaborate translation process each time they run. What they get translated into is "machine language," the only thing a computer can understand and act upon. And that takes time. Programs that exist in machine language are already "there," and practically no translation is required. Consequently, they run much faster. When fast response is important, as in a word processing or database program, machine language software will usually be much easier to use and perform more effectively than programs written in some other language.

---

For that matter, it would be nice to know why programs written for one brand of computer can or cannot be run on another brand. And what's all this hoopla about CP/M? Why do so-called "integrated" software programs, like those designed to run on Apple's Lisa or in conjunction with something called "VisiOn" on the IBM/XT, often require more RAM ("random access memory") than other programs? And why does a "16-bit" machine permit software that is easier to use and more "user friendly"?

Answering these questions requires the kind of understanding of a computer's physical workings mentioned above. And that's what we'll set about building next. Later we'll use this foundation as a basis for looking at specific types of programs and the actual features and capabilities each type can (or should) offer. Taken together, this general and specific information will give you the tools you need to select, evaluate, and buy software—*with confidence.*

## How Personal Computer Software Really Works

*Here's the Plan*

The information that follows has been selected on the basis of "what you need to know" about the physical workings of a computer to be a smart software buyer. This is the kind of information that computer owners typically acquire in shreds and pieces over a period of years, if they acquire it at all. Indeed, in the past it has been impossible to find all of the key concepts presented and explained in a single place. The following section is designed to remedy that situation.

By pulling together the important information, organizing it, and presenting it as a unified whole, we hope to make it easy to see where everything fits—from a software perspective. We've also made every attempt to avoid burdening you with a lot of unnecessary details. If you're a new computer owner, however, it won't always be apparent just how the following information can help you pick the right word processing, spreadsheet, or other program. Here we must ask you to make a leap of faith.

The problem is similar to trying to learn how to raise a healthy plant without knowing anything about sunlight or water. An explanation of either by itself may not seem to be all that important—until you realize how they can affect your garden. If you stay with the program, we guarantee that you'll emerge at the end of the chapter with an understanding of your computer and your software you may not have thought possible. And who knows? You may even have some fun along the way.

Since it will be helpful to have some mile markers along the way, here's where we're going and what we're going to do:

- First we'll see a computer for what it really is—a machine for manipulating the flow of electricity. And we'll show you how software is really nothing but a collection of instructions concerning how a computer's switches should be set to control that flow.
- Then—using a little Rube Goldberg device we've cooked up— we'll look at the microprocessor chip or "CPU" (central process-

ing unit) at the heart of your computer. Most of the switches here are permanently locked into position. Believe it or not, it is this simple fact that makes software possible. It's also the reason why you can't run an IBM program on a Commodore or an Apple program on a TRS-80.

- Next, we'll enter The Operating Theater of Dr. C. P. Ewe for a somewhat fanciful look at how the programs you buy force the good doctor to do some useful work.
- Then it's on to doorbells and data buses and a brief look at how the CPU stretches forth its hands to beckon your program's switch setting information into its chamber.
- Why does everything about a computer seem to come in multiples of two? The numbers 16, 32, 64, 128, and their relatives are always popping up. We'll find out why.
- Next we'll look at how information and programming is stored in your machine by some cute little switches called "flip-flops," and we'll help you see why static electricity can cause your software to misbehave.
- Finally, we'll look at "memory" in a computer—what it consists of and the crucial role it plays in determining not only the software you can run on your machine, but also how easy that software will be to use.

### Broadway and Baklava

The most important thing to remember when trying to understand how a computer physically works is in the concept of *layers*. It's something you run into again and again. One thing laid on top of another and another and another. A simple BASIC program statement, like $X = A + 1$, may pass through anywhere from 10 to 100 layers before being turned into a much longer collection of *1*'s and *0*'s symbolizing the switch settings that the computer can accept and act upon. And, to use some terms that we will explain later, the ROM (read-only memory) that gives a computer its personality is laid on top of the CPU (central processing unit) that performs the actual computing. The operating system is laid on top of the ROM and the program on top of the operating system.

When you think about it, it is both ironic and fitting that the paradigm of this concept should be the microchip itself. Not only do microchips make a personal computer possible in the first place, the chips themselves are made up of layer upon layer upon layer of interconnected circuitry and microscopic switches. The concept of *layers* is thus at both the physical and figurative heart of all personal computers.

Have you ever had a serving of baklava, the Greek dessert pastry? If you have, then you know that the top crust is made up of hundreds of thin, translucent layers. Taken individually, each layer doesn't amount to much. But when you combine them, piling one on top of another, you have a complete and quite meaningful dessert.

Computers and software are a lot like baklava. Most of us rarely see any but the topmost layer and hardly suspect that so many other layers exist. The majority of books on the subject begin several layers above the bottom and laboriously work their way up through a lot of material that is irrelevant to all but professional programmers. Yet it is the lowest level—those switches—that is crucial to understanding how the machine and the software physically interact. And that's what we're going to dig into now.

We're going to start on Broadway in New York City, with any show in any theater you care to name. In years past, stage lights were controlled from banks of switches on the walls of the wings to the left or right of the stage. But if you look at many theaters today, you're likely to find a small booth at the back of the house with row upon row of switches and other controls. (Increasingly, you're also likely to find a computer, but we'll pass over that for the moment.) During the performance, the booth will be occupied by a technician who follows the script carefully and throws the switches needed to create the desired pattern of light onstage for each scene.

For the sake of simplicity, let's assume that there are 25 shiny toggle switches arranged in a row across the desk of the lectern. Each one controls a particular colored light hung up out of sight above the stage. If it's supposed to be nighttime on stage, only a few will be on. If a daylight pattern is required, only a few will be off. And if a sultry seduction scene is supposed to take place, some will be on and others will be off to create the proper mood.

In every case, if you were to look at the row of switches, the positions of the switches themselves will form a pattern. The question is, How does the person in the booth know which pattern of switch settings to create—which switches to turn on and off—for each scene? An experienced operator would probably have many of the patterns memorized, but someone who is new to the job would have to consult a list:

Act II, Scene III
In M'lady's Chamber (Seduction Scene)


Switch 1–On


Switch 2–On

Switch 3–Off

Switch 4–On

(etc.)

The operator may not realize it, but that list is pure software. The fact that it gets loaded into the person's brain through the eyes and activates the hands is immaterial. The important thing is that the list-software contains the information needed to set the switches in a particular pattern, and that doing so causes a corresponding pattern of light to appear on the stage.

---

**SoftTip:** The world's first personal computer, the Altair 8800, came out in 1975. Or more accurately, the build-it-yourself kit came out at that time. The machine consisted of a rectangular box with some 36 lights and 25 metal toggle switches on its front panel. Users entered programs by flipping the appropriate switches into a particular pattern and then "depositing" the pattern in the machine with another switch. It was very slow going, to say the least, and it called for a lot of switch flipping. In fact, so much switch flipping was required to get the machine to perform even the simplest tasks that some individuals had to wear rubber gloves to keep their fingers from bleeding.

---

There are some things going on here that may seem obvious, but they're worth bringing out because they correspond so closely to the way software and computers interact. First, notice that a single set of equipment—lights, wires, and switches—can be used to produce completely different effects. (Daylight, nighttime, or seduction—word processing, accounts payable, or *Zork—The Underground Empire.*) Second, the various patterns can be duplicated, performance after performance, by following the software guide to switch settings.

Finally, and perhaps most important of all, the switches themselves have no control over how they are set. Their settings are in fact meaningless and random, until they are acted upon by an outside force determined to set them into a desired pattern. This collection of switches is like the keys or valves of a musical instrument, which are completely at the mercy of the musician who plays it. And, for the sake of illustration, we could say that the musician is merely the mechanism for transmitting the musical "switch settings" or notes from a page of sheet music software to the instrument. The only difference is that the result is a pattern of sound instead of a pattern of light.

It is impossible to overemphasize that a computer by itself is an inert machine, dependent on someone or something to set its switches in a particular way to produce a useful pattern. When every book, manual, and authority tells you that "software comes first," you can begin to see why it's advice worth heeding.

### Flow Control

The next step requires a little mind twiddle, similar to the twiddling you do when you look at a simple map and can't immediately tell what part is supposed to be land and what part is ocean. In some cases, you can twiddle your perception back and forth so that the same map appears one way and then the other. The map does not change, but your way of looking at it does.

Do the same thing now with an electric switch. Instead of thinking of it the way you normally do, as a device for turning a light or appliance on or off, think of it as a device for *controlling the flow of electricity.* "I want to send electricity up to that light on the ceiling, and to do so, I throw this switch on the wall. Now I want to stop the flow, so I throw the switch the other way."

From this viewpoint, the fact that the electricity fires up the bulb causing it to give off light is irrelevant, since generating light is not the main goal. All the light bulb does is serve as a signal that the electricity you sent has indeed arrived.

This concept is important because at their most basic level, computers are essentially machines designed to control the flow of electricity. If the electricity ends up at one spot, it may cause a letter to appear on your video screen. If it ends up someplace else, it may cause the same letter to be printed on your printer. The switches in the computer are what control where the electricity ends up.

### Of Mazes and Garden Hoses

For the moment, let's put electricity aside and substitute something we can see, like water. And let's forget about microscopic circuits and semiconductors and substitute something we can touch and feel, like wood. Specifically, a wooden typesetter's box of the kind Ben Franklin might have used.

If you've ever seen one of these boxes, you know they contain little compartments designed to hold lead type. There's a compartment for capital *E*'s, and one for lower-case *e*'s, and so on throughout the alphabet. All in all, a lot of compartments. Now let's dump the type out (this *is* the computer age!) and prop the box up so that we can look at it as rows and columns of compartments.

And let's make a few alterations. We'll bore large holes across the top and label them *1* through . . . let's say *26*. (See Figure 1.1.) Then we'll do the same at the bottom, but label them *A* through *Z*. Finally, we'll leave the frame (the top, bottom, and sides of the box) as it is, but we'll cut the connections between each horizontal and vertical crosspiece and drive a nail through their centers so that they pivot freely. As a result, the tops, bottoms, and sides of each little compartment within the frame of the box can be pivoted to an opened or closed position.

## ——— Figure 1.1. Typesetter's Box "Computer" ———

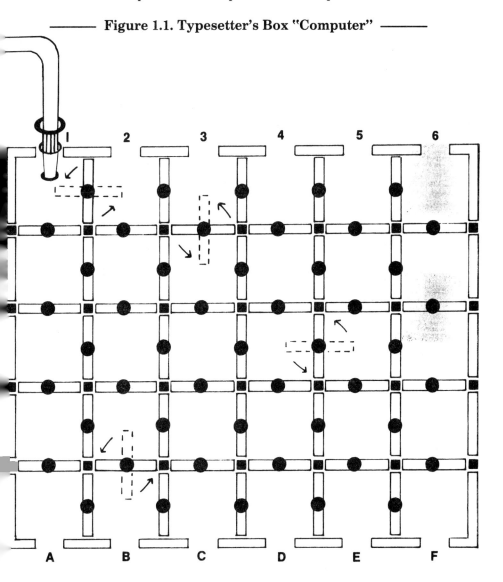

These pivoting pieces of wood are our switches, and we'll assume that we've driven the nails in hard enough so that the wooden pieces will stay in whatever position we set them. All that remains is to haul out the garden hose and set the switches.

But how should the switches be set? The answer depends on what you want to accomplish. If you want to plug in the hose so that water enters this "maze" through the top hole labelled *1* on the far left and exits through the bottom hole labelled *Z* on the far right, it's a simple matter of opening and closing the appropriate switches to guide the water's flow.

What's more, there are any number of switch settings that will produce the same results. You could arrange things so that the water flowed in a more or less diagonal line, from *1* downward to *Z* like this:

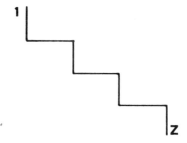

Or, if you were an inefficient programmer, you could send it all the way to the right, then all the way to the left, and repeat this pattern so that the result was a zig-zagging stream leading to *Z* like this:

You could even set things up so that the water you pump in at *1* or *5* or any other location exits the box at *both Z* and the hole labelled *M*.

This gives you tremendous flexibility. You can use the same modified typesetter's box to produce a whole range of *A* to *Z* results from a whole range of *1* to *26* inputs. All you have to do is set the switches in the pattern that will control the water's flow in the desired way. Here again, as with the lighting control panel in the theater, *the list of how each switch should be set to produce a particular result is "software."* And again, it is this versatility that allows you to play a game one moment and calculate your taxes the next—though many authorities would concede that there's not much difference between the two activities.

*Two Types of Software*

The system we have just described can be compared to the internal circuitry of a computer, as you may have suspected. When you load in a program, you are setting the switches up in a pattern such that a particular input will produce a particular output. Once a program has been loaded, hitting a key on your keyboard is like turning on the hose. It causes electric current to flow through the switch pattern so that it ends up producing a letter on your video screen or printer, or generating some other output.

That is something we take for granted. But it's important to realize that there's no reason why hitting the *A* key, for example, should always produce an *A* on the screen. With a different pattern of internal switch settings, it could easily be made to produce a *Z* or a smiling "happy face" graphics character or anything else.

Everything depends on the switch patterns, and software is what creates these patterns inside a machine. The software, or programming, which a computer uses can be of two types. It can be loaded in by the user or it can be a permanent part of the machine. When it is permanent, the switch settings are said to be "hard-wired," and for this reason, software of this type is called "firmware."

The best example of firmware is your collection of video game cartridges. Each time you plug a cartridge into your Atari, Coleco, or Intellivision console and turn on the power, you are pumping current through firmware to produce a particular result on your TV screen. Each cartridge contains a different hard-wired switch pattern that determines where the electricity goes and what it does once it gets there.

Computers use both firmware and the regular software that you load in from a floppy disk or cassette tape. They thus have two types of "typesetter's boxes" at their disposal. In one type, the wooden switches are movable and can be set by you or your program. In the other type, the switches are glued in place to form a permanent hard-wired pattern.

*Glue and the CPU*

*Permanent* switch settings are a vital part of your machine's most vital component: the central processing unit or CPU. The CPU *is* the computer. It is a tiny chip of silicon measuring no more than a quarter of an inch on a side, and everything—absolutely everything—in a computer revolves around it. The CPU is the only thing in the whole box that does any "computing." It is the only unit that actually changes or processes information by adding, subtracting, or comparing it to some other piece of information. Virtually everything else—all the other layers of switches and circuitry—is designed either to store the information that the CPU needs, transport it to and from the CPU, or respond in some way to the CPU's output.

A real CPU is divided into a number of sections. Some of its 20,000 or so switches are changeable and some are hard-wired. Most of the hard-wired ones exist in the CPU's "control" section, and using the model of our typesetter's box, that's the section we want to look at now.

We've seen how water that is pumped in at any top location or "port" from *1* to *26* can be guided and directed so that it flows out of any bottom location from *A* to *Z*. Now let's hard-wire the box by gluing the switches into a pattern so that whenever water is pumped into port *1* it *always* exits through port *Z*. We could hard-wire a second or third box into different patterns to produce different results. But suppose we're really clever and are able to combine the various patterns into a single box. Perhaps we set up an "in at *18*, out at port *K*" path in addition to our *1*-to-*Z* pattern. And maybe we add some other paths as well.

Next, let's twiddle with our way of looking at this hard-wired unit for a moment. Let's suppose that whenever water flows out of *Z* it causes a bell to ring. And every time water flows out of location *K*, it causes a whistle to blow. Suppose that instead of focusing on the flow of the water itself, we thought in terms of the bell and whistle. How would you "tell" the unit to ring the bell? How would you "tell" the unit to blow the whistle?

The answer, of course, is that you would pour water into port *1* if you wanted to hear the bell and into port *18* if you wanted to hear the whistle. By doing either of these things, you would be telling the unit to execute a particular preprogrammed, hard-wired *instruction*. We can say, then, that our bell-and-whistle unit contains two instructions in its "instruction set."

Obviously, a unit that contains instructions for ringing a bell and blowing a whistle is more desirable than one that can only ring a bell. But it's not going to be as desirable or as powerful as a unit with *four* instructions that permit it to ring a bell, blow a whistle, hit the cymbals, and bang a drum.

In the world of microprocessor CPUs, the number and nature of the instructions each contains is one of the primary things that distinguishes one microprocessor chip from another. CPUs typically have an ensemble of from 40 to 200 instructions hard-wired into them. Usually the more instructions a chip can execute, the more powerful it will be.

> **SoftTip:** The number of instructions a chip can have is related to the number of "bits" it can handle at one time, something we'll soon get into. For now, it's enough to know that each instruction must have a name, and the number of possible names is limited by the number of bits the CPU is designed to handle. Most 8-bit CPUs can handle up to 64 different instructions, while 16-bit CPUs typically handle 100 or more.

Instructions are what the CPU uses to actually perform its work. They are the pure "machine language" we keep hearing about, and they are very, very elementary. They are also very specific, both in what they tell the CPU to do and in terms of the particular CPU itself. For example, chip-making companies give their products different model numbers to distinguish one from another. Thus there is the 8088 from Intel, the Zilog Z80, the 6502 from MOS Technology, the 68000 from Motorola, and so forth. Each of these CPU chips has its *own* unique instruction set.

Now, let's combine several thoughts. First, all software programs must ultimately be translated into machine language, the only thing that a microprocessor can accept. The words in the machine language every program ends up as consist of individual CPU instructions. *But every CPU has a different vocabulary.* Each CPU's instruction set is unique. Consequently, a software program cannot include anything that will be translated into a machine language word or an instruction that is not in the CPU's instruction set vocabulary.

To put it another way: *Software must be written to be used by a* **particular** *CPU.* That's not to say that a program can't be converted to run on a different CPU. But you can never take a program written for the 6502 chip in an Apple II and run it without alteration on a TRS-80 Model III, a machine built around the Z80A, a faster working version of the Z80.

> **SoftTip:** Because it makes sound business sense to do so, chip companies frequently take pains to make sure that, in addition to new instructions, their new chips also contain most or all of the

*SoftTip continued*

same instructions found in previous models. This means that software written for the Motorola 6800 chip can easily be adapted to run in its replacement, the Motorola 6809. The same thing is true for the Texas Instruments 9900 chip and the newer 9940. The older software may not be able to take advantage of the new chip's new features, but it will usually run.

This is called "upward compatibility," and older software that will run on a new, more powerful chip is said to be upwardly compatible with the chip. Microchips with the same or compatible instruction sets are often considered to be part of the same chip "family."

## The Operating Theater of Dr. Ewe

One way to gain a better appreciation of a CPU's instruction set and how a programmer uses it to create the software you use is to visualize a surgeon's operating theater. Our lone programmer is sitting in the first row of the balcony looking down into the operating room itself. He's dressed in faded jeans, Nike running shoes, and a tee shirt, and right now he's stroking his beard as he contemplates the operating room's sole occupant: Dr. C. P. Ewe.

The good doctor is known as the "Lone Ranger of the O.R." because he operates completely by himself. He may issue orders to have things brought in and taken out, but only Dr. Ewe touches and uses the gleaming scalpels, forceps, and other instruments in his instruction-set tray. The doctor has another unusual characteristic as well: He likes to operate on two patients at the same time. Indeed, it's been whispered along the hospital corridors and in the staff lounge that something strange seems to take place in Dr. Ewe's O.R. Inevitably, two patients go in. But only one ever comes out. And that one often doesn't look much like either of the two who disappeared behind the O.R.'s swinging metal doors.

There's another thing as well. In addition to being something of an egoist, Dr. Ewe is not very bright. Not only could he not walk and chew gum at the same time, he couldn't even get a stick of gum out of its wrapper unless someone gave him step-by-step instructions.

As it happens, step-by-step instructions are our programmer's stock in trade. Looking at him now, we see that he's scribbling on a piece of paper. He tears the sheet off his tablet, folds it into a paper airplane, and sends it sailing down to Dr. Ewe. The doctor walks over and picks it up. He looks at it and sees that it says, "Go get the first patient."

The doctor knocks on the operating room door and beckons for the nurse to wheel in the patient called Data One. The nurse complies, and the doctor stops. Meanwhile the programmer has been scribbling madly.

The next paper airplane sails down, and the doctor goes over to pick it up. It reads, "Wheel Data One over to location seven against the wall." The doctor complies and stops.

Next instruction: "Go get the second patient." The routine is repeated, as a similar series of paper airplanes results in the patient called Data Two being wheeled over to location eight.

Yet another airplane zooms down: "Pick up the scalpel." And another: "Make an incision in . . . " And . . . we can safely leave the rest to the imagination.

Though Dr. C. P. Ewe doesn't seem to mind, this is clearly a tiresome process for the programmer. But the next time the identical operation must be performed, things will be easier. If he's smart, the programmer will have put a number on each paper airplane. When the current operation is over, he can retrieve the planes he's launched and use them in the same sequence again.

*Correspondence*

Like the good doctor, CPUs operate alone. And they typically operate on two pieces of data at a time. That is, they add one piece of data to another, or subtract it, or compare it to a second piece of data and take a particular action based on the results of that comparison. Each has a finite number of instructions to work with, and each must be told step-by-step what to do to accomplish a given task.

Fortunately for the programmer, it is rarely necessary to write out each instruction individually in the machine language the CPU needs. There are many types of translation programs that enable someone to write $X = A + B$ without having to write: "Go get A." "Move A to location seven." "Go get B." "Move B to location eight," etc.

*Pause and Regroup: The Story So Far*

You may not know as much about a computer as about your stereo yet, but you already know quite a bit. For example:

1. Computers are machines designed to manipulate the flow of electricity.

2. Software is the collection of switch settings that determines where that electricity will go.

3. There are two types of software switch settings: hard-wired and what, for now, we'll call "flexible."

We haven't looked at the flexible type, the type that responds when you load in a program. But we know that the hard-wired settings are 100% predictable. A given input will always produce the same output, something that's particularly valuable in the computer's CPU.

4. Indeed, when hard-wired switch settings are grouped together in a CPU, they form that unit's instruction set—the basic tools the CPU uses to perform its operations.

5. We've also learned that all software programs must ultimately be translated into one or more of these instructions before the CPU can act. Usually it's more—a *lot* more—since the CPU must be told what to do every step of the way.

Since the instructions are different for every CPU, a program must be written for the particular CPU on which it is to run.

6. Typically, the CPU operates on two "things" or pieces of data at a time by adding, subtracting, or comparing them to each other.

7. Remembering the Operating Theater of Dr. Ewe, we've also seen that the CPU accepts *two* kinds of input. It accepts and acts upon instructions from the programmer. And it accepts and operates on data that are wheeled in from another location.

Computers can be viewed as "the CPU and everything else." All the various components, all the floppy and hard disk drives, all the banks of memory chips, the keyboard, the video screen, the printer—everything is designed for one purpose: to bring instructions or data *into* the CPU and to transport the results *out*, displaying them in a human-readable form.

The CPU is a little quarter-inch chip of sand sitting at the heart of and connected to a massive collection of hardware. It occupies barely a tenth of the square-legged, black-backed "caterpillar" that surrounds it and plugs into the computer's circuit board. A butterfly could carry it away. Yet it can control the machinery to move mountains—if it is programmed correctly.

*The Next Step*

These ideas lead naturally to a number of important questions, namely:

• How does the computer move data and instructions in and out of the CPU?

- Where does this information come from?
- What does it consist of?
- How is it stored?
- How—in general—does the CPU operate on it?
- And how does everything work together when you load in a program?

To look at the answers to these questions, we have to leave the land of flowing water and enter the realm of flowing electrons. We can start with a common doorbell of the sort you may have made or studied in a junior-high science class. What makes a doorbell ring when someone comes to call? Electric power suddenly flowing through the doorbell "system," of course.

The whole thing's based on someone's discovery that if you wrapped wire around a shaft of iron you could turn the iron into a magnet by feeding electricity through the wire. Better yet, you could turn the magnetism on or off at will by turning the power on or off. (See Figure 1.2.) That's exactly what happens with a doorbell. The clapper is attached to a spring, so it's normally held away from the iron core. But when power is fed through the system, the sudden magnetism of the iron core pulls the clapper toward the bell.

### ———— Figure 1.2. A Simple Relay Switch ————

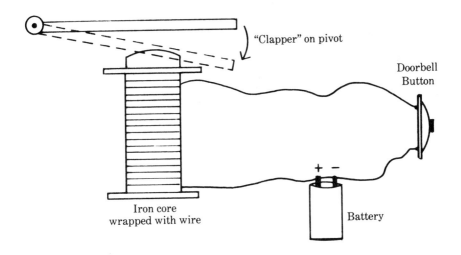

"Clapper" on pivot

Doorbell
Button

+ –

Iron core
wrapped with wire

Battery

As it happens, a doorbell is wired up so that the motion of the clapper breaks the circuit leading to the magnet, turning it into ordinary iron again. The clapper's spring snaps it back into its normal position, causing it to complete the circuit again and again be attracted to the now magnetized iron. It's a classic approach/avoidance complex on the clapper's part, but that's not important here. What is important is the fact that the clapper is pulled toward the electromagnet.

In quasi-technical terms, the electromagnet and the circuit in the doorbell are known as a "relay." But the central thing to remember is that—because of the electromagnet—someone standing at your front door can press a button and cause the clapper to move. That's the essence of a relay: It enables you to throw a switch in one location and cause something to *move* at some other location.

---

**SoftTip:** The world's first large-scale automatic digital computer, the Mark I, was built in 1939 by IBM and Howard Aiken at a small college in Cambridge, Massachusetts. The machine could execute only five to ten instructions per second, and it made a tremendous racket. But it was an important first step because it established the fundamentals of digital computing. Its primary component: relay switches.

---

Now suppose you replaced the bell with a piece of wire connected to a second circuit. And suppose you stuck the other wire for that circuit on the clapper. Then when you pressed the doorbell button, the clapper would move, the two wires would touch, and the second circuit would be complete. It would be as if by pressing the doorbell button you had caused the clapper to throw a switch.

Notice that two separate circuits are involved here: the doorbell button circuit and the clapper or "target" circuit. The first circuit controls the second through the action of the electromagnet. But because the clapper never touches the iron core—it merely moves toward it—there is no electric connection between the two circuits. This is a great arrangement because it lets you use a low-powered battery-driven doorbell-type relay to control the flow of much more powerful current through the second circuit. Since there's no contact between the two circuits, you never have to worry about the powerful current burning up the battery.

All of this sounds terribly industrial, and it is. Many machines, including most of the telephone switching equipment still in use today, operate with mechanical relays of this sort. A complete discussion is beyond the scope of this chapter, but you should know that the idea of using a small amount of electric current in one circuit to control the flow of current through a second, independent circuit is the bedrock upon which vacuum tubes, transistors, and microchips are based. The physics are different, but the idea is the same.

There's no better example of this than the technique the CPU uses to bring information into itself from some remote location and to send it back out again. A typical microprocessor CPU will have at least three lines connecting it to the rest of the machine. There's a control line, a line for data, and a line for memory addresses. The lines actually consist of many individual wires or printed circuit paths. They're known as the "control bus," the "data bus," and the "address bus."

When the CPU wants a piece of information needed to execute one of its instructions, it locates the correct memory address, sends a control signal to that specific location in the computer's storage area, and says, "Come to Papa." Sending the control signal is like pushing the doorbell button. It causes a second circuit to close, permitting electricity to flow from the selected storage location into the CPU. Typically, that second circuit is the data bus. The doorbell-like control relay is called a "gate." In describing this process, computerists say that "information is gated onto the data bus."

When the CPU has finished operating on the information, it will send the results out the same way, possibly to a different location. Just about every kind of input and output by the CPU is handled in a similar way. When the CPU needs a programming instruction, like "Load internal register A," it will find where that instruction has been placed in the machine's memory by your software and gate it onto the bus. When it needs data, like today's date or the Social Security number of an employee, it will do exactly the same thing.

---

**SoftTip:** One might ask how instructions get into the CPU if there are only two buses, one for addresses and one for data. The answer is that the data bus works in both directions and is used to carry both instructions and data. To a microprocessor, instructions and data look the same. Both are composed of combinations of the same two electric signals. What distinguishes them is their "memory location." When a program starts up, it "tells" the CPU where in the computer's memory its instructions begin and end. So the CPU knows that if it gets signals from one of those locations, the signals are to be interpreted as instructions, even though they are brought in on the same wires used to transport data.

Now that we have a general idea of how information is moved in and out of the CPU, we want to take a closer look at what that information consists of and how it is stored in the system. To do that, we'll look at how computer information is represented electrically.

### No Computation without Representation!

In the Sham Shui Po district of Hong Kong, there's an open-air market on Apliu Street filled with exactly the kind of exotic sights and smells you'd expect in the Orient. Fresh fruit and strange vegetables with even stranger names fill the stalls. Sacks of rice, cellophane noodles, headless chickens strung up by their feet, and live snakes and frogs ready for the wok are available wherever you look. Everywhere there's the hustle and bustle of Hong Kong and the fried-oil aroma of Chinese cooking.

If you were to take a stroll down Apliu Street on a hot summer's day, though, you'd be in for something of a surprise. Because sandwiched in between the vegetable vendors and butcher shops you'd find stalls selling personal computers and electronic components: mounds of chips, jelly-bean-like piles of color-coded transistors, stacks of disk drives, power units, circuit boards, video displays, anything you want—including complete computers that look and behave like Apples or some other brand, but aren't.

If you were to watch while someone inquired about one of these counterfeit machines, the chances are that you'd see a young man doing the selling. But when negotiations progressed to the final deal stage, you might see the salesman's father, or grandfather, or uncle suddenly appear. And after some more haggling, when it came time to total a bill, you might be surprised to find the older man ignoring the illicit electronic splendor surrounding him in favor of his trusted abacus.

As his fingers fly over the beads, the irony of the situation might strike you: Here's a guy using what is probably mankind's earliest computing tool to calculate the price on one of the very latest. Beads on a bamboo shaft, for heaven's sake!

The abacus is important because it is primarily a device for representing numbers (or "data," or "information"). It is not a computer. All of the computing or CPU functions are done in your head. But since it's constructed out of beads on a shaft, it makes it easy to represent numbers by moving the beads from one location to another. There is no in-between point for an abacus bead. If it's in one position, it is not counted. When it's in another, it is. Thus, to add three to a number represented on the abacus, you move three beads to their counting position. To subtract three, you move three beads to their noncounting position.

*The "Tagged" Current Connection*

For our purposes, the key thing about the abacus is this: Each bead has two and only two possible positions or "states," and this fact makes it possible to represent numbers by setting up a particular pattern of beads and to manipulate numbers by changing the positions of the beads.

So far, we have talked a lot about moving electricity around within a computer. But we haven't looked at *why* anyone would want to do that. The reason is that electricity can be "tagged" so that you can tell one flow from another. And, while it is technically possible to use many different "varieties" of electricity, the electricity used by a computer—like abacus beads—comes in just two types.

This fact makes it possible to *symbolize* numbers. And once you've got a number symbolized, you can add, subtract, multiply, divide, or compare it to another number by manipulating those symbols.

*Ampersands and Asterisks*

How is it possible to represent all numbers with just two symbols? It's done by using a different set of assumptions about what the symbols and their locations in the expression you write mean. The symbols themselves don't matter. You could use ampersands (&) and asterisks (*), or *A*'s and *B*'s, or any other characters that suit your fancy. What's important is, How many symbols do you have to work with and what do their positions mean?

Thus the number one-hundred-and-one could be written *101*. And it would be meaningful as long as the person looking at it was aware that there were eight other symbols (*2* through *9*) that *could* have been used. The person must also be aware that the digit to the far right symbolizes a certain number of ones, the next digit symbolizes a certain number of tens, and the next one after that symbolizes a certain number of hundreds.

Someone else looking at that same expression *(101)* with a *different* set of assumptions—assumptions based on the "binary number" symbolizing system, for example—would interpret it much differently. To keep things interesting, binary numbers are usually read from right to left, like Chinese. So that would be the person's first assumption. In addition, if the person assumed that the symbol *1* and the symbol *0* were the only possibilities and that the digit to the far right represented ones, that the next one represented twos, and the next represented fours, he would say that *101* symbolizes the number five, not one-hundred-and-one. To him, the expression *101* would mean "a single one, no twos, and a single four, added together makes five." Notice, however, that under this system, *three* characters are required to symbolize what we normally symbolize with a single character *5*.

This "binary" or "base-two" system was invented by Gottfried Wilhelm von Leibnitz (1646–1716), a fellow who caused a lot of controversy by (some would say) beating Sir Isaac Newton to the discovery of calculus. All you really have to know about the binary system can be summarized by the following points:

- Given the right assumptions, it is possible to represent *any* number with just two symbols, and once you've got the numbers symbolized you can add, subtract, multiply, divide, and compare them.
- Using only two symbols, however, means that you're going to have to write *more* characters to symbolize the same number than someone using ten symbols (*0* through *9*) would have to write.
- And if someone for some reason says, "Sorry, you can only use *eight* characters," that puts a limit on the largest number you can symbolize at any one time. In the system we normally use, a row of eight nines would represent ninety-nine million, nine hundred and ninety-nine thousand, etc.

In the binary system, a row of eight "one" symbols would translate as two hundred and fifty-six.

### *"64 . . . 128 . . . 256 . . . Hike!"*

Computers, of course, use the binary system to symbolize and manipulate numbers. (This is not because it is the only system available to them. Some computers have been built to use five or ten symbols, each represented by a differently "tagged" electric current.) The reason is that of all the available systems, the binary system is the least complicated. After all, you can't represent all numbers using just one symbol. Two is the absolute minimum.

The fact that computers use the binary system explains many things, like why you keep bumping into numbers like 64, 128, and 256 when you read about them. All of these frequently encountered numbers are multiples of 2. Or more accurately "powers" of 2.

The fact that the binary system requires so many characters to represent most numbers is also one of the main reasons why the original electronic digital computers were so huge. To represent the number 256 in the binary system, you need *eight* switches. Multiply that by the number of numbers a computer needs to do its work, and you can easily end up requiring tens of thousands of switches for the simplest tasks. To accomplish anything really worthwhile, *hundreds* of thousands of switches are needed.

As we said at the beginning of the chapter, *64K* of computer memory actually consists of 524,288 switches. And by personal computer standards, *64K* is often the minimum requirement for performing useful work.

---

**SoftTip:** You don't have to know anything about binary arithmetic and the rules a computer uses when manipulating the *1*'s and *0*'s of binary numbers. However, if you are interested in this kind of thing, you'll find an explanation of all the pertinent facts in:

> *An Introduction to Microcomputers:*
> *Volume 0—The Beginner's Book*
> by Adam Osborne and David Bunnell
> OSBORNE/McGraw-Hill    $12.50

Adam Osborne, of course, is the man who introduced the first transportable computer. David Bunnell was instrumental in founding both *PC Magazine* and *PC World*. They know what they're talking about. (Be sure to get volume "zero." Volume 1 is considerably more advanced.)

---

*"Tagging" Electric Current*

In a computer, the *binary digits* or "bits" used to symbolize numbers consist of two voltage levels of electricity. A computer does its work by shuttling these two types of current around between switches that are *sensitive to voltage levels*. When one of these switches "receives" one voltage level, it reacts one way. When it "receives" another it reacts another way.

Frequently, you will see the two types of current a computer uses represented as electric circuits that can be either "on" or "off." Usually there will be a drawing of a light bulb included in the diagram to illustrate the point. This approach often proves confusing. If you get rid of the light bulb and lead the wires into the CPU instead, it's not too difficult to see how turning a switch "on" would send current into the CPU. But what happens when the switch is "off"? There's no current flowing, so how does anything get pumped into the CPU? How do you send an "off" signal?

What the books don't tell you is that it is not the electricity that is being turned on and off. What's actually happening is that the voltage level is being changed. Voltage is one of a seemingly unending stream of terms used to talk about electricity. But, for our purposes, we can think of it as the amount of "push" that forces electrons through a wire. When a bit of information is "gated onto the data bus" using a separate control switch as described earlier, a circuit is connected to a line leading into the CPU. If that circuit generates one voltage level, it means one thing to the CPU. If it generates another level, it means something else.

The key to the whole operation is the switches inside the CPU and elsewhere that are designed to be "voltage sensitive." These switches could be designed to respond to a positive voltage of 5 and a negative voltage of 10, or any other pairing of two different levels. As with the binary system itself, as long as there are two different "things" to symbolize a number, the things themselves don't matter.

Although voltage levels of +5 and −5 volts have been frequently used in the past, most modern personal computers use the levels of +5 volts and 0 volts to "tag" the electric current they shuttle around when doing their work. And, because of this, and because of the voltage-sensitive switches they use, the absence of voltage on a line (0 volts) is just as important as the presence of voltage (+5 volts).

Unless you hope to find work as a circuit designer, however, there is no reason why you can't think of a computer as using two different kinds of current, and switches that respond one way to one kind and another way to the other kind. Thus, if you've got three circuits lined up and three separate lines coming out of them, you can easily symbolize the number five in the binary system. As you will recall, the symbol *101* is used to represent a five in binary. If we decide that the symbol *1* will correspond to a high level of voltage and the symbol *0* will correspond to a low level of voltage, we can set the three switches to generate that pattern.

---

**SoftTip:** This gets technical, but if you want more information on the electric aspects of computers, the key word to look for is *TTL*. That stands for "transistor-transistor logic," and refers to standard electronic component (microchips) input/output signal levels. It specifies, for example, that an output signal must be between 2.4 and 5 volts and contain at least 400 microamps when representing a certain state. When representing the other state, the signal voltage must be between 0 and 0.4 volts and be capable of sinking 16 milliamps of current. Other specifications apply for input signals.

Assume for the moment that the 5-volt signal is a *1* and the 0-volt signal is a *0*. Under the TTL standard, when the CPU outputs a *1* it sends out or "sources" current to a memory cell or other device. But when it outputs a *0* it absorbs or "sinks" current. In this case, power is flowing from the memory cell into the CPU— even though the CPU is "outputting" a *0*. The reason this works is that the switches in the memory cell respond one way to the sinking of current flowing *from* them toward the CPU and another way when the current is flowing *toward* them from the CPU.

You can thus think of the CPU as generating either a strong wind or a strong vacuum. As long as the memory cell switch is free to "move," an electric wind will push it into one position, while an electric vacuum will pull it into its other position.

It is worth pointing out that there is absolutely no reason why ones and zeroes have to be used in the binary system. In fact, since we are all conditioned to think of the symbol *1* as something that comes before *2*, it's often difficult to make the mental transition to thinking of *1* and *0* as meaning something entirely different in the binary system. Using high and low voltage levels as our guide, we could symbolize the number five (binary *101*) like this: HLH (high, low, high). In that case, HLH + HLH would equal HLHL, or ten. (Reading *right to left:* No ones, a single two, no fours, and a single eight—added together makes ten.)

Unfortunately, the mathematicians got hold of this before the liberal arts majors, and as a consequence we're stuck with *1*'s and *0*'s, confusing as they may be. On the other hand, the math people *did* invent the thing, so they clearly have certain proprietary rights. Fortunately, they're the only ones who have to use the *1*'s . . . and *0*'s.

*Flip-Flops*

The name sounds like a pair of Japanese beach sandals, but the switches that a computer uses to represent and store binary digits really *are* called "flip-flops." (They're also called "bi-stable devices," a more accurate but considerably less colorful term.)

The essence of a flip-flop switch is this: It has *two* stable states so when you punch it one way, it stays punched until you hit it again to set it the other way. In the days of vacuum tube computers, each flip-flop consisted of two tubes wired together in a special way. One tube was used to represent a *1*, or high voltage state, and the other, a *0*, or low voltage state. Both had access to a single output line, but only one of them could be connected to it at a time.

If there was a *0* on the output line of a flip-flop and the computer wanted to use the switch to store a binary *1*, then it would send a signal to the unit. Because of the way the circuit was wired, that signal would cause the *0* tube to be cut off and the *1* tube to start conducting. A *1* or a high voltage state would then exist on the output line. The switch would remain that way (stable) until the computer sent it another signal causing it to flip-flop into its opposite state and output a *0* once again.

Sending a flip-flop a signal that causes it to output a *1* is called "setting" it. Sending it a signal that causes it to output a *0* is called "resetting" it. Thus, when you hit the RESET button on your computer (if you have such a button), you are actually causing your machine's flip-flops to be cleared and "reset" to *0* output.

---

**SoftTip:** A single flip-flop can represent only one binary digit. So if there were two vacuum tubes in each flip-flop, how many tubes would be required to symbolize the number five in binary form *(101)*? You'd need six. With six tubes the biggest number you could represent would be a binary seven *(111)*. If you want to represent larger numbers, you'll need more tubes—quite a few more.

ENIAC (Electronic Numerical Integrator and Calculator) was the first computer with electric switching. Produced in 1946 at a small school in Philadelphia to aid the Army in calculating artillery shell ballistics, it occupied 1,500 square feet, weighed 30 tons, and contained 19,000 vacuum tubes—one of which blew every 7½ minutes. That necessitated the hiring of a two-man maintenance crew whose sole job it was to locate and replace them as they burned out. It also consumed enough electric power to drive a locomotive. The thing whizzed along at 5,000 operations a second, more than 1,000 times faster than the relay-based Mark I.

A TRS-80 Color Computer, an Atari 400, and many other inexpensive machines available today come from the store with more than *16* times the memory of ENIAC. Some portable, notebook-sized computers like the Radio Shack Model 100 or the Epson HX-20 provide *32* times the memory of ENIAC and run on four AA penlight batteries.

---

The tubes have long since disappeared, and with them the huge rooms needed to house a computer and the gigantic air conditioning systems they required to dissipate the heat generated by all of the glowing wires within the tubes. But the flip-flop concept is very much alive.

Without pushing the analogy too far, you can think of a collection of flip-flops as that first typesetter's box in which the wooden switches could be moved. By mentally placing this flip-flop box above the hard-wired CPU box (whose wooden switches were glued in place) and coupling the two with "data bus" tubes, you can get a very rough view of how a program works on the CPU.

Let's suppose that we set the flip-flop switches so that water pumped into the top of the box flows downward and exits through flip-flop port *D*. (See Figure 1.3.) If port *D* happens to be connected to the hole labelled *1* on the CPU, the water will continue through the CPU and leave at the unit's *G* port—where it will cause a bell to ring. That's one of the CPU's preordained, hard-wired instructions.

If we reach into the flip-flop box and change the switches so that water exits through a port connected to hole number *18* on the CPU, the water will flow downward along a second path that causes a whistle to blow when it leaves the CPU at port *H*. That's another of the CPU's hard-wired instructions.

The key point here is this: When the output from one flip-flop pattern is poured into the CPU, it causes the CPU to execute one of its instructions. The output from another flip-flop pattern causes the execution of another CPU instruction. If you knew what flip-flop patterns caused what CPU response, and could set them rapidly enough, you could cause the CPU alternately to ring a bell, blow a whistle, bang a drum, etc., fast enough to create what might pass for music.

Fortunately, in a real computer there's no need for you to change the flip-flop patterns rapidly because your software has stored the patterns in the machine's memory. And, thanks to a built-in "chain reaction" effect, made possible by the way a computer is wired up, things proceed automatically.

## The Chain Reaction Effect

This chain reaction concept is almost as important as the idea of layers. On a conceptual level, you can think of computers as elaborate chain reaction machines. For example, we've talked about our water box CPU being turned into something of a one-man band by rapidly changing inputs from the flip-flop box above it. Without worrying about how it's done, imagine what would happen if the first flip-flop instruction to the CPU not only caused a bell to ring, but *also* caused a new flip-flop pattern to appear, one that would order the CPU to blow the whistle. And what if the CPU's execution of the whistle instruction automatically caused the flip-flop pattern to change to the *next* instruction: "bang the drum"?

If things could be set up that way, all you'd have to do would be to feed the CPU the first instruction. After that, everything would run automatically. Quite literally, one thing would lead to another and another and another.

The circuitry is very complex, of course. And it may encompass tens of thousands of CPU switches. But conceptually, this really is the way a CPU works. Like a Slinky© falling down stairs after you give it an

—— **Figure 1.3. Bells and Whistles** ——

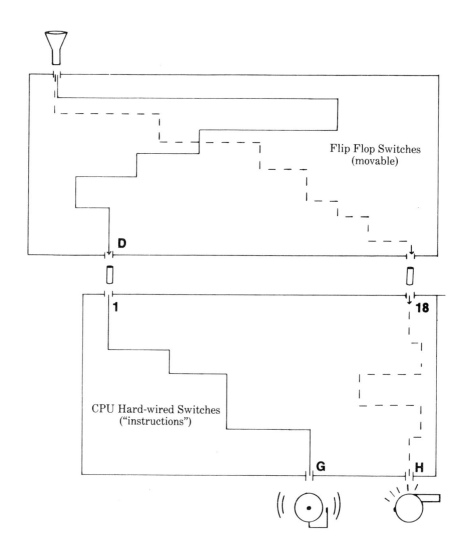

initial push, the CPU is designed to continue executing instructions in what can sometimes appear to be an infinite, self-sustaining chain reaction.

---

**SoftTip:** Today we take for granted the idea of loading a program into a computer's memory and telling it to act upon it. But it wasn't always so. Back in the days of ENIAC, programs were entered one bit at a time by flipping switches on the machine's front panel and by laboriously wiring things together on a "patch panel."

During this time, a brilliant mathematician named John Von Neumann had a better idea. Working at Princeton University's Institute for Advanced Study, Von Neumann published a paper in which he suggested that computer programs be entered and stored in the machine's memory instead of being entered by hand. In the same paper, Von Neumann also suggested that computers be designed to communicate in "parallel" (several bits flowing down several wires all at once) as opposed to the "serial" (one bit flowing down one wire) technique used at the time. Both ideas were incorporated in subsequent machines and have proved essential to the development of the modern computer.

---

It is as if you took lots of the doorbell relays we looked at earlier and wired them all together in a long chain stretching from your living room to your neighbor's house—and then pressed a *single* button. The motion of the clapper in the first relay would throw a switch to activate the clapper in the second relay, which would do the same thing to the third relay, and so on. Clunk–clunk–clunk–clunk . . . across your front yard, all the way to your neighbor's door.

You could even wire things up so that chains of relays branched off in various directions, circled back, and branched off again like one of those elaborate domino constructions that people create to get themselves in the *Guinness Book of World Records*. At its peak a construction like this will have several chain reactions going on at once. You can almost hear the clicking and clacking in your head.

You can't hear the switches opening and closing inside the CPU, but if you could, they'd sound much the same way, only much, much faster.

The actual chain reactions taking place in the CPU may involve alternately gating instructions and data onto the data bus, bringing the voltage patterns into the CPU, doing something with them, and sending them back out again. Of course, whatever it's doing, the microprocessor is so small that it needs lots of off-site storage space to hold its instructions and data.

## *RAMulan and ROMulans—No Klingons*

In a computer, the flip-flops or their microchip equivalents are the primary components of RAM, which is short for "random access memory." The fact that they can be changed from one state to another makes it possible for the CPU to "read" instructions or data out of them or "write" the same kinds of things into them. The same thing happens when you hit a key on the keyboard or when your floppy disk drive comes on and loads in a program.

The "random" part of the name comes from the fact that RAM is arranged like a bulletin board, allowing you to read any notice that's posted there in any order you please, without having to read one notice after another until you get to the one you want. A record on a turntable works somewhat the same way. You can put the stylus down on any cut whenever you want to hear a particular tune without starting at the beginning of the record. That's "random access." With a cassette tape, in contrast, you've got to wind the tape forward or back until you reach the song you want. This is called "serial" access, and it makes it impossible for you to get at it immediately.

The hard-wired switches mentioned earlier exist in a different type of computer memory called ROM, short for "read only memory." A computer can only read instructions (and in some cases, data) out of ROM; it can't write anything into it. Both types of memory offer a computer random access to their contents.

RAM is often said to be "volatile," because the flip-flops it contains depend on electric current to hold their information. When you "power down" and turn your machine off for the day, the flip-flops all shout "Quittin' time!" and reset to 0. The same thing can happen, involuntarily, when there is a surge of electricity or a voltage spike on the power line you've got your machine plugged into. And, because RAM is made up of voltage-sensitive switches, it's the RAM that gets zapped when you walk across a carpet and a spark of static electricity flies from your fingers the moment you touch your machine.

---

**SoftTip:** Studies have shown that the typical power line in the United States receives about 113.3 voltage spikes a month. That's an average of about one every six-and-a-half hours. In reality, more of them are likely to occur during peak usage hours than during the late evening and early morning hours. Conditions vary, but you may not need to invest in a separate surge suppressor. Radio Shack says that they build a surge suppressor into their machines. IBM says that their computers are designed to handle surges up to 15% above normal household line voltage. And Atari and Apple claim that nothing short of a direct lightning strike will affect their machines.

Still, not even the experts know what causes all voltage surges or when they will occur. So, if you find that your computer suddenly locks up on you (keystrokes no longer cause letters to appear on the screen) for no apparent reason; if a program that has worked perfectly in the past begins to malfunction; if your printer suddenly spits out characters when it should be idle; then the voltage surges or "transients" on your power line could be the culprits.

The best way to defend against these problems is to install a voltage spike eliminator or surge suppressor. You plug these devices into the wall socket and then plug your system into them. They cost around $100. A bit more if they have the capability of filtering out the electric noise generated by AC motors running off the same power line. You don't have to worry about what the following specifications mean, but you should look for a surge suppressor with "reaction time" of between 50 and 100 nanoseconds. And many authorities say it should be able to handle peaks of between 30 and 100 Joules or 4,000 to 5,000 amps.

If you can't find one of these units at your local computer store, you might check the ads in computer magazines or try one of the data processing catalogs like *INMAC* (2465 Augustine Drive, Santa Clara, CA 95051).

---

**SoftTip:** Static electricity can also cause similar problems. If your winters are cold and dry, you might install a humidifier in your computer room and turn it on when static electricity is particularly bad. You might also use an antistatic spray, like Alberto-Culver's Static Guard. You can find this at your grocery store next to the laundry detergents. Some office equipment manufacturers recommend periodically using it to spray lightly the keyboard, your chair, the area around the system, and even the screen.

As a last resort, you might look into a special antistatic floor mat. These mats have a ground wire for bleeding off charges before they get to the zapping level. At between $80 and $125, they're not cheap. But you will find them in Radio Shack computer catalogues. The 3M Company offers an even wider selection. Call the firm's Data Recording Products Division at (800) 328-1300; in Minnesota, (612) 736-9625, for more information.

A company called Computerware, Inc. at 315 South Third Street, Stillwater, MN 55082 sells a product called TouchMat

## Memories, Words, and Location! Location!

*The Flip-Flop Gangs*

As we saw earlier with telephone-type relay switches, when the CPU
"gates information onto a bus" from a particular address location, it
sends a control signal to that location to throw a switch and make a
connection. What actually gets connected to the bus is the output line
from each flip-flop. Once the connection is made, the CPU can tell
whether a unit is putting out a high or a low voltage signal, a *1* or a *0*.

We know we need flip-flops and we know that each one can store or
represent a single binary digit or bit. But how *many* of them do we
need and how should they be arranged within the machine?

One way to decide is to ask, What is the largest number we want to
be able to symbolize in binary form? That is, how many *1*'s and *0*'s—
how many flip-flops—will the binary version of the biggest number we
would like to be able to write all at once, contain?

If you focus on the things you want the computer to print out or
display, you can come up with a pretty good approximation of that number. For example, the only way to get a computer to display the letter
*A* is to convert it to a binary number that the computer can deal with.
With that as a starting point, we can assign a number to each letter of
the alphabet for a total of 26. But that's just for the capital letters. We
need a second group of 26 numbers for the lower-case letters, for a total
so far of 52. And don't forget the digits from 0 through 9. That's another
ten. Punctuation marks and mathematical symbols add an another 23 or
so, bringing us up to 85.

Here's the point: The biggest binary number you can write using six
digits is 63 *(111111)*. To symbolize a number like 85, you've got to use
*seven* digits *(1010101)*, or seven flip-flops for each number.

The largest seven-digit binary number *(1111111)* translates to 127 in
our standard decimal system. When you include the number *0000000*,
you've got a total of 128 possibilities to work with. That gives you
plenty of room to accommodate everything you need, with numbers left
over to symbolize commands to cause the printer to advance the paper

one line (a "line feed") or cause the printing element to return to the far left (a "carriage return") and other "device control signals." But . . .

What if you want to be able to write a plus or minus sign next to a number to signify that it's positive or negative? What if you want to use a lot of unique graphics characters? And what if you want to develop an error-checking procedure built around an extra bit attached to each character?

The answer to all of these questions is that *you need an eighth bit.* That, of course, is the system that has been adopted. All microcomputers, even most of the newer "16-bit" machines like the IBM/PC, have their flip-flops arranged in 8-bit units. A special code called the American Standard Code for Information Interchange, or ASCII ("az-key"), has been created to assign each letter, digit, punctuation mark, and device control signal a particular number, and all microcomputers use it.

---

**SoftTip:** You'll find more information on ASCII and other points dealing with how data is represented and communicated in:

*The Complete Handbook of Personal Computer Communications: Everything You Need to Go Online with the World* by Alfred Glossbrenner (St. Martin's Press, New York)

---

*Nibbles, Bytes, and Other Words*

The eight-digit binary number is so important in the world of computerdom that it has been given a special name: "byte." Because a byte is used to represent a letter or a decimal number, it is also called a "character." There are other, related, terms as well. As evidence that computerists are not without a sense of humor, a four-digit binary grouping, or half a byte, is called a "nibble." And as evidence that computerists are not without a penchant for confusing people, a byte or character is sometimes called a "word."

---

**SoftTip:** Occasionally, a "word" consists of not one, but two bytes. It's not worth worrying about, but the reason for the apparent inconsistency lies in the CPU. Central processing units are built to handle a certain number of bits at one time. However many bits that may be, that's what constitutes a "word" as far as that particular CPU is concerned. Really old machines could handle only four bits at a time and so had a "4-bit" word. Modern machines deal with eight bits and thus have a word length the same as a byte. Even more modern machines deal with 16 bits at a time, and for them, a word contains 16 bits or two bytes.

*A Good Location*

Real estate agents are fond of saying that three things determine the value of a property: Location, location, and location. Well, location is equally important to a computer's flip-flop memory circuits, both in terms of having any kind of location at all and in terms of exactly where the location is.

If you're going to represent characters and other data in eight-bit cells consisting of eight flip-flop circuits, there's got to be a way to make each cell an individual unit. After all, if you had 64 or more flip-flops all lined up, some set as *1*'s and some as *0*'s, how would you tell where one byte ended and the next one began?

It is for this reason that a computer's internal memory is organized into discrete locations, each of which contains the eight flip-flop switches needed to represent a byte of information.

Memory locations are often described as being similar to a wall of post office boxes. And that's quite accurate. But it doesn't begin to convey the scope of things. To store all of the characters, spaces, and punctuation marks on this page, you could easily need three *thousand* or more "post office boxes" inside the computer. To run some software programs, you would need 64,000 of them—minimum. The boxes in that case would form a wall three stories high and 80 yards long. And these days, 64K is not a lot of memory for many personal computers to have.

For the moment, let's think of memory that way—as a huge wall of discrete boxes that rises three stories or more and stretches in either direction as far as you can see. We can even add a nimble little man with a moustache, a floppy hat, and a red bandanna. To pick a name out of nowhere, let's call him "Mario" and give him an electric cart equipped with an accordian style lifter to help him reach the higher box locations.

It's Mario's job to make sure that the CPU gets the data and instructions it demands from various locations in memory. Every box looks like every other box, but fortunately each has an *address* that keeps it from being just another byte in the wall. When the CPU wants something, it first sends Mario the address of the box containing what it wants. Mario clambers into his cart and drives to the correct part of the wall.

We can look over Mario's shoulder as he identifies a box by the address number the CPU gave him. If you were to peek inside a box as it is opened, you would find eight flip-flop switches giving off a pattern of high and low voltages. And if you were to reach over Mario's shoulder and poke your hand in, you'd find that you could set those switches to a new pattern if you liked.

Mario works with the CPU to identify the correct box location and make sure that its contents get transmitted back via the data bus. Needless to say, when the CPU is running full tilt, Mario is very busy.

*How Many Locations? How Many Addresses?*

In a real computer, you've got your CPU; you've got your banks of memory boxes; and you've got your control lines and buses. What actually happens is that when the CPU wants a piece of information, it sends the address number for that location down the address bus to a unit like Mario. Like everything else in a computer, the address consists of a number represented in binary form by a pattern of high and low voltages.

When the Mario-unit has located the right box, the CPU sends a signal down its control line to open the box and gate its contents onto its data bus. That's called a "read" operation, and it has no effect on the switch pattern storing the data. The little flip-flops simply duplicate their voltage pattern on the bus. A "write" works in a similar way: the address of the target location is sent to Mario on the address bus; a control signal connects the box to the data bus. But this time, the flip-flops are first reset to 0, or cleared, by a control line signal. Then data flow into the box to create a new pattern of high/low settings among the eight flip-flops.

Now, given these facts, if someone were to ask you what determines the largest amount of memory a computer can have, what would you guess?

The amount of memory a computer can use is determined by *how big an address* it can write.

Every memory location has an address number. And every CPU has an address bus designed to communicate that number to a unit like Mario. The address bus for most computers that are built around an eight-bit CPU consists of 16 lines. So even though an eight-bit computer can create an address out of two bytes (16 bits), the total number of possible addresses is still limited by the 16 address bus lines. How many possibilities? Two to the 16th power, or 65,536. In binary form, that includes all possible numbers from 16 zeroes in a row to a solid row of 16 ones.

Because the numbers are so large and take so long to write and pronounce, computerists use the abbreviation $K$ when referring to memory sizes. The $K$ stands for "kilobytes" or "units of 1,000 bytes." Actually, 1K is equal to 1,024 bytes, but no one quibbles about the extra 24 bytes. Thus, by convention, 65,536 bytes of memory is referred to as *64K*, even though the expression is not precisely accurate.

*Because an eight-bit CPU has 16 address lines in its address bus, the maximum amount of "addressable memory" it can have is 64K.*

**SoftTip:** There is a relatively new technique that enables some eight-bit computers with 16 address bus lines to use up to 128K of memory—but not at the same time. The technique is called "bank switching," and it enables the computer to divide 128K into two 64K-chunks or banks. Each bank has an identical set of addresses, but the CPU decides whether it wants to use an address in bank one or bank two.

For more information, write to Commodore's MOS Technology Division and ask about the 6509 chip:

> MOS Technology
> 950 Rittenhouse Road
> Norristown, PA 19401
> (215) 666-7950

*Software: It's Not the Bits. It's the Bus.*
Newer personal computers, like the IBM/PC and its many clones, are built around a 16-bit CPU chip, which means that they can manipulate data in 16-bit or two-byte chunks—once they get the information inside. But, the fact is that the chip used in the IBM/PC has the same kind of eight-bit data bus found on older computers. It may be able to handle the data faster once it brings it in, but it can only bring it in in single-byte chunks. Consequently, for most people, the extra internal speed made possible by this particular 16-bit chip and others like it isn't all that important.

**SoftTip:** For more information on how a 16-bit microprocessor can use a 20-bit address bus, as well as many other excellent technical explanations, see:

*Inside the PC: Access to Advanced Features and Programming* by Peter Norton (Robert J. Brady Co.)

If you can't find the book at the bookstore, write to:

> Mr. Peter Norton
> The Norton Utilities
> 2210 Wilshire Blvd. #186A,
> Santa Monica, CA 90403

*Note:* Mr. Norton does *not* own a gas, electric, or water company. The utilities referred to are special programs written to perform routine chores with an IBM/PC.

What's important is the memory it can address. The Intel 8088 chip at the heart of the IBM, for example, has not 16 but *20* lines on its address bus. This means that it can address two to the 20th power or—get ready—*1,048,576* discrete memory locations. That's 1,024K or, in computerist's terms, a *megabyte* of storage.

What does this increase in memory addressing ability mean to you as a software user? It means that if you had equipped your machine with a "meg" of memory, you'd have enough room to load in a word processing program, a spreadsheet program, a list handling program, a spelling checker program, and one or two other things—*all at the same time.* Once all of these programs were loaded, you'd be able to switch from one to the other without fiddling with a bunch of floppy disks. With the additional software to tie all of these functions together, you'd just hit a few keys to go from "What if?" of a spreadsheet to the "What's this?" of a spelling checker.

This "integrated" approach to software is probably the most significant development since the invention of the personal computer itself, for it will ultimately make your machine much, much easier to use. A number of techniques are already available. We'll look at three of them in Chapter 7 (Apple's Lisa computer, VisiCorp's VisiON package, and a program called DesQ from Quarterdeck Office Systems). In Chapter 18 we will look at two more: the leading "all-in-one" packages, Lotus 1-2-3 and Context MBA.

Software integration is made possible by the conjunction of three things:

- Tumbling memory prices
- The amazing memory-addressing capabilities of 16-bit, 20-address-line CPUs
- The fact that software can be written to take advantage of these facts and handle several programs at once

---

**SoftTip:** It's important to note that you don't have to buy all of the chips necessary to make up a megabyte of memory to benefit from the capabilities of one of the newer CPU chips. That's just the upper limit. The point is that with a new machine, the old 64K constraint no longer applies. Thus you can have 64K, 96K, 128K, 256K, etc., whatever you can afford.

---

*Instructions, Data, and Quality Software*

If you think back to the Operating Theater of Dr. Ewe, you'll remember that the good doctor accepted two kinds of input: data patients wheeled in through the O.R. door and paper airplane instructions from the programmer in the balcony. As we know, both types of input are essential to a computer. Both look alike (*1*'s and *0*'s). And both are stored in memory box locations.

So how does the CPU know the difference? How can it tell that a particular string of *1*'s and *0*'s means "Load your internal A register" and not "Put a character on the screen"? It tells by *where the input came from in memory*.

When you turn on your personal computer, all of the little flip-flops in the thousands of memory locations in your machine are reset to zero. Blank. Zip. Nothing. But they don't stay that way for long. When you load in a program, a certain amount of memory is immediately set aside to hold instructions for the CPU, while other locations are set aside to hold data.

If you remember Mario and the wall of post office boxes, it's as though someone dropped a red ribbon from the top of the wall and said, "Okay, everything stored on this side is to be interpreted as CPU instructions, and everything over there is to be considered data."

As a software user, it will make no difference to you where a program is stored in your machine's memory. Because it has no visible effect on how you use the program, the memory locations are "user transparent." What *does* matter is how much of your memory a program appropriates for itself. The more memory a program occupies, the less you have to work with when using the program.

The following principles apply to almost every software package, but we'll look at word processing as an example. When you use a word processing package, some of your machine's memory is going to be used to hold the program instructions and some is going to be set aside to hold the pages that you write. The characters and spaces you type are data, and a separate memory box is needed to store each of them. Obviously, the more boxes the program itself takes up, the fewer boxes you'll have to use for storing characters in at any one time.

This limitation can have a noticeable effect on how convenient the program is to use. If you can only store, say, four pages of text in memory, what do you do when you're on page 10 and want to go back and look at page 3? Your only choice is first to hit the keys needed to record the pages currently in memory on your floppy disk. Then hit some more keys to tell the system to find the recording of page 3 on the disk, read it into the machine's memory, and display it. When you're finished with page 3, you'll have to go through the same process to get page 10 back on the screen.

This is inconvenient and time consuming. There are two solutions: Either go out and buy more memory so that you can store more pages at one time, or use a word processing program that requires a smaller amount of the memory you already have. Or, better yet—and here is where this book comes in—be sure to look at how many pages a particular word processing program will let you work with before you buy it.

## All Code Is Not Alike

At this point it is reasonable to ask, Won't a program that occupies less memory space have less power and fewer features than one that requires more? The answer is that it might and it might not. It all depends on how carefully and imaginatively the program was written or, in computer terms, how "tight" or "efficient" the code is.

As a software user, you will probably never see the programming instructions or "code" that makes a package run. But it is very, very important to realize that software, like a novel or a movie, is the result of a creative effort. A really imaginative programmer can find ways to write a program that will do all of the things another package will do but use only two-thirds or half the memory. Other firms or individuals, either for lack of skill or to get a product on the market, may elect to do things the "quick and dirty" way.

## The Logic of the CPU

The only major thing we haven't covered is, What happens to instructions and data after they enter the central processing unit? To which the answer could safely be, The instructions get acted upon and the data get processed. Next question.

The details of the inner workings of the CPU are really of interest only to programmers, and in fact only to certain kinds of programmers who are skilled in writing code that is very close to the *1*'s and *0*'s of machine language. For our purposes, we can say that the CPU consists of a lot of different kinds of switches. There are switches similar to the flip-flops the CPU uses to temporarily store the information and instructions it brings in from outside memory locations. There are also switches that can add or subtract (and thus multiply or divide) two binary numbers and output the result. There are the hard-wired switches and circuits of the CPU's instruction set. And there are special switches called "logic gates."

"Logic" is a term that you encounter frequently when dealing with computers, particularly when you're using a database management system (DBMS) like dBASE II, or other software that offers a sophisticated search function. Computer logic is built around the rules of Boolean logic (named for George Boole 1815–1864), which in turn is built around the concepts of AND, OR, and NOT.

Thus, "logic" is what makes it possible for you to command your DBMS to "give me a list of all of my customers who live in New York AND Los Angeles AND have bought a Widget OR a Wumpus from me in the past year but have NOT bought the new Diamicrom II."

To select the target customers in the above example, the CPU must make many comparisons. But we'll take a quick look at just one. Imagine that you want to find just those customers who live in New York. When you type "New York" in your command line, imagine that you are setting up a pattern of bits representing those characters in the CPU's temporary memory. The CPU holds onto this and then brings in each customer's state address in turn so that it can compare its bit pattern to the pattern of "New York." When the *1*'s and *0*'s of the two patterns match, the CPU selects the customer. When they don't, it goes on to the next one in the file. In this case the logic circuitry tests to see if "New York" AND the customer's state address are the same.

In an actual computer, *many* circuits must be used to perform this comparison. But looking at a single, very simple circuit will give you all you need to know for a conceptual understanding of computer logic switches. Here's what's called an AND gate:

We can think of the selector mechanism as a machine that is designed to pull address cards from a deck containing all of a firm's customers. As you can see from the diagram, the machine will swing into action only if both switches A AND B are closed to allow the power to flow.

When the CPU compares "New York" to a customer's address, it in effect closes switch A, then says to the address, "Okay, let's see what you got." It pumps this information into the circuit. If the bit pattern of representing the information on the card causes switch B to close, power will flow and the "address card" will be selected. If not, it's "Next customer, please."

In an actual operation, many circuits are involved, and instead of "pulling cards" a computer's selector mechanism will do something else to identify the target customers. But, in very general terms, this is how CPU and other logic circuitry work.

There are only three other points to make here about computer logic:

- Like Dr. C. P. Ewe, logic circuits operate on *two* inputs at a time and produce a result based on how those inputs compare.
- There is a separate logic circuit for each bit in a number. (Remember, letters get converted to ASCII numbers before a computer deals with them.) If you're going to compare two binary numbers, each of which is eight digits long, you need eight logic circuits—one for each pairing of bits.

• There are *many kinds* of logic gates. For example, without too much trouble it should be possible to see how wires could be added and things could be moved around into a parallel arrangement so that the selector mechanism illustrated above would be activated if either switch A OR B were closed.

---

**SoftTip:** For more information on how the various logic circuits physically work, you might want to read:

*Basic Digital Electronics*
by Ray Ryan
TAB Books, Inc. $7.95

Also recommended are just about any of the books published by Radio Shack in cooperation with the Texas Instrument Learning Center. (Look for the TI logo on the cover or spine.) Most are well written and profusely illustrated‚ and at prices ranging from $2.95 to $6.95 for full-length books, they're one of the great bargains in computerdom. They're much too technical for a bookstore's normal customers, but you should be able to find them at most Radio Shack outlets.

---

*Onward and Upward*

The "Questions for Review" sections that textbook publishers love to put at the end of each chapter surely rank with the "Preface to the Third Edition" pages that scholars put at the front of a boring tome as one of the least-read blocks of text ever published. No one wants to read a rehash of a long and detailed chapter, and we won't put you through one.

However, since we've been dealing with the "sunlight" and the "rain" and other background information and only briefly touched on how they affect the software "plants," one or two "points for review" might be in order. For example, later on (in Chapter 4) we're going to talk about something called "print spooling." This can be an important feature to look for in many programs because it lets you work with your computer while it is simultaneously printing out "hard copy." You might not know what the term means right now, but if someone told you that a print spooling feature set aside a certain portion of your computer's memory as a "holding tank" to store text before it is sent to the printer, you'd have a fairly good idea of what it meant.

Similarly, if you owned an Apple II and were to read a software ad that proclaimed the product suitable for "any Z80 machine!" you would certainly think twice before placing an order since your computer is built around a 6502 CPU chip. If you were considering software for your IBM/PC, you now know why it is important to ask whether a particular program takes full advantage of the memory addressing capabilities of your computer's 16-bit processor, or whether it is merely a translation of a program originally designed to run on an eight-bit machine.

These are only a few of the ways that you will be drawing on what you've learned in this chapter. Now that we've got the groundwork laid, we can move right into that most misunderstood category of software: computer operating systems. In the next chapter we'll see how an operating system works with your machine's hardware to give it a "personality." More importantly, though, we'll find out why it is that this kind of software, like the CPU, ultimately determines what other programs you can run.

# ...2...

# Operating Systems:
## *The Center of the Software Universe*

*Softwaria est omnis divisa in partes tres*

Generally speaking, all software is divided into one of three broad categories: *system* software, *applications* software, and *programming languages*. Applications software includes programs for word processing, spreadsheet analysis, database management, personal finance, games, and the like. You might think of it as software that lets you *apply* your machine to a particular task. Programming languages like BASIC, FORTRAN, Pascal, COBOL, etc., are the various collections of words and rules that let human beings "talk" to the computer's CPU. System software includes the programs that are directly concerned with your computer, how it operates, and how its various resources (memory, video display, disk drives, etc.) are organized and made to work together as, well, a "system." As such, system software is the *sine qua non* of computerdom. All applications programs and all programming languages must be designed to work with it or under its control.

System software is usually sold as a one- or two-disk package, but there is no widely accepted definition of all the programs that such a package should include. Often, it includes program modules that are not strictly "system software," but have come to be placed under that rubric. For example, the package may contain a program module to let you edit the programs or text you write line by line like a word processor. It may have a "linker" module to paste one piece of programming to another. And it may include a "debugger" to test a program that you have written and aid you in identifying programming mistakes and other "bugs."

Unless you're really into programming, however, there's not much need to concern yourself with these modules. It's always nice to feel that you're getting more for your money. But after a cursory glance, many software buyers rarely even look at the editor, debugger, or

45

linker sections of the instruction manual that comes with the package. These modules have nothing to do with your ability to run applications programs.

*You Gotta Have a System*

The system software that matters—and matters profoundly—is the collection of both hard-wired and disk-based programs that makes up what is called the "operating system." Naturally, being a computer term, this collection of programs is abbreviated as "OS." The OS is what makes sure that each key you strike gets displayed on the video screen or that the text you've written gets dumped to the printer instead of or in addition to the screen. All computers must have an OS of some sort.

If you have one or more floppy disk drives, however, your system software will be called "DOS" ("doss") for "disk operating system." (Only rarely is it called "the" DOS.) It is DOS that swings into action when you want to see what's recorded on a disk. And it's DOS that makes it possible for you to pull the letter you just wrote to Aunt Erma out of your machine's internal memory (RAM) and record a copy of it on a floppy disk.

Although there is technically a difference between an OS and a DOS, they are closely related and, in actual practice, the term "DOS" is frequently used to refer to both modules. Thus it is DOS that works with whatever applications program you're running so that when the *program* says, "Print this text," your computer does what it is supposed to do. This is such an important point that it is worth stating again: *No applications program can run on a computer without some kind of operating system.* This is what makes a computer's DOS so vital, and it's what makes operating systems in general the center of the software universe.

As we explore this subject further, we're going to run into some terms and ideas that will probably be unfamiliar. With all of the different modules and names flying about, it can sometimes be difficult to see where everything fits. But the following "software map" should help:

**Software Map—Version 1.0**

    I. System software
      A. Operating system (OS)
      B. Disk operating system (DOS)
      C. "Extras" for programmers
        1. Line editor
        2. Linker
        3. Debugger
        4. Etc.

II. Applications programs
 A. Word processing
 B. Games
 C. Electronic spreadsheet
 D. Database management
 E. Etc.

III. Programming Languages
 A. BASIC
 B. Pascal
 C. FORTRAN
 D. COBOL
 E. C
 F. Forth
 G. Etc.

## Understanding Operating Systems

*Why Bother?*
Unless you're going to be doing some serious programming yourself, there is no need to understand exactly *how* a given operating system works. As Gary Kildall, the creator of the operating system called CP/M has said, "Probably 80 or 90% of the applications that use CP/M make CP/M really transparent. You see it only when you get into the programming environment."

The same comment might apply equally well to most other operating systems. As a software buyer, however, there are at least three good reasons for developing an understanding of what an OS is, why it's needed, and what it does. First, since all applications programs must be written to run under the control of an operating system, the operating system you select will determine what specific programs you can run on your computer.

Second, operating systems are the key to software "transportability." If two different brands of computers can run the same operating system, then many times they can both use a program written to run under its control. The best-known example of an OS making it possible to "port" (transport) a program from one computer to another is Kildall's CP/M®, a registered trademark of Digital Research, Inc. From a user's standpoint, transportability often means a wider selection of programs for your equipment and potentially lower costs.

Finally, operating systems may be a special kind of software, but they are still software. And, like any other software package, different operating systems offer different features. One of the best examples of this is something called UNIX (covered in Chapter 6). Most microcomputer operating systems are designed to let one person use the machine at any given time. In some cases, however, a UNIX or UNIX-like OS such as Microsoft's XENIX can take the same machine and make it possible for several people to use it at the same time and for several programs ("tasks") to be run simultaneously. These are called "multiuser" and "multi-tasking" features.

*Without Me, There's Nothing*

The best way to understand what an operating system is and does is to imagine what a computer would be like without one. This is a little difficult to do since all computers come with a very basic part of an operating system built in. This primitive bit of programming is hardwired into a ROM chip and it is activated as soon as the power is turned on. Consequently, you can never see what a computer would be like *without* operating system type programming.

But where reality fails, imagination can step in. Without too much trouble, we can visualize what a computer *sans* any form of OS would be like. It's not a pretty sight. Basically, without operating system programming, if you were to turn on your computer *nothing would happen.* Electricity might flow through some of the switches, but the screen would remain blank, the printer wouldn't print, and the computer would not respond to anything you typed on the keyboard. Nothing would work until something or someone set the computer's switches to tell it what to do.

Without the proper switch settings to channel electricity in the right directions, Dr. C. P. Ewe would just sit there in splendid isolation, a patient quarantined behind a glass wall with no way to get information or instructions in or out.

Obviously, this is an unacceptable situation, and no manufacturer is going to produce a machine that just sits there like a lump of cold spaghetti when you "power up" (turn the computer on). Consequently, everyone builds at least some part of an operating system into their machines. Usually, the portion of the operating system that gets built in is designed primarily for getting information in and out of the computer. At the very least, for example, when a computer is turned on you want to be able to "talk" to it from the keyboard and see the results displayed on the screen.

In computerese, these input and output operations are abbreviated as—what else?—"I/O" (pronounced "eye-oh"). Better yet, the portion of an operating system responsible for these functions is often called the BIOS ("buy-o's") for "Basic Input/Output System."

**SoftTip:** Some manufacturers do not use the term BIOS when referring to this module as it exists in their machine. Regardless of what it is called, there will be some module designed to perform BIOS-like functions in every computer.

At this point, there are three important things to remember about a machine's BIOS. First, it is a *module*, meaning that it performs certain functions but is also designed to be connected to other modules to form a complete system. Second, it normally "resides in ROM." That is, the BIOS usually consists of hard-wired switch settings in a read-only microchip inside the machine. Third, the BIOS *is* programming. Before the ROM is created, the BIOS programs it will contain are written out line by line, just like any other program. As we saw in Chapter 1, the fact that these programs end up as permanently recorded firmware, like a video game cartridge, doesn't change the fact that they are still programs.

It's important to emphasize that the BIOS and other operating system modules consist of line after line of computer programming because it highlights once again the fact that a computer must be told what to do every step of the way. In some respects, this is a double-edged sword. On the one hand, the need to specify absolutely everything can be extremely tiresome. But, on the other hand, the need to specify everything can also be viewed as an opportunity to specify many *different* things and so produce many different results with the identical hardware. This is why it's possible to run several operating systems, each with different features, on the same computer at different times.

*The BIOS in Action*

When you turn on your computer and hit a key on the keyboard, the corresponding character immediately appears on your video screen. It happens so fast and seems so natural that most of the time we take the process for granted. That is exactly as it should be. However, it *can* be important to have some idea of what's involved in getting that character on the screen and the many steps that the BIOS program must perform to make it happen. A brief look at some of those steps will not only give you an idea of how this particular process is executed, but it can also serve as an example for how *all* operating system programming works.

Let's assume that you've turned your computer on. The little block called the "cursor" is blinking in the upper left corner of your video screen, and you have just hit the letter *A* on your keyboard. In very general terms, here's what happens. As soon as you turn your machine on, the BIOS programming in ROM begins to "watch" the spot where the keyboard is plugged into the system. Whether your keyboard is attached to your computer by a cord or whether it's built in, you know that somewhere inside the machine it's connected to the computer.

As soon as you strike the *A* key, the keyboard sends a pattern of *1* and *0* bits representing the ASCII code number for *A* to that spot in the machine. The BIOS notices it immediately and says, "Uh-oh, a character from the keyboard. Now where's it supposed to go?" In the absence of any instructions to the contrary, the BIOS will probably put the character on the video screen, instead of, say, the printer.

Before that can happen, though, the BIOS has got to go through a little catechism:

- Where does the video screen plug into the system?
- Is the screen in a 40-column mode, calling for large letters? Or is it set for 80 columns, meaning smaller letters?
- Where is the cursor located right now? What row (line) and column?
- Is the cursor at the end of a line? If it is, I've got to skip down and put the *A* on the next line.
- Is the next line beyond the bottom of the screen? If it is, I've got to scroll the screen up one line. Meaning I've got to take everything that's currently displayed off the screen, get rid of the uppermost line, and then rewrite (display) the rest of the stuff in new line locations.

Clearly, getting a character on the screen is not a simple process, even though it appears to be instantaneous. There are exceptions to almost everything, and there *are* other ways to get things onto the screen. But for now we can assume that each time a character is to be displayed on the screen, steps like these must be followed. And when you think about it, it really makes sense. How *else* could a system know where to put a character on the screen if it didn't first check to see where the cursor was located and run through all of the other questions noted above?

There are two important points to make here. First, the same general routine must be followed for all other input or output devices connected to the computer. The input could come from a light pen, from a joystick, a floppy disk drive or cassette player, or from a telecommunications port hooked up to a modem. The output could be to the printer, to a built-in speaker, to a modem, or to a floppy disk. In every case, there must be a particular package of hard-wired programming to get the system to pick up characters or other information, check the output unit, and then take the appropriate action. In computer parlance, the programs that do these things are called "device drivers."

## *The Original Microcomputer Operating Systems*

Device drivers formed the basis of the very first microcomputer operating systems. And that's the second point. Because the only way to get a keyboard character displayed on a screen or a printer is through a driver program written to tell the system what to do, early micro users had to include drivers in all of their programs. For example, they might write a program to calculate the value of *pi* to umpteen places. Well, in addition to all of the program instructions needed to perform the calculation, they also had to include many lines of programming to tell the computer how to handle both its keyboard and its display I/O.

Back then, the keyboards that were used were frequently teletype terminal-printers. They were old and they were slow, but they represented a big improvement over the front panel toggle switches that had to be flipped by hand, one bit at a time. There were no video monitors. And the disk drives that existed were far too expensive, even if they could be successfully "interfaced" (connected to) the computers. Many machines were programmed by means of punched paper tape, with each hole or absence of a hole representing a bit.

It was hard enough being a computerist under these circumstances. Any technique that would lighten the load and save time and effort was clearly welcome. And so computerists began to develop operating systems out of the device drivers they had been writing. After all, why should someone have to reinvent the wheel every time he wrote a program? As long as you didn't plan to do anything fancy with the hardware or attach a unit that would need a customized device driver program, there was no reason why you couldn't use the same set of drivers every time you wrote a program for your machine. Before too long the necessary drivers were hard-wired into ROM chips and thus were available instantly whenever the computer was turned on.

This was the beginning of the personal computer operating system as we know it today. Once the device driver programs were made a readily available part of the machine, programmers obviously no longer had to concern themselves with including them in their software. Thus, operating systems were designed as a *convenience to programmers*, not to end users of the applications software the programmers would create. It is cold comfort to anyone who has ever struggled with a complex and "unfriendly" OS, but this programmer orientation lies at the heart of such travails.

Nor was there any thought at first of using an operating system as a means of running the same program on different machines, the way

CP/M is used today. That came later, principally for the *convenience of the hardware manufacturers and software houses*. (Again, the end user was not the main consideration.)

The existence of an operating system was not only convenient, but it also made it possible for programmers to forget about "talking" to the machine directly when creating their programs. Software no longer had to explicitly tell the system, "Check the position of the printing element on the printer . . . move it to location X . . . advance the paper up one line . . . print the letter *A* . . . " and so forth.

With even a crude operating system installed, the programmers could say, "Print this character on the printer," and let the OS worry about the position of the printing element and other details. In effect, software could now be written *to talk to the operating system*, which then would talk to the hardware itself.

We'll look at the implications of this later, but here's a brief glimpse of what it makes possible. If you have two different brands of computer, each with its own distinctly different hardware (printers, video displays, keyboards, etc.), it may still be possible to run a given program on either one of them—if both computers can run the same operating system and if the program is written to talk to that operating system. For example, a program might include an instruction to "put this character on the screen." As long as it issues that instruction to the operating system, the program (and the person who wrote it) doesn't have to worry about the fact that one computer is equipped with a Panasonic black-and-white television, while the other is using a high-resolution Amdek color monitor. The two types of video displays are very different and have very different requirements that must be met to get them to do their stuff. But the program can let the operating system worry about that. All the program has to do is say, "Put this character on the screen."

The program thus becomes "portable," because it can be run—without changes—on any machine equipped with the same operating system. In the best of all possible worlds, that would mean a wider market for the program, a larger number of sales than if it were wedded to just one brand of computer, and lower prices for software consumers.

In the real world, of course, it doesn't always work that way. Certainly, software portability has increased the number of programs computer owners can choose from. But the software market is still young and highly entrepreneurial, and software houses are inclined to charge whatever the market will bear whenever they can. Thus, all too often, program portability simply means less work, lower costs, and larger profits for the software company, instead of lower prices for you. In addition, in the real world a program may not be able to be "ported" from one machine to another without making a few changes. But the potential for lower prices is there, thanks to the relatively standardized "interface" offered by most leading operating systems.

## The BIOS Is Not Enough

As we've seen, each of the device driver programs that make up the BIOS is designed primarily to facilitate information input and output. But what happens when a computer is forced to deal with more than two kinds of input or output at the same time? Suppose, for example, that you hit a key on your keyboard while your disk drive is on and programming or data are being read into your computer's memory. What should your machine do? Should it ignore the keyboard input and keep the disk drive turning, or should it stop the drive and pay attention to the keyboard? Which source of input should get priority?

Again, a computer has no way to make this decision on its own. It needs programming to set conditions and responses to tell it how to handle situations like these. And the simple device-driver routines in the BIOS simply aren't up to it. A piece of programming must be written to tie everything together and to make decisions about which device gets priority, what tasks will be performed in what order, and so forth.

The operating system module that performs this function is called a *monitor* program. It's the "traffic cop" you may have heard described elsewhere. The keyboard driver in the BIOS may be responsible for channelling into the machine the bit pattern symbolizing the key you hit, but it's really the monitor program that looks at that input and decides what to do about it.

For example, if your disk drive is on and you should happen to fall asleep and pitch forward so that your face lands on the keyboard, the monitor program would look at all of the keys you had inadvertently pressed and probably allow the disk drive to continue on its merry way. The monitor would, in effect, ignore that keyboard input.

However, should you be sitting there and suddenly decide that you didn't want to continue with the task currently under way and thus wanted to stop the disk drive, you would probably press a special key or a special combination of keys. The monitor program would take notice. And because it was programmed to respond to this particular bit pattern, it would shut down the disk drive and await your next instruction.

## The BIOS and Monitor Are Not Enough

We know what the BIOS does, and we have a general idea of what the monitor does. Now, how does the computer know how to handle its disk drives? Suppose you've typed a letter with a word processing program and want to record it on a floppy disk so you'll be able to retrieve it later. The information exists inside your machine. It's all set to go. But how does the machine know where to start physically recording on the disk? How can it be sure that by recording the letter you wrote today it won't be writing over—and thus eliminating—the first draft of that short story you were going to send into *Playboy*?

The specifics are different, but in general, the problems are of the same type faced by the machine when you want it to display a character on the video screen. It can't just *do* it. It's got to be told how to do it and where to do it. It's got to check to see what's already been recorded on the disk, find space for your letter, and command the disk drive read/write head to move to a certain location and begin the recording.

Once again, we run into the inability of a computer to do anything without explicit programming instructions. And once again, special modules have been created to handle the chore. This is where the "basic disk operating system" or BDOS (pronounced "bee-doss") module of the DOS package fits in. (If you've got a cassette recorder instead of a floppy disk drive, you're not off the hook. The specifics are different, but the problems are the same and must be handled by a cassette or tape operating system.)

Floppy disks are more complex than video screens and keyboards and thus cannot be handled by a simple "disk drive driver" program. And, as mentioned at the beginning of the chapter, the term "DOS" is frequently used by computerists to refer to the operating system in general and not just to the BDOS or disk-related portion of it.

*By His Bootstraps*

There is one final problem to be solved and that's the fact that typically only the BIOS is hard-wired into a ROM inside the computer. All the other operating system modules—the monitor, DOS, and some small programs we haven't considered—normally reside on a floppy disk and must be brought into the machine shortly after it is turned on.

We should point out here that it doesn't have to be this way. There is no technical reason why the entire operating system couldn't be hard-wired into one or more ROM chips. Indeed, in most notebook-sized, battery-powered computers, that is exactly how things are handled. But a "desktop," "home," or "personal" computer is a different product. It is designed to provide a wide range of flexibility. Hard-wiring a complete OS or DOS into the machine wouldn't eliminate the possibility of using a different operating system. But, as we'll see later, there are many reasons why it usually makes more sense to put just the BIOS in ROM and "bring in the rest of the system from disk."

**SoftTip:** It's a minor point, but you might as well learn the lingo. Computerists frequently speak of "going out to disk," "writing a program to disk," or bringing something "in from disk." Just as the word *the* is rarely used when referring to DOS, the word *a* is rarely used when referring to disk I/O.

The operating system module responsible for bringing the rest of the system in from disk is called a "bootstrap loader." Like the BIOS, it is hard-wired into ROM, so it is activated as soon as the power is switched on. It's a very simple program that essentially says, "Start Disk drive *A* (or *0* or *1* . . . whatever). Look for the first system program on the disk, and start reading it into memory."

That's all the bootstrap loader does. Typically, the first program brought into the system will then take over and pull in other modules. The operating system programs hit the system like a commando team parachuting behind the lines to seize an enemy bridgehead. They get in there, mesh with the BIOS, and they *take charge:*

"Kieling! Can you handle the video over there?"

"Let's see, lieutenant . . . 80-column . . . memory mapped . . . standard controls. Sure, lieutenant, I can drive this sucker."

"Very well. Put Grawbowski on the printer and Jackson on the keyboard. I'll get down to the BASIC. And Kieling . . . "

"Yes, lieutenant?"

"Be sure to check back with me every nanosecond or so. Let's go."

Once the operating system is in control, the computer is ready to start executing programs. The system—in this case the computer and all its peripheral equipment—is "up and running" and ready to go. What has happened, of course, is that the machine has virtually pulled itself up by its bootstraps. And if you haven't guessed it already, this is where the term to "boot the system" or to "boot a program" comes from.

*The Software Map—Version 1.1*

We're now in a position to update and expand the software map outline presented earlier. So here it is:

### Software Map—Version 1.1.

I. System software
A. Operating system
  1. BIOS (basic input/output system)
    a. Hard-wired into ROM chip
    b. Consists of various device drivers

*The Software Map—Version 1.1 continued*

 2. Bootstrap loader
  a. Hard-wired into ROM chip
  b. Responsible for turning on disk drive and bringing in other OS modules
 3. Monitor program—the "traffic cop"
 4. BDOS (basic disk operating system)
 5. Other system modules (not discussed)

B. Disk-related "utility" programs
 1. Programs often loaded in at the same time as DOS
  a. Format a disk
  b. Copy a file or a disk
  c. Print or display a complete file on screen
 2. Programs residing on disk and brought in as needed
  a. Check disk capacity
  b. Compare two disks
  c. Etc.

C. "Extras" for programmers—strictly speaking, not system software. Typically brought in from disk as called for.
 1. Line editor
 2. Linker
 3. Debugger
 4. Etc.

II. Applications programs
A. Word processing
B. Games
C. Spreadsheet
D. Database management
E. Etc.

III. Programming languages

### Operating Systems and Software Selection

Entire books have been written on microcomputer operating systems, how they work, and what they do. But unless you plan to do a lot of programming yourself, they probably won't be of much interest to you. For the majority of computer users, there is rarely any need to see, work with, or even be aware of the operating systems their machines are using.

The only times you really need to come into contact with an operating system are when you are doing things like copying material from one disk to another, ordering the system to display and/or print out the contents of a file, requesting a "directory" (table of contents) of a disk, and performing other routine chores. The specific commands may differ, but all operating systems include these functions, and they all work in pretty much the same way.

For most people, the most important consideration regarding any operating system is the question, *What applications programs are available to run under its control?* From a software user's standpoint, an operating system can and should be viewed as a means to an end:

"You say that hot new personal finance program that's been getting rave reviews in all the magazines will only run under the control of the LDOS operating system on the Radio Shack Model III? Okay, fine. I've got a Mod III. How much is LDOS and what other programs will it let me run?"

"Yes, I'm sure there are important differences between LDOS and the TRSDOS system that came with my computer. But frankly, it really doesn't matter to me. I'm much more interested in what applications programs have been written to run under each operating system."

*Money-saving "Run Time" Packages*

Operating systems, like all other software programs, vary in price. The *T*andy *R*adio *S*hack Model III computer comes with TRSDOS® ("triss-doss") as part of the package. TRSDOS is the Model III's "standard" operating system. LDOS® ("ell-doss"), a trademark of Logical Systems, Inc., is one of a number of other operating systems designed to run on the Model III. LDOS lists for about $170 and, like all other non-TRSDOS systems, it is not supplied with your computer but must be purchased separately. The same situation exists for virtually every other brand of computer.

Fortunately, it is not always necessary to buy a complete operating system package in order to use a particular applications program. Some software houses supply what are called "run time" versions of the operating system their software is designed to be used with. Run time packages are normally placed on the same disk that contains the applications program. At the time you run the program, they are brought in by the bootstrap loader just as any other OS is. The difference is that run time versions can only be used with that particular program, and usually they contain only those portions of the complete operating system that the applications program needs.

This is a very sensible, consumer-oriented approach. The only problem is that not enough software houses use it. One of the reasons for this is cost. A company that wants to provide a run time version of some other firm's operating system must pay that other firm a licensing fee or a royalty for each copy of the program it sells. That, of course, adds to the price of the first company's software, making it appear more expensive than competing products. In the highly competitive software market, even the appearance of a higher price is not something to be taken lightly by a firm.

---

**SoftTip:** If you look at the total cost, however, a slightly more expensive applications program that comes equipped with a run time operating system will almost always end up costing less than an equivalent program selling for less but requiring you to buy a complete OS in order to run it.

---

*The Crucial Question: Will the Program Run on My Machine?*

When you're considering buying a particular program, the main thing you want to know is whether you can use it on your computer. Unfortunately, there isn't always a simple answer to that question. Ads and reviews will almost always tell you what computer(s) the program is written for and what operating system is required. (If they don't, the copywriters and reviewers should be unceremoniously shot at dawn.) But the printer, the video display, and other hardware you are using can be a major factor. There are so many different hardware configurations that it would be impossible to cite each one individually.

Then too, some of the requirements that are cited can be a bit cryptic: "Requires Apple II with Microsoft SoftCard . . . " "Runs on the IBM/PC with a XEDEX Baby Blue card . . . " "For Commodore PET computers equipped with a SoftBox from Small Systems Engineering." What on earth are they talking about? (We'll see in a moment.)

There is also the problem of "media compatibility." Media is whatever material the program is recorded on. It could be a cassette tape, a floppy disk, or a firmware cartridge. Obviously, if your system doesn't have a disk drive, a program must be available as a cartridge or on cassette tape in order for you to be able to use it.

Not so obviously, but just as important, is the fact that even if the program is issued on a floppy disk, you may not be able to run it on a disk-drive-equipped machine. We won't go into detail here, but it's important to realize that a "standard" 5¼-inch floppy disk must be "formatted" before anything can be recorded on it. Magnetic signals must be placed on the disk to divide up the available space in a certain way—and there are about 95 different ways or different formats in use today. If the program is only available on disks using a format your machine cannot read, the media would not be "compatible" with your system.

*Upside/Downside*

Clearly all of this is absurd—particularly in an industry that, according to a recent study by International Resource Development, expects to have sold over 50 million personal computers by 1992. It's almost as if the Red Queen in *Alice in Wonderland* had dreamed up the ground rules for an entire industry.

It is true that if you stick with widely used—and therefore widely supported—hardware from major manufacturers and if you limit your software purchases to programs produced by well-established software firms, you can reduce the confusion and avoid most potential problems. Yet even if you take the major manufacturer/major software house route, there still is no guarantee that you'll be able to run absolutely everything.

That's the negative side of the software market as it exists today and as it is likely to remain for several years to come. On the upside, there is the innovation and excitement of a burgeoning market so full of fresh ideas that it sometimes appears as though nothing is impossible. No sooner will some authority state that you can't do thus and so for such and such reasons than some clever programmer will find a way around the problem. Unfortunately, things are moving so fast and developments are so widespread that even full-time professional computer experts have a difficult time keeping up. There is a price to pay for all of this innovation: lack of uniform standards, lack of assured software compatibility, and the previously noted absurd degree of confusion.

To boil it all down, any time you buy anything—be it hardware or software—there are two major paths you can choose to follow: the tried and reasonably true or the innovative and potentially uncertain. If you go with major manufacturers and software houses, you will reduce the confusion about whether a program will run or not to a minimum. But major firms can be slow to adopt new ideas. (IBM, the quintessence of "tried and true," did not enter the personal computer market until November of 1981, nearly seven years after the first Apple computer was introduced.) Consequently, you may not be able to do everything that you want to do with your computer using just major sources.

If you choose the second alternative, you will probably be able to find the hardware and the software to do just about anything you want to do with your computer. And if it's not available today, wait. An ad for it will probably appear in the next issue of *PC World, Personal Computing*, or any of the dozens of other microcomputer magazines and publications. Unfortunately, connecting the hardware or "implementing" (running) the software may not be easy. You may have to deal with many confusing points and questions before you reach your goal.

The two paths are not mutually exclusive, of course. Either way, though, you'll have to ask and understand certain basic questions. And

that brings us back to where we started. One of the first questions you must ask when considering a program is, what operating system does it run under?
Other key questions include:

- Is there a version of that operating system available for your brand of computer (operating system and microprocessor compatibility)?
- Is your hardware configuration compatible with the program (hardware compatibility)?
- Is the program available or can it be placed on a disk or other media that your computer can read (media compatibility)?

**Operating System and Microprocessor Compatibility**

*The Tyranny of the CPU*
In discussing personal computer operating systems, the one thing we have not considered up to this point is where the machine's CPU fits in the scheme of things. As with everything else about a computer, it sits smack dab at the center. One must never forget that the microprocessor CPU chip *is* the computer.

As we mentioned in Chapter 1, an applications program must be written with a particular CPU chip in mind. The program cannot demand that the CPU do something it's not capable of. It can't tell the chip to execute an instruction that is not part of its instruction set. The same rule applies to operating systems and, for that matter, to most programming languages. At the very least, an existing programming language must be modified (expanded, contracted, edited, or rewritten) to match the requirements of each computer's CPU. But since they're even more intimately involved with the CPU and what it does, operating systems, like applications programs, must usually be written from scratch for a particular microprocessor.

That fact has lots of implications. Among other things, it means that if you're an electronics company and you want to manufacture a computer, the operating system that will run on that computer must be a major consideration from the very start. Actually, personal computers tend to be "assembled" as opposed to "manufactured" by the firm that markets them. The only major component of the IBM/PC that's actually manufactured by IBM, for example, is the keyboard. Everything else—disk drives, monitors, printer, memory boards, etc.—is made by some other firm and shipped to a plant in Boca Raton, Florida for final assembly by IBM workers and technicians. The same could be said of many other brands.

Of all the decisions a manufacturer makes when designing a new machine, the selection of the CPU chip is undoubtedly the crucial one, because the chip will influence all subsequent decisions about how the machine is to be designed. And, in addition to questions of cost, an assured source of supply, and the chip's capabilities, the question of an operating system will play an important role in the decision.

In effect, a computer company has two choices. Either it can build its machine around a particular microchip and write its own operating system, or it can purchase the right to use a preexisting operating system and design it into the machine almost as if the OS were a disk drive or some other component part of the final assembly.

If the company decides to license a preexisting operating system, it will naturally want to evaluate it the way it would any other piece of "equipment." Does it take full advantage of the powers of the CPU? How well is it likely to work with the hardware and peripherals the system will contain? What are its strengths? What are its weaknesses? And so forth.

The prime question, however, will always be, *What applications software is already available to run under the operating system?* For a computer manufacturer, nothing is more vital than the answer to this question. It's far more than a matter of avoiding the cost of producing and offering its own programs. Today, the success or failure of the computer as a product will usually hinge on what and how much software is immediately available for it to use. With so much at stake, it's no wonder that most manufacturers opt for a preexisting operating system and build their machines around the chip it was designed to work with.

*The "Adaptor Plug" Approach*

We'll look at the preexisting, "off the shelf" operating systems most manufacturers choose, products known as CP/M and MS-DOS, later. Right now, it's important to consider how a computer company "implements" an operating system once it has made its choice.

There are many ways it can be done. As mentioned earlier, with notebook-sized computers, the entire OS is usually hard-wired into a ROM chip. That's really the only practical way to do things, since notebook-sized computers like the Epson HX-20 or the Radio Shack 100 are meant to be ready to use instantly, the moment the power is switched on. They're intended to be used as portable "peripherals" for full-sized personal computers and thus have neither the disk drives nor the flexibility of their larger brethren.

---

**SoftTip:** Battery-powered, notebook-sized computers could be one of the most important personal computer developments in years. Certainly they are already one of the most remarkable. They have lots of uses, but here's just one example. If you were on a trip you might use one to write memos and other correspondence. Then, once you were back in the office, you could "dump" the material you've written into your main personal computer for "massaging" and printing by a word processing program.

Many notebook-sized computers are also capable of communicating over the telephone, meaning you could transmit what you'd written back to the office once you arrived at your destination. Or you could access a remote database to obtain the information you need or pick up your "electronic mail." Of course, you could access your firm's mainframe computer as well. And, while it may not be terribly practical, many machines will also let you write and run BASIC programs.

With a notebook-sized computer you can carry what amounts to a major portion of your main system around with you in a briefcase. And, unlike the Osborne, Kaypro, Compaq, and other full-power "transportable" computers, you never have to worry about finding a place to plug it in.

---

A full-sized personal computer, in contrast, *must* offer a wide range of flexibility and choice. Consequently, manufacturers usually avoid putting the complete system in ROM. Instead, they use what might be called "The Adaptor Plug Approach." If you think of the little adaptor plug you use when you want to put a three-prong plug into a wall socket with only two slots, you'll grasp the idea immediately.

Typically, computer manufacturers will design the BIOS so that one "end" of it "plugs into" the computer's CPU and hardware. This "interface" between the hardware and the BIOS is always highly customized, for as we've seen, the BIOS must mate and deal with the specific requirements of the various devices that make up the computer.

The other end of the BIOS is where the operating system proper will "plug in." If the computer company is going to use a preexisting operating system, it will make every effort to keep this BIOS/OS interface as standardized as possible. Although every preexisting operating system must be "configured" or slightly modified to run on a given model of computer, ideally these changes will be kept to a minimum.

So far, we have the BIOS plugged into the hardware and one end of the operating system plugged into the BIOS. Now the question is, What plugs into the other end of the operating system? The answer is, Just about anything you want. This is the place where you as the user "plug into" the computer, telling the operating system to tell the BIOS to tell the hardware to print a character or display it on the screen or do something else.

This particular spot is called the "user interface," and it's where, at last, man meets machine. More importantly, it is where man's *programs* meet the machine. Software written to run under a particular operating system "plugs into" that operating system on your machine at this point. Thus, if a programmer is familiar with the user interface of a given operating system, he or she can write a program to run under that operating system without worrying about the specific hardware requirements of each brand of computer. Any model or brand of computer capable of running the OS will be able to run the same program.

---

**SoftTip:** That at least is the theory. And in many cases, it is the reality as well. Unfortunately, however, you can't assume, just because your machine can use, say, the CP/M operating system, that any CP/M-based program will work on your computer. Everything depends on the specific program.

If the program needs 64K of RAM to do its job, for example, it won't run "as is" on a computer with only 32K. If the program occupies 160K of space on a floppy disk, and your computer formats disk so that 90K is the maximum disk space available, the program will not run on your machine. These points are fairly obvious. But many far less obvious "incompatibilities" can make it impossible to run such a program. A good example is the VisiCalc spreadsheet program for the Hewlett-Packard 125 computer. Although it is CP/M-based, the program cannot be run on other CP/M machines because it is written to use the second microprocessor the HP 125 contains for putting characters on the screen.

Generally, it is best to view operating system compatibility as an indication that a program *may* work on your machine. But under no circumstances should you automatically assume that every program written to run under CP/M, MS-DOS, or some other OS will run "as is" on your particular equipment. Thus, whenever possible, you should insist on actually seeing a program run on your brand or model of computer before you buy.

---

*OS "Versions" and Upward and Downward Compatibility*

If you've already got a computer, you have most assuredly already interacted with your machine's operating system and its user interface.

If you don't have a system yet, all you really need to know is that the user interface consists of a number of commands that call upon utility modules designed to accomplish certain tasks.

For example, suppose you want to find out how much room is left on a floppy disk. If you were running CP/M, you would type in the STAT (for "status") command. If you were running MS-DOS, you would type in CHKDSK (for "check disk"). If you were running TRSDOS on a Radio Shack computer, you would type in FREE (for "Free Space"). The output generated by these commands varies slightly—some give you more detailed information than others—but basically they all accomplish the same thing. Each one will tell you how much room is left on a particular floppy disk.

The user interface contains lots of other commands as well, each of which will be explained in your operating system manual. The important thing for our purposes here, however, is not the commands themselves but the fact that they always remain the same. Or, to put it another way, an operating system's user interface tends to remain relatively constant.

In many respects, the software companies that produce the operating systems computer manufacturers license for their machines view the user interface as sacred. And the reason is simple. If a software house were to come out with a completely new user interface, none of the programs written for the old user interface would work with it. Programmers depend on the user interface for a given operating system remaining the same.

That's not to say that operating systems can't be updated. It happens all the time. But when the originator of an operating system comes out with an update, the important changes usually involve adding *more* commands and *more* features, not changing the commands that already exist. Whenever any change is made to the user interface, the company will signify the update by changing the "version" number.

Version numbers are usually written in the form "N.N." Typically, "Version 1.0" means that this is the very first commercially available version of the product. If you saw the designation "V. 1.1" for the same product, you could assume that some minor changes had been made in the original 1.0 version. However, if you saw "V. 2.0," you could assume that *major* additions had been made since V. 1.0 came out.

Here's a good example. When the IBM/PC was introduced in the fall of 1981, it came with PC-DOS (a.k.a. MS-DOS) Version 1.0. By about the middle of 1982, however, PC-DOS V. 1.1 was announced. This was identical to the first version, but among other things, it made it possible for someone to use double-sided disk drives with their IBM computer.

**SoftTip:** As its name implies, a single-sided disk drive unit reads and writes on only one side of the disk. A single-sided drive on the IBM lets you store 160K on each disk. A double-sided drive has *two* read/write heads and can put 160K on each *side* of each disk, for a total of 320K per disk. This is no mean feat, and commands and programming had to be added to the operating system to make it possible.

In early 1983, PC-DOS 2.0 (pronounced "two point oh") was announced. This represented a major modification. In addition to including new programming to support a "hard disk" drive capable of storing up to 10 *million* bytes (10 megabytes) or more, PC-DOS 2.0 included so many new features and commands that the size of the instruction manual more than doubled.

It's important to emphasize, however, that all of the commands that formed the user interface in PC-DOS 1.0 were still part of the user interface of Version 2.0. The newer version simply had more commands and features. This meant that applications programs written to run under 1.0 would still run under 2.0. They just wouldn't be able to take advantage of all of the new features.

**SoftTip:** As you may remember from our discussion of microchip families, any time something older works with something newer and more powerful, the older item is said to be "upwardly compatible" with the new item. For the sake of simplicity, we haven't gone into all of the details of upward compatibility. You might find, for example, that newer DOS versions format disks in a different way. Apple DOS 3.3 allows for 16 sectors per track, whereas Apple DOS 3.2 permitted only 13. Similarly, PC-DOS 2.0 formats disks to store about 10% more information than PC-DOS 1.1.

Generally, this is nothing to worry about. Apple provides a program called MUFFIN to let you make the conversion. And PC-DOS 2.0 can read and write to disks formatted under 1.1. Upward compatibility may thus not be quite as simple as one would like, but one way or another, it will almost always be maintained.

The same notation is often used for applications programs. There are versions 1.3, 2.1, 3.2, etc., of many programs. And, as with operating systems, usually a change in the number to the left of the decimal point indicates major changes or "enhancements," while the number to the right of the point indicates minor improvements and tinkerings. In any case, there are no hard and fast rules about what constitutes a "major" or a "minor" change. Nor does any independent organization or body govern these matters.

## Hardware Compatibility

*Brand Names and Briggs & Stratton*

Have you ever noticed how many different brands of power mowers use the same Briggs & Stratton engine? They may be rotary or reel mowers, they may be "rear baggers" or side-discharge; they may be "self-powered" or the type you have to push. But they are all built around the *same* engine. With computers, it's the differences in the hardware that surrounds the same CPU engine that makes each machine different, and it's the operating system's job to smooth out those differences so that each computer presents an identical face to the world when under the OS's control.

Unfortunately, however, the fact that your machine has the microprocessor chip and the operating system that an applications program needs is no guarantee that it will run on your computer. That probably makes things sound worse than they really are, since if you've got microprocessor and operating system compatibility, there are lots of programs you'll be able to run. Still, it is important to be aware that hardware *can* be a hang-up with some programs.

For example, some programs require a certain amount of RAM and won't run if you don't have it. Here are a few other examples:

- Some programs, like the IBM/PC version of the popular integrated spreadsheet program Lotus 1-2-3®, will work only if your machine has double-sided disk drives. Other programs may work with two single-sided drives.
- A graphics program may produce beautiful pictures and charts on your screen, but if your printer isn't designed for graphics printing, you won't be able to generate a hard copy of what your program has produced.
- Some programs require video monitors and printers capable of displaying 80 characters per line (80 columns), and some will work with either 40 or 80 columns.
- A program that takes advantage of special keys on the keyboard of one computer will obviously present problems if you were to run it on a machine that lacked any of those keys.

*How to Deal with Hardware Hang-ups*

There are other hardware incompatibilities, of course, but many of them can be overcome one way or another. What you want to avoid is buying a program, opening the package, and only then discovering that it won't work on your machine as it is currently equipped or "configured." If this happens, you may have a hard time getting your money back. Because programs and instruction manuals can be copied, software retailers and mail order houses generally frown on giving refunds for opened software packages. They take much the same view that a merchant selling stereo records would take if you were to ask for a refund on an album that had been opened.

Of course, just because a program won't work on your current equipment configuration doesn't mean that you can't add the necessary hardware. But you don't want to spend six or seven hundred dollars on a software package only to discover—surprise!—that you'll have to invest a like amount of money in a brace of double-sided disk drives or other hardware.

So how can you tell before you buy? The answer is that *you* shouldn't have to. The manufacturer or the retailer should be the one doing the telling. Every ad, every piece of product literature should include a section labelled "System Requirements" that lists everything a computer must have to be able to run a particular program.

If this information is not provided, a little alarm should go off in your head. Not a major alarm, just a prudent note of caution. When the system requirements are not included in an ad, it may be simple carelessness on the part of the copywriter. The lack of information may be the result of an assumed minimum "standard" system configuration for a particular brand of computer—one disk drive and 48K, two drives and 64K, whatever "most people" tend to buy. There could be other, less savory reasons as well. Some merchants are not above advertising a software package as a "come on" in hopes of selling you the (unmentioned) hardware you need to run it once you bite on the ad.

Ads are one thing. Product literature is something else. There is no excuse for a software house not including system requirement information in the brochures it publishes describing its product. And there is no excuse for a computer store salesperson not being able to tell you—in detail—what hardware is necessary to run a program he or she wants to sell you.

---

**SoftTip:** In any case, as we'll see in Chapter 8, your first question should *always* be, What hardware is required to run this program?

*"Installing" a Program*

Sometimes the software you buy will include a special piece of programming designed to overcome certain hardware hang-ups by letting you customize the program to your computer configuration. These are usually called "installation" modules or programs and they typically deal with printers and video displays. They can usually be found in software that makes extensive use of either of these devices.

For example, a truly full-featured word processing program will take advantage of all of the special features a printer offers: underlining, bold print or "overstrike," compressed or expanded characters, super- and subscripts, etc. This involves much more interaction with the printer than the uncomplicated printouts required by many other applications programs. Consequently, the program can't simply say, "Print this character on the printer." It must say, "Print this character and print it in compressed print mode."

To get a printer to print compressed letters, you or the program must send it a special code that says, "Okay, until you hear otherwise, print every letter in compressed form." The problem is that different brands of printers "need to see" different codes to get them to do compressed printing or to take advantage of any of their other features. And that's where the installation program comes in.

The first time you boot some word processing programs, you will be presented with a listing or "menu" of various brands of printers and asked to enter the number that corresponds to your own printer. The disk drive containing the program disk will then come on for a bit while the module containing all of the proper printer codes for your machine is "plugged into" the main program.

---

**SoftTip:** What do you do if the printer you own is not among the choices offered by the installation program? The easiest thing to do is to ask the people who sold you the program. Indeed, if you purchased the program at a retail store and paid full price for it, then you have every right to insist that the retailer install the program for you before you leave the store. This kind of service is part of what you're paying for when you buy a program at list price. If the dealer balks, you should walk out of the store and take your business elsewhere. His refusal is a good indication that he won't be willing to answer your questions as you use the program or provide any of the other support to which you're entitled.

If you bought the program at a discount through a mail order house, you may be able to contact them with your question. They may or may not be willing to help you. It all depends upon the firm, its policy, and even who happens to pick up the phone when you call.

As a last resort, you might try installing each printer module and testing the results until you find one that (with luck) matches your own printer's requirements.

---

Video display installation modules work the same way, though they're necessary for somewhat different reasons. Remember all the rigamarole the BIOS has to go through to put a character on the screen? Well, that "Where's the cursor? What's the position of the next line? Who's on first?" interrogatory routine is fine for some programs, but it takes too much time for a VisiCalc-like program or a word processing program. Consequently, many programs like these cut the BIOS out completely and "talk" directly to the video display.

This means that such programs do not use the operating system to smooth out the differences among the various brands of video displays. Instead, the programs must be able to "talk" to each brand of display in its own language. When this is necessary, the video installation module will present you with a menu of major brands of video displays or monitors.

Here again, you should ask about what video displays the program supports before you buy. If you don't, you may find yourself in a position similar to a writer who was once asked to review a word processing program for a computer magazine. The program arrived, he put it into his machine, and the program's copyright notice and other text appeared on the screen. The only problem was that the text was completely unreadable. Something was obviously there, but it was impossible to make it out.

There was nothing wrong with the monitor. It worked perfectly with other programs. Clearly a call to the software house was in order. The customer service representative who answered the phone was unable to understand the problem, let alone suggest a solution. But a second phone call to the vice president of marketing produced the answer: Although the program "supported" (was designed to work with) several brands of video monitors, the BMC brand monitor the writer was using was not among them. But, of course, the VP hastened to add, "future versions of the program will fully support the BMC and most other monitors."

## Media Compatibility

Even if everything else is copacetic, your plans to run a particular software program can still be derailed if the program is not available on a recording medium that your system can read. As mentioned earlier, gross media incompatibilities are obvious: You can't run a program that's available only on a floppy disk unless you have a disk drive; you can't run an 8-inch disk on a machine equipped with 5¼-inch drives; you can't run a double-sided disk on a single-sided drive.

---

**SoftTip:** You might think that if you had enough internal memory, you could place a double-sided disk in a single-sided drive, read the contents of one side into memory, and then flip the disk over and read the contents of the second side into memory. What makes this impossible is the fact that double-sided drives read and write to each side alternately. They'll put one piece of information on the first side and a companion piece of information on the second side. They don't start at the beginning of one side, go straight through until it's full, and then switch to the second side.

---

What's not so obvious is that while a handful of 5¼-inch floppies may all appear to be identical to the human eye, to a computer each can look quite different. The differences concern the way each disk has been formatted. As you probably know, floppy disks come to you from the factory completely blank.

Before you can use the disks on your computer, each must be properly "formatted," and it's easy to see why. If you put a completely blank disk into your machine and told the system to record some information on it, how would the computer know where to begin? To the computer, the blank disk would represent a vast uncharted sea of milk-chocolate-colored magnetic oxide. It would have no idea where to put something and probably couldn't find it again if it did.

The disk formatting program that all disk operating systems include solves this problem by setting up a framework on the disk. The framework consists of recorded magnetic signals that mark the disk off into concentric tracks resembling the circular waves you see when you toss a pebble into a pool of quiet water. The tracks themselves are marked off into sectors of a uniform size. The sectors act like pigeonholes. Each has a given and easily identifiable location on the disk and each can store the same amount of data.

Finally, the formatting program will set aside certain sectors on every disk to hold special information. Some sectors may be used to hold the operating system programming, if you choose to place the system on the disk. And some sectors will hold the disk's "directory" or table of contents. The directory will always be put in the same location on every formatted disk. This way, the computer always knows right where to go to update the directory whenever you record or erase a file on the disk.

---

**SoftTip:** If a disk's directory gets "bombed" (erased or destroyed) due to a program or computer malfunction, you will not be able to read or use the files the disk contains even if they are intact. This can be a minor tragedy, but there may be hope. Sometimes a disk's directory can be rebuilt by hand. This requires a skilled computerist and may not be worth the effort. But it is a possibility you might look into if the files on the disk are irreplaceable. Before giving up, check with your computer retailer or users group to see if you can find someone to help you.

---

These are the essential things that must be done to any disk to prepare it to accept information. Where incompatibilities arise are in the specific way each computer sets up the disk format. Different formats put the operating system and disk directory in different sectors on the disk. And the number of tracks and sectors can vary widely. For example:

- The TRSDOS operating system on the TRS-80 Model III formats disks by dividing them into 40 tracks with 18 sectors per track, each of which is large enough to store 256 bytes of information.
- PC-DOS on the IBM/PC might take the identical floppy disk and format it to have 40 tracks with only 8 sectors per track, each of which can store 512 bytes of information.
- The Osborne 1 uses 40 tracks and 10 sectors of 256 bytes each, while the Apple running under Apple DOS 3.3 uses 35 tracks and 16 sectors of 256 bytes.

---

**SoftTip:** If you ever need to find out how many kilobytes of information a disk can store, multiply the number of tracks by the number of sectors by the number of bytes per sector. That's all there is to it. From the information above, for example, you can tell that disks formatted for the TRS-80 can hold 184,320 bytes (180K) and those for the IBM's single-sided drives, 163,840 bytes (160K).

**SoftTip:** The figures in the text above all refer to single-density disks. We'll look at the difference between single and double density in the next chapter. But if you include both forms, the number of tracks that different formats use can range from 35 to 80. There can be from 10 to 16 sectors. And the number of bytes per sector can range from 128 to 512. As technology improves, these numbers will undoubtedly increase.

*Why Are There So Many Formats?*

Earlier we said that there are probably 95 different formats in use for 5¼ floppy disks, none of which is likely to be compatible with any other. The most significant reason for all of this variety is undoubtedly the variety in disk drive hardware. Like printers and video displays, disk drive units have different capabilities and limitations.

Given the proper programming, some disk drives can read and write to disks in several formats. But other brands are physically incapable of creating and using more than one format. This is one hardware interface that an operating system cannot smooth out. The only alternative is to obtain a copy of the program on a disk that has been formatted to match the disk drive's requirements.

*Dealing with Media Incompatibility*

Most major software firms make their products available on disks formatted for many different machines. So as long as you make sure that you buy the disk that's right for your machine, you won't have a problem. If the format you need is not among those listed in the ad or product literature, you still may not be out of luck. Owing to space limitations, some firms cite only the most popular brands of computers when describing their software. In those cases, you might contact the firm, the mail order house, or your local dealer to see if a copy of the program is indeed available for your machine.

*The Data Communications Solution*

If you come up empty handed there, you may *still* not be out of luck, thanks to a relatively new software distribution technique. Because all of the various floppy disk formats are as big a headache for the software house as they are for you, some firms have begun shipping their products to dealers on a standard 8-inch disk. (Unlike the 5¼-inch variety, there *is* a standard and widely used format for 8-inch disks.) The package will also include an instruction manual for each copy of the program the dealer has agreed to purchase from the firm.

When you want to buy the program, the dealer will ask you what system you will be running it on and what disk format you need. Assuming he has your model of computer in the store, he will connect it by cable to a computer capable of reading the 8-inch program distribution disk and transmit a copy of the program to your type of computer. The program will thus be recorded on a disk your machine can use, and that's the disk you'll take home with you, along with one of the instruction manuals.

This technique has yet to gain widespread use, and the jury is still out on whether it will become the standard way of doing things in the future. The important thing is, though, that it can be done and is being done at various retail outlets. If the dealer doesn't have your particular model of computer, you may be able to bring your own system into the store. The major caveat is that your own machine will have to be equipped for data communications. Any dealer who offers this service will be able to tell you what that means.

### "Standard" Operating Systems: CP/M and MS-DOS

It is impossible to leave the subject of operating systems and software/hardware compatibility without looking at the matter of "standard" operating systems. Earlier, we said that, faced with the need to offer an operating system with their equipment, computer manufacturers could choose between writing their own or licensing a preexisting system for use on their machines. But it's important to point out that this choice has not always existed. In fact, by any time standards but those of the computer industry, it is a very recent development.

For example, the Apple II computer is built around the 6502 microprocessor chip manufactured by MOS Technology. When the first Apple II was manufactured in 1977, however, the firm really had little choice but to write its own operating system. But Apple had the advantage of being practically the only game in town, and if software was going to be written, much of it was going to be for the Apple II.

It is a fascinating aspect of the software market that most of the programs originally written to support the Apple II (and many other personal computers) were written first by hobbyists and then by hobbyists-turned-entrepreneurs. VisiCalc, the popular electronic spreadsheet program, which more than anything else is responsible for the success of the Apple computer, was created by Dan Bricklin and Bob Frankston, two men in their late twenties. It was introduced in 1979 and marketed out of a third-floor Cambridge, Massachusetts apartment belonging to Bricklin's Harvard Business School classmate, Dan Flystra. No one guessed that the firm would shortly become a multimillion dollar company.

At about the same time, other hobbyists and amateur programmers were playing with machines built around the Intel 8080 microprocessor chip and experimenting with floppy disk drives that had recently become available for their often home-built computers. A disk operating system was clearly needed, and for many individuals a system called CP/M for "Control Program/Microcomputer" filled the bill.

As mentioned earlier, CP/M was created by a young man named Gary Kildall. Kildall worked for Intel and wrote CP/M in his spare time, but when he offered it to his employer, he was told that it had no commercial possibilities. So he formed a company originally called Intergalactic Digital Research and began to market the system to the nation's computer hobbyists at $70 a copy. That was in 1975, and at the time CP/M was the only microcomputer DOS on the market.

Opinions vary widely on CP/M. Some individuals condemn it for its all but incomprehensible user's manual and for the fact that it was originally written for a paper tape (as opposed to a floppy disk) based system and still retains vestiges of those earlier versions. Others are equally passionate in support of CP/M, and in truth, any operating system that calls its debugging module "DDT" ("Dynamic Debugging Tool") can't be all bad.

Regardless of one's opinion, however, it is no slight to say that CP/M was clearly the right software in the right place at the right time. Consequently, it became, to use the stock phrase, the "de facto standard"—in the world of 8-bit personal computers.

*The Eight-Bit DOS of Choice*
The hobbyists and computer buffs adopted CP/M and wrote their programs to run under its control. In a matter of months, there was a large library of CP/M programs. (In Chapter 12, we'll show you how to obtain over 2,000 of them free of charge.) Taking notice of this fact, more and more computer manufacturers began to build their machines around the Intel 8080 or its cousin, the Zilog Z80 microprocessor, and to license CP/M as their standard operating system. Today, there are more than 300 different models of computers capable of running CP/M and CP/M-based applications programs. And, as at least one authority has said, "You couldn't offer an eight-bit computer system today without a CP/M base—it would be suicidal."

*Z80s, SoftCards, Baby Blue, and CP/M for Word Processors*
Wait a minute. We've been talking about CP/M and the Intel 8080 chip. Where'd this "Z80" come from?

It came from a phenomenon that's apparently endemic to Silicon Valley and other high-tech hangouts. The microchip industry has a long history of companies dividing like cells going through mitosis. First there was the 8080 chip from Intel. (The name is a compression of the words "Intelligent Electronics.") Then three of the designers of that chip left Intel to form a company called Zilog.

The firm's first product? The Z80, of course. And you can imagine what other chip it resembled, and resembled so closely that much of the software written for the 8080 can run "as is" on a Z80-based system. Running 8080-based CP/M on a Z80 is thus not much of a problem. To add to the fun, CP/M will also run on a computer built around an Intel 8085, a combination chip that incorporates a complete 8080 microprocessor in its design.

To summarize, CP/M, or CP/M-80 as it is now officially known, is written to run on the Intel 8080, the Intel 8085, and the Zilog Z80 microprocessor chips. So where does that leave you if you've got an Apple II or a Commodore PET, both of which are built around the MOS 6502 chip and you want to access the vast numbers of CP/M applications programs? Out in the cold, that's where—unless . . . unless you can somehow get one of those CP/M CPUs into your machine.

There is so much CP/M software available and the demand is so great that a number of companies have produced plug-in circuit boards or "cards" containing a Z80 or an 8080 microprocessor. Perhaps the best known of these is the SoftCard™ offered by Microsoft Corporation for Apple computers. A firm called Small Systems Engineering offers a similar Z80 board called a SoftBox for Commodore PET owners. Memory Merchant offers the Shuffleboard III for TRS-80 Model III owners. (The Mod III already contains a Z80 chip, but for technical reasons, it can't be directly used by CP/M.) And XEDEX Corporation sells a Baby Blue board for the IBM/PC.

---

**SoftTip:** These are only a few of the board makers. Your computer retailer should be able to provide more information on such products, but if not, here are the addresses of the firms mentioned above:

Microsoft Corporation
10700 Northup
Bellevue, WA 89004

Small Systems Engineering
222B View Street
Mountain View, CA 94041

Memory Merchant
14666 Doolittle Drive
San Leandro, CA 94577

XEDEX Corporation
1345 Sixth Avenue
New York, NY 10105

Most plug-in CP/M boards also include additional memory chips and all come with the software necessary to activate them. When activated, the Z80 chip takes over the computer, either ignoring the machine's primary chip or putting it to a different use. List prices vary from a low of about $300 for the Shuffleboard III to a high of $895 for the SoftBox.

---

**SoftTip:** Those prices are virtually guaranteed to drop and may already be doing so. Still, even at a lower price, you should think long and hard before investing in one of them. In the first place, as eight-bit processors, they represent old technology. The current trend is clearly toward 16-bit machines. Second, virtually all worthwhile eight-bit software has been or is currently being "brought over" to the 16-bit "environment." Unless there is an eight-bit CP/M program that you've got to have immediately, or unless you've got so much tied up in your present equipment that replacing it is out of the question, it might make more sense to sell your eight-bit machine and replace it with a new model capable of running 16-bit CP/M.

---

*Dedicated Word Processors and CP/M*

Manufactured by such firms as Lanier, Wang, Xerox, CPT, NBI, and IBM, dedicated word processors can be thought of as personal computers with special keys, features, and software designed to make writing and editing especially easy. They are still computers, however, and many of them can be used to run CP/M software.

The procedure differs with the manufacturer, but generally there are two main approaches. If the word processor uses one of the CP/M chips (8080, 8085, Z80), as is the case with CPT word processors, then running CP/M is a relatively simple matter of purchasing a CP/M operating system disk and loading it into the machine. If the word processor does not have one of the CP/M chips, then the manufacturer (or some other vendor) will supply a plug-in circuit board similar to those discussed above.

---

**SoftTip:** A word of caution is in order here. The sales literature for CP/M packages designed to run on dedicated word processors will undoubtedly highlight the "vast library" of CP/M programs and imply that they will all become available to you. As we've seen, however, there is the matter of disk format and media compatibility to deal with. The programs may exist, but they may not be available on a disk that your word processor can read. In that case, you could find that you're limited to running just those CP/M programs sold by the manufacturer of your word processor.

In some cases, this is exactly what the word processor manufacturers have in mind.

---

**SoftTip:** Digital Research has combined forces with The Source to offer an online information service for CP/M users. To access this feature, select the Command Level from the first menu you see when you sign on to The Source. When you see the Command Level prompt (->), type MICROLINE. The following menu will then appear:

1 WELCOME TO MICROLINE

2 DIGITAL RESEARCH PRODUCT INFORMATION

3 INDEPENDENT SOFTWARE VENDOR (ISV) INFORMATION

4 MICROCOMPUTER HARDWARE INFORMATION <<* COMING SOON *>>

5 NEWS & UPCOMING EVENTS (Press releases, trade shows, seminars, etc.)

6 RESOURCES (USERS GROUPS, REFERENCE MATERIALS, ETC.)

Select an option or enter help: 6 <---We entered "6"

RESOURCES

1 USERS GROUPS

2 REFERENCE MATERIALS AND RECOMMENDED READING

3 THE EXPERTS SAY . . . (Comments from the industry leaders)

4 DIGITAL RESEARCH TECHNICAL SUPPORT SUBSCRIBER SERVICES

Select an option or enter help:

*Note:* To return to The Source Command Level, type QUIT. To return to The Source Main Menu, type QUIT and then type MENU when the Command Level prompt appears. For more information on using The Source, see *The Complete Handbook of Personal Computer Communications* by Alfred Glossbrenner.

---

*In the 16-Bit World*

It will be several years before one can say for certain, but it is possible that in the future, the period from 1975 through 1981 will be viewed as the Age of the Eight-Bit Computer. And it is possible that the Age of the 16-Bit Computer will be seen to have begun in November of 1981 when IBM introduced its personal computer.

As you know from the first chapter, computers that are built around a 16-bit microprocessor with 20 address-bus lines have the advantage of being able to use over a million bytes of memory, compared to the 64,000-byte maximum of an eight-bit machine. All indications are that this is the wave of the future and that the only development capable of derailing the trend toward 16-bit machines would be the introduction of affordable 32-bit computers.

The IBM/PC was the first major personal computer to be built around a 16-bit microprocessor, the Intel 8088. Like any other computer, the PC needed an operating system. Because it was IBM and because there was no "standard" operating system for 16-bit computers at the time, the company elected to take what was in effect the "in-house development" route. Actually, what IBM did was to commission Microsoft, the Seattle-based firm whose BASIC is the most widely used computer language in the world, to develop a 16-bit operating system on its behalf. The code was written by Tim Paterson, then a brilliant 23-year-old who had already written a preliminary OS when IBM came to call.

The resulting product, when purchased from IBM, is known as PC-DOS. But it is also sold by Microsoft under the name MS-DOS and by a firm called Lifeboat Associates as SB-86. All three products are the same. Today, any company wanting to build a computer around the Intel 8088 microprocessor has the option of licensing MS-DOS or SB-86 or writing its own operating system. But just as with CP/M in the eight-bit world, there really isn't much choice. A computer company using the Intel 8088 is virtually required to offer MS-DOS as its standard operating system, and for a very simple reason: IBM

It will come as no surprise to anyone that the three most magical letters in all computerdom are *I-B-M*. The firm has such clout, such marketing muscle, and is held in such high regard by potential computer buyers that when the company fired the first shot in what has been called the "Autumn Revolution" by announcing its PC in November of 1981, it reverberated around the world. Professional and amateur programmers alike immediately began to write software to support the PC. In many cases, individuals completely dropped the eight-bit projects they were working on to focus exclusively on the IBM.

And, of course, the operating system everyone began writing applications programs for was MS-DOS, the IBM "standard." It is doubtful that any other company could have done what IBM did—unilaterally set the standard for an entire generation of computers. Certainly, no one else could have accomplished it as quickly.

*What Happened to CP/M?*

When IBM announced its machine, a battle was immediately joined to determine whether CP/M or MS-DOS would become the de facto standard operating system of the 16-bit world. As the DOS chosen by IBM, MS-DOS clearly had a leg up. But Digital Research produced CP/M-86 and was not without certain advantages.

---

**SoftTip:** By now you may well be "chipped" to death and wonder why Intel, Zilog, and all the rest can't call their products "Joe" or "Sally" or at the very least name them the way automobiles are named. Anything but these endless strings of numbers. It's not possible to say when a computer will be built around a chip called "Joe" or "Firebird," but there *is* an explanation for all the *86-ing* that seems to be going on regarding the IBM and its Intel 8088 (CP/M-86, SB-86, etc.).

The Intel 8088 *is* an Intel 8086. The only difference is that the 8088 is limited to bringing in instructions and data in eight-bit chunks, while the 8086 can pull in 16 bits at the same time. Once the bits get inside, everything works the same.

---

The Intel 8088 chip chosen by IBM is similar enough to the Intel 8080 that CP/M was originally written for to make it relatively easy to translate many eight-bit CP/M programs. In fact, the bulk of the work can be performed by a special translation program. So the juggernaut of available CP/M software looked as if it might again be a deciding factor in establishing CP/M as the standard. IBM even offered CP/M-86 as an option, though it wasn't available until six months after the PC was introduced and at $240 was six times more expensive than MS-DOS.

---

**SoftTip:** Although the situation is rapidly changing, much of the software made available by independent vendors for the IBM and later, for other 16-bit machines, consisted of nothing more than translations of eight-bit programs. In the beginning, when there was very little 16-bit software around, that wasn't so bad. At least, it gave computer buyers something to run, and not incidentally, offered software vendors a chance to cash in on the growing popularity of the PC. It didn't much matter that an eight-bit program is still an eight-bit program and thus incapable of taking advantage of the increased memory addressing and other features that a 16-bit machine has to offer.

Today things are different. There is plenty of software written specifically to take advantage of the power and capabilities of a 16-bit microprocessor, and if you've got a 16-bit machine, you shouldn't settle for less. But with all the eight-bit stuff still on the market, how can you tell?

*SoftTip continued*

There is no pat answer, but one of the first things to do is check the reviews in the major computer magazines. Catalogue-type publications usually won't be able to tell you. It's not always the case, but often, if the program is being sold by a major software house, there's a good chance that it's a true 16-bit program. If the ads for the program mention a 64K *maximum* anything, then that may be an indication of eight-bit origins. Finally, the surest test is to see if an eight-bit version exists and compare the two side by side.

This is not to say that you should necessarily avoid all translated eight-bit programs. Sometimes you won't have a choice. But if your machine has 16-bit capabilities, you should make sure that the software you buy takes advantage of the fact whenever possible, particularly since software vendors won't charge you any less for an eight-bit program to run on your 16-bit machine.

The battle between CP/M-86 and MS-DOS raged for all of 1982 and on into 1983. Then somehow the conviction began to grow within the industry that CP/M had lost and MS-DOS had won. There were no major announcements, no clear-cut events one could point to. Perhaps the number of computer manufacturers adopting MS-DOS as their standard operating system and the amount of software issued to run under MS-DOS simply reached a critical mass. For whatever reason, this was the collective opinion of the industry. Not even Digital Research's decision in the spring of 1983 to offer CP/M-86 on its own at a price much lower than IBM could reverse the trend.

**SoftTip:** There is a story that people in the personal computer industry tell about IBM, CP/M and Digital Research. It exists in several versions and is presented here without documentation. It may or may not be true. But regardless of its accuracy, clearly something similar *could* have happened and undoubtedly does happen all the time.

It seems that IBM's first inclination regarding an operating system for the personal computer it was building was to ask Digital Research to develop CP/M for the new machine. But when the men from Big Blue dropped in at Digital's Victorian home headquarters in Pacific Grove, California, to discuss the matter, none of the firm's executives was in. An alternate version of the story has the IBMers waiting patiently on the airport tarmac while Gary Kildall was off flying his plane.

Whatever actually happened, the IBM folks got tired of waiting and simply went on up the coast to Bellevue, Washington, to Microsoft Corporation. Bill Gates, the chairman of the firm, and his executives *were* in and, of course, were more than eager to discuss whatever IBM had on its mind.

And so it goes. Regardless of the veracity of this particular tale, there can be no doubting that fortunes can be won or lost in the personal computer industry on the basis of just such elements of chance. Prior to the introduction of VisiCalc, for example, the Apple was regarded as little more than a toy. It's pure speculation, but if Bricklin and Flystra hadn't met at the Harvard B-School and if Flystra hadn't already been involved selling a chess-playing game for Apple computers, VisiCalc might have been introduced for some other machine (probably an 8080-based computer running CP/M) and the Apple computer company might never have become what it is today.

*Amaze Your Friends . . . Confute Your Enemies*

You now own a substantial portion of the background information you need to be a smart software consumer. Better yet perhaps, you've got the terms and the concepts at your disposal to sling computer jargon with the best of 'em.

Want to start an argument? Ask a CP/M user how he or she feels CP/M-86 compares to MS-DOS. Users of MS-DOS tend to be less fanatical than CP/Mers, but you might try the same question on them. Ask a computer store salesperson whether the program you are considering includes an installation module. You might also consider salting your conversation with references to "a Z80 board," "the 8088," and "the 6502." (Note that the word "chip" is rarely used when referring to specific microprocessors. Also, "8088" is pronounced "eighty-eighty-eight," and "6502" is pronounced "sixty-five-oh-two.")

In the next chapter, we will leave the lowest level of computer operations behind and begin looking at the highest level. As mentioned in Chapter 1, the layers in between can safely be left to programmers and computer professionals.

# ...3...

# Programming Languages and Applications Software: *A Basic Primer and Bluffer's Guide*

Computer programming languages are like typesetting machines and printing presses. They are a means to an end, and you don't have to know how to operate them to enjoy and use what they produce. It is true that few things are more satisfying to many new computer owners than to write, run, and debug a simple BASIC program. And it's true that programming can be an engrossing, time-annihilating hobby. But computer literacy of this degree is not required to run most application programs and may not even be particularly helpful.

When you select an applications program, the most important things to consider are how the features it offers correspond to your needs and whether the program is available for your particular computer. For reasons that will become clear, the language of creation usually has no effect on your ability to run the program. And since it is extremely rare for one company's program to be produced using two different languages, you normally will not have a choice.

The language used *can* be a factor, however, when you are considering similar programs produced by different companies. An accounting package written in one language may respond much faster and perform much better than a competitive product written in another language. Language can also be an important consideration if the program is designed to be modified or customized by the buyer. And it can be an indication of whether running the program will require the purchase of a special "interpreter" or other software component in addition to the program itself.

*Three Areas of Impact*

There are thus three major reasons why it can be important to know what language was used to create an applications program:

82

- As a means of comparing competitive applications programs on the basis of probable speed and performance.
- As an indication that you will be able to modify or customize the program either now or in the future as your needs change.
- As an indication that you may need something other than just the program itself to make it run.

The most important language-related point to consider when comparing two competitive products is whether one or both of them are written in "assembly language." When Ashton-Tate, the producers of the popular dBASE II database management system, advertises its product as being written in "assembly language," what it is telling you is that the program runs exceptionally fast and is designed to make maximum use of your machine's capabilities.

Speed is a very important feature in a program of this type because one of the things it is designed to do is to search through hundreds of records for the piece of information you want. Database management systems (DBMS) are also used to sort records into a particular order (alphabetically, by ZIP code, by invoice number, etc.). The actual time required will depend on the total number of records involved, but in some cases a sort requiring only five minutes for an assembly language program to complete could take another program five or more *hours* to finish.

That's an accurate but extreme example. It is doubtful that any commercially available DBMS would compare so unfavorably to its competitors. Nevertheless, ads for DBMS packages frequently focus more on the number of records they can handle than on execution speed. Information capacity is a very important consideration, to be sure. But the speed with which the program lets you get at and manipulate that information can be equally crucial.

Since the slower program may be the only one with all the features you want, the speed of assembly language may not be the determining factor. Still, any time you are considering a program that will deal with large quantities of data, it is worth finding out what language it was written in. If nothing else, the information will serve to corroborate or confute any manufacturer-supplied speed specifications.

Most software houses would rather not have their customers in the programming game. It's bad for business. Thus, most applications programs are issued in a form that is either impossible or extremely difficult for a user to change. On the other hand, given a choice between two very comparable products, one of which could be customized and the other of which was unalterable, which one would you choose?

You may not know anything about programming and have no desire to learn. But who knows what will happen in the future? Everything else being equal, the option of customizing the program or adding other modules and programs to it may prove irresistible. By offering this feature, a software producer may be able to get a leg up on the competition. As we'll see later, whenever the phrase "source code supplied" is used in an ad or review, you can assume that it will be possible to customize or change the program.

Finally, if you see an ad that describes a program as being written in UCSD Pascal or Forth, or refers to something called the "p-System," it is an indication that you *may* not be able to run the program by itself. Such programs could require a special "interpreter" package, or operating system, that is not provided with the applications program. Then again, they may not. Unfortunately, the ads that include these terms do not always make the requirements clear.

Because of this, it is usually a good idea to investigate further whenever you see a language other than assembly language mentioned in a software ad or a review. Citing the language may be nothing more than computer snobbery. Pascal, for example, is very much in style and the firm may simply want the world to know that it is keeping up with the trend. Or the citation may be aimed at experienced programmers who are aware of the subtleties of different languages. Or, most important of all to you, it may indicate that the program will require an additional software component in order to run.

---

**SoftTip:** Lest all this talk of languages prove confusing, it is important to emphasize from the start that you usually do *not* have to own a copy of the language used to create a program in order to run it—any more than you have to own a printing press to read a book. The languages available for your computer are sold as separate software packages, and they are designed to be used by people who want to *write* programs. They have nothing to do with your ability to *run* an applications program.

---

### The Essence of Programming Languages

As a software buyer, there are only a few things you really need to know about programming languages. And here is the most important of them: Every computer programming language is designed to translate human ideas and desires into a collection of instructions that will tell the machine's CPU what to do. As you know from the first chapter, each microprocessor has a clearly defined instruction set and each instruction consists of a pattern of switch settings. Symbolized by *1* and *0*, the two electric voltage levels produced by the switch settings are the only kind of input a CPU can accept. They are the only things that will set off the chain reactions within the CPU that ultimately result in useful output. Sometimes the patterns of *1*'s and *0*'s of a CPU's instruction set will be referred to as that particular chip's "native language" or "native code."

Where computer languages differ is in the techniques and approaches they use to translate human instructions and ideas into the CPU's native language. Producing *1*'s and *0*'s is the object of all computer languages, but each of them approaches that goal differently. There are two major points that characterize the way a computer language achieves its ultimate goal. The first is the structure of the language itself, and the second is the method used to convert the written words of the language into a chip's native code.

A discussion of the structure of computer languages and the differences between them is far beyond the scope of a book about how to buy applications software. However, you should know that, like human languages, computer languages consist of words and rules for combining those words in meaningful ways. A typical computer language may only have from 100 to 400 words. The rules for how the words may be put together are called the language's "syntax."

There are many differences among languages—both human and computer—that make some more suitable for certain tasks than others, though one of the major differences centers on the language's vocabulary. For example, in the Eskimo language there are more than 30 words for *ice*. There is a word for "the thin crust of ice that forms over small pools at the onset of winter," and there is a word for "the ice that is riddled with holes caused by melting in the summer sun."

The important thing to keep in mind is that the Eskimo language can express in a single word an idea that requires many English words to convey. Clearly, if you want to talk about ice, Eskimo is the language to use. English simply doesn't have the vocabulary to do the job efficiently and precisely. Needless to say, the same types of differences exist among computer programming languages.

*Layers and Languages*

Now let's look at the three major techniques used to convert a programming language into a chip's native code. We should start by saying that it *is* possible to program a computer by typing in the native code directly as nothing but a series of *1*'s and *0*'s. This is the modern day equivalent of physically flipping individual switches on an early computer's front panel. And except for the fact that it reduces wear and tear on your fingers, programming in "machine language," as the *1*'s and *0*'s are called, is just as tedious and error-prone.

Consequently, virtually no one does any extensive programming in machine language. Instead, people use an "assembly language" created for each particular CPU chip. This language lets them type in expressions like *MOV* for *move* instead of something like *01111110;* or *LD* for *load* instead of *00100001.* When the program is finished, a translation module called an "assembler" is used to convert all the *MOV, LD, ADD, XOR,* and other words into the *1's* and *0's* of machine language. Like the assembly language, the assembler must be specifically written to translate things into the instructions in a particular CPU's instruction set.

Here's an example of assembly language programming designed to tell the CPU that $X = X + 1$ where $X$ is an eight-bit number stored in address location $Y$:

```
LD    H,Y
MOV   A,M
ADD   1
MOV   M,A
```

And here is the machine language that might be produced when the above program is run through an assembler:

```
00100001
01111110
11000110
00000001
01110111
```

The assembly language program is called the "source" program or "source code." When it passes through the assembler, it gets converted into machine language or "object code." (If you remember that producing machine language was the "object" all along, it will be easy to keep the two terms straight.) Once a program has been assembled, the object code can be run as is. The assembler is no longer needed.

**SoftTip:** Technically, "machine language" and "assembly language" are different. But the terms are often used interchangeably. Thus, a program advertised as being written in machine language may actually have been created with an assembly language and translated with an assembler. Notice in the example given above that the four lines of assembly language translated into five lines of machine language, indicating an almost one-to-one correspondence between the two. Because of this high correspondence, programming in assembly language is almost like using the *1*'s and *0*'s of the CPU's native code. The only difference is that each byte is given an easily remembered name or "mnemonic."

*Assembly Language and Software Prices*

Because assembly language is only about one step removed from the computer's native code, it is considered a "low-level" language. That's not a pejorative term. It simply means that the language is very close to the CPU's native language. A "high-level" language, in contrast, is much closer to English and is thus many steps removed from machine code.

As we saw in Chapter 1, the CPU must be told what to do every step of the way, and when you are as close to the CPU as you are with assembly language, there is no way to escape that burden. This makes assembly language rather difficult to learn and work with and means that assembly language software requires more of a programmer's time to produce than similar programs written in a higher-level language. And more time translates into higher costs, and possibly higher prices.

If the program becomes popular, the software house will be able to spread its development costs over many copies of the software and so keep prices down. If it doesn't become popular, you may have to pay more for an assembly language program. The question is whether it's worth it.

As mentioned earlier, assembly language programs are fast because there is very little translation to slow things down. In addition, because assembly language is so closely related to a CPU's native code, it's relatively easy for a programmer to directly manipulate the computer and the chip to fully exploit its inherent features and capabilities. Higher-level languages usually do not permit this kind of direct access to the CPU.

Unfortunately, there is no rule of thumb about how much—if anything—the costs of programming in assembly language add to the price of applications software. Since each program designed for the same application can have its own unique features, it is difficult to compare them on the basis of language and price. There is also the question of how often you plan to use the program. If you plan to use it only occasionally, then high-speed response and execution might not be as important to you as they would be to someone who will be using it every day. (See Chapter 18 for more on how assembly language programs like Lotus 1-2-3 compares with a program written in UCSD Pascal, such as Context MBA.) About all that can be said for certain is that, as with any other product, you will probably have to pay more for high performance. But only you can decide whether it's worth it.

### *"Compilers": A Second Route*

Another way to translate computer languages into machine code is to use a "compiler" program. Though there are some important differences, basically a compiler is very much like an assembler. It is a translation program that is loaded into the computer when it is necessary to convert a program into machine language object code. The difference is that a compiler is designed for use with a higher-level computer language. Examples of compiled languages include FORTRAN (FORmula TRANslator), COBOL (COmmon Business Oriented Language), and in some cases, Pascal (named for the seventeenth-century French mathematician/philosopher, Blaise Pascal). As with assembly language, the program itself is called "source code," and the machine language results generated by the compiler/translator are called "object code."

A compiled language frees the programmer from having to specify absolutely everything for the CPU and lets him or her write and think in a more natural, English-like way. When the program is finished, it is relatively easy to run it through the compiler and so produce the *1*'s and *0*'s of machine language. As with an assembler, once the compiler has performed its translation, it is no longer needed. The object code it produces can be recorded and run just as if it had been written in machine language.

---

**SoftTip:** Many commercial software packages are supplied on a floppy disk in object code form. Since they have already been compiled or assembled, you do not need a compiler or an assembler to run them on your machine. Usually, you will not be able to look at the object code that has been recorded on your software disk—at least not by any of the standard ways of displaying a disk file.

And even if you could, it probably would not do you much good. Object code is very difficult to "disassemble" or translate back into its source code. Consequently, there is really nothing you can do to alter or customize an object code program. This is why manufacturers whose products offer the option of user customization provide the source code. Of course, if you plan to customize a compiled program by altering the source code, then you *will* need to own the appropriate compiler.

That means that a compiled program will run almost as fast as an assembly language program. The reason for the "almost" qualification is that, as a general purpose tool, a compiler has to make certain compromises. A compiler can produce the machine code that will get the job done. But the machine code instructions it generates may not be the quickest, most efficient way for the CPU to do things in every case. Similarly, the generalized approach used by the compiler may mean that it will not be able to fully exploit the CPU's capabilities the way assembly language can.

**SoftTip:** Since the whole idea of a computer language is to produce *1*'s and *0*'s for the CPU, and since the CPU doesn't care where those *1*'s and *0*'s came from, there is no reason why compiler-produced object code and assembler-produced object code can't be combined into the same program. Software companies frequently write the bulk of a program in a compiled language, but use assembly language to add certain features that exploit the particular CPU. After the appropriate parts of the program have been compiled or assembled into *1*'s and *0*'s, they are identical to the CPU.

Because a program written in a compiled language can't be run until the whole thing has been converted into machine language, identifying and fixing program bugs can be a time-consuming process. Typically, a program will be written, compiled, and run to check for bugs. When a bug turns up, the programmer will have to fix it in the source code, *recompile* the program, and run it again. The process continues until everything runs perfectly. But because the compilation process can require anywhere from several minutes to several hours each time, it can represent a major inconvenience.

*"Interpreters": The Third Route*
One way to eliminate this problem is to approach the machine language goal via a third route. Suppose, for example, that instead of converting an entire high-level language program into machine language before running it, you set things up so that only one line of the program was "converted" and run at a time. You could then let the program run until it hit a snag and stopped, fix the bug, and tell it to continue running. That, of course, is the way BASIC (Beginners All-purpose Symbolic Instruction Code) works.

BASIC is an "interpreted" language, and it requires a BASIC interpreter to run. The BASIC interpreter consists of a collection of small programs written in machine language, each of which corresponds to a particular statement or command in the BASIC language. Thus, when your computer executes a BASIC program, it looks at the first line of code and checks with the interpreter. The interpreter checks its list of machine language "subroutines" and selects the ones that correspond to the instructions you have written. Then it sends these subroutines to the CPU for execution. By that time, the system is ready to look at the next line of programming.

BASIC is easy to use and modify, but by both computer and human standards, it is very, very slow. All of that checking with the interpreter consumes a huge amount of time. Consequently, relatively few professionally produced applications programs are written in interpreted BASIC.

Unlike an assembler or a compiler, the BASIC interpreter has to be available at all times. You can run an assembly language or a compiled program "as is," but you cannot run a BASIC program without a BASIC interpreter. Because of this and because BASIC is so popular with computer owners, most manufacturers build the interpreter into the machine by putting much of the necessary programming into one to four ROM chips.

Because the ROM BASIC may not have all of the features and power you need, you will probably be able to buy a BASIC language package that mates with and "extends" the BASIC in your machine's ROM. Typically, the extended or advanced BASIC will be supplied on a floppy disk or cassette and be loaded into the machine whenever you want to write or run BASIC programs.

There are many "dialects" (versions) of BASIC, many of which may be available for your machine. Each has different features and capabilities that may be of interest to you if you plan to do any BASIC programming.

**SoftTip:** Is there a "standard" BASIC? The answer is yes and no. The American National Standards Institute (ANSI) is an industry group that codifies and publishes standards for everything from floppy disks to computer languages. Thus, as with COBOL, FORTRAN, and others, there is an ANSI standard for BASIC. But it is rarely used.

The real standard is Microsoft BASIC, a version of the language created by the Microsoft Corporation of Bellevue, Washington. Microsoft BASIC has been adopted by so many computer manufacturers, software houses, and users that it has become the most widely used computer language in the world.

Before buying any other BASIC dialect, however, you owe it to yourself to explore the BASIC supplied with your computer. Some manufacturers, like IBM, supply an extended BASIC with their standard disk operating system packages. And that's fine. But unless you are already familiar with BASIC, you should not let a salesperson talk you into purchasing any other BASIC package when you are buying your computer. Conceivably, the manufacturer's BASIC may be all you will ever need. If it isn't, you can always buy a different dialect later.

---

**SoftTip:** There are many books designed to introduce their readers to the BASIC language. For a general, non-machine-specific introduction, you might want to consider:

*Basic Basic* by James S. Coan (Hayden, $11.50)

Regardless of whether you own an IBM/PC, you might also want to look at:

*Learning IBM BASIC* by David A. Lien (CompuSoft® Publishing, $19.95)

Lien writes with exceptional clarity and humor, as readers of his manual for the Epson MX-80 printer and his *Getting Started in TRS-80 BASIC* can attest. If you can't find this book at your local store, you can order it directly by calling (800) 854-6505 (24 hours) or (714) 588-0996 in California (8:00 AM to 5:00 PM). Or you can send $19.95, plus $1.65 shipping and handling, to:

CompuSoft® Publishing
P.O. Box 19669
San Diego, CA 92119

---

**SoftTip:** Although BASIC programs are usually interpreted, there is no reason why the same program cannot be compiled into machine language. Many companies now sell compilers for the various versions of BASIC running on most major brands of personal computers. These software packages typically cost between $150 and $400. Compiled BASIC programs usually run from five to ten times faster than interpreted versions.

*UCSD Pascal and the p-System*

Primarily because of the advantages it offers software producers, a growing number of products are being written in a language called UCSD Pascal. Unlike other applications programs, most of which are written to be used with CP/M, MS-DOS, or some other standard operating system, these products may require a separate OS called the p-System.

"UCSD" stands for "University of California, San Diego," the school where Kenneth Bowles and his students developed both the language and the operating system. The p-System™ is a registered trademark of the Regents of the University of California. The outstanding feature of this language/OS pairing is the ease with which applications programs written in it can be transported from one computer to another. UCSD Pascal and the p-System make it possible to use identical applications programs on the IBM/PC, the Apple II, or any other computer, in spite of the fact that each uses a different microprocessor chip CPU.

That's quite a trick, as you can imagine. But it wasn't accomplished without making certain compromises that can be important to you as a software buyer. The overall idea is similar to the layers used to make CP/M and other operating systems easy to transport from one computer to another. It also involves *both* a compiler and an interpreter.

Here's how it works. A program written in UCSD Pascal is first run through a compiler. But unlike most compilers, this one does not generate machine language for an Intel 8088 (IBM/PC), a MOS 6502 (Apple II), or any other widely available CPU chip. Instead, it generates a special code for an idealized CPU or *pseudo*-machine. This is called "p-code" or "intermediate code." When the program is to be run on a real computer, a p-code interpreter is used to translate the programming into instructions for that computer's particular CPU.

The key point is that *only the interpreter must be customized* to the specific computer. Because customized interpreters are fairly easy to create, the same UCSD Pascal program can easily be made to run on a wide variety of computers. This is what makes UCSD Pascal and the p-System so appealing to many software houses.

As a trade journal ad from SofTech Microsystems, the licensed vendor of the product, states, "There was a time when . . . you had to sink significant time and money into programming. . . . The p-System is portable across virtually any micro made anywhere today. . . . So you can broaden your customer base quickly. . . . The p-System allows you to reuse program components . . . over and over again."

The p-System is clearly terrific for software producers. Unfortunately, it may not be so good for software users. It is true that feeding pseudo-compiled programming to an interpreter makes a program run as much as 10 times faster than one that feeds BASIC-like text to an interpreter. However, it is also true that the extra steps of the interpretation process cause such programs to run from 10 to 40 times *slower* than assembly language programs.

Whether this slower speed is significant or noticeable largely depends on the program. For example, when you use a word processing program, even if you are a whirlwind typist, your computer's CPU spends most of its time waiting for you to enter the next keystroke. Consequently, if the CPU takes a bit longer to do its job the difference may not be very noticeable. When you ask the program to find a particular word in your text or to perform other CPU-intensive chores, the difference may be more apparent. The same is true with engineering, scientific, and other programs requiring the CPU to do a great deal of "number crunching" computational work. Here the processing delays inherent in the p-System may be unacceptable.

The other major point that will affect your purchase decision is whether or not you will need to buy the complete p-System OS/interpreter package in order to run the program. This may be necessary for two reasons. As is always the case, an applications program is written for use with a particular operating system, and you must have that OS in order to run the program. Second, as with programs written in BASIC and any other interpreted language, the necessary interpreter must be available whenever the program is run.

Fortunately, some programs written in this language may be available in two versions. One version may include a "run time" package and the other version may require you to have your own copy of the p-System. If you buy a run time version, everything you need to use the program will be included. (Look for a phrase similar to "UCSD p-System—Run time provided" in ads and catalogue listings.) Because the software house must pay a royalty for the right to include the run time package, this version will probably be more expensive than one without it. More than likely, though, it will be less expensive than the total cost of buying your own copy of the system and the non-run time version of the program.

If you think you will be buying only one or two p-System-based programs, then "run time" is clearly the way to go. However, the extra royalty cost tacked on to each run time program can mount up if you buy several programs. In that case, it may be more economical to take the plunge and purchase your own copy of the p-System for your machine.

**SoftTip:** The p-System is available for the IBM/PC or Display writer, and computers made by Apple, DEC, Hewlett-Packard, Osborne, Phillips, Radio Shack, Texas Instruments, and others. The principal licensed vendor is:

SofTech Microsystems
16885 West Bernardo Drive
San Diego, CA 92127
(619) 451-1230

**SoftTip:** Pascal, or more properly UCSD Pascal, is closely bound up with the p-System. Usually, a programming language is created or adjusted to match an operating system. But in this case, the operating system was built around the language. (The p-System was actually written in Pascal.) This close association can lead to confusion about Pascal.

Pascal is a separate language designed to be used with a Pascal compiler, the way any other compiled language is used. The fact that a program is billed as being written in Pascal does *not* mean that it has anything to do with the p-System. The only time the p-System is a consideration is when a program is written in *UCSD* Pascal.

*When in Doubt—ASK!*

It is worth emphasizing once again that when choosing software, the most important things to consider are the features the program offers and how well those features perform. If the program works well, the language used to create it will be of little concern to you and probably won't even be mentioned in most ads and reviews.

When you want or need to know the language of creation, or when the ad does not make clear whether you will need additional software like the p-System to run the program, there are a number of ways to find out. The surest and simplest way is to phone the software house itself. Unlike virtually any other industry, it is customary for a software firm to offer direct access to consumers. So you shouldn't be shy about phoning. Most companies are prepared for calls of this sort, and some are so small that the individual who picks up the phone may be the person who actually wrote the program you are considering.

Phoning is economical if an "800" number has been provided or if the company isn't too far away. Sending a letter is another possibility, of course, but many firms are better prepared to answer the phone than the mail. You might also check with your retailer. If the store carries the product, it should have a copy of the instruction manual for you to examine. Often a software producer will include a "technical specifications" section in its manual that will contain the information you seek.

Finally, while you should *always* read two or more reviews of a product whenever possible, the reviews published in magazines like *InfoWorld, Creative Computing, Byte,* and *Dr. Dobbs* can be especially helpful when you need specific information about how a program was written or the techniques used to implement its features. The reviews published in these and similar magazines have a more technical orientation than those published in magazines aimed at more general audiences and thus are more likely to cite the language used to create the program.

## The Bluffer's Guide to Programming Languages

Several years ago the ebullient Englishman, David Frost, M.C., produced a series of "bluffer's guides" to art, literature, history, etc., containing choice morsels for the reader to drop into cocktail party conversations to impress fellow guests. As we have said, you don't have to know anything about programming languages to use a personal computer effectively. Still, should the occasion arise, you may find the following facts will have the desired effect if artfully worked into a conversation with your boss, business associates, or golfing partners.

### COBOL and the DOD

The United States Department of Defense (DOD) is the largest buyer of data processing equipment in the world. In the late 1950s, it got fed up with receiving all of the software it commissioned in unalterable assembly language form. So the DOD funded the development of COBOL (COmmon Business Oriented Language) and insisted that COBOL compilers be provided with every computer it bought. Needless to say, computer manufacturers hastened to comply. Then, since they had this language on their hands anyway, manufacturers began to offer it to their commercial customers. As a result, COBOL became the most commonly used language for business applications programs. Normally, those programs are designed to run on large computers, but a "subset" of the language is available for a Softcard-equipped (Z80 microprocessor) Apple II, the Heath computer, Radio Shack computers, and others.

## Ada and Charles and Daddy George

COBOL was introduced in 1958, but by the 1970s, the DOD had begun to promote a new Pascal-like language called Ada. The DOD would like to have all of its computers use programs written in the same standardized language, instead of the hodgepodge of languages that are used now. Ada™ is a registered trademark owned by the DOD, and only language packages that strictly conform to DOD standards are permitted to use it.

Ada is named for Ada Agusta, Countess of Lovelace (1816–1852), and daughter of George Gordon, Lord Byron, the famous Romantic poet. She is reputed to have been "the world's first programmer." This came about because she joined forces with a man named Charles Babbage, a professor of mathematics at Cambridge, who set out to build the first automatic computer long before there was even a practical adding machine.

Babbage basically laid the foundations for modern computer science. His "analytical engine," as he called it, contained three sections: the *store* to hold the data needed for computing, the *mill* to perform the actual computations, and the *control* to provide automatic supervision. The whole thing was supposed to run on cams and toothed cogwheels.

One of Ada Agusta's most important contributions was to see the connection between the punched cards used to control the Jacquard automatic weaving machines that had been introduced in France and Charles's analytical engine: "Why not put the programming for your analytical engine on punched cards, Charley?"

Babbage liked the idea and immediately incorporated it in his plans. If the analytic engine had been built, it would have been larger than a football field. Unfortunately (as is always the case), Babbage couldn't get the parts. The technology of the day simply couldn't produce the wheels and other components with the degree of precision he needed. It took 100 years for technology to catch up with his ideas.

For her part, Ada Agusta, Countess of Lovelace, isn't even listed in most encyclopedias and biographical dictionaries. So it is immensely fitting that she be remembered by having her own computer language.

## Forth

Forth is a language that has many fanatical followers in the programming community. Like FORTRAN it is particularly well suited to solving complex mathematical equations and so is often used to create engineering and scientific applications programs. Unlike FORTRAN, however, Forth can be extended by the user, allowing the programmer to add his or her own commands and statements. The language was supposed to be called "Fourth" for "fourth generation," but the computer on which it was developed would only permit filenames that were five characters long—hence, "Forth."

## C

Like Pascal, the C language is one of the up and comers in the microworld. It offers many of the advantages of assembly language but is much easier to use. It is also rather easy to "port" from one machine to another. Developed at Bell Labs by Dennis Ritchie, C is the language that was used to create the UNIX operating system, another microworld cause célèbre. That is probably its principal cachet for nonprogrammers. Because C compiles into the native code of a particular CPU, programs run faster than UCSD Pascal/p-System programs and their pseudocode. The language is called "C" because it was developed as part of a series, the previous units of which were designated "A" and "B."

## APL

A similar burst of creativity was shown when the name "APL" was chosen for a language developed by Kenneth Iverson at the IBM Watson Research Center. "APL" stands for "A Programming Language." Actually, that was supposed to be a temporary name or working title. But it stuck. APL is used extensively to create statistical applications software. It also has a lot of Greek letters in its vocabulary.

## LISP

LISP stands for "LISt Processing language." The most important thing is that LISP programs have *the ability to modify themselves.* LISP programs treat everything in the computer's memory, including the program itself, as data that can be manipulated and changed. In a limited sense, that means a computer can "learn" from past experience. For this reason, virtually all "artificial intelligence" programs—programs that attempt to make a computer imitate human thought—are written in LISP.

## Other Terms

"Tiny" anything, as in "Tiny C" or "Tiny Pascal," means that the product referred to is a diluted and usually considerably less powerful version of the main language, designed to run on a computer with limited memory.

A "structured" programming language requires the programmer to define all of the variables or pieces of information that the program will use right up front in the first few lines of code. Pascal is perhaps the best example of this in the microworld. Developed in the early 1970s by Professor Niklaus Wirth of the (Swiss) Federal Institute of Technology in Zurich, Pascal was originally intended as a tool for teaching good programming habits, like thinking about what you are doing before you start writing code.

BASIC was likewise developed originally as a teaching tool by John Kemeny and Thomas Kurtz at Dartmouth College in 1965. BASIC is probably the best example of an "unstructured" programming language. A BASIC programmer can more or less wing it, defining his variables as he goes along.

*LOGO and Turtle Graphics*

Although LOGO is a fairly powerful general-purpose language, it is particularly well suited to teaching programming concepts to young children. For example, it makes it easy to see how complex programs can be built up by combining many smaller modules.

"Turtle graphics" is a general term for a technique that makes it easy to draw pictures on your screen. Usually, though not always, turtle graphics involves a subset of the Logo language. As a subset, turtle graphics products do not contain all of Logo's commands and features. Instead, they contain just those commands and words needed to use this drawing technique.

A stylized cursor is used to represent a "turtle" on the screen. The turtle is thought of as having dipped its tail in paint. Consequently, whenever you move it, it paints a line in its wake. It's a neat way of looking at things, particularly for children. But the most important feature of turtle graphics is how easy it is to get the little terrapin to do its stuff. You simply tell it to move a certain distance left, right, up, down. This is much, much easier than the conventional procedure of specifying numerical $X$ and $Y$ coordinates and entering a command to draw a line between them.

*Ready—Set—Go!*

You've now got all the basic background information you need. In the next chapter, we'll show you how to start applying it as you begin reading software ads and reviews of personal computer programs. As you read succeeding chapters, you'll find yourself constantly drawing on what you've learned in Chapters 1, 2, and 3. And as new products and programs are issued, you'll have a pretty good idea of where each fits in the overall scheme of things.

Right now, however, I'd like to suggest a little experiment. Before you dig into Chapter 4, pick up one or two computer magazines and randomly read a few software ads. Put a paper clip on the advertising pages so you'll be able to find them again, and read Chapter 4. When you finish, return to the ads and see if they make more sense the second time around. I think you'll be pleasantly surprised at what you find.

# ...4...
# How to Read Software Ads and Reviews: *A Quick-Start Guide*

In "The Prologue" to *The Canterbury Tales*, Geoffrey Chaucer writes of the Wife of Bath that:

> She learned much by wandering along the way
> Gap-toothed she was, the truth to say.

If a writer today were to describe a character as having teeth set widely apart, the most that a modern reader might conclude would be that the person's parents should have taken her to an orthodontist when she was young. But Chaucer's fourteenth-century audience understood that a character's physical attributes were an emblem for the inner self, and would recognize the gap-toothed Wife of Bath as bold, gluttonous, and above all, lecherous—characteristics later borne out by the tales she tells.

Physiognomy was part of the common body of knowledge of Chaucer's time, and 200 years later, the Wife of Bath herself had become part of that same common body of knowledge. Thus, Shakespeare could have Petruchio say in *The Taming of the Shrew*, "Be she as foul as was Florentius' love . . ." confident that his audience knew he was referring to a "Canterbury Tale" told by that redoubtable lady. An American writer could use a phrase like "George Washington's cherry tree" and be equally confident that readers understood the reference without further explanation.

There is a common body of knowledge in computerdom as well, and the writers of software ads and reviews are equally free about taking advantage of the fact. Consequently, you can pick up any computer publication and be almost certain of encountering phrases like these:

- Spooler software
- Will store up to 54 files, each with over 200 records and user-definable field lengths

100

- 8087 coprocessor required
- Disk-based tutorial provided
- ISAM file structure

Unfortunately, knowledge of these and similar obscurities is not nearly as common as software reviewers and copywriters sometimes assume. Thus, many readers have no choice but to run hard to catch up. This chapter will give you a head start. Developed by culling the most frequently encountered terms from hundreds of software ads and reviews, it is necessarily eclectic in its approach. The explanations are not intended to be comprehensive. Instead, they're designed to give you a basic understanding of what the terms mean and why they are important from a software buyer's viewpoint.

Parts II and III of this book will look at the terms, features, and details associated with specific types of applications programs, why they're important, and why what ads for these products *don't* say is often as important as what they do. Here, however, we will be dealing with things that can apply to or affect many applications programs, regardless of what each is designed to accomplish. We'll look at three main areas: the general components and features of applications programs, the special hardware that can sometimes be required to run them, and the significance of—Allah be praised—ISAM.

## Applications Programs: General Components and Features

*File, Record, and Field*

If you were a contestant on a special computerist edition of "The Family Feud" quiz show—perhaps one that featured the Apple family versus the Franklins—you can bet your disk drives that three of the words most likely to appear behind the answer board would be *file*, *record*, and *field*. As the three major divisions of information storage and processing, they are about as fundamental to a personal computer as software itself.

Fortunately, they are not difficult to understand. The classic explanation is to think of a collection of cancelled checks. The collection as a whole can be thought of as a *file*. Each check within the file is a *record*. And each piece of information on each check (the date, the amount, the payee, etc.) is a *field*.

Thus, if you were using a software program to keep track of your favorite recipes, you might have a file for "main dishes," for "vegetables," and for "desserts." Within each of those files, you would have several individual recipe records. And on each record you would find fields for the ingredients, cooking times, and other preparation information.

It's important to point out that you won't encounter all three divisions in every program. All programs contain files. (Indeed, the programming itself is stored as a file.) But a file doesn't have to contain discrete records, per se. And a record doesn't have to contain specific fields. A good example would be a letter you create with a word processing program. To save the letter, you'll normally record it on disk as a file. While technically that single letter can also be called a record, it's usually thought of and referred to as a file. Similarly, if you look at the letter you probably won't find anything that corresponds to the idea of fields.

Generally, while the concept of a file is universal and found in every program in some form or another, the more specific divisions of record and field are used mainly in programs that do more formalized information processing and management: a mailing list program that will sort addresses by ZIP code; a personal finance program that will locate, total, and graph your entertainment, food, shelter, and other types of expenses; a personnel management program that will locate every employee who has a birthday in the month of August, etc.

Because the actual information placed in a field will differ from one record to the next, it's usually referred to as a *variable*. You may have an address file consisting of 10 address records. And each record may have a field for name, street number, city, state, and ZIP code. Those fields remain constant for each record, but obviously the actual information or variables will differ in each case.

From a software buying standpoint, the two most important considerations regarding files, records, fields, and variables are "How many?" and "How long?" Some programs will let you create a larger number of files than others. Some may permit fewer files, but let you put more records in each one. Some may allow variable fields that are only 10 characters long, while others may give you 32 characters of space or more.

These characteristics determine the capacity and much of the flexibility of any program designed to produce results by manipulating information. While you may not need the maximum capacity available, it is still one of the first points you should check when evaluating a program of this sort.

---

**SoftTip:** Something that really brings the effect of field lengths home (literally) are the address labels used for junk mail. If you have a relatively long last name, for example, it isn't uncommon for it to be printed on one of these labels with several of the last letters clipped off. The computer program used to generate the labels obviously doesn't permit variables in the last name field to be any longer than eight or ten characters.

A junk mail company doesn't care. But you might. Particularly if you're going to be using a mailing list program to send letters to customers or friends on your Christmas card list.

## Column and Row

Among the terms of computerdom that seem needlessly strange and potentially confusing are "column and row," "support," and "documentation."

Columns are the columns of numbers or letters that run from the top to the bottom of your screen. There's nothing wrong with that term. But why the term "rows" must be used to refer to what human beings think of as "lines" on a page or on a screen is a mystery.

These terms are used with programs in which the way information is displayed and/or printed is important. They have little relevance for game programs, but they are of vital concern when dealing with word processing, electronic spreadsheet, and similar software. Again, they are a measure of capacity and flexibility, and again, the question to ask is, How many?

For example, since standard 8½" × 11" letter-sized paper will accommodate 85 characters per line when using pica type (10 characters to the inch times 8½ inches = 85 characters), and since it's customary to leave a margin of 10 characters on each side, virtually all word processing programs will allow you to write 80-character lines. Assuming that your computer can display 80 columns on the screen, it will be convenient and natural for you to write standard-sized letters. But if you have a wide-track printer and plan to create text that will extend more than 80 characters left to right, then the number of columns the word processing program permits will be an important consideration. You may need a program that gives you 132 columns or more.

## "Support"

The word *support* in the common body of computerdom knowledge is a rather elastic term. As indicated previously, it generally means "to work with." One might say that WordStar™ "supports a wide variety of printers" and mean that whether you've got an Epson, an Okidata, or a Prowriter printer, you'll be able to use it to generate hard copy of the text you create with that program. As you might expect, there are degrees of support. "Full support" in this case would mean that the printer can produce everything the program throws at it (bold print, underlines, all the whistles and bells). "Partial support" could mean that the printer will type out the characters but may not be capable of doing all the fancy stuff WordStar makes possible, at least not without a bit of software modification.

"Support" can also mean things like "having the parts and accessories for," as when a computer retailer supports a particular brand of computer by stocking everything you need to use it and possibly even maintaining a repair shop to fix it when it breaks. In a related sense, "support" can mean "stands ready to provide customer service." As in any other business, customer service can cover a wide range of things, and every dealer would probably define it a bit differently.

In the software industry, it is supposed to mean that the dealer will do all that he or she reasonably can to make sure that you are able to use a program successfully. That can include everything from properly "installing" the program so that it works with your printer and video display to taking the time to show you how to use the program and answering any questions you may have at a later date.

*"Documentation"*

"Documentation" is a term that comes straight from the lexicon of computer programers. It has no place in the real world where people pay real money for programs to make their lives or their work easier, not when there's a perfectly good phrase that means exactly the same thing: "instruction manual." Programers are supposed to "document" what they have done when they write or change a program the same way you or your attorney might "document" an important conversation or meeting. So, technically, software "documentation" is a summary of the steps that were followed and the features that were added to a program in the course of its development. Thus, it's not too difficult to see how the term came to be applied to instructions for using a program and its features.

*"Tutorials"*

In addition to documentation, some programs include some kind of "tutorial" material. Generally, tutorials are designed to give you "hands-on" experience in using what you've learned from the instruction manual by working through sample applications. The tutorial material itself may consist of several pages at the end of the manual or all of the text may be on disk. It may include sample files containing information for you to use as you get to know the software, or it may involve an "interactive" program that requires you to key in information in response to what you see on the screen.

## "User Friendly"

The term "user friendliness" is to software producers what respect for motherhood, apple pie, and the American flag used to be to an old-time politician. It is something they all claim to have, but something no one ever investigates too closely. Nor, save for a few perceptive editorial writers, does anyone ever point out how ironic it is that such a term should be needed in the first place. Essentially, "user friendly" is supposed to mean "easy to use." But it is applied without rigor. Consequently, about all you can reasonably be sure of is that a user-friendly program probably won't require graduate work in computer science to master.

## "Menu Driven"

One gauge of user friendliness is the degree to which the program is "menu driven." This typically means that when you first boot the program you will be presented with a range of numbered choices. You make your selection by keying in the appropriate number and are then presented with a second menu that has other choices. The process continues until you reach whatever point you were aiming at when you started.

The principal advantage of a menu-driven program is initial ease of use. Some programs are so conscientious about providing menus every step of the way that you don't have to know anything about the program to begin using it immediately. Other programs are only partially menu driven and at a certain point leave you to your own devices as far as what you key in next.

The main disadvantage of a menu-driven program is that once you master the program, it becomes tedious to have to step through all those menus. Realizing this, the creators of many fully menu-driven programs either make it possible for you to "turn off" most of the menus and use commands that will take you directly to the section of the program you want to use, or they write the program so that it will accept such direct commands in addition to numbers from the menus.

## "Prompts"

Program "prompts" are another aspect of user friendliness. A prompt is anything that appears on the screen asking you to enter information. It could be something like "Please enter today's date . . ." or it could be "Please enter selection from menu above. . . ." Generally, the more specific the prompt is about what the program wants you to do, the easier the program will be to use.

For example, some programs may prompt you to "Enter filename:".

That's adequate and certainly something you can live with. But suppose that filenames on your system consist of two parts: the actual name (like "LETTER") and an "extension" indicating what type of file it is (like ".TXT" for "text"). Given the prompt above, what are you supposed to enter? "LETTER" or "LETTER.TXT"? A better prompt might be, "Enter filename and extension:" or "Enter filename (no extension):".

The differences are merely a matter of cosmetics. Substituting one prompt for another has absolutely no effect on the program or how it runs. But it can make a big difference in how easy it is to use. The problem is that all too often things like this are left exclusively in the hands of the programmers. The programmer knows that the user must enter the name of a file at a certain point, and so he or she simply writes the prompt and includes it in the program.

This is not to slam programmers, most of whom are highly trained specialists and many of whom are creative geniuses. It is rather to point out that programmers have a lot more on their minds than cosmetics and that a software shopper interested in selecting a product that the manufacturer has tried to make easy to use can tell a lot from such details as the actual wording of the prompts.

*"Single and Double Precision Floating Point Arithmetic"*

This term is like J. P. Morgan's view of owning a yacht: "If you have to ask how much it costs, you can't afford it." More than likely, if you don't already know what the term means, you don't need the features it describes. Normally, it is important only for mathematical and scientific applications where it is necessary to deal with very long numbers.

"Precision" refers to how many digits are in a number. The number *25* has two digits, the number *75,147* has five digits. In a perverse twist of language, precision has nothing to do with the accuracy of the number itself. Precision is a measure of the exactness with which a number can be calculated. So a number can be precise to 10 figures and still be inaccurate.

"Single precision" refers to the maximum number of digits the computer normally uses when working with or displaying a number. "Double precision" refers to an ability to handle nunbers that are twice as long. The actual number of digits possible in each case varies with the computer, though seven digits is typical for single precision numbers, and for technical reasons 16 digits (as opposed to 14) is typical for double precision numbers.

"Floating point arithmetic" is based on the technique of expressing numbers with exponents. As you may remember from high school science classes, when dealing with numbers that include lots of zeroes it saves time if you write them as a power of 10. For example, *1,574,000* can be written as *1.574* × *10⁶*. But the same number can also be written as *.01574* × *10⁸*. The decimal point "floats" to the left or right depending upon the power of 10 that is used.

The important thing about the floating point format is that it lets you or the computer add, subtract, multiply, and divide lengthy numbers by performing the operations on the digits and the exponents without ever having to write the numbers out completely. To add two numbers, for example, you first make the decimal points float so that both numbers are expressed using the same exponent or power of 10. Then you just add the digits. Multiplication is even easier. You simply multiply the digits and *add* the exponents, even if they are different (e.g., $10^3 \times 10^2 = 10^5$.

Whether these features are offered or not is sometimes a function of the computer, but often it's a software matter. A program written in "integer BASIC," for example, will only let you use whole numbers (no decimal points, floating or otherwise). A program written in a more advanced BASIC or other language, will let you enter numbers in a floating point format and will produce results with single or double precision. Both programs can usually be run on the same computer.

*"Spooling"*

In the absence of special programming or additional hardware, most personal computers sold today can only do one thing at a time. Computers are so fast that usually this isn't much of a problem. Where difficulties arise, however, is when the computer is forced to "wait" on a piece of hardware that operates much more slowly than it does. The hardware that slows things most often is the printer. If you tell the computer to "print this letter," both you and the computer may have to wait until the printout is finished before doing anything else. This makes it impossible, for example, to print one letter while simultaneously composing the next one.

There are two major ways to get around this problem, and they both involve memory chips. The more expensive way is to buy a "buffer box" and hook it up between your computer and your printer. A buffer box is little more than a lot of memory chips designed to be used as a temporary "holding tank." When you want to print something, you order the computer to dump the information to the buffer box.

As far as the computer is concerned, that's the end of it. The machine will immediately be free for you to use in writing something else or running a different program. While you're doing that, the buffer box will be feeding text to the printer at whatever speed it will accept. The computer itself is no longer involved.

The second solution is to use the memory chips that are already in your machine as a buffer box. This can be done in software. The feature is called "print spooling." In Chapter 1 we discussed how a program can mark off a computer's memory into sections reserved for CPU instructions and programming and sections for data and information. A print-spooling program does much the same thing. It says, "Okay. All the memory locations from here to there are to be used as a buffer box for the printer."

The CPU is then instructed to continue with whatever program it is that you are running and to send information from the internal buffer to the printer only when it has a bit of spare time. In human terms, the amount of time between the keystrokes entered by a high-speed typist seems almost nonexistent. But to a CPU it can seem luxuriously long. There is so much CPU time that with print-spooling software it can appear that the machine is really doing two things at once, accepting your keyboard input and printing out a previously composed piece of text.

You may find print spooling as a built-in feature of an applications program or you may find that you can buy a "spooler" program separately for use with many different applications. Some newer operating systems, notably MS-DOS 2.0 for the IBM/PC, even include a print-spooling feature as part of the standard DOS package.

The advantages of this feature are clear. Yet you should be aware that there are some limitations. Obviously you've got to have enough RAM in your system to spare for use as a spooling buffer. The actual amount will vary with the system, but you will probably need something close to 64K. It may or may not be important to you, but a spooled printout can take longer to produce than one to which the CPU is giving its full attention. (It all depends upon the other demands you are making on the CPU's time.) Finally, and probably most important of all, if you buy a separate print-spooling program, you may not be able to use it with all applications programs because the applications program may need the memory space the spooler normally uses. As separate "outboard" memories, buffer boxes don't suffer from this limitation.

---

**SoftTip:** Whenever a computer does two things at the same time, it is said to be performing "background" and "foreground" tasks. The foreground task is the one that has first priority as far as the computer is concerned. In the example above, if it had to choose between accepting a character from your keyboard and sending a character to the printer at a particular moment, the CPU would handle your input first since the word processing is taking place in the foreground.

## "Piping"

This term is a relatively new addition to the microworld, but as more and more 16-bit computers and operating systems capable of supporting the feature are sold, it will become increasingly common. A program that offers a piping feature is designed to accept input from a number of different sources. If you have a graph-generating program, for example, you obviously have to give it the numbers or statistics it needs to draw pie charts, bar graphs, trend lines, or other types of output.

In the past, this has normally meant that you or someone else must type in each statistic by hand. A piping feature can eliminate that inconvenience, for it allows you to "pipe in" the data from a number of sources. The data could come from a file that you have created on disk. Or they could come from the keyboard as in the past. Most important of all, as long as piping is supported by the operating system, data can also come from another program.

To put it another way, piping permits two programs to be chained together so that the output of one becomes the input of the other. Among other things, this means you could enter raw data into a program that would analyze the information and automatically dump the results to a graphics program for display on your screen.

## Other Important Terms

### "Patch"

A "patch" is a relatively short piece of programming that is added to the main applications or other program. As its name implies, sometimes a patch will be designed to fix some problem with the main program. But, more often than not, a patch will add some additional feature or enable the program to do something that it could not do without the patch.

A good example is a word processing program that will not support a particular brand of printer in its "as is" state. In that case, the manufacturer of the printer or the vendor may be able to supply a patch to the main program. Applying the patch is similar to the installation procedure discussed in Chapter 2. The computer takes the patch program off disk and does a little processing to incorporate it into the main program.

### "Overlay"

An overlay is a piece or module of an applications program that does not get loaded into the computer's memory when the program is booted. Instead, it stays on the disk and is loaded in only when you call for the functions it is designed to provide. It's called an overlay because when it is brought in it "overlays" (replaces) whatever other programming happens to be in the machine's memory at the time.

As you know from Chapter 1, a computer cannot execute a program until its internal memory switches have been set to patterns that tell the CPU what to do. Were it not for overlays, the programs you could run would be limited by the amount of memory your machine contained. But by figuratively emptying the tub and filling it with fresh programming, overlays let you use programs with more power and more features than would otherwise be the case.

That's the main advantage of overlays. But it is also the main disadvantage. Any time information or programming must be brought in from disk, there is an unavoidable delay in the program. The disk drive has to be turned on and brought up to speed; the read/write head has to pick up the information and dump it to RAM; the CPU has to look at RAM and reassure itself that the programming it needs is there; and so on.

Admittedly, this only takes a few seconds, but during that time you as the user must wait for the system to finish before doing anything else. After a while, this can be annoying. Fortunately, you can get around the overlay delay with a "RAM disk" or "electronic disk drive," a feature we'll look at in the next chapter.

### *"Default"*

Of all the words in computerese, this may well be the most difficult one to become accustomed to. The word *default* has such negative connotations in standard English that it's hard to think of it in a nonpejorative way. In computerese, "default" is an adjective, a verb, and a noun. In all cases it means "in the absence of instructions to the contrary."

Thus when a manual says that Drive A or Drive 1 or Drive 0 is the "default drive," it means that this is the disk drive a program or a computer will turn on and begin reading—unless you tell it otherwise. When a communications software program "defaults" to 300 baud and even parity, it automatically institutes those settings—unless you tell it otherwise. Similarly 300 baud is the program's "default."

It would be wonderful to be able to say that you don't have to acknowledge or accept this term. But unlike "documentation," there isn't an equivalent word or phrase you can conveniently substitute for it. And "default" is an important and necessary concept when dealing with software and computers.

### *ASCII Files*

The short explanation of an ASCII file is that it is a file stored as text. When you look at it by causing it to be displayed on the screen or printed on the printer, the words and punctuation marks—all the ASCII characters described in Chapter 1—will be there for you to read. This seems completely unremarkable until you realize that an ASCII format is not the only way information can be stored or filed by a computer. Indeed, most computers default to a machine language filing scheme for programs that tend to take up less room than a full ASCII format.

You will find more information about ASCII versus machine language files in your computer manuals. (Check your BASIC manual and see if it doesn't include commands to let you save a program in either format.) For now, all you need to know is that ASCII files are easy to read, and more importantly, easy to send and receive over the telephone or directly to some other computer. One computer may not understand another computer's machine language, but all communicating computers understand ASCII-represented English.

*DIF Files*

To most of us, a file is a file is a file. As long as the information we expect appears on the screen when we call for a particular file, we don't want to get involved. That is absolutely the way it should be. But having said that, it *is* important to be aware that files don't appear through magic. There is a lot going on beneath the surface that we never see.

For example, it's natural to assume that a letter you've written with a word processing program and recorded on disk as a text file consists of nothing more than the words you've written: "Dear Mom, How are you? I yam fine . . . It is lonely hear at camp and . . ."

But there's a lot more in the file than that. There might be a section called a "header" at the front of the file. The header holds information about what the file contains, and its job is to say, "Psst. Hey, System. Yeah, that's right, you over there. Listen, this file contains $X$ number of bytes. It consists of this piece of information here, that one over there, and another one someplace else."

As software users, we don't see any of this stuff. But it's there, and it's important. And it is subject to many variations. There are lots of ways a file can be stored on disk, and many different formats, none of them compatible. The DIF format is an attempt to establish a standard.

DIF® stands for "*Data Interchange Format*," and it is a trademark of Software Arts, Inc., the company that created VisiCalc. If a program is designed to accept and use files stored in the DIF format, it won't care where those files came from. That means that you can create a file with a mathematical problem-solving program like TK! Solver™ and use the resulting file as the input for a VisiCalc or other electronic spreadsheet—without having to type in any data. (See Chapter 15 for more details.)

**SoftTip:** If you would like more information on the DIF format, write to:

DIF Clearinghouse
P.O. Box 638
Newton Lower Falls, MA 02162

Be sure to enclose a check for $6.00 with your request for a copy of the "Technical Specifications" describing the format and the "Program List" that includes many of the applications programs that can exchange files in the DIF format. You will also receive a reprint of an article from the November 1981 issue of *Byte*, which describes the technical aspects of the DIF format.

## Hardware-Related Terms

*Mouse*

Throughout history humans have tended to view mice (of the furry rodent variety) with feelings of fear and dismay. Thus it seems a bit ironic that the name "mouse" should be applied to a mechanical device designed to help humans overcome those same feelings when they encounter a computer. It isn't clear where the name came from, perhaps from the fact that a computer mouse is small and meant to be moved around. It is generally agreed that the first mouse was designed in 1967 by Douglas Engelbart, a scientist at the Stanford Research Institute.

A mouse is a hand-held device that is used to move the cursor on the screen. It can be used the same way you might use the directional arrow keys on your keyboard if your machine has them. But it really comes into its own when used with software that allows you to run several programs at once and displays portions of each program in overlapping "windows" on your screen. (See Chapter 7—VisiON, DesQ, and Lisa.) A mouse lets you easily point to the portions of one program that you want to insert into another program.

Mice have long, thin cords for tails and they can be connected to your computer in a number of ways. Perhaps the most common is to plug the little bugger into a standard RS-232 communications port. Some firms sell interface boxes designed to accept both the mouse and the plug on your keyboard cable. The interface box is then plugged into the computer at the keyboard port.

There are two types of mice—"mechanical" and "optical." A mechanical mouse moves the cursor the way a trackball moves the aiming point crosshairs in Missile Command or other video games. In this case, the trackball-like mechanism is on the underside of the mouse, and you move it by rolling the mouse around on a table. An optical mouse requires a special pad that's been marked off with dots or lines. Measuring about 18 inches on a side, the pad lets the mouse optically count the marks to figure out how far it has moved and in which direction. It then translates the result into an onscreen cursor movement.

**SoftTip:** An important specification used with both mechanical and optical mice is "resolution"—or, "How far must the mouse be moved to move the cursor a given amount on the screen?" If an optical mouse had a resolution of 100 and a mechanical mouse had a rating of 200, the optical mouse might have to be moved twice as far to produce the same cursor movement on the screen as the mechanical one.

The numbers refer to measurable "events" per inch of mouse movement. With an optical mouse, an "event" is a dot or a line that it counts as it moves over the pad. Thus an optical mouse's resolution can be increased by using a different pad with more dots per inch. "Events" for a mechanical mouse are different, but you may be able to change the resolution through the software that senses mouse motion.

Mice also have one or more buttons. After you've got the cursor where you want it, one button may be used to activate some aspect of the program, like entering a selection from a menu. Depending on the software used with the mouse, a second button may allow you to scroll through the contents of an on-screen window at varying speeds. ViSION, among others, supports this feature.

Mice can cost anywhere from $200 to $350. But unless you have a specific use in mind, you probably shouldn't buy one. Since different mouse-supporting software products may have different mouse requirements—one, two, or three buttons, for example—it would be better to wait and make sure that the one you get can be used with the program. In some cases, you may even be required to purchase a mouse as part of the software package.

*Cursor-addressable CRT*
This term is used less and less frequently today. If you see it in an ad, you can probably assume that it's not something you have to worry

about. On many older computer terminals the cursor was limited to moving back and forth on the same line and could not be moved to various parts of the screen. The lines you typed in would always appear near the bottom of the screen and would scroll upward whenever you hit <ENTER> or a "carriage return." But you couldn't move the cursor up to add a word to a line you had already typed.

Today, virtually all personal computers have the ability to "address" the cursor, telling it to move to whatever location you specified with your joystick, mouse, or by hitting some key or combination of keys on your keyboard.

*Coprocessor or 8087 Coprocessor*

A few sophisticated applications programs require a "coprocessor" of some sort, and you'll see the term used in connection with the Z80 Softcard for the Apple and similar plug-in boards mentioned in Chapter 2. But the term is most frequently used in connection with the IBM/PC, as in "8087 coprocessor required."

A coprocessor is a second microprocessor chip designed to work with the main microprocessor CPU in your computer. Like the CPU, it has an instruction set and a certain amount of "intelligence." But often it has been "optimized" to perform certain tasks particularly well. The best example of this is the Intel 8087 cited above, a chip particularly well suited for performing calculations and fast number crunching.

When the IBM/PC was introduced in November 1981, the computer industry required about three hours to tear the machine apart and begin speculating about the "empty socket" IBM had left on the mother board (main circuit board) next to the machine's Intel 8088 main processor. Clearly some "future enhancement" was planned, but what could it be? It took less than three hours for many experts to conclude that the socket was designed to accept an Intel 8087 coprocessor chip.

Adding an 8087 to an IBM/PC or adding any coprocessor to any computer can increase the machine's power. By dividing the workload between two chips, it can also make the computer run faster. However, since the software must be written to take advantage of that extra power, there is usually no point in installing a coprocessor chip or board unless you need it to run a specific program.

---

**SoftTip:** One company that has taken the coprocessor concept and really run with it is Sritek. The firm sells its 256K VersaCard™ for the IBM/PC at a suggested retail price of $995. The card is unique, for not only can you boost the memory to 512K by plugging in RAM chips, but you can also insert a MicroCard™ equipped with any of the following processors: Z80, 8086, 68000, iAPX-286, or

16032. Working with the 8088 at the heart of the IBM, these coprocessors have the effect of turning a PC into many different machines capable of running many different kinds of software, including a complete 68000-based UNIX™ or Microsoft XENIX™ operating system.

For more information, contact:

> Sritek
> 10230 Brecksville Road
> Cleveland, OH 44141
> (216) 526-9433

*S-100 Bus*

You'll frequently see references to the S-100 bus or "S-100" systems. A bus, as you will recall, is the collection of electric lines that transport the voltage levels used to represent memory addresses, data, control signals, keyboard and disk drive input and output, and other types of information within a computer. The bus determines where the signals will be sent and which "pins" (connecting points) will carry what information.

Ideally, a bus will be standardized so that software writers and hardware manufacturers can create products that will work equally well on any computer that uses the bus. The RS-232C interface used for communications between a computer and a modem, printer, mouse, or video display is an example of one of the oldest standard buses. And so is the IEEE-488 interface found on the Commodore 64 and other computers.

When microcomputers were first introduced, however, there were no such standards for their internal bus arrangements. Like the CP/M operating system, the S-100 bus appeared on the scene at a time when everyone was desperately searching for some kind of standard. It was designed by the now defunct MITS, Inc. for use in the Altair, the world's first microcomputer. It was then adopted by IMSAI and things simply grew from there.

Like CP/M, the S-100 was never intended to become a "de facto standard" and consequently is generally agreed to have many weaknesses. It has since been codified as standard IEEE-696, a clear acknowledgement of its position as the most widely used busing scheme in the microcomputer industry.

## Indexed Sequential Access Method (ISAM)

This one's not as bad as it sounds. "ISAM" refers to a technique for recording information so that your computer can find it again quickly.

Because storing and retrieving all kinds of information—part numbers, addresses, invoices, baseball statistics, you name it—are things computers do superbly, the *way* that information is stored and retrieved is at the heart of many applications programs. It influences how they perform, how easy they are to use, how closely they conform to the way *you* want to do things, and more. ISAM represents one widely used solution. You'll find that it's a pretty neat solution, once you understand the problem.

The whole thing is based on the fact that information takes up space. Every letter, number, punctuation mark—even every blank space on a line—has a unique ASCII code number and every one of those ASCII codes must be recorded if you ever want to see your information alive again. The central thing to keep in mind, though, is that pieces of information vary greatly in length. The last name "Jones" takes up only five characters of space, while "Trachtenberg" requires 12 characters of space.

A computer has no difficulty recording either of these names on a floppy disk or other medium. The question is, How should it do the deed? If you assume that Jones and Trachtenberg are two names on a mailing list, then each address will constitute a record in your mailing list file. Wouldn't it make sense to simply record the names and addresses one right after the other? Sure it would, and many programs do just that.

The problem is that the record for Jones is shorter than the record for Trachtenberg. Even if they both live at the same address and their records are identical in every respect except the number of characters in their names, the records are *still* different and will still require a different amount of space to store. Programs that allow you to enter all the information in one of your records, regardless of the amount of storage space each one ultimately occupies, are said to use "variable-length records." (The word "variable" here is used as an adjective, meaning that the records can vary in length, not as the noun that refers to one of the fields in the record. The confusion is unfortunate, but that's the way computerese is.)

Variable-length records have two main advantages. First, you don't have to worry about how long each record is and whether all the stuff you want to enter will "fit." Second, since each record is written to disk one right after another, there is no "wasted" space on the disk. (Hold onto that thought. The significance will become clear in a moment.)

The main disadvantage of variable-length records is that they are difficult to locate again once they've been recorded. The only way a computer can tell where one record ends and the next one begins is to start at the beginning and read and reject each record until it finds the right one.

If you had 500 names (records) in your file and you wanted to look at record 206, the computer would have to start at record number 1 and read a total of 204 additional records until it knew that it had located record 206. This is called *sequential access*, because each record must be read in sequence. It's fine when all of your records will be processed in one continuous stream, but it is slow when the program calls for skipping around.

So slow that some time ago the computer industry concluded, "There's got to be a better way." What they came up with was the concept of "fixed-length" records. This amounted to a compromise, for in effect any program that uses fixed-length records says to its users:

"Congratulations! You have just purchased the finest (blah . . . blah . . . blah) . . . And, oh, by the way, you will be able to access your records with record speed. But in return for this speed, we must insist that you limit last names to no more than ten characters."

And so, "Mr. Trachtenberg" becomes "Trachtenbe." Actually, many programs that use fixed-length records will allow you to decide how long each record will be. Thus, you could probably accommodate Mr. Trachtenberg. *But you would have to plan to do so beforehand.* When you are deciding how long each record—or each field in a record—should be, you must think ahead to allow enough characters of space to accommodate the longest piece of information you plan to enter.

This need to plan ahead is the main disadvantage of a fixed-length record scheme. But there is another negative point as well. If the program says, "Okay, we're marking things off so that all records will be 256 bytes long," what happens when you've got a record that is shorter than that? What happens when you enter information for Ms. Jones?

The answer is that some of the space that has been set aside is not used. If things have been set up to permit 12 characters in the last-name field, then 12 characters of space will be reserved for every record. Whether Ms. Jones becomes Ms. Jones-Smith or remains Ms. Jones, her record will still occupy the same amount of space on disk.

*On the Plus Side*

The advantage of storing information in fixed-length records is a considerable one: *random access.* Each record has a number. And since each occupies the same amount of space on the disk, each can be given a specific address. If the computer keeps a separate little file containing all the record numbers and their corresponding disk addresses, then locating any given record is a snap. "You want record 206? Okay, let's see, that record is at disk location da-de-da. Pow! You got it."

The little list of record numbers and disk addresses the system keeps is called an *index*, and files constructed for random access of this sort are sometimes called "indexed files." They work quite well and are quite fast. There's just one problem: How do you locate Mr. Trachtenberg's record? How do you find Ms. Jones?

You could guess. That is, you could call for record numbers you think are close to the ones holding the desired names and start your search from there. But that's no fun. And it wastes time. It's much easier to keep a printout of all of your records by number and all of the information they contain. That way you can leaf through the pages until you find that the record for Ms. Jones is record 107, while Mr. Trachtenberg's is record 234. You can then type in the specific record number, make the additions, corrections, or changes you want, and save it to disk.

This is a powerful feature. But if you need to look at and deal with more than a few records, it can be a real nuisance to have to thumb through the printout looking for the correct record numbers. It would be much easier simply to tell the computer, "Find me Ms. Jones's record," or "Print out Mr. Trachtenberg's record." And that's where ISAM comes in.

Under the ISAM system, the computer keeps its little index file. But in addition to containing record numbers and their corresponding disk addresses, this list *also* contains information on what's in each record. That information is called a "key." "Key" is short for "search key," which itself is short for "the keyword on which the search will be conducted." As you might imagine, an index file that contains keywords is sometimes called a "key file."

They may not always say so in their literature and ads, but filing programs, database management programs, and many others use some variation of the ISAM approach. Basically, the thing to remember about this technique is that it allows you to locate information on the basis of key words, rather than record numbers.

---

**SoftTip:** For information on other puzzling terms, please see The Computerese and Jargon Interpreter at the back of this book. The items you'll find there have been selected on the basis of the terms you are most likely to encounter when reading software ads and reviews.

For a broader focus that encompasses both hardware and software, you might want to get one or more of the computer dictionaries listed at the beginning of that part of the book. You should know, however, that none of the dictionaries available at this writing is comprehensive. And none focuses exclusively on the personal computer world. All of them contain terms that are applicable only to mainframes and minis. As a recommendation, you should probably start with *Webster's New World Dictionary of Computer Terms* by Laura Darcy and Louise Boston ($5.95). This was published in 1983 and appears to contain a higher percentage of personal computer terms than most.

Although it may not yet have been published at the time you read this, keep your eye out for a dictionary/glossary book by Steve Rosenthal. Mr. Rosenthal writes a regular glossary column for *InfoWorld,* "the newsweekly for microcomputer users." His definitions are excellent and he focuses exclusively on those that apply to personal computers. His columns are sure to be published in book form sometime in the future.

# ...5...

## The Media and the Message
## *How to Make Any Program Easier to Use*

The speed with which an applications program does its job, the way it handles information, and the features it includes are for all intents and purposes "set at the factory." They are a function of how the program was designed and how the code was written, and usually there is nothing you can do to change them. However, while you can't alter the software, there are at least three things you can do to make *any* program easier, faster, and more convenient to use. You can:

- Equip your system with disk drives capable of storing more information on a single disk.
- Install additional RAM chips and use a special program that will let your computer treat the extra memory as a disk drive.
- Install or add on a super-capacity "hard disk" or "Winchester" drive.

Of course, you can also make sure that your system includes these options when you buy it and thereby eliminate the need for any postpurchase installation. One or more of these three options is available for most major eight-bit and 16-bit computers, but since each involves machine-specific hardware, the precise details will differ with your particular brand. In addition, since they can add anywhere from $250 to $2,500 or more to the cost of your equipment, you should ask yourself, Do I need this? Is the extra cost worth it to me? when considering any of these alternatives.

Having said that, however, you should also be aware that high-capacity floppy disk drives, RAM-based "electronic" drives, and hard disk systems can enhance speed and ease of use so dramatically as to become

120

almost irresistible. Fortunately, with memory and hardware prices constantly falling, in the near future they may become irresistibly affordable as well.

*Mass Storage Basics*

As you know, before a CPU can run a program, tens of thousands of internal memory switches must be set to generate the voltages that represent either the chip's instructions or the data it will use as it executes the program. And as you also know, one of the major advances in early computer development was the concept of storing instructions and data on some kind of "media" that would make it easy to pour them back into the machine whenever you liked.

The various techniques used to store programming and data can have a major impact on the convenience, capabilities, and ease of use of the applications software you buy. This area of computerdom is called "mass storage," and over the years many devices have been developed for this purpose.

Today, almost all mass storage techniques are based on the same general ideas found in an audio or video tape recorder. A piece of Mylar® or some other "substrate" material is coated with a substance like iron oxide (a fancy name for highly refined rust), and brought into contact with a read/write head capable of generating or responding to tiny magnetic fields. A magnetic field that is polarized in one direction is used to represent a *1* and a field polarized in the opposite direction is used to represent a *0*. Basically, that's all there is to it.

Many variations have been played on this theme, of course, and the considerable differences among them can be quite important to you and the software you run. In the broadest sense, the type of mass storage device you use will affect you in three areas:

- The speed with which you can use a program. (Will there be a delay between the point when you enter a command and the action the system takes, or will things appear to happen instantly?)
- The amount of data and other information that will be conveniently available to you and your program at any one time. (Will you be able to look at any page of a 100-page report whenever you want, or will you have to do some fiddling first?)
- The total cost of your system.

These three points—speed, capacity, and cost—are inextricably linked, and an increase or decrease in one usually has the same effect on the others. At the bottom of the scale are cassette tape recorders— painfully slow, of limited capacity, but about as cheap a peripheral as you'll find. At the top are "hard disk" systems—incredibly fast, capacious, and very expensive. In between, are several types of "floppy disks."

### Predisk Systems: Cassette Systems and Firmware Cartridges

Some people would disagree, but it is difficult to avoid feeling that "serious software" and "cassette system" are mutually exclusive terms. Many personal computers, including the Atari, the Commodore VIC, the Radio Shack, and even the IBM/PC offer you the option of using a tape recorder as a mass-storage device for programs and data.

On the surface, that seems like a good idea. After all, tape recorders sell in the $50 to $75 range and disk drives go for upwards of $200. What a great, inexpensive way to get into personal computing. And it is. If you don't have a lot of money and if your main goal is to play computer games or learn about computers and programming, then a cassette system may make sense. But if you plan to *use* your computer in any significant way, you would be better off waiting until you could afford a floppy disk drive. That wait may not be too long. There will probably never be a $75 floppy disk drive, but prices *are* coming down.

Leaving aside the hassle of getting the tape wound to just the right spot and the frequent need to fiddle with the tape recorder's volume control, the main problem with cassette systems is speed. They are painfully slow. Equally important, since everything is stored on one long piece of magnetic tape, you cannot get at information immediately. You must wait for the tape to turn forward or back until it reaches the file you want.

If you have never sat in front of a computer waiting and waiting and waiting for a cassette-based program to load in, you owe yourself this experience before deciding to use a tape recorder as a mass storage device. Ask a salesperson or a friend to give you a demonstration. Perhaps the best thing that can be said about a cassette tape recorder is that it is so cheap that you won't be out all that much money when you get fed up and replace it with a floppy disk system.

Firmware cartridges of the sort designed to be plugged into Texas Instruments and Atari home computers do not use magnetic media. Instead, they contain ROM chips with permanently entered, hard-wired programming. They are thus very fast, because as far as the computer is concerned, the programming is instantly within its grasp. Thus, there is no need to load it in from some external device.

Unfortunately, firmware cartridges have two major disadvantages. Most of them contain programs designed to be run on a system with minimal memory, and therefore are not very powerful. They will have little more than the most basic applications program features. Second, once you've used such a program to write a letter or work out your household budget, how do you record what you have produced? More than likely, on a cassette tape recorder.

## Software Impact Statement

To summarize, cassette systems and firmware cartridges can serve as an excellent, inexpensive introduction to personal computing. But they are far too limited and make too many demands on the user, the most serious of which is "Please wait."

**SoftTip:** A number of manufacturers have attempted to overcome many of the limitations inherent in a tape-based system while preserving the advantage of low cost. The most promising and possibly the most significant of these attempts may be the high-speed tape device that is a part of the Adam computer manufactured by Coleco, a leading home video game company. As with everything else in computerdom, seeing is believing, so be sure to get a complete demonstration of the mass-storage system used by the Adam or any other computer before you buy.

## Disk Systems—Tools for Modern Times

The most fundamental advantage offered by a disk-based mass storage system is random access. As noted elsewhere, random access allows you to grab any piece of information or programming at any time the way you "access" any cut on a record by moving the tone arm and lowering it to the record. Thus, a disk can be thought of as a cassette tape that has been melted down and recast in record-album form. There are two major categories of disk systems—"floppy" and "hard"—and we'll look at both from an applications software perspective.

## Floppy Disks: SS/SD, SS/DD, DS/SD, etc.

It probably goes without saying that the most obvious distinction among floppy disks is one of size. There are disks measuring 8 inches across and disks measuring 5¼ inches across. Both consist of very thin circular pieces of plastic encased in a protective square of cardboard. When information or programming is to be read from or written to the disk, the read/write head of the disk drive is pushed onto the revolving disk. Some personal computers use 8-inch disks, but most use the 5¼-inch size.

**SoftTip:** In the not too distant future, a third size is destined to become widespread if IBM, Sony, Matsushita, Hitachi, Verbatim, and other firms have their way. The disks will measure 3, 3.25, 3.3, or 3.9 inches across and the battle to establish one of them as the industry "standard" has already begun. Regardless of who is successful, a new acronym describing this media appears likely to enter the language: CFD for "compact floppy disk."

Floppy disks differ in other ways that cannot be seen with the naked eye. For example, all floppy disks are designated as either "single density" (SD) or "double density" (DD). The density is determined by the thickness of the magnetic oxide coating. The actual figures vary with the machine, but if we disregard the need to store disk-formatting information, a single-density disk might be able to store 80K of programming or data.

Since one double-spaced typewritten page occupies about 2K, there's room to store a 40-page document or any combination of documents, programs, spreadsheets, and the like totalling 80K. A double-density disk, however, could store twice that amount: 160K, or 80 pages.

The second major invisible distinction among disks is whether they are single sided (SS) or double sided (DS). In reality, *all* disks are double-sided and can be used in double-sided drives. The difference is that a double-sided disk is certified by the manufacturer to be error free on both sides, whereas only one side is certified for the other variety. As their names imply, a double-sided disk can store twice the information of a single-sided disk.

### The Drive Dictates the Disk

As you can see, the amount of information that can be stored on a floppy disk is a function of its density and whether it is single or double sided. But neither of these characteristics means anything if you don't also factor in the disk drive. If you want double-density storage, for example, your computer must be equipped with a double-density disk drive. If you want to take advantage of double-sided disks, your drives must have two read/write heads, one for each side.

**SoftTip:** Double-density disks cost between 10% and 20% more than single density. One might think that their thicker magnetic coating would make them perform better even in a single-density drive, but that is not the case. The extra coating has no effect on performance in a single-density system, so save your money if you have single-density drives.

Working in conjunction with your DOS, the disk drive or drives in your system will also determine the *actual* number of kilobytes that constitute single or double density. To the Tandon TM 100-1 drives in the IBM/PC, double density means 160K per formatted disk. To the drives in the Osborne Executive, it means 200K.

Information is stored in concentric circles or tracks, and the more tracks the read/write head can put on a disk, the more information it can store. There are other factors involved, but you might think of the read/write heads as pens. The head in one drive might be a Flair® felt tip, while the other is more like a Pilot Razor Point® pen. The "finer point" head is going to be able to "draw" more tracks on the same disk.

Until recently, the maximum number of tracks possible has been about 96 tracks per inch. Since a band measuring less than an inch is the only part of the disk's surface that is actually used, that translates into 80 tracks per side. However, drives capable of 150 tracks per inch (about 125 per side) are expected in the near future.

---

**SoftTip:** Sometimes you will hear the term "quad-density" applied to floppy disks. Unfortunately for the sake of consistency, this does not refer to the thickness of the magnetic coating. Instead, a quad-density disk is a regular double-density disk that has been formatted to have 96 tracks per inch. Consequently, it can store quadruple the amount of information stored on a *single*-density disk that has been formatted to have the more standard 48 tracks.

---

*Hard and Soft Sectors*

Floppy disks are also designated as being "soft sectored" or "hard sectored," though most personal computers use the "soft" variety. The two terms refer to the presence or absence of punched holes in the disk. All floppy disks have an index hole in the cardboard envelope that surrounds them. You'll find it near the disk's hub, and if you were to rotate the disk, a corresponding hole in the medium would eventually appear there. The disk drive uses this hole as a reference point. Every time the hole in the medium appears, the drive knows that one full rotation has been completed.

Disk sectors, as you know, are portions of the concentric tracks that are placed on the disk when it is formatted for use by your system. You can think of sectors as arcs. Better yet, imagine cutting a pie-shaped wedge out of an archery target. The portion of each of the colored target rings in the wedge is a sector.

With a soft-sectored disk, the location and number of sectors is determined by the operating system that does the formatting. One operating system might format the disk to have 10 sectors per track, while another DOS might create 16 sectors on the same disk. A hard-sectored disk, in contrast, does not permit this kind of flexibility.

Hard-sectored disks have from 10 to 16 index holes punched into the medium for each sector. The principal advantage of a hard-sectored disk is that the index holes eliminate the need to record much of the formatting information on the disk. That saves space and allows a hard-sectored disk to store more useful data. Hard-sectored disks are only effective on drives designed to use them.

*Software Impact Statement*

The type of disk drives you use in your system affects the software you use in two ways. First, you've got to make sure that the program is available on a disk that your drives can read. Double-density drives can usually read disks designed for single-density drives, but it doesn't work the other way around. By the same token, you will not be able to use a program that has been recorded on a double-sided disk in a single-sided drive, regardless of density. So, before you buy a program, be sure to ask about this point.

The second area of impact has nothing to do with the program itself. Instead, it concerns the information the program generates and uses. In almost every case, the more information your disk drives can store and retrieve, the more convenient the applications program will be to use. Word processing programs are a good example, though the same idea applies to any program.

If you had written something that totalled 160 double-spaced typewritten pages, approximately 320 kilobytes of disk storage space would be needed to record it. If you were using a SS/SD disk drive, you might be able to fit about 40 pages on a disk. Thus, you would need four disks to store the entire manuscript. A single-sided, double-density drive would let you put twice as much on a disk and reduce the number to two disks. But with a double-sided, double-density drive you could put the whole thing on a single disk.

Now, suppose that you had this manuscript and that you wanted to make some changes on page 78. Which of the three disk alternatives is going to be easiest to use? Clearly, the one that gives you the greatest capacity per disk. With a DS/DD drive and disk, the entire manuscript is "online" (available to the computer). Any page can be looked at and changed without having to locate one of two or four disks. You merely insert it into the drive, find the target page and make the changes, record the results on the disk, and then repeat the process to look at or change another page.

There are many other examples, but clearly the more storage your disk drives provide, the more convenient a program will be to use. We'll look at the cost issue in a moment. But first, let's consider the current apotheosis of disk drive technology—the hard disk.

*Hard Disk or "Winchester" Drives*

The Cadillac of mass storage is the hard or "fixed" disk drive. Sometimes called "Winchesters" after the code word IBM used when developing the first hard disk system, these units consist of rigid aluminum platters coated with sumarium cobalt (Who knows what it is? It sounds wonderful.) or an equally sensitive material sealed in a metal box. The platters typically rotate at 3,600 r.p.m., or more than 10 times the speed of a floppy disk. The high speed of rotation creates a cushion of air that lifts the read/write head off the disk's surface as it turns.

When formatted, hard disks can hold anywhere from five to 160 *megabytes* (Mb) of information, or more. The 10-megabyte hard disk originally supplied with the IBM/XT, for example, occupies no more space than a standard floppy drive, but can store more information than 60 single-sided, double-density floppy disks. It can locate your files 10 times faster than a floppy drive and it can pour them into the computer or onto your screen at a rate of five million bits per second—compared to only a quarter of a million bits per second for floppy disks. In human terms, that means virtually instant access.

*Software Impact Statement*

From a software standpoint, there are at least three points to bear in mind regarding hard disks. First, the operating system you use must support a hard disk. Like floppies, hard disks have to be formatted before they can be used. And, like any piece of hardware, they have to be "interfaced" to the rest of the system. Those jobs are the responsibility of the operating system and the DOS you use must be able to perform them.

Second, since hard disks mean speed, virtually any applications program placed on a hard disk will run better and faster than its floppy disk version. If the floppy-disk-based program you buy permits you to make unlimited "backups" (copies), transferring the program to a hard disk can be as easy as making a floppy copy. However, since many software houses use one or more "copy-protection" schemes to keep users from duplicating their disks, "installing" such a program on a hard disk could be a problem.

**SoftTip:** There is no clean solution to getting a copy-protected program onto a hard disk, though in the computer industry, few things are truly impossible. The question is always whether the game is worth the candle. If you have a good relationship with the retailer who sold you the hard disk or the hard-disk-equipped computer, and if you are purchasing the applications program from him, then he may be able to arrange to install the program for you.

In addition, it is not unheard of for a customer to ship a hard disk unit to a software house, along with a purchase order for the program. The software company can then install the program and send back the disk unit. Obviously, detailed arrangements must be made beforehand. And, since hard disk units are rather delicate, they must be carefully packed and insured.

The third software/hard disk consideration concerns the need to make backups of your data. More than one company has had its entire mailing list wiped out because the computer operator mistakenly erased the wrong hard disk file. With a hard disk system, it is as easy to obliterate 10,000 names, payroll records, or accounts receivable as it is to erase one. Good computer practice has always dictated making backups on a regular (daily) basis. The problem with hard disk drives is that there is so *much* to back up.

Inserting and dumping files to 60 or more floppy disks each day is clearly out of the question. Many companies, after performing this process once, keep track of and back up only the files that have been changed during the day. With a special interface board and software it is also possible to use a standard video tape recorder to back up a hard disk. The time required is between two and four minutes per megabyte, or roughly half an hour to back up a 10-meg hard disk.

The more modern solution, though, is to use a special hard disk backup unit with removable hard disk or high-speed tape cartridges. These units can copy the contents of a hard disk in as little as two minutes. The cartridge can then be removed and stored in a safe place, like an "archival copy" of a floppy disk.

Hard disks are expensive. They start at around $1,375 for a 5-meg system and rapidly increase to the $3,000 range for disks of larger capacity. But, as we'll see in a moment, they are quite cost effective, and for many businesses with large mailing lists, inventories; payrolls, accounts receivable, and the like, they are a virtual necessity. A DS/DD 320K floppy disk might be able to hold no more than 1,700 typical inventory records, whereas a 5-meg hard disk could hold 26,000.

It is difficult to imagine a home or small business application for which the storage capacity of a hard disk system would be essential, or the expense worthwhile. But that doesn't mean that you can't have hard-disk-like speed and a more affordable price. There is another solution.

*RAM-based Electronic Disk Drives*
For speed and relative affordability, you can't beat a RAM-based disk drive. You will hear it called many things, including RAM disk, Flash disk, E-disk (for disk emulator), virtual disk drive, pseudo- or hyper-drive, and C-drive. But all of these terms refer to the same thing: a technique for fooling your computer into thinking that a portion of its internal memory is actually a floppy disk drive. Performing this bit of prestidigitation can boost the speed with which your applications software performs by 60%, 70%, or more, giving you the benefits of hard disk response without hard disk costs.

The general concept is to install enough RAM in your system to equal or approximate the amount of storage available on a floppy disk. To use this feature, you first run a special RAM drive program to "tell" your system that this memory is to be treated as a disk drive. Then you copy the applications program and data files "onto" that "drive."

Since all bits look alike to your computer's CPU, it doesn't care where they actually came from. But you will. Particularly when you are using a program (such as WordStar™) that makes extensive use of overlays.

When you run WordStar without first copying the program into a RAM drive, it frequently has to go out to disk to get the program module it needs to respond to your commands. That means that the disk drive must be turned on and brought up to speed. The target module must be located and read into memory. And the CPU must execute the necessary instructions. With a RAM drive, the response is almost instantaneous. In fact, the improvement in response time is so dramatic that many people will not use WordStar any other way.

Some type of RAM drive can be installed for almost all personal computers, but it is often easier to implement on a 16-bit machine because the ability to accept large amounts of additional memory is built into its design. There are two major ways that a RAM drive can be installed on most 16-bit computers. Both require a plug-in memory expansion card that has been "populated" (filled in) with a sufficient number of RAM chips and a special software program to fool the system.

Many memory board manufacturers include RAM drive software as part of the package, though you may be able to buy a different RAM program elsewhere. There may be a good reason for doing so, since, like all software, different RAM drive programs offer different features. Some will let you create RAM drives of up to 320K, while others permit "drives" of up to 2.5Mb, and still others will let you divide your extra memory into two RAM drives. A lot depends on your particular computer, so be sure to investigate thoroughly. And to keep expenses down, be sure to look at the *minimum* amount of memory that can be treated in this way by the program. You may not need all the RAM necessary to hold everything on a floppy disk.

The memory boards available also differ with the computer. Some offer nothing more than slots to hold additional RAM chips, but increasingly the trend is toward including things like a battery-driven clock, and a communications (RS-232) and printer interface as well. Because of this they are sometimes called "combo (combination) cards." And because of their different features, they can be difficult to compare in price.

There are two main techniques used to create a RAM drive. The only difference is one of convenience. Using one approach, you must flip some switches on the combo card that have the effect of setting aside 160K or some other amount of memory as a "permanent" RAM disk drive. PC-DOS for the IBM, for example, has a function that can be used to ask the system to report how much internal memory it has. With your combo card installed, you may actually have a total of 320K of RAM in your computer.

But if you have flipped the switches to set aside 160K of that for use as a virtual disk drive, the system will not be able to "see" it. Consequently, it will report that you have 160K when you enter the proper DOS command. Should you ever want to run a program that requires more than 160K of internal memory, you can do so. But you must reset the switches on the combo board first. Removing the computer's cover and reaching in with a small screwdriver to flip the tiny switches is not something that you will look forward to doing on a regular basis.

The second technique is much more convenient. The extra memory you add is normally considered part of the computer's main memory. However, the RAM disk software is able to set aside a certain portion of it as a virtual disk drive. If you had 320K of RAM, for example, you could use the special software to set aside 160K of it as a disk drive for one program, but use the full 320K for some other program without ever having to reset the switches on the combo board.

Having all of your extra RAM available as directly accessible machine memory when it is not in use as a RAM drive can dramatically reduce the time required for an applications program to sort information. It can be important if you are using a software print spooler. And it can allow you to work with much larger files. VisiCalc will let you use up to 256K and SuperCalc can use up to 512K to create massive spreadsheets.

## Software Impact Statement

RAM drives are thus very similar in performance to hard disk drives. The main differences are that they have a much smaller capacity and they cannot be used to store programs and data permanently. When you power down, the volatile RAM chips immediately forget whatever it was they were holding. Consequently, it is crucial to remember to copy your files back onto a floppy disk before turning off the machine. Indeed, since RAM is vulnerable to power surges and voltage spikes, it may make sense to install a surge suppressor (see Chapter 1) and to frequently copy files onto a floppy disk throughout the day.

As with a hard disk, your computer's operating system must be capable of supporting all of your drives, RAM and floppy. If you already have two drives in your system and your DOS will only support two drives, then you may not be able to use a RAM drive, at least not without applying a DOS patch. The RAM drive software may include the necessary patch, but it's something you should check.

The limitation on using copy-protected applications software with a hard disk applies to RAM drives as well. If the program cannot be copied, you probably will not be able to transfer it into RAM. The answer may depend on the particular copy-protection scheme used by the software producer, so it pays to ask.

For example, Philadelphia's MicroCorp uses an especially interesting technique to copy-protect its Intelliterm™ communications program. The master program disk contains what can be thought of as a software "key." Whenever the program begins to run, it looks for that key on the master disk. Everything except the key, however, can be copied.

This means you can copy the entire program into a RAM drive. When you run the program, it quickly looks for the key on the floppy disk. But once it has found it and started to run, the master disk is no longer needed and can be removed, freeing your floppy drive for other purposes.

## Which Option Should You Choose?

It is axiomatic in computerdom that regardless of the amount of memory or storage in your system, it will always be at least a thousand bytes less than you need. This is something of a variant of Parkinson's Law, which states that the amount of work will always expand to occupy the amount of time available to complete it. In short, if you've got a high capacity floppy drive, a RAM drive capability, or a hard disk system, you'll use it and be glad that it's there.

But should you buy one of these options in the first place? That's the question likely to strike terror into the heart of your Visa card. If you work for a corporation, it may make sense to buy the biggest, fastest hard disk drive you can bury in your marketing or expense budget without raising eyebrows around the firm. If anyone asks you about it, assuming they understand what it is in the first place, you can easily cost-justify it on the basis of increased operator productivity. No time wasted looking for floppy disks; instant access to critical information; the possibility of a future "local area network" linking several computers; that sort of thing.

If you are in business for yourself, it makes sense to buy the most capacious system you can afford. Coming up with the cash may be difficult, but you should know that there's a reward every April 15th when the government lets you write off substantial portions of your investment in computer hardware. Check with your accountant for details and to see if it would be better to buy a hard-disk equipped computer or add a hard disk at a later date. If you've got partners to persuade, don't overlook the "room for future expansion" argument. You may only have 1,000 customers now, but in the future, who knows?

If you plan to use your computer at home, it's important to be aware of the seductively sexy nature of "massive" memory capacity. No one gets worked up over a 320K or even a 500K disk drive, but there is something magical about having 196K or 256K or more RAM in your system—even if you regularly use less than 64K of it to play "Cosmic Crusader" or "Castle Wolfenstein." More memory and a high capacity disk drive will make many of your programs easier and more enjoyable to use. Just be sure you'll use it.

*A Second Floppy Drive or a RAM Disk?*

If you have a cassette-based system, your first decision will be what kind of disk drive to add. But since many people begin with a single-drive system, the more frequently encountered question is whether to buy a second floppy drive or the plug-in board and memory chips needed for an RAM disk. Because combo cards offer other features in addition to more memory, it is difficult to compare the cost of a RAM drive to a floppy drive.

However, to use the IBM/PC as an example, a single-sided, double-density floppy drive and disk might sell at a discount for about $200. With one drive already in the system, there would be no need to purchase a disk controller card, so that would be close to your total cost for 160K of storage. The memory expansion board sold by the Seattle Computer Company might sell for about $240. At that price, the board would come with 64K of RAM. But it would also include an RS-232 communications port, a device IBM sells for about $120.

To compare the two on the basis of storage provided, you'd have to subtract $120 from the price of the Seattle board. That would mean that the board and your first 64K of memory would cost $120. The RAM disk software is included, and it can be used to turn that memory into a 64K RAM drive.

---

**SoftTip:** A RAM drive of 64K is not large enough to accommodate a word processing program like WordStar or Select™, so those programs will not run any faster. They will still have to go out to disk to bring in their overlays. However, a 64K RAM drive can still be a boon because you can use it to store and work with whatever you happen to be writing or editing.

By loading your document into the RAM drive, you will be able to call up and display any page or piece of text instantly. If the document were stored on a floppy disk, you would have to wait for the system to turn the drive on and read it into memory before you could work with it. That convenience alone might make it worthwhile for you to buy a 64K board instead of a second 160K floppy drive.

---

Fortunately, after your initial investment in the board, you can add memory in 64K chunks by plugging in more RAM chips. The chips sell, at a discount, for about $50 per 64K of memory. Usually, you must add 64K at a time, but for the sake of comparison, let's assume that you can add two 64K chunks ($100) and a 32K chunk for $25 to bring the original 64K board up to 160K. The total cost of the board would then be $365. But since we are assuming that $120 of that is for the communications port, the total cost for 160K of RAM would thus be $245—only $45 more than a floppy disk drive and disk.

---

**SoftTip:** Since PC-DOS for the IBM comes with a free communications program (COMM.BAS), you won't need any additional software to begin using the communications port on a combo board immediately. There are free or inexpensive communications programs available for most other computers as well.

Since most combo boards include a communications port, you need spend only about $70 more for a 300-baud modem and connecting cable to begin using the nation's free computer bulletin boards to obtain hundreds of free programs.

We'll go into more detail in Chapter 12, but inexpensive communications alone can be a powerful inducement to buy a combo board instead of a second floppy drive.

*Floppies, RAM Drives, and Hard Disks—A Cost-per-K Comparison*
One way to compare these three program-improving storage options is on the basis of what it costs to store 1K of information in each of them. The following table includes real prices, but a number of caveats apply. First, all hardware is for the IBM/PC. The costs of comparable equipment for non-IBM computers will undoubtedly vary, just as the prices given here will almost certainly have changed. The thing to focus on is the relationships between the various options, for these are likely to be similar for any brand of computer and remain fairly constant over time.

The table assumes that you already have one disk drive and therefore do not have to purchase a disk controller card. And prices of the combo boards have not been adjusted to reflect only the cost of the memory. The approach used can be characterized by the question, What would I actually have to pay per kilobyte to add more memory to my system, even if I had to buy extra features to get it?

**A Comparison of Storage Costs**

| Description | Capacity | Total Cost | Cost per K |
|---|---|---|---|
| SS/DD drive and floppy | 160K | $200 | $1.25 |
| DS/DD drive and floppy | 320K | $250 | $0.78 |
| Seattle Board (includes comm. port) | 64K | $240 | $3.75 |
| Seattle Board (includes comm. port) | 256K | $400 | $1.56 |
| Davong Hard Disk System | 5Mb (5,000K) | $1,375 | $0.275 |
| Davong Hard Disk System | 10Mb (10,000K) | $1,775 | $0.178 |
| Davong Hard Disk System | 15Mb (15,000K) | $2,175 | $0.145 |

*Demand a Demo!*

Cost comparisons and explanations are important, but only a live demonstration can give you the information you will ultimately need to make your decision. You can never fully appreciate the ease, speed, and convenience these options can add to any applications program until you see them in action. As a suggestion, you might visit your computer retailer and ask a salesperson to demonstrate the word processing examples described in this chapter. The retailer will almost certainly have a copy of WordStar and be able to show you how it runs on floppy, RAM, and hard disks. You will be amazed at the difference these options can make.

# ...6...
# Secondary Operating Systems and UNIX™:
## *A Change in the "Environment"*

Virtually all computers come with a standard operating system of some sort. But since system software *is* software, there is usually no reason why you can't buy it and choose it the way you would any other type of software—on the basis of the features each program provides. The difference is that the main purpose of any operating system is to give you access to the applications programs written to run under its control. It is thus usually a means to an end, not an end in itself.

Nevertheless, operating systems are something special. Many of them offer "features" in the way that a word processing program or a spreadsheet program does. But some of them go beyond that. Because operating systems are concerned chiefly with the computer's physical resources (internal memory, disk drives, video display, etc.), they have the power to alter and control the "environment" in which a program runs. That can have a major effect on the features the applications software itself is able to offer. Equally important, it can affect the way you interact with your machine. Increasingly, new system software is the focus of a major drive to make personal computers much easier to use.

*OS's and Window-Making Add-ons*
Classification schemes are always tricky, but generally it seems fair to say that there are now two types of system software: operating systems and operating system "add-ons." An operating system is and always will be necessary to run an applications program. An "add-on" can be thought of as a chunk of system programming that fits between the operating system and the applications program to produce a special effect—like dividing your screen up into overlapping windows, each of

136

which displays a spreadsheet, a memo, a graph, or a portion of some other program currently loaded into your machine. Two of the best examples of these "window makers" are VisiON™ and DesQ™. We'll consider them, as well as Apple's implementation of windows on its Lisa computer, in the next chapter. For the present, the only thing you need to know about them is that by themselves VisiON and DesQ and "window makers" from other firms cannot run an applications program. An operating system is still necessary.

## DOS Divided by Four

For their part, operating systems can be divided into perhaps four categories. First, there is the standard DOS that has received the official blessing of your computer manufacturer. Examples include TRSDOS for Radio Shack products, PC-DOS (MS-DOS) for the IBM, and DOS 3.3 for the Apple. Most software written for your machine will be designed to run under its standard operating system.

Next, there are what might be called "secondary operating systems." These are DOS's written and sold by independent software companies, though your computer manufacturer may offer them as well. There are basically two reasons to consider a secondary DOS. Either it will give you access to a large number of programs not available for your regular DOS, or it will be just like your regular DOS but include more convenience features.

The best example of the first type is CP/M for the Apple, the IBM, or any other computer where CP/M is not the standard system. Examples of the second type include LDOS, MultiDOS, or any of the dozen other operating systems sold for use with Radio Shack equipment. Because of all the extra features they include, these products typically sell for considerably more than the standard DOS, but they will run virtually all of the same applications programs.

Third, there are operating systems that are able to bring off a fundamental change in the way you use your computer and your applications programs. The best examples of these are Concurrent CP/M or "CCP/M," and a multiple-user DOS called MP/M. Both of these are products of Digital Research and both are designed to let you run CP/M software. The difference is that with CCP/M you can have several programs in your machine at the same time and switch among them as you please, and with MP/M several people can use the same computer at the same time.

Finally, there is the "It's-a-whole-new-ball-game!" type of operating system, which holds the potential for bringing minicomputer and mainframe power, features, and capabilities to the microworld of personal computers. There is really only one operating system in this category—

UNIX from AT&T's Bell Laboratories. Although it is not yet widely available for personal computers, UNIX is clearly where the micro-world is headed, and you will be hearing much more about it in the years to come.

In this chapter, we will first look at some of the things you will want to consider when buying an operating system that is compatible with, but more feature filled, than your standard DOS. Then we'll look at the "multi-tasking" and "multi-user" features offered by DOS's in the third category. And finally, we'll show you what UNIX is all about and what it will eventually mean to you.

## Secondary Operating Systems

*The Main Components of Any DOS Package*

It is important to emphasize once again that almost every DOS is sold as a package and that the package typically contains three main components:

- Pure system software that is essential for running applications programs. Includes modules to mate with and extend the BIOS or its equivalent in your computer, the BDOS, and other modules.
- Utility programs intended to help you handle housekeeping chores like formatting a blank disk or copying files from one disk to another. Not needed to run applications programs.
- "Extras" for programmers. Line editors, linker modules, and the like intended to be used when writing programs. Again, not needed to run applications programs.

The different "utility" programs and features offered by different DOS packages can be very desirable, since they can make using your computer easier and more convenient. To take just one example, Multi-DOS by Cosmopolitan Electronics (P.O. Box 234, Plymouth, MI 48170) loads into a TRS-80 Model III in about one second, compared to the nine seconds required for TRSDOS, the machine's standard system. Multi-DOS also includes a print spooler and a "RESTOR" command that "un-erases" erased files (as long as nothing else has been written on top of them). Neither of these features is offered by TRSDOS.

MultiDOS is far from being the only additional operating system for the Mod III. Among others, there are NEWDOS, NEWDOS/80, DBLDOS, and LDOS. Much the same could be said about any other popular machine. In fact, you may find that there are a dozen or more different operating systems available for your particular computer.

Each offers different features that can be important if you use your machine heavily at the system level. But for many computer users, the main importance of any DOS is the applications programs it will let you run. Still, those little extra touches and features offered by "nonstandard" (and thus more expensive) DOS packages can be nice to have, once you've acquired a little experience.

---

**SoftTip:** Additional operating systems can cost anywhere from about $80 on up to $400 or more. They can also make using your computer more complicated. You may have to maintain several sets of programs and data disks, one for each operating system. And, while the producers will usually try to use most of the same commands found in your machine's standard operating system ("KILL" or "ERASE" to wipe out a file; "DIR" to call for a directory of a disk; etc.), all of them will include *additional* commands needed to activate their special features.

That's the kind of complexity a new user definitely does not need. Don't make things hard on yourself. Wait until you're comfortable with your computer's standard operating system before you even consider an additional DOS. Familiarity with your machine's standard system will make any new DOS you eventually purchase easier to use. It will also make it easier to buy, since you'll have something to serve as a reference point and thus have a much better idea of the features you want.

---

In discussing the kind of features you can expect to find, we won't consider the special features designed for programmers. Instead, we'll look briefly at utility programs to give you a flavor of how DOS's differ in this area. You can think of "utilities" as general tools for using your system. They normally function outside of any applications program.

### Typical DOS Utility Programs and Features

*Disk Formatting and File Management*

Every DOS includes commands for formatting a blank disk so that your computer can put information on it. Actually, since putting information on a disk is DOS's responsibility, the disk's format is completely within its domain. DOS is rather like the opening of the 1960s TV show "The Outer Limits." Instead of saying, "We can control the vertical. We can control the horizontal. For the next hour we will control all that you see and hear and think . . . ," DOS says, "I control the read/write head. I control the drive speed. And I control how many tracks will be placed on your disk." The more tracks on the disk, the more information it can store. Consequently, different DOS's can differ in the amount of information they will let you put on a disk.

Every file has got to have a name, and DOS will control the conventions that are used. Some DOS's, for example, will let you do some pretty fancy things in the naming department. You may be able to give the file an invisible name, making it impossible for anyone else to see that it is on the disk. You may be able to use various types of "protection" by using some sort of secret password when you name the file. These features are called "attributes," and, to take one example, they can let you create a file that can be used by others but can only be changed or erased by someone who knows the password.

*Directories and Listings*

All disk operating systems will also include commands to let you see what files a particular disk contains, to display the contents of those files, and to copy, erase, or rename them. To look at the contents of a disk, with most systems, you type in DIR for "directory." Some DOS's will let you add something to that command telling the system to pause when the screen becomes full. Others will let you ask to have the files displayed in alphabetical or some other order.

If you want to see what's in a file, you might key in a command like TYPE or LIST, followed by the file's name. Here again, you may be able to tell the system to pause whenever the screen gets full. And you may be able to tell the computer to list the contents of a file directly to your printer to give you immediate hard copy. This can be convenient because the alternative is to load a word processing program and print the file from there.

*Global and Wildcard Features*

Often you will want to put a copy of a file on a different disk, give it a new name on the same disk, or erase it to make space for new files. Again, all operating systems include utility programs to perform these functions. But some DOS's include features that make them easier to use. Two such features are "wildcard" filenames and "global" commands.

To appreciate these commands, you need only know that files are typically given both a filename and an "extension." Depending upon your computer, a file might be called TEST.BAS or TEST/BAS. The filename is TEST, and BAS is the extension. Usually, whenever you want to copy or erase a file, you must type in its full name. That can be inconvenient when you want to do the same thing to several files.

For example, if you had three files named OLD-A.TXT, OLD-B.TXT, and OLD-C.TXT and you wanted to erase all three of them, you might be able to use a DOS-supported wildcard feature to do the job. You could tell the system to erase OLD-?.TXT. The question mark is the wildcard and it means that any letter or number can occupy that position in the names of the files to be erased.

A global command is even more sweeping. Under PC-DOS, for example, if you told your computer to erase *.TXT, it would erase any file that had TXT as its extension. That would be fine in some circumstances, but it would not be the specification to use if the files NEW-A.TXT, NEW-B.TXT, and NEW-C.TXT were also on the disk and you did not want to erase them.

## Dealing with DOS: A New User's Guide

We've looked at a few of the ways DOS's can differ. There are many more. But, as mentioned earlier, none of them should concern you if you are a new computer user. Far more important is learning how to use the DOS that came with your machine. And, at first, you will probably only want to learn enough about it to be able to run applications programs.

Like the software they produce, many of the people who write disk operating systems for computer manufacturers tend to be more technically oriented than are applications program producers. And, unfortunately, the instruction manuals they prepare show it. Many manuals simply list the available DOS commands in alphabetical order and fail to provide any guidance on which commands a new user should concentrate on and which should be left for a later time.

If you find yourself in this situation, the following list will help. Scan the manual to get an idea of its layout. Then zero in on the commands that will let you do the things listed below.

## The Six Most Crucial DOS Commands

1. *Format* a blank disk. You won't be able to do anything with your system until you've done this. If there is an option to "put the system" on the disk, use it. This will allow you to insert the new disk and boot your computer without using the DOS disk.

Only DOS can format a disk, so if you are in the middle of an applications program and you need a fresh disk, you could be in trouble. At best, it will be inconvenient, since you would have to leave the program, bring in DOS, format a new disk, and reload the program. At worst it can be disastrous, for you may find yourself with a screen full of work and no way to record it. All that work will be wiped out if you leave the program in order to format a disk.

Thus, it's a good idea to format several disks at once, and always be sure to have several empty ones handy.

2. *Change disk drives.* If you have a single drive system, this doesn't apply. But if you have two or more floppy drives, there will be a command to tell the system to switch its attention from one to the other. The drive on which the system is focused at any given time is often called the "default drive" or the "logged disk drive."

3. *Copy* a file or copy a disk. As the manual will probably point out, one of the first things you should do is to make a backup copy (duplicate) of your operating system disk and put the original in a safe place.

You will also need to know how to make backup copies of your applications programs and how to copy the individual files they create.

4. Call for a *directory.* This is usually the simplest of all DOS commands. As mentioned earlier, it will give you a table of contents of your disk.

5. *List* or *Type* the contents of a file. You may also want to see if you can make the listing pause every 24 lines or so instead of continuing to scroll up and off the screen. And you may want to see if the listing can be sent to the printer so you can have an immediate hard copy.

File listings are unformatted. They don't include margins, line spacing options, and the other niceties of word processing software. Indeed, this type of command will not let you alter or add to a file. It's designed to give you a quick look and nothing more.

6. Check the amount of *free* space remaining on a disk. If you are about to begin an applications program, it is often a good idea to see how much room you've got on your data disk(s). Otherwise, you may be in the middle of a program and suddenly find that you're out of space.

Some DOS's will tell you what *percentage* of your disk space is available. Other, less user-friendly DOS's give it to you in bytes. The figure is meaningless if you don't know how many bytes your disk can store. The figure will be in your manual someplace. And when you find it, you can use a pocket calculator to convert the number of free bytes into a percentage of the total.

**SoftTip:** One thing to check before buying any DOS is the amount of "overhead" it requires. "Overhead" is another way of saying "disk space" or "memory space." Even if you leave the nonessential utility programs on another disk, the basic system itself can occupy so much space that you may not be able to fit all that you want on the disk. The same holds true for internal memory. If the system soaks up a large portion of your available RAM, then your applications programs may run more slowly.

In some cases, there may not be enough room inside your machine for both the new DOS and your applications program. IBM/PC-DOS 2.0, for example, requires 24K of RAM, twice the 12K required for Version 1.1. If you have a 64K system and use a program that just barely fits inside your machine under PC-DOS 1.1, you probably won't be able to use 2.0 without adding more memory. The same thing applies to other computer brands and DOS's.

## Mini- and Mainframe Manifestations: Multi-everything

*Productivity through Superior Micropower*

When MITS, Inc. introduced the eight-bit, 8080-based Altair assemble-it-yourself, front-panel programmable computer in 1975, mainframe computers were selling for hundreds of thousands of dollars, and minicomputers went for several tens of thousands of dollars. It is hardly likely that anyone at the time seriously entertained the notion that the Altair's descendents would one day rival their mainframe and mini brethren in capability, capacity, and operating features. Yet it only took six years for this to become a practicable reality. When IBM introduced its 16-bit computer in 1981, only a few months were required for software houses to begin offering products that incorporated mainframe- and minicomputer-like capabilities.

Today, many experts would agree that putting a mainframe or a mini on the desktops of American managers in the form of a microcomputer is one of two major goals in the personal computer revolution. The other goal, as we'll see in the next chapter, is to make all that power easier to use than it has ever been before.

The key to achieving both of these goals is the greatly expanded memory-addressing capabilities of a 16-bit microprocessor equipped with a 20-line address bus. As you know from Chapter 1, such a chip can address over one million bytes of memory, compared to only 64,000 bytes in older machines. When equipped with a hard disk and double-sided, double-density disk drives (See Chapter 5), a $10,000 to $15,000 micro really can give a pretty fair imitation of a mini or mainframe costing several times as much—if it has the right software.

To "emulate" (fake it) a mainframe or a minicomputer, a personal computer needs a special operating system. This kind of system software can cost $350, $650, or more. Even leaving aside the expense of the hard disk ($2,300+) and other equipment, this tends to put mainframe and minicomputer emulation out of reach for most consumers and smaller businesses—for now. In addition, it is not clear why such computer users would ever *need* this kind of power. For relatively large firms, however, the expense may make sense, particularly if it can eliminate the need to buy a $30,000 minicomputer.

Nevertheless, you will see terms like CCP/M-86, MS-DOS 3.0, and references to UNIX in many software ads and reviews. And it can be helpful to have at least some idea of what they're talking about.

*Mainframe and Mini Characteristics*

There are two principal features found on mainframe and minicomputers that many software houses are striving to bring into the microworld. Both fall under the general rubric of "time-sharing," but can be more specifically described as "multi-tasking" and "multi-user" capabilities.

In days of old, which is to say, less than 10 years ago, all computing power was housed in a central location. The only way a person could access the power was either to consult with one of the DP (data processing) priesthood charged with tending the machine, or go through a terminal. A terminal is essentially just a keyboard and CRT connected to the main computer with a wire. (Because they have no processing power, these devices are called "dumb terminals.") If several people are going to be using the central computer via terminals, then the computer must be able to (a) handle several jobs at once, or at least give the appearance of doing so (multi-tasking) and (b) serve several terminals (multi-user).

Because these features are so intimately involved with how a computer's hardware resources and CPU time are managed, they are naturally the province of the machine's operating system. In addition, with several users to serve and several tasks to perform, both features require a machine with a considerable amount of internal memory to hold the various programs being executed and a considerable amount of disk-based storage space to hold programs and data. And the operating system must be able to manage these things as well.

One operating system that fills this bill quite nicely is called UNIX™, a trademark of Bell Labs. UNIX was designed for minicomputers (DEC's PDP-7 and PDP-11), and offering versions of UNIX, or DOS's with UNIX-like features, is clearly the direction in which most 16-bit system software is headed. We'll look at UNIX in more detail later. For now, it's important to briefly point out some of the steps that have been taken in its direction.

## Multi-tasking: CCP/M and MS-DOS 3.0

The first step toward large computer capabilities has been multi-tasking. Because there is only one user or source of primary input to worry about, this is the easier from a programming standpoint and the cheaper for the user. (No additional CRTs, keyboards, or interface cards needed.) Among others, two operating systems that offer this feature are CCP/M-86™ (the extra *C* stands for "concurrent") from Digital Research, and MS-DOS 3.0 from Microsoft. Both are available for 8086-based systems like the IBM/PC, the DEC Rainbow, and computers made by Sony, NEC, NCR, Fujitsu, and many others.

An operating system that offers multi-tasking or "concurrency" essentially does one primary thing. It carves up a computer's internal memory into sections, each of which can accommodate an applications program. If you recall the wall of post office box memory locations in Chapter 1, this is equivalent to having the operating system say, "Okay, the boxes from here to here will be occupied by WordStar. That group of boxes over there will be used by dBASE II; and SuperCalc goes over here."

From a user's standpoint this means a number of things. It means that you need a minimum of 256K of RAM. (CCP/M-86 itself, for example, has an overhead of 90K.) Although you may be able to get by with two floppy disk drives, you will probably also need a hard disk capable of holding 10-million bytes (10 megabytes) or more to accommodate data and programming. And, of course, you'll need the applications programs themselves in addition to the operating system.

In return for this not inconsiderable investment, you will be able to load your main applications programs all at once and then put the disks away. In contrast to single-tasking systems, you will not have to repeatedly close your word processing files, boot a spreadsheet, develop the information you want, and then reboot the word processor to add the information to whatever it was you were working on. With "concurrency," you can switch from word processing to spreadsheeting to accessing your database to using your communications or other programs at will by entering a few keystrokes.

## Key Points Re: Multi-tasking

In addition to aiding the industry in achieving the goal of putting mini-like features into a micro, multi-tasking also is a crucial part of the second goal—making the machines easier to use. VisiON, DesQ, Lisa, and "integrated" applications software like Context MBA and Lotus 1-2-3 all rely on multi-tasking. They couldn't exist without it. But, as explained below, they also offer other important features.

One point to keep in mind when considering a new operating system with multi-tasking features is that the applications programs must be compatible. In addition, the total number you can use at any one time will be determined by the amount of RAM your machine has. According to Gordon Eubanks, General Manager of Digital Research's Commercial Systems Division, there is technically no upper limit to the number of programs CCP/M-86 can handle. Memory is the crucial factor. "If you figure that each program takes about 80K and you have four programs, that's 320K. If you have large programs doing a lot of work, pretty soon you're up to a half megabyte of memory."

Also, it's worth pointing out that a microprocessor can't *actually* do two things at once. Like a print spooler, multi-tasking simply makes better use of a CPU's time. While it is waiting for you to hit the next key on the keyboard, the CPU can be cycling between sending text to the printer, performing calculations, and doing other things to fill in the idle nanoseconds.

The illusion holds up best when the machine as a whole is performing tasks that are heavily "I/O bound," meaning that a lot of the time is spent pulling information off disk or accepting it from the keyboard. These chores don't require much of the CPU's time. "Compute-bound" tasks, such as those requiring the CPU to roll up its sleeves and perform some serious calculations, are another story. Here you can expect to notice some degradation of response time when using your programs.

Finally, there are at least two features that distinguish VisiON-type system software from these products. First, they do not offer multiple on-screen "windows." CCP/M-86, for example, displays one complete screen at a time, with a little reminder at the bottom of each indicating which other applications programs are currently up and running. Mice need not apply.

Most important of all, however, is the fact that multi-tasking *qua* multi-tasking does not mean that you will be able to "pass data" between programs. Unlike integrated software and "window makers," you may not be able to insert the output of an electronic spreadsheet into a graphing program and insert the results of both into the text of a report you are preparing. At least you won't be able to do it with a few keystrokes or a few twists of a mouse's tail.

*Multiple Users: MP/M-86*

Once you've got multi-tasking going, the next step on the way to minicomputerhood is making it possible for several people to use the same micro at the same time. The operating system known as MP/M-86 (*Multi*Programming/*M*onitor) from Digital Research is probably the best known example of this feature. MP/M-86 can be run on virtually any 8088 or 8086 computer with a minimum of 128K RAM. Theoretically, it can support up to 16 different users at the same time, though more memory and one or more hard disks would be necessary to make this practical. A separate communications interface and terminal for each user is also necessary, of course.

With a properly equipped microcomputer running a multi-user operating system, one person could be preparing a letter with a word processing program while someone else was accessing a remote database. A third individual could be running an accounting package and a fourth could be entering data for a graphing program. All at the same time. All using the same disk drives, printer(s), and CPU.

*The "Impersonal" Personal*

That's the general idea behind multi-user systems. But just why one would want to have such a system isn't exactly clear. Unlike a multi-tasking capability, this feature does very little, if anything, to make a computer easier to use. Indeed, depending on the nature of the programs the other users are running at the time, it can actually cause the machine to be less responsive. A CPU may be fast, and it may have a lot of time on its hands under most circumstances, but there are limits.

In addition, a multi-user approach is antithetical to the whole idea of a *personal* computer. There seems to be an application for everything, and undoubtedly some companies will appreciate the fact that a multi-user system makes sure that everyone uses the same data in the same centralized files. That can be quite important for the company as a whole. But as good as the software and hardware may be, it is difficult to believe that any multi-user setup could ever be as convenient for each *individual* as a single-user system. At the very least, it makes the personal computer as impersonal as a mini- or a mainframe.

## UNIX™—What the Microworld Is Coming To

Multi-tasking and multi-user features are vectors pointing in the direction of large-machine capabilities for microcomputers. As such, they are one of the latest manifestations of the trend in the industry for power and features to migrate downward to smaller, less expensive machines. As technology makes it possible to put more capability into smaller and smaller packages, and as economies of scale and other economic forces come into play, this trend becomes all but inevitable.

In the microworld today, the central processing units with the ability to address vastly expanded memories are in place. The RAM chips that comprise those memories are widely available and have fallen in price so rapidly that they are now quite cheap compared to what they cost only a short time ago. The hard disk drives and other mass storage devices are affordable. All the hardware components needed to provide minicomputer capabilities and capacity are here today. The only major component that remains to be added is an operating system to tie everything together into an efficient, highly effective unit that people can use to exploit fully the power now within their reach.

*Striving for UNIXity*

Virtually every authority in the industry agrees that such a system already exists. It's called UNIX ("you-nix"), and it is something you will be hearing much more about in years to come. Many software houses and hardware firms are pushing to make UNIX *the* standard operating system in the 16-bit (and eventually 32-bit) world. And many more think they are on the right track.

---

**SoftTip:** UNIX is either the progenitor of or model for a number of microcomputer operating systems, among them Xenix™, QNX™ (formerly Qunix), and CROMIX™. An OS called Oasis-16™ is also part of this group, though its cachet is that it has been optimized and configured especially for business use. When computerists talk about "UNIX," they often mean "an operating system modelled on UNIX," rather than a specific system.

---

*The Significance of UNIX*

Much of the hoopla about UNIX is coming from and directed to professional and amateur programmers. Except as an indication of things to come, UNIX has next to no significance right now for the average computer user. The system has yet to become widely available. While it is already having an influence on some products, most notably MS-DOS 2.0, it will be some time before the full impact is felt by the end user. And when it is felt, it will be in the applications programs—the features they provide, the way you can use them, and the way they use your system—which UNIX will make possible, not as an operating system for the sake of an operating system.

That much appears certain. Far less certain is whether software houses will be motivated to pass along the considerable savings in program development costs UNIX makes possible in the form of lower prices. Yes, Virginia, it *could* happen. But don't hold your breath.

What will UNIX mean—eventually? It is difficult to say exactly. Since there is relatively little microcomputer software available to run under UNIX, one can only guess at the direction future applications programs will take. Undoubtedly, they will be more powerful and easier to use. Undoubtedly, they will require more internal memory and more capacious mass storage than most users currently own.

There is one other thing that can be said with certainty. UNIX is an incredibly powerful and versatile programming tool. (When many programmers visualize heaven, they tend to think in terms of "kernels" and "shells" and other UNIX-related concepts instead of golden streets and pearly gates.) If the brief history of the microcomputer industry to date is any guide, when you put a tool like this in the hands of tens of thousands of programmers, there's no telling what resourceful and imaginative applications they'll come up with. It is entirely possible that *the* most important application for UNIX has yet to be conceived or is only now taking shape in the mind of some soon to be famous (and wealthy) programmer.

In any case, it's a safe bet that every major software house in the country currently has one or more UNIX-related project under way. By looking at some of the points that are significant to them, we an get a better idea of how UNIX will affect the software we all use in the future.

*A Mature System*

From a programmer's viewpoint, one of the most important things about UNIX is that it is a mature system. It has been under development and available for use on minicomputers for well over a decade. This is in sharp contrast to CP/M, MS-DOS, and other operating systems that began with particular microprocessors and are still in the process of evolving upward toward more minicomputer-like capabilities. UNIX supporters point to it as a proven commodity, written by programmers for programmers, and filled with the kinds of features and tools that make for a superb programming environment.

The first version of UNIX was written in 1969 by Kenneth Thompson of Bell Laboratories for use on the PDP-7, a minicomputer manufactured by Digital Equipment Corporation (DEC). From the very beginning, a primary goal was to bring the power of expensive mainframe computers to relatively inexpensive ($50,000 to $80,000 at the time) minicomputers. Shortly thereafter, Dennis Ritchie, also of Bell Labs, created the C programming language, and UNIX was converted from Thompson's B language into C.

This was a crucial step, for because of the way C is designed, it is particularly easy to transport programs from one machine to another.

Thus, as new minis like the PDP-8 and PDP-11 came out, UNIX and the programs developed to run under its control were easily brought over. More features and more programming "tools" were added, to the point where UNIX in its standard form offers over 100 different modules designed to aid program development. No other operating system offers a programmer such an extensive range of features.

*Multi-tasking, Multi-user, and a B-Tree Directory*

Of these features, three of the easiest to understand are the multi-tasking and multi-user capabilities discussed earlier, and what might be called "hard disk directory support." How many files could a hard disk hold if a hard disk could hold files? A lot. An awful lot. A 10-meg hard disk can store the equivalent of 60 or more single-sided, double-density floppy disks, or about 5,000 typewritten pages. That's equivalent to five or six books the size of this one.

If a typical file were five typewritten pages long, that would mean a total of 1,000 files on your disk—and the names of every one of them would appear each time you called for a directory of the disk. No one wants to search through 40 screens full of filenames to locate a particular file. UNIX offers a better way.

In ads for UNIX-like DOS's, you will frequently see the term "B-tree" (binary tree), "inverted tree," "hierarchical tree structure," or some similar term. All of these terms refer to a technique that has important ramifications (so to speak) for hard disk users. The key word in each of them is *tree*, because that implies branching and a branching directory is exactly what UNIX offers.

The technique is somewhat complicated, but here is the general idea. When you call for a directory of a floppy disk, every file the system displays is a work file consisting of programming or data. Under an inverted tree setup, however, there's an additional category: directory or index files. In other words, some of the files contain programming, some contain data, and some are subdirectories or indexes that consist of nothing but lists of filenames. Each of the files named in a subdirectory can in itself consist of programming, data, or a sub-subdirectory of more filenames. And so on and on ad infinitum, or at least until you run out of disk space.

The most important thing to remember about a hierarchical tree-structured directory is that it allows you to organize your files by classifications and categories, much as a subject might be organized in outline form with large Roman numerals (I.), followed by capital letters (A.), followed by numbers (1.), etc. Under this system, each of these categories is a "directory." If you know the name of the category containing the file you are looking for, you can go right to it by specifying the correct "directory." If not, the tree system makes it relatively easy to chart a path through the various directories, subdirectories, and sub-subdirectories until you reach your destination. You might think of these directories as separate disks, each with its own table of contents and recorded files.

### The Kernel, The Shell, C, and Transportability

The terms may be strange, but if you remember how an operating system like CP/M or MS-DOS meshes with a computer you already have a pretty good idea of how UNIX works. There are some very important differences, however—differences that make UNIX and UNIX-based programs about as close to 100% transportable as it is possible to be. This is one of the main reasons that so many software houses are so interested in UNIX. Once a program has been written for the UNIX system, it can easily be converted to run on virtually any computer capable of running that system. That's *any* computer, not just different brands built around the same CPU chip, as is the case with CP/M or MS-DOS. Clearly this has sweeping implications for software producers and software buyers alike. At the very least, it means ultimately lower prices and it means wider and faster availability of outstanding programs for everyone.

There are two major reasons why UNIX can make this possible. The first is the way it is constructed and the second is the fact that it is written in C. At the programming level, UNIX consists of a collection of programs and device drivers called the "kernel" and a user interface called the "shell." These components are usually illustrated as two concentric circles: a small one for the kernel and a much larger one for the shell, rather like a diagram of the Fat Man atomic bomb.

Circles or no, it is still possible to view these components as "plugs." The kernel is the portion closest to the computer's CPU and hardware, and, like the BIOS, it must be specifically written to plug into each machine. The shell plugs into the other end of the kernel via a standardized interface and can thus be machine independent. Applications programs plug into the shell, and they too can be machine independent.

It sounds just like CP/M, and as previously noted, it's essentially the same idea. (Layers again!) However, there are some important features about the shell that make it easy to quickly string together small programming modules so that they form a rather sophisticated piece of work. More importantly, though, the entire system, kernel and shell, is written in the powerful and easily transportable C language.

*C Versus Assembler*

To appreciate this fact and what it implies, you need know only a few details. As mentioned in Chapter 5, C is a *compiled* language. That means the programs are written in a high-level language and then translated into the *1*'s and *0*'s of machine code before they are run. This is a crucial point because the translator (compiler program) gives you control over what the high-level program is translated into. By changing the compiler, you can change the translation and make it possible for one uncompiled program to be converted into the native language of many different microprocessors.

CP/M and MS-DOS, in contrast, are written in assembler. That is, each version of these two DOS's is written in the native language of a specific CPU. To port them to a different CPU, virtually 100% of the code must be rewritten. Because 90% of UNIX is written in C, only 5% to 10% of it must be rewritten to make it run on a different chip. At worst, a compiler for the target machine would have to be created as well, but that's a relatively straightforward, one-time-only job.

How is all this different from UCSD Pascal and the p-System, another contender in the transportability sweepstakes? It is different because p-System-based programs are first compiled into p-code (pseudo code) and then interpreted at run time. The C language, in contrast, compiles into native machine code. Because no interpretation is necessary, C-language programs run much faster.

Admittedly, they may not run quite as fast as assembly language programs written to take advantage of a specific CPU, and since they have already been translated, they are much "denser" (take up more memory) than p-System programs in their uninterpreted form. However, these drawbacks are more than compensated for by their transportability. And as an operating system, the p-System is not considered at all comparable to UNIX.

---

**SoftTip:** For more information on the technical aspects of UNIX and how it works, you might want to buy:

> *A User Guide to the UNIX System*
> by Rebecca Thomas and Jean Yates
> Osborne/McGraw-Hill
> 508 pages; $15.99

---

*Licensing Arrangements and Work-alikes*

UNIX is owned by AT&T, and the 1982 consent decree between that firm and the Justice Department is likely to have profound implications for UNIX in the microworld. Part of the deal was that in return for spinning off its local operating companies (the phone companies you write your checks to each month), AT&T would be free to market its products in a much more competitive (read: "aggressive") way. In June 1983, Western Electric Company (WECO), AT&T's manufacturing/marketing arm, announced that it had licensed Intel, Motorola, and National Semiconductor to build (hard wire) UNIX into one or more of their microchips. Industry analysts speculate that one of those chips, known as either the Intel 286 or the XENIX 286, will eventually form the heart of a yet-to-be-announced IBM personal computer. According to one spokesperson, WECO also plans to create versions of UNIX "for the full range of computers from personal computers to mainframes." Hotline services, regular technical seminars, a newsletter, and other elements of a massive marketing push are also said to be in the "pipe," so to speak.

The complete UNIX with all of its programming and system development aids requires a minimum of 128K of RAM to house the kernel and the shell and a 5-meg hard disk to store the modules. That's obviously not practical for micro users. Consequently, in addition to marketing the complete UNIX system, WECO licenses software companies to create versions of UNIX. Since these versions typically do not contain the communications, typesetting, games, electronic mail, and other UNIX modules, they cannot use the UNIX name. But some of them come close.

The largest distributor of UNIX for microcomputers is Microsoft, creators of MS-DOS. The firm sells a system called Xenix™ for computers made by Tandy Radio Shack (Model 16) and Fortune (32:16), among others, as well as for Apple's Lisa computer. Xenix runs on the Intel 8086 chip (an 8088 with 16 data bus lines instead of eight) and the Motorola 68000. Future versions for other chips are a certainty.

Other officially licensed versions include VENIX (a single-user version of Xenix for the IBM/PC) from VenturCom Corporation, ZEUS, ONIX, and IS-1. Other software firms have chosen to imitate rather than license UNIX, and their products include Cromemco's CROMIX, Whitesmith's IDRIS, Alycon Corporation's REGULUS, COHERENT from The Mark Williams Company, and Quantum Software Systems's QNX, sold as part of a complete software package called The Quantum System. Other firms produce systems that include UNIX-like features, but are not closely related to UNIX. Some of these products are MARC, Unica, and MicroShell. All in all, there are probably close to 50 different operating systems that are either licensed by, modelled on, or incorporate features found in UNIX. There will certainly be more in the future.

**SoftTip:** Of all the licensing arrangements Western Electric ever initiated, the most important may have been its decision to virtually give UNIX away to colleges and universities. At a time when commercial license fees were as high as $43,000 for the source code and $6,700 for each additional computer using the system, WECO set the licensing fee for educational institutions at $200.

The result has been a generation of computer science majors trained in UNIX and accustomed to its power. Faced with the current limitations of microcomputer operating systems, many of these individuals are demanding system and development software with the tools they learned to use in school. It is difficult to say for certain, but without this kernel of trained UNIX programers in the microworld, it is doubtful that the system would have developed such momentum so quickly.

*UNIX and You*

As UNIX becomes more widespread, it is likely to have a number of implications for software buyers. If nothing else, it should make good software available much faster. A company can convert a UNIX-based program to additional computers and have the package on the market in as little as three months, compared to the more typical 18-month lag with non-UNIX software. Although one can't necessarily expect the initial prices for UNIX-based applications programs to fall, UNIX-based transportability will enable companies to spread their development costs over a much wider market and so reduce the cost to each individual user.

There is also the fact that a great deal of micro software is currently being written in C. UNIX is not required in order to run such programs, but when the time comes they should be relatively easy to convert for UNIX systems. In addition, there is a strong possibility that at least some of the software now running under UNIX on minicomputers will become available in some form for micros. Since conversion is easier and cheaper than starting from scratch, this too bodes well for software selection and lower prices.

Programs written for UNIX will undoubtedly offer multi-tasking and multi-user capabilities. But the most important UNIX-based feature may be the system's ability to pass data from one program to another, the way the integrated packages like Context MBA and Lotus 1-2-3 do today. As noted elsewhere, this feature is called "piping," and it's easy with UNIX because it is an integral part of the system's design.

*Three Final Points*

At times, it seems as though there is a demon in the microcomputer industry whose sole responsibility is to prowl the air-conditioned corridors of software and hardware companies, sowing perplexity and switching things around to deliberately confuse the public (and not a few computer professionals). Such a demon was afoot when Bell Labs changed their UNIX designations from version numbers to "system" numbers.

Prior to licensing UNIX for use on microcomputers, the latest edition of UNIX was called "Version 7." The next generation, however, the one that Microsoft and other firms have licensed, is "System III." (This is the term you're most likely to see in ads and reviews.) To make matters even more fun, an internal version called System V already exists at Bell, and System VII is either finished or soon will be. If Bell Labs didn't have such an excellent reputation as one of the leading research facilities in the world, one might look askance. As it is, it is probably best not to look at all and assume on the basis of past performance that they know what they're doing.

Second point. Don't let anyone sell you a UNIX-alike system to run on an eight-bit personal computer. At least not until you have checked it out thoroughly. Genuine UNIX power requires a 16-bit or 32-bit microprocessor. However imaginative or cleverly implemented, eight-bit UNIX can be only a very diluted version of the original. Unless the package has features that you want in and of themselves, save your money for a bigger machine capable of running a truer version.

Finallly, will UNIX make your current operating system obsolete? Ultimately, yes. Or if not obsolete, at least less desirable than it is now—because of the applications software UNIX will eventually offer you access to. Before UNIX becomes widely available in the microworld, it is likely that new versions of standard operating systems will be issued incorporating many UNIX-like features. Time will also be required to adapt current programs so that they can make full use of the possibilities UNIX presents.

In any case, according to Jean L. Yates, president of Yates Ventures of Los Altos, California, by 1986 the total number of copies of MS-DOS sold will be close to 4.5 million, followed by eight-bit CP/M (2.3 million copies), 16-bit CP/M (2.0 million), and officially licensed UNIX with 1.3 million.

UNIX is definitely on the way. But it will take a while to get here.

# ...7...

# VisiON™, DesQ™, and Lisa™:
## Branches in the Stream

Not long ago, whenever you opened a computer magazine you could be virtually certain of encountering a nine-page, four-color ad for Apple's new Lisa computer. Part of that firm's push to introduce its product to the world, the ads focused on a startlingly crisp computer screen that had been divided into several "windows." Sitting with his back to the camera was a young man clad in an appropriately conservative pinstripe suit manipulating a mouse. It's tough to tell from the back of someone's head, but the picture bore a striking resemblance to other photos of Steven Jobs, the founder and chairman of the firm.

Elsewhere in the same magazines, one might encounter Dan Flystra, chairman of VisiCorp, discussing his firm's new VisiON "operating environment." Prominently featured: more computer screen windows. Less crisp than Lisa's, the windows still clearly showed portions of spreadsheets overlapped by part of a bar graph overlapped by part of a memo. In Flystra's hands was a mechanical mouse.

Around the same time, one could also encounter articles featuring Mitchell D. Kapor, president of Lotus Development Corporation, sitting at a computer and explaining his firm's phenomenally successful Lotus 1-2-3 software package. The computer's screen would be divided into two sections showing parts of a graph and parts of a spreadsheet.

Aside from the fact that they were all born *after* 1950 and that the combined sales of the companies they founded total well over $250 million, what do these three men have in common? Or, more to the point, what are they trying to tell you (and sell you)?

*The Master Goal*

Joined by many other leading figures in the industry, all three are saying the same thing: In the very near future, personal computers will be much easier to use. *That* is the main objective. That is the Master Goal hardware and software producers are burning the midnight oil to

156

achieve as quickly as possible. It's even more important than bringing mini- and mainframe power to personal computers. It is what the market demands, and many firms know that if they don't achieve it, they probably won't survive.

This goal may seem obvious, but it's important to keep it firmly in mind as you read the magazines and investigate your software options. With all the talk of "integrated packages," with all the media attention being devoted to multiple-window, "desktop-like" screens, and with all the mice sold with a fully equipped computer attached to their tails, it is easy to get distracted. As interesting, "sexy," and innovative as they may be, these things are the sizzle, not the steak.

The real meat of the matter lies elsewhere, and it can be rendered in three points. Suppose you had used a personal computer for about a year, and someone came to you and said, "We can do three things to make your machine easier to use. What should they be?" How would you respond? Overcoming the temptation to present a 10-page laundry list of improvements, you might be able to pare things down to speed of response, multi-tasking capabilities, and the ability to transfer information easily from one applications program to another.

These are the three battlefields upon which the next revolution in personal computers will be fought. Each must be achieved to make the Master Goal a reality. The thing to remember is that Jobs, Flystra, Kapor, and several others all have different ideas about the best way to go about it. The armies have been marshalled and the battles have been joined. It may be years before the outcome is clear.

In the meantime, it can sometimes be difficult to tell the players apart, let alone choose a side, without a program. In this chapter, we'll look at the main issues involved and at three of the approaches being used to address them: Lisa, VisiON, and an approach typified by a program called DesQ. Each of these deals with things at the system level. In a later chapter, we will consider the "integrated" approach that deals with things at the applications level, an approach exemplified by Mr. Kapor's Lotus 1-2-3, Context MBA, and other products.

*Speed and Multi-tasking*

To be easy to use, a computer should respond instantly to a person's commands. You want to go from page 2 to page 10 of a report? Bang! You should be able to get there right away, without laboriously scrolling through all the intervening pages. You want the machine to perform a complex calculation? Zap! It should hand you the answer immediately, without making you wait while it cogitates. The same is true if you want to switch from word processing to telecommunications to spreadsheet analysis to graphics. The switch should take place in a twinkling.

That is the ideal, at least. We humans are a demanding lot. If a donkey could talk, many of us would be critical of what it said instead of marvelling that it could speak at all. Nevertheless, computers are our creations and they will jolly well perform the way we want them to or we simply won't use them. As we've seen in previous chapters, great strides have been made in the direction of speed. Abundant, inexpensive internal memory. Capacious, fast-access hard disk drives. Coprocessor microchips to speed up the main CPU. And programming languages that can be compiled into fast-executing machine code. All of these hardware and software components play a part in everyone's approach to the Master Goal.

Multi-tasking, as you know from the previous chapter, refers to the ability of a computer to appear to be doing two or more things at once, allowing you to switch from one to the other whenever you please. The effect is similar to being surrounded by separate computers, each running a different program, and swivelling in your chair to use one, then the other, then back to the first one, and so on.

It is hard to fully appreciate this feature if you haven't used a computer very much. If that's the case, then ask others who have. They will undoubtedly outline the inconveniences of having to insert program disks into the machine to boot and reboot the same programs over and over again as they move back and forth among them during the day. If their programs are on a hard disk drive, the process will be less time consuming, but they will still have to close up one program before they can switch to another. And over the course of the day, even that can add up to a major inconvenience.

*Data Transfer—The Most Crucial Issue*

Most inconvenient of all, however, is transferring information developed in one program into something you are developing with a second program. For business users in particular, this is the single most important aspect of the Master Goal. It is what the multi-window screens and the mouse are *really* all about. As with so many things about personal computers, to appreciate the significance of this feature, you have to know what the alternative is.

To take a simple example, let's suppose you've got to produce a report detailing your division's sales projections for the next quarter. In addition to the insightful comments and boilerplate C.Y.A. material you plan to include in the text, you also want to incorporate a spreadsheet to show the projected impact on sales if the plant doesn't produce enough product, if it produces enough product but is several weeks late, if the advertising budget is boosted by 20%, if your expense account for entertaining prime customers is increased by 30%, etc.

Here are the steps you might have to follow:

1. Load the word processing program.

2. Write the report.

3. Record it as a file (SALES.TXT) on disk.

4. Load the spreadsheet program.

5. Enter your equations and data and produce a result.

6. Save the spreadsheet as a file (SHEET.TBL) on disk.

7. Reload the word processing program.

8. Bring SALES.TXT onto the screen.

9. Scroll through the report until you find the place where the spreadsheet is to be inserted.

10. Use your word processing program's commands to merge SHEET.TBL into SALES.TXT at the target point.

11. Pray that it works and that SALES.TXT and SHEET.TBL use a compatible file format.

12. Save the newly endowed SALES.TXT and print it out.

The exact details will differ, and in some cases, incompatibilities will make it impossible to insert a spreadsheet into a text file. But one way or another, this is clearly a cumbersome, time-consuming process.

Here is what might be called the Multi-tasking, Multiple-window, Master Goal Alternative:

1. Load both your word processing and spreadsheet programs into the machine at the same time.

2. Use a mouse to move the cursor to a menu and select word processing.

3. Create your document.

4. Use the mouse again to select the spreadsheet.

5. Create your spreadsheet.

6. With portions of the spreadsheet and the report overlapping each other on the screen, use the mouse to identify the parts of the spreadsheet you want to move.

7. Use the mouse to move into the word processing/report window and to scroll the text until you locate the desired spot.

8. Use the mouse to tell the system, "This is the place. Please insert the previously identified portions of the spreadsheet here."

9. Wait for the insertion to take place.

10. Save the report to disk and print it out.

Again, the details may differ, but this is the general idea. There are several things to notice about this alternative. First, although a multitasking capability plays an important part, this alternative involves much more than that. Second, the text for the report and the figures for the spreadsheet must still be typed in just as if you were using these programs separately. And third, you don't have to worry about file compatibility. The system takes care of that, and if it says that you can insert spreadsheets—or graphs or picharts or the output of some other program—into the report, that's all you need to know.

### How Do They Do It?: Three Different Approaches

This is the general framework of what we have labelled the Master Goal. As noted earlier, there are at least three different ways to achieve it. Apple's Lisa depends upon a combination of software and special hardware (the Lisa itself). VisiCorp does it with software, by inserting VisiON between your operating system and VisiCorp applications programs. The firm refers to VisiON as an "operating environment" and uses it to provide a common interface and an easy connection between its other software. Quarterdeck, a new Santa Monica, California software house, offers DesQ ("desk"), a program designed to do what VisiON does with off-the-shelf (your's or your retailer's) applications software.

These three are not the only firms in their respective areas. The Xerox Star system is the acknowledged conceptual parent of both Lisa and

VisiON. Micropro's Starburst package, Executec's Business User's Solution (Execu/BUS), and an entry from Microsoft Corporation use a VisiON-like approach. There will undoubtedly be a number of DesQ-like packages as well.

In the following section, we'll use Lisa, VisiON, and DesQ as models demonstrating how the Master Goal can be achieved. Then we'll look at five major points to be considered and some things you might want to think about before spending any of your firm's money, or your own.

*Apple's Lisa*

"Lisa" stands for "Locally Integrated Software Architecture." The result of a $50 million project, the machine represents Apple's bid to snare a large portion of the professional/managerial/office market away from its traditional sources of supply, principally IBM. The machine is built around Motorola's MC68000 microprocessor. This is significant because the 68000 is a speed demon. This chip was introduced after the Intel 8086 and the Zilog Z8000. (The IBM/PC runs on an 8088, a chip that is virtually identical to the 8086.) It is a 16-bit processor with many of the same speed-enhancing features of a 32-bit chip, and it can directly address 16 megabytes of internal RAM-based memory. (The IBM/PC can directly address one megabyte.)

The initial hardware configuration includes a meg of memory, two disk drives capable of storing 860K per disk. (IBM's disks typically store 320K—double density, double sided.) Also included is a five-megabyte hard disk drive. (The IBM/XT comes with a 10-meg drive, standard.) There is also a crisp 364 by 720 display. (The highest resolution typically available on the IBM is 640 by 200, or about half that of Lisa.)

---

**SoftTip:** The numbers used to describe the sharpness or resolution of a display refer to "pixels." These "picture elements" are separate dots of light, each of which may be individually controllable. The greater the total number of pixels, the sharper the onscreen images will be. For information on why the numbers are written in the order they are, see the "How to Buy Graphics Programs" chapter.

---

This exceptionally high resolution allows Apple to display little pictures called "icons" on the screen to represent various commands. A tiny trash can, for example, represents the command to erase a file. You identify the file you want to erase by moving the cursor with the supplied mouse; then you "mouse" on over to the trash can to tell the system you want to junk the whole thing. The system was originally introduced at a price of about $10,000 but is now sold for $8,200 or less. It includes the following fully or semi-integrated applications programs:

LisaWrite (word processing)

LisaGraph (graphing)

LisaDraw (paint pretty pictures)

LisaList (database management-like lists)

LisaProject (project management)

LisaCalc (spreadsheet)

LisaTerminal (communications)

*VisiCorp's VisiON*

Apple's approach is designed and tooled into the system, and the only way to get Lisa's features is to buy the whole package. VisiCorp's approach can be characterized as, Why do in hardware what you can do in software? Why pay thousands for a Lisa when we can sell you a package for $1,710 to run on your IBM or DEC or other computer? To which Apple might reply, It's not the same thing.

The $1,710 includes the cost of VisiON, three applications packages, and a mouse. But it doesn't include the 256K RAM (minimum), the two double-sided, double-density disk drives, the graphics adaptor card, the RS-232 card and port (for the mouse), and the hard disk card and drive VisiON requires when used on an IBM/PC. If you didn't have these components, they could easily add as much as $3,000 or more to the total cost of being able to run VisiON. In addition, on the IBM at least, the graphic resolution isn't high enough to allow VisiON to use icons. It must use words instead.

But it's got the multi-tasking, multi-window data transfer capabilities of Lisa. It too uses a mouse. And its help function will instantly give you relevant instructions when you run into trouble. While it may not have everything that Lisa offers, it comes close. VisiON will eventually be available on the IBM/PC, the DEC Professional, and computers made by Wang, Honeywell, Xerox, and others. VisiCorp is clearly betting that VisiON will come close enough to win a large share of the business and professional market.

VisiON uses a kernel and shell approach similar in concept to that of UNIX. (VisiON was designed and developed using UNIX.) It involves four different layers of software. At the bottom of the heap, closest to the CPU chip and hardware, is your standard operating system (MS-DOS, CP/M-86, whatever). Next is a module called VisiHost. This is the "kernel" that represents about 25% of the VisiON system, and it's the most machine specific. Written largely (70%) in assembly language, its job is to plug into the operating system. The VisiON module itself, the shell in this particular game, plugs into VisiHost via a standardized, non-machine-specific interface. The applications programs (word processing, graphing, etc.), all of them written in the C language, plug into VisiON.

According to Roy Folk, Marketing Manager for Systems Products at VisiCorp, VisiON can run any number of programs on a multi-tasking basis and display any number of them in on-screen windows (though naturally there are the limitations imposed by available memory and what one can reasonably deal with on the screen at any one time). The system includes nine VisiON commands, each of which is available at any time, regardless of the applications program you are running. These include commands to adjust the size of the various windows you are displaying, to save files, and to transfer data between programs. In addition to these commands, the commands needed to use whatever applications program you are focusing on at the time are also displayed.

Data transfer is accomplished by responding to the following prompts with your mouse:

Transfer from which window?

Start of region to transfer?

End of region to transfer?

Transfer to which window?

Where to put transferred region?

In addition to a mouse ($250) and the VisiON Application Manager (VisiHost and VisiON itself—$495), the package includes VisiCalc, Visi-Word, and VisiPlot, each of which has been rewritten and rechristened for use with the system:

VisiON Word ($375)

VisiON Calc ($395)

VisiON Graph ($195)

More software will be available as well. Virtually all of VisiCorp's eight or nine other major packages can be expected to eventually run under VisiON, for example. And in May 1983, Digital Research announced plans to work with VisiCorp in adapting VisiON programs for CP/M systems. Other hardware and software vendors will surely follow.

*Quarterdeck's DesQ*

Possibly the biggest drawback to the VisiON approach is that the user must run specially prepared VisiCorp (or VisiON-supported) programs. You cannot use Micropro's WordStar, Ashton Tate's dBASE II, or Peachtree Accounting with it. Equally significant, you will not even be able to use *files* created by these and other programs with VisiON, or vice versa. VisiHost imposes a different filing structure on your operating system, forcing it to store things in a different, VisiON format.

A new company founded by Theresa Myers and Gary Pope, both formerly with the Axxa Corporation, thinks it has a better way. Its product is called DesQ, and like VisiON, it can be thought of as a "software integrator." Unlike VisiON, however, DesQ gives the user multitasking, multiple windows, mouse control, and data transfer using virtually *any off-the-shelf* program.

The program sells for $395 and requires a minimum of 256K RAM, one double-sided floppy disk drive, an RS-232 communications port, and a five-megabyte hard disk. While it's important to note that all prices quoted here are naturally subject to change, DesQ is likely to remain the program with the lowest price. Certainly, it is the least demanding in the hardware department. As with VisiON, however, it is important not to overlook the other costs. DesQ was originally issued for the IBM and does not require a color graphics adaptor on that system. (It's nice, but you don't need it.) Still, all that hardware could easily cost $2,000 to $2,500 or more if you had to add it. And, unlike VisiON, DesQ does not include any applications software.

What Quarterdeck is counting on is that most of its initial customers will own an IBM/XT, the "extended," 10-meg hard-disk-equipped version of the IBM/PC. Equally important, it is banking on the fact that most customers will want to continue to use their own software instead of chucking the lot and replacing it with VisiCorp products. Thus, if VisiCorp can be seen as nipping at the heels of Apple's Lisa, Quarterdeck can be seen as squarely targeting VisiCorp. Clearly, being in the computer business these days is to "live in interesting times."

Can a $395 package deliver all that a $8,200 computer and a $1,710 "operating environment" can? Probably not. But as Adam Osborne, the man who popularized and profited from the idea that "adequacy is enough," might say, "That is not the question." Indeed, it isn't. The question is whether the DesQ approach will take the user close enough to the Master Goal to conclude that the differences aren't worth the extra cost. Judging from the crowds that packed the aisles every time

DesQ was demonstrated at COMDEX in May 1983, Apple and VisiCorp should probably avoid looking over their shoulders: DesQ may be gaining on them.

Written in a proprietary language developed by Quarterdeck, DesQ loads in on top of the operating system. Applications programs load in on top of DesQ. The number of applications programs one can use is limited only by available memory. But each must be run through a menu-driven installation module before it can be used with DesQ the first time.

When everything has been installed and the system has been booted, DesQ presents you with a screen that can be divided up into windows and mouse (or keyboard) activated commands to select your programs. When you move the cursor to tell the system that you want to open a dBASE II file, DesQ issues the appropriate dBASE II command string. When you do the same thing with Peachtree Accounting, DesQ issues the file-opening commands Peachtree requires. In every case, all the user must do is tell the system to open a file in a particular program. DesQ does the rest.

Once you are into a given program, you may use it just as you would had you booted it separately. All the commands you originally learned will still apply. The full complement of DesQ commands are available at any time. DesQ handles the tricky and all-important job of transferring data among programs by converting the files from DIF format to simple ASCII and back as needed.

DesQ, like VisiON, offers online help when you get stuck using the system. And both programs include the option of recording the keystrokes needed to accomplish a particular task as a file and then issuing the entire sequence to the system by touching a single key. When used with a color monitor, DesQ windows can be "color coded." The system will also allow you to use internally integrated packages like Lotus 1-2-3.

## What to Look for When Making Your Choice

When trying to choose among various software packages, it is obviously ideal to be able to compare them side by side in a hands-on demonstration. If that isn't possible, the next best alternative is to use each of them separately. With other applications programs, you may be able to make your decision solely on the basis of the reviews you read, though a live demonstration is always important. With the kinds of programs and hardware discussed here, though, it is absolutely crucial. For here, ease of use is the main focus and the only way to tell for sure which approach best suits your needs is to wrap your hand around a mouse. As you take a whirl at these approaches, there are at least five things you'll want to consider.

*1. How easy is it to use?* Ultimately, this must be a completely subjective judgment. That being the case, if you will not be using the system yourself, it clearly makes sense to bring along the person who will be. It is impossible to overemphasize the effect a particular "user interface" can have on a particular user's productivity. (Unfortunately, it is probably also impossible to quantify, time and motion studies not withstanding.) Little things can be enormously important.

Does the system "feel" right? Is it well designed for the way you would use it? What about the mouse action—is it as easy to use as you would like? Does the online help function provide the kind of quick assistance you need? Details like these, while important, will have a different significance to each user.

One point that will be important to everyone, however, is *speed.* How long does the system take to switch from one applications program to another and another and another? How quickly does the spreadsheet respond to a new entry? Are you able to scroll through the word processing program text rapidly enough?

*2. How powerful are the applications programs?* In all the excitement over multi-window screens and mice, it is important not to lose sight of programs that will be doing the actual work. How convenient are they to use? What features do they offer? Have any important (to you) features been left out? Do they run smoothly? Do they have the capacity you think you'll need? (Is the spreadsheet big enough? How many files will the database management system support? etc.)

Guidelines for choosing these and many other programs can be found elsewhere in this book. It would be a mistake not to apply the same standards and selection criteria to the programs offered by Lisa and VisiON that you would to any other applications software of the same genre. Apple and VisiCorp are both top-flight companies, so you will probably find everything you need. However, if you find anything lacking, it might be wise to wait before buying since more and better and improved versions of the applications software are a virtual certainty.

*3. Can you use your present software?* This is something of a loaded question, since only DesQ permits the use of off-the-shelf programs. Yet it is an important consideration for anyone who has invested money in a collection of programs and spent time learning how to use them. One advantage offered by both Lisa and VisiON is a unified command structure, which is another way of saying that you can use the same basic commands whether you are running a spreadsheet or setting up a graph. For someone just getting started with computers, this can be a real advantage.

It is also extremely important to think about the future implications of buying either Lisa or the VisiON package. In itself, a $1,700 investment in VisiON, or even a $10,000 investment in Lisa, may not be all that significant. But over time, as you acquire more and more software—none of which can be used on any other system—you may find that you or your firm have considerably more tied up in Lisa or VisiON than you had originally planned. That can make switching vendors an expensive decision.

*4. How flexible, comprehensive, and easy is the data transfer?* This is the question you should grab hold of and not let go until you get complete answers in whatever level of detail you demand. You may find, for example, that LisaCalc can only transfer data to the word processing and graphing program; that you cannot "paste" the output of the graphing program into the report you are writing with the word processor; and that LisaList, the "electronic personal database," can't transfer data anywhere. To paraphrase Mark Twain, "Reports of complete integration may have been greatly exaggerated."

*5. What is it going to cost YOU?* There are so many factors involved that all one can say with certainty is that your total cost will be different from everyone else's. The key question is, What is it going to cost *me* to install and use this capability? If you don't already own a computer, your cost will obviously be much higher than that of someone who does. If you own a large amount of software that will no longer be used, it may be important to account for it as an asset that has been replaced. How much of your time or your staff's time will be needed to learn to use the system effectively and what's it worth? It is possible to spin cost considerations out into infinity. The main point, of course, is that it's important to avoid getting caught up in the hoopla and to look beyond the simple retail price.

### A 10% Savings?

Finally, one should also look at the upside. A recent issue of *Business Week*, for example, reports that a Citibank vice-president who tested VisiON felt the system reduced the amount of time he had to spend with his computer by an average of four or five hours a week. If you assume that an executive at that level receives about $80,000 in salary and benefits, a four-hour per 40-hour week savings amounts to 10% of that compensation, or $8,000 a year—more than enough to justify the purchase of VisiON or Lisa.

## When You Go to the Computer Store . . .

You may not have the time to be as thorough as you would like, but since these Master Goal approaches are so closely bound up with how you will interact with your system each day, and since they are so different from the programs you may be accustomed to buying, it would be worth your time to plan right from the start on making at least two visits to your retailer.

Make the first one an initial "get acquainted/general overview" visit. Let the salesperson give the spiel. Ask for a demo. And ask if there is any literature on the product that you may take with you. Basically, try to get a feel for Lisa, VisiON, DesQ, or whatever other approach you are considering.

Then come back later and put the system through its paces—on your own. In the interim, try to visualize how you would actually use the system. What are the tasks you typically have to perform in the course of a day? How would the particular system make those tasks easier? Depending on the amount of time you have to spend, it would be an excellent idea to put together some sample tasks and use them as the basis for testing the system on your second visit.

---

**SoftTip:** It is not reasonable to expect a retailer to loan you a copy of a software program to use on your own, though if the potential order is large enough, some stores may oblige. But if you are seriously considering buying five to ten or more Lisa computers for your firm, there is nothing unreasonable about asking—even insisting—on a "loaner" for a specified period of time. Many retailers lease computers on a monthly or even a weekly basis. The worst that could happen would be that you would have to lease a Lisa, though if you eventually buy several systems, the retailer should be willing to credit your lease payment toward the final purchase price.

---

## A Word about Windows

Submitted for your consideration: magazine copy synthesized from the Twilight Zone of parroted press releases and misinformed media.

The multiple windows displayed by Program DUMB make your screen resemble an ordinary desk in an office, with many overlapping papers and open files. In the course of a normal day, you might be working on a spreadsheet and be interrupted by a phone call. While you are talking on the phone, you might move the cursor into the word processing area and jot down a memo regarding an upcoming meeting. Based on information received on the phone, you might access the spreadsheet area to insert some new assumptions. Then return to the memo. And so on throughout the day. "DUMB™ does away with the desk!"

Can you see yourself actually using a computer this way? Can you visualize yourself in an austerely furnished office with nothing but a computer sitting on a thick slab of glass supported by stainless steel tubes? Maybe. But it seems much more likely that managers will use computers the way they use a desk clock to check the time, the telephone to make a call, or a calculator to work out an equation.

In other words, a computer will be used like any other appliance or decision-making tool—on an as-needed basis. From at least one perspective, the enthusiastic assertions that multi-window capabilities will soon have managers working at their computers the way they now work at their desks are like fashion designers proclaiming that transparent cellophane dresses are the next new "look." In both cases, a lot of looking will be involved, but neither assertion has any basis in reality.

Multiple windows are new, and they have commanded a great deal of attention. But when the dust settles, it seems likely that many people will find them really good for only two things. First and most important, they make it very easy to tell your computer that you want to move this column of figures to that location in your report. And second, they serve as a visual reminder of what programs you have going on a multi-tasking basis and where you are in each.

When it comes to actually using the machine, it is unlikely that anyone would do any serious work with the screen in a multi-window mode. It is much more natural to expand the window containing the application until it fills the entire screen. Windows (and mice) are an extremely important convenience feature. But the fact that they make a computer screen resemble a desktop does not mean that managers will call the movers.

# Part II

# —TECHNIQUE—

# ...8...

# Surveying the Field:
# *How to Locate Programs and Software Reviews*

"There are eight million programs in the Naked City . . ." Well, no, there aren't. But sometimes it seems that way. It depends upon whom you talk to, but by most estimates there are somewhere between 30,000 and 40,000 programs available today for personal computers. Tomorrow there will be tens of thousands more. To most of us, even 100 programs is a lot. Thinking of 500 causes an immediate outbreak of symptoms indicating an acute case of "over-choice." And once you begin thinking about choosing from among 1,000 programs, you might as well throw in the towel. It is so difficult to conceive of 1,000 of anything that it makes little difference whether the actual number is thirty or forty thousand . . . or eight million.

---

**SoftTip:** Still, we can give it a try. If each page of *Popular Computing* or *Personal Computing* magazine represented one software program, 30,000 programs would require a stack of 120 magazines measuring two-and-a-half feet high. On the other hand, if Ziff-Davis's *PC Magazine* were used, the total copies required would be about two.

At 642 pages and weighing in at just under three pounds, the June 1983 issue of *PC Magazine* was at the time the largest single issue of any magazine ever published. It is said that Ziff-Davis is now offering reader insurance in case you drop an issue on your foot. For more information, contact the publisher.

---

*Dealing with the Deluge*

Clearly, one needs some kind of method to counter the madness of the software marketplace. And that's what we will look at in this chap-

173

ter and the two that follow it. The first thing to do is to develop a list of possibilities: "I want a communications program for my TRS-80 Model 4. What specific brands of programs do I have to choose from?" The next step is to narrow the field to a list of main candidates based on price, features, capabilities, etc. And here you will find the software reviews published in various books, magazines, and newsletters invaluable.

In Chapter 9, we'll focus on the third step—getting your hands on the documentation and arranging for demonstrations of your main candidate programs. At that point, you'll want to zero in on the actual details of how each program operates, how easy it is for you to use, how useful the features it offers are likely to be, and so forth. Finally, in Chapter 10, we'll look at the various ways you can buy that software once you've made up your mind.

You may not feel inclined to follow each of these steps rigorously in every instance. They make sense for a $250 electronic spreadsheet or a $700 database management program, but admittedly, for a $30 game program the process is probably overkill. The amount of money you plan to invest, though, shouldn't be the only consideration. If you plan to use a program frequently, it can be worthwhile to investigate your options thoroughly, regardless of what the software costs. No program is perfect. Each will have its own little quirks and minor irritations. If you're going to spend $150 on a program, you might as well get the one whose quirks bother you the least. And the only way to do that is by a little investigation.

In any case, whether you decide to be a "method" software buyer or feel like being a bit more eclectic, the upcoming sections will give you a good idea of the resources at your disposal. We have divided information options into two large categories: conventional sources and electronic, online sources that can be used by anyone with a personal computer equipped to "talk" on the telephone. As we will see, both offer you the opportunity to develop a list of "possibles" and to obtain the product reviews and user reports you need to narrow your focus and begin making your decision.

### The Four Programs Every Computer Owner Should Buy

For many people, there is an even more fundamental step than developing a preliminary list of program titles. And that is deciding what *kind* of program to buy. The "Toolchest" chapters in Part III of this book will give you a good idea of what is available and of the types of things your personal computer can do for you. But before throwing yourself into a massive "needs identification and program evaluation" effort, there is something you should know.

There is a myth that has grown up in the computer industry implying that you need a separate, single-function program for each job you want your computer to perform. No one deliberately tries to foist this idea on computer owners, but the huge numbers of single-purpose programs, the constant flow of ads promoting them, and reviews that describe them make this conclusion all but inevitable. Fortunately, for most individual users, this is simply not the case.

If you are interested in buying nongame applications software for use at home, there are really only four programs that you need. And you should probably acquire them in this order:

- Communications
- Word processing
- Electronic spreadsheet
- Filing or database management program

With these four programs, that computer you bought or are thinking of buying can make a real diffference in your life. The *total* cost for these four can be as low as $300, and once you've got them, you can accomplish almost everything that ten or more single-purpose programs can do.

## The Building Block Approach to Software Buying

These four types of software can be thought of as the "building block" programs, for they should form the basis of nearly everyone's software collection. Again, leaving aside game and educational programs, they are the programs you should buy first. Later, once you've got a better handle on your computer and a clearer idea of what it can do, you can branch out and acquire more specialized software.

There is something else worth considering as well. And that is the way the four building block programs can work together to accomplish what you want. For example, a personal filing or database management system can do a crackerjack job of keeping track of a list of addresses. And, if it can interface with your word processing program, it can be used to create customized form letters, inserting the appropriate address at the beginning of each letter. There is no need to buy a mailing list program.

A word processing program can be used to print your checks each month, eliminating the need for a personal checkbook program. (See Chapter 21 for tips and details.) And a spreadsheet program can be used to analyze both your home budget and your stock and bond portfolio, making it unnecessary to buy separate programs for these two functions.

*Why a Communications Program?*

No other program is likely to have a greater impact on your life than one that will let your computer talk on the telephone. And if the software is well written, none requires less effort on your part to use. In most cases, you'll be able to just load it in, dial the phone, and go online with the world. You'll need a plug-in communications card (about $100) and a peripheral device called a "modem" in addition to the program itself. But, as explained in Chapter 17, modems can be had for as little as $70 and most memory expansion boards are equipped with communications "ports," thus eliminating the need for a separate "comm card." In some cases, as with Andrew Fluegelman's "PC-Talk III" for IBM personal computers, the communications program can cost as little as $35.

Once your computer can be connected to the telephone, you will find that vast resources of information and communication are suddenly open to you. As we'll see later in this chapter, for example, you will be able to use your computer to search for and obtain information and reviews of *other* building block programs. You will be able to get advice and tips on using your equipment from experts and online users' groups. And, as we'll see in Chapter 12, you will be able to have thousands of *free* games, utility, and other programs pumped directly into your computer. For these and many other reasons, a communications program is clearly the best type of software to buy first.

*Why a Word Processor?*

A word processing program goes hand in hand with a communications program. It will let you edit, erase, and reformat the free programs and other information you receive online. It will also save you money. The Source, CompuServe, and the other databases mentioned in Chapter 17 charge by the amount of time you spend connected to their systems. You *can* write a letter while you are connected. But it usually makes more sense to prepare the letter with a word processing program before you "go online." You can then transmit the file containing the letter at "machine" speed instead of typing it in at human speed.

Of course, using your word processing program in conjunction with your communications program is but one application. As you will see in Chapter 13, anything you now do with a typewriter, you can do with a word processor and a printer. In fact, since a computer printer is more versatile than even the most expensive typewriter, you will be able to print letters, memos, reports, etc., with bold print, italics, and some interesting graphic effects.

*Why a Spreadsheet?*

A paper spreadsheet is essentially anything with rows and columns of numbers. It could be a home budget or checkbook register. It could be a list of stocks, what you paid for them, and what they are now selling for. Or it could be an invoice, an accounts receivable file, or some other accounting document. What makes an *electronic* spreadsheet so special is that if you had prepared a spreadsheet for your household budget and decided to add an item to your list, the program would automatically recalculate everything that depended upon that number and display the results. It could also automatically indicate what percentage of your income is budgeted for each expense.

Spreadsheets can do many other things as well. (Some people even use them as stripped-down word processors.) So many, in fact, that they are really the ideal type of software for almost any job requiring arithmetic or other kinds of calculation. Unfortunately, because spreadsheets have traditionally been closely associated with business and because business people are the largest users of this type of software, many individuals never consider electronic spreadsheet programs for use at home.

In reality, however, an electronic spreadsheet can be the perfect "engine" to drive almost any kind of household or personal finance application. And thanks to prewritten, inexpensive instructions or "templates" that can be loaded into a spreadsheet the way you load a regular program, there is no need for you to fiddle with formulas. As explained in Chapter 15, you just load the template, enter your budget or checkbook or other figures, and you're done. Spreadsheet programs are available for as little as $50.

*Why a Personal Filing System?*
In addition to crunching numbers and talking on the telephone, one of the things computers do exceptionally well is filing, finding, and generally keeping track of things. And with a personal filing system or a larger, more powerful (and more expensive) database management system (DBMS), that is exactly what yours will be able to do. Whether it's a list of addresses, recipes, or "Notes to Myself," if you've filed it with one of these programs, the computer will be able to find it, usually on the basis of a key word or two entered by you. More than likely, it will also be able to sort your information as well. ("Put all recipes with 'main dish' in them in one file and all the 'desserts' in another.")

**SoftTip:** You will find many possible uses for a filing program around the house. But there is an important caveat: A computer can't find information unless you first sit there and type it in. This is a necessity many people overlook in their enthusiasm for computing power, and to a lesser extent it applies to electronic spreadsheets as well. Any time you want your machine to "process

*SoftTip continued*

data" of any sort, remember that a "data entry" process must take place first.

Can you see yourself sitting down and typing in all of the Campbell's Soup recipes you have painstakingly pasted to three-by-five cards over the years? Do you think you will really take the time to enter every record album in your collection, typing in the artist, the title, and the name of each cut on both sides? If you do and are willing to pay this hidden price for instant information access, then by all means buy a personal filing program or a DBMS. For when it comes to retrieving information, "nobody does it better" than a computer. If this does not sound appealing, you may want to forego a filing program. Or at least wait until you are completely comfortable with your other software.

*Working with the Building Blocks*

Now let's take each of the four programs in turn and look briefly at how you can apply them and thus avoid buying a clutch of specialized programs. Communications is unique in that if you want to go online, you need a single-purpose program to do it. (Incidentally, if you are an IBM/PC owner using DOS 1.0 or 1.1, you already have a communications program on your DOS disk. It's called COMM.BAS and you load and run it from BASIC.) Your main decision here concerns the features you want and how much you want to spend.

If you have a word processing program with a "search" feature, you can easily use it as a filing program. If you were to type in all of the information for your record collection, you could tell the system to find all of the albums that include recordings of "Eine Kleine Nachtmusik," probably by simply typing in "Eine."

In terms of versatility and sheer power, the real workhorse of the four is the electronic spreadsheet. It can be used for personal budgets, checkbook balancing, and all other personal finance applications; for general ledger, accounts receivable, and most other accounting functions; it can analyze your investment portfolio and help you make informed decisions on what house to buy (and how much the sellers will have to come down in price for you to be able to afford it).

Now, lest you get the wrong impression, spreadsheets don't normally come with all of these "setups" built in. You may have to create them yourself. But if that does not appeal, and it very well may not, you can buy a book of templates to set up home budgets, checkbook balancing, loan amortization, and other applications. Such books sell for about $15 and contain as many as 50 different templates for you to type in. Alternatively, you will be able to buy prepared templates on disk that involve no typing whatsoever. These normally sell for $30 to $50—compared to $150 single-purpose programs designed to do the same thing. (See Chapters 15 and 21.) You will also find spreadsheet templates available for free on computer bulletin board systems, The Source, CompuServe, and possibly some other databases.

Finally, as mentioned earlier, a personal filing program or DBMS will let you keep track of and manipulate information. Unlike the word processing filing system suggested above, a filing system will do more than merely locate every occurrence of a specified word in a file. Its search function will be much more powerful, allowing you to specify "every recording of 'Eine Kleine Nachtmusik' conducted by Eugene Ormandy but *not* played by the Philadelphia Orchestra." Or you might specify everyone on your club mailing list who has not paid dues for the current year. With some programs you will be able to say, "Find me all of those deadbeats and print out an address label for each one." The more powerful DBMS programs will even let you interface with your word processing program to tell the system to print out a form letter and stick the address from the DBMS file into each one.

*Limitations*

Of course, there are many things the building block programs cannot do. They cannot check your spelling, though some word processors come with a spelling checker program as part of the package. They cannot generate high quality graphics from the figures that you hand them, though some of the more expensive spreadsheets have "character" graphics (points are represented by an asterisk). And, of course, they can't do the kinds of things found in game or education programs.

In addition, while they will have an equivalent or even greater amount of power and capacity (the number and length of files, the amount of data they can handle), they will probably require more preparation and "setup" work before they will be able to do the jobs that a single-purpose program can handle right out of the box.

Finally, the building block programs will not have what is known as a "front end." The front end of a program consists of the menus, special prompts, and possibly the help functions and help files that are laid on top of the main program to make it more user friendly. It is the front end that makes a program "interactive," which means that the program asks you for a menu selection or some other piece of information; it goes away and does something or responds in some way; then it asks you for something else.

The alternative is for you to sit at your console and issue commands, the way you do when using DOS. Naturally, to be able to issue commands, you must remember what they are and what they do since there is no interactive menu to lead you. When you use a building block program to accomplish a single-purpose program type of task, you will not have the menus normally offered by the single-purpose program to rely on. That can make the task more difficult to accomplish. But then again, as we will see, it may not.

*Advantages*

The strongest argument in favor of the building block approach is that there is no need to learn a separate set of commands and procedures for each application. With four programs to concentrate on, you can take the time to master each thoroughly. And although you must take it on faith at this point, once you master a good program, you will be amazed at what you can do. Useful applications and ideas will occur to you unbidden, and you will know almost instinctively how to accomplish them with the programs at your command.

Finally, there is the matter of cost. We've already indicated that the building block approach can save you money. But let's look at it from a slightly different perspective for a moment. Let's suppose that you have decided to spend a certain amount of money on software this year. For whatever amount of money you plan to spend, you might be able to buy several single-purpose programs or a single, full-featured, building block program.

Your choice will naturally depend on how extensively you plan to use the program, for clearly it doesn't make sense to pay for more power than you will need or use. But, in some cases, buying a full-featured database management system for $400, for example, might give you more power, capacity, and capability than buying a $150 personal filing system and a $250 mailing list program. The money is the same in both cases. But you may be able to do more with the DBMS than with the other two.

---

**SoftTip:** It is impossible to overemphasize this point: If you plan to use the building block approach, make sure that each program you buy offers the adaptability and flexibility you need. The points to look for are cited in the Software Buyer's Quick Reference Checklists at the end of each chapter in Part III. For example, make sure that your spreadsheet will accept templates and make sure that your database management program or personal filing system can be used with your word processing program. Buying software with the idea of building a foundation that can be used for

---

many different applications thus calls for a slightly different or expanded perspective from what might be appropriate for a single-purpose program.

*For Business Users and Professionals*

The building block approach has considerable merit in business as well. But much depends on your situation. If you are an executive with a large firm and you have your own computer at your office, the first program you will want to buy will be a full-featured electronic spreadsheet. A communications program to allow you to tap commercial databases for marketing and other business information or to let you access your firm's mainframe computer would probably be the next piece of software you would want. And you may want a graphics program to display and manipulate the information developed on your spreadsheet or captured from the various databases. It all depends upon your job and your individual needs, but many managers find that the new "integrated" packages that combine many of these functions in a single program are perfectly suited to them. (See Chapter 18.)

If you are running a business, or if your are a doctor, lawyer, dentist, consultant, or other professional, you will probably want dedicated accounting and time management software, as well as one or more of the building block programs. Much depends on how extensively the software will be used and who will be using it. For a small business, an electronic spreadsheet with a suitable set of templates can handle most of your accounting, invoicing, sales reporting, and other chores. A DBMS can be used to track inventory and generate customer lists. And a word processing program is a *sine qua non*.

For a larger business, one or more interrelated accounting programs may provide the features and convenience you need. With a dedicated package, you can say, "Give me an aged billing report listing all customers who have yet to pay their bills," and the program will print it out. You can get the same kind of report using one or more of the building block programs, but somewhat more effort will be required since the necessary steps may not be built into the program(s). (See Chapter 16 for information on how a "relational" database management program can be used for accounting.) If clerical staff will be using the software, the kind of convenience and front-end user friendliness offered by the best dedicated programs can be very important.

The building block programs can be quite useful to a professional, but there is no practical way to use them alone to run a professional office— taking care of client scheduling, handling your billing, keeping track of supplies, etc. For these applications, the professional programs discussed in Chapter 23 are essential.

---

**SoftTip:** Communications can be particularly useful to professionals. Attorneys have long used the LEXIS and NEXIS databases maintained by Meade Data Central, and now that a leased Meade terminal is no longer required, usage will increase. Generally, medical professionals have used online services considerably less. But now that many physicians and dentists are converting their offices to computers, this may change. Fisher-Stevens, a pharmaceutical industry marketing service company in Totowa, New Jersey, has announced "Phycom." Offered in conjunction with GTE Telenet's Minet service for health care professionals, Phycom allows doctors to search for and retrieve information on pharmaceuticals by pressing a few keys on their communications-equipped computers. The service is free, thanks to online advertising sponsorship.

---

*What Should You Do?*

Regardless of whether you want to use the building block approach or not, you will almost certainly want a communications program or an electronic spreadsheet, if you are a business user. These are programs that you would probably buy in any case, and they are an excellent place to start. Similarly, you would probably also buy a word processing program. Again, this is a low-risk choice since it is something you are virtually certain to use. You can't go too far wrong if you buy a basic $50 word processing program, even if you decide later that you want a more powerful piece of software. The only "commitment" you will have to worry about is whether to buy a dot-matrix or a letter-quality (typewriter-like) printer, though in some cases they will be nearly comparable in price, if not in versatility and speed.

Conceivably, communications and word processing software will be all you need, at least for a while. If you later decide that you want to do other things with your computer, you can once again consider the building block approach or a single-purpose program. At that point, however, after working with your machine for a while, you will be in a much better position to decide which path is best for you.

---

**SoftTip:** There may be an added bonus to building your software collection gradually over time: falling prices. *ISO World*, a microcomputer industry publication, recently quoted executives from ComputerLand Corporation and several major software houses as saying that software prices may drop as much as 50% in the near future. The reason is the growing number of "inexpensive" ($1,000 and under) personal computers aimed at the home market. "With the advent of less expensive hardware systems," says a vice president at Microsoft, "and with companies thinking about mass merchandising software for these systems, it is inevitable that the price is going to go down." The executive went on to say that programs that in the past have sold for $250 to $350 are likely to have their prices cut to fit within the $100 to $150 range.

## Locating the Right Program

As mentioned at the beginning of this chapter, a sensible first step is to develop a list of "possibles"—programs that are compatible with your computer and are capable of doing what you want. Although you might want to weed out some of the products at this point on the basis of price, this is generally not the time to begin worrying about specific features. Try to reduce the overwhelming number of programs to a manageable number. It could be 5, 10, 15, or 25. It all depends on what is available for your desired application.

Probably the best place to start is with the appropriate "how-to-buy" chapter in this book. The chapter will give you a good idea of what the software can do. Read it over once to get the general idea. Later, you can read it again when you get down to deciding on a specific program. Another good first step is to visit your local bookstore and pick up several copies of the computer magazines they now carry, paying particular attention to any that are devoted to your brand of equipment.

**SoftTip:** Your bookstore will also undoubtedly have a selection of the new software catalogues that are sprouting up like mushrooms after a thunder shower. Some of them may also be available at your local library. And you will find a number of catalogues—as well as hard-to-find newsletters and magazines—listed in the appendices of this book. Clearly, the more listings a catalogue has for programs that you can run on your machine, the more useful it will be to you.

**SoftTip:** Whenever possible, make an effort to copy down the name, address, and phone number of the software house that produces the program. Because of its limited distribution channels, the software industry can be thought of as an hourglass. On the

*SoftTip continued*
producing side, there are thousands of software firms. On the consuming side, there are millions of computer owners. But in the middle, where the glass pinches to wasp-waist restrictiveness, there are the computer and software stores. Limited in number (though rapidly growing), each store has only so much shelf space and only so much money to invest in software inventory. Selections are thus often quite limited.

For this reason, there is no other industry in which direct customer-vendor (software house) contact plays such a key role.

### A Pleasure Visit to the Computer Store

Computer and software stores also sell magazines and catalogues. But they have the added advantage of having literature from manufacturers. And, of course, they have programs for you to look at—though in many cases you will be surprised at how few programs they actually stock. Computer and software stores also have salespeople, and that can be a problem, for more than likely a salesperson who is a "fast closer" will try to sell you whatever is on the shelf, in spite of your protestations that you are just looking.

Ask for a demonstration, examine the various software packages, ask for any product literature—but resist the sales talk and the pressure to buy. Don't purchase anything at this point. If you have made it clear to the salesperson from the beginning that you really *are* just looking, neither of you has any reason to feel bad when you leave without buying anything. If the salesperson is smart, he or she will be as accommodating as time will allow, fully aware that most customers make several visits to a computer store before actually making a purchase.

**SoftTip:** You might also ask to look at the catalogues the store has on file from various software suppliers. Stores can not stock everything the suppliers offer, but they can usually obtain it for you. Ask for the salesperson who does the software ordering for the store and then ask that person if you might look at the catalogues kept behind the counter or in a backroom office.

### Join a Users Group

Users groups and clubs dedicated to a particular machine, or to computing in general, are the wagon trains of the software world. Affordable personal computers may represent the crowning triumph of the free enterprise system, but the territory is so new and uncharted that everyone who owns a machine is in some sense a pioneer. By pooling their resources, their knowledge, and their experiences and making them available to all members, members of users groups can help protect you from the hazards of your journey. They can help you identify the programs you seek and alert you to potential problems and clinkers.

Probably the best way to find out about users groups in your general area is to ask at the computer store where you bought your machine. If that store can't help you, some other store may be able to. If there is a college or university or even a high school nearby with a computer course, you might also contact the instructor or some of the students.

---

**SoftTip:** Begun in 1980 as the first "software locator service," a firm called SOFSEARCH maintains a database of over 30,000 different computer program products from over 12,000 software producers. This is one of the most comprehensive lists of micro, mini, and mainframe software anywhere, for as the firm points out, if it were to count every available version of each product as a separate program, its database would total over 100,000 items.

You can ask the firm to search its database using a wide range of criteria. Search Reports are shipped within 48 hours. Costs range from $40 to $75 per search request, but quantity discounts are available. Discounts on the software you buy may also be available. For more information, contact:

SOFSEARCH International, Inc.
P.O. Box 5276
San Antonio, TX 78201
(800) 531-5955
(512) 340-8735, in Texas

---

**SoftTip:** A firm called ITM will conduct a search of its database for you *for free.* The database contains over 2,000 programs and, with the guidance of a telephone consultant, you can ask for a search on the basis of one or more of over 300 criteria. Naturally, ITM hopes that you will buy from them, and they offer software for as much as a third off the list price.

A spokesman indicated that most major programs are kept in stock for immediate shipment, though specialized programs may take a bit longer. ITM offers a full refund policy if you are not

*SoftTip continued*
satisfied with the product you order and return it within 30 days.
A free catalogue is also available. Contact:

ITM
Software Division
936 Dewing Avenue, Suite E
Lafayette, CA 94549-4292
(800) 334-3404
(415) 284-7540, in California

*Narrowing the Field: Read the Reviews!*
At this point, you will have developed a list of "possibles" and be ready to tighten your focus. In the course of assembling your list, you may have already begun to narrow things down. But now it is time to compare seriously the features offered by the various products remaining. The idea is to come up with two or three candidates that you can have demonstrated at a computer store. A thorough demonstration requires some preparation on your part and may take an hour or more. It simply is not practical to have more than about three main candidates.

The software reviews published in computer magazines, books, and newsletters are vital to this process. They can give you a feeling for the program, how it works, what it can do, how easy it is to learn and use. And they can alert you to problems that you might never discover on your own—until it's too late.

The most serious problem you will face concerning software reviews is locating reviews of the particular products you are interested in. Magazines naturally try to review the latest products, though the long period between the time magazine issues are written and the time they appear on the stands or in your mailbox makes them somewhat less current than you might expect. But what if one of your main candidates has been on the market for a while? What if all the reviews appeared six months ago, before you knew you were interested in the product and possibly before you even owned a computer?

In that case, you'll need to find out which issue the review appeared in and you'll need to somehow obtain a copy of it. The answer may be as close as your local library. There you will find a series of *Readers Guides to . . .* books that index most major magazines. Ask the librarian for help in locating both these books and the magazines they refer to.

If you cannot find the information you want at your library, consider contacting the magazines themselves to see if they publish cumulative indexes. *Creative Computing,* for example, offers a six-year (1974 to

1980) index of every article, software review, and program listing the magazine has published, classified by subject area and title. Other magazines may have similar publications. Send $2.00 to:

> *Creative Computing*
> 39 East Hanover Avenue
> Morris Plains, NJ 07950

Another publication to look for at the library, or possibly order yourself, is the *Microcomputer Index*. This publication includes a comprehensive index of *Popular Computing*, *Personal Computing*, and some 20 other personal computing magazines. The *Microcomputer Index* is published quarterly (annual subscription: $30), and each issue contains over 1,300 entries. Back issues may be available at a cost of $22 for each year. Contact:

> *Microcomputer Index*
> 2464 El Camino Real, Suite 247
> Santa Clara, CA 95051

*Note:* This publication is also available online through DIALOG and The Knowledge Index. See the next section of this chapter for details on using your computer to search it electronically.

You should also consider the *Periodical Guide for Computerists* published by Applegate Computer Enterprises. This is a continuation of a guide begun in 1975 by Eldon Berg, and it is issued in the fall every year. The guide includes 15 categories (games, graphics, software, communications, hardware, etc.) and covers most major computer publications. To order a copy, send $11.95, plus 75¢ for postage and handling to:

> Applegate Computer Enterprises
> P.O. Box 288
> Applegate, OR 97530
> (503) 846-6742

---

**SoftTip:** The above publication is one of at least two indexes that are also available on floppy disk for use with a database management or personal filing system. When used with a DBMS, you can have your computer search for and produce a list of all the articles in the index containing one or more key words ("communications" and "modems," "games" and "children," etc.). The Applegate index is available for use with dBASE II. (It is also available for use

*SoftTip continued*

with MBASIC or CBASIC, though the searches cannot be as sophisticated.)

Bill Roach at Elliam Associates also maintains an on-disk magazine index called MAGART.DB ("magazine article database"). Your first disk is $20, updates are issued approximately every three months at $10 each. Thanks to a proprietary program, Elliam Associates can supply MAGART.DB in virtually any format required by your computer. The firm also sells software and can make available over 2,500 public domain CP/M programs at a cost of about $10 a disk. (There are about 90 disks worth of programs from the national CP/M users group and about 117 disks from SIG/M, another national CP/M group.) Ask for the Elliam catalogue. To use the magazine index, you will need a copy of Superfile ($195), from F.Y.I, Inc. (see Chapter 16).

For more information, contact:

Elliam Associates
24000 Bessemer Street
Woodland Hills, CA 91367
(213) 348-4278;
Evenings, 7:00 PM till "any time";
weekends, including Fridays,
any time. (CA time, of course.)

and:

F.Y.I., Inc.
4202 Spicewood Springs Rd., #204
Austin, TX 78759
(512) 346-0133
(Superfile runs under CP/M and IBM/PC DOS.)

**SoftTip:** Primarily for business people, Hyatt Research Corporation offers a publication called *PC News Watch* that serves as something of a current index of articles on the computer industry and software drawn from 20 or more publications *(ISO World, Mini-Micro Systems,* the *Wall Street Journal,* etc.). Each monthly issue provides a headline and brief summary paragraphs of important articles, followed by information on the issue and the page on which the article appeared. The cost is $185 a year. Ask for a sample issue and contact:

> Hyatt Research Corporation
> P.O. Box 662
> Andover, MA 01810

*Getting Copies of Reviews*

Discovering that an article or review exists is half the battle. The other half is finding a copy of it. Again, your library is a good place to start. But there are so many computer magazines, and library budgets tend to be so tight, that you may not be able to find the issue you need. The next stop should be your local users group. Some groups and clubs maintain libraries of computer magazines. If yours does not, the chances are good that one or more of the members will have the magazine in a private collection.

If you are still unsuccessful, you might consider contacting the publisher of the magazine to see about obtaining the back issues you need. McGraw-Hill's *Popular Computing*, for example, offers back issues of its predecessor, *onComputing*, as well as *Popular Computing*. The cost per issue (including postage and handling) is $3.25 in the United States; $3.75 for Canada and Mexico. Since magazines rarely reprint issues, supplies are limited to whatever they happen to have in the warehouse. Thus, you may or may not find the copy you seek. For *Popular Computing*, contact:

> *Popular Computing*
> Back Issues
> P.O. Box 328
> Hancock, NH 03449

**SoftTip:** Whether you subscribe to one or more computer magazines or make a monthly trip to your newsstand to pick up the latest issues, follow this simple rule:

KEEP YOUR MAGAZINES INTACT!

Unless you buy two copies of each publication, one to be cut up and one for archival storage, resist the temptation to tear out interesting articles and reviews. Computer magazines are an absolutely invaluable resource. Unlike *Time* or *Newsweek*, they should

*SoftTip continued*
not be disposed of when you're finished reading them. Instead, you should save them in an organized fashion the way you might store an encyclopedia that you purchase on a one-volume-per-month basis.

By keeping them intact, you will be able to use the year-end indexes that most of them publish, and you will be able to take advantage of other publications that direct you to particular issues. In short, treat your magazines as a reference work, for that is how you will be using them, possibly for years to come.

*Getting the Most Out of Software Reviews*
Software reviews play a crucial role in helping you identify the programs that are right for you. They will explain the product's features, highlight its strong points, alert you to weaknesses and potential problems, and generally tell you what it is like to use the program. However, there is one very important point to keep in mind when reading such an article: Like movie and book reviews, software reviews are ultimately one person's opinion of the merit or value of the product. And just as one movie reviewer can praise a film that another one panned, so it is with software.

For this reason, it is important to read at least two reviews of any program you are seriously considering. And if you can do so without feeling overwhelmed, three or more reviews would not be out of the question. Leaving aside the matter of the reviewer's opinion, there is a very good practical reason for this. Different reviews will focus on different aspects of the same program. One article might go into detail on some of the features, while another article might devote a similar amount of space to a completely different set of features. Generally, the more reviews you read, the more complete will be your picture of the program.

It must also be noted that reviews do vary in quality as well as in thoroughness, partly because of the lack of standards on what points a software review should include. Many publications neglect to insist that their freelance and other reviewers adhere to a format. Consequently, the reviews they publish tend to be "free form" at best. At worst, they consist of nothing more than someone's half-formed thoughts and personal impressions of the software under consideration. Some may find this impressionistic approach valuable, but others are frustrated by the lack of organization.

*The* InfoWorld *Standard*
One publication worthy of special note for its efforts in establishing

and enforcing reviewing standards is *InfoWorld.* You can always count on finding the following labelled sections in any *InfoWorld* review:

- Features
- Performance
- Ease of Use
- Error Handling
- Documentation
- Support
- Summary

---

**SoftTip:** *InfoWorld* is a weekly magazine that offers is one of the best ways to keep your finger on the pulse of the microcomputer and software industry. Unfortunately, it may be a bit expensive for many computer owners. Major bookstores like Dalton's and Waldenbooks have begun stocking it in their magazine racks, so you can buy a sample copy before you subscribe. For more information, contact:

InfoWorld
375 Cochituate Road, Box 880
Framingham, MA 01701
(800) 343-6474
(617) 879-0700, in Mass.

$31 in U.S., $65 in Canada, Central and South America, $100 in Europe and $170 in all other countries.

*Note:* You can also reach *InfoWorld* on The Source at TCX939 and on CompuServe at Y0001,1150. *InfoWorld* also has a special section on CompuServe. Type GO INF-1 at the exclamation (!) prompt to read online editions of *InfoWorld* software reviews.

---

This is an excellent format to keep in mind when you are reading *any* software review. You can use it as a framework for organizing the points the reviewer makes, regardless of where they actually occur in the article. What does the review say about ease of use? Does it mention error handling? Does it talk about the support you can expect from the software producer? If these or any of the other points in the framework are not mentioned, then you can conclude that the review is not complete.

You will also want to use the Software Buyer's Quick Reference Checklist at the end of each "Toolchest" chapter to see what the review has to say about specific features for each type of program. The items on the Checklists will alert you to important points the reviewer may have forgotten or been unable to include, such as the number of pages of text a word processing program can handle. (Some are limited to 15 or 20 pages; others have no effective limit on the size of the document you can create.)

*The Qualifications of the Reviewer*

Even the editors of *InfoWorld* would probably be willing to admit that a good strong review framework is no guarantee that the article will provide all of the information you as a software buyer need. Though it is fair to say that virtually all reviewers make a valiant attempt, some are simply better qualified than others. The fact is that in the past there have not been enough qualified reviewers to go around. Many magazines are under such pressure to produce editorial copy—articles and reviews—to slip in between all of the ads that they are sometimes less than stringent about whom they ask to review software and hardware products. In some cases, if you can put two words together and own a computer, you can be a software reviewer. Just produce the copy and get it here by Tuesday. Other publications are more selective, realizing that it is in the best interests of their readers (and thus, in their own best interests as well) to ask someone with an accounting background to review an accounting package, or to have an attorney review a law office management program.

This is not to denigrate software reviewers as a group. There are many fine writers who labor long and hard at their machines to put a program through its paces and to give you the kind of information you need. Instead, it is to suggest that you should not necessarily accept every review as the last and authoritative word on the product.

The need for quality also makes it important to pay more attention to the name of the person who wrote the review than you would for most magazine articles. If the author is identified as having a background in the applications area you are interested in, it is at least an indication that the individual may have the desired qualifications. It is too early to say whether "star" software reviewers will emerge the way "star" movie reviewers have developed. But clearly, if you find a review informative and—based on your experiences after buying the product—accurate and complete, then you will want to look for the reviewer's name on future articles.

---

**SoftTip:** One thing that seems worth taking with a small grain of salt is a reviewer's reports of how the software house responded to the kinds of questions a user might ask. If you were a software house and someone called up saying, "This is John Smith and I'm reviewing your product for *Megabyte Magazine*," you might be inclined to respond with more alacrity than if John Smith, Software Buyer, were on the phone. A better source of information regarding the quality of support you can expect might be a friend or fellow users group member who has actually had occasion to call the firm.

(The time to really start worrying is when the reviewer calls for support, identifies his or her publication, and *still* does not get a satisfactory response. If the firm won't respond to *Megabyte Magazine*, how do you think you'll fare?)

## Online Electronic Resources

If your computer is equipped to talk on the telephone or if you are considering giving it this capability in the near future, you're in for a real surprise. Some might even call it a thrill. Whatever you call it, the fact is that whether you are at home or in your office, you can search through over 20,000 software product listings, magazine article references, and online software reviews without ever leaving your chair. You can summon up a list of all programs for the Apple IIe that deal with accounting applications or just general ledger or something else. Simply tell the database what you want.

You can electronically scan two or more collections of magazine references for all word processing articles or all reviews of specific word processing programs. Just tell the database what you want.

You can contact other individuals who have bought the product and ask for their reactions and advice. You can chat electronically with the editors of *Computers and Electronics* magazine at regular weekly electronic confabs. You can read *InfoWorld* software and hardware reviews. And you can read and respond to online newsletters sponsored by major computer manufacturers. There are even users groups dedicated to exchanging tips on using specific programs like the PIE Writer word processing program for the Apple or WordStar. And Digital Research has recently begun a group for users of CP/M and other DR products. (See Chapter 2.)

The cost for this abundance of information riches? As little as $6 an hour, plus whatever you have spent on your modem and communications software. In the following section we will be assuming that you have already equipped your computer for communications and that you have a subscription to one or more of the database services mentioned. Chapter 17 will help you choose the communications software you need, and Appendix C includes addresses and subscription information. A more extensive explanation of how to get your computer to talk on the phone and what you can do once it has this capability can be found in my book, *The Complete Handbook of Personal Computer Communications* (St. Martins's Press, $14.95).

## Software Resources Available on CompuServe *

*Magazine Index*

If you were to sign on to CompuServe and type GO PER-1 at the exclamation (!) prompt, you would see the following menu on your screen:

```
             Compuserve        Page PER-1
             Computer Periodical Guide
          1 Clubs        11 Microcomputers
          2 Commun.      12 Microprocessors
          3 Computers    13 Music/Sound
          4 Education    14 Networks
          5 Games        15 Programming
          6 General      16 Publications
          7 Hardware     17 Robotics
          8 Art. Intel.  18 Shows/Exhibits
          9 Languages    19 Software
         10 Law
```

This is the menu used to access CompuServe's database of magazine article references, and you can use it to locate any recently published article in most of the major computer magazines. For example, here are some of the items that appeared when we selected PUBLICATIONS (16) as the category of interest. No other keywords were used, but any of these listings would have appeared had any of the words in capital letters been entered as a search criteria:

```
                      Publications
         PUBLICATIONS              NETWORKS
         Title: $75 BILLION HOME MARKET
         Author:
         Magazine: INFOWORLD      Issue: My1280    Page: 1

         PUBLICATIONS                    80
         Title: ANNUAL INDEX TO ARTICLES
         Author:
```

* Page numbers on the CompuServe system are subject to change. Consequently, the ones cited here may no longer apply. Everything discussed in this section, however, can be reached via the CompuServe menus, regardless of the specific page number. Aim for the "Personal Computing Section" (PCS) as you work your way through the menus.

Magazine: 80 MICRO          Issue: D81          Page: 402

PUBLICATIONS              BOOKS
Title: BASIC HANDBOOK
Author:
Magazine: SOFTALK          Issue: 081          Page: 86

PUBLICATIONS              TRS-80
Title: CIRCUIT DESIGN PROGRAMS
Author:
Magazine: PERS. COMP.      Issue: Ju81          Page: 104

PUBLICATIONS              MAGAZINES
Title: CLOAD MAGAZINE INC
Author: HATFIELD,J
Magazine: DR. DOBBS        Issue: Mr81          Page: 38

Now, here are the results of a more tightly focused search. We wanted to locate articles published about the best-selling electronic spreadsheet program, VisiCalc. We entered 19 (SOFTWARE) from the previous menu and typed "spreadsheet" and "VisiCalc":

        CompuServe      Periodical Guide
                  Software
            . Category: Spreadsheet
            . Title: VisiCalc
            . Author:

Searching . . . CompuServe              Periodical Guide

                  Software
        14 Items Selected
        1 BREAK EVEN ANALYSIS WITH VISICALC
        2 BREAK EVEN ANALYSIS WITH VISICALC
        3 SOFTWARE ARTS VISICALC
        4 VISICALC
        5 VISICALC
        6 VISICALC
        7 VISICALC & T-MAKER
        8 VISICALC A SOFTWARE REVIEW
        9 VISICALC FROM SOFTWARE ARTS
        0 VISICALC PLUS FROM HP
        . Input a number or key
        <ENTER> for more choices. =!

        CompuServe      Periodical Guide
                  Software
        14 Items selected.
        1 VISICALC REVIEW
        2 VISICALC REVIEW

```
3 VISICALC SPAWNS PRODUCTS
4 VISICALC:REASON ENOUGH FOR A COMPUTER
. Last menu page. Key digit
or M for previous menu. . = !
```

By selecting any of the items on the first or second menu reporting the results of the search, a listing similar to the ones we've just seen would have appeared. With that kind of information (publication, date, article title, author, and page), it would be relatively easy to locate the article via any of the conventional routes described earlier.

InfoWorld *Software Reviews—Online*
For actual software reviews, we could have typed GO INF-1 at the CompuServe prompt and seen the following page. Notice the menu selections we entered at each exclamation point to specify first Atari and then IBM/PC software reviews. Page INF-102 lists reviews of specific Atari products. Page INF-106 does the same for the IBM. Either page can be accessed directly as soon as you sign onto the system.

```
        CompuServe              Page INF-1
             InfoWorld On-Line
             Software Reviews
          1 What is InfoWorld
          2 Software Reviews On-line
          3 Subscription Information
          4 Advertising Information
          5 Software Review Book
          6 Talk to InfoWorld (FEEDBACK)
          . Last menu page. Key digit
          or M for previous menu.. = !2


        CompuServe              Page INF-6
                InfoWorld
             Software Reviews
          1.Apple           6.IBM
          2.Atari           7.TRS
          3.Commodore       8.TI
          4.CP/M            9.Timex/Sinclair
          5.Heath/Zenith
          . Last menu page. Key digit or M for previous
          menu.. = !2


        CompuServe              Page INF-102
                ATARI
             SOFTWARE REVIEWS
          1.Atari Word Processor
          2.File Manager 800 v.3F
```

```
3.Crossword Magic
4.Data Perfect
5.S.A.M.
6.Legionnaire
. Last menu page. Key digit or M for previous
menu.. =!M (Intervening menu not shown.)

CompuServe                    Page INF-106
                IBM—PC
           SOFTWARE REVIEWS
1.Pascal & Pascal MT+6
2.Personal Investor
3.QADB01
4.Desktop/Plan
5.Bonus Accounting System
6.Easywriter II
7.Wordix 1.1
8.Edix
. Input a number or key <ENTER> for more
choices. =!
```

Other reviews and particularly insightful comments can be found in CompuServe's electronic magazine, *The Micro Advisor*, written and edited by Eric Balkin. Again, simply type in the page name (GO TMA-1) at the CompuServe prompt:

```
CompuServe               Page TMA-1
. . . . . . . . . . . . . . . . . . . . . . . . . . . . . . . . . . . .
           THE MICRO ADVISOR
Copyright 1981, 1982, 1983
Battery Lane Publications
. . . . . . . . . . . . . . . . . . . . . . . . . . . . . . . . . . . .
1 Software Reviews
2 Hardware
3 Book Reviews
4 Miscellaneous articles
5 Micro Business Commentary
. Input a number or key <ENTER> for more
choices. =!
```

If you own an RCA, a Commodore, or Tandy Radio Shack computer, you will also find special newsletters on the CompuServe system. (Key in GO PCS-10 for the main newsletter menu.) Here, for example, is the table of contents for a recent Tandy Newsletter:

```
CompuServe               Page TRS-1
           The Tandy Newsletter
1 Tandy News Releases
2 MOD I/III/4 Information
```

```
3 MOD II/12/16 Information
4 Color Computer Info
5 Pocket Computers Info
6 Model 100/Portables
7 Educational Information
8 Terminal/Modem Info
9 Computer Supplies Info
10 Peripherals
```

And here is the main menu for the extensive communications and information network that Commodore maintains on the CompuServe system, followed by a sample of the "Tips" and the "Questions and Answers" menus. (Intervening menus are not shown.)

```
Commodore                    Page CBM-1
COMMODORE INFORMATION NETWORK'S
             MAIN MENU
    1 Introduction
    2 Survival Kit
    3 Hotline (Ask Questions)
    4 Product Announcements
    5 Bulletin Board
    6 Commodore Magazine Articles
    7 Directories
    8 Commodore Tips
    9 Commodore Product Line
   10 User Questionnaire
   . Last menu page. Key digit
   or M for previous menu.. = !8
```

```
CompuServe                   Page CBM-500

Commodore Tips
    1 Questions and Answers     <---- See page CBM-510,
    2 Software Tips                    below.
    3 Technical Tips
    4 Descriptions
    Last menu page. Key digit
    or M for previous menu.. = !3
```

```
CompuServe                   Page CBM-800

Technical Tips
    1 Adding Sound to PET
    2 6845 Video Controller
    3 IEEE-488 Bus
    4 DOS Versions
```

```
 5 DOS 1.2 Problems
 6 Relative Record Bug
 7 CBM 8032 & DOS 2.0
 8 DOS 2.1 & 2.5 Bugs
 9 2 Tape & Disk File Hints
10 Compiler Comments
11 SuperPET RS-232 PORT
.Last menu page. Key digit
or M for previous menu.. = !
```

Or, if you had entered a *1* at page CBM-500, to call up "Questions and Answers," here's what you'd see:

```
CompuServe              Page CBM-510

Questions and Answers

    1 PET (2000, 4000 Series)
    2 CBM (8000 Series)
    3 SuperPET (9000 Series)
    4 VIC
    5 Disk Drives
    6 Printers
    Last menu page. Key digit
    or M for previous menu.. = !
```

**SoftTip:** In the electronic universe of online communications, users' groups are called SIGs (Special Interest Groups). Members are located all over the country and sometimes all over the world. Most SIGs are open to everyone, though a small membership fee may be charged to cover expenses. On CompuServe, SIG members can "meet" and chat in large numbers via the "CB" section of the system. On The Source, conversations take place over time via an online conferencing facility. SIGs on both systems maintain bulletin boards to alert members to new products, software bugs, and other information. And in both cases and places, SIGs maintain online libraries of articles, free software, commentary, advice, etc.

The magazine *Computers and Electronics*, formerly *Popular Electronics*, operates a Special Interest Group and online magazine on CompuServe called CEMSIG. Shown below is the main menu, followed by a list of regularly scheduled events. At the designated times, any member can sign on and enter a conference headed by the "SYSOP" ("System Operator"). Communication takes place as if you were talking on a CB radio. The only difference is that you type in your questions and comments from your personal computer. It's a great way to "talk to the experts" and is similar (but much better) than an instant "Letters to the Editor" column in a magazine.

```
            CompuServe              Page CEM-5
            COMPUTERS + ELECTRONICS MENU
            1. NEW PRODUCTS ROUNDUP
            2. COMING ATTRACTIONS
            3. CEMSIG—THE USER'S GROUP


            . Last menu page. Key digit
            or M for previous menu.. = !3



            CompuServe              Page CEM-6
```

CEMSIG—The Computers & Electronics Users Group. This is the area where people with an interest in any branch of Computers or Electronics can ask questions, or have interactive contact with experts, or other hobbyists. To get into the CEMSIG area, type Go CEM-450 or Press <ENTER>. .

```
            WELCOME TO THE CEMSIG CO AREA!
            ****************************************
                 Regularly Scheduled Events
            --------------------------------------------------------
            MONDAYS at 10:00 PM EST
                SOFTWARE Conference
                with SYSOP/Randy
            TUESDAYS at 10:00 PM EST
                TI Conference
                with SYSOP/Jim
                (and/or SYSOP/Randy)
            WEDNESDAYS AT 7:30 Pacific
                TIMEX and Commodore Highlights
                Featuring
                SYSOP/Pat (SPERA P.M.)
                ->TIMEX-SINCLAIR<-
                    and
                ----SYSOP/JD----
                -->CBM Computers<--
            ****************************************
```

In addition to the *Computers and Electronics* group, there are also SIGs devoted to many major brands of computers. Membership may be free or a small ($15) fee may be required to help defray online storage costs for the SIG library of free programs and software reviews. Here is a recent list of the SIGS on CompuServe:

```
                 Personal Computing SIGS

            1 CP/M SIG              11 PowerSoft's
            2 HUG (Heath)           12 Programmer's
```

```
 3 MAUG (Apple)          13 CEM SIG
 4 MNET-11 (HII)         14 Author Forum
 5 MUSUS p-sys.          15 Commodore
 6 RCA micros            16 Atari SIG
 7 TRS80 COCO            17 IBM PC SIG
 8 Panasonic             18 OSI SIG
 9 MNET80 TRS80          19 Instructions
10 LSI Users             20 Descriptions
Input a number or key
<ENTER> for more choices=!
```

Most of these names are self-explanatory. However, MAUG stands for the MicroNET Apple Users Group. (CompuServe used to be called "MicroNET.") MUSUS is a group sponsored by the UCSD p-System Users' Society (USUS) (again, the "M" for "MicroNET"). RCA is a technical group for users of RCA 1800. "COCO," of course, stands for Tandy's Color Computer. LSI is a group interested in the multi-featured LDOS operating system for the TRS-80 (The "L" stands for "Logical Systems, Inc.," the firm that wrote the software.) PowerSoft is an alternative TRS-80 users' group. The Programmers' SIG is for programmers, and the Authors' SIG is devoted to exchanging information and news about writing articles for magazines. Authors of microcomputers software for all brands of machines are also members of this group.

## Software Resources on The Source

The Source also has extensive resources guaranteed to be of interest to any prospective software buyer, particularly owners of Apple and IBM personal computers. For example, in the PUBLIC area of The Source you will find a number of newsletters, product review sections, and software catalogues. "SAUG" in the listing below stands for "Source Apple Users Group." To access any of the following sections, type in PUBLIC at The Source command level prompt (->), followed by a space and the number in the center column. You can also reach these sections by following The Source menus to the World of Personal Computing area, an advisable first-time approach since the numbers in the middle column may change. The numbers in parentheses in the right column are The Source mail addresses of the individuals who manage each section.

```
APPLE CITY               172    (TCD912)
APPLESOURCE              115    (TCF369)
IBM PC GAZETTE           114    (TCA257)
MR. SOFTWARE'S CATALOG   171    (TCE523)
PRODUCT REVIEWS          117    (TCY617)
```

| SAUG MAGAZINE | 116, 133 | (TCA265) |
| SAUG BASIC LIBRARY | 23 | (TCA265) |
| SAUG PASCAL LIBRARY | 24 | (TCA265) |
| SIGOP LIBRARY | 21 | (TCV176) |

Here is a sample of what you can expect when you enter the PRODUCT REVIEWS section. The List Times column tells you how long it takes to receive the file at a rate of 300 baud, an important consideration since you are charged by the amount of time you spend connected to the system. We have greatly shortened the list to include just the more easily recognizable programs. The actual list you will see is much longer. Any of these reviews can be read by keying in the FILE number:

PRODUCT REVIEWS

| FILE # | FILE NAME | LIST TIME |
|---|---|---|
| 1 | Introduction | 5:43 |
| 4 | Templates | 8:01 |
| 6 | Diablo-630 | 8:10 |
| 7 | Grappler-H-A | 2:53 |
| 15 | Move-It | 5:23 |
| 16 | Data-Capture-4.0-A | 4:50 |
| 17 | WordStar | 15:17 |
| 19 | Proof-Reader | 8:07 |
| 22 | SpellBinder | 14:17 |
| 25 | VersaForm | 5:41 |
| 28 | DB-Master | 20:41 |
| 29 | PFS | 7:20 |

**SoftTip:** The Source Apple Users Group has a great deal to offer, but as with any users group, one of the most important aspects is the sharing of tips and useful information. Here, for example, is a copy of a notice posted on the group's internal bulletin board. (Note that the free membership offer is subject to change.):

If you are an Apple PIE or PIE Writer word processor user with an Apple ] [ or / /e, then you will be interested in a new Users Group now forming:

Apple PIE Writers

As the name indicates, we plan to support all Apple versions of PIE. This support will include tips, tricks, modifications, help, and just about anything to enhance your use of the already outstanding PIE word processor.

If you have made some modifications to PIE let us know; maybe others would be interested. If you have questions ask the Group; somebody will have the answer. This is your Users Group, we are just the clearinghouse.

Right now membership is free so if you are a PIE user send us your name, Source or CompuServe ID, and your US Mail address. Include which version of PIE you use: Apple PIE or PIE Writer, 40 or 80 column (specify your board), and ] [ or / /e.

Send to:  Apple PIE Writers
          Source: CL1312                         CompuServe: 74405,764

For IBM owners, there is the *IBM Gazette*, an electronic magazine featuring product reviews, prices, software, and a compiled listing of all the notices that have appeared on The Source IBM Bulletin Board (POST) in another section of the system:

<------IBM PERSONAL COMPUTER GAZETTE VIA THE SOURCE------>

TABLE OF CONTENTS

1 INTRODUCTION  = Objectives, Publications & User Groups
2 PRICES  = At IBM's Product Centers (for reference)
3 PC MAGAZINE  = Charter Issue Index
4 SOURCES  = OF SOFTWARE, HARDWARE & PERIPHERALS
5 VISICALC  = VisiCalc Models for the PC
6 POST SCAN IBM  = Collected POST items in date sequence
7 SCAN BY ID  = POST SCAN sequenced by ID for reference.

There is also *Real-Times Magazine*, yet another source of software reviews, columns, tips, and advice for computer owners of every persuasion. You can access *Real Times* by typing PUBLIC 117, The Source command level prompt, or following the menus to the personal computing area. Here, slightly modified for reasons of space, is the kind of thing you can expect to see:

|  |  | Read-Time |
|---|---|---|
| COLUMN | CONTENTS | 1200 baud |
| 1 | Welcome to REAL-TIMES Magazine | 0:19 |
| 2 | /MENU/ COMDEX Computer Show Reports | 11:40 |
| 3 | Report on Digital Research's CP/M-83 Show | 1:49 |
| 4 | /MENU/ Product News Editions | 2:47 |
| 5 | /MENU/ In-Depth Product Profiles | 1:45 |
| 6 | COMEDY: "Sex and Silicone in Las Vegas" | 1:48 |
| 7 | /MENU/ "SOURCE-AIDE"—Advice on Source Usage | 1:46 |
| 8 | ESSAY: Micros—History, Perspective & Use | 1:59 |
| 9 | SPECIAL: The new IBM-XT Hard Disk Computer | 1:20 |
| 10 | GUIDE: Buying a micro word processor | 4:10 |
| 11 | ESSAY: "RAM DISKS"—All about disk emulators | 1:15 |

**SoftTip:** All of The Source features discussed in this section fall under the category of User Publishing. The files are maintained by individuals or groups of individuals. All of them can be read at normal Source rates. But to compensate the club and magazine organizers for their efforts, The Source pays a royalty ranging from 10% to 17.5% of the billable connect time individuals spend accessing these files. If you have an idea for a magazine of any sort (not just computers and software), you might want to contact The Source about offering it online. See Appendix C for the address.

The Source does not currently have a direct equivalent to CompuServe's CB, so users cannot engage in multiple simultaneous conversations. Nor does it have so many well-developed SIGs. However, it has a superb "computerized conferencing" system, and information similar to that found in CompuServe's SIGs can be found here. The system is called PARTI (short for "Participate"). Subjects are considered in "conferences," and any Source subscriber who belongs to a conference can read the messages written by other users, comment on them, add new messages, etc. This doesn't begin to describe PARTI and how it works, so for more information, type PARTI at the Source command level. (Or follow the menus.) Here is a partial list of the conferences you may find on the system that deal with software and computers:

### Selected PARTI Conferences on The Source

"SYSTEMS"
"WORD PROCESSING"
"UCSD"
"MICRO ACCTG SYS???"
"QUASAR HHC"
"POST SOFTWARE"
"PRINTERS"
"UNIX"
"CP/M USERS GROUP"
"APPLE II"
"APPLE/ / /"
"IXO TELECOMPUTER"
"SOFTWARE"
"BUG REPORTS"
"SMALL BUSINESS"

"LOGO AND THE IBM PC"
"LAN"
"APPLE CLASS HELP"
"COLLEGE SOFTWARE"
"GAMENET"
"APPLICATIONS"
"LISP"
"COMPUTERS & LAWYERS"
"COMPAQ PORTABLE"
"FAMILY & COMPUTERS"
"COMPACT DISC"
"DEC RAINBOW USERS"
"EPSON QX & HX USERS"
"IBM PEANUT"
"TRS-80"

## Software Resources on DIALOG's Low-Cost Knowledge Index

It would be hard to imagine a more complete and powerful weapon in a software buyer's arsenal than a subscription to The Knowledge Index. The initial cost is $35 to open an account, and the price includes two free hours of online searching. After that the cost is $24 an hour, including Telenet and Tymnet charges.

DIALOG is a massive "encyclopedic database" offering an unbelievable amount of information on an equally unbelievable range of subjects. The Knowledge Index is the firm's low-cost, after-hours service specifically designed for personal computer owners. The service is available after 6:00 PM until 5:00 AM (your local time) on weekdays. On Saturdays, it is available from 8:00 AM until midnight; on Sundays, from 3:00 PM until 5:00 AM Monday morning.

*The International Software Database*

The Knowledge Index includes an impressive array of information, but if you are interested in software, there are two main sections to focus on. One is called the International Software Database. This is the electronic edition of the printed work called the *International Microcomputer Software Directory.* Updated monthly, it contains information on over 10,000 computer programs, and every one of them can be located by a wide variety of key words. (See Appendix A for information on how to obtain the print version.)

The monthly updates and the fact that you can specify key words makes this database an invaluable resource. For example, you can say, "Give me a listing of all electronic spreadsheet programs that run on the IBM/PC." Figure 8-1 shows some of the results of just that search. (Don't worry about the terms and abbreviations. The documentation that comes with your subscription to "KI" will explain them.)

---

**SoftTip:** Any program listed in the *International Software Directory* can be ordered directly from Imprint Software's One Stop Soft Shop. Contact:

Imprint Software, Ltd.
1520 South College Avenue
Fort Collins, CO 80524
(800) 525-4955
(303) 482-5000, in Colorado

*Surveying the Field*

—— **Figure 8.1. Searching the International Software Database on KI** ——


We have placed in italics the commands you would type. All other text comes into your computer from the database itself.

*?Begin Comp2*

MM/DD/YY 00:00:00 EST
Now in COMPUTERS & ELECTRONICS (COMP)) Section
Intl. Software (COMP2) Database
(Copyright 1983 Imprint Software Ltd.)

*?Find SPREADSHEET and IBM*
      38 SPREADSHEET
     2246 IBM
S1   16   SPREADSHEET AND IBM

*?Display SI/L/1-2*

Display 1/L/1
011135    81270100
THE THINKER
TEXASOFT
1028 NORTH MADISON AVE
DALLAS, TX 75208
IBM PERSONAL COMPUTER/5¼-INCH DISK/49.00$/49.00$
Country of Currency: USA
Source Code Available: NO
Integrated Packaging: NO
Updates: NO
Warranty: YES

This is an electronic spreadsheet program for the IBM PC.

1/L/2
010777    78900900
THE WEDGE
SYSTEMS PLUS INC
1120 SAN ANTONIO RD
PALO ALTO, CA 94303
(415) 969-7047

Distributors for: SOFTWARE DIMENSIONS, DIGITAL
IBM/5¼-INCH DISK/48K/199.00$/199.00$
CP/M (DIGITAL RESEARCH)/5¼-INCH
DISK/48K/199.00$/199.00$
MP/M 1.1 (DIGITAL RESEARCH)/5¼-INCH DISK /48K/199.00$/199.00$
TURBO DOS (SOFTWARE 2000)/5¼-INCH DISK /48K/199.00$/199.00$

Country of Currency: USA
Source Code Available: NO
Integrated Packaging: NO
Updates: YES     Update Cost: 000050.00
Date of Release: 800600     Warranty: NO

An electronic spreadsheet program that is compatible with CPM and MPM. The quick reference cards allow the new end-user to quickly understand and use the power of the Wedge to manipulate his data. It supports 52 columns and 400 rows and has a unique file storage routine which allows very large directory names for storing and retrieving spreadsheets. It interfaces with Accounting Plus. Formatted for most 8" and 5¼" systems. For specific system requirements contact Systems Plus.

*The Microcomputer Index on KI*

The online Microcomputer Index is a database of more than 15,000 citations from more than 40 computer publications from 1981 to the present. Publications include *Byte, Interface Age, InfoWorld, Personal Computing, Popular Computing, Softside,* and *Dr. Dobb's Journal.* The 40 main publications are indexed cover to cover, but the database also includes selected references to other magazines and journals likely to be of interest to its users.

The database is updated quarterly and corresponds to the previously mentioned print publication by the same name. As with any KI database, the electronic version can be searched many different ways. (For an example of a search for articles mentioning software for the Commodore 64 computer, see Figure 8-2.) For more information on the printed version, contact:

> Microcomputer Information Services
> 2464 El Camino Real, Suite 247
> Santa Clara, CA 95051
> (408) 984-1089

**SoftTip:** If you can't find the articles or software reviews you are interested in at your local library or elsewhere, there is good news: You can order a photocopy of it while you are connected to the Knowledge Index. The system will convey your request electronically to the information provider. The service is not cheap ($4.50 per article, plus 20¢ per page copied), but you can't beat it for convenience.

———— **Figure 8.2. Searching for Articles on the "64"** ————

As in the previous figure, we have placed in italics all of the commands that you would type. The database contains 177 articles with the word *Commodore*, and 35 with the word *64*. There are 18 articles in which both words appear. By entering "Find S1 and SOFTWARE," we were able to say, "Look through those 18 articles for any reference to software." We then displayed the abstracts for two of them.

*?Begin Comp3*

MM/DD/YY 00:00:00 EST
Now in COMPUTERS & ELECTRONICS (COMP) Section
  Microcomputer Index (COMP3) Database
  (Copyright 1983 Micro Info. Serv. Inc.)

*?Find COMMODORE and 64*

```
                177 COMMODORE
                 35 64
        S1       18   COMMODORE AND 64
```

*?Find S1 and SOFTWARE*

```
                3637 SOFTWARE
        S2        3   S1 AND SOFTWARE
```

*?Display S2/L/1-2*

```
3/L/2
041003    8241009
  Commodore 64 leads the way: First hand reports on new units
  Baker, Robert, Microcomputing,    Oct 1982,    v6 n10 p20-22,  3
  pages  ISSN: 0744-4567
```

Languages: English
Document Type: Column
Geographic Location: United States
PET-POURRI column reports on some new products introduced at COMDEX;  two favorable reviews for Millipede and Wallbanger (arcade games) for the VIC-20; describes a bug in VIC-20 BASIC that happens when PRINT# output to a device is used.

Descriptors: *PET; *VIC-20; *BASIC; *COMMODORE 64
Identifiers: Millipede; Wallbanger; On LIne Software; EasyCalc; EasyPlot; EasyTools; EasyScan

3/L/3
039570    8236133
Sprite graphics and sound synthesis on the Commodore 64
Halfhill, Tom. Compute!, Sep 1982, v4 n9 p106-110, 5 pages
ISSN: 0194-357X

Languages: English
Document Type: Article
Program Listing in BASIC
Geographic Location: United States
Presents the last article in a series that has covered the Commodore 64. This installment
includes game programming examples and includes the latest news on the software and pe-
ripherals available for the Commodore 64.

Descriptors: *Graphics; *Sound Effects; *Programming
Instruction; *Commodore 64

---

**SoftTip:** What else is available on The Knowledge Index? Here's a brief non-computer overview of some of the databases you might consider once you've finished looking for software:

- AGRICOLA—Information from over 600 agricultural journals and publications.
- BOOKS IN PRINT—Same as in the bookstore or library.
- ABI/INFORM—Information from over 500 business and management journals and magazines (*Forbes, Futurist, Money, Technology Review, Vital Speeches,* etc.)
- INSPEC—Information from over 2,300 engineering and technical journals.
- STANDARD & POOR'S NEWS—Updated weekly.
- ERIC—Material from more than 700 education-related periodicals.
- MAGAZINE INDEX—More than 370 of the most popular American magazines.
- INTERNATIONAL PHARMACEUTICAL ABSTRACTS— Over 700 international journals.
- NATIONAL NEWSPAPER INDEX—*New York Times, Wall Street Journal,* and the *Christian Science Monitor.*
- and more, of course . . .

---

**SoftTip:** For information both general and specific, you might want to sample *The Computer Cookbook* and *The Computer Cookbook Update* by Bill Bates. *The Computer Cookbook* is available in print form from Prentice-Hall. (The third edition was issued in 1983.) And both publications are available for keyword searching on the NewsNet system. The "Update" is revised and expanded each week by the author, and is a NewsNet exclusive. NewsNet also offers online access to over 150 newsletters from various industries. The monthly subscription is $15, credited against usage. For more information, contact:

NewsNet
945 Haverford Road
Bryn Mawr, PA 19010
(800) 345-1301
(215) 527-8030, in Pennsylvania

---

*Conclusion*

Whether you use the conventional resources or the new electronic resources, or a combination of the two, obtaining a list of the programs suitable for your machine and the application you have in mind and then narrowing your choices on the basis of reviews and other information can be crucial. The more you know about a particular type of software (word processing, spreadsheet, etc.) and the more you know about the specific programs on your list, the better. With the kind of information discussed here under your belt, any demonstration of the product in a computer store will be much more meaningful. Computer stores and judging the quality of specific programs is what we will consider next.

# ...9...

# Documentation and Demonstration:
## How to Put a Program through Its Paces

I n this chapter, we'll assume that you have developed a list of possibles and narrowed it down to two or three main candidates. Now it's time to move in and take a really good look at the programs themselves, what they offer, the documentation they provide, and several other factors. This chapter will show you what to look for when examining a program's instruction manual and explain why you should do your best to "break" a program in the course of an in-store demonstration. (We'll give you suggestions for some tricks you might try.)

*Software Quality in a Single Point*
Before delving into the details, however, it is worth knowing that the quickest indication of software quality is . . . money. Not the money you have to pay to buy the program, but the money that was spent to produce and package it. It takes money to hire the best programmers and documentation writers. It takes money to produce an attractive, typeset manual, complete with tabbed sections, extensive index, glossary, tutorial lessons, and a pull-out "quick command reference card." And it takes money to offer the kind of knowledgeable telephone "hotline" vendor support that many of today's software buyers expect and need.

This is said in the full realization that one can't always judge a program by its packaging. And most assuredly one can find bad programs in beautiful boxes. It is also true that if money is used as the main selection criterion, you will miss out on excellent programs that may do a better job of meeting your needs than the better-packaged, more widely advertised competition. But the logic of money is inescapable. If you want the solution with the lowest risk, you have no choice but to buy a well-heeled, well-financed program from one of the large software suppliers.

The days when a brilliant programmer, working with home-built equipment in his garage, could develop a product, type up a few pages of *pro forma* instructions, pack them with a disk in a Baggie, and strike

211

it rich are rapidly drawing to a close. As Philip Aiken, president of Philadelphia's MicroCorp points out, "Today it takes a million dollars just to play. You simply can't get into the game for less." By the time equipment costs, salaries, production, packaging and distribution expenses, and the extensive advertising needed to break through to the consumer are added up, a million dollars may seem an almost insignificant sum of money. Indeed, it is said that Lotus Development Corporation initially spent more than a million dollars a *month* on advertising alone during the time it was introducing its Lotus 1-2-3 integrated program. The advertising paid off. Six months after it was introduced, it had become the best-selling business program with over $12 million in sales.

The huge amounts of money are necessary because of the fundamental change that has taken place in the software market in the past few years. The typical customer is no longer a computer-sophisticated hobbyist who actually enjoys poking around among the hexidecimal addresses of a machine's internal memory to get a program to work. For such an individual, five stapled pages of smeary "instructions" were not only adequate, they were largely unnecessary. Today's customer wants and needs user-friendly programs that are well packaged, well documented, and well supported by vendor and dealer, and widely distributed. And all of that takes money.

The lone programmer will not become a thing of the past. But he probably will not develop a product and start his own company. Instead, he will sell or license his work to a major company with the resources to package and market the program. This is already happening today, and the trend will undoubtedly accelerate in the future as software becomes more and more like a commodity and less like a highly wrought specialty product.

### What Does It Mean to You?

A single programmer or a small two- or three-person firm with a good idea for a personal computer program has two main places to go for the money to develop the product. They can ask a major firm for backing. Or they can seek venture capital from groups of investors willing to accept the risks in hopes of large future profits, and usually in return for part ownership of the company as well.

By and large, neither a big company nor a group of venture capitalists is going to invest in a product or an idea without completely analyzing it and thoroughly investigating the capabilities of the individuals who plan to produce it. A large computer company will have its own in-house staff of experts. A venture capitalist group will usually hire an expert consultant. If trained specialists have examined the product and seen fit to back their opinions with investment dollars, you can assume that the product has merit. In many respects, they have done some of your work for you.

## Dealers, Documentation, and Demonstrations

*The Controlling Factor*

Whether you buy a bare-bones program or the most expensively produced software in the store, there is one fact you must be aware of. Though it is something experienced computer owners take for granted, it may not be obvious if you have just bought a machine. The controlling factor in the whole software selection process—the reason why you must be so careful—is that software is *nonreturnable*. The store might not post a sign over the cash register, but every retail outlet operates under the motto: You bought it—you own it.

If a couch does not fit your living room, you may be able to persuade the department store to take it back. But if a program does not fit your needs, you will either have to live with it or write it off as a loss and buy a different product. Nor is there much of a market for "used software" the way there is for "pre-owned" furniture.

As mentioned elsewhere, the reason retailers, vendors, and mail order firms take such a tough attitude on returns is that software, like books, can be copied. The difference is that copying a book may involve an hour or more at a photocopier and cost you a dime or more a page. A program, in contrast, can be copied in about 30 seconds and cost no more than $3.00 for a floppy disk.

---

**SoftTip:** Is it ever legitimate to copy a program? Possibly yes, if the manufacturer has not included an extra or backup copy for you to store in a safe place, or if such copies are not readily and easily available to you even as a registered user. But it is difficult to accept the justifications offered by individuals who copy programs to avoid paying for them in the first place: "Software prices are too high." "Everyone is doing it." "The companies are making plenty of money as it is." In a way, this is little different from breaking into the unoccupied home of the person whose creative effort went into the program and stealing money out of a dresser drawer.

---

*You're Not Buying a Program: You're Buying a Package*

The most important thing to remember when you start getting down to cases about the specific program you want to buy is that you are not buying *just* the program. You are buying a complete package that consists of at least four elements: the documentation, the program, support from your dealer, and support from the vendor (the software house).

For example, whom do you call if you are having difficulty using the program? Who will solve your problems if you find that you have a defective program disk, or if you inadvertently spill coffee on it? What happens if the vendor issues a new and improved version of the product—can you obtain a copy for free or at a reduced price? What good are all of the program's powerful (and expensive) features if you can't figure out how to use them because the documentation is so poor?

Whether you buy from a dealer and pay the full retail price or buy at a discount through the mail, whether the vendor offers hotline support or not, whether the documentation is as clear and free flowing as a mountain stream or so dense you couldn't cut it with a chain saw—you must consider the four elements cited above. You may ultimately choose to buy a program that does *not* satisfactorily meet your criteria in all these areas. But it would be a mistake not to at least consider them.

*Seven Steps along the Software Trail*

If you are an experienced computer user (and when you eventually become one), you may be able to forego dealer support in return for the savings you can realize by ordering from a reputable mail order firm. We are going to assume, however, that you are just getting started and are interested in buying one of the building block programs (communications, word processing, spreadsheet, and database management) mentioned in Chapter 8. If you are buying a computer game, or possibly an educational program, you can probably afford to be much more casual in your approach.

In picking the right program for your needs, you may find it helpful to follow these seven steps:

- Locate and evaluate a knowledgeable dealer or salesperson.
- Thoroughly examine the documentation for the programs you are considering.
- Arrange for a demonstration of the program(s).
- Prepare for the demonstration before you go in.
- Put the program through its paces.
- Evaluate the quality of support you can expect from the dealer.
- Do the same thing for the vendor.

## Step 1: Finding a Knowledgeable Dealer

A knowledgeable computer or software store owner—someone who really knows his or her stuff—is as good as gold, and nearly as rare.

There are many hard-working, competent dealers in the microworld. Indeed, a large percentage went into business precisely because of their competence and because they loved what they were doing. But there are also men and women who have opened computer stores the way others used to open McDonald's franchises, and for the same reason. Fast food has leveled off, but computers and software are hot new growth areas. Some of these individuals will themselves grow in knowledge and competence; others will always remain best qualified for assembling burgers.

---

**SoftTip:** One can open a franchised software-only store for an investment of approximately $150,000 to $170,000, half of which is usually required in cash. Market research studies indicate that in the very near future, software stores will be opening at the rate of 1,000 a year. *Caveat emptor.*

---

This may sound like a harsh assessment. There is, after all, a tremendous amount to learn, and things are constantly changing. But before you let incompetent dealers off the hook completely, keep in mind that they are asking you to pay them anywhere from $200 to $700 for a single program. Of that amount, their gross profit will be between 30% and 50%, with an average in recent years of between 35% and 40%.

In return for that money, you have a right to expect them to know their products and to be able to offer well-informed advice to guide you in your selection. You also have a right, within reason, to expect dealer support and assistance in getting started with the program and helping you over any rough spots you encounter in the initial phases. If a dealer doesn't supply these kinds of services, if the individual is just an order-taker, you might as well give your order to someone over the telephone and save 20% to 30% in the process.

---

**SoftTip:** If you need help in locating a qualified dealer or a consultant to help you, you might contact either of the two following organizations:

Association of Better Computer Dealers
861 Corporate Drive
Lexington, KY 40503
(606) 223-3804

Members are dealers who specialize in service and support. Dealers must meet rigorous standards to be admitted.

*SoftTip continued*
Independent Computer Consultants Association
P.O. Box 27412
St. Louis, MO 63141
(314) 567-9708

Members specialize mainly in advice on acquiring hardware; but they are a likely source of software information as well.

There are at least two other associations of computer dealers:

National Association of Computer Dealers
Box 6877
Towson, MD 21204
(800) 237-8400, ext. 450

National Association of Computer Stores
196 North Street
P.O. Box 1333
Stamford, CT 06004
(203) 323-3143

*The Salesperson as Consultant*
Of course, "dealer" means more than just the store owner. It also means the store's sales, support, and technical staff, as well as its software inventory. Thus, you will want to consider whether the store is likely to have a demonstration copy of the program you want to look at. Do they have a selection of programs in several different price ranges, or do they stock only the "big ticket" ($250+) items? Is their stock primarily games, or do they have programs for every major application?

You may be unpleasantly surprised at how thin the software selection is at even major computer chain stores. As more software-only stores begin to open, the number of locally available programs will grow. But until this happens, you may want to look at the software inventories of several existing stores, beyond just the one nearest your home or office.

Ideally, the store with the most extensive inventory would also have the most knowledgeable and helpful sales staff. But that isn't something you can count on. Probably, given a choice between a well-stocked store and a competently staffed one, you should go with competence. A good salesperson can be like a personal software consultant and advisor and, as such, be worth every dime of commission. A pro like that will take an interest in your business or application and in the details of the problems you want your computer to solve. If you have done no research, then you will be able to get recommendations on one or more products. If you have developed a list of main candidates, such a salesperson will be familiar enough with the application to be able to alert you to points you may not have considered, even if he or she is not familiar with the specific program.

Finding someone like this can take some doing. But it will be worth it in the long run, particularly if you plan to be using your computer for a number of applications and buying more software in the future. Here are some things to ask yourself when evaluating a salesperson:

- Do you hit it off?
- Does the person seem knowledgeable in general? Does he seem to know what he's doing?
- How much does he know about your business or profession and the problems you want to solve? Does she ask about your specific needs? Or is it, "A word processing program? Coming right up. That'll be two hundred dollars, please." Ideally, the individual would interview you the way a doctor or a lawyer does when you have a medical or legal problem.
- Does the individual voluntarily recommend several products in different price ranges? Or does he immediately begin selling the highest priced program in the store, packed with features that you will never use?
- This is a judgment call, but based on your conversations, does the individual have your best interests at heart? Is he or she striving to get you the best possible program for your needs or just to get you to buy a program?

You might also consider asking the salesperson a question about a program to which you already know the answer based on your previous research. Look at the Software Buyer's Quick Reference Checklist at the end of the appropriate "how-to-buy" chapter in this book and choose something that you feel a salesperson ought to know. Be careful, of course, to avoid letting on that you already know the answer. No one likes to feel that they are being tested. But given the ineptitude of some salespeople, and given the fact that you are going to be spending your hard-earned money on a product, you may not have a choice.

A question dealing with the program's capacity is both reasonable and fair. For example: How many pages long can a document be with this word processor? Can I use a nine-digit ZIP code with this mailing list program? How many different kinds of graphs will this business graphic package produce?

If the individual does *not* know the answer, you shouldn't necessarily hand out an "F'" on this test. There is so much to know, so many details to keep track of, that no one can remember everything. The key question is, What does he or she do then?

An individual who shrugs and says, "I don't know how many records you can have in this database system, but you'll have plenty of room," is someone to avoid. Someone who is not motivated to find the correct answer *before* you buy is unlikely to be any more responsive when you call up with an important question that you *don't* know the answer to. Even more dangerous is a salesperson who doesn't know but tries to fake it. A quick, but incorrect, answer followed by a lot of computerese is often an attempt to intimidate you and to forestall further questions. Again, such a salesperson is not likely to be much help after you purchase the product.

---

**SoftTip:** What do you do if you walk into a store with five salespeople, four of whom are busy with customers, and as the fifth comes toward you, you know instinctively that you are not going to hit it off?

Tell the person that you are "just looking," which, in fact, you are. Then make a point of strolling around the store and listening to the conversations of the other salespeople. Lunchtime is a particularly good time to do this, since the store will probably have more customers and you can pass virtually unnoticed.

Should you find someone who sounds knowledgeable and seems personally compatible, politely interrupt the conversation to get a name. You can then come back to the store at a later time and tell anyone who approaches you that you wanted to talk to "Joe," or "Judy," or whomever.

Under no circumstances should you allow yourself to become someone's permanent customer simply because you happened to have walked through the door at a time when that individual was free. The role of the salesperson is too important to leave the choice to chance.

---

### Step 2: Evaluating the Documentation

Once you've decided on a salesperson and dealer, the next step is to review the documentation thoroughly. It might be helpful to see a quick demonstration of the program first, since this will give you something to which you can compare the explanations in the documentation. But any full-scale demonstration will be much more meaningful to you if you have had a chance to look at the documentation first.

Depending on the program and how thorough you want to be, reviewing the documentation can take an hour or more. Usually, it is not something you want to do while standing at a store counter. So ask the dealer if you might borrow a copy of the manual overnight. If the store is nervous about this, tell them to write up a Visa or MasterCard charge slip and hold it as security.

While you can probably count on the dealers' cooperation, you cannot assume that they will have a copy of the program. And, of course, if you are buying through the mail, there will be no dealer to turn to. The answer in both cases may lie in purchasing a copy of the documentation from the software vendor. Many firms will sell you a copy, usually for between $15 and $50, and credit the amount against the price should you later decide to buy the program. You can probably buy a copy through your dealer, through a mail order firm, or by contacting the vendor directly.

*The Truth about Documentation*

Most software documentation is appalling. It would be one thing if this were the software industry's "dirty little secret." But it's not. The poor quality of the documentation available in recent years is more on the order of a proclamation from the rooftops that the industry is not yet ready to serve the general public. Indeed, if there is any single factor that could kill off the computer boom, it is the lack of complete, easily understood instructions for using software.

Ironically, poor manual quality—even virtual impenetrability—has not stopped sales. CP/M-80, WordStar, and dBASE II have been the best-selling programs in their respective fields for years, and as many reviewers have pointed out—and as company officials have acknowledged—the manuals for each program are well below par. That these and other products could succeed in spite of their documentation may be a tribute to the quality of the programming. Or it may be the result of desperation for software on the part of the buyers. Either way, as a software seeker you may have no choice but to put up with the absurdity of paying perhaps $700 for a program and then paying anywhere from $30 for a book to $175 *a day* (!) for a three-day seminar that will teach you how to use it. You could probably earn several college credits for less.

Why is software documentation so bad? According to many experts and individuals who have written documentation, it is bad because it is almost always done as an afterthought, particularly in firms run by programmers (which includes most in the market today). As consultant Jeffrey Hill points out, "Computer programmers live in their own worlds, often far removed from the needs of the typical computer user. Neglecting this critical aspect of software development is common."

There is also the undeniable pressure to get a product on the market and so, hopefully, begin earning a return on all the money that has been invested in the project—whether or not the documentation is up to snuff.

---

**SoftTip:** Software firms like to claim that documentation is constantly improving (as if this were justification for selling expensive, complex products without instructions on how to use them), and although many computer owners don't think those improvements are happening fast enough, there does seem to be hope.

If you have a chance, ask your dealer to show you a copy of the documentation for Lotus Development's Lotus 1-2-3 integrated software package and the manuals for dBASE II or WordStar. Compare them side by side. Even if you are interested in none of these packages, open each manual at random and read a paragraph or two. Be sure to look at the Lotus "Customer Assurance Plan" at the back of the manual and at its equivalent in the other manuals.

One can hope that dBASE and WordStar will have improved their manuals by the time you make this comparison. But more than likely you will agree that the Lotus documentation is superb. You might even want to use it as a standard against which to compare all documentation, regardless of the application the program is intended for. Significantly, the Lotus project was one of the best organized, best financed ever to take place in the microworld.

---

*How to Examine Software Documentation*

If you read between the lines of some software reviews, you will hear the writer saying, "The documentation for this product stinks. But what can you do? If you want software for your computer, and if you want this program in particular, you have no choice but to put up with poor or inadequate instructions."

There is a certain degree of truth to this, alas. Consequently, when someone tells you (as we are about to) what to look for in software documentation, it's important to factor in the reality of the situation. You probably will not find a single program with documentation that meets all of the standards listed below. At the very least, however, these standards will help you identify weaknesses and potential problem points before you buy. If a program's documentation is exceptionally weak, for example, you will want to make sure that dealer and vendor support is exceptionally strong.

The first things to consider are the reasons why it is important to carefully examine a program's documentation, even before you see the software demonstrated at your dealer's. The documentation should be looked at from two perspectives: as a window on the soul of the program and as a discrete component of the complete software package.

Viewing things from the first perspective means treating the documentation as an extensive product brochure that you are examining to get detailed information on the program, its features, its capacity and capabilities, etc. The second perspective means evaluating the documentation in much the same way that you would the program itself, as a tool that you plan to use. How complete is it? How easy is it to locate the instructions you need? Is it written in computer gobbledygook, or can you easily understand what it is saying?

### The Documentation as Product Brochure

In actually going over an instruction manual, you will undoubtedly want to look at it from both perspectives at once. An excellent way to do this is to make gathering information about the program your main goal. As you page through the manual or use the index (if it has one) in quest of the program's particulars, you will automatically gain a sense of how effective it is likely to be as a tool should you purchase the program.

You might want to make a photocopy of the Software Buyer's Quick Reference Checklist at the end of the appropriate "Toolchest" chapter in this book and use it as your guide. Take a moment to look at the manual's table of contents, index, glossary, and general organization. Then see if you can find the answer to a question on the Checklist. You might start with a question that has been answered by your previous research, then try to find out something that you don't already know.

One thing to be particularly cognizant of is the tendency of some manuals to thoroughly explain the most elementary of the program's features, but to do only a cursory job of telling you how to use the more advanced features.

### The Documentation as Useful Tool

The officially approved way to begin mastering a program is to review the manual and then load the program and begin working your way through the various chapters learning commands and their usage along the way. Since some manuals also include "tutorial" sections, you are supposed to work your way through them as well. In practice, almost nobody follows these procedures. For most people, the tendency is to jump in and immediately begin "playing." That's an excellent thing to do, because it gives you something to relate the manual's instructions to later. Just don't mix serious work with playing, since you might end up hitting a wrong key and wiping out everything that you had typed in.

Whether you begin playfully or methodically, however, there will come a time when you must dip into the manual to find out how to do something, such as record your file on disk, or generate a hard copy from the printer. When that time comes, you will be thankful for a manual that makes it easy to locate the information you seek quickly. You will want to be able to use the documentation as a tool to help you accomplish things with the program.

In deciding how effective a tool the manual is likely to be once you buy the program, there are four main characteristics to concentrate on: physical format, content, writing style, and whether or not the manual includes a tutorial. The following checklist presents the main things to look for in each of these areas.

## Documentation Evaluation Checklist

*Layout and Format*

- Typeset or typewritten? Even for best-selling programs, it is not uncommon for a manual to be typewritten and printed on a photo-offset press (possibly to save money). Typographically speaking, this is probably *the* most difficult kind of printing to read.

- Tabbed sections? If manual chapters are separated by die-cut tabs or tabbed inserts, you will be able to locate target chapters much more quickly. If a manual is not tabbed, you can add your own tabs. Go to a stationery store and ask for an AICO Index Tabbing kit. The kit contains blank labels and clear plastic, pressure-sensitive tabs that you can cut to any length. The cost is about 60¢.

- Subheads in bold print? This is another design element that enhances readability and lets you locate information faster.

- Screen images? The better manuals will say, "When you enter this command, your screen should look like this:" and follow up with a reproduction of the screen. This serves as sort of an electronic biofeedback to let you know that you have done things correctly.

• Two-color printing? Black counts as one color. Any color used to high-light passages, subheads, and important commands is a second color. This is one of those nonessential-but-nice features since it enhances readability. It also costs more to produce a two-color manual since the pages must be run through the press a second time.

• Foldouts? Like a *Playboy* centerfold, a foldout will give you the big picture. It may present a drawing of the keyboard with arrows indicating what functions the program assigns to certain keys. It may consist of a flow chart, showing you the steps you must follow to accomplish certain tasks. Or it may show you boxes with the various program modules and how they fit together. It's a nice feature, but usually not essential.

• Three-ring binder or easel? Software documentation has traditionally been issued in three-ring binders. This undoubtedly got started because three-ring binders are traditional in the mainframe and mini-computer worlds as well. And for a very good reason: updates. With a three-ring binder, it is easy to pull out the old and bring in the new whenever additional features and their supporting pages are added to a program. Three-ring binders also lie flat when you have them next to your computer as you are using the program, making it unnecessary to hold them open with an empty coffee cup or ashtray. Some documentation comes in an easel binder, with a foldout back support that allows you to prop the book upright on your worktable, like a medieval alchemist.

## Content

• Understandable "installation" instructions? Often a program will have to be installed for your system. It may be necessary to tell it what kind of monitor you are using and what kind of printer. Usually the program will handle this by presenting you with a menu listing major brands or types in each case. Installation can be as easy as choosing the appropriate menu item and hitting <ENTER>. The disk drives will come on as the program inserts the correct piece of programming from its library into the main program, enabling it to run on your equipment.

  If you are buying through the mail, the clarity of the instructions will be very important since you will be performing the installation yourself. If you are buying from a local store, the dealer should install the program for you. The manual should include a reproduction of any installation menus. Check them carefully to make sure that your equipment is listed. If it isn't, this is one of the first things you will want to ask about before buying the program.

• Table of contents. No question mark, since all but the crudest manuals will at least attempt a table of contents. The "ToC" is really important only if there is no index or if the index is inadequate. The best tables of contents will provide not only the chapter title, but also a fairly complete listing of the topics the chapter contains.

• Overview? Forget about the letter from the firm's president congratulating you on your purchase of his product. Does the manual begin by clearly outlining the capabilities of the program and suggest how you will be able to use them? In other words is there an indication that the writer used any form of organization at all?

In the best manuals, you should be able to see the writer's organization as clearly as a skeleton that glows in the dark. It should virtually jump out at you, showing you where everything fits—even if you don't know what "everything" means at the present time. The inclusion of an overview section that performs this function is a very good sign.

• Does it have a good index? There are indexes and there are indexes, and when you are first getting to know a program you may not be in a position to tell whether the index is complete enough to be useful or whether it is largely symbolic. One fairly good rough-and-ready approach is to look at how many pages it occupies. A two-page index in a 300-page manual, for example, is not likely to be terribly complete or precise.

• Command summary and/or quick reference card? When you are using a program, particularly a powerful and complex program, you will not always be able to remember instantly all of the commands needed to accomplish various tasks. It can be helpful to have a page or two that summarizes the commands you need, or a pull-out reference card to refresh your memory.

• Trouble-shooting guide? What to do when things go wrong . . . go wrzayea . . . gxs@$%6qrng . . . The best trouble-shooting guides say, "If you see *this* on your screen, then here's what probably went wrong, and here's what you should do about it." By making it easy to identify and correct problems, a trouble-shooting guide can save you a great deal of time.

• List of error messages? This is similar to a trouble-shooting guide, though usually it is less elaborate and complete. In some cases it may be next to useless. Some software manuals from one major computer manufacturer, for example, will give you only the error code number (13), the abbreviation (TM), and the error ("Type mismatch") without telling you what you should do to get out of trouble. Other manuals are more helpful.

Since even experienced computerists make errors, you can assume that you will need some quick way to diagnose and correct the problems you run into. If a manual doesn't include an error message list, you may want to create one for your own use.

• A technical section? A section that explains file structures, hexidecimal memory address, and how the software works at the bits and bytes level may not be important to you personally. But it can be helpful to anyone you later ask to make a particular printer, video monitor, or other piece of hardware work with the program. It can also be essential should it be possible to have someone customize or alter the program for your particular needs.

Usually, technical information will be available from the software vendor, but it is obviously more convenient to have it right there in the manual. In addition, the inclusion of technical information, when appropriate, is an indication that the software house is well organized.

• Glossary? Another quick-reference aid. For use mainly when you are reading a chapter of the manual and come across a term that was defined earlier. A glossary saves you flipping back to look for the original definition.

*Writing Style*

• Is the documentation written in a conversational tone? Use the presence or absence of a conversational tone as the master criterion. Open the manual at random and read a few paragraphs. If the paragraphs sound like diplomatic correspondence or a legal contract, or if you run into sentences that begin, "It is assumed that the reader is thoroughly familiar with . . ." you know you're in trouble.

On the other hand, if the text reads as though the writer were talking to you personally ("It may take a little while to get used to dividing your attention like this. Don't worry. The program is infinitely patient."), you are probably in good hands.

*Tutorial Section*

- Is a series of "lessons" presented in the manual? The most beneficial lessons are those that manage to provide explanations of the program's main features and commands while showing you how to accomplish a definite goal. A tutorial on creating a business letter with a word processor, one taking you step by step through the creation of a mailing list in a database management system, and instructions on creating a variety of graphs for a mythical company with a business graphics package are all examples of definite goals.

  Tutorials that merely explain each command in turn are less helpful because they fail to demonstrate how the program's features are related to one another and how they can be used together to accomplish a certain task. Look for the tutorial that flows the way you will be using the program once you master it.

- Are there sample files on disk? Having sample files filled with imaginary data on disk can save you the trouble of going through an elaborate setup procedure and plumbing your brain to come up with data before you can begin learning about and using a program's features. You can't practice sorting or listing a file of addresses, for example, unless such a file exists. A sample address or other file on disk would save you the tedium of creating one before learning those commands.

- Is there an on-disk tutorial? As software manufacturers become more sophisticated, more and more of them will begin taking advantage of the computer itself to teach you how to use their programs. The best-known firm in this area is Select Information Systems of Kentfield, California [(415) 459-4003]. The firm produces the Select word processing system and a user-friendly "front end" program for CP/M users. In both cases, much of the instructive material is on an additional disk supplied with the program.

  On-disk tutorials are "interactive"—the system asks you to type in something and it responds based on what you enter. When you use the Select "Teach" module, for example, you are presented with a menu of 26 of the most frequently used commands, plus an option for starting the course from the beginning. When you choose a command lesson, the screen clears and you are presented with the headings COMMAND:, WHAT IT DOES:, and HERE'S HOW:, followed by appropriate information. There will also be the phrase, "It's your turn for some practice . . . PRESS RETURN."

  When you press <RETURN>, the system gives you step-by-step instructions and asks you to execute them. When you finish, you press the <ESCAPE> key. If you have been successful, you receive a congratulatory message. If not, it's "Have you ever felt like the ship was sailing without you? Please go back and give it one more try."

There is much to recommend the interactive on-disk approach. It won't teach you everything you will eventually need to know about a program. But it can serve as an excellent—even exciting—introduction to using the basics. At the very least, it indicates regard for the end user. An effective on-disk tutorial can also be important if you are buying a program that will be used by clerical staff and temporary workers since it can eliminate the need for lengthy instructions and constant supervision while the individual is learning to use the program.

- Is the tutorial section separate from the rest of the manual? You might not think this would matter. And one should probably be grateful for any tutorial material, regardless of whether it is accompanied by a separate section describing commands and features individually. Nevertheless, when properly done, tutorials and command descriptions are two types of writing with two different goals. A tutorial is designed to teach and command descriptions are designed both to inform and to serve as a ready reference. If most of the information explaining a command is buried somewhere in a tutorial, you may have difficulty finding it.

*Clearly Defined Customer Support Statements*

At the end of a manual, you may find information relating to the software supplier's stated obligations to you as the purchaser and its policy regarding customer service. We'll use the Lotus 1-2-3 manual as an example. This manual includes the following items:

- Statement of customer support policy. The manual affirms "continuing support in the form of telephone advice and other assistance" and suggests that you first check your manual if you are having problems and then call your dealer. If you need more help, a telephone hotline number is provided.

- A customer registration card. Unlike the registration cards that come with refrigerators and other major home appliances, software registration is not chiefly a device to get your name on a list so the firm can later sell you a maintenance contract or sell your address to a mailing list company.

With a major software product, registration can be vital for it is the only way you can be assured of learning about program updates and the only way you can easily get a replacement copy of your disk should something evil happen to it.

- A product upgrade plan. This section explains that upgrades incorporating new features will be regularly introduced and assures you that you will be notified by mail and be given the option of purchasing the upgrade at a "special price."

- A product replacement plan. Here you will find a clearly stated policy on replacing defective or user-damaged program disks. If you are a registered user, you can return the original disk and obtain a new copy for $15.

- Replacement order card. This is the card you fill out and mail in to obtain a replacement disk.

- Limited warranty. The firm states that it will replace any registered user's program disk free of charge during the first 90 days.

As mentioned earlier, you will probably not find all of these various qualities in any single piece of documentation. But hopefully, comparing a program's manual to the ideal described above will alert you to potential weak spots. It is also important to point out that there *are* sheep in wolves' clothing. The fact that a manual looks sleek on the outside is a strong indication that it will be a useful tool. But it is not a guarantee. The DOS and BASIC manuals issued by IBM for the Personal Computer, for example, set a new standard for documentation format and packaging. They were beautiful. And close to useless. If you weren't already familiar with the function of an operating system and the BASIC language, you would have a challenging time figuring out how to use this software.

---

**SoftTip:** Because of the inadequate documentation supplied by many software vendors, it is a good idea to see if there are any books on how to use the product before making your final decision. For example, various publishing houses have books that will help you use WordStar or dBASE II or some other program. In addition, you might check to see if there are any newsletters or other software-house-sponsored publications. Stoneware, Inc., creator of the database program DB Master, for example, publishes "Stoneware Age" (first year free to registered owners, $6 annually thereafter) for users of its product. Ashton-Tate, creator of dBASE II, has a similar publication. Software Arts, creator of VisiCalc, offers

SATN ("Software Arts Technical Notes") for users of VisiCalc and the firm's TK! Solver program. (See the spreadsheet and database chapters for subscription information.)

The existence of program-specific books, newsletters, and other resources can be as important as the documentation itself, for in some cases you may really be unable to use a program if forced to rely upon the documentation alone.

## Step 3: Arranging for a Demonstration

You may be able to simply walk into a store and say, "I'd like to see a demonstration of SuperCalc, please." In fact, if the store is not busy and they have the program, you can almost always do this. However, whether you are buying as a business person or as a private individual, you may want to make an appointment. Obviously, it is best to have established a relationship with a salesperson first, but usually anyone at the store will be happy to serve you.

Making an appointment for a software demonstration is not at all unusual and it can be especially important if the store is located in a city and gets a large amount of traffic. The time you allot will depend upon the complexity of the program and what you plan to do with it, but more than likely you should plan on spending about an hour.

**SoftTip:** When making your appointment, try to ascertain whether you will be able to see the program demonstrated on a computer system that *exactly* matches your own: the same model, type of disk drives, printer, monitor, etc. One of the things you hope to learn in a demonstration is what it will be like to use the program on a day-to-day basis. For example, if you see it demonstrated using a hard disk system, and you don't have a hard disk, you could easily get the wrong impression about how fast the program will run on your own system.

**SoftTip:** Although it will not be possible with every program and may not be possible at all where you live, there could be a way for you to demo a program on your own equipment. A firm called Soft-Link has a unique system that could represent the wave of the future in software retailing. The company sells the local dealer "locked" or "crippled" copies of major programs, which the dealer then sells to you for about $50. You take it with you and load it into your own system.

*SoftTip continued*

Since the package has been crippled, it may not let you print anything or it may only allow the creation of one or two files. But you will be able to test and experiment with all of the features and develop an excellent feeling for the way the program works. If you don't want to buy, you can return the disk for full credit. If you do, the dealer telephones Soft-Link and receives the code number or software "key" needed to unlock that particular copy of the program. Soft-Link debits the dealer's account and the dealer charges you the purchase price of the software.

Recently available Soft-Link programs have included SuperCalc (I and II), SpellGuard, MicroPlan, Condor III, T.I.M. III, Spell-Binder, Profit Plan, and other programs from major software suppliers. For information on your nearest dealer offering Soft-Link programs, contact:

Soft-Link
3255 Scott Blvd., Bldg. 2
Santa Clara, CA 95051
(408) 988-8011

*Note:* The Soft-Link also plans to offer locked programs on hard disk systems available from your local computer dealer. You would be able to try the program, and if you liked it, contact the dealer to have it unlocked.

---

**SoftTip:** There's another technique that is becoming increasingly popular among software companies. A number of them will now make available a two-disk package. One disk is designed to allow you to demonstrate the program on your own. You will be able to use it just as you would the actual program—except that you will probably not be able to generate a printout and may find that the information you can store is extremely limited.

The disk containing the complete program will be supplied in a sealed envelope. If you like what you see on the demonstration disk, you can break the seal and use the program. But if you decide that you do not want to keep it, you will be able to return the whole package for full credit—as long as the seal on the envelope has not been broken. (Most envelopes of this sort are sealed with a warning sticker.) This is a very sensible approach and one can hope that more companies will use it in the future.

## Step 4: Preparing for a Demonstration

You may not want to be this thorough, but you will definitely get more out of a demonstration if you do a little preparation beforehand. If you have had a chance to look over the documentation, for example, you will already have a general idea of what the program is all about and how it works. There may be some features that you want to be sure to try. Or there may be something that you don't quite understand and want to check on. If you have read the reviews, you will probably also be aware of one or two things that the program does not do well.

Make a list of these "Be-sure-to-check" items and take it with you to the store. Generally, if you can take an active role in a demonstration you will get to know a program faster and better than if you are passive and let someone else push the buttons or decide what you will be shown next.

Many experts also recommend bringing actual work materials with you to use as you test a program. If a word processor will be used to type short letters and memos, bring a few real ones along and see how easily you can enter and print them. If you are buying an electronic spreadsheet, pull together or invent some figures you can use on one of the reports you will want the program to generate. Since you won't be able to take the program back to work with you, bringing your work to it is the next best thing. You can be assured that the sample files supplied by the manufacturer to help sales personnel demonstrate a program will work like a dream. The real test is to see how the program handles the kind of thing you will be throwing at it every day.

---

**SoftTip:** It can be important to have something to *do* when demonstrating a program. If you are unable to bring work with you or if, as with a communications program, the software is not intended for data entry, ask the salesperson if there is a manufacturer-supplied "demo disk" of some sort. You may also want to consider planning to work through one or more of any tutorial lessons in the manual. A demonstration in which you attempt to accomplish something will be much more revealing than one in which the salesperson says, "Well, there's this feature and here's how it works . . . then there's this other feature, and . . ."

---

## Step 5: Putting a Program through Its Paces

A demonstration takes a salesperson's time and it takes advantage of the hardware and software resources and other overhead items paid for by the store. It is an act of bad faith for anyone to arrange a demonstration at a retail store while planning to buy through the mail all along. By the same token, you should not feel that a demonstration of a product in any way obligates you to purchase it, any more than a test drive of a new car obligates you to buy it. In fact, if a program does not meet your needs or satisfy your requirements, most salespeople would rather not sell it to you, for they know that you will be phoning them frequently for support.

A software demonstration can be like buying a new car in other ways as well. The salesperson will show you the basics, give you some sales talk, and then, ideally, leave you alone. The salesperson should remain within questioning distance in case you have a problem. But you are not likely to feel comfortable or have a chance to get to know the product if the individual insists on hovering over you. If that happens, politely suggest that there are some things you'd like to try, and would the person mind if you "soloed" for a bit.

## Program Demonstration Checklist

*Verify the Hardware*

- Is the demonstration computer configured identically to your own? The best possible way to demonstrate a program would be to take it back to your home or office and see how it runs on your own equipment. But since this will not normally be possible, the next best alternative is to make sure that the computer used in the demonstration exactly matches your own. The type of video monitor, printer, and model of computer will all be obvious. The things to watch out for are the boards and other equipment that may be tucked away inside the machine.

  For example, there is usually no way to tell from the outside whether the machine has single- or double-sided disk drives. You will be able to see from the screen whether an Apple computer has a card that allows it to display 80 columns instead of 40. But you won't be able to tell from the outside whether it or any other brand is equipped with a Z80 card to allow it to run CP/M-80 programs. You might also be unaware of the need for a special card to display the graphics the program generates. Since the salesperson may assume that you are aware of these points, he or she may forget to mention them. So be sure to ask.

  Unless you own or plan to buy a hard disk or an add-on memory board to be used as a RAM-based disk drive, you should try to avoid using this equipment in a demonstration. They can make a program run so much faster that, if you aren't aware that they are being used, you may be in for a disappointment when you run it on your own floppy-based system. Because it consists of a plug-in circuit board, a RAM-based disk drive will not be visible from the outside. A hard disk drive, however, should be fairly obvious. (See Chapter 5.)

• Do you have to buy more than meets the eye? A distinction should probably be made between hardware that is nice to have and hardware that is essential to using the program. If you have done your research, you should be aware of any CP/M, graphics boards, communications cards, and modems the program may require. You will probably also be aware of whether or not you will need a secondary operating system, a language package, or any other additional software. But it never hurts to ask. The software reviewers may have left something out, or the product suppliers may have neglected to include a point or two in their literature.

Whether additional hardware and software is a matter of speed and convenience or a requirement for using the program, what you want to avoid is the unpleasant, budget-smashing experience of deciding to buy a program and only then discovering that you must spend additional money to make it work or make it run the way you want it to.

---

**SoftTip:** Salespeople like to demonstrate programs using either a RAM drive or a hard disk because this equipment shows a product off to best advantage. There is no reason, however, why a demonstration must be conducted this way. If the salesperson tells you that the program is already on hard disk, and you have a floppy-based system, ask the individual either to locate the original floppy disk or copy the program from the hard disk onto a new floppy. It may represent a slight inconvenience for the salesperson, but there is no technical reason why this cannot be done.

---

*The "Going Bare" Test*

• Can you begin using the program without reading the instructions? It isn't reasonable to expect to be able to use all the features of a powerful program without reading the instructions. However, the ease with which you can immediately begin working with the program and the number of things you can accomplish without referring to the manual are an excellent measure of the product's user friendliness. It is thus a good idea to give all programs the "going bare" test. Simply load the program and see if you can use it—or how much of it you can use—without referring to the manual.

If you have already reviewed the manual, this can be an even more accurate test. More than likely, when you bring a program home you will boot it immediately, play with it for a while, review the documentation, and return to the program in earnest to really learn how to use it. It is in the "learning in earnest" stage that you will begin to discover hidden flaws and problems. By reviewing the manual before the demonstration, you will already have progressed to that point and be in a good position to put a program through its paces for real.

• Is the program menu-driven and, if so, how extensively? The key point that makes it possible to use a program without referring to the manual is whether or not it is menu-driven. Using a program that is *not* menu-driven is very much like using DOS. The program boots up and puts a title line on your screen, asks you for the date, and then presents you with a simple dot or a question mark or some other program prompt. At that point, you are on your own. The program is waiting for you to enter a command to tell it what to do and, obviously, you must be familiar with the commands to use it. This type of program is thus said to be "command-driven."

As explained in Chapter 4, a menu-driven program will present you with a list of initial or Main Menu options. In a word processing program, for example, there may be an option to start a brand new document, to edit an existing document, to print a document, etc. Entering a choice from the Main Menu will take you to the portion of the program that will let you accomplish the desired task. The key question is, What happens then?

Any program offering a Main Menu can technically call itself "menu-driven." But, with some, the Main Menu is the only menu. Once you enter your initial selection, you are once again on your own. More extensively menu-driven programs will display a series of subsidiary menus once you have made your initial selection. Some programs may be so "fully menu-driven" that you may never have to type much more than menu selections and filenames.

---

**SoftTip:** A fully menu-driven program will be the easiest to learn and use initially. But you may pay for this advantage later. After you have learned the program, menus will no longer be so necessary. At that point, they can actually impede your use of the program, for you will have to work your way through them even if you already know the correct command. The idea program is one that offers you the option of using either a menu or a command approach.

• Are "Help" screens available? "Help" screens are a lot like menus. In fact, they are often called "Help Menus." The difference is that menus are normally used to guide you to a certain section of the program, and help screens serve as an onscreen reminder of the commands available for your use once you get there. You may use a menu, for example, to get into the section of a program that will enable you to type a letter. And once there, you may find a list of the commands to use for setting your tabs, line spacing, page length, etc.

Micropro, Inc., the creator of the "Star" line of software products (WordStar, CalcStar, SpellStar, DataStar, etc.) has developed help screens to a fine art. Whenever you use one of these programs, you have the option of always having a help menu displayed at the top of the screen. Some of the commands on the menu are designed to have an immediate effect on what you are writing. Others call up additional help menus with more commands. There is another nice feature as well. The software gives you the option of three different levels of help menus: extensive, abbreviated, and none. You can set the program to default automatically to any of these levels when it loads in. This can be important once you have learned the program's major commands, for by eliminating or shortening the help menus, you will be able to view more text or data on your screen at any given time.

## Cosmetics and Ease of Use

• Are the program prompts easy to understand and follow? The clarity and readability of the prompts and error messages a program displays at various points are indicative of two qualities. First, it is obviously going to be much easier to use a program that says, "The disk is too full. Please insert a blank, formatted disk," than a program that says, "Error condition 07."

Second, the nature of the prompts can be an indication of the care with which the program was written and tested. You should know that the prompts a program displays are pure cosmetics. The programmer simply includes a line of code that tells the machine to "Display this prompt:" and types in whatever he or she wants the prompt to be. The cosmetics of a program are usually one of the last things to be "cleaned up" before the product is shipped. And the fact that someone has done so is a good sign because it means that, more than likely, other details that you may not encounter in a demonstration have been reviewed and taken care of as well. You might think of it as an indication of the firm's quality control.

• Do the prompts always appear in the same place on the screen? It is nice to be able to count on finding prompts and instructions at the same spot on the screen all the time. If a lot of data are displayed on the screen, you don't want to have to search saying, "Let's see where did the programmer put the prompt this time?"

• Do the commands seem logical and easy to remember? A programmer can usually set things up so that any given key can be used to call a particular function. A program will be much easier to learn and master if logical key assignments are used: *H* for "Help," *P* for "Print," *Q* for "Quit," etc.

• Does the program take advantage of your computer's function keys? The IBM/PC was one of the first computers to be designed with ten auxiliary "F-keys" or "function keys." They are arranged in two columns to the left of the main keyboard. Unfortunately, many programs originally brought over to the IBM, and other F-key-equipped computers, came from computers that did not have this feature. Other software was issued as well that failed to support the function keys, and some of it is still on the market.

If the program supports them, function keys can be convenient because you will be able to hit a single key instead of several keys to issue a command. For example, to set the right margin in WordStar, you must normally hold down the <CONTROL> key on the IBM/PC and then hit the <O> and the <R> keys. But if the IBM's function keys are supported, you may be able to simply hit the <F4> key. With the Select word processing program, you can load entire paragraphs into function keys to be recalled and inserted into a document whenever you press one of them. Non-word-processing programs that support function keys will usually allow you to load them with frequently used strings of commands. This is sometimes called a "macro" feature because a single keystroke generates such a relatively large number of characters.

---

**SoftTip:** If you own a program that does not support your computer's function keys, or if you are considering buying one, ask your dealer or the members of a local users' group whether or not the program can be "patched" to support this feature.

---

• Does the computer display something on the screen at all times? Even to experienced users, a computer screen that goes blank or does not change while the computer is loading a program, signing onto an electronic database over the phone, or simply performing calculations, can be disconcerting. Since you may not know how long a process should take, you might wonder whether something has gone wrong. Should you reboot and start over, or give it another minute or two?

To save you from such dilemmas, a program should be "human engineered" to give you constant feedback on what the machine is doing: "Now loading communications module . . . Now logging onto Dow Jones News/Retrieval Service . . ." or "Sorting file MAIL.LST . . ." or "Formatting text for printing . . ." etc. These messages let you know that everything is all right. If they don't appear, you can assume that something has gone wrong.

## How to "Break" a Program

What can you do to a program to throw it for a loop? How does it respond when you deliberately make a mistake or do something that you are not supposed to do? Does it take things in stride and respond with an error message and suggested correction, or does it suddenly stop working and just "hang" there or "lock up" on you?

In this part of the demonstration, your role is that of an inspector from Scotland Yard assigned the task of investigating a murder committed at the home of an old family friend. You hope you don't find anything to indict the program. But you've got to investigate with your customary thoroughness nonetheless. It's a nasty business, but someone's got to do it.

In the course of your investigation, you are actually matching wits with the programmer. Did he or she think to disable all but certain keys when a menu is presented? Let's find out by hitting a key not offered as a menu selection. Does the computer issue a warning "beep"? Does the program lock up, or go spinning off into some unintended direction?

Here are the errors you should deliberately make to try to break a program:

- Hit a wrong key when offered an onscreen menu.
- Place your whole hand on the keyboard to hit several keys at once at various opportune moments. Try to pick a time when the program is doing something important, like calculating or accessing a disk drive. These can be its most vulnerable points.
- Narrow your focus and hit just the <BREAK> [<SHIFT> <BREAK>, on some machines] key at various unexpected times. Do the same thing with the <ESCAPE> key.
- The explanation of this one is slightly technical, but once a computer has "opened" a disk file, it usually must "close" it properly in order for you to be able to use it again. When you "quit" or "exit" a program, it should automatically close all files. The process involves placing some signals on the disk.

So what happens if you hit the <RESET> key, or its equivalent on your machine, without formally "quitting" the program? If the programmer was on the ball, he or she will have included instructions to tell the software to automatically close all files.

Test it by creating a short file and recording it on disk. Bring it in again and begin using it. Then hit <RESET> to cause the program to stop and reboot. Then see if you can bring the file in again or whether you get an error message.

- Try entering letters when the program calls for numbers and vice versa.
- What happens if you type in a filename that is longer than the program will permit?
- Ask it to load in a disk file that you know does not exist.
- Deliberately leave the data disk out of its drive and ask the program to load a data file. Does the program notify you of your error, or does it simply stop working?
- Will the program run if the printer is not connected and turned on? Amazingly, some of them won't. Test it both ways. If the program requires the printer to be online, what will you do when your printer is in the shop for repairs?
- Does the program choke if you type your commands rapidly? If it does, the programmer has neglected to set aside a portion of memory as a "keyboard buffer" to store keystrokes until the program can act on them. (This could be caused by a lack of sufficient memory in the computer itself.)

A well-written program will be very difficult to break. Certainly, you won't be able to confuse it by hitting wrong keys, entering incorrect letters or numbers, leaving the data disk out of the drive or committing any of the other errors a person might normally be expected to make. The programmer will have anticipated all of these eventualities and written "error trapping" routines to catch and handle them, usually by informing you of the problem and suggesting a solution.

---

**SoftTip:** As pointed out on appropriate Software Buyer's Checklists, one of the most dreaded of all error messages is one that informs you that your "Data disk is full." If this occurs in a word processing program, you may discover that the program will be unable to record any text currently in memory—even if you insert a new, blank disk. Since this is difficult to test in a demonstration, be sure to check the documentation and ask the salesperson how the program handles this problem.

*Program-Specific Tests*

The Software Buyer's Quick Reference Checklists at the end of the various "how-to-buy" chapters will give you ideas on how to test particular applications programs, what to watch out for, where their weaknesses may lie, etc. As mentioned, you may want to make a photocopy of it and take it with you to the demonstration. In the course of reading the reviews of a particular product, you may also have developed a list of points you want to be sure you investigate. If it is not possible to test a feature in the course of a demonstration, at least ask about it before you leave.

You may also want to pay special attention to how fast a particular program runs. If you are new to computing, you will need some basis of comparison. If possible, ask your salesperson for the name of the fastest running progam in the same applications area as the one you are considering and see if you can get a brief demonstration. Then compare the program you are considering. Speed may not seem important to you right now, but the more you use a program, the more you will appreciate it.

Also, make sure that you have a chance to print something on the printer. Because your main attention is focused on the program itself, you may be inclined to take the printing function for granted. You may assume that because a printer can generate a variety of typestyles and other special effects, the program will naturally let you use these features. Many programs will not. You may also assume that getting the program to print will be a fairly straightforward procedure. But again, this is often not the case. Since printed "reports" (loosely speaking, any program output, be it a mailing list, a general ledger, or an invoice) are usually the goal of your endeavors at the keyboard, it is worth paying extra attention to how the program handles and produces them.

*Data Transferability*

You will find more information in the applications program chapters, but the ability of one program to use files created by another program can be so important that it is worth emphasizing here. For example, suppose you are in business and you have got to put a large mailing list into a database management program so that it can be sorted and otherwise manipulated in some way. Your problem is that while you have five computers, each with a word processing program, and five clerical assistants, you only have one database management program. And you don't have very much time.

Conceivably, the only way to accomplish the job would be to have one assistant type in all of the names using the DBMS program. However, if the DBMS can use files created by the word processing programs running on the other four computers, then all five assistants can help with the job. When all names have been typed in, you would combine everything into one master file and the database program would never know the difference.

This is a simple example. At other times, you might want to be able to enter data in a DBMS and transfer selected items or numbers to an electronic spreadsheet. When you were finished with the spreadsheet, you might want to transfer the results to a business graphics program to look at the information visually. Then you might want to incorporate both the graphs and the spreadsheet in a report created by your word processing program, print it out, and possibly even transmit a copy over the telephone to a distant colleague with your communications program—all without ever retyping any of the data you originally entered in your database management program.

If these are the kinds of applications you are interested in, it is obviously crucial for all programs to be able to use the same data files.

*The Latest Version?*

As you know, the better software companies are constantly updating and upgrading their products. Sometimes a new version will merely contain "fixes" that correct previously unidentified bugs. Sometimes it will include additional features. The version number of a given copy of a program should be easy to find. It will either be on the disk label or it will appear on the screen when you use the program.

The problem is to discover the number of the latest version ("V. 1.1"? "V. 3.2"? etc.). The reviews you read may be able to help you. But there is a problem here as well. The September issue of a magazine may "close" in May or June, and after that date it may be impossible for reviewers to change their copy. If a new version of a program is issued in the meantime, there may be no way to inform the reader. It is also possible that a dealer might not be aware of the latest version or may even deliberately try to sell an outdated copy.

The surest way to discover the latest version number is to call or write the software firm itself. Some will have toll-free hotlines listed in the documentation for their products.

---

**SoftTip:** If you later learn that the copy you bought was not the latest version, you should be able to get an updated copy from the software vendor. Unfortunately, it probably will not be free, though you might try your powers of persuasion and explain your situation. You will almost certainly have to return your original program disk for updating, and that can be inconvenient, to say the least.

The important thing is to make sure that you send in your registration card as soon as you buy the program. As explained earlier, registering your software is vital. It is not the same as a small-appliance registration card that you probably throw away.

## Step 6: Evaluating Dealer Support

Dealer support is part of what you are paying for when you buy a program at the full retail price. Unfortunately, the nature and extent of the support you can expect from a dealer is rarely spelled out. For this reason, it can be important to establish a clear understanding of exactly what the dealer will do for you before you buy.

If you pay the full list price for a program, here is what you have a right to expect:

- The dealer should be willing to "install" the program for you.

If the program has an installation module, getting it set up for your brand of printer and video monitor is usually a quick process. As mentioned before, it may be a simple matter of choosing items from a menu. Having the dealer do it saves you the time and trouble of reading the instructions and lets you begin using the program immediately.

Dealer installation can be especially important, however, when your brand of printer or video display is *not* among those on the installation module menu. The dealer will know which of the menu choices is equivalent to your equipment and—equally important—what to do if none of the choices will work. At the very least, this will save you phoning the dealer should you encounter the problem when trying to install the program yourself.

- There should be at least a superficial amount of instruction on how to use the program.

Much of this may have been covered in the demonstration. The amount of help you need here will depend on your past experience. Some dealers report that their customers learn to use programs faster when given just the basics and allowed to explore on their own, as opposed to sitting through a long and detailed explanation. This may work quite well for you. Or it may not. Either way, be sure to get the amount of information you feel you need.

• The dealer should also be available to answer your questions after you begin using the program.

This is the single most important element of dealer support, for you *will* have questions. A dealer may be only a local phone call away. He or she may be familiar with both the program and your equipment. And if you are having really serious problems you can go in for a personal chat.

Software is unique in that there is probably no other product in which the retailer is expected to be so heavily involved after the sale. In a typical store, the sales staff may spend as much as two to three hours a day responding to customer questions.

Now for the ticklish question: How much "hand-holding" (support) can you reasonably expect? There is no answer. Indeed, this is one of the reasons why some dealers avoid spelling out support commitments. The dealer is in something of a bind. On the one hand, he wants to keep you as a satisfied customer and hopes that you will continue to buy from him. But, on the other hand, he knows that he could easily end up spending all day on the phone answering questions.

To protect themselves, many dealers will leave the amount of time they will spend answering your questions undefined. This way they can decide on a case-by-case basis where to draw the line. This is certainly more sensible than saying, "You can ask ten questions." Or, "You are entitled to half an hour of support." From a customer's standpoint, a loosely or undefined amount of support can be advantageous. It may not commit the dealer, but it doesn't limit you either.

As a rule of thumb, it is reasonable for you to expect the dealer to answer your questions on the program's features and how they operate, and to help you get out of trouble if you've made a mistake and can't figure out how to solve it. At some point between 30 and 90 days after you purchase the program, the dealer has a right to expect you to have learned enough to be self-sufficient.

Where things become hazy is when you are seeking advice on how to use the program for a particular application. For example, you can expect a dealer to explain how to operate an electronic spreadsheet, but you cannot expect him to design a form that will let you keep track of your home budget with the program. Technically, this request falls under the heading of "consulting," not "support."

As with any other type of consulting, it is quite legitimate for a dealer to charge for his time and expertise. Some highly skilled dealers, for example, offer consulting services to businesses at a rate of anywhere from $40 to $100 an hour. That's not to say that you won't be able to persuade the dealer to give you this kind of help. But it is not something a software buyer has a right to insist on receiving for free.

**SoftTip:** Before phoning a dealer or a salesperson, do them the courtesy of at least trying to find the answer in your manual first. You may not be successful. And certainly, given the impenetrable quality of many manuals, you should not spend an inordinate amount of time. But if you have made a legitimate attempt to find the answer on your own, you will find that your conversation with the dealer will probably be more productive.

- You should also be able to return a program that does not work.

Clearly, if a program disk is defective, you have a right to return it for a new copy. You can usually do this through the dealer or by contacting the vendor directly as mentioned earlier. After determining that the disk is indeed defective, many dealers will be willing to give you a new copy and handle the return themselves. Others may only be willing to send the disk "back to the factory" for you and notify you when the replacement arrives.

The more frequently encountered situation is that of a customer buying a program and discovering that it will not run on his or her own machine. Unless the dealer has guaranteed that the software will run on your equipment, technically you may be stuck. The dealer may be under no legal obligation to accept your program as a return. In actuality, many dealers will try hard to diagnose and correct the problem, even going so far as having you bring your computer and printer into the store.

The dealer may assign one of the technical people in the service department to take a look at it. And someone may phone the software company. Unless you have mistakenly picked up a program intended for the TRS-80 and tried to run it on your Commodore 64, there will usually be a way to solve the problem.

The one thing you can't do is return a program because you have decided that you don't like it or because you have belatedly discovered that it will not do everything that you want. The dealer may make an exception if you are a particularly good customer. But it is not something you can count on.

## Step 7: Evaluating Vendor Support

Because of the huge number of customers and software houses and the small number of dealers, and because many dealers are not qualified to support fully every program they sell, it is important to investigate the kind and quality of support you can expect from the vendor. Since some software firms are quite small, not all of them offer every feature listed below. In some cases, smallness can be a customer advantage, for when you dial the hotline number you may end up speaking to the person who actually wrote the program you have bought.

Here is what to look for when gauging vendor support:

• A customer registration card or form in the documentation. This is a good sign because it indicates that the firm probably has at least some kind of organized customer support program. Again, registering your copy of the program is the only way a firm will be able to notify you when updates are issued.

• A clearly stated policy for replacing damaged disks. A software house is under no obligation to replace a damaged disk unless it agrees to do so in writing. Usually, you will have to return your original disk and you may have to pay a small ($20) fee. Or replacements may be issued free of charge.

• A policy regarding program updates and registered users. Technically, a firm is not obligated to offer you an update of the program at a reduced price. But it is obviously good business to do so. A good example is VisiCorp. When the firm announced its more powerful Advanced Version of VisiCalc at $400, it offered registered users of the original version ($250) the chance to buy it at half price.

• A customer support hotline. Regardless of size, any software firm that wants to have respectable sales must of necessity offer telephone support to its customers. The number may be toll free, or you may have to pay for the call. A hotline is so important and such an accepted part of the software business that you should be extremely skeptical of any firm that does not publish either its phone number or its hotline number.

If you buy a program from such a firm, you'll have the devil's own time getting answers out of a post office box.

• A warranty. (See below).

*A Word about Warranties*

Warranties can be a hazardous area for software firms, and many do not offer them at all. What they are afraid of is that someone will use their product and for one reason or another find that it does not work or works ineffectively for their application. You can hardly sue a software firm for "strain and mental suffering," though if you could, a lot of firms would constantly be in court because of their poor manuals.

On the other hand, someone who claims that the program wiped out his mailing list or that the software incorrectly calculated his firm's taxes, leaving him open to IRS penalties, might bring suit against the company for "programming malpractice," or some such misdeed. Consequently, firms that include warranties generally cover themselves seven ways from sundown.

Lotus Development Corporation, for example, warrants that the disk material and user's manual for Lotus 1-2-3 are not defective; that the program has been properly recorded on disk; that the user's manual is "substantially complete" and contains all information the firm feels is needed to use the product; and that the program functions "substantially as described" in the user's manual. The warranty statement goes on specifically to exclude any guarantee of the product's fitness for a particular purpose and limits the purchaser's "remedy to return of the software and User's Manual to the dealer or to Lotus for replacement."

By explicitly limiting liability, warranties have more to do with protecting the software firm than the customer. Aside from the guarantees cited, warranties are largely symbolic as far as a software buyer is concerned. Given the complexity of many programs and the wide variety of uses to which they will be put by tens of thousands of users, it is difficult to see how they could be otherwise.

*Conclusion*

We'll do our own version of a warranty right here and clearly state that the author and publisher cannot guarantee that anyone who follows the seven steps set forth in this chapter will automatically meet with success. But we will guarantee that you will have a much better chance of choosing the program that is right for you and your needs. In the next chapter, we'll consider the main ways to actually buy a program once you've made your choice.

# ...10...

## Where to Buy Software: *From Your Local Dealer or through the Mail?*

The most perplexing question software buyers must face after they have chosen the program they want is whether to purchase it from a local dealer at the full retail price or buy it at a discount through the mail. There is no single "right" answer to this question. Whatever you decide, it is obviously crucial to know what you can save, and what you will have to give up in return for those savings. That's what we'll look at now.

The main advantage of buying from your local dealer is the opportunity he or she offers for you to see the program demonstrated before you buy it and to get support after the sale. The main disadvantage is that none of these things is free. Although you may be able to negotiate a discount if you are buying several copies of the same program for your company, most of the time you will have to pay the full list price. The current prices may be different, but for purposes of comparison, that might mean buying VisiCalc for $250, WordStar for $500, and dBASE II for $700.

These same programs may be available through the mail for $170, $325, and $430, respectively, for savings ranging from $80 to $270. Similar savings are available for hundreds of other programs as well. In light of this, the question you've got to ask yourself is, How much support do I need and what is it worth to me?

As we said in the previous chapter, it is important to make sure that both you and the dealer have an understanding of exactly what "support" will consist of before you buy. But generally, in return for mail-order savings, you would probably have to rely exclusively on the reviews of the program when making your selection. You would have to take full responsibility for ensuring that the software will run on your equipment. And since a dealer will not be eager to help you if you have purchased the program through the mail, you will probably have to solve any hardware incompatibility problems yourself. The software company may have a customer-support hotline, but it probably will not be as convenient as calling your local dealer. Basically, if you buy through the mail, you're on your own.

This is not necessarily a major drawback, for as one mail order company's headline puts it: "If you know what you want . . . Why pay more?" If you know enough about a program and its capabilities from your research, and if you are confident of your ability to use it effectively on your own, it may make little sense to pay for the support and other services built into a local dealer's full retail price. Ultimately, only you can decide, and even among experienced computerists, the answer may vary with the specific program. Here are some points to consider when making your decision:

• What is the actual dollar amount you can save? Mail order firms report that a discount of anything less than 15% fails to attract many buyers. Typical discounts range from about 25% to 40% off the list price.

• Is that amount worth three to five or more hours of your time? Even if you are an experienced computerist, you will be able to learn to use a program faster when you have a knowledgeable dealer or salesperson to explain it to you or answer your questions. In some cases, this can save you literally hours of work trying to learn the program with only the manual to help you.

• How complex is the program? How powerful? Clearly, the more complicated the program, the more help you are likely to need in mastering it. Full-scale database management systems, some electronic spreadsheets and word processing programs, and some integrated packages can be quite complex. Less powerful and less expensive versions, as well as game and educational software, will be much easier to use.

When a dealer is particularly knowledgeable about a complex program, even an experienced user might happily pay the full retail price to be able to take advantage of the person's advice.

In many cases, there is something of an unpublished, almost underground, body of knowledge about how to use some programs. To an experienced computerist, few things are more gratifying than to hear a dealer/expert say, "Oh, yes. That's not in the manual, but here's what you should do."

• What do the reviews say about how easy the program is to use? The best software reviewers will be sure to tell you how easy a program is to master, how good or bad the documentation is, whether the package includes a tutorial, etc.

• Does the software firm have a customer-support hotline? Since this is likely to be your sole means of support if you buy through the mail, it is obviously an important thing to consider. If a hotline is not mentioned in a review or an ad, you might consider contacting the firm itself to ask. Buying any program without an easy means of contacting the vendor or a dealer for help is always risky.

• How much experience have you had with software? General software knowledge is both cumulative and highly transferable. Consequently, the more programs you have purchased and used on your computer, the more likely it is that you will be able to master a new program on your own, even if it is for an application that is new to you.

  In answering this question, it would be a good idea to first see if there are any books or other publications designed to teach you how to use the program. For example, books exist for a number of popular spreadsheet programs, database management programs, word processing, and others.

  Computer magazines may also carry articles that can be of help, so you might want to check your back issues. It is quite possible that with these resources, your own experience, and a software house hotline, you will not need any additional support.

• What programs are available? Sometimes the *only* way to obtain a particular program is by ordering through the mail. Dealer inventories may be limited to games and just a few best-sellers. It may not be possible for a given dealer to obtain a copy of the program, and if he orders it for you, you will probably be committed to buying it. At other times, because of the large quantities mail order houses purchase, even best-selling programs may temporarily be available only through them.

• Are you willing to wait or do you need the program immediately? Sometimes things work exactly the opposite from what was described above. A dealer may have a product on his shelf and instantly available. A mail order firm—despite what its ads say—may not have it in stock and have to back order it for you. This can take two to three weeks or more.

- Is the program one that has been widely reviewed and offered by a major software house? It goes without saying that the only programs that can be safely ordered from a mail order house are those offered by major software manufacturers. It is true that you might get lucky and find an unknown program by some very small firm at a very low price that turns out to be a real gem. But the odds are heavily against you.

---

**SoftTip:** According to a 1983 report published by the market research firm Frost & Sullivan, the average personal computer owner buys $608 worth of software when he or she purchases a computer and then spends an additional $439 on software during the first year. Mail order sales account for 39% of software sales, making it the largest single distribution channel, followed by computer-product chain stores (30%) and independent specialty retailers (22%). The chain stores and specialty retailers can be considered "dealers," meaning that the dealer-sold software accounts for a total of 55% of the market.

At the time of the study, book and department stores account for less than 2%, though the report concluded that it is in these areas that the greatest future growth will take place. The report is number 1134, *The Personal Software Market in the United States* ($1,275). Contact:

> Frost & Sullivan, Inc.
> 106 Fulton Street
> New York, NY 10038
> (212) 233-1080

---

*Recommendation*

If you are interested in a game or an educational program that has been well reviewed, you will be fairly safe buying it from a reputable mail order company, even if you are new to personal computing. You won't have the instant gratification of racing home from your dealer's and immediately booting the disk. But such programs will not be difficult to learn to operate and since the total amount invested will probably be small ($20 to $50), there is not much risk. The only real problem would be a defective disk that you would have to send to the software house for replacement.

Similarly, if you are a business person interested in buying additional office copies of a program you already own and know how to use, it doesn't make sense for you to pay the full list price since you will not need the support. You might see if you could work out a discount with your dealer. Since you will not be asking for his support, his total costs will be comparable to those of a mail order house and he might be interested in giving you a similar price. If that isn't possible, buy through the mail.

However, if you are a new user interested in buying a reasonably powerful "building block" (communications, word processing, spreadsheet, and database management) or other "serious" software, then you should definitely purchase your first program from a dealer who is able and willing to support you. Conceivably, you will learn enough and become so adept at using software that you can confidently buy all subsequent programs through the mail. But you will never know until you try your first "serious" program. To do so without the support of a knowledgeable dealer is to risk being penny wise and pound foolish.

## How to Choose a Direct Mail-Order Firm

If you decide to order your software through the mail, it can be important to choose the firm you deal with as carefully as you select a dealer. Starting a mail order firm is a relatively easy and inexpensive undertaking in most cases, and new ones are springing up—as others fold up—all the time. Consequently, the most important thing to look for is continuity. Page through six months' worth of the same issue of a major computer magazine and see what mail order firms have ads in every issue. (Some magazines include an advertiser's index at the back of each issue to make it easy for you to locate specific firms.)

Continuity of this sort can be a good sign, indicating that the firm is probably not in business to make a quick dollar and close its doors as soon as it has sold out its inventory. It can mean that the firm is profitable and successful, something that is difficult to achieve over time without satisfied customers and repeat business. Perhaps most important of all, it can indicate that the magazine carrying the ad has received no major complaints from readers on the firm's policies, products, or service.

A magazine may not have a definite policy ("Ten complaints and we won't accept any more ads from these guys . . ."), but most major computer magazines are sensitive to reader complaints and will probably refuse an ad if the number grows too large. Other magazines will accept any kind of ad, as long as the firm pays up front in cash.

As you are fanning through back issues you might also look at the letters columns many magazines carry. See if any readers have written in to complain about a particular firm. And you might contact the magazine itself to ask if any complaints have been registered, what they may know about the company, etc.

Additional options include contacting the Better Business Bureau or the Chamber of Commerce in the mail order firm's home city to ask about complaints. You might also write to the Direct Mail/Marketing Association, an industry group that tries to police the activities of its members, to see if the mail order firm belongs. It is a good sign if the firm does belong, but not necessarily a bad one if it doesn't since there are many reputable firms in all industries that do not belong to trade groups. Here is the address and phone number of this association:

> Direct Mail/Marketing Association, Inc.
> 6 East 43rd Street
> New York, NY 10017
> (212) 689-4977

**SoftTip:** If you were to pursue all of these options, you would have an excellent chance of identifying reputable firms and avoiding the bad ones. The trouble is, all of this investigation will take time, time you could otherwise be spending at your computer or doing other things. To short circuit the process, ask the members of your local users group for their suggestions. See Chapter 8 for information on how to locate a computer users group in your area.

**SoftTip:** If you're going cross-eyed reading the fine print and pricing information in software ads to locate the lowest price, you might consider subscribing to a publication called "Computer Price Alert." Issued every two weeks, this publication surveys and compares the prices of the best-selling computer hardware, software, and supplies offered by over 75 major discounters and mail-order firms.

Each entry in "Computer Price Alert" includes the product name and manufacturer, the list price, and the three lowest prices found during the two-week survey period. Naturally, it also includes the name, address, and phone number of the mail-order firm offering each price, as well as the forms of payment acceptable to the firm and other information. The publication carries no advertising.

For more information, contact:

*SoftTip continued*

> COMPUTER PRICE ALERT
> Box 574
> Harvard Square Station
> Cambridge, MA 02138
> (800) 824-7888, 24-hours a day, ask for Operator 71
>
> *Subscription:* $29 per year (20 issues)—Introductory rate; regular price is $35 per year

## What to Look For

Mail order houses can differ in a number of ways. The first and most obvious difference is the nature and tone of their ads. Allowing for the fact that they must somehow grab your attention, some firms' ads are clearly much better and more useful than others. For example, an ad that scatters product information all over the page and blares at you like a grocery store ad in a newspaper makes it difficult to locate the program you are interested in. Far better is an ad that presents products in columns organized by computer type (IBM, Apple, TRS-80, Commodore, etc.). And better still is one that also includes both the legitimate list price of the product (verifiable from the reviews you have collected) and the discounted price.

Other points to look for include the following:

### Tips for Reading a Software Ad

• Price. Most mail order houses will sell the same products at prices that are within about $10 of each other. You can take a nickel and dime approach if you like and always order from the firm with the absolute lowest price, but once you have found a mail order firm that you like, it is much more sensible to stay with it, as long as its prices are generally in line.

• Toll-free ordering number. This is such a standard feature that, if it is not offered, it is reason enough to use a different firm.

• Information number. In most cases, only the ordering line will be toll free. But it can be helpful if the firm also offers a phone number for you to call to get some information about the firm's policies, about the status of an order you have placed, and possibly a small amount of information about the programs themselves.

This can also be useful since many firms cannot fit all of the products they sell into a single ad. They may have just the program you want but for one reason or another have not featured it. (See if you can get away with calling the toll-free ordering number first, but don't be surprised if you are referred to the information number.)

• Clearly stated returns policy. The better mail order firms will at least leave the door open for you to return a product, usually for replacement, if you have some problem. But you can't count on it. A returns policy may not be stated. And if it is, it will usually indicate that returns will be handled on a case-by-case basis. You will probably have to phone the firm for a return authorization number. Also, if you return a package, the firm may charge you 15% of the price you paid.

• Clearly stated terms. You will get the fastest service and the lowest prices if you pay by cashier's check or money order. The service will be equally fast if you pay by major credit card, but most firms add an additional 3% for credit card purchases.

Paying by personal or company check usually takes the longest, for the mail order firm may wait two to three weeks for the check to clear before shipping the product. Some firms state how long they will wait, others simply say, "Please allow time for check to clear."

Sales tax. No sales tax should be charged on any item if you are ordering from a firm in another state.

• Shipping charges. Some firms may charge $2.50 per item ordered. Others may indicate that there will be a minimum shipping charge of $2.50, regardless of what you order. Clearly, this is something you will want to watch. If the shipping charge for five game programs at $2.50 each is $12.50, for example, buying them through the mail may not be such a bargain.

• Technical support phone number. In the past it has been relatively rare for a mail order house to offer any kind of technical support. But a number of them have begun to do so. It is really not a bad idea on a mail order firm's part since offering this kind of help could be a deciding factor in whether someone buys from them or somebody else.

Unfortunately from a software buyer's standpoint, there is really no way to gauge the quality, value, and extent of this support beforehand. Unless you know someone who has good things to say about it and until you have tried it yourself, you will probably be safest if you treat it as a nice but non-vital feature.

## Tips for Buying through the Mail

• Get the name of the telephone order salesperson you deal with. This can be very helpful later on if you want to check on the status of your order or if you have some problem. In addition, you may find that some representatives are more helpful and pleasant to deal with than others. If you chance upon someone you like, it makes sense to stick with him or her. Some telephone representatives work on a commission basis and will *want* you to request them when you call again.

• Get a confirmation of the shipping date when you place your order. If the mail order house does not have the item in stock, it will have to back order it. That can take one to three weeks in many cases. If you don't want to wait, you may decide to order through another firm, though if a product is hard to come by, all firms are likely to be in the same position.

Some salespeople will automatically tell you whether an item is in stock. Others may not know or not volunteer this information. Be certain to ask.

• If a product must be back ordered, find out whether and when you can cancel the order. You may want to try to find the program elsewhere. Or you may simply change your mind. Either way, you should ask when and how you can cancel an order before you actually place it. Since you are likely to be buying a program that the mail order firm would normally stock anyhow—as opposed to something they are ordering just for you—there is little reason for the company not to allow you to cancel a back order before it is shipped.

• Be sure you know the total price, including shipping, before you place your order. Any firm that cannot tell you what your total cost will be when you place your order is not a firm you should deal with. Similarly, although most ads carry the legend "All prices subject to change," if the salesperson indicates that the program will cost significantly more than the advertised price, do not place an order.

This may or may not be an example of the illegal tactic of "bait-and-switch," and there may be legitimate reasons for a higher price. But you owe it to yourself to check—either by calling the software firm or by calling another mail order house.

• If you have any questions about the status of your order, feel free to call back in a week or so to check on it.

- Include your phone number on all written orders and suggest that a telephone salesperson write it on your order.

- Ask if the firm has a printed catalogue and request a copy. You might also ask to be placed on the company's mailing list. Since a catalogue will offer many times the room of a magazine ad, the company will be able to list many products not featured in the magazine. Though the prices will probably change, a catalogue can serve as a handy reference the next time you want to order a program.

- Develop a list of two or more mail order firms that you trust. The need for this will depend upon how much software you plan to buy. But it can be convenient to know of more than one reputable mail order firm. When one is out of stock, for example, you will have someone else to call.

Whether you decide that it would be best for you to buy from your local dealer or through the mail, the important thing is always to seek the most reputable establishments and the best-qualified people. They're out there, but you may have to do some looking to find them. Whatever effort you spend in this endeavor will be well worthwhile, for in the long run it will save you time, money, and aggravation. Most important of all, it will enable you to use your computer effectively with a minimum amount of frustration. And that, after all, is what good software is all about.

---

**SoftTip:** What do you do if you purchase a program and later discover that it is not well suited for your needs? Or suppose you get tired of a game and would like to trade it in for something else? It's very unlikely that your dealer will give you credit, but there may be another alternative, thanks to the National Software Exchange (NSE).

For an annual fee of $75, NSE will run an unlimited number of notices in its monthly newsletter for people wanting to sell or swap personal computer programs. The notices include your system, the software you have and what you want for it, your name, address, and phone number. Members are free to contact each other directly, or NSE will arrange a sale or swap for $5 per transaction. For more information contact:

> National Software Exchange
> 700 Bloomfield Avenue
> Montclair, NJ 07042

*Delivering Software over the Phone: A Look at the Future*

In years to come, according to some companies, the choice you will face as a software consumer will not be which local dealer to buy from or which mail order house to deal with—it will be which number you should dial to have the programs you want instantly delivered to your personal computer over the telephone. These firms foresee you sitting down at a computer, connecting your modem, and dialing an online software store. Once logged on to the store's database, you will see a menu on your screen listing any number of software products.

You key in your credit card number, the computer says, "Standby for software download," and after you tell it you're ready, it sends you the program over the phone. Once the software has been captured in your machine, it is recorded on a floppy disk. You sign off, tell the modem to hang up the phone, and immediately begin using the program you have bought.

This might be considered an interesting idea with certain limited applications were it not for the unbelievable projections that are being put forward. In a study called "Downloading & Teledelivery of Computer Software, Games, Music & Video," International Resource Development, Inc. (IRD), a well-respected market research firm, projects that the software sales will double every year for the next 10 years, rising from $9.1 million in 1983 to $20.2 billion by 1993, for a total growth of 2,200%. Of that $20.2 billion, the study projects that fully 75% will result from personal computer software sold and delivered over the phone.

---

**SoftTip:** The above-mentioned market study is report number 558 and is available for $1,850 from:

International Resource Development, Inc.
30 High Street
Norwalk, CT 06851
(800) 243-5008
(203) 866-6914, in Conn.
Telex: 64-3452

---

*The Pros as the Pros See It*

Conceivably, the teledelivery of programs from the software house directly to the consumer could be the industry's ultimate response to the choke point presented by today's limited retail distribution channels. Software producers would no longer have to engage in the brutal battle for retail shelf space for their products. Since a single copy of each program, duplicated innumerable times over the telephone, would be all that was necessary, there would be no inventory costs to worry about, no shipping charges, and no floppy disks and disk duplication services to pay for. What's more, by cutting out the middleman, the software firm could charge more than its current wholesale prices but less than what a program would normally retail for—producing more profits for the firm while offering lower prices to consumers.

*Cons and Conundrums*

All of this sounds wonderful from the industry's viewpoint and supporters may have good reason to be excited. Critics would claim, however, that the extravagant projections for the success and eventual dominance of teledelivered software amount to a monumental case of self-inflicted blindness. Principally, blindness to the needs of software consumers, a group whose viewpoint is rarely considered when the subject of teledelivery is discussed, and a group upon whose cooperation and enthusiastic support these plans depend.

The technical problems of sending computer programming—every bit of which must be accurately received for the program to work properly—over today's snap-crackle-pop telephone lines are being solved. Indeed, as early as 1978 some Apple owners were receiving software (worldwide!) via short-wave radio. Transmitted by Dutch Radio from a base station in Hilversum, North Holland, programs were successfully received as far away as the United States and Australia.

But while the technical difficulties may not pose a problem, there is still the matter of documentation and the cost and time required to transmit it. At a rate of 1,200 baud (the fastest speed most conventional telephone lines can handle), a 90K program like WordStar would require nearly 10 minutes to transmit. The WordStar user's manual, occupying the equivalent of 344 typewritten, double-spaced pages, would require more than an hour and 15 minutes to transmit.

At least that much time would also be required to print out a hard copy. And, more than likely, that copy would contain none of the keyboard diagrams, charts, and boxed sections that are largely responsible for whatever understanding you can glean from that densely written tome. With telephone companies charging customers on the basis of connect time for even local calls, in accordance with the AT&T antitrust settlement, downloading a program and a lengthy instruction manual over the phone may not be a financially attractive proposition.

*The Telephone Software Connection, Inc.*

Edward Magnin, founder of the Telephone Software Connection, Inc., one of the country's first teledelivery services, disagrees. Mr. Magnin feels that most software documentation could be considerably reduced in size if the programs they described were written to trap most user errors, eliminating the need for instructions that tell the reader what *not* to do. He also feels that if a program is properly written, most of the instructions a person needs can be embedded within it in the form of "Help" messages and files. The Telephone Software Connection uses sophisticated "error checking" techniques to make certain that its products are transmitted accurately, and it provides high-quality support for users who call with questions about the programs they have purchased. Customers often have the opportunity to talk with Mr. Magnin himself.

The software offered by Mr. Magnin's firm is written either by on-staff programmers or commissioned from independent consultants. Programs are currently available only for Apple owners, though the Telephone Software Connection and the companies that will follow its lead will support more computers in the future. In the meantime, if you call up the Telephone Software Connection's computer with your own machine, here is the kind of thing you can expect to see on your screen:

TELEPHONE SOFTWARE CONNECTION, INC
PO BOX 6548, TORRANCE, CA 90504

24-HOUR MODEM LINES—(213) 516-9432

OFFICE (213) 516-9430 / TELEX 46935

WELCOME TO AN EXCITING NEW WAY TO
PURCHASE FULLY DOCUMENTED AND TESTED
SOFTWARE FOR YOUR APPLE.

TO BE ABLE TO ORDER AND RECEIVE
PROGRAMS INSTANTLY THROUGH THE PHONE
ALL YOU NEED IS AN APPLE II WITH:

    A MODEM

    A DISK

    APPLESOFT

    A MAJOR CREDIT CARD

WE CURRENTLY HAVE 65 PROGRAMS FOR THE APPLE ][
COMPUTER. (ALL SOLD 'AS IS'.

NO WARRANTIES OR REFUNDS. LIABILITY
LIMITED TO REPLACEMENT OF PROGRAM.)

DEPARTMENTS:

```
SOFTWARE..................................1
ACCESSORIES...............................2
SPECIAL SERVICES..........................3
EXIT SYSTEM...............................4
```

WHICH? #1

SOFTWARE:

```
BY PROGRAM TYPE..............................1
BY PROGRAM NUMBERS...........................2
DESCRIPTIONS.................................3
TAKE FREE SAMPLE.............................4
PURCHASE PROGRAM.............................5
RETURN TO MAIN MENU..........................6
```

WHICH # 3

FROM PROGRAM #1
TO PROGRAM #7

```
#1  CALL TSC...............................................$  FREE
```

USE THIS PROGRAM NEXT TIME YOU CALL US.
WILL AUTOMATICALLY DIAL OUR NUMBER AND
LOG YOU ON. (REQUIRES MICROMODEM OR
APPLECAT WITH ROM)

[Intervening text not shown.]

```
#4  PICTURE TRANSFER PROGRAM............................$ 35.00
```

WATCH HI-RES GRAPHICS PICTURES AS THEY
ARE SENT FROM ONE APPLE TO ANOTHER—
ABOUT 1 MIN SET UP THEN SENDS PICTURE
IN 4.5 MIN.—AUTOMATICALLY SAVES TO
DISK—REQUIRES MICROMODEM OR COMCARD.

[Intervening text not shown.]

```
#6  ANALOG CLOCK .........................................$  FREE
```

A TIMELY GIFT FOR THOSE WHOSE WHO HAVE EITHER
THE APPLE CLOCK OR THE SUPERCLOCK II.

Other Telephone Software Connection programs and prices include:

```
ANSWERING MACHINE ............................ $ 35.00
DESK CALCULATOR II ............................ $ 30.00
DESK CALENDAR II ............................... $ 35.00
UPDATE DESK CALENDAR II ....................... $ FREE
DESK CALENDAR II TUTORIAL ..................... $ FREE
TERMINAL PROGRAM .............................. $ 35.00
TIME & MONEY METER ............................ $ 25.00
GIANT GRAPHICS ................................. $ 35.00
CHECKWRITER ................................... $ 40.00
CHECKWRITER TUTORIAL .......................... $ FREE
DESK CALCULATOR II ............................ $ 30.00
DESK CALCULATOR II TUTORIAL .................... $ FREE
DOUBLE DOS ..................................... $ 18.00
DOUBLEBOOT FOR LANGUAGE CARD .............. $ 15.00
LOST FILE RETRIEVER ........................... $ 35.00
```

The company asks for your credit card and address information as soon as you sign on. So after you have read the description of the program and decided that you want to buy it, you choose the appropriate selection from the menu and tell the system you want to download. The system will then send your Apple some programming that effectively takes control of the machine and implements the error checking procedure. You will then be asked to insert a blank, formatted disk and signal when ready to receive. (Programs are transmitted as text files as opposed to machine language.)

---

**SoftTip:** If you have an Apple equipped as the online information above states, initialize your modem, get its attention by hitting Control-A and set it to "full duplex" with Control-F. Then get its attention again and tell it to dial with a Control-Q and type the number for the Telephone Software Connection:

IN#3      (OR YOUR MODEM SLOT #)
CTRL-A    CTRL-F
CTRL-A    CTRL-Q 1-213-516-9432

*Note:* The company will probably offer you a free program of some sort whether you purchase anything or not. For *voice* communications, call: (213) 516-9430.

## Conclusion

It seems unlikely that most software buyers will ever be satisfied buying major programs over the telephone. In addition to the cost of transmission and the problem of providing adequate documentation, the advantages of being able to buy a program at any hour of the day without ever leaving your home or office do not outweigh the desire to see, demonstrate, and shop for a product before buying it.

There is also the "pig in a poke" problem of having no idea of what you are buying. It is just possible that the most important problem the software industry must face is not the retail store bottleneck at all, but the staggering number of programs on the market. Even if each and every one of the 40,000 or more personal computer programs were to be described thoroughly in published reviews, there is still a limit on how much a person can absorb and how many different brands of programs one can consider.

Placing a computer in a retail store and connecting it by a high-speed line to a centrally located machine containing copies of programs for sale may be the most logical role for teledelivery technology. It would eliminate both the financial and storage problems of carrying a large inventory, permit customers to demonstrate a program before they buy, and ultimately make a wider selection of software available than would be possible with floppy disks. In addition, a popular program would never be out of stock. (IBM has already begun to move in this direction by installing IBM/XT's in retail stores carrying its computers and using them to transmit pricing and product information, news, and electronic mail between the store and a central location.) The only thing this approach does not do is cut the middleman out of the loop, which is probably a bad idea in any case.

From a software buyer's standpoint, the most likely benefit of the teledelivery phenomenon will be a wider selection of relatively inexpensive programs. Conceivably, if the cost and telephone charges are low enough, you might be inclined to buy and try programs that you would not consider under other circumstances. There is also the fact that, if the company is on its toes, the program you buy will always be the latest version. And, as Ed Magnin of The Telephone Software Connection points out, teledelivery makes it easy to update older versions belonging to previous customers.

The Telephone Software Connection has been in business for several years and gives every indication of being a highly reputable and innovative firm. If the predicted explosion in teledelivered software really does take place, however, it will be important to be as cautious as you would be when choosing a mail order company. Only more so. Effective laws protecting your rights as a teledelivery customer have yet to be written. And, while it is somewhat difficult for a mail order company to disappear overnight, the teledelivery "firms" of the future may consist of nothing but an easily transportable auto-answer modem and a hard-disk-equipped computer.

# ...11...

# The Twelve Sure-Fire Rules for Software Success

With a little help from your friends, a good computer magazine or two, the material in this book—and most of all, with experience—there is no reason why you can't buy personal computer software as confidently as you buy stereo equipment, kitchen appliances, or power tools.

The best way to approach a computer program is the same way you approach a book or a movie. All three represent the creative efforts of a group of people or an individual. There is nothing magical about any of them. Most important, just as there are good, bad, and absolutely awful movies and books, there are good and bad programs and some that are real stinkers.

After you begin to use computer software, you can be sure that neither the product itself nor the ideas behind it will remain unfamiliar. In a very short time, the strangeness will wear off and you will become comfortable. Before long, you will become critical—wondering why this program doesn't have a certain feature, or why that one works so slowly, or even coveting a new package offered by such and such a firm.

At that point, you will no longer need this book. You can put it on the shelf above your machine, next to your growing collection of three-ring binders and slip-cased software, using it merely as a reminder of what you already know. Meanwhile, the twelve rules listed below can help you along your way.

### The Twelve Sure-Fire Rules of Software Success

• Rule 1. Don't take *anything* for granted.

If the advertisement or literature says the program will run on an Apple IIe, an IBM/PC, or Radio Shack TRS-80 Model 4, or some other machine, treat it as a strong *indication* that you can use the program if you own one of those machines—but not as fact. The program may require double-sided disk drives, a plug-in graphics card, a special printer, or some other hardware configuration not mentioned in the ad. Similarly, it may require a secondary operating system, a copy of some computer language, or even a newer version of your machine's standard operating system in order to run. These requirements may not be spelled out in the literature.

• Rule 2. *You're* not the stupid one.

If a program turns out to be hard to understand or difficult to use, it is because the program's creator has not lived up to his or her responsibility to you. The same is true of the software house and the author of the manual that accompanies the program. If a novel began, "It was a dark and stormy night . . ." and proceeded to introduce wooden, two-dimensional characters and a completely unbelievable story line, it is doubtful that you would react to it with feelings of personal inadequacy. You'd say, "This is a really stupid book written by someone who didn't know what he was doing." The same is true of a poorly written, hard-to-understand manual.

Don't ever let yourself feel foolish when looking at, reading about, using, or otherwise dealing with a computer program. If its creators haven't lived up to their responsibility, it is their fault, not yours.

• Rule 3. How many? and How long?

If you will develop the habit of asking these two questions at every conceivable point as you consider a program, you can probably eliminate 60% or more of the unforeseen problems and disappointments new software buyers encounter: How many names can I put in that file? How long can each name be? How many accounts will fit on a single disk? How long a document can this word processing program handle?

Asking questions at every turn is particularly crucial with programs intended to accomplish something that you now do by hand—like addressing envelopes, handling business accounting chores, or creating a household budget. With these programs, there's a tendency to assume that the software will do things pretty much the way you do them now, with all the flexibility that this implies. It's such a natural assumption that it may not even occur to you to ask. But that can be fatal.

When you address an envelope, for example, you never have to worry about the length of the person's name or how many lines the address will contain (name, title, corporate division, suite number, office building floor, etc.) Nor do you have to worry about having enough room to use a five-digit or a nine-digit ZIP code or adding

CANADA or U.S.A. But, with a computer mailing list program, these details are a major concern.

As we've seen repeatedly, when you are dealing with a computer *everything* must be specified. If the author of the program has not specified enough address lines or allowed room for enough characters in each line, you will be in for an unpleasant surprise. The first time you try to address a letter to:

> Mr. Tamburino T. Marangopoulos
> Senior Vice President
> Drum and Cymbal Division, Suite 405
> Acme Peerless Percussion Products, Ltd.
> 7987 Effingham Avenue
> Carmarthenshire, ME 12345

You may find that it comes out looking like this:

> Mr. Tamburino T. Marangopoul
> Senior Vice President
> Drum and Cymbal Division, Su
> Acme Peerless Percussion Pro

Similarly, some programs will come to a full stop if you try to enter a number larger than 99,9999.00. A home budget program could be limited to only 14 categories of expenses. A word processing program may be limited to documents no longer than 15 pages.

Nothing brings a program's limitations to the surface faster than the questions, How many? and How long?

• Rule 4. Forget about the sizzle and focus on the steak.

In every case, it is advisable to take what might be called the "Watergate Approach" to software evaluation. Only instead of asking, What did he know, and when did he know it?, ask, What is the program designed to do, and how well does it do it? It is so easy to be distracted by all of the whistles and bells with which many programs are tricked out that many software buyers lose sight of their goal. And if you are new to the game, there is a tendency to give equal weight to every feature.

What is the fundamental purpose of the program? What is it designed to *do?* It may be nice that a spelling checker can tell you exactly how many words are in your document and how many times you used each word. But how well does it check your spelling? An educational program may use wonderfully imaginative graphics and sound effects, but what does it really teach and how well does it teach it?

Software firms are particularly interested in highlighting the sizzle, for it can make their products appear to be different from the competition. And sometimes the little extra features can make a world of difference in how easy, effective, and enjoyable a program is to use. A communications program capable of automatically issuing your password and other information needed to sign you on to a database at the touch of a button is a good example. But it's an "extra" feature and is a lot less essential than how well the program does its main job of sending and receiving information.

Sometimes a loudly proclaimed list of "extra" features can even be a smokescreen intended to cover up fundamental inadequacies in the program. If a program was written in haste or if the author was less than skillful, it may soak up far more of your machine's memory than software of similar capabilities, making the software less convenient to use. Or the program may be laden with extra features, but run with all the speed and responsiveness of a water snake on a winter's day.

Software reviewers and article writers are also partially to blame for inadvertently focusing your attention on the nonessentials. It is easy to sympathize with a writer who has reviewed so many word processing programs that he begins a new review with the sentence, "This program contains all the standard word processing features," and then launches into a detailed description of the program's unique whistles and bells. But such a review is of little help to you as a software buyer seeking a word processing program.

There *are* no widely agreed-upon "standard" features of any program. If a review is to be of any real use to you, it must focus on what the program was designed to do and how well it does it. The extra features should come later, both in the review and in your consideration of the program.

• Rule 5. Whenever possible, make an effort to *visualize* yourself using the program.

This is not as difficult as it may sound. If you are considering a communications program, for example, you will probably have some idea of what you can do with it. You may be planning on buying a subscription to The Source, CompuServe, Dow Jones, or some other database. Or you may intend to explore the world of free computer bulletin boards. When do you plan to use the program to do these things? How will these activities fit into your present schedule? Will you go online after dinner to chat with your electronic friends instead of watching TV? If you can't see yourself using the program, perhaps you shouldn't buy it in the first place.

Do you think you might be using the program several times a week or only occasionally? If you're going to be a frequent user, the little conveniences and extras in a full-featured program will be important and well worth the additional cost. Otherwise, a less expensive, "barebones" package may be quite adequate.

The same idea applies equally well to all computer software. When do you see yourself or your family playing a computer game? If you are thinking of buying a typing tutor or other instructional package, do you see yourself using it with the regularity required to accomplish its goals? How much work will be involved putting all of your books, records, or magazines into database management files? Will you be willing to enter each new book or record, or are you likely to let things slide?

The best way to do this is to make a detailed list of every step involved in the job and ask yourself how the program would handle it. For example, suppose that you are in business and you want to use a database management program to handle your personnel records. You already know from reading about this type of program that it can be used for this purpose. But instead of stopping there, *visualize* the process. You'll need a form for each employee containing blanks for each item of information you want to enter. How will you use the program you are considering to create that form? What will it look like when you're done?

What are the items of information you want to enter? Name, address, phone, Social Security number, department number, supervisor, etc.? Do you normally enter both a home phone and "contact in case of emergency" number? How will the program handle that? Do you normally keep performance reports and evaluations in each employee's file? How will you deal with that aspect once you begin using the program? Does it give you room to enter these things?

Is there a way to allow your clerical staff to enter personnel information while preserving the confidentiality of employee evaluation reports and supervisor comments? A well-planned program will include this feature. But it's something you might not consider if you do not visualize the entire process, step by step.

A program that does not include this feature will not be unusable, but neither will it allow you to take full advantage of computerizing your personnel records. This can be particularly annoying because a program that *does* include a "confidentiality" feature might not cost any more and probably wouldn't involve any more work to set up. This specific example may not apply to you or your business, but the same thread runs through all software. It will take a little work, but the more completely you visualize the various steps involved in accomplishing a task and the more you know about how a given program will deal with (or not deal with) those steps, the greater the chance that you will be happy with your purchase.

• **Rule 6. Read at least two reviews of any program before you buy.**
Software reviews are invaluable, but, as you will discover, they tend to be just as personal as movie and book reviews. Often, they take the form of a war correspondent's report from the front lines: "I did this . . . I tried that . . . I watched helplessly as the program systematically wiped out all my files . . ." This is useful when it tells you something you might not be able to find out any other way, namely, what it's like to actually use the program.

Needless to say, however, different people react to the same thing in different ways. Some movie critics thought *My Dinner with André* zipped by in a twinkling; others sighed with relief when the coffee and dessert were finally served. Software reviewers likewise will highlight different aspects of the same program. To one, the lack of a feature may represent a serious omission, possibly even sufficient reason to avoid buying the program. But a different reviewer might note the missing feature in passing, saying that "it would be nice to have . . ." A third reviewer might not mention it at all.

Because reactions can differ so, it is important to read *at least two* reviews of a package before you buy.

• **Rule 7. Get a demonstration on the identical computer, configured *exactly* as the one you will be using.**
As every computer owner knows, the number and variety of possible hardware incompatibilities is beyond bewildering. Software is the same way: "This program will work with that printer, but you won't be able to do underlining. And the program won't work at all with that monitor. And you'll need a Whiz-Bang plug-in card, but you'd better make sure you have enough empty slots inside your machine because you'll also need 64K more memory. Actually, 128K would be even better and . . ." And, forget it!

You can cut through all of this nonsense and save yourself time if you make an effort to have the program demonstrated on equipment that exactly matches your own. Let the dealer worry with the bits and bytes, the program patches, the installation modules, and the like. You don't have to know or be concerned about any of these things. All you need to know is, When I walk out of the store with this program, will it work, and work completely, on the equipment I own?

The only way to be absolutely certain of the answer is to actually *see* it work on a machine configured exactly the way yours is: same printer, same amount of memory, same type of disk drives, etc. Unfortunately, you cannot always take a salesperson's word for it. In all innocence, the individual may believe that it will work. But without actually testing it, there is simply no way to be certain that you won't run into some unsuspected problem.

When it is not possible to conduct a demonstration on equipment identical to your own, it is vital to pay attention to the hardware and exactly how it differs from your system. Run down the differences point by point, asking, How will this affect the way the program works on my computer? in every case. The difference may have no effect whatever, but at least you will know that this is the case.

• Rule 8. Life will be easier if you stick with proven products offered by major hardware and software firms.

This is said with certain wistful reservations, for one of the exciting qualities of the microworld is the decentralization of power and the fact that, for a very modest investment, *anybody* can write a program. At the same time, however, one cannot in good conscience recommend any but the "major brand, big company" approach to buying either software or hardware. This automatically eliminates whole battalions of programs, many of which will undoubtedly more closely match your needs. It wipes out warehouses of computers and computer hardware, much of which could be well suited to your situation. And it makes it extremely difficult for a small hardware or software firm with a brilliant idea to achieve the success it deserves.

But the logic is inescapable. The computer industry is choking on its own innovation and the seemingly limitless variety and incompatibility it has spawned: 95 to 100 different disk formats, none of them compatible; an untold number of ways to store information, making it impossible for one program to use the data developed in another; an endless stream of printers, graphic plotters, and peripherals, not one of which can you be sure of using with each and every program.

It is no wonder that the entire industry breathed a collective sigh of relief when IBM at last entered the market late in 1981. At last, there would be at least some kind of standard. If nothing else, perhaps IBM could do for 5¼-inch disks what it did for their larger, 8-inch brethren: set a formatting standard that nearly everyone uses. That hasn't happened yet, but there can be no question that the industry is moving toward standardization, whether it's IBM's standards, or those of some other firm.

For example, most programs now fully support the best-selling Epson MX-80 printer and other members of the Epson line. The Hewlett-Packard 7470A graphic plotter is on its way to becoming the standard that all business graphic programs must support. And all major communications programs fully support the Hayes Smartmodem. If you happen to own any of this equipment, you will have far fewer worries about getting your program to run. Actually, you do not even have to buy the "leading brands." As long as whatever you do buy is fully compatible with the standards they set, you will have no major problems.

Software is following suit. Few companies today would even consider issuing a *major* program that wasn't designed to run under MS-DOS (a.k.a. IBM/PC-DOS). Other operating systems might be supported as well, but MS-DOS will be the first one offered. In the future, anyone with a computer that can run MS-DOS will have the best selection of the best programs. In the eight-bit world, the same thing can be said of CP/M-80.

In the area of applications software, you find users groups forming to share information about VisiCalc, SuperCalc, and other best-selling spreadsheets; WordStar, PIE Writer, and other leading word processing programs; and dBASE II, the top-selling database management program. Publishers are issuing books to tell you how to get the most out of these same programs. Thus, if you happen to own one, you will find a wealth of tips and tricks from fellow users, a selection of independently marketed add-on modules, customizing program patches and application templates on free computer bulletin board systems, newsletters and support publications, and a greater number of knowledgeable dealers and salespeople.

These programs may or may not be the best available. They may not suit all of your needs. Or they may be "overqualified" for the applications you have in mind and thus be more complex and cost more than you really want to spend. But for one reason or another, they are becoming "standards," and if you don't own them, you will not be able to tap these resources.

We should hasten to add that all of this depends on what programs are available for your particular machine and upon how extensively you will be using your software. If you will be using a word processing program to write an occasional note or two, any well-reviewed program will be fine. But if you do a lot of writing, you cannot afford to ignore the support that has grown up around the major word processing programs. If you will be using an electronic spreadsheet to figure your home budget, you won't need a program with more rows than the Superdome and more columns than the Roman Forum. But if you will be using a spreadsheet every day, you cannot afford to ignore the greater number of books, users groups, and templates available for the best-selling programs. The same considerations apply in one degree or another to every major non-game, non-educational category of software.

• **Rule 9. Buy only the four "building block" programs to start.**
This does not apply to games and educational programs, of course. But if you are among the growing numbers of people who are becoming interested in what is sometimes called "productivity software," then you will probably be best off if you start with just the four building block programs described in Chapter 8: communications, word processing, electronic spreadsheet, and personal filing or database management. If you are a business person and use your computer a lot, it will probably make sense to buy these programs as an all-in-one (including business graphics) "integrated" package, of the sort described in Chapter 18. But if you are buying as a private individual, you will probably be able to do virtually everything you want with just these four programs.

For many people, it makes sense to get one of the best, most feature-filled programs available in each category, since the more features and power the program offers, the more flexible it will be. But unless you have a crucial need, do your best to resist the temptation to load up on all four building blocks at the same time. Buy them separately and plan to learn how to use one before adding the next program to your collection. Not even an experienced computerist can learn four new programs all at once without getting confused. You'll master each program faster and more completely if you concentrate on just one at a time.

• **Rule 10. Don't drive yourself crazy trying to get something to work: ASK!**
When you run into a brick wall and there seems to be no way to get the program to do what it is supposed to do, you can assume that you're missing a piece to the puzzle. It may be in the documentation, and certainly you should look. But documentation is generally so poor that it may not be there—or if it is, you may not be able to find it. When this happens to you, and it happens to *everybody*, don't bloody your head against the wall—bow to the inevitable and phone your dealer or the software vendor's hotline to get help.

There is no better example of this than the comments made by a regretfully unbylined writer in a discussion of his attempts to buy a computer and a word processing program several years ago. After noting that the documentation was written wittily but that it was dangerously incomplete, he said:

I worked for two hours to get from one mode to another without losing the text. I eventually called the computer store. The response I got was, "Oh, yeah, he left that out. Just hit the space bar twice." I wasn't pleased. And I didn't buy the machine, the software, or the store's attitude.

• **Rule 11. Nothing is impossible. But the game may not be worth the candle.**

It used to be thought that an eight-bit processor could address no more than 64K of memory. But then someone invented the technique of bank-switching, and voilà—the maximum was suddenly doubled to 128K. An Apple computer couldn't run CP/M and could display only upper case letters; then several companies began offering plug-in boards to solve both problems. The versatility even extends to otherwise incompatible hardware. The plugs and cables may not be designed to fit, but with a soldering iron, the right components, and an intimate knowledge of the equipment, almost any printer can be connected to any computer. The result will inevitably be a "kludge" ("clue-juh")—computerist slang for any inelegant, chewing-gum-and-baling-wire hardware lashup—but it can usually be done. Whether it's worth it is another story.

The same versatility exists in software. Can't get color in DOS on the IBM/PC? Want to generate characters that aren't on your Radio Shack keyboard? Want to print out a report, a poster, or a spreadsheet *sideways?* No problem: There are programs to do all of these things and many, many more.

A program written in one dialect of BASIC for one computer can be translated into the dialect your machine needs. There are even programs capable of performing most of the translation automatically. And the fact that you have erased a file doesn't necessarily mean that you can't get it back again. As long as nothing else has been recorded in the disk space that it occupies, you can usually recover it, by using either a program designed for that purpose or a "zap" program to display the contents of each disk sector on your screen and changing a few key bytes by hand.

Computers and software are so versatile that you can accomplish just about anything you want. With the exception of running a program written for one microprocessor's instruction set on a machine built around a different chip, there is almost no instance where someone can say legitimately, "No. You absolutely, positively cannot do that." That does not mean, however, that the goal will be worth the time, effort, and money required to achieve it. And it certainly doesn't mean that you should do it yourself.

But it does mean that if you have a problem, an idea, or a goal, you shouldn't take no for an answer. You may have to contact a large number of people to get the information you seek. And here a communicating computer, a list of good bulletin boards phone numbers, the PARTI conferences on The Source, and the SIGs on both The Source and CompuServe can be a godsend. After learning how much effort and money you will have to invest, you may decide that it isn't worth it. But more than likely, it *can* be done, because with computers and software, virtually nothing is impossible.

- Rule 12. Whenever you can—WAIT!
  You can only gain by waiting until you need or are ready for a program before you make a purchase. There are at least five reasons why this makes sense. First, you don't want to be a pioneer. You don't want to be among the first to buy a new program.

Statistics undoubtedly exist relating the number of lines of code to the probable number of bugs in a program. But all programs have them. And major software vendors will admit as much. Let someone else discover them and wait for the vendor to issue a revised version of the software in which the bugs have been corrected.

The second reason also concerns vendor improvements. When a reputable software house issues a version of a program with major improvements, added features, etc., it will make the product available to registered users of the previous version at a reduced cost. But the total amount of money those users will have invested in the software will probably be greater than if you walked into a store and simply bought the new and improved version.

Third, as mentioned both in this chapter and elsewhere, it is a mistake to purchase several major programs all at once. It may be fun to walk out of a bookstore with an armful of books for your summer reading, but if you follow that same practice with software, you will quite frankly be overwhelmed.

If you *do* buy several programs at once, you'll miss out on the fourth benefit of waiting. And that is that new and more user-friendly programs are on the way. Freed of the constraints of even a bank-switched eight-bit processor, more and more programmers are taking advantage of the megabyte memory-addressing capabilities of the 16-bit chips to make their creations both more powerful and much easier to use. There is no way to know exactly when such a program will be issued for the application you have in mind. But by waiting, you increase your chances that it will be available when you are truly ready for it.

Finally, software prices are coming down. This may be the most important reason of all for waiting whenever you can. It simply doesn't make sense to buy four programs and leave three of them sitting on the shelf while you master one. Not when there's a chance that the identical software may be available for considerably less money by the time you're ready to master it.

In short, make the rapidly changing software marketplace work *for* you. Buy a program, master it, then buy another on your own schedule. But don't buy them all at once, even if you can afford to. You have everything to gain and nothing to lose by waiting.

# ...12...

## Free Software:
## How to Get Thousands of Programs over the Phone

They are known by names like RCPM, CBBS™, FORUM-80, Net-Works, PMS, AMIS, HOSTCOM, ST-80, BULLET-80, and The Greene Machine and there are literally hundreds of them across North America. They serve as an electronic meeting ground, as message exchange systems, and as online users groups. They are one of the best sources of computer tips and problem-solving advice available anywhere. They are also repositories of vast libraries of free, public domain software. Best of all, they are available to you today for the cost of a telephone call—if your computer is equipped for communications.

Generically, these facilities are called "bulletin board systems," or "BBS's." You will also hear them called CBBB's The C is for "computer," of course.), but this term has recently been trademarked by Ward Christensen and Randy Suess, the two individuals who created the world's first personal computer bulletin board system in 1978. Similarly, sometimes they are also referred to as PAMS (Public Access Message Systems).

We will use the term BBS, but whatever you call them, the systems all consist of the same basic components: someone's personal computer that has been equipped to answer the telephone automatically and sign you onto the system as if you were accessing The Source, CompuServe, or some other commercial database. In some cases, private individuals or computer users groups have been able to "bring up" (make available) a BBS for a total investment of about $500. But a more typical system will contain three or four floppy disk drives and/or a hard disk for truly massive storage, for a total cost of between $4,000 and $7,000 or more.

In addition to a modem (see Chapter 17) to connect the computer to the telephone line, there will also be special bulletin board software to

275

make the computer act like a commercial database. When everything is ready, the computer and the modem will be turned on and the software will be loaded. Then the machine will simply sit there waiting for you to call. When you do call, the modem will automatically answer the telephone and connect your computer to the "host" computer. The software will take over then and you'll be asked for your name and probably your city and state.When you finish typing in that information, you will be "into the system" and free to leave messages, read the files stored on disk, or "download" any of the free programs the BBS may offer.

**SoftTip:** Like most areas of computerdom, telecommunications has a terminology all its own. The "remote" or "host" system, for example, refers to whatever computer you happen to be calling with your own machine. "Online" in this field refers to being connected to the BBS or other computer. And "download" means to issue a command causing the other computer to send you one of its files over the phone. Your computer "captures" the file and records it on floppy disk or prints it out as it comes in. "Uploading" refers to the process of sending a file from your computer to another. And the SYSOP of a BBS is the "System Operator," the person responsible for managing it.

*Applying the Concept*

Those are the basic mechanics of how bulletin board systems work. Now, before looking at what you will need in the way of hardware and software, let's see how the idea can be applied. Anyone contacting a BBS can leave a message for other callers to read. The messages are given numbers and scanned the way you might scan the notices on a real cork-and-thumbtack bulletin board, and often they contain information you might never discover any other way.

For example, the following messages were downloaded from a BBS specializing in information on the IBM/PC. To fully appreciate the problem the first person is asking about, you have to know something about the IBM/PC. But the question itself is not important here. What's important is the exchange of information, and the free software suggested to solve the problem.

```
Msg- 2784
Date-00/00/00 18:21:42
From- Joe
To- ALL
Sub- COLOR IN DOS
```

Does anyone know how to get color in PC/DOS. I have a color graphics card and I can get color in BASIC, but I can't seem to do so in DOS.

Msg- 2793
Date-00/00/00 02:46:44
From- GEORGE
To- JOE AND ALL
Sub- ANSWER TO COLOR IN DOS

I have just the answer for you. I've written a program that will allow any color card equipped-PC to display all possible colors in DOS. Actually there are three programs: COLOR.HEX & COLOR.ASM & COLOR.DOC . . . All available on either Rich's or Larry's BBS.

---

**SoftTip:** If you own an IBM/PC and want a copy of COLOR.HEX and the other programs mentioned above, you might write to Mr. James Johnson to see if it is still available. Enclose a self-addressed, stamped envelope:

> Mr. James Johnson
> 402 Beech Street
> Fort Washington, MD 20744

---

If you wanted to obtain this or some other program, you would locate the correct BBS number, call up the system, and download it directly into your computer. Once you were offline, you could look at the software again and use your word processing program to edit out all the non-programming information. Then you could record the now clean file to disk and load and run the program as if you had entered it yourself or bought it from the store. The ".DOC" file would contain the documentation and instructions you need.

In this chapter, we will be focusing on the free programs and related files available on computer bulletin board systems. (If you are interested in the message exchange and other non-software aspects, see *The Complete Handbook of Personal Computer Communications*.)

*A "Board" for Every System*

The IBM/PC is far from being the only type of BBS available. In fact, only a very small fraction of the 400 to 500 systems in North America—no one knows exactly how many there are—are dedicated to IBM software. There are "boards" for users of Heath/Zenith, TRS-80 Models I and III, TRS-80 Color Computer, Atari, and North Star equipment. And there are literally hundreds of Apple bulletin boards or "ABBS" (Apple Bulletin Board System, pronounced "abbies"). For example, here is part of what you will find when you sign a bulletin board run by the Commodore Computer users group in Kansas City, Missouri (816-257-2502; available 24 hours a day):

THE COMMODORE USERS GROUP BULLETIN BOARD

\*\*\*\*\*\*\*\*\*\*\*\*\*\*\*\*\*\*\*\*\*\*\*\*\*\*\*\*\*\*\*\*\*\*\*\*\*\*\*\*\*\*\*\*\*\*\*\*\*\*\*\*

GOOD NEWS

There is a version of the Vic-20 Upload—Download software on the BBS. Get a hold of one of your friends with a 64 or Pet and have them download it for you. The user group will have a copy to give out within the week.

\*\*\*\*\*\*\*\*\*\*\*\*\*\*\*\*\*\*\*\*\*\*\*\*\*\*\*\*\*\*\*\*\*\*\*\*\*\*\*\*\*\*\*\*\*\*\*\*\*\*\*\*

The address of KCPUG is:
KCPUG
P.O. Box 36492
Kansas City MO   64111

The Hot Line is:
(816)-252-7628   24 hrs a day.

Greetings and welcome to KCPUG Bulletin Board.
The Kansas City Pet User Group is one of the largest Commodore user groups in the U.S., and we welcome any user of the Commodore line. The group is a nonprofit group with no ties to any computer company.

Program Up-Load Down-Load
--------------------------------------------------------------------------------

Being able to take programs you have written, put them on a public distribution system, or load other peoples' programs off this system is what microcomputer owners have been waiting for a long time. For the time being, this service is FREE OF CHARGE to anyone with the appropriate Terminal Program (which is also available free of charge). If you are interested in obtaining one of these programs, they are available for IEEE and RS232 modems (Livermore Star, Commodore 8010, Novation Cat, and others). Simply leave me, SYSOP, a message on the bulletin board system under the subject Terminal Programs, and be sure to leave a phone number at which you can be reached.

## What Hardware and Software Do You Need?

To access computer bulletin board systems, and download and use the software they offer, you will need the following:

- A plug-in communications card with an "RS-232C" plug. (Don't worry about the *C* since it is often dropped.)
- A modem (short for *modulator/demodulator*) to connect your computer to the telephone lines.
- A cable to connect your RS-232 plug to the modem.
- Communications software. Sometimes also called a "terminal package." (See Chapter 17.)
- A word processing program to edit and "clean up" the files you download so the programs will run without bombing.
- A telephone, of course.

Please note that these are the requirements for *most* computers. Your own needs may vary. With the Commodore VIC-20 and 64 you will not need a separate communications card but you will need a Commodore modem. With the Apple, you may be able to buy an "all-in-one" communications card with modem and simply plug your phone into your computer. Check with your local dealer in every case.

*A Direct-Connect Modem*

There is no difference in price between a direct connect modem that plugs directly into your telephone jack and an acoustic coupler with rubber cups to hold your telephone handset. But there is a major difference in performance. A direct connect modem is less error prone, and often includes a feature enabling it to dial the telephone automatically. If you can afford it, you should also seriously consider a modem capable of working at both 300 and 1200 baud. An audo-dial feature that lets you send the modem the number you want to dial from your computer is also an important feature, for you are likely to be doing a lot of dialing.

---

**SoftTip:** One of the least expensive direct connect modems on the market is the Volksmodem from Anchor Automation ($70; 300 baud). The firm's direct connect Mark 12 (about $265 at a discount) offers both 300 and 1,200 baud, auto-dial, and many other features. Both are designed to work with a wide variety of computers. But be certain to get the connecting cable that is right for your brand. For your information contact:

> Anchor Automation, Inc.
> 6913 Valjean Avenue
> Van Nuys, CA  91406
> (213) 997-6493

---

*Get a Really Good "Comm" Package*

You will not need a sophisticated word processor to edit the programs and files that you download. (We have recommended a word processing program because you will probably find it much easier to use than a program editor.) However, if you can afford to do so, it may be worth buying more than just a "bare-bones" communications package. Any communications program can be used to access a BBS, but there are a number of features that are especially important:

- The most important feature is one that allows you to capture incoming data in a "buffer"—a portion of your machine's memory that has been set aside by the program as a holding tank. Once captured, you must then be able to write the information to disk. (More advanced programs will automatically write incoming information to disk.)

  Without this feature, you will have to turn your printer on as the program comes in. Then you will have to retype the whole thing.

- A "dialing directory" is another important feature for anyone seriously interested in tapping the wealth of available BBS information. With a dialing directory and modem capable of dialing the phone, you will be able to call up a BBS by pressing a single key. This is an important convenience feature since BBS phone lines are often busy. (Some programs also include a "redial" feature to let you automatically redial the same number. And some advanced programs will let you tell your modem to keep dialing a number until it gets an answer.)

- Though it is not essential, it is also convenient to have a program that will easily let you change your communications settings "on the fly" (while you are connected to the remote system). Please see Chapter 17 for more information on communications settings.

- Finally, a program that supports the Ward Christensen file transfer protocol (also called XMODEM) can also be important. This is the most widely used protocol (set of agreed-upon rules) for sending and receiving programs written in machine language, as opposed to the "text files" of a BASIC program. Either the XMODEM or some other protocol is needed to make sure that noise on the telephone line doesn't ruin the program. And both your system and the remote system must use the same one.

**SoftTip:** There are many excellent communications packages for virtually every brand of computer. But if you own an IBM/PC, you are especially fortunate since you will be able to use PC-TALK III by Andrew Fluegelman. It is a miracle of rare device: a full-featured program at an affordable price. The original version was the first program to be distributed under Mr. Fluegelman's "Freeware" concept whereby users were encouraged to make copies and pass them around. If you liked the program, and most people did, you were asked to send a small donation ($25) to the publisher. Because PC-TALK has been so widely distributed, and because it is written in easy-to-customize BASIC, users have written a number of enhancements and add-on modules and made them available on IBM/PC bulletin boards. If you know a bit of BASIC, you can download these offerings and incorporate them into your own copy of the program.

PC-TALK III is available in both interpreted and compiled BASIC. Most new users will want the interpreted form. (Later, you can buy a BASIC compiler program, if you like, and compile it yourself.) The documentation is excellent and is all on the disk for you to print out. To receive a copy, send a blank-formatted floppy disk to the address below. The requested contribution is $35. Write to:

> PC-TALK III
> The Headlands Press, Inc.
> P.O. Box 862
> Tiburon, CA 94920
>
> Source: TCP204
> CompuServe: 71435,1235

*What's the Next Step?*

Once you have read your modem and software documentation and have your system up and running, the next thing to do is to dial a BBS number and see if a computer answers. You will find a list of several hundred bulletin board numbers for systems all over the country in Appendix D of this book, but you will undoubtedly want to start with a system nearby since the long distance charges will be lower. Long distance charges will always be a major consideration, but when you become more adept at using bulletin boards, you won't have to spend precious cross-country connect time reading instructions on how to use the system.

**SoftTip:** Many bulletin boards will have files listing other BBS phone numbers for you to download. However, since BBS's are maintained as personal hobbies by their SYSOPs, they do tend to come and go. The most reliable list of BBS's is the one compiled by Jim Cambron for his *On-Line Computer Telephone Directory*. Mr. Cambron collects BBS numbers and uses a proprietary testing program to have his computer automatically dial every one. If a modem answers, the computer puts the number in its update file. If the phone has been disconnected, or if there is an indication that the board is no longer functioning, the number is removed. The publication contains command summaries and instructions for using various systems—so you don't have to spend money collecting them yourself—as well as news of the BBS world. To subscribe to the "OLCTD," write to:

OLCTD
P.O. Box 10005 (That's "ten thousand and five.")
Kansas City, MO   64111-9990

One year (4 issues): $9.95
Two years (8 issues): $15.95

CompuServe: 70040,414

*How Bulletin Board Systems Differ*

Bulletin board systems are usually referred to by the specific type of BBS software they use. Most of the names cited in the first sentence of this chapter, for instance, are actually the names of the commercially available BBS programs the SYSOPs use to create their boards. Because the software is different, the commands you must enter when using various systems differ widely. Fortunately, this is less of a problem than it may at first appear, for virtually all BBS's will offer to display a "Help" file listing the needed commands as soon as you sign on. Thereafter, you may be able to request the list again should you get stuck in the system. You will also find that, while the commands required to activate them are different, most boards offer certain basic functions and features.

For example, there will be a command to scan descriptive information about messages that have been posted on the system, to stop and read those that interest you, and to enter a message or request yourself. In many instances, there will also be a command to request a "Main Menu" of the board's files and features. If the board has free software to offer, it will be listed in this "directory," along with instructions on what you must do to download it.

---

**SoftTip:** You will probably be able to use a BBS the first time you sign on. But you will get more out of it and hold down your long distance charges if you familiarize yourself with its commands first. It is thus a good idea to check the list at the back of this book for the different types of systems that are nearest to you, sign on, download the instructions, and print them out. This is the least expensive way to obtain the documentation you need. Since any board using the same software (ABBS, FORUM-80, PMS, etc.) will also use those commands, you will be well prepared when you dial up a long distance system of the same bulletin board "family."

---

*How to Set Your Communications Parameters*

You'll have to check your manual or Chapter 17 to know what all of the terms mean, but most BBS's can operate at 300 baud, and many can handle both 300 and 1200 baud. The higher speed can be important if you will be doing a lot of downloading. At 1200 baud, you will be able to receive a file or program four times faster than at 300 baud, so your long distance charges will be lower. Many lists of BBS numbers will tell you whether a particular system can handle 1200 baud. If no baud rate is given, the first time you call you should set your system for 300 baud. Your modem should be set to "Originate."

Follow the instructions in your software documentation to set your communications parameters to:

300 or 1200 baud
Full duplex
8 Data bits
No parity
1 Stop bit

If those settings don't work or if you find that you are receiving a lot of nonsense characters, try the following settings:

300 or 1200 baud
Full duplex
7 Data bits
Even parity
1 Stop bit

*Making the Connection: Nulls, Line Feeds, and WRU?*
When the bulletin board's modem answers the phone, you will hear a high-pitched tone and your modem will respond with a tone of its own. At that point, you will no longer be able to hear the tones and you will probably begin to see some information appear on your screen. If you don't, hit your <ENTER> key once or twice to let the remote system sense your baud rate and communication parameters and to announce your arrival.

One of the first questions you will be asked before you can get down to business will probably be, "HOW MANY NULLS DO YOU NEED?" A "null" is a time-wasting signal of about 30 milliseconds that is transmitted by the host system at the end of each line to give the printing element on a teletype-like terminal a chance to return to its far left starting position before printing the next line. If you are using a personal computer, you don't need any nulls, so type in *0* and hit <ENTER>.

Next, you may be asked whether you need "line feeds." A line feed is a signal sent at the end of each line to make it scroll up the screen or to "feed" an additional line to your printer. Either you or the host system must add a line feed, or the text of one line will be printed right on top of the previous line. Check your software documentation to see if your system can be set to add its own line feeds or if it adds them automatically.

The system will then ask you to type in your name and where you are calling from. At that point you will be signed on. The next thing you see will probably be a welcoming message from the SYSOP, followed by some information about the board and how to get help and instructions. As mentioned earlier, it is a good idea to download all of the instructions for a particular type of BBS, print them out, and save them for reference the next time you call a member of that BBS "family."


*RCPM Systems: You Are the Console*
The bulletin boards we have discussed so far are true bulletin board systems. That is, they present you with menus and allow you to move around, read files, leave messages, and download software by entering your menu selections or simple commands. There is another type of system, however, that can best be described as one that lets you take control of the host computer and run it just as if you were sitting at its keyboard instead of your own. The vast majority of these facilities are called "remote CP/M" systems or RCPM's. And almost all of them have free CP/M software files for users to download. Here is the kind of thing you can expect to see when logging onto an RCPM:

Welcome to MYSYS of Anytown, USA!

The system uses the PMMI modem, with baud rates of 110, 300, 450, and 600. This system has 4 drives (A thru D), with open User Areas 0 thru 9. Feel free to "explore."

Most public-domain software distributed by both CPMUG and SIG/M (the two major CP/M-compatible software libraries) is available on request. Leave a note for SYSOP telling which files you want and they'll be there as soon as possible.

Booting system . . .

Anytown, USA  RCPM System Ver. 2.6F

[Requests for name and location not shown.]

Pleased to meet you!

To learn the CP/M commands, type "CPMINFO".

To learn more about this system, type "HELP".

To locate files, TYPE the file INDEX.DOC
Note that filenames consist of 2 parts, which should be separated by a period in commands.

Entering CP/M . . .

Welcome to my remote Z-80 CP/M system. On this system you are now the CONSOLE.

A0>

When you see this last prompt (A0>), you are ready to enter any legal CP/M command. If you have been on the system before, you may know which drives and user areas contain what material. But if you don't, you can type INDEX.DOC or a similar filename to tell the system to run the desired program. (Notice that you are actually commanding the remote system to display a file or load and run a program, as opposed to choosing an item from a menu. The effect will be the same, but the menu-driven systems may be easier to use.) Here is the kind of thing you can expect to see when you ask for an overview of the disks and user areas:

        A0>TYPE INDEX.DOC

            ——> LISTING FILE: INDEX.DOC

This is a general index of where various types of files are stored on this system. User numbers are shown in the left column, and the four drives across the page. Files are located by type or source as shown, but the arrangement is subject to update as contents change. This is current as of MM/DD/YY.

| Usr ! Drive A | ! Drive B | ! Drive C | ! Drive D |
|---|---|---|---|
| 0 ! System, Help & ! BBS Numbers | ! SIG/M Vol 10 ! | ! Misc new files ! | ! Newsletters, ! More .DOC |

| Usr | ! Drive A | ! Drive B | ! Drive C | ! Drive D |
|---|---|---|---|---|
| 1 | ! SQ/USQ/FLS file | ! SIG/M Vol 9 | ! SIG/M Vol 26 | ! SIG/M Vol 11 |
| 2 | ! CPMUG Vol 48 ! ("C" Programs) | ! SIG/M Vol 18 | ! CPMUG Vol 49 | ! RBBS Progs. |
| 3 | ! New "C" Modem ! program "YAM" | ! CPMUG Vol 23 ! (STOIC) | ! CP/M Enhances | ! Modem progs. |
| 4 | ! UNIX C files | ! SIG/M Vol 6 | ! Misc stuff. | ! Smartmodem ! programs |
| 5 | ! Temporary Area | ! BDS-C Util's | ! SIG/M Vol 39 | ! Ham & Packet |
| 6 | ! SIG/M Vol 43 | ! SIG/M Vol 19 ! Pascal-Z V1 | ! SIG/M Vol 56 ! Music System | ! |
| 7 | ! FORTH programs ! (assorted) | ! | ! | ! |
| 8 | ! | ! | ! | ! |
| 9 | ! | ! | ! | ! |

See the next section for an explanation of CPMUG, SIG/M, and Volume numbers.

**SoftTip:** For an exceptionally complete listing of the RCPM systems that are up and running in North America, you might want to subscribe to a publication called *User's Guide to CP/M Systems and Software.* Contact the following address for more information:

TUG, Inc.
Box 3050
Stanford, CA 94305

*Over 2,500 Free CP/M Programs*

There is no way to know how many free programs are available on the hundreds of bulletin boards in North America. However, it is known that there are at least 2,500 free CP/M programs, and as pointed out in the opening message for MYSYS of Anytown, USA, most of them are available for the price of a phone call to an RCPM system. The reason it is possible to get something of a handle on the number of CP/M programs is that at least two national users groups collect and catalogue software written and made available to the public by their members.

Since reviewing the names of the programs and their descriptions in a printed catalogue is likely to be less expensive than reading about them while you are online, you might want to contact these organizations and ask about their latest catalogues of free CP/M software. The groups are CPMUG ("CP/M Users Group") and SIG/M ("Special Interest Group/ Microcomputer") and both catalogue their programs in "volumes." In this case, "volume" refers to a unit of magnetic storage (i.e., a single floppy disk), but you can think of them as "book" volumes. Both groups have over 100 volumes in their libraries.

**SoftTip:** Since each program is assigned to a particular volume, you will always know where to find it. Thus, if you knew the contents of SIG/M Vol. 43, you could count on finding the same programs in that volume, regardless of the RCPM system you happen to be using at the time. The two groups have most of the same programs, but the volumes in which they are located are different. Here is a rough and ready way to make the translations:

### Volume Number Cross Reference Table

| SIG/M | CPMUG |
|-------|-------|
| 1 | 55 |
| 2 | 56 |
| 11 | 57 |

*Note:* From here on add 54 to the SIG/M volume number to determine the CPMUG volume with the same programs.

Here are the addresses to write to obtain a catalogue of the volume listings. The publications may cost from $6 to $10, though prices may have changed since new volumes are constantly being added, swelling the size of the catalogues. These groups can also supply their volumes on disk for a nominal charge, but you should verify that disks are available in a format your computer can use. Be sure to enclose a stamped, self-addressed envelope when you contact them:

CP/M Users Group (CPMUG)
1651 Third Avenue
New York, NY   10028


SIG/M
Box 97
Iselin, NJ   08830

*Note:* SIG/M *programs* are available on eight-inch disks. The cost is $6 for the first disk; $5 for each additional disk in the same order. Add $3 per order for overseas shipping.

Most programs are written to run under what is now called CP/M-80, the original version of CP/M for eight-bit computers. However, at least one organization has converted or otherwise translated many of these to run under MS-DOS and PC-DOS. Over 100 volumes of CP/M-80 software and more than 20 volumes of translated MS-DOS software are available from the New York Amateur Computing Club. CP/M-86 programs are also available. (The IBM/PC and MS-DOS volumes are in the "PC-Blue" collection and are available on disk for about $6.) For a 200-page catalogue, send $10 ($15 for overseas shipment) and a stamped, self-addressed envelope to:

> New York Amateur Computing Club
> P.O. Box 106
> Church Street Station
> New York, NY 10008

---

**SoftTip:** One of the most extensive and immediately available collections of CP/M software can be found on a system in Toronto. The board has over 25 megabytes worth of files online at all times. The annual membership fee to access this vast library is $30. The board has two numbers: (416) 231-9538 and (416) 231-1262.

Much of this software is also available at a nominal cost on disk. And a printed catalogue may be available as well. Contact:

> SYSOP
> MICROCOMP Services
> 4691 Dundas Street West
> Islington, Ontario M9A

---

*What Kinds of Programs Are Available?*

A great deal of the public domain CP/M software consists of system utility programs—helpful routines that can make working with your computer more convenient. For example, a program called COM-PARE.COM will compare any two files byte for byte, enabling you to make sure that the two copies match perfectly. FIND.COM lets you search for occurrences of words or phrases ("strings") in any of the documents (ASCII text files) you have written. A program called UN-ERA.COM will "un-erase" a file that you have erased, as long as nothing else has been added to the disk. PASSWORD.ASM allows you to "password protect" any file. The file will show up on the directory of the disk, but no one will be able to access it unless they key in the password you have assigned.

A sampling of other public domain CP/M files you may find useful or interesting includes:

**Description**

*CP/M File*

ADVENT-X.COM     The popular game, *Adventure* (X-pert level). Other files are required for the full game. A "B.COM" (beginners' level) version is also available.

CHESS.COM     Just what you'd expect. Also known as ZCHESS or Z80CHESS.

FILEFIND7.COM     Find any filename, regardless of drive or user area.

LABELS.BAS     Prints labels (one or two across).

MBREM.BAS     Removes "REMark" statements in BASIC programs to save disk storage space.

XMODEM.DOC     How to download programs from RCPMs.

*MODEM7 and On-Disk Copies of CP/M Programs*

As mentioned earlier, when you are downloading BASIC or other programs that exist as text files, you will not need to use any special file transfer error-checking protocols. A standard communications package will be fine. If there is an error in transmission, you will be able to spot it relatively easily by simply looking at the listing of the program.

However, when a program on an RCPM exists in binary form as "machine" or "assembly" language, then a sophisticated error-checking protocol is essential. Any file with an extension of ".COM" or ".ASM," for example, requires this kind of transmission verification. Both you and the remote system must be using the same communications program with the same protocols in order for things to work correctly.

The communications/file transfer program most RCPM systems use is called MODEM7, and it's free. This is the seventh version of the original MODEM program written by Ward Christensen to implement what have become known as "the Ward Christensen file transfer protocols." MODEM7 was written by Mark M. Zeiger and James K. Mills. Other, earlier versions are also available, as are versions that have been customized for particular computers. All are compatible with each other.

You can use a standard communications program to obtain a copy of MODEM7 from most RCPM systems, but this involves some sophisticated file manipulation. It is much better to obtain a copy on disk from a local users' group, from one of the national CP/M groups mentioned earlier, or from one of the sources listed in the following section. In most cases, your only cost will be the price of the disk and perhaps a small duplication charge. If you get it from a users' group, even those expenses will be eliminated.

---

**SoftTip:** Sometimes you will find a system that uses another file transfer program/protocol instead of, or as well as, MODEM7. Don't worry about it now, but should you ever encounter "REACH," "COMMX" or "AMCALL," you will be able to obtain the software you need on disk from:

REACH
The Software Toolworks
14478 Glorietta Drive
Sherman Oaks, CA   91423

(About $20; for Heath and Zenith systems.)

COMMX
Hawkeye Grafix
23914 Mobile
Canoga Park, CA   91307

(About $100; for all CP/M computers.)

AMCALL
Micro-Call Services
9655-M Homestead Court
Laurel, MD   20810

(About $95; for all CP/M computers.)

---

*Where to Get MODEM7 and Other Free CP/M Programs*
CPMUG and SIG/M can usually supply MODEM7 and most CP/M

programs in a number of different disk formats. But you may also want to contact the individuals and companies listed below for your particular brand of computer. As a courtesy, send a self-addressed, stamped envelope with your information request. There may be a small duplication charge, but where the cost is unknown, you might consider sending a blank, formatted disk and return postage. Some sources may send back the disk with the program you want and a request for a small amount of money to cover expenses. Sending a disk beforehand may speed up the process.

*TRS-80*

Mr. J. Cramer
Box 28606
Columbus, OH   43228-0606

Catalogue of free CP/M and free non-CP/M programs to run on Radio Shack computers.

*Heath/Zenith*

Mr. Robert Todd
1121 Briarwood
Bensalem, PA   19020

Complete CPMUG, SIG/M, and CP/M for IBM/PC owners with "Baby Blue" Z80 boards in virtually all Heath/Zenith formats. Write for details.

*Osborne*

The Software Anthology
Workman Associates
112 Marion Avenue
Pasadena, CA   91106

Refined and improved public domain CP/M programs for purchase.

FOGHORN
Box 3474
Daly City, CA   94015

Monthly newsletter of a large First Osborne Group. Annual subscription: $24. Be sure to ask for the most recently updated back issue containing Osborne CP/M library listings. It may be November 1982 or a more recent issue. Also, the April 1983 issue contains names and addresses of many Osborne users around the country with software collections for you to send for.

*Kaypro/Xerox 820*

Mr. John Palmer
Sheepshead Software
P.O. Box 486
Boonville, CA   95415

Complete CPMUG library (90 + volumes). $2.00 for complete catalogue listing. $10 per disk volume (you specify). Assembled, ready-to-run MODEM7, on request with Volume 84.

*Vector Graphic*

L. M. Hammer
San Mateo Camera and Photo Supply
1933 South El Camino Real
San Mateo, CA   94402

MODEM7 for Vector Graphic computers.

*Intertech Data System Superbrain*

Mr. David Steidley, President
Omnitech
50 Baltusrol Way
Short Hills, NJ    07078

MODEM7 on disk for $7.50. Other Superbrain programs as well.

*DEC computers*

Mr. Larry Cole

10228 Parkwood Drive
Kensington, MD    20895

A version of MODEM7 for DEC computers. Send $5 for disk, copying, and postage.

*NEC computers*

Mr. James Love
Awm American Micros
3493 North Main Street
College Park, GA    30337

MODEM7 and several public domain programs. Contact by mail only.

---

**SoftTip:** There are two minor difficulties involved with obtaining free CP/M software on disk. One is the need to get the correct disk format. The other concerns the fact that most of the programs are distributed in "volumes." You may not be interested in all of the programs on a particular volume, but you may have to buy several volumes to get the programs you do want. Elliam Associates, however, may be able to help you. The firm can make most public domain CP/M software available in almost any disk format. And it offers "collections" of the most popular programs drawn from several volumes.

Prices range from $10 to $22, depending upon the size of the collection and the type of disk required. Elliam also offers a disk conversion service. Send them your disk and they will put a copy of its contents on any other type of disk for $5 and return both the copy and the original. Brand name software is also available. For a free catalogue, contact:

Elliam Associates
24000 Bessemer Street
Woodland Hills, CA    91367
(213) 348-4278

*Note:* See Chapter 8 for information about the on-disk computer magazine index offered by the same firm.

*Free MS-DOS and PC-DOS Software for the IBM*

Although there are as yet no libraries of free IBM/PC software to rival those of the CP/M groups, the number of programs available on IBM-dedicated BBS's is already large and rapidly growing. Here are just a few of the free programs you can expect to find on various bulletin board systems:

### A Sampling of Free IBM/PC Software

| Program | Description |
| --- | --- |
| SD20 | Sorted directory lister for DOS 2.0. |
| 123PATCH | Documentation to unlock Lotus (123.EXE) for copying to hard disk. |
| JPGHEX. | Converts binary files to/from a readable ASCII format. Use this program if you want to transmit or receive a .COM or .EXE file. |
| SDHEX | Diskette directory sort utility for DOS 2.0. |
| SDDOC | Documentation for SDHEX. |
| DIABLO | Interface to support a serial printer. Example: Diablo 1620 or 1640. |
| SCROLOCK | Supports the Scroll Lock key, a much more desirable alternative to CTRL-NUMLOCK. See SCROLDOC for documentation. |
| MAIL1 | Basic mailing list generation program. |
| GRAFNEW | Lets you plot curves on an Epson or other dot matrix printer. |
| PEEKPOKE | Tips for peeking and poking around in PC memory locations. |
| FASTDISK | A BASIC program used to generate SPEEDUP. COM. Only needed if you are still using DOS 1.0. |
| BIORHYTHM | Charts your biorhythm on the printer or screen. |
| PACMAN | You guessed it! |
| HOST | A BASIC program to let your computer answer the phone and allow the caller to use your system. |
| SPOOLER | A print spooling program to let you print one file while you work on another. |

**SoftTip:** The PC Software Interest Group (PC-SIG) offers at least 38 disks full of public domain programming for the IBM Personal Computer. There are over 400 programs, including a RAM-disk print spooler, games, utilities, spreadsheet templates, graphics, financial calculation, education, database retrieval and filing, and communications. The software has been collected from users groups and bulletin boards and sells for $5 per disk.

You can get a printed directory of the programs each disk contains for $3; order a set of the 10 most popular disks for a total of $50; or buy the whole 38-disk collection for $180. For more information, contact:

PC Software Interest Group
1556 Halford Avenue, Suite 130P
Santa Clara, CA   95051
(408) 247-6303

**SoftTip:** If you own a Texas Instruments home computer and you subscribe to The Source, you will find a special TI users group called TEXNET with over 150 downloadable programs. TI computers can receive special graphics information when using The Source, but you must tell The Source that you are using a TI machine when you open your account. Contact your local TI dealer or phone the Communications Marketing Department at The Source (800) 336-3366 for more information.

*Free Programs for Apple Users*

There are over 3,000 free programs for Apple computers. As with most other major brands of computers, many of them are available for downloading on Apple-dedicated bulletin board systems. And most are obtainable on floppy disk. Possibly the most complete list of what is available and where is the *Catalog of Public Domain Software for the Apple*, available for $2 from the Apple Avocation Alliance in Cheyenne, Wyoming. This firm also makes the software available on disk (there are over 100 disks, plus 10 volumes of Pascal programs). Blank disks are sold in packages of 10 for $1.80 apiece and there is a $1 copying charge per disk.

The disks are arranged by subject and include Art (and graphics), Business and Finance, Education and Schools, Math and Statistics, an Apple Tutor, a *Demon Adventure* game, and a variety of utility programs. As with all free software, the quality is variable. But at these prices, you've very little to lose. The $2 for the catalogue may be deducted from the first order of $20 or more. An annual subscription for the monthly catalogue is $3. Contact:

> Apple Avocation Alliance, Inc.
> 2111 Central Avenue
> Cheyenne, WY   82001
> (307) 632-8561

A firm called Appleware Inc. also offers public domain Apple programs on disk at about $1 per program. Since each disk contains 60 programs, the cost is $60 apiece. Disks 1 through 3 contain Business, Education, Music, Data Base, Graphics, Finance and other programs. Disk 4 is devoted to Games, Disk 5, to Utilities, and Disk 6, to Graphics. Other disks may also be available. Discounts are offered for the purchase of three disks or more. Contact:

> Appleware, Inc.
> 6400 Hayes Street
> Hollywood, FL   33024
> (800) 327-8664
> (305) 987-8665, in Florida

A firm called American Software Publishing offers over 2,500 public domain Apple programs on disk in its Freeloader 500 Software Library. Disks are packaged in seven three-ring binders, each of which contains up to 10 disks. Each binder is devoted to a separate subject (Business and Finance, Graphics and Sound, Utilities, Games, Education, Home Management, and Adventure), and each sells for $75. The entire seven-volume collection is available for $500. There is a $20 source book containing program listings (for you to type in yourself) of each binder's contents. Contact:

> American Software Publishing, Co.
> 1010 16th Street NW
> Washington, DC   20037

*Bulletin Board Etiquette*
Whenever you use a bulletin board system, it is important to remember that it is offered to you and to everyone else out of the goodness of some individual's heart. The amount of work, let alone the financial investment, required to bring up a board and keep it running is stagger-

ing. Yet unbelievably, some sick individuals make a practice of calling bulletin boards and deliberately trying to erase files, causing the host program to crash, or otherwise wreaking havoc with the system. Less virulent but equally noisome are the legions of callers who do nothing but download programs and files without ever offering anything in return. On some systems, the "takers" outnumber the "givers" by 20 to 1, according to SYSOP caller logs.

Although that is probably a reasonable approximation of the ratio of takers to givers in most other areas of life as well, it need not apply to BBS's. If you are like most computer owners, you probably are not a trained programmer and thus may not be able to upload a program of your own. No one expects you to. But at the same time, ask yourself, What can *I* contribute to the board?

It might be a program you found on some other BBS that you think other callers would be interested in. It might be some tip you've discovered in using your hardware or software or a source or person to contact for hard-to-find information that could be of help to others. It could be a good joke, a poem, a recipe, or even a short story or essay. Whatever you can give will be enough. But give something.

# Part III

# —TOOLCHEST—

# ...13...

# How to Buy a Word Processing Program

If personal computer software is a jungle, then word processing and word-related products undoubtedly constitute its thickest and possibly most hazardous part. There are so many things to consider, so many ways to go wrong. It's so easy to get bogged down in nonessentials that, if you aren't careful, you can easily end up buying a program with far more features—at a far greater price—than you will ever need or use.

Truly, you can buy a word processor for $50 or a best seller for $500 and *never notice the difference*. It all depends on how you plan to use the program. The two products will not be equivalent. Far from it. But if you aren't going to be flying to Paris, there's no point in buying a Learjet when a little two-seater, single-engine plane will do. Equally important, the two-seater will have a much simpler control panel and be much easier to learn and to fly. On the other hand, if your computer will be used intensively for a wide variety of word processing tasks, you'll want all the features and power that can be packed onto a floppy disk.

*The Most Popular Application*

Virtually every computer owner eventually buys a word processing program, and it's easy to see why. You may not have any use for an electronic spreadsheet, a database management system, or other specialized programs, but almost everyone needs to write a letter or a report now and then. Even an inexpensive word processing program with fairly limited features can make those chores much easier. Sometimes, word processing can even make them enjoyable as well.

This chapter will show you how to pick a word processing program that will best suit your needs. We'll look at the features that are available and what they can mean to you, and we'll focus on the critical points to look for when reading an ad or talking to a salesperson. Because word processing has such wide appeal and because the concept may be new to you, we have also included a section designed to show you what it's like to actually use one of these programs. Then, in the following chapter, we will look at two other word-related programs: spelling checkers and mailing list programs.

299

## What Is It Good For?

Next to telecommunications and the ability to access remote databases, word processing is the best reason to buy a personal computer. For many individuals and companies, it may be *the* best reason. There is no other application that so decisively places a computer's power in your hands. Nothing else can boost an office worker's productivity by 200%, 300%, or more—immediately. And nothing else can make it so easy for a manager, an executive, a student, or a writer to communicate with fellow human beings.

That may sound a bit cosmic, but it is an aspect of word processing that must not be overlooked. Pencils, pens, and typewriters are a vast improvement over the writing implements that preceded them. But each still represents a barrier that must be overcome by anyone who wants to put something on paper. How many ideas, suggestions, and proposals have gone unrecorded because of the unappealing prospect of writing everything out by hand? How many letters have gone unwritten because typing a first draft, making corrections, and then typing the entire text again was such an involved process?

*Superconductors of Thought*

Just as different metals resist the flow of electricity to varying degrees, so does every writing implement offer some kind of resistance to the free flow of ideas from your brain to the physical page. But the resistance offered by word processors is several orders of magnitude less than anything else you can use. A word processing program can turn your personal computer into nothing less than a superconductor of thought. It can't ensure that you'll always have something to say, but it will make communicating it virtually effortless. Once you have used one, you will never, never go back to a typewriter.

*Getting a Handle on Word Processing*

On a more mundane note, perhaps the easiest way to answer the question of what word processing software is good for is to say that it will enable your computer and printer to do everything that a typewriter does—and much, much more. Like a typewriter, a word processor can easily be used to produce reports, memos, order entry forms, and letters. Unlike even the most advanced typewriter, however, a word processor will let you do the following:

- Include bold print or italics, or any of 20 or more typestyles in the same document without ever changing the printing element.

- Assemble a document from several stock paragraphs without re-typing a single word.
- Produce a first draft, make corrections, and produce a final draft, retyping only the corrected material.
- Use your computer as a typesetter and save up to 40% of the cost of conventional typesetting.
- Prepare memos, reports, and letters to be sent across the country or around the world in seconds over ordinary telephone lines through "electronic mail." Send and receive Telex and TWX messages the same way.

There is much more, of course. Taken together, the features offered by this kind of software are so extensive that calling them "typewriting programs" is woefully inadequate. A new term clearly had to be invented. Thus, with its etymological roots firmly planted in the more numbers-oriented "data processing," the term "word processing" seemed logical.

## The Main Idea

The concept that unlocks the many splendors of word processing is the "captured keystroke." With a conventional typewriter, when you hit a key, a corresponding character appears on the page and that's the end of it. With a word processor, the character appears on the screen, and once that happens, you're in business. The two keystrokes require exactly the same amount of effort. But because the keystroke on the computer generated a pattern of electric bits instead of putting ink on a page, the character it produced can be manipulated, or in computer terms, "processed."

The character can be moved around as though it were floating on a film of oil. It can be pushed to the right or left to make room for another character. It can be picked up and moved to a new location. It can be sent out over the telephone line. But, most important of all, it can be "captured" by being recorded on a floppy disk. Once captured, there is never again any need to enter a keystroke for that character.

The character can also be sent to a dot matrix printer. Since each letter or "character" has a specific ASCII number, the printer will always know what to produce when it receives a particular bit pattern. Send it an $A$, and it will print an $A$. However, if the printer has been told, "Print everything in italics until you hear otherwise," the machine will print the $A$ in italics. Similarly, if the printer is told, "Here's a $2$, but print it half a line below the $H$ in $H_2O$," that's what it will do. The printer has to have these capabilities built into it, of course. The point here is that the same bit pattern is always sent to the printer for a particular character, but the printer can make it appear in many different styles.

That's it. That is all there is to the basic idea behind word processing, or for that matter, to virtually everything else a computer does. Where things get complicated is in the number and variety of manipulations it is possible to perform once the keystroke has been captured.

### *What's It Like to Use a Word Processing Program?*

The best way to understand word processing software and learn the special vocabulary used to describe its features is to compare the steps you would follow using a typewriter to those you would follow using a word processor in producing the same letter or report. With a typewriter, there are usually three stages. The first draft is typed. Then someone goes over it, crossing out words, drawing arrows to rearrange paragraphs, changing phrases, and possibly even clipping paragraphs from another report and taping them to the current one, along with cryptic instructions regarding what the typist is supposed to do with them. Finally, everything gets retyped in its final, and ideally, error-free, form.

With a word processor there are three stages as well: typing, editing and formatting, and printing. One of the advantages of word processing is that you may type, edit, and format at the same time. For the sake of clarity, we will look at each process individually.

---

**SoftTip:** Word processing programs are sometimes described as "text editors" and are said to have three modules. The modules are the text editor, formatter, and output or printing. Unfortunately, "text editor" is a very slippery term since it is also used to describe products or DOS modules that are used for writing programs. As such, they have none of the features of a real word processor. If a program is described as a "text editor," proceed with caution. It may not be what you're looking for. The only way to be certain is to check carefully the features the program provides.

---

**SoftTip:** Since word processing is the one type of software that virtually every computer owner will be interested in, it seems appropriate to go into a bit more detail than might otherwise be the case. The following section assumes that you know next to nothing about word processing. If you are already familiar with the basic concepts, you may want to jump ahead to the "Extra Features" or the "Critical Points" sections.

## Getting Things Set Up

*Typewriter*

After you turn a typewriter on and twirl in a sheet of paper, the next step is to check the margin and tab settings and the line spacing. When setting the margins, you are obviously limited by how wide the typewriter is. With a word processor, you boot the program and select an option from a menu to tell the system that you want to begin typing. The screen will clear to represent a blank piece of paper. There may be a menu listing some of your options outside of this typing area, and more than likely there will be a margin line (also called a *ruler line*) at the top.

Tabs and margins may be set by moving the cursor to the desired point on the ruler line and pressing a key. But, more than likely, you will enter a command and be prompted to enter the desired numbers on the line. You might do the same thing for the line spacing. Some programs also display a *status line* to keep you informed about the name of the file you are working with, the amount of memory remaining in the machine, whether the "caps lock" is on, etc. One particularly valuable feature to look for on a status line is a counter to tell you what line and what column the cursor is on. The numbers should change automatically as you move the cursor.

*How a Word Processor Differs*

*Commands and Help.* To set the margins on a typewriter, you physically move the margin markers on the machine. Since you can't do that on a computer, you have to issue a command to the system that says, "I'd like to set the left margin now." This is an important point, for, with the exception of straight typing, everything you do with a word processor is usually preceded by a command. One of the major differences among programs is the ease with which you can enter commands: How many keys do you have to hit? How easy are they to remember? Does the program provide a "Help" menu to remind you of what commands are needed to accomplish what you want to do?

*Number of Columns (Characters) on a Line.* In addition, word processors differ in the number of characters they will let you type on a single line. Some are limited to 80 columns. Others may give you as many as 256 columns. Since a screen can't display more than 80 columns at once, a *horizontal scroll* feature is necessary to see what has been written beyond the eightieth column. Usually, you just hold down the space bar to make the cursor keep moving to the right. As it moves, text scrolls off the screen to the left, just as it moves off the top or bottom of the screen when you scroll vertically.

For most letters and reports produced on 8½″ × 11″ typing paper, 80 columns are fine. But particularly in businesses, there are many times when more characters per line are essential. When that's the case, the firm will buy a wide-track printer capable of producing perhaps 132 characters or more per line.

So what's the benefit of a program that gives you 256 columns? The answer: *compressed printing.* Most dot matrix printers are capable of producing regular pica-style letters just like a typewriter. But many can also produce compressed letters that let you put more characters on a line. The best-selling Epson MX-80 can only use paper that is 8½ inches wide. In its normal mode, it will print 80 pica-sized characters per line. But in its compressed print mode, it will produce 132 characters per line.

*Is What You See, What You Get?* Another important difference among word processors concerns the line spacing you choose. Some programs will let you select single, double, or triple spacing before you begin typing and display the text in exactly that way. Others don't give you that option. Instead, they display everything as single-spaced text. If you want the printed copy to be double spaced, you must tell the printer to print it that way at the appropriate time.

This distinction carries over into other aspects of the program. The terms are not at all helpful, but a word processing program that is *character oriented* will not show you what the final text will look like. One that is *screen oriented* will display text with the paragraphs indented, with double or single spacing, with the text divided into pages, and so forth.

---

**SoftTip:** You might think that by not including all those empty lines, copy produced with a character-oriented word processor would take up less space on disk. But that is not really the way it works. In both character-oriented and screen-oriented word processors, text is stored as a continuous stream of ASCII numbers.

There are no blank lines. The difference is in the programming itself. A screen-oriented word processor has instructions built into it or recorded with the file that tell it to display a certain number of characters and then scroll up one, two, or three lines before displaying the next line.

Unless the price is absolutely irresistible, there are two main reasons to *avoid* buying a character-oriented word processor. First, it is obviously much easier to work with text when you can see what it will actually look like in its printed form. Second, treating text as a block that is formatted only when it is printed is the way computers in the past have usually handled things. The fact that a word processing program uses this approach may be an indication that its author is a hard-core computerist. And since such writers do not typically produce easy-to-use programs, a character-oriented approach can serve as a warning that the rest of the program may not be user friendly.

**SoftTip:** Some programs compromise on this feature, which is almost worse than not offering it at all. With such a program, you may see an approximation of what your text will look like when it is printed. But you may not be able to tell where the pages will be divided or exactly how the text will be adjusted. The acid test is to enter a page of text, print it, and then compare it to how the file appears on the screen—before you buy the program.

### Centering and Entering the Text

*Typewriter*
When you're ready to roll with a typewriter, one of the first things you may do is to center a title on the page. Normally, you'll tab over from the center of the margin line and backspace once for each two characters in the words you want to center. Then you'll start typing, hitting the <RETURN> key at the end of each line and hyphenating words as necessary. To underline a word, you type it, backspace, and hit the underline key the appropriate number of times. To go back to the top or down to the bottom of the page, you turn the platen. To return to a previous page, you remove the one you are working on and twirl in the page you want.

*How a Word Processor Differs*

Centering a title on a word processor is a simple matter of typing the text and entering a command. The computer automatically figures out where the title must go to be centered between the margins you have set. To begin entering text with a word processor, you usually hit the tab key if you are going to indent the first paragraph and then you just start typing.

An experienced typist will notice the difference immediately. The keystrokes are the same, but the letters appear so much *faster*. There is no need for a typing ball or letter stalk to move forward and strike a ribbon. The response is (or should be) instantaneous.

Companies that produce word processing products shy away from making any specific claims regarding speed improvement. But a first-rate typist can easily double and probably triple his or her speed. This is an often overlooked aspect, but it is one of the major factors that make word processors such superconductors. It is one of the reasons why their resistance to "thought flow" is so low.

The speed with which a character appears is a function of many things. Some programs may be fast enough by themselves. But since some computers are limited in how fast they can display characters, many word processing programs will be equipped with a *type-ahead buffer*. This means that the program will accept characters as fast as you can type them, even if it can't quite get them on the screen as fast.

---

**SoftTip:** Because the speed with which a word processing program responds is so important, it may be a good idea to try to find a program written in assembly language, or better yet, an assembly language program written specifically for your machine. This will give you the maximum amount of speed and will usually ensure that the program takes advantage of any unique features or capabilities found in your brand of computer.

---

When you reach the end of a line while entering text on a word processor, you do not have to hit the <RETURN> key. You merely keep on typing. The system will automatically move the cursor back to the left and down to the next line. This feature is called *word wrap* because the words automatically wrap around the margin and onto the next line. The only time it is necessary to hit the <RETURN> key is when you reach the end of a paragraph. That will cause the system to scroll the text up and put your cursor on a fresh line.

With most word processors, you do not have to worry about hyphenation. Most have an *autohyphenation* feature that will cause the words to break at the proper place and insert the hyphen for you. (Though it's always a good idea to check to make sure that the system has done it properly.) Usually, you will be able to turn the feature on or off at will.

*"Hard" and "Soft" Carriage Returns and Hyphens.* As you know, everything you see on your computer's screen has its own ASCII code number. But there are also ASCII codes for things that you don't see. They are invisible within the word processing program, but they are there nonetheless. A good example of a hidden ASCII code is what happens when you hit <RETURN> or <ENTER> at the end of a paragraph. Most systems will tack two invisible codes onto the last line. One code is called a "Carriage Return" and the other is called a "Line Feed." Though neither may be visible, the system knows they are there, and it knows that they mean "Move the cursor all the way over to the left (carriage return) and scroll up one line."

In the language of word processing, this is called a *hard carriage* return because it is "permanent" until you remove it. The system will always respect it. This is in contrast to a *soft carriage* return of the sort that are caused by word wrap. There are also *hard* and *soft hyphens.* Both look alike on the screen. But the ones added automatically by the system are represented by a different ASCII code than the "hard" ones you type in from the keyboard. The machine will always respect a hard hyphen. But it will remove its own soft hyphens and rejoin the words as necessary when text is adjusted.

---

**SoftTip:** If you ever want to see what your word processing program is hiding, create a text file and save it to disk. Then go into DOS and enter the command to list or type the file. You will see all manner of strange things, never revealed by your word processor. If you consult your computer manual, you will find that each strange character on the screen corresponds to a particular ASCII code.

---

The concept of everything on the screen, visible and invisible, having an ASCII code number is crucial to understanding word processing software and the features it offers. It is particularly important because of the way ASCII codes can control your printer. For example, if you want your printer to print a word in boldface type, you've got to send it an ASCII code (or codes) that says, "Begin bold printing." By the same token, when you want it to stop bold printing, you must send it a code that says, "Okay, that's enough. Back to normal type, please."

Most word processing programs let you enter these control codes just as you would regular letters. Usually, all you must do is hold down a key marked <CONTROL> and hit whatever letter your program uses to signify the start of the end of bold printing. Called *control characters*, these codes appear on your screen immediately before and immediately after the words you want to have printed in bold, or italics, or some other special type style. What actually appears on the screen will differ with the program, but it will usually consist of a letter preceded by a caret or some other character to set it off from the rest of the text. They will not appear on the printout and they will not occupy a space. Because they are embedded in your text, they are often called *embedded codes*.

---

**SoftTip:** Because one embedded code turns a feature on and the other turns it off, it is important to use the codes in pairs. Otherwise, an entire page or more may end up being underlined or printed in italics. A few programs will help you avoid this by informing you that the "off" code of the pair is missing. They will then tell you where the "on" code is and possibly take you to that point. You can then insert the correct code.

---

**SoftTip:** One frequent use of embedded characters is to tell the printer to underline a section of text. Unlike a typewriter, it is usually not possible actually to show underlining on the screen. The reason is that an underlined character, be it on a typewriter or a computer, consists of three keystrokes: the character itself, a backspace, and the underline character. The problem is that, on a computer, backspacing wipes out the character. You can display a character, you can display an underline by itself, but you cannot display an underlined character. Hence, the embedded printer codes.

---

*Printer Compatibility.* Control codes are important for a number of additional reasons. First, and most important, they may *not* be standardized. The software house can decide to use any control code it pleases to signify the start and end of bold print, for example. That has next to no effect on you as you use the program, but the specific control codes chosen are of vital concern to your printer. If the program uses one ASCII number (or combination) to signify bold print, but the printer expects to see something else to activate that feature, then the word processing program and the printer will be incompatible.

Printer/computer/software incompatibilities have probably been responsible for more frustration and wasted manhours than any other aspect of personal computing. The example given above doesn't begin to indicate the depth and complexity of the problem. Fortunately, you may never have to delve into it. For most people, it is enough to be aware that the potential exists and therefore to proceed with extreme caution.

---

**SoftTip:** If you are ever in a situation where you cannot get a printer to work, don't waste your time entering the labyrinth of control codes and default values. Pick up the phone and immediately call your dealer. If that is not possible, call the software house and politely ask them for detailed instructions on what you should do.

Most firms will be happy to oblige, but one firm in particular deserves special mention. Camilo Wilson, author of *Volkswriter 1.2* ($195) for the IBM/PC and president of Lifetree Software, has announced that his firm will support any printer not already supported by the program. The user need only mail in the printer manual to:

> Lifetree Software
> 177 Webster St.
> Monterey, CA   93940
> (408) 659-5531

---

Word processing software producers overcome many of the incompatibilities with "installation modules." As described in an earlier chapter, these modules let you "configure" the program for a particular brand of printer before using it the first time. Essentially, the installation module translates the word processing program's codes into the specific codes a particular printer must receive for those features. Usually, it is merely a matter of selecting your brand from an onscreen menu and allowing the installation program to do the rest.

If your printer is not on the menu, one of the brands listed may have identical requirements and you may be able to install the program for it instead. When that is not the case, the software company may provide a "patch" to the main program to create the configuration you need.

If this sounds like something that you as the buyer should not need to become involved with, you're absolutely right. That's what dealers are for. When you buy a program at the full retail price, having the dealer "install" it or apply the necessary patch for you is part of what you are paying for. You have every right to insist. You should not allow a salesperson to convince you that "it's so easy, you can do it yourself." That may very well be—but "easy" is a relative term, and what if it turns out not to be "easy" at all as far as you're concerned?

---

**SoftTip:** Once a program package has been opened, even by the dealer when performing an installation, "you bought it." That can lead to unpleasantries should you discover afterwards that the software will not produce all of the effects it is supposed to produce with your printer, installation module notwithstanding. Consequently, before you make any move toward your credit card, it is always advisable to actually see how the program works with your brand of printer. Bring your printer into the store if need be.

---

*Cursor Control and "Navigation."* One of the most fundamental conceptual differences between using a typewriter and using a word processor is the way both you and the two machines "think" of the text you create. Instead of treating a report as a collection of separate pages, word processors "look at" the entire report as a single, continuous stream of text. At first, this seems quite strange to someone accustomed to the single-page orientation of a typewriter, but the ability to treat text this way is really one of the secrets of a word processor's power.

Imagine the pages of a typewritten report taped together into one long sheet, and imagine stretching it out on your lawn so that you can read any page or any paragraph by simply walking over to the right location. That's the way most word processors see things. There are a few other details, but for now we can think of them as holding the entire document in your computer's memory. That makes it easy for the program to shoot any page or paragraph onto the screen whenever you like.

One important area where word processing programs differ, however, is the ease and speed with which they allow you to do this. All of them will let you move the cursor around on the displayed page—up a line, down a line, possibly down a paragraph, etc.—using either directional arrow keys on the keyboard or some combination of keys if your keyboard doesn't have arrows. This is called *full-screen editing*. But suppose you are working on page 5 and want to go back to check page 1.

With some programs, you can enter a command that will take you to your destination immediately—the screen will blink and page 1 will appear. With others, you may enter a command, but the system will page backwards, momentarily displaying each page between page 5 and page 1.

Clearly, the instant response version is much more desirable. Equally desirable is a feature that will let you instantly return to the place you started from, after moving to some other location. These features may not always be available on the program you want, but they are definitely something to look into before making your final decision. The commands used to move around on the document are usually called *navigational commands.*

## Correcting Mistakes and Typing Headers

*Typewriter*

When using a typewriter, you may routinely begin each page after the first with a *header* like "Sales Report—Third Quarter." You would then type in the page number and continue typing text. Should you make a mistake in your typing, you may have to erase it and retype the word correctly, or you may be able to use a self-correcting feature to backspace and lift the wrong character off the page. With some advanced typewriters, you may even be able to get rid of a line at a time in this manner.

*How a Word Processor Differs*

*"Programmable" Keys.* A word processor makes both of these tasks so easy, it's almost sinful. There are many ways to avoid having to type the same header (or footer) over and over again. If your computer has "function keys" the program may let you "load" one or more of them with text. This way, whenever a header is called for, you merely hit a function key and the computer automatically inserts the text. On machines that have no function keys, the program may allow you to do the same thing by holding down the <CONTROL> key and hitting some character. In computer terms, these are sometimes called *macro* features because they permit a "macro expansion" from a single keystroke. Still other programs will let you specify the header when you want to print the document. In this case, you type it in once and the machine automatically inserts it at the top of each printed page.

The same function key technique can also be used to insert entire paragraphs. You might create 10 paragraphs and record each as a sepa-

312 . . .     *How to Buy a Word Processing Program*

rate file on disk. Then you could load each file into one of your function keys. Once that was done, you could create an entire letter by merely hitting the function keys. You might send paragraphs 1, 3, and 5 to one person and paragraphs 1, 4, 7, 9, and 5 to someone else. In either case, assembling the letter would involve only three to five keystrokes. In some cases, as when you want to include "stock" or, in office slang, "boilerplate" paragraphs in a letter, proposal, or contract, this is called a *boilerplating* option.

*Delete, Insert, Search, and Replace.* Removing unwanted characters is usually a simple matter of backspacing over them. Or there may be a key you can hit to erase characters as the cursor moves from left to right. If you need to put a phrase, a comma, or a word into a line that has already been typed, there is no need to erase the whole line. Instead, you move the cursor to the target point and hit activate the *insert* option. Different programs handle this in different ways, but the end result is always the same. The text to the right of the target point simply slides to the right to make room for the insert. If that causes it to hang over the right margin, it is easy to adjust the paragraph so that everything moves to accommodate the additional words.

Another incredibly powerful error-correcting feature found in many programs is a *global search* option. This feature will typically let you locate any specified word or phrase wherever it occurs in your text. That can be handy if you know you were last working on a section where you mentioned a particular phrase or name, but can't remember just where it was. But it is even more useful when it is coupled with a *replace* feature. If you like, you can usually tell the system, "Search for and find this word. Then replace it with that word."

The system will perform the task and usually automatically move the text around to account for any difference in the number of characters of the new phrase. With a word processor, there is never any need for someone to retype an entire report because a set of figures or a name or anything else must be changed. The software and the computer can take care of it in a flash.

## Editing and Formatting: Typewriters Need Not Apply

There is no typewriter equivalent for the second major phase of using a word processor—editing and formatting. If you want a report to be typed using different margins or if you want it to contain paragraphs from some other document, your only choice with a typewriter is to retype the whole thing. As we said at the beginning, typing and editing and formatting with a word processor are typically done at the same time.

For example, many programs will automatically *right justify* your text so that every line occupies the same amount of space and every line ends with the last letter of a word, as opposed to the *ragged right* margins produced by a typewriter. Usually, right justification is a feature that can be *toggled* on or off by entering a command. Adjusting and *formatting* usually refer to setting the margins and commanding the system to adjust the text accordingly. This makes it possible for you to look at how the text would appear if printed with different margins. But it also lets you use different margins within the text, as when you want to type a single-spaced quotation or other paragraph with narrower margins than the rest of the document.

---

**SoftTip:** An ability to record margin and tab settings within the text is especially important if you will be creating charts, tables, and other blocks of text that require different settings than straight typing. If the margin and tab settings cannot be recorded, you will have to reset them every time you return to the document to edit the table or chart.

---

*Block and Column Moves*

This feature may also be referred to as *cut and paste*, for it enables you to clip a paragraph, a column of figures, or some other "block" of text out of a document and move it to another location. Typically, the feature requires you to mark off the text you want to focus on with *block markers*. These are usually special characters that let you tell the machine, "Everything from marker number one to marker number two is to be considered a block of text." In reality, depending on the program, a block may be a word, a line, a paragraph, a column of numbers, or several pages.

Once a block has been identified, the program may display it in shaded or *reverse video*. On a monitor with a black screen and green letters, "reverse video," causes letters to be displayed as black cutouts surrounded by green boxes. At that point, you may move it anywhere you like. Or, again depending on the program, you may be able to delete the whole thing or save it to disk as a separate file.

## Printing

When you have finished writing and editing your text, the next step is to save the entire body of copy to disk. Some programs do this for you automatically as you go along. Some force you to save the file before you can print it, and some allow you to print it right away. Only by getting to know more about a particular word processing program can you judge which course is best for you to follow, but generally the rule is "Better safe than sorry." Compared to the amount of time required to recreate or retype text that somehow gets zapped before you have a hard copy in your hands, the time required to record it on disk is almost insignificant.

A dot matrix printer is an amazingly versatile piece of machinery. As you may know from investigating computer hardware, the printing element consists of a rectangle of closely packed wires, each of which makes a dot on a page when it is pushed forward and into a ribbon. Because virtually any combination of wires can be pushed forward at any time, this makes it possible for the printer to produce a wide range of characters of varying sizes.

Because the printing element is on a pully-like mechanism, it does not have to be moved a set distance each time it prints a character. Instead, it can print characters closer together or further apart as desired. Finally, the mechanism that advances the paper is equally flexible. It is not limited to moving the paper up a certain amount of space each time. This makes it possible for you to print text with almost any amount of space between lines.

Letter-quality daisy wheel or thimble printers have many of these same capabilities. They cannot produce different fonts without first stopping to let you change the wheel or the thimble, but they produce a finished copy that is indistinguishable from that produced with a typewriter.

Dot matrix or letter quality, it all adds up to a lot of flexibility . . . and complexity when it comes time to tell the printer how you would like the text to appear. For example, because of the precision with which the printer can be controlled, many programs offer *microjustification*. Under regular justification, words are strung out on a line in such a way that each line ends with a character in the rightmost column. This is an unnatural way of printing, however, and large gaps are often left between words to make it possible, which can make the text appear strange and difficult to read.

Microjustification takes advantage of a computer's computing ability to stretch things out more evenly. Instead of adding or subtracting space in character-sized chunks that usually measure one tenth or one twelfth of an inch, it distributes space in units as small as one one-hundred-and-twentieth of an inch.

*Proportional spacing* is yet another option. It can be characterized as "to each, according to his size . . . " For mechanical reasons, every letter on a typewriter must occupy the same amount of space. But word processors and printers have much more flexibility. Thus, since the letters *M* and *W* take up more space than *l* or *j*, the computer can be instructed to print them accordingly. This is the technique used when copy is professionally typeset, and that is the main reason for using proportional spacing.

### How Do You Tell the Program What You Want?

Fortunately, most word processing programs have built-in *default values* that can save you from worrying about all of your choices at first. These are usually standard settings that produce text in the same format used by a typewriter. No fancy line spacing, no elaborate justification or spacing schemes.

To take advantage of more advanced printing features or to change the default values, most programs have you embed commands in the text itself. The command will be preceded by a character like a slash (/) or by a period (.), usually called a "dot" in the trade. The dot will be followed by a letter or a number or a combination of the two that tells the computer what you want it to do. Because they were popularized by the best-selling WordStar program, commands like these are often generically referred to as *dot commands*, even though they may actually contain a slash or an "at sign" (@), or some other character. The commands will not be printed, but they will be recorded with the text so that they are always there. Usually, they are put at the top of the first page, though they can be inserted anywhere to change the printer's instructions in the middle of the text. Some word processors will let you record a string of dot commands as a file so that you do not have to retype them for each new document. You need only insert the file at the appropriate point.

One dot command of particular interest concerns "page breaks." Since there are 66 conventional lines on a piece of typing paper, it is customary to put about 55 lines of text on the page and divide the rest between the top and bottom margins. The text thus starts about an inch down from the top and ends an inch from the bottom. Since that is the normal default setting for a word processor, every time you finish typing about 55 lines, many programs will usually scroll up about five lines and display some kind of dividing line signaling a page break. If a program does not do this, it is an indication that what you are seeing on the screen will not be exactly what appears on the printer.

Because this page break occurs once the 55-line condition has been met, it is called a *conditional page break*. However, you may usually enter a dot command to change the conditions. If you were printing on legal-sized paper, for example, you would want to change things to reflect the longer (84 lines) page length. There are also *mandatory page breaks*. These are used when you want to make sure that every line on a table appears on the same page, or to prevent the last page of a letter from containing nothing but "Sincerely yours,".

Finally, when all of the dot commands have been embedded and the text looks just the way you want it, you tell the system that you want to print the file. Most programs will then present you with a menu allowing you to specify things like how many copies of each one you want, whether you will be using continuous-form tractor-driven paper or single sheets. This option tells the system to stop after each page to let you insert a new piece of paper.

A similar-sounding, but quite different option will let you command the printer to stop at a particular point so you can enter text from the keyboard. This can be useful if you want to enter an inside address for a business letter without going back into the word processor and adding it to the file. You may also be able to specify *background printing*. As you may remember, this is a print spooling function that will let you use the word processor to create a new file while another file is being printed.

Two of the most important features that may be offered at this point are options to tell the system which pages you want it to start and end with and an option to abort the printout at any time. Without the first feature, you may have to print the entire file each time. And if there is no abort function, you may find that the only way to stop the printout is to turn the computer and printer off and reboot.

## The Basic Features of a Good Processing Program

You should now have a fairly good idea of what word processing is all about. It's important to emphasize, however, that not all programs have all of the features described above. Some are very rudimentary and cheap ($20) and some are quite sophisticated and expensive ($500 to $700). Some even include and require a coprocessor board with a special ROM chip and 64K of memory. There isn't always a direct correlation between features and price, and as always, the program you pick should be the one that best meets your needs at a price you can afford.

Because individual needs vary so widely, it is difficult to say that there are certain features every program *must* have. After all, if you only want to produce text, you may find that the line editor module that probably came with your DOS package will be quite adequate. You may also find that you can use some feature of a completely different applications program to accomplish what you want. Some people, for example, use their VisiCalc or other spreadsheet programs for writing short letters.

However, from one perspective at least, it is possible to conclude that if you are going to buy a word processing program, you should buy one that will let you do *real* word processing, a program that will let you take advantage of all the power sitting there in your machine. Programs of this class typically cost between $100 and $200, and most of them offer many powerful "real word processing" features.

With a moderately priced program as a guide, here are the basic features of a word processing program:

- Ability to set up an initial margin, tab, and line spacing format.
- Rapid display of text on the screen, with no discernible delay under most conditions.
- Display text *exactly* as it will be printed; "screen oriented."
- Word wrap, automatic hyphenation, right justification, automatic page breaks.
- Full-screen editing, ability to move cursor all over the screen.
- Navigational commands to go instantly to top or bottom of text or any number of pages forward or behind your current position.
- Insert or erase words or phrases and reform text to accommodate the change.
- Identify and move blocks of text from one part of the manuscript to another or record on disk as a separate file.
- Insert a separate file or files within the current text; "boilerplating."
- Programmable function keys or other keys; loaded with text that is automatically reproduced when you hit the key.
- Global search option to find or find and replace words or phrases wherever they occur in the document.
- Full support of your printer, enabling you to use all or most of the machine's special print functions (bold, italic, and underline, for sure; possibly compressed and expanded as well).

Should you avoid buying a moderately priced program because it lacks one or more of these features? Not at all. You may not need the features it lacks. Yet it can be important to use the points listed above as a framework for evaluating any word processing program. After all, the advertisements are not going to tell you that a product *lacks* certain features.

This general framework is important for another reason as well. As you read various ads and reviews, you can easily feel overwhelmed with all of the many features a product offers. But not all features should be given equal weight. The ones listed above are the ones that are really important. With the exception of spelling checkers and mailing list options considered in the next chapter, virtually everything else a program contains is derived from this basic framework.

## "EXTRA" FEATURES

Though not strictly essential, some of the "extra" features many programs include can be very nice to have. Others are just plain ridiculous. Examples of the former are the "Help" menus most programs include and a feature that automatically tabs in for you to start the next paragraph.

An example of the latter is a feature that lets you correct transposed letters, like *hte* for *the*, by moving the cursor under the *t*, holding the <CONTROL> key down, and typing <A>. As one reviewer put it, "Entering this command causes the word *the* to appear so fast that you can't see it happen." Considering how much easier it would be merely to retype the word, many people may not see the need for the feature either.

It would be impossible to list all of the extra features provided by the various microcomputer word processing programs. But here are a few that may be of interest to you:

*Outline Formatting*

This feature automatically sets up the correct tabs for creating an outline. Usually, it will also automatically produce the Roman numerals, the capital letters, and other designators for the various levels of the outline. Perhaps most important of all, most such features will automatically renumber or reletter an outline if you insert an additional point after preparing the first draft.

*Typewriter Mode*

This option acts like a direct pipeline from your computer keyboard to your printer. Hit a key, and it is immediately printed on the paper. It is useful for addressing single envelopes because it is quicker than preparing a file with the word processor's other features. It may also be useful for filling in the blanks on preprinted forms.

*Split Screens*

Some programs will let you divide the screen into two or more sections and display a different file in each one. The files can usually be scrolled separately. This can be convenient when you want to check a paragraph in another file before inserting it into the document you are working on. In most cases, the feature will allow you to transfer blocks of text easily from one file to another.

*Math Mode*

Some programs include a calculation feature that will let you add columns of figures right on the screen, without pulling out your pocket calculator. Usually, the function is limited to the four arithmetical operations.

*Wildcard Search*

One point on which various programs differ is in the sophistication of their search function. With some, you can specify only a few characters as your target word. Sometimes a program will find a word regardless of whether it contains a capital letter and sometimes, if you are looking for "Word," but type in "word" as your target, the program will fail to find it.

The most sophisticated search functions allow you to enter an asterisk or other character in place of a specific letter. The asterisk is your way of telling the system, "I don't care what the character is, I want you to find it." If you wanted to eliminate all references to 1980, 1981, and 1982, you might tell the system to search for every occurrence of "198*".

## Critical Points

The features a software house cites in its ads don't always tell the full story. Sometimes it is necessary to look at the specifications almost as if the program were an automobile to get a complete picture. For example, a program may be advertised as having a "block move" feature. But once you buy it and begin to use it, you may discover that the size of the block you can move is limited to only five or six lines. A good software reviewer will usually pick this up, but you can't always count on it. It is one more reason for reading *several* reviews of a product and then asking your own questions of the retailer or looking at the documentation before you buy.

A good procedure to follow when trying to find a word processing program is first to evaluate your needs and then look for programs with the features that match them most closely. Once you have things narrowed down, investigate the features, their limitations, how they work, etc., more closely. Listed below are some of the most critical points to check at this stage.

*Ease of Use*

Although it is largely subjective, the ease with which you can use a word processing program that contains the features you need may well be the most important criteria. If you will not be using the program yourself, be sure to consult the person who will be. There is no other genre of program that involves such close and constant interaction with the user, and when things are that "intense," even the little things can be crucial.

As vague as it is, the question, How does it *feel?* can be of prime importance. For example, you can sit behind the wheel of some cars and immediately sense that they have been thoughtfully and intelligently designed. With other automobiles, the impression is one of gloss and glitter, with components thrown together in a workable but somewhat thoughtless manner. Again, because you will be so closely involved with the program when you are using it, this is one case where there can be no substitute for a hands-on demonstration.

*Speed*

Speed is one of the main advantages of word processing, and there are at least four areas where it can be critical. The first and most obvious is how quickly the program displays the characters you type. Ideally, they will appear instantaneously. But where that is not the case, there should be a type-ahead feature. Under no circumstances should even the fastest typist have to wait for a program to "digest" a burst from the keyboard before permitting the person to continue. The only time any delay is acceptable is when you have the computer doing background printing, a process that can slow it down.

Second, there is the speed with which the program adjusts the text after you have made additions or deletions. Since this involves rewriting the entire screen, it can take three seconds or more. The maximum acceptable time will vary with the individual, but this is definitely something to test before you buy.

The third speed-related area concerns the program itself and the way it performs its different tasks. Since programs like WordStar use overlays, there will always be a delay when you switch from one function to another. The advantage of using overlays is that a program too large for many memory configurations can still be used by the computer owner, if the person is willing to put up with the delays.

As mentioned in Chapter 5, the overlay delay can be overcome by loading the complete program into an electronic disk drive. A hard disk drive may also be used, but in both cases if the program is copy protected, it cannot be used in this way.

Finally, there is speed of "navigation." How fast can you get from one page to another? Does the system take you to your target instantly, or do you have to wait while the intervening pages scroll by? If you have never used a word processing program before, you may not mind this kind of delay. But as you grow more accustomed to word processing, it can be a real nuisance to have to wait.

*Number of Columns*

How many characters can you put on a line: 80? 132? 256? And, considering the compressed printing option, how many are you likely to need?

*Block Size*

What is the maximum number of lines that can be included in a block? Since these figures may be expressed in number of characters, simply divide by 80 to determine how many lines are involved. Remember, these are characters, not words. Spaces count the same as letters. Some programs can handle only about 1,000 characters per block. With others, a block can consist of several pages. This is a function of the amount of RAM you have in your system. Putting more kilobytes at a program's disposal can greatly expand the number and size of the blocks it can use.

Almost as important is the question of how many blocks you can designate at one time. It may be one, it may be four, it may be an unlimited number.

*Maximum Document Size*

Some programs cannot handle and will not permit documents any longer than 15 pages. Others are limited to 25 pages. And still others don't care. With the last group, document length is limited only by the amount of disk space. It all depends on how the program is written and how it manages its files. If you plan to use the program primarily for correspondence, then most length limitations won't affect you. But if you intend to write long reports, novels, short stories, etc., then the imposition of a maximum length can be a nuisance. It can be overcome by dividing a 30-page report into two separate files, but that is obviously not an ideal situation.

*What Happens If your Disk is Full?*

Some programs are designed to hold your text in internal memory until a certain number of characters have been entered. At that point, they record the characters on disk, empty the memory, and start the count again. Others hold the entire text in memory and record it on disk at your command.

In either case, problems can occur if the program tries to write to disk but finds that there is no more room. Unfortunately, if the programmer has not anticipated this situation, you may not be able to solve it by simply inserting a blank disk. Some programs will simply stop if they fail in their first attempt at writing to disk. That can be disastrous. Not only do you lose everything that is still in your computer's memory when a program locks up, but you may also not be able to recover the material that has already been recorded since the file will not have been properly closed.

It is always a good idea to check the amount of remaining disk space before you begin. You can do this with a DOS command or possibly with a command in the word processing program itself. Nevertheless, the program should be capable of handling a full-disk situation. Ideally, it should prompt you after failing in its attempt and advise you to hit a particular key that will cause it to close out the current disk file properly. After that, it might prompt you to insert a fresh disk and hit a key to tell it that it is free to record the material in memory.

This way you will be safe. You can easily go into DOS after you are finished and use its commands to combine the two files at a later time.

*File Compatibility with Other Programs*

File compatibility is something that one can easily overlook when evaluating the features a word processing program offers. As long as you use the program by itself, there is no need to worry about how it formats and stores its files. But should you want to prepare a document and insert a VisiCalc or SuperCalc spreadsheet or a file from dBASEII or some other DBMS program, you may find that you've run into an unexpected brick wall. The same is true if you want to run the file through some spelling checker programs or use it with a mailing list program. File incompatibility can also be a problem if you want to prepare a letter for transmission to The Source, CompuServe, or some other electronic mail service, or prepare text for transmission to a typesetting firm.

The document files created by word processing programs may have unusual header information recorded in front of the text. Although you do not see it, the program may need this information in order to do its work. In addition, many programs store special ASCII characters at the end of each line or word. These are necessary to indicate things like soft hyphens and soft carriage returns. Again, you will not see them in the text, but the program needs them.

Without going into detail, it is enough to know that all of these things can cause unexpected problems. Some of them can be solved relatively easily. Some are impossible to get around. If you think you might want to insert files created by programs other than your word processor or transmit files over the telephone with a communications program, be sure to ask your dealer whether this can be done. Then ask for information on exactly *how* one might do it, the steps that would be followed, etc.

If the word processing program is written in FORTH or Pascal, you should be particularly wary. The FORTH language, for example, is really both a language and an operating system. And the version of Pascal that is used may require the p-System. These programs may run on your machine with no problem, but more than likely the files they produce will not be compatible with your machine's standard DOS and the spelling checker, mail merge, or communications programs written to run under its control. The question to investigate is whether the program stores text in the same format used by your standard DOS. And if it doesn't, does the program include a function for *translating* its own files into DOS-compatible files?

### Spelling Checker and/or Mail Merge

Some programs include modules that will read through your text searching for misspelled words. Some may also include a mail merge feature to let you produce customized form letters. If these modules are not included, they may be available from the same vendor as an extra-cost add-on. Or you may be able to find a program produced by another firm that is designed to be compatible with your word processor. Both types of software are discussed in detail in the next chapter.

---

**SoftTip:** One of the advantages of using your computer as a word processor is the possibility of loading your printer with continuous-form paper, telling the system to print out a batch of letters, and simply walking away while the machine does its stuff. But what if your personal or corporate letterhead is not on a continuous form? In the past, that could pose a problem, but as the demand has grown, more and more stationery companies have begun to offer custom imprinting services.

Today it is possible to order continuous-form letterhead and envelopes of the same quality you may now be using (20-pound, 25% rag content, laid finish or plain, etc.). Typically, the perforations in the paper will be exceptionally fine, leaving no trace when the sheets are separated and the pinhole strips are detached. Here are firms you may want to contact for a catalogue and more information:

*SoftTip continued*

Moore Computer Forms
P.O. Box 20
Wheeling, IL   60090
(800) 323-6230
(800) 323-4185 (Alaska/Hawaii)
(312) 459-0210 (Illinois)

Quill Corporation
100 South Schelter
Lincolnshire, IL   60069
(312) 634-4800

Prices depend on paper quality and quantity ordered and start at around $65 for 500 sheets. The minimum order from Quill is 500 sheets, but paper selection is somewhat limited. Moore offers a wider selection but has a minimum order of 1,000 (about $90 for the least expensive bond). Prices drop rapidly as the size of the order increases.

**SoftTip:** Would you like a powerful, multi-featured word processing program for free? If so, Bob Wallace of Quicksoft may have just the program for you. Called "PC-Write," the program runs on the IBM/PC and supports the hard disk features of PC-DOS 2.0. It allows you to edit 62K files, has a windowing feature, and allows you to redefine keyboard controls. It also includes word wrap, block move operations, text reformatting to different margins, and text justification. Additional enhancements are planned.

Wallace, a former programmer for Microsoft—he helped develop Microsoft's version of Pascal—makes the program disk available for $10. The documentation is on the program disk. The program is copyrighted, but Wallace and his firm give the user permission to copy the disk and freely share the program with others. If you like the program, you are asked to send $75 to Quicksoft to become a registered user.

Registered users receive a printed copy of the instruction manual, telephone support, a warranty, the Pascal and assembly language source code (so you can make alterations), and a copy of the latest version of PC-Write. (Wallace plans to eventually make the program a true "what you see on the screen is what you get on the printer" word processor.)

Here is the address to write to for more information. But there is a caveat. Bob Wallace has said that he will treat PC-Write as an experiment. If he can make a living under the "freeware" concept, he will continue. If not, he will offer PC-Write commercially. Contact:

Quicksoft
219 First Avenue North #224
Seattle, WA  98109

## Software Buyer's Quick Reference Checklist

*—Word Processing Programs—*

The following checklist provides a brief summary of the most important points to consider when buying word processing software. It is designed to guide you in choosing a moderately priced ($100 to $200) program that will offer complete word processing power. A less expensive ($50 to $75) program may be perfectly suited to your needs. Alternatively, your application may require features found in only the most expensive ($250 to $700) software.

Whichever word processor you choose, however, it is important not to let yourself be distracted or overwhelmed by all of the little features and variations every program will include. Focus on the most important points, and you'll have an excellent chance of buying a program that suits both your needs and your budget.

### Preliminaries

*Version*

☐ Is the software you are considering the latest version of the program? If you are in doubt, check the most recent reviews in the computer magazines, or call the software producer.

*Hardware*

☐ How much RAM does the program require?

☐ Will larger amounts of memory improve the program's speed and performance?

☐ Can the program deal with more than 64K?

☐ How many disk drives are required?

☐ Does the entire program load into your machine's regular memory or must the program disk always be "online" and occupying a drive? A program that can be completely loaded into regular memory cannot be as large (or as powerful) as one that uses overlays.

☐ Can the program be loaded into a RAM disk or onto a hard disk drive to make it run at top speed? If the program is copy protected, this may not be possible.

### Software
☐ What operating system is required?

☐ Does the program use your machine's standard operating system, or will you have to buy a secondary system and possibly a coprocessor board, as when equipping an Apple or an IBM to run CP/M programs?

☐ Does the product require any non-operating system software, such as Apple Business BASIC, in order to run?

## Compatibilities

### Printer
☐ Does the program let you use *all* of the features your printer provides? If not, which ones will it not support? At a minimum, the program should be able to make your printer produce underlined words, bold print, and italics.

☐ Check the program's documentation to see if your brand of printer is supported and whether there is an installation module to apply the necessary patches to the program.

### Monitor/Terminal
☐ As with printers, display monitors have different requirements and the program may have to be patched with an installation program to make it support your particular brand. Usually, this poses no problem.

☐ Most programs expect to use a monitor capable of displaying 80 columns across and 24 or 25 lines down. But if you have a TRS-80 Model III that has been modified for CP/M, you may find that portions of a program's menu and other lines will be lopped off at the right. As always, it is best to test a program with the *exact* equipment configuration that you will be using.

## File Structure

☐ Does the program produce text files that are compatible with your standard operating system? Or does it use a "foreign" (FORTH or Pascal p-System) format?

☐ Can the files be transmitted over the telephone using one of the communications packages available for your computer and standard operating system? Will you be able to use a spelling checker or mail merge program with the files?

## Essential Features

☐ A *minimum* of 80 columns (characters per line); more if possible.

*Note:* If you will be inserting a spreadsheet generated by your spreadsheet program into documents created with a word processor, make certain that the word processing software can display all of the spreadsheet's columns.

☐ Rapid display of text on the screen. No discernible delay under most conditions; "type-ahead buffer."

☐ Word wrap, automatic hyphenation, right justification, automatic centering, automatic page breaks.

☐ Full-screen editing. Move the cursor all over the screen at will.

☐ Navigational commands to take you to top, bottom, or elsewhere in the text instantly.

☐ Insert or erase words and phrases and reform text to accommodate the change.

☐ Block moves. Mark off sections of text to be moved to another location or to be recorded on disk or deleted.

☐ File insertion. Insert a separate file or files within the current document. "Boilerplating."

☐ Programmable keys. Load function or other keys with sentences, paragraphs, or files for instant one-keystroke insertion into text.

☐ Global search and locate/search and replace. Find words in a document or find and replace them with something else.

## Critical Points

*Document Size*

☐ What is the maximum document size? Are you limited to documents no longer than 15 pages? Or can a document be as large as your available disk space?

*Speed*

☐ Is the program fast? Is it written in machine or assembly language? Was the version written for your particular computer?

☐ How quickly can you scroll (not jump) down to the bottom of the page? How quickly does the program reform paragraphs after an insertion or deletion?

*Error Recovery*

☐ What happens if you run out of disk space? Does the program prompt you through the procedure of closing out the current file and inserting a new disk? Or does it lock up and force you to reboot, losing everything you have entered since the last disk write?

*What You See . . .*

☐ Will the program print the text *exactly* as it appears on the screen? Can you tell exactly where the page breaks will occur in the printout?

*Block-Move Features*

☐ What is the smallest block possible? A word? A sentence?

☐ What is the largest? A full page? Several pages?

☐ How many blocks can you mark at one time? Can the blocks be recorded as separate files on disk?

☐ Are larger block moves possible with more RAM?

*Recording Margin Settings*

☐ Is it possible to record margin and tab settings within the document so that you do not have to reset them each time? Does the program make it convenient to edit tables and other "tabular matter"?

*Header and Footer Limitations*

☐ If the program allows you to use headers and footers, is there any limitation on how long they may be? Are they limited to one line each, for example? Is it important to you?

*Inserting Other Files*

☐ Will it be possible for you to insert files created by your spreadsheet, database management, or graphics programs into a document?

## Hands-on Demonstration

When picking a word processing program, there simply isn't any substitute for a live, hands-on demonstration. After you have narrowed your focus to perhaps two or three programs, take several pages of the kind of text you normally produce with your typewriter with you to the store. Ask the salesperson if he or she would demonstrate the program for you and then allow you to "play with it" for a bit.

You won't be able to learn or test all of a program's features. But the dealer should be able to show you how to set your margins, enter text, save the document, and print it out. Be sure to compare the printout with how the text you entered appears on the screen.

If possible, try to use the search feature to find and/or replace some word in your document. You might also try the block move feature, though this might be too involved for an in-store demo.

It is also a good idea to sample at least two different programs, even if you are not seriously considering one of them. This will give you at least some basis of comparison.

Finally, try to make certain that the demonstration takes place on equipment that is as close to being identical to your own configuration as possible. You might want to see how the program runs when an RAM drive or hard disk is used, but if you don't plan to buy that hardware, do not let the dealer use it when actually demonstrating the program.

*Convenience and Ease of Use*

☐ How convenient are the program's control commands? How much work is required to enter the commands? How many keystrokes?

☐ Are they easy to remember? And, if not, is a help menu displayed?

☐ How convenient are the navigational commands? Can you quickly jump to the top of a document? The bottom? Some place in between?

☐ Can you advance the cursor a line at a time? A paragraph at a time? A word at a time?

☐ Does the text adjust to the margins automatically after you have inserted or deleted a phrase? Or is it necessary to enter a special command? Are both options available?

☐ What steps do you have to follow to erase a hard carriage return? The hard carriage return at the end of one paragraph must be removed to blend that paragraph with another.

☐ What are the limitations of the search feature? How long a word or phrase can you search for at one time? Is there a wildcard search option?

☐ Can you use the search feature either to locate a target word or to replace it automatically with some other word?

*Printing*

☐ Can you print a range of pages, or must you print the entire file?

☐ Can you abort a printout without having to shut off your computer?

☐ Can you tell the system to pause for you to enter information from the keyboard or to change paper?

☐ Can it print in the background while you continue to use the word processor in the foreground (Spooling)?

## Extra Features

Here are some of the extra features that some programs offer. Their value will vary with your particular needs. But as with everything else about applications software, it is important to know what is available and what options are open to you.

☐ Outline formatting.

☐ Split screen editing.

☐ Typewriter mode.

☐ Math mode.

☐ Mail merge option (see Chapter 14).

☐ Spelling checker (see Chapter 14).

# ...14...
## How to Buy Spelling Checkers and Mailing List Programs

A s we saw in the previous chapter, once you convert a letter or a word into a pattern of voltage levels that a computer can understand, all kinds of wonderful possibilities open up. Word processing is one. Data communications (sending text over the telephone) is another. But since computers are particularly good at comparing patterns of switch settings, there is no reason why they can't check your spelling as well. This is especially helpful to those of us who suffer under the tyranny of Noah Webster. For, as Peter McWilliams, author of several best-selling computer and word processing books has pointed out, "He's the one who started it all. He's the one who came along 198 years ago and gave us only one way to spell words. The right way. *His* way."

Computers are also good at manipulating bit patterns, a fact that can save you a lot of money if you are a business person and have the right mailing list program. In the past, the only way a small business could avail itself of the power of direct mail was to rent a mailing list from one of the many commercial "list houses" in the country. The problem is, the minimum order from such firms is usually about 5,000, far more names than many businesses need. Commercial lists can also be expensive, and you can only use them once. To mail to the same list again, you must re-rent the list.

Today, however, there is no reason why a small business with a personal computer can't build its own mailing list from existing customer files, responses generated by advertising, telephone books, trade publications, and other sources of prospective customers. Once the list has been created, it can be used again and again. And, with the right software, the computer can sort the mailing by ZIP code to take advantage of special post office discounts. It can also produce labels and letters for just those prospects or customers who meet certain criteria and so reduce mailing costs while ensuring a higher response rate.

In this chapter, we'll look at both spelling checkers and mailing list programs. As always, it is important to have as clear an idea as possible of how you will actually use the program and what your specific needs are. This chapter will show you what to look for in each case.

## How to Buy a Spelling Checker

Some word processing programs include "spelling checkers" as part of the whole package. With others, an add-on module from the same software house may be available at extra cost. In many cases, there will also be several independently produced programs designed to be compatible with various word processors. When purchased separately, the programs can cost anywhere from $20 to $200 or more.

### The Main Idea

A spelling checker is a program that reads every word in your text and compares it against an electronic lexicon or "dictionary." Words that do not match are considered *suspect*. The program collects or marks these words in some way and presents them for your consideration. This is something all such programs have in common, but naturally they differ in the ways they go about it.

At the bottom of the heap in terms of convenience and power are programs that simply generate a list of suspect words on your printer and force you to use your word processing program's search feature to locate them in the text. Next are programs that vet your text and create a duplicate of it on disk with all suspicious words marked, often with a "pound sign" (#). You must then go through each page of the file examining each suspicious word and either correcting it or allowing it to stand.

Other programs take a different approach. After reading the file, they present you with a list of suspicious words, one at a time, and allow you to decide whether you want to have the word marked in the text or not. This type of program has two disadvantages. First, it will usually give you just the suspect word without showing you the "context" or the rest of the sentence in which it was found. That can make it difficult to decide whether the word is correct or not. Second, you are still required to return to your text to make the corrections yourself.

The third and most convenient type of spelling checker also presents you with a list of suspect words. But it will also show you the context in which it was used, if you like. And, most important of all, it will make all necessary corrections in the text automatically, if you tell it to.

*Critical Points*

*Dictionary Size.* The dictionary used is the heart of any spelling checker program. Some have dictionaries as small as 10,000 words; others offer 50,000, 60,000, or more. It is possible to get caught up in competing dictionary size claims, but it is worthwhile to stop and think about how many different words you normally use. If you never use the word *piquancy*, for example, does it really matter whether the word is in your spelling checker's dictionary or not? If it's not there, the worst that can happen would be that the program would identify it as a suspect. In that case, you might add it to the dictionary yourself to prevent it from coming up again, if the program has that feature. There is also the fact that dictionaries with more words can take longer to vet your text. For most people, a dictionary of around 20,000 to 30,000 words is probably sufficient.

*Dictionary Construction.* The dictionaries spelling checkers use exist as a separate disk file, and two techniques are used to create that file. As you might expect, the simplest and easiest technique is to list every word, spelling it out completely. This is called a *literal* dictionary. The main drawback to a literal dictionary is that it requires so much space. Remembering that one byte is required to store a single character, and assuming that the average word contains seven bytes, a 30,000-word dictionary would require 210K of disk space. If your system's disk drives use 160K disks, you could be out of luck.

For this reason, a second technique called "hashing" is often used. The technical details are not important. It is enough to know that this allows the dictionary to be compressed so that less space is required for each word. For example, a dictionary that occupies perhaps 176K in its literal word form can be squeezed down so that it fits into only 56K. Dictionaries of this type are often called *root word* dictionaries because they often consist of root words followed by the most frequently used prefixes and suffixes and a set of rules about how they can be legitimately combined.

Although a root word dictionary will require less disk space and so permit a longer list of words, it is usually not as reliable as a literal word dictionary and may let more misspelled words slip through. Therefore, if a software house uses a literal word dictionary, it will usually say so in its ads. Firms using root word and compression techniques will tend to highlight the enormous number of words their products contain.

Since there are many different ways to handle data compression and create root word dictionaries, some products will perform more reliably than others. Consequently, it is always a good idea to read two or more reviews. If the product has the number of words and the other features you want and if the reviewers find that its reliability is high, then you will probably be satisfied with the product.

*Can You Add Words to the Dictionary?* This is a particularly important feature. Since it would be impossible for a software dictionary to include all the proper names, place names, and technical and other terms you use in the course of your writing, it is vital to be able to "educate" the dictionary by adding those words to its list. Whenever the program encounters a suspect word, you should be given the option of "updating" the dictionary.

Other important considerations include:

• What is the maximum number of words you are allowed to add? With some programs, it may be 250, with others, 3,000 or an unlimited number.

• Can you add words independently of a spelling check session? With some programs, you can sit down and simply begin keying in the words you want to add. With others, you can only add the words the program identifies as suspect in the course of a checking session.

• Can you add Arabic numbers, asterisks, graphics and other characters, or are you limited only to words? This can be important if you want to check foreign language and scientific documents.

• Can you tell the program to print out only the words that you have added? Can you do this at any time, even months after buying the program or can you only do it before the words are actually written into the dictionary?

• Can you list the entire dictionary or parts of it to see what it contains?

• Can you delete words? And if you can, which ones? Only the ones you have added or any word in the dictionary? This can be important if you have mistakenly entered a misspelled word or if you want to reduce the space your backup copy of the dictionary occupies by eliminating words.

• Can you create special dictionaries of your own for use with the program? If you occasionally write about aviation, for example, you might create a separate dictionary filled with aviation terms. By segregating these terms in a separate dictionary file, you can avoid increasing the size of your main dictionary and possibly slowing down the speed with which the program operates.

*How Fast Does It Work?* One program might require two-and-a-half minutes to read 150 words (about three quarters of a double-spaced typewritten page), but another might do the same job in less than 30 seconds. Again, this is something that the faster programs will usually highlight in their ads, but the slower programs will somehow forget to mention. Typically, the faster programs are more expensive.

One point to look into is whether the program lists every occurrence of a word when it presents its list of suspects. If it does, you could be forced to deal with the same word over and over again. The better programs collect their suspects and then go through the list to eliminate duplicate words before presenting the list to you.

*How Accurate Is the Program?* In addition to the reliability considerations of whether the dictionary is a literal or root word type, it is important to look into how the program deals with hyphens and apostrophes. For example, a program should be able to distinguish between a soft hyphen entered by your word processing program and one that is necessary to the proper spelling of a word. It should also be able to deal with contractions and not report *doesn* as a suspect when what you actually wrote was *doesn't*. Any control codes you have embedded in the text to activate special printing and other functions should pass through the spelling checker without comment.

*Maximum Document Size.* It is also important to find out whether there are any limits on the number of pages or words the program can check at one time. Some programs are designed to handle documents of virtually any size, while others can manage only about 1,600 words (six to eight pages) at a time. In the latter case, you would have to divide a longer text file into several separate files totalling no more than 1,600 words and pass each through the spelling checker separately. Clearly, that's not an ideal situation.

*Word Processor Integration.* Though not essential, it can be very convenient to be able to 'call" (activate) a spelling checker while you are using your word processing program. When the spelling checker is supplied as part of the complete package, this is no problem at all. The same is true if you buy a word processor and later add a spelling checker module offered by the same firm. Usually, it is a simple matter of making sure the program is "online" (loaded into one of your disk drives) and entering the correct command.

If you buy your spelling program from another vendor, however, you may still be able to integrate it with your word processor. The vendor may supply patches that can be used to connect its checker to your brand of word processor. Obviously, it is important to make sure that the vendor supports your particular word processing program. Finally, there are packages which are meant to be used separately. Here it is important to make sure that the checker can read and work with the text files that your particular brand of word processor creates.

---

**SoftTip:** Patching a spelling checker into a word processing program is usually not a difficult job. Often the routine is handled the way an installation routine is handled: You just select an item from a menu and the program does the rest. When that is not the case, your dealer should be able to apply the patch for you.

One word of caution, however. If your word processing program has *already* been patched to make it support special printer options or function keys or to add some other enhancement, you may not be able to patch successfully in a spelling checker. Since there is *no way to be certain* beforehand, take a backup copy of your word processing program to the dealer and have the patches applied and tested before agreeing to purchase the spelling checker.

---

*Extra Features*

*Word and Frequency Counter.* Some programs will tell you exactly how many words a text file contains. This can be especially helpful to a writer who is paid by the word, but it can also be useful to anyone trying to determine whether a piece of text will fit in a given amount of space. A feature that will tell you how many times you used each word may also be available. This might be useful as an educational tool to help students broaden their vocabularies, but it is difficult to imagine any other genuine application.

*Close but No Cigar.* Instead of blindly telling you that a word is suspect, some programs helpfully offer suggestions by presenting several words that contain the same letters in the suspect arranged in their properly spelled order. This is as if the program were saying, "Excuse me, but *thier* is not correct. Could you possibly have meant: *tier, thief,* or *their?*"

*Lookup Feature.* Realizing that if you can't spell a word in the first place, you will have trouble finding it in a dictionary, some software companies include a "lookup" option. This allows you to key in the word as you think it should be spelled and causes the system to display either the correct spelling of the target word or several words that are close.

---

**SoftTip:** Checking your spelling isn't the only thing your computer can do. With the right program, it can also check your grammar and even your writing style. Perhaps the best known program of this sort is Grammatik ($75) from Aspen Software Company. Designed to work with the firm's Proofreader ($50) or some other spelling checking program, Grammatik will not only identify mismatched quotation marks and parentheses and spot doubled words like *and and* or *can not*, it will also flag wordy phrases and suggest alternatives. If you were to write "in the range of," for example, Grammatik might flag it and suggest replacing it with "in between." The program doesn't like clichés either. It is available for the IBM/PC, the TRS-80, and CP/M systems. For more information write to:

> Aspen Software Company
> P.O. Box 339
> Tijeras, NM   87059
> (505) 281-1634

---

## Software Buyer's Quick Reference Checklist
*—Spelling Checkers—*

*Compatibility*
☐ Is the software compatible with your word processor? Can it read the files the word processor creates?

*Dictionary Size and Construction*
☐ How many words are in its dictionary? There should be between 20,000 and 30,000 at minimum.

☐ Does the program use a *root word* dictionary or a *literal word* dictionary?

Root word products are usually recorded in compressed fashion, allowing more words per disk. Literal word products require more space, but are generally more accurate.

☐ Can you create your own special dictionaries? How and how many words?

## Program Operation
☐ Does the program merely mark words in the text or present you with a list of suspects words? Or both?

☐ Does it eliminate duplicate suspect words before presenting you with a list?

☐ Can you elect to view the context or part of the sentence in which the word was used?

☐ Will the program automatically change a misspelled word wherever it occurs in the text?

☐ What is the largest-sized document you may use with the program?

☐ How long does the program take to read and check a single page of double-spaced text (about 200 to 250 words)?

## Dictionary Management
☐ What is the maximum number of words you can add to the dictionary?

☐ Can you add words independently of a spelling checking session?

☐ Can you include numbers, punctuation marks, foreign language symbols, and graphics characters?

☐ Will the program list out the words you have added at any time or only just prior to inserting them into the dictionary?

☐ Can you list the entire dictionary? Can you edit out words?

☐ Will the program find doubled words like *and and*? How does it deal with apostrophes and hyphens?

## Extra Features
☐ Word and word frequency counters.

☐ Word approximation feature: lists several words that are close to what you may have meant.

☐ Lookup feature to let you use the program instead of a paper dictionary.

## How to Buy Mailing List Programs

There are two basic types of mailing list programs. First, there are programs that will not only generate address labels, but will also perform some of the functions of a database management program. It will let you sort records or print out labels based on some particular piece of information, such as the person's ZIP code, or the size of his or her contribution to your political campaign. This is the kind of software that is usually meant when someone speaks of a *mailing list program.*

The second type of program in this category is one designed to interface with your word processor to generate "customized" form letters. Because the process of creating form letters involves merging a list of addresses with a master letter, this is often referred to as a *mail merge* program. With a mail merge program you may be limited to simply inserting a person's name and address into the inside address section of a form letter. More powerful programs will let you insert an address that begins "Mr. Robert Smith," but open the letter with something like "Dear Bob." However, these programs do not usually offer database management type features.

Mailing list programs sell for anywhere from about $80 to $300. Although we have divided the programs into two categories, in actuality the distinction among such programs may not be all that clear. Some mailing list programs, for example, not only provide address sorting and other list management features but can also be used to create form letters. Others may be limited to producing labels or addressing envelopes. Generally, though, a mail *merge* program or module will not be as sophisticated as a full-blown mailing list program.

As with spelling checkers, you may find that a mail merge option is either included in your word processing package or available as an extra-cost add-on from the same firm. You will definitely find mailing list software available as free-standing programs.

### The Basic Idea

In both cases, you begin by creating a list of names and addresses. The list is made up as a separate file containing any number of address records, but the real action centers around the fields that each record contains. For example, instead of typing in "Mr. Robert Smith," you would probably break the phrase up into three different fields: one for title (Mr., Mrs., or Ms.), one for the first name (Robert, William, or Joan), and one for last name (Smith, Parker, Trachtenberg).

This is an important concept in many, many computer programs because breaking things up into fields gives you (and your machine) a large degree of flexibility. Basically, it lets the computer narrow its focus and allows you to tell the machine where to look in each record to find the particular piece of information you are interested in.

As a simple example, suppose you have a list that you would like to have sorted alphabetically on the basis of each person's last name. If each last name were not separated from the rest of the address by being placed in a "last name" field, the computer would have a difficult time locating the information. Computers, as we've seen, have to be told *everything*. They don't know a last name from "The Last Waltz." All they understand is, What's the character, and where is it located? Thus, it is easy to tell a machine, "Look at the first character in the 'last name' field and alphabetize the list on that basis." It is not so easy to tell it to figure out where the first name ends and the last name begins.

Thus, when you want to type in the first address on your list, the program may present you with a standardized format or *data entry form:*

```
        Customer Address List     Record:1
        MR/MS:
        FIRST NAME:
        LAST NAME:
        ADDRESS:
        CITY:
        STATE;
        ZIP:
```

You might fill in this form with the information for Mr. Robert Smith, record the record and be presented with an identical data entry form differing only in the fact that the upper right hand corner would now read "Record:2."

This is the easy way to do things. The mail merge options available for many word processors may merely give you instructions for creating a form to their specifications. You might have to type the information like this: Mr., Robert, Smith, 206 Nassau Street, Oshkosh, NE, 12345. If you forget a comma, forget it. The program won't work properly because the commas are used to designate the information fields. You could end up producing a letter addressed to Mr. Robert Smith 206 Nassau Street."

Where programs differ is in how long they allow each field to be, the number of standard fields they provide, and in the number of fields you yourself can add. For example, a program that permits only five characters in the ZIP code field could become out of date should the U.S. Postal Service begin to *require* nine-digit ZIP codes. Similarly, if you frequently address mail or send letters to corporate executives, you would not want to use a program that made no provision for a person's title (Vice President, Comptroller, Chief-Cook-And-Bottle-Washer). The same idea applies if you want to use a formal address and an informal greeting. There must be a field for both "Robert" and "Bob."

Unlike many word processor mail merge modules, virtually all mailing list programs include a sort feature of some sort. Since the post office will give you a discount if you presort your mail by ZIP code, this can be a money-saving feature. But suppose you want to target your mail more precisely. Suppose you want to send a new product announcement just to your best customers. Or what if you do not want to send a Christmas card to somebody who either didn't send you one last year, or sent you one but included one of those cloying "family newsletters," something you don't want to encourage in the future?

In such cases, it can be very useful to be able to include a "user-defined" field or two in your address list. Programs that include this option may give you two or three fields (FIELD1, FIELD2, etc.) or a dozen or more, each of which provides room for one to two characters. You may be able to assign any designation to these fields that you like, based on your own coding scheme.

Depending on how you set things up, a letter *A* in FIELD1 could signify a "best customer." A letter *B* could indicate, "Pays within 30 days but buys infrequently." And so on. The second field could be used to designate the range of the person's average purchase. An *A* might indicate $1,000 or more. A *B* might indicate $500 to $1,000, etc. It is important to point out that the program will not be involved in this at all. You will have to keep your own list of what the fields and codes stand for.

Other programs might allow you to specify the actual dollar amounts in the field. Or you may be able to enter some comment that would not print with the label but would be a part of the customer's record. Such a comment would appear any time you called up the record on your screen.

The more user-definable fields a program offers, the more flexible and powerful it will be. Given the right program, for example, you might be able to say, "Program, I want you to go through my customer file and print out labels for just those customers whose average purchase totals $1,000 or more." With a powerful enough program, you may even be able to say, "Program, do everything I just said, but limit the list to people with ZIP codes between 12345 and 12356."

> **SoftTip:** Since database management systems (DBMS) usually offer even more powerful features, and since many of them let you create mailing lists, you may want to consider one of them instead of a mailing list program. Much depends upon the sophistication and precision of address retrieval you need, but if highly specific mailing lists are a goal, you should definitely look into a DBMS program. (See Chapter 16.)

*Mail Merge and Form Letters.* Once you have created your address list, it is often easy to merge it with a form letter created with your word processor. Essentially, all you need to do is to create a master letter that contains the fieldnames used on your address list in place of real names. A mail merge program simply substitutes the actual information for the fieldname in each copy of the letter. Here, for example, is what the inside address on a master form letter might look like:

```
@M@ @FNAME@ @LNAME@
@TITLE@
@ADDRESS@
@CITY@, @STATE@  @ZIP@

Dear @NICK@:
```

Here FNAME is the fieldname for "First Name," LNAME is the fieldname for "Last Name," and NICK is the fieldname for "Nickname." As long as these fieldnames correspond exactly to the fieldnames used on the address list, the program will be able to merge the letter and the addresses with no problem. In most cases, the information will be adjusted properly on the printed page so that you needn't worry about the length of the actual first and last names that are being inserted.

A more sophisticated mail merge program will usually allow you to insert "variable" information in the body of the letter as well. For example, Emily Post would have some sharp words on the subject, but a newly married couple sending thank you notes for wedding presents might be able to create an address list with a field labelled PRESENT. They could then create a form letter that included the sentence, "Thank you so much for the @PRESENT@. It was most thoughtful of you." Obviously, a business could do the same kind of thing with a field called PRODUCT.

*Critical Points*

*Capacity.* Some programs can handle only about 200 addresses, while others can deal with 3,000 or 30,000. Still others are limited only by the amount of available disk space. With the right program and an eight-megabyte hard disk to work with, you might be able to have a list containing up to 65,000 names, for example.

*Number of Fields.* The number of individual pieces of information you can include with each address can range from 8 to 100 fields or more. Eight fields is really the absolute minimum since it provides space for first name, last name, title, company name, street address, city, state, and ZIP. If you want to use a nickname in a letter, you would need an additional field.

*Fixed, User-Defined, and Field Length.* With a database management program, you can usually decide exactly what fields a record will have, what they will be called, and how many characters each will contain. Since a mailing list management program will probably come with pre-defined fields, it can be important to look carefully at what they include. For example, in addition to all of the standard address information, the program may offer from 1 to 12 or more fields for you to use in entering single letter codes. As mentioned earlier, the program views these merely as FIELD1, FIELD2, etc. It is up to you to decide what they will signify.

It is also a good idea to check how long each field may be. A last name field might have a maximum length of 25 characters or it may permit 40 characters. Is there a field you can use for a telephone number, and if so, does it give you enough room to include the person's extension? Is there a "comment" field for you to enter any kind of information you please, and if so, is it limited to 80 characters, 300 characters, or unlimited? (Remember, these are characters, not words.)

*Data Entry and List Management.* When addresses and other information on your list change, you will want to be able to correct the out-of-date record. Consequently, it is worth checking to see how the program handles this. Can you selectively edit the fields (change only the address, but leave everything else the same)? Or must you reenter all of the information? Is editing done within the mailing list program itself, or do you have to use a word processing program?

Does the program have the power to purge duplicate records? If you are building a mailing list on the basis of customer inquiries and responses to your ads, this can be a particularly important feature. Over a period of time, for example, it is quite possible that some of the same individuals will respond to different ads. When that happens, it can be much quicker simply to enter all responses without worrying about whether the same person is already on your list. Then let the software eliminate the duplicates.

*Printing Capabilities.* Some programs are rigidly limited to printing just one label and advancing the paper four lines to begin the next label. Others can print "three up" (three labels at a time) and will allow you to specify printing parameters the way a word processing program does.

It is not a make-or-break weakness, but you might also check to see if the program "hangs up" (stop dead) if you tell it to print and the printer is not on. In such cases, you will have to reboot and begin again. More carefully written programs will give you an error message and wait for you to get the printer ready before continuing.

*Word Processor Interface.* If you plan to use your mailing list program to produce form letters, you must obviously make sure that it will work with files created by your word processor. As with any add-on module, if you buy the program from the same firm, compatibility will be no problem. You will even be able to call the mail merge program while you are using the word processor. With independently produced stand-alone programs, you will have to verify word processor compatibility.

*Extras*

The main "extras" found in this type of software center around their database management functions, principally *sort* and *search* features. A search function may let you generate a list of all the records that meet some criterion you have specified. You might ask for everyone on the list with a specific ZIP code, everyone who lives in Alabama, everyone with "Ms." in one of the address fields, etc. There are at least three things to look at when evaluating a search feature:

1. Which fields can be searched? Only the address fields, or every field in the record? Some programs will even let you search for a particular phrase in a comment field ("likes golf," "W.C.T.U.," "slow pay," etc.)

2. Can you search for a *range* of information such as every ZIP code from 10010 to 10015? Or can you only search for records with a single ZIP code?

3. Is there a *wildcard* feature? Can you ask for every record with a ZIP code reading 1001**, where the asterisks may be any number?

When you sort a list, the program will disassemble it and rewrite each record in the order you have specified. You might want to alphabetize a list or, as mentioned before, sort by ZIP code. One consideration here is what fields can be used as *sort keys*. That is, which fields can you specify as the basis of the sort? For some users, a ZIP code sort may be enough. For others, it may be convenient to be able to sort by one of the fields they have defined to identify good customers or for some other purpose.

The most sophisticated programs will allow you to sort on the basis of two or more keys, which means you could tell the program to sort by ZIP code, but within each ZIP code category to sort the names alphabetically. Again, if you need that kind of power, you'd be better off buying a database management system instead.

Finally, there is the matter of speed. Disassembling and rewriting a complete address list can take a good deal of time. One program, for example, may take six to eight minutes to sort an address list of only 30 names, while another may be able to sort a 100-name list in only a few seconds. The time factor can be important if you frequently add new names to your mailing list, since you will probably want to resort the list each time.

As always, machine or assembly language programs work much faster than programs written in higher level languages, but they may carry a higher price. The amount of time required can also be based on the amount of RAM in your machine. Since sorting takes place in memory, a larger memory may enable the program to sort larger chunks of the list at one time.

## Software Buyer's Quick Reference Checklist
### —Mailing List Programs—

*Categories and Compatibility*

☐ Do you want a program that will simply generate address labels?

☐ Do you want list management capabilities (sort, search, update, etc.)?

☐ Do you want to use a list for customized form letters generated by your word processor? "Mail merge?"

☐ If you want a mail merge program, is it compatible with files generated by your word processor? Can the program be called from within the word processing program?

*Capacity*
☐ What is the maximum number of records (addresses) you can have? It could be 200, 500, 3,000, or unlimited.

☐ Is the maximum number limited by the program or can you expand the number by using a larger capacity floppy drive or a hard disk?

☐ How many fields may you have on each record? Eight is the absolute minimum, but not recommended.

☐ How many characters can you put in each field? Compare these figures with the addresses you normally use.

*Predefined and User-Defined Fields*
☐ What predefined fields does the program use, if any?

☐ Are there any fields you yourself can define? How many characters will each accommodate?

There may be two user-defined fields; there may be 100. The key question is whether there are enough to let you enter all of the codes you want to use. Most will offer one or two characters of space apiece.

☐ Is there a comment field for you to add your own free-form comments? How many characters?

*Ease of Use*
☐ How easy is it to create a mailing list with the program? If you will be using a lot of addresses and plan to merge the list with form letters, you may be better off buying a separate mailing list program that can be used with your word processor instead of a mail merge module. Mail merge modules are more difficult to format and use.

☐ How easy is it to add a new name? Delete an old one? Enter updated information?

☐ Will the program automatically purge duplicate records?

*Printing Capabilities*
☐ How many labels across can the program print? One, three, more?

☐ Can you specify the line spacing between labels? Can you specify other printing parameters?

*Sort and Search*

☐ Does the program have a sort feature and, if so, which fields can it sort on?

☐ Is the sort fast?

☐ Does it have a search feature and, if so, what fields can be searched? Is there a wildcard feature?

---

**SoftTip:** If you simply need to print address labels or continuous-form envelopes, you could create an address file with your word processor in which each page would contain a certain number of addresses, properly spaced for label printing. Indeed, if you only do occasional mailings, this is probably the alternative you should choose, since even the least expensive word processor will probably be able to do this.

Either way, if you need labels you may find that your local stationer has a rather limited selection. If you need more alternatives, you might contact Moore Computer Forms or Quill, mentioned in the previous chapter. Or you might contact a firm that specializes in continuous-form labels. The one listed below, for example, offers over 750 different kinds of continuous-form labels. For information and a catalogue, contact:

> Mail Advertising Supply Co., Inc.
> P.O. Box 363
> 1450 S. West Avenue
> Waukesha, WI   53187
> (800) 558-2126
> (414) 549-1730 (in Wisconsin)

# ...15...

# How to Buy Electronic Spreadsheet Programs

On St. Martin's Eve (November 10) in 1619, the French mathematician and philosopher René Descartes (1596–1650) had a dream that revolutionized mathematics for centuries to come. He had never been blessed with robust health and from an early age had developed the habit of spending much of his time in bed, a place he found particularly conducive to doing his best thinking. The previous day, as he lay there speculating on the nature of Man, the World, the existence of God, and other weighty matters, he had idly watched a fly flitting from one place to another on the ceiling of his rented room in Neuberg, Germany.

As he went to sleep that night, his subconscious went to work and he suddenly realized that if lines were drawn along two perpendicular sides of the ceiling and if numbers were equally spaced along the lines, then the location of the fly at any given point could be expressed as two numbers—one for its "horizontal" coordinate and one for its "vertical" coordinate. This was the beginning of analytical geometry and a host of other innovations, the most familiar of which are the X/Y axes and graphs of high school fame.

Nearly 360 years later, another young man had another "graphic" dream, only this time it was a waking dream designed to solve a particular problem. It was 1978, and Dan Bricklin, an M.I.T. graduate who had enrolled in the Harvard Business School, was spending the spring days inside, laboring at the mind-crunching task of working through the spreadsheets required by the "case studies" the Harvard B-School is famous for. He had only two alternatives: do the work either with paper, pencil, and pocket calculator or on one of the time-sharing mainframe systems at the school.

The disadvantages and error potential of working through multiple calculations by hand are obvious. But in terms of total time, convenience, and ease of use, the mainframe alternative wasn't much more attractive. With a heavily used mainframe system, it is usually necessary for users to put their programs in line—drop them off and come back later for the results. If the program bombs, you must make corrections and get in line again. In addition, the traditional way to input spreadsheet data to a mainframe computer is to create a long list of numbers, equations, labels, and other programming specifications. That can make it difficult to *visualize* what you're doing.

With the classic words, "There's got to be a better way," Bricklin invented the electronic, microcomputer-based spreadsheet. His metaphor was not a fly on the ceiling, it was "an electronic blackboard and electronic chalk in a classroom." By the summer of 1978, he had programmed the first working version of his concept. It consisted of five columns and 20 rows, and, being close to Boston's Route 128 complex, Bricklin thought he might be able to peddle the program door to door to the high-tech firms concentrated there.

At about the same time, however, he realized that the fact that the program required more than a passing knowledge of computer programming made it considerably less than user friendly. To punch it up a bit and give it a more human demeanor, Bricklin enlisted the aid of Bob Frankston, a fellow M.I.T. alumnus. Frankston took to the idea and was eventually able to expand the program and pack the code into a mere 20K of machine memory, making it both powerful and practical enough to be run on a microcomputer.

At about that time, another M.I.T./Harvard Business School graduate, Daniel Flystra, entered the picture. Flystra was looking for products to offer through a small software publishing company he had founded and he suggested that if the Bricklin/Frankston program could be run on the Apple, the three of them might have something. The young men formed a company called Software Arts in January 1979. And, in April of that year, Flystra christened the program "VisiCalc," a compression of the words "visible calculator" and a reference to the fact that, unlike doing spreadsheets on a mainframe, all the elements of a VisiCalc spreadsheet were visible.

This triumvirate then proceeded to set the business world and the budding personal computer industry on its ear. No other program in history has sold so many copies (over 300,000) or been directly responsible for so many sales of microcomputer systems. Like the telephone, VisiCalc opened up possibilities and fulfilled needs that business people didn't even know they had until they saw what it could do.

Corporate planners, who were accustomed to preparing at most two spreadsheets based on differing assumptions before making their decisions, could now change assumptions and produce spreadsheets in minutes instead of hours or days. Executives who were reluctant to use corporate mainframes because of the inevitable delays could get the answers they sought instantly, in the privacy of their offices where there was no DP professional to smirk if they made a mistake. And, by corporate standards, the Apple computers the program ran on were cheap enough to be buried in research, expense, and advertising budgets—much to the consternation of said DP professionals.

In an ironic twist—and a grassroots affirmation that "Software comes first!"—for a while Apple computers were known as "the VisiCalc machines" in the executive suites of corporate America. Bricklin's inspiration may not have the lasting effect of Descartes's, but few authorities would disagree that if it were not for VisiCalc, Apple computers and the personal computer revolution as a whole would not be where it is today.

*Competition and the Start of a Trend*

VisiCalc is now marketed by VisiCorp, a company started by Flystra, while Bricklin and Frankston continue as principals in Software Arts. And, although all three members of the triumvirate would probably disagree with the statement, it is difficult to avoid concluding that they made a serious error: They left a gaping hole in the market by not converting VisiCalc to run on CP/M-based machines. When asked about this, Bricklin notes that to run properly, VisiCalc must be fine tuned to each brand of computer, CP/M or no. And clearly that represents a major effort.

Nevertheless, the fact that there was no CP/M-based electronic spreadsheet prompted Sorcim Corporation to offer SuperCalc in August 1981. Designed to run as on any CP/M machine, SuperCalc contains many improvements over the original VisiCalc and in benchmarked tests has been shown to run much as 40% faster. VisiCalc has been improved many times in succeeding versions, and both a standard and advanced version are now available. But the trend is clear: With each improvement and each new "VisiClone," electronic spreadsheets become both more powerful and more convenient to use. (They also end up requiring more RAM, but as noted in previous chapters, RAM has fallen in price to the point where it is considered quite cheap.)

This trend has profound implications for business users and personal users alike. It is a computer industry truism that when programs are easier to use, more people will use them. One of the latest manifestations is MultiPlan from Microsoft Corporation. MultiPlan incorporates all of the features of VisiCalc and SuperCalc, but it goes them at least one better. You will better understand the significance of this in a moment, but MultiPlan makes it possible for people to use real-word labels when telling the spreadsheet to add total "Sales" and multiply by

"Rate" to generate "Commission." With either VisiCalc or SuperCalc, the same instruction would require you to refer to the numbers as coordinate locations by typing in something like this: $+F1.F10*G39$.

As spreadsheets have become more user friendly, considerably less expensive versions have also appeared on the market. Today it is possible to buy a very powerful "home" spreadsheet program for about $50 (see Chapter 21), compared to "business" spreadsheets that sell for $250 to $400 or more. At first, that may not sound terribly thrilling. After all, how often do you in your private life have to calculate "net present value" or "discounted cash flow" or use a spreadsheet in any of the other ways it is used in business? But, as we'll see, there are aspects of spreadsheeting and the inherent versatility of the concept that can make the programs as important to you when using your home computer as when using the one you may have at work.

*What Is a Spreadsheet?*

If you already have a pretty good idea of what a spreadsheet is, you might want to jump ahead to the FRAMEWORK section later in the chapter. But if you are not a business person or if you are not involved in the upper levels of corporate management, there's a good chance that you may never have heard the term "spreadsheet" prior to your entry into the microworld. It is not a word that comes up frequently in polite conversation among non-accountants. The terms "financial modeler" or "decision support system" (DSS) are also applied to this kind of software, but they're not much help either.

In the conventional sense, a spreadsheet is basically a piece of paper—usually a *large* piece of paper—that lays everything out for you. It spreads all of the costs, the taxes, the interest rates, the income—everything—on a single sheet for you to look at when making a decision. Typically, the most important part of a spreadsheet is "the bottom line," because it represents the "final outcome," "the end of the story," "the whole enchilada," "the go/no-go decision," "the 'I'm-talking-Grade-triple-A-municipal-bonds, Ted,'" and "the big picture."

The closest most non-business people ever come to the spreadsheet concept is when calculating their income taxes each April 14. ("Let's see, if I claim my Golden Retriever as a dependent, my taxes will be . . . ") But you probably use the same ideas when trying to figure out whether you can afford the latest Z car or Porsche. In either case, the bottom line is what you are most interested in. But the bottom line is usually the result of adding several figures, each of which is the result of *other* calculations.

The bottom line on whether you can afford a particular house, for example, depends on the total amount of money you have to borrow.

And that depends on the size of the down payment you can afford to make. The bottom line also depends on the interest rate that you will be charged to borrow the money and the number of years you have to repay. Balloon payments, local property taxes, the money you'll have to spend to put in a new kitchen, and literally dozens of other financial factors can be a part of the bottom line.

Given the complexity and interdependence of the figures, you would probably have to be very serious about a particular house before you would go through this effort with a pocket calculator and a pencil. The thought of doing it for two or even three houses could be enough to persuade you that the flaking paint and the outmoded plumbing in your current abode aren't so bad after all.

Problems like this are not very different in kind from the type that businesses face every day. But while no one cares if you work your figures out on the first scrap of paper that happens to be at hand, corporate vice presidents take a dim view of having the numbers for a multi-million-dollar plant expansion handed to them on the back of an envelope. Hence, the more formal and more elaborate "spreadsheet."

With a spreadsheet, things can be organized neatly into labelled columns and rows and then added up to make a total, bottom line figure. But a spreadsheet is much more than a simple column of figures to be added. It's really more like a 1040 long form federal income tax return spread out on a large sheet instead of being printed on both sides of a piece of letter-sized paper. If you've ever filled out one of these forms, you know that many of the figures that ultimately get added, subtracted, and multiplied on the form actually come from someplace else.

The number you ultimately write in the Total Income box, for example, is the sum of "wages, salaries, tips, and other employee compensation" plus "interest income" plus "dividends"—but here we have to stop for a moment. Before you know what to enter in the dividend box, you must first take your total dividend income and subtract $100—the dividend exclusion allowance. Then enter the remainder in the box. After that, you can continue through business income (attach Schedule C), capital gains (attach Schedule D), pensions and annuities (attach Schedule E), and so on, until you get to the good stuff—the deductions. And again, there will be schedules to attach and calculations to perform before you know what amount to enter in each block.

This is exactly the kind of thing that a traditional spreadsheet contains, including attached schedules and explanations to tell the reader how the figures in the columns were derived. To understand immediately why *electronic* spreadsheets are so popular, you have only to imagine that you have your income tax return all filled in when you suddenly remember that you forgot to deduct the $500 you paid in interest on a credit union loan and the $100 you gave to your college to get them to stop sending you Annual Giving notices.

Deducting those two figures will affect the bottom line amount on Schedule A—Itemized Deductions. And since that figure is entered on the main 1040 form, it will mean that nearly every figure that follows it on the 1040 will have to be recalculated until you come up with a new tax refund or balance due amount.

Clearly, that's going to be a lot of work. And it's just the kind of work that electronic spreadsheet programs were designed to eliminate. With VisiCalc, SuperCalc, Multiplan or any other similar program, all you would have to do would be to type in $500 on one line of Schedule A and $100 on another line. The program would automatically perform all of the recalculations.

### How Does It Work?

The concept behind an electronic spreadsheet is elegantly simple, yet extremely powerful. The program puts a line at the top of your screen and a line running down the left side. The top line might contain the letters of the alphabet and the side line might contain numbers starting with *1* and stretching all the way down your screen (see Figure 15.1).

As with the fly on Descartes's ceiling, this arrangement makes it possible to precisely locate any spot on the screen by referring to its coordinates. In effect, a spreadsheet program divides the screen up into easily identifiable chunks. In spreadsheet parlance, these chunks are called "cells." We won't go into it now, but a cell can be anywhere from three to 63 characters or more wide. And when you specify a particular width, the letters at the top of the screen move closer together or further apart to compress or widen the width of the column they head.

In Figure 15.1, the cursor is at cell *D5*. The columns are set to be seven characters wide. On a VisiCalc screen, the cursor will be represented as a filled-in block. Notice that the cursor is as wide as the column, and that its location is printed in the upper left corner of the bar across the top of the screen.

### A Window on the Spreadsheet

A computer screen isn't big enough to display the whole spreadsheet at one time. In fact, the most you can look at is about 21 columns and 21 rows. However, when you move the cursor to the right, the screen will scroll horizontally. New column letters will appear as the *A*, *B*, *C*, etc., columns scroll off to the left. Moving the cursor down past row 21 causes the screen to scroll vertically, revealing more numbers while rows 1, 2, 3, etc., scroll off the top of your screen. The screen can thus be thought of as a window that you move around over a spreadsheet

——— **Figure 15.1** ———

**An Empty VisiCalc Screen**

| D5 |
|----|

|     | A | B | C | D | E | F | G | H |
|-----|---|---|---|---|---|---|---|---|
| 1   |   |   |   |   |   |   |   |   |
| 2   |   |   |   |   |   |   |   |   |
| 3   |   |   |   |   |   |   |   |   |
| 4   |   |   |   |   |   |   |   |   |
| 5   |   |   |   | [ ] |   |   |   |   |
| 6   |   |   |   |   |   |   |   |   |
| 7   |   |   |   |   |   |   |   |   |
| 8   |   |   |   |   |   |   |   |   |
| 9   |   |   |   |   |   |   |   |   |
| 10  |   |   |   |   |   |   |   |   |
| 11  |   |   |   |   |   |   |   |   |
| 12  |   |   |   |   |   |   |   |   |
| 13  |   |   |   |   |   |   |   |   |
| 14  |   |   |   |   |   |   |   |   |
| 15  |   |   |   |   |   |   |   |   |
| 16  |   |   |   |   |   |   |   |   |
| 17  |   |   |   |   |   |   |   |   |
| 18  |   |   |   |   |   |   |   |   |
| 19  |   |   |   |   |   |   |   |   |
| 20  |   |   |   |   |   |   |   |   |
| 21  |   |   |   |   |   |   |   |   |

that extends 63 or more columns to the right and 254 rows or more from top to bottom.

*The Setup*

To use a spreadsheet program, you type the column labels you want to use into a number of cells at the top of the sheet (or anywhere else), and you label the line items. In both cases, your labels may stretch across several cells. You can add lines and other characters as well, just as you would when using a word processing program to create a chart (see Figure 15.2).

Once you have labelled your worksheet's rows and columns, you're ready for the really important part: entering the formulas you want to use for various cells. For example, in Figure 15.2, the cursor is parked at cell *E8*. If you were doing the sales report by hand, you would multiply the Quantity times the Unit Price to figure out what should go in cell *E8*, but VisiCalc or another electronic spreadsheet can do this automatically.

All you have to do is tell the program what you want. You move the cursor to the target cell and use the program's commands to enter a formula. In this case, you would type in: +*A7*C7*. (The asterisk or "splat" is the symbol for multiplication.) The formula will appear just below the status bar at the top of the screen, and when you hit <ENTER> it will disappear. However, the program will attach it to cell *E8*.

——— **Figure 15.2** ———

**Simple VisiCalc Set-Up**

| EB |
| --- |

+A7*C7

|   | A | B | C | E |
| --- | --- | --- | --- | --- |
| 1 | Sales Report |  |  | Date: |
| 2 |  |  |  |  |
| 3 | --------------------------------------------------------------------------- |
| 4 |  |  |  |  |
| 5 | Quantity | Item | Unit Price | Total Price |
| 6 | =========================================================================== |
| 7 |  |  |  |  |
| 8 |  |  |  |  |
| 9 |  |  |  |  |
| 10 |  |  |  |  |
| 11 |  |  |  |  |
| 12 |  |  |  |  |
| 13 |  |  |  |  |
| 14 |  |  |  |  |
| 15 |  |  |  |  |
| 16 | =========================================================================== |
| 17 |  |  |  |  |
| 18 |  |  | Sub-total: |  |
| 19 |  |  | Discount : |  |
| 20 |  |  | ------------------- |  |
| 21 |  |  | Grand Total: |  |

Now when you are writing up your sales report, you have only to type the quantity in cell *A7*, add an Item description if you want, and type the unit price into cell *C7*. When you hit your <ENTER> key after entering the Unit Price, the correct amount will automatically appear in Total Price cell *E8*.

When you move your cursor to Subtotal cell *E18*, you can enter a formula to tell the program to add up all the figures in the Total Price column. You would use the same process for Discount cell *E19*, only here you might have even more flexibility. You could tell the program to multiply the Subtotal by a flat 7% and put the result in the Discount cell.

But if you wanted to make the discount percentage increase as the total sales figure increased, you could do that as well. This is done by telling the program to compare the Subtotal amount to the values on a "look-up" table you have created elsewhere on your worksheet. The look-up table would say, in effect: If the subtotal is less than $100, do not give a discount. If it's between $100 and $300, give a 7% discount. And if it's over $300, give a 10% discount.

Of course, spreadsheets can be saved and they can be printed. If you wanted to, for example, you could get everything in the Sales Report set up and record it on disk as a "master form." Then each month you could call the file into the system again, and enter a new date and the month's sales data. You could then save your work under a different filename, and tell the program to print it out.

## The Electronic Spreadsheet as a Software Engine

*The Magic of Spreadsheet Templates*

This is the basic concept of an electronic spreadsheet and how it works. As you can imagine, though, the details vary with the particular program. We've already mentioned that Microsoft's Multiplan will let you enter formulas using column names instead of cell coordinates. Thus, the formula for Subtotal might be written: Quantity*Unit Price. We'll look at a number of other variations in a moment.

Right now, if you are afflicted with math anxiety and if all this talk of formulas (a.k.a. "equations") is making you short of breath, there is good news. The major work in using a spreadsheet comes in planning and laying out the form and in deciding what formulas to enter at appropriate points. But thanks to something called "templates," you may not have to do any of these things to apply a spreadsheet to a problem.

When you create and save a worksheet, what is actually stored on disk is a series of instructions to the VisiCalc or other spreadsheet program. The instructions say, "Put this label in cell *A1*, and enter this formula in cell *E8*, etc." When you load one of your worksheets into the program, the system reads and acts upon these instructions. Thus, if someone in your office or computer users' group has gone to the trouble to lay out a worksheet and its formulas, it is easy for you or someone else to use it. All you have to do is get a copy of the individual's saved worksheet file and load it in when using your own program. The programs must be compatible, of course. Either that or your program must have a file conversion feature to put the file into a form it can use.

Here is part of a 128-line VisiCalc template that was downloaded (captured) from a free computer bulletin board system (see Chapter 12). The only cost was the price of the late evening long distance phone call.

```
——Start of VisiCalc BREAKEVEN Model——
. . Delete these first 2 lines before using . .
>L46:/FR
>D21:+C21*B6*(.01*(100-B19))-(B11+(B18*C21))
>C21:+C20+B21
>B21:2000
>A21:"    UNITS
>D20:+C20*B6*(.01*(100-B19))-(B11+(B18*C20))
>C20:+C19+B21
>B20:"ENT IN —
>A20:"— INCREM
>D19:+C19*B6*(.01*(100-B19))-(B11+(B18*C19))
>C19:+C18+B21
>B19:20
>A19:"%DISCOUNT
>D18:+C18*B6*(.01*(100-B19))-(B11+(B18*C18))
```

The characters like *L46* and *D18* are easily recognizable as VisiCalc cell coordinates. The colon (:) is the symbol that tells the program to "put the following characters, value, or equation into this cell." It serves the same function as the <ENTER> key. The only thing that is not obvious is why the template doesn't begin with a cell like *A1* the way you might when creating a worksheet. The answer is simply that VisiCalc recreates its models from the bottom up, beginning at the lower right corner and ending in the upper left.

The template is not signed, so it is impossible to credit the author. But clearly someone spent some time and effort laying out a worksheet and figuring out what formulas should be entered for which cells. As the recipient of such a template, you have only to use your word processing or other editing program to delete the first two lines as instructed, save the edited version to disk, and load it into your VisiCalc screen.

**SoftTip:** The partial template you've just seen can be viewed and transmitted over the telephone because it is a *text* file. VisiCalc and other spreadsheets record their worksheets in this regular

ASCII character format. Other programs, however, save their worksheets in "binary" (machine language) form. Templates for these programs cannot by typed in by the user. And, although they can be sent over the telephone, you may need communications software with a special error-checking protocol (see Chapter 17). If you think you might want to enter your own templates or use those found on computer bulletin boards, you should buy a program that either normally saves its worksheets as text files, or includes a feature to make this possible.

*The Unexpected Culmination?*

It may not be obvious, but the scenario just described is of tremendous importance to you as a software buyer, for it may ultimately lead to considerably less expensive programs and far more of them. In so doing, it may turn out to be the least expected and most significant result of the invention of the electronic spreadsheet.

There are three main factors to consider. The first is the versatility of an electronic spreadsheet program. We haven't discussed many applications yet, but with different templates an electronic spreadsheet can be used to monitor your investment portfolio, perform all of the important business chores (cash flow analysis, depreciation schedules, balance sheet, income statement, etc.), serve as a personal checkbook balancer, a home budget program, a home accounting program, and do many other things now performed by single-purpose programs. Some people even use spreadsheets as rudimentary word processors, and at least one engineer uses them to lay out electric wiring diagrams.

The potential applications appear to be endless, and they will undoubtedly increase as newer spreadsheet versions add more features and power and take fuller advantage of the expanded memory made possible by the newer 16-bit machines. (The standard VisiCalc for the IBM/PC is a translation of the 8-bit Apple version. The Advanced Version of VisiCalc is a true 16-bit program.) Thus, with the right selection of templates, the electronic spreadsheet could become an "engine" that will drive an unlimited number of applications.

The second point concerns the relative ease with which a spreadsheet application can be developed. As we saw when building the sales report model, no knowledge of computer languages or computer programming is required. The more complex templates require a firm grasp of arithmetic and algebra, but that is something that many people have, compared to the number of individuals conversant with computer programming. In addition, electronic spreadsheet models are much easier to create than computer programs. You can *see* exactly what you are doing and obtain test ("debugging") results immediately. Because templates can be created so quickly, the firms that create them will be motivated to charge lower prices than they currently charge for "dedicated" programs that accomplish the same things.

This leads to the third point. As electronic spreadsheets increase in power and user friendliness, more people will be using them. And more templates and applications will be created, either for sale or offered gratis via computer bulletin boards and other outlets.

*Limitations and Possibilities*

Clearly, it will take some time before electronic spreadsheets and templates rival dedicated, single-purpose programs. Menus and extensive help functions could be a problem, for example. But, as noted, spreadsheets are constantly increasing in power. Some programs already have the ability to "chain" together several different spreadsheets, and many already offer an "IF . . . THEN . . . ELSE" function.

Additional programming would be required, but conceivably, the first worksheet screen you see could contain a menu with instructions to move your cursor to a particular cell. The cell could have a formula "attached" to it that said, "If this guy enters a *1* here, then bring in Worksheet A, otherwise (ELSE), bring in Worksheet B."

It is also true that there are some tasks that a spreadsheet will never be able to perform as well as a dedicated program. Communications, database management, business graphics, and word processing are all non-spreadsheet applications. (See Chapter 18 for information on integrated packages that combine all of these functions.) But any "number crunching" application such as portfolio management, budgeting, and personal finance is ideally suited for an electronic spreadsheet/template combination.

This means that, in the future, instead of spending hundreds of dollars to obtain a dedicated program for each of these applications, you may be able to buy a single spreadsheet program and individual applications templates at perhaps $20 apiece. Or you may be able to buy a book containing a series of template listings that you can type in yourself.

Actually, you can already do this today. The field is just getting started, so the selection of templates, while impressive, is still relatively limited. None of them provides all of the extra features, "front-end" menus, and other cosmetics found in dedicated programs. But the core of the program is there, with all the power of the spreadsheet concept. Given the difference in price between a single-purpose program and a free or inexpensive template, the current limitations of spreadsheet templates may be more than acceptable.

**SoftTip:** Here are four template packages offered by SpreadSoft for use with VisiCalc on the Apple II or III (other computers may also be supported as well):

*Business Bookeeper™ ($48)*
Six templates to create
a mini-accounting system
for a small business.

*Money Marketor™ ($48)*
Twenty templates
Discounts
Yields
Effective return
etc.

*Business Basics™ ($76)*
(2-disk package)
  Cash flow
  Breakeven
  Sales goals
  Contracts bidding
  Project analysis
  . . . and more

*Business Budgeting™ ($48)*
Eight templates;
  Master budget
  Advertising
  Cost of goods sold
  Operating costs
  etc.

For information on home budgeting and personal finance templates, see Chapter 21. For more information on the above products, contact:

Spreadsoft
P.O. Box 192
Clinton, MD   20735
(301) 856-1180

---

**SoftTip:** You will find a growing number of books at your book and computer store containing spreadsheet templates for you to type in yourself. Two particularly good books are:

*VisiCalc: Home and Office Companion*
by Castlewitz, Chisausky, and Kronberg
Osborne/McGraw-Hill, 1982, $16 (50 templates and instructions)

*The Power of VisiCalc*
by Robert Williams and Bruce Taylor, 1981, $14.95

*SoftTip continued*

(Step-by-step guide to creating worksheets)
Management Information Source, Inc.
1626 N. Vancouver Avenue
Portland, OR   97227
(503) 287-1462

Similar books, some by the same authors, exist for SuperCalc,
Multiplan, and other spreadsheet programs.

## How to Create and Use a Spreadsheet Template

Many manuals, including some VisiCalc manuals, make no mention of
templates and how to use them. If you find this to be the case in your
situation, the following steps will show you what to do. These instructions apply to VisiCalc on the IBM/PC, so you may have to translate
them for use with other spreadsheets and computers. Use them as an
indication of where to look in your own manual for the commands
needed to accomplish similar tasks.

1. Create your worksheet, including all labels and cell formulas. Then
   save it to disk as a regular VisiCalc file. Entering "/S" followed by
   "S" will cause the program to prompt you for the filename you want
   to use. Enter a drive designator and colon like "B:" and type in the
   name. Do not add an extension, as the program will automatically
   save the worksheet as "FILENAME.VC" on the drive you have
   specified.

2. There is no way to look at the file while you are in the VisiCalc
   program. So leave the program with the /SQ command, and respond
   with a "Y" for "yes" in answer to the program's question as to
   whether you really want to leave so soon.

   This will drop you into DOS and the A> prompt will appear. Call for
   a directory of the disk to which your worksheet has been saved.
   FILENAME.VC should be on the list.

3. To take a quick look at the file, enter "TYPE," followed by FILE-
   NAME.VC. A listing similar to the Break Even model cited earlier

will rapidly scroll up your screen. (You can get an instant hard copy as well if you toggle on the IBM Print-Screen function before entering the TYPE command.)

4. To edit your own file or to remove any unwanted lines in a template you have received from a computer bulletin board, you will need your word processing program.

Boot the program and bring in FILENAME.VC just as if it were a letter or memo. You can then edit, add, delete, print it, or do whatever else is necessary. The only rules are that you must preserve the format: flush left, single-spaced, each line beginning with a greater-than symbol (>) and ending with a hard carriage return.

5. VERY IMPORTANT. When you are finished editing, be sure to save your work to disk under a filename that ends with the VisiCalc (.VC) file extension. If you don't do this, you will not be able to load the worksheet template into your VisiCalc program.

---

**SoftTip:** You may have read about DIF (Data Interchange Format) files and how they can be used to transmit VisiCalc information over the telephone. To avoid confusion with the template files discussed above, you should know that a DIF file records *only* labels and numbers. It does not record the formulas you need for an automatically running template. (See the "Data Transfer" section later in this chapter.)

---

### Framework

With all the claims, counterclaims, advertising, and general hubbub that surround electronic spreadsheets, it is easy to become confused about all of the standard features, let alone the "new and improved" versions. Often, it is difficult to know where each feature fits, especially if you have had little or no experience with this type of software. Fortunately, the major steps you must follow when using a spreadsheet divide naturally into about five categories:

- Layout and labeling

- Entering formulas

- Entering and viewing data

- Printing spreadsheets

- Transferring data

Virtually all of the features and functions of an electronic spreadsheet program can be placed under one of these categories. The nature of these features, their power, and the ease with which they enable you to accomplish necessary tasks are the major points on which spreadsheet programs differ. In the following section, we'll look at each category briefly. Then we'll use the same framework for the Software Buyer's Quick Reference Checklist at the end of the chapter.

*Layout and Labelling*

There are two major points that often concern spreadsheet users when preparing their forms. The first is, How good can I make it look? and the second is, How easily can I accomplish that goal? Concern about appearances may sound a bit vain, but it really isn't. Whenever you read about spreadsheets, the function that is invariably emphasized is the "What If . . . ?" decision support feature. Nonspreadsheet users may never realize that the worksheets—be they sales or inventory reports, personnel records, checkbook registers, or anything else—are intended to be printed, and in a corporate environment, distributed as well.

Consequently, it can be important to make the spreadsheet look as though it was created on a typewriter or word processor. You wouldn't think that would be too difficult, but the fact is that the program's dependence on clearly defined rows and columns can cause problems. If the columns cannot be made wide enough, for example, the titles used to identify them may be split, leaving unattractive gaps on the printed page. If numbers cannot be preceded by dollar signs ($) or if numbers larger than 999 cannot include commas, the figures can be difficult to read and understand. It can also be nice to be able to underline a title to give it added emphasis. The newer programs include many of these features, but not all programs will allow you to do each of these things.

Another good example is the flexibility of the column expansion features. Suppose you need 14 characters to fully accommodate the title you want to use in the first column. But in the second column, you need only five characters. Ideally, you should be able to make the first column 14 characters wide and the second column five characters wide. But, until recently, that has not been possible. When using the regular version of VisiCalc, for example, if you want one column to be 14 characters, then *all* columns must be 14 characters. There is no provision for variable column widths.

This limitation presents a very unappealing choice. Either the first column will be wide enough to accommodate the complete title (and since every other column must be the same width, your figures will be spread out all over the page), or you must find a way to abbreviate the first column title so that it will fit within a narrower column. The Advanced Version of VisiCalc, Multiplan, SuperCalc, and other spreadsheets now offer variable column widths.

The ease with which you can create a spreadsheet to your specifications is also important, particularly if you plan to use the program a lot. Thus, it can be convenient to change the width of all columns with a single "global" command, should you want to do so. A global "search and replace" feature of the type found in better word processing programs can enable you to tell the program to locate a particular title or word and replace it with something else. A feature that automatically right, center, or left justifies your titles (and data) can also be important, since it saves you counting characters to do this yourself. A "replication" feature will let you enter a dashed line or some other characters in a single cell and tell the program to duplicate the entry in a specified range of cells, across or up and down the spreadsheet. The ability to insert columns or rows at any given location can be important. Again, programs differ on the features they offer in this area. (Some will allow you to insert columns but not rows, some will do both, and others will do neither.)

*Entering Formulas*

The formulas or calculation "rules" you can enter are the heart of any spreadsheet's power. But the ease with which you can enter them and error-prevention features are also very important. In the power category, you can expect a spreadsheet to offer all arithmetical functions (add, subtract, multiply, and divide), of course. But after that, the sky's the limit. Depending on the program, you may be able to enter formulas to calculate absolute values, exponential powers, logarithms, square roots, the trigonometric functions (sine, cosine, tangent, etc.), averages, standard deviations, depreciation, percentages, and many more.

There may also be "logical" operators and Boolean functions enabling you to tell the program "IF the value in cell *A1* is 'true,' THEN put that value in this cell, ELSE (otherwise) put another value here." You might say, for example, "If the value in cell *A1* is greater than 50, then put that value into this cell, otherwise put something else here." Logical operators like these can also be used to print different text messages. Suppose you used a spreadsheet to produce sales reports for several individuals. You could use an IF . . . THEN . . . ELSE function to tell the program to print "Congratulations on a job well done!" at the bottom of every report in which the Month's Total figure was greater than $5,000. If the figure was less than $5,000, you might print a different message.

Entering formulas will probably be easier if you can use complete words like "Balance" or "Rate" instead of cell designations. In addition, programs differ in the cell coordinates they use. SuperCalc and VisiCalc use letters and numbers like *F5* ("column F, row 5") to refer to a location. Micropro's CalcStar uses just numbers separated by a comma *(5,6)*. Multiplan uses numbers and *R* for "row" and *C* for "column"— *R5C6* ("row 5, column 6"). Some people will find one format easier to use and remember, others will have the opposite opinion.

With many programs, like VisiCalc, there is no easy way to look at the formula that has been attached to a cell after you have entered it. VisiCalc's Advanced Version and others, however, include this feature. In some programs, to change a formula, you may have to retype the entire thing, or you may be able to edit it as you would with a word processor.

---

**SoftTip:** Apple II Plus and Franklin Ace owners may be interested in a special plug-in keypad designed to make it especially easy to create VisiCalc models and enter data. Called "Keywiz," the unit has keys for the most frequently used VisiCalc commands. Hitting the "Save" key, for example, automatically issues the "/SS" sequence VisiCalc needs to record information. There are also cursor arrow keys. Keywiz-83 lists for $300 and includes a numeric keypad. Contact:

> Creative Computers
> Aztec Environmental Center
> 1044 Lacey Road
> Forked River, NJ    08731
> (609) 693-0002

---

Finally, there is the matter of error prevention. Virtually all programs will prevent you from entering a formula that calls for division by zero and other mathematical impossibilities. But perhaps the most important error-prevention feature is the option to "protect" a cell. Once a formula has been entered for a cell, there is usually nothing on the screen to indicate that a formula is there. Consequently, if you come along and type something else in that cell, the first formula will be erased. You might not discover the fact until you tried to use the program.

Newer spreadsheets may allow you to put a marker in the cells that contain formulas. And many will let you tell the program that it should prevent you or anyone else from typing anything in a cell that would wipe out or alter its formula. Typically, numbers can be added or erased as usual. But any labels or text in the cell, as well as any formulas, will be protected until you "unprotect" them.

---

**SoftTip:** The protection feature can be especially valuable to managers who want to prepare worksheets for use by clerical staff. This can reduce the possibility that the model will be damaged or rendered inaccurate by an inexperienced user. In some cases, it may even be possible to buy a program that requires a special software "key" to unprotect a cell. The key can be kept in the manager's office, thus reducing the possibility of deliberate tampering with the worksheet.

One such product is Wondercalc (99 columns, 998 rows) from Westico. The full program costs $395, but an "inhibited version" for use by clerical workers is available for $195. Contact:

Westico, Inc.
25 Van Zant Street
Norwalk, CT   06855
(203) 853-6880

24-hour computer bulletin board
(300 baud): 203-853-0816

---

*Entering and Viewing Data*

The prime considerations here are convenience and ease of use. Many programs will let you enter a "GOTO" command to take you instantly to the cell you specify. When using a large worksheet, it can be very important to be able to look simultaneously at two or more sections while entering numbers in a third. Almost all programs include some kind of "windowing" feature that lets you hold a column or row on the screen while displaying another section of the sheet that would not normally be visible at the same time. Thus, you will be able to divide the screen horizontally or vertically along whatever lines you please.

More elaborate windowing functions may also be available. It might be possible to divide the screen into as many as eight windows, each of which would scroll independently whenever you placed the cursor within them. Or you might be able to link the windows together so that causing one to scroll made the other one scroll as well.

One feature many people will find particularly convenient is the option of turning the automatic calculation function on or off. Usually, when you enter a number in a spreadsheet cell, the program immediately recalculates and enters new figures for every cell that depends on that number. While this is taking place, you cannot continue to add numbers. You've got to wait until the program is finished. In a complex spreadsheet with many interlocking cells, this can be a nuisance. Consequently, many newer programs will let you enter all of your data and then tell the program to perform all of its recalculations at once.

The ability to sort columns and rows in ascending or descending order is another nice feature found in some of the newer spreadsheets. Some programs include a "Help" function or menu. CalcStar offers onscreen help menus similar to its famous relative, WordStar.

**SoftTip:** In addition to onscreen help, Multiplan includes a unique "proposed response" feature in which the software tries to anticipate your desires. If you tell the system that you want to split the screen vertically, for example, the program will ask if you want to divide it exactly in half. You are free to enter a different response, of course. But if the program has guessed correctly, you have only to hit <ENTER>. Over a long session, this can save you a considerable number of keystrokes.

**SoftTip:** VisiCalc is not able to sort spreadsheet columns, but a number of independent firms sell utility packages to give the program this and other capabilities that it lacks. For Apple II Plus, TRS-80 (Models I and III), and IBM/PC users, there is V-Utility from Yucaipa Software. The package sells for $130 and includes sorting, printing, statistical analysis, and several templates as well. Contact:

> Yucaipa Software
> 12343 12th Street
> Yucaipa, CA   92399
> (714) 797-6331

There is also Versacalc from Versacalc Enterprises, Inc. Available for the Apple II, Commodore PET and CBM, and IBM/PC at prices ranging from $100 to $150, it includes a number of other functions as well. Contact:

Anthro-Digital Software
P.O. Box 1385
Pittsfield, MA   01202
(413) 488-8278

These utilities are fine, but if you have not yet purchased a spreadsheet program, they do not make very sound economic sense. Most people would be much better off buying a single spreadsheet that incorporated these features for $275 to $400 than buying both VisiCalc ($250) and a hundred-dollar utility program to provide features VisiCalc lacks.

---

**SoftTip:** Perhaps the ultimate VisiCalc add-on is a program called StretchCalc from MultiSoft Corporation. Among other things, this program gives the standard IBM/PC version of VisiCalc the ability to utilize the IBM/PC function keys, to store keystrokes, to produce eight types of graphs, and to sort on the basis of a single key. VisiCorp has licensed StretchCalc and offers both it and VisiCalc as a package called "VisiCalc IV." By doing so, the firm hopes to compete with the Lotus 1-2-3 integrated package (see Chapter 18).
    If you already own VisiCalc, you can purchase StretchCalc from MultiSoft in one of two configurations. With the graphics module it sells for $99. "Little StretchCalc" (no graphics) is available only by ordering directly from MultiSoft ($49). Contact:

StretchCalc
MultiSoft Corporation
140125 S.W. Farmington Road
Beaverton, OR   97005
(800) 322-4110
(503) 626-4727, in Oregon

---

*Printing Worksheets*
    Given the emphasis that is often placed on an electronic spreadsheet's "What If . . . ?" capabilities, many software buyers fail to pay close attention to a given program's printing features. But, of course, the ease and flexibility with which you can send a worksheet to your printer

are very important. All programs will allow you to print everything contained in the worksheet, whether you can see it all on the screen or not. But they go about it in different ways.

For example, you may have to print a large worksheet in sections. This is often done by moving the cursor to cell *A1* (or some other location) and then entering a command to tell the system that you want to print something. The software will assume that the cursor is positioned at the upper left location of the worksheet or portion that you want to print. It will then ask you to type in the cell coordinates for the lower right location. At that point, you may be able to enter any special commands to tell the printer to print in bold print or in compressed type. The printing is then started by hitting <ENTER>.

This doesn't sound too bad, and it does give you the flexibility of printing just a portion of an entire worksheet, though it can be inconvenient if you do not remember the cell coordinates for the lower right corner. But what if you want to print the entire worksheet? And what if the worksheet extends more than 80 characters off to the right? If the maximum number of pica characters your printer can print left to right is 80, you might find yourself following instructions like these:

> Calculate how many columns of the worksheet (characters) can be printed at a time, then divide the worksheet into the number of rectangles required to print the full width. The separate printed copies can be taped together to reproduce the worksheet.

This is no fun, to say the least. The above quotation is taken from the IBM/PC VisiCalc manual, but VisiCalc is far from being the only program that requires this procedure. Newer programs (or VisiCalc add-on utilities) eliminate much of the inconvenience. With these products, you may only have to tell the system that you have an 80-character printer and that the pages are 66 lines long. The software will then perform the necessary calculations to determine how large a section of the spreadsheet can be printed at one time.

---

**SoftTip:** The VisiCalc manual does not mention the possibility of using compressed printing to squeeze spreadsheets measuring 132 characters across onto a letter-sized page. (Compressed printing is activated with a Setup command.) The only other way to avoid counting and dividing characters is to buy a wide-track printer. With pica-sized type, you will be able to print 136 characters. In compressed print mode, 233.

As you know, when a spreadsheet is saved to disk, it is often recorded as a file that includes all of the cell locations, data, and formulas the software needs to recreate your worksheet on the screen. However, there are usually other options as well. As we will see in a moment, you will probably be able to save a worksheet, without its formulas, in the DIF format. But you will usually be able to record what you see on a floppy disk the way you would record a report, memo, or other piece of text created with your word processing program. The VisiCalc program calls this "printing to disk," but other programs may use a different term. Again, only the titles, labels, and data are saved, not the formulas.

The main advantage of this option is that it lets you use the worksheet you have created in a word processing program. As long as both your spreadsheet and your word processing program use the same operating system, and thus record data with the same file format on disk, this is usually no problem. Once you bring the file into your word processing program, you can manipulate the characters just as you would any other chart or table. When you are finished, you can save the file again or print it out, or both.

---

**SoftTip:** Being able to load a worksheet file into a word processing program makes it easy to include the worksheet in the body of a report. But for many software buyers, it has an even greater significance. Once you get the spreadsheet into the word processing program, you can underline words, print some of them in bold or compressed print, add expanded print titles, italics, dollar signs and percent signs, add superscripts and subscripts, and use other features that the spreadsheet program itself does not offer. Using two programs to produce a final report may not be convenient, but no spreadsheet offers the full range of features found in a major word processing program.

*Very Important:* If you plan to use a word processing program to dress up your worksheets, make certain that the program can read and display the worksheet file created by the spreadsheet program. Second, and equally important, find out how many characters the word processing program will display horizontally. (What is the maximum right margin setting?) The Select word processing program, for example, will allow no more than 80 characters per line. WordStar works best with a maximum of 240 characters, but will accept lines as long as 32,000 characters. Other word processing programs have other limits.

---

**SoftTip:** With VisiCalc and other programs, once you "print a worksheet to disk" you cannot bring it back into the spreadsheet program to be printed. (The program cannot read text files other than those in the special template format.) Consequently, you will have to print the worksheet with a word processing program.

For this reason, and because a worksheet printed to disk contains no formulas, it is a good idea to print a worksheet to disk *and* record a copy of it in the system's standard template-style format. With VisiCalc, that means creating a .VC file (template) and a .PRF file (printing). This is easy to do since the original worksheet remains on the screen throughout both saving processes.

---

*Transferring Data In and Out*

In business it is often especially important to be able to view data in the form of bar or line graphs, pie charts, and other graphic representations. Graphs make it much easier to spot trends and to quickly grasp relations than do column after column of mind-numbing figures. Although some spreadsheets have very elementary graphics capabilities, it is usually necessary to use a separate business graphics program of the type discussed in Chapter 19. (The integrated programs discussed in Chapter 18 combine spreadsheet and full-featured graphics capabilities in a single software package.)

If you want to use such a program, the first problem you will face is transferring the numbers from your spreadsheet into the graphics program. To do this you might have to print out the spreadsheet and type in all of the relevant numbers by hand. But often, there is a much easier way. Thanks to the Data Interchange Format (DIF) standard established by the creators of VisiCalc, you may be able to effect the transfer by pressing only a few keys.

*What Is the DIF Format?*

As you know, computers use many different techniques for recording information on a floppy disk. We've seen elsewhere, for example, how different operating systems divide up the available space in different ways and how the files created by one DOS cannot usually be read by a program running under the control of another DOS. The DIF format has *nothing* to do with these DOS-related file formats.

What DIF deals with is the *order* in which the information is recorded and the way it is formatted in the file. The DIF format stipulates that the first word in the file will be TABLE, followed by information regarding the size of the spreadsheet. The words VECTORS, TUPLES,

DATA, and BOT (*Beginning Of Tuple*) will also be used, followed by appropriate numerical information in each case. Though the words have other meanings in other contexts, in the DIF format, "vector" is a fancy name for "column" and "tuple" (pronounced "two-pull") is an equally fancy name for "row." As a software user, you don't have to know anything about this, however. When you record a worksheet in the DIF format, the program automatically adds these terms and numbers to produce a file that starts out like this:

```
TABLE
0,1
""
VECTORS
0,58
TUPLES
0,26
DATA
0,0
""
-1,0
BOT
1,0
"New Year's Budget"
(etc.)
```

Any graphics program that "supports DIF file transfer" will include special programming that enables it to make sense of words like TABLE, VECTORS, TUPLES, DATA, and BOT. The graphics program will thus know where to look within the saved worksheet file for the numbers you want to put on a graph. The same is true of a statistical program for use in analyzing the figures on your spreadsheet. Indeed, you can transfer spreadsheet figures saved in the DIF format to any program that is capable of accepting DIF files.

DIF works the other way as well. If you have developed a set of figures with another program and then want to put them into your spreadsheet, you can usually do so. As long as there is a way to put the figures into the DIF format, it can be an easy matter to load them into your spreadsheet as you would any other spreadsheet file.

**SoftTip:** The ability to transfer data into a spreadsheet can be especially useful if you use your communications program to access the Dow Jones News/Retrieval Service for the latest stock quotes and other investment information. The same is true of information you might download from your firm's mainframe computer. The trick, of course, is to convert the numbers into the DIF format.

*SoftTip continued*

Fortunately, there are a number of conversion programs available that make it easy to do just that.

With a product called VC Loader from Micro Decision Systems, for example, you would first capture the information you want and record it as a file. Then boot the VC Loader program and tell it that you want to load that file. When the file is displayed, you have only to move the cursor to the figures, column headings, etc., that you want to have recorded in the DIF format. When you are finished, you can boot your spreadsheet and load in your stock quotes or other information from this newly created file. The program is available for Apples and IBMs. For more information, contact:

Micro Decisions Systems
P.O. Box 1392
Pittsburgh, PA   15219

*Text Files and the Telephone*

There are three other things to be aware of regarding DIF files. The first is that the key word is *data*. Data Interchange Format files do not record the cell formulas on your spreadsheet the way a template does. They contain only the column and row labels and the associated figures. Thus, if you are going to save a worksheet in the DIF format, be certain to save it in the standard template-like format as well.

Second, since they are text files (as opposed to binary or machine language files), they can easily be transmitted over the telephone or via some other communications link. For example, if you have a business associate with a TRS-80 Model 16 and you own an IBM/XT, you will not be able to use each other's floppy disks. But if your associate has developed figures on a spreadsheet and saved the work in the DIF format, he or she can easily transmit the data to you over the phone. Again, because of the DIF format, you will then be able to immediately transfer the information into your own spreadsheet program without rekeying any data.

The third point concerns the way DIF files are used to insert data. If you have your spreadsheet with all of its formulas on the screen, you can load another file (DIF or other spreadsheet) in on top of it. Wherever there are numbers or letters in the same cell locations of both worksheets, the numbers in the worksheet you are loading in will replace those in the first worksheet. Everything else will remain unchanged. The new, combined worksheet can be saved under a new filename, of course.

**SoftTip:** One application of DIF files is likely to be of special interest to executives and professional investors. In the fall of 1982, VisiCorp and Data Resources, Inc. (DRI) signed an exclusive agreement to make information available in the DIF format. DRI is an online database that, among many other things, maintains files on virtually all publicly held companies in the United States. With VisiLink, VisiCorp's $250 communications and DIF formatting program, subscribers to DRI's database can now receive the information they need over the phone and immediately use it with their VisiCalc spreadsheets.

For more information contact:

Data Resources, Inc.  
29 Hartwell Avenue  
Lexington, MA   02173  
(617) 861-0165

VisiCorp  
2895 Zanker Road  
San Jose, CA   95134  
(408) 946-9000

## Consolidating Models

It can often be important to be able to combine several worksheet models into a single consolidated form. A good example would be a firm with several departments. If you maintained a sales report worksheet for each department, at the end of the month you could combine them into a single corporate sales report without rekeying any of the data. The ease with which you can do this can be an important consideration when deciding which spreadsheet program to buy.

With VisiCalc and the Advanced Version of VisiCalc, for example, there are two main ways to effect a consolidation of several reports. The first way would be to create the worksheets for each department in such a way that they will fit together like pieces of a puzzle and save them all in the DIF format. Since a master worksheet can be put on the screen and DIF files loaded in on top of it, as long as one department's DIF-saved worksheet does not overwrite another's when they are assembled into a single consolidated form, they can be easily combined. The master worksheet would contain all of the formulas needed to manipulate the data, generate totals, etc.

The second approach is to purchase an additional program that will automate the process for you. A good example is VIZ.A.CON from Abacus Associates ($120). This program basically does two things. First, it enables you to record the keystrokes you would use to perform the consolidation described above. If you go through the process once, recording the keystrokes, you need never do it again. The next time you want to consolidate worksheets, you merely tell the program to take its marching orders from the file containing your keystrokes.

The second thing the program does it to perform all the necessary addition. This means that there is no need to create each department's worksheet like puzzle pieces to keep them from overwriting each other when you load them all into a master worksheet. As long as each worksheet is identical in format, VIZ.A.CON will add up all the figures and display them on your master form. For more information, contact:

> Abacus Associates
> 6565 West Loop South, #240
> Bellaire, TX   77401
> (713) 666-8146

---

**SoftTip:** A similar program called MergeCalc ($125) will also consolidate VisiCalc work sheets. Contact:

> Cypher
> 121 Second Street
> San Francisco, CA   94105
> Phone: 800-SMARTWARE
> (415) 974-5297, in California

---

**SoftTip:** If you use Sorcim's SuperCalc or some other CP/M-based spreadsheet, you might be interested in an add-on called Con-Calc from Sunwest Software. This $125 program consolidates up to 256 worksheets and includes logic for "rate of return" calculations. It is supplied on an eight-inch disk and requires CP/M and MBASIC. A test disk and manual are available for $15. Contact:

> Sunwest Software
> 2000 S. Logan
> Denver, CO   80210
> (303) 777-9400

---

Microsoft calls its Multiplan a "second generation" spreadsheet, and one of the points the firm highlights in support of this claim is the program's automatic consolidation feature. Using the program's "Xternal" command, one can link several spreadsheets together in such a way that changing a number on one spreadsheet automatically changes every other number that depends upon it, regardless of what spreadsheet(s) it happens to be on. Thus, you might go through and update each department's sales report worksheet and then bring in your consolidated worksheet. The moment your master worksheet is brought in all of the totals or other figures on it that are affected by the updates on the other worksheets will automatically be updated as well.

## A Word about Memory

Electronic spreadsheet programs and worksheets gobble memory the way a beer drinker snarfs up salted peanuts—by the fistful. And the more powerful the program, the more insatiable its appetite. Because worksheets are usually held in RAM until you tell the program to record them on disk, the amount of memory in your computer can directly affect the size and complexity of the worksheets you can build. Since RAM chips are relatively inexpensive, it is not likely that you would want to buy a less powerful program than you need. But it is important to be aware that you may have to add extra memory to your computer in order to use your spreadsheet program effectively.

There are two things to consider here. The first is, How much internal memory does the program itself need and how much does that leave you for use in creating worksheets? If your machine is equipped with 64K and the program itself soaks up 48K of that, only 18K will be left to hold your spreadsheet. The significance of this will depend on the size of the worksheets you normally create, but many business users would find 18K very restrictive.

The second consideration is, Does the spreadsheet program have a built-in limit on the amount of memory it can address at any one time? Because the microchips in eight-bit computers can only address 64K of memory, for example, most spreadsheets designed to run on them can only use 64K for both the program and the worksheets. In other cases, the program may be limited to 64K, regardless of whether you are running it on an eight-bit or a 16-bit machine. Some programs, for example, can be run on a computer equipped with 320K of RAM or more but can use 64K of that memory to hold both the program itself and the worksheets you create. Other programs have the ability to address all of the memory in your machine directly, regardless of how large it happens to be.

## The "Virtual" Solution

For home users, an absolute limit on the amount of memory a program can address may not be all that important, though it is something that business users should avoid. Yet in many cases the fact that a program can address only 64K at any one time may not be a crippling factor, thanks to something called "virtual memory." A program that uses virtual memory techniques has the ability to "swap" information from RAM to disk and back, and as such the real limit on worksheet size is the number of free bytes on disk.

For example, assume that you are currently looking at a portion of a worksheet that fills your screen with eight columns and 21 rows. You add some figures or formulas and decide that now you want to make the screen scroll so that you can look at another portion of the worksheet. If you were using a program that took advantage of virtual memory techniques, the program might say, in effect, "Just a sec. The portion of the worksheet you want to see is not in RAM right now. It's recorded on disk. Let me record what we've got so far and bring in and display the desired portion." The program thus treats portions of the worksheet as overlays (see Chapter 4). Indeed, overlays—whether comprised of programming or of data such as worksheets—are central to the virtual memory concept.

### The Hard Disk Speed-Up

The main disadvantage of using a program that uses virtual memory compared to one that can address an unlimited amount of RAM is the time required to go out to disk and bring in the section of the worksheet you want to look at. While the program is doing this, you will have no choice but to wait until it has completed the task. If the program is accessing a floppy disk, the delays can be a major nuisance.

Often, installing a hard disk in your system is the ideal solution (see Chapter 5). Hard disks work so fast that you will probably not notice any delays caused by the frequent disk access that virtual memory techniques can involve. In addition, hard disks offer a large amount of storage, making it possible for you to create quite sizable and complex worksheets.

**SoftTip:** Because Apple II and Apple II Plus owners have frequently been frustrated by the limited memory available to them once VisiCalc loads in, a company called Saturn Systems created a software/RAM board combination called VC-Expand. The software utilizes the technique of "bank switching" mentioned in Chapter 1 to enable the Apple to address more than 64K. With VC-Expand you can boost the 18K of VisiCalc workspace available on a 48K Apple to a maximum of 177K. The software costs $100 ($125 for the 80-column version). RAM boards (available from Saturn) are extra and are available in a variety of memory configurations. Contact:

> Saturn Systems, Inc.
> P.O. Box 8050
> Ann Arbor, MI 48107
> (313) 973-8422

---

**SoftTip:** Omega Microware has a RAM board/software package they call the Super Expander Plus for Apple owners. The software adds variable column width capabilities and a number of other features to the standard VisiCalc program. When used in conjunction with the software, the firm's Ramex-128 boards ($499) allow Visi-Calc models as large as 136K (one board) or 255K (two boards). Contact:

> Omega Microware, Inc.
> 222 South Riverside Plaza
> Chicago, IL 60606
> (312) 648-4844
> Credit card orders only: 800-835-2246

---

### Software Buyer's Quick Reference Checklist

*—Electronic Spreadsheet Programs—*

*General Considerations*

☐ *Very important:* Versions of spreadsheet programs vary with the brand of computer they run on. VisiCalc on one machine, for example, may not have all of the features of VisiCalc on another machine. Make certain that the version of the program you are examining is the same one that you will actually use on your machine.

☐ Nothing is forever. But you should be aware that full-featured spreadsheet programs can require anywhere from 20 to 40 hours or more to master, and once you've learned a program, you will be reluctant to start over with another product. For this reason, it can be worthwhile to spend a little extra time to get to know a program before getting married to it.

☐ The documentation accompanying the software will show you how to use its features. But it may not tell you much about how those features can be *applied*. For this reason, it can be important to look at what books, templates, teaching programs, and other information are available concerning the product and its various uses.

Check the bookracks in the computer store and the shelves at your bookstore. You might also consult the R. R. Bowker guides to *Books in Print* and *Forthcoming Books in Print* at the library or your bookstore.

☐ Do you plan to use the spreadsheets you create with graphics, word processing, statistical, database management, or other programs? Will this be possible with the spreadsheet you are considering?

If this is important, perhaps you should consider one of the integrated packages described in Chapter 18.

Alternatively, you might consider compatible programs produced by the same software house. Micropro (CalcStar), VisiCorp (VisiCalc), Microsoft (Multiplan), and other firms either have or are developing word processing, graphics, and other programs for use with their spreadsheets.

☐ Will you be sending and receiving spreadsheet data over the telephone or via some other communications link? If so, can the program save data in the DIF format? Or is some other text format acceptable?

☐ Is it possible to use templates to create predesigned worksheets?

☐ Is there an onscreen "HELP" menu or some other kind of built-in "HELP" feature? Does the documentation include a separate quick reference card?

☐ Does the vendor offer direct telephone support? If so, how much does it cost? Prices can range from $50 a year to $50 an hour.

☐ Memory: How much memory does the program occupy once it has been loaded in? And how much does that leave you, given your present configuration?

Is there a limit on the amount of RAM the program can address at one time? If so, does it utilize virtual memory techniques to let you create any size spreadsheet?

If the program uses virtual memory, it would be a good idea to have it demonstrated with both a floppy disk and a hard disk. This will help you decide whether you need a hard disk system.

*Note:* You can always add a hard disk later if you find that a floppy-based system involves too many delays. You might ask about the possibility of putting the program itself on a hard disk.

*Capacity*
☐ What is the maximum number of columns? Many spreadsheets offer between 60 and 63 columns, so this can probably be considered "average."

☐ What is the maximum number of rows? Here, "average" is between 200 and 254 rows (lines).

☐ What is the widest you can make a column? How many characters? The "average" varies: SuperCalc is 127, VisiCalc is 77, CalcStar is 63, etc.

*Layout and Labelling*
☐ Can you mix numbers and letters in your column and row labels? Some programs will permit this; others will let you use either letters or numbers but not both in the same heading.

☐ Can the program automatically justify headings left, right, or center?

☐ Can column widths be set *independently* or must all columns be set the same width?

☐ Can you write a title across several columns?

☐ Will the program let you use commas, dollar signs, plus ( + ) or minus ( − ) signs, percent signs (%), or CR (credit) and DR (debit) notations? Will the program follow the standard business format of printing negative values in parentheses?

☐ Can you enter super- and subscripts or footnotes? T/Maker II for CP/M based machines (Lifeboat Associates, 1651 Third Avenue, N.Y., NY   10028) is one of the few programs that includes this feature.

☐ Can you underline words in your titles?

## Predefined Functions

All spreadsheets include a number of predefined functions that you can include in formulas to take the square root of a number, to round off a number, calculate the net present value of future cash flows, etc. All of the functions listed below can be found in at least one spreadsheet program. However, it isn't likely that you will find a single program that offers all of them. Consequently, you should view the following list as an indication of what is available. If you need one of the functions, you should search for a program that offers it.

*Entering Formulas and Data*

☐ How are cell locations referred to? As row and column coordinates *(A1)* or can you use words ("Sales")? Which do you prefer?

☐ Is there a "replicate" or "copy" command to let you easily move labels, formulas, and numbers from one part of the worksheet to another?

☐ Can you move a column? A row? An entire block of the spreadsheet?

☐ Can you insert columns or rows between existing columns and rows?

☐ Is there a way to determine whether a formula has been attached to a particular cell? Any special symbol on the screen?

☐ How can you tell what formulas have been used? Is there any easy way to relieve them, or must you save the worksheet and look at the template with your word processing program?

☐ Can you edit formulas a character at a time? Or must you always retype the entire formula whenever you want to change a single character?

☐ Is there a way to protect a cell from being changed by clerical personnel or by accident?

*Arithmetic and Other Functions*

Absolute value

Average

Constants

COUNT (returns number of nonblank cells in a list)

Exponentiation (raises a number to a power, calculates roots)

Greater than, less than, not equal to, etc.

Integer (lops off everything to the right of the decimal point)
Logarithms (base ten)

Logarithms (natural)

LOOKUP (obtains values from a table)

Maximum (largest value on a list)
Minimum (smallest value on a list)

Modulo

Percent

Pi

PRECISION (degree of precision possible varies with the program)

Round off (to specified application)

Slope

Square root

Sum (add up a list)

Sum of the squares

Weighted average

| *Financial Functions* | *Trigonometric Functions* |
|---|---|
| Interest rates | Sine |
| Internal rate of return | Cosine |
| Net present value | Tangent |
| Payments | Arc sine |
| Depreciation | Arc cosine |
| | Arc tangent |

*Logical Operators*
*and Boolean Functions*
TRUE
FALSE
IF. . .THEN. . .ELSE
AND. . .OR. . .NOT

*Statistical Functions*
Linear regression
Standard deviation

*Entering and Viewing Data*
☐ Can the program store a series of keystrokes to let you enter the whole string by pressing a single key?

☐ If you insert, move, or delete rows and columns, what is the effect on your labels? Are there large gaps, or does the program close things up?

☐ Can you scroll in all four directions (up, down, right, left)?

☐ Is there a split-screen option? Will it split both vertically and horizontally?

☐ How many separate windows can you have: two, six, eight? Can they be made to scroll independently or together at your option?

☐ Is there a global search and locate and/or search and replace feature?

☐ Does the program use reverse video or blinking values?

☐ Does the program take advantage of a color monitor to display negative numbers, protected data, or any numbers you designate in different colors?

☐ Is there a sort feature? If so, can you sort both columns and rows or only columns?

*Printing Reports and Program Output*

☐ What is the maximum number of characters you can print across the page? Surprising as it is, some programs (Magic Worksheet from Structured Systems and Micro Plan from Chang Laboratories, for example) can create large spreadsheets but cannot print out more than 132 characters (not columns) per page. With other programs, the character width is limited only by your printer.

☐ Will the program allow you to use a compressed printing feature to put more characters on a single line of page?

☐ Can you use bold print, underlining, italics or other special printing features? Or must you put the spreadsheet through a word processing program first?

☐ Can you tell the program to print just what is visible on the screen for a quick, hard-copy "snapshot"?

☐ When printing a spreadsheet that cannot fit on a single page, must you figure out where the blocks should be divided? Or will the program ask you for the length and width of the page and automatically figure things out for you?

☐ Can the program generate any kind of graphics by itself (bar graphs, histograms, etc.)?

☐ Can you "print to disk" to record an image of the worksheet exactly as it appears as if you were using a word processing program?

*Transferring Data*

☐ What provisions are there for transferring the data you have developed with a spreadsheet into another program?

☐ Exactly how would this work?

☐ Can the program create DIF files? Can it use DIF files created by another program or even another brand of spreadsheet?

☐ Is it possible to link several spreadsheets together so that a change on one will automatically effect changes on the others?

☐ What options are there for consolidating several worksheets into one master file? Exactly how would this be done?

---

**SoftTip:** There are at least two excellent sources of information on getting the most out of VisiCalc. One is the VisiCalc user's group known, of course, as "Visigroup." The other is a newsletter called SATN (*Software Arts Technical Notes*) published by the creators of VisiCalc. (A separate edition is also available for people using the firm's target seeking, "what would it take?" TK! Solver program.) Here are the places to contact:

Visigroup
P.O. Box 254
Scarsdale, NY   10583
($25 annual membership;
includes newsletter)

Software Arts Technical Notes (SATN)
P.O. Box 494
Cambridge, MA   02139
($30 for six issues; back issues may
be available at $7 each.)

TK!SATN Subscriptions
P.O. Box 100
Newton, MA   02162
($30 for six issues; $50 for 12)

**SoftTip:** There is even a magazine dedicated to electronic spreadsheets. Called *The Power of ES*, or simply *ES*, it deals with spreadsheets of all persuasions as well as integrated programs containing spreadsheets. Published by Management Information Source, Inc., the same people who publish the book, *The Power of VisiCalc* ($14.95), and other *Power of* . . . titles cited earlier, it is issued six times a year. Although it contains good information, the first few issues were a bit short (30 to 50 pages), but that may change.

Copies may be available at your local computer store. For subscriptions, contact:

> Management Information Source, Inc.
> 3543 N.E. Broadway
> Portland, OR  97232
> (503) 287-1462

Cost for six issues: $18.00 in the United States; $25 in Canada; $40 air-delivered to Europe; $56 air-delivered or $30 surface mail to all other countries. MasterCard; Visa; check in U.S. dollars.

---

**SoftTip:** A collection of templates, tips, how-to articles, etc., originally published in *Spreadsheet*, the "international VisiCalc user's newsletter," is now available as *VisiCalc—By the User for the User* ($10). Contact:

> Intercalc Users Group
> P.O. Box 4289
> Stamford, CT  06907

---

**SoftTip:** Finally, for a feature-by-feature rundown on 32 electronic spreadsheet programs, you might be interested in "All About Electronic Spreadsheets" by Alan Hirsch at McGraw-Hill's Datapro Research Corporation. The cost is $19. Contact:

> Datapro Research Corporation
> 1805 Underwood Blvd.
> Delran, NJ  08075
> (800) 257-9406
> (609) 764-0100, in New Jersey

# ...16...

# How to Buy Personal Filing and Database Management Systems

O
f all the various categories of software for your personal computer, none has a more intimidatingly computeristic name than "database management system" or "DBMS," which sounds as if it is straight out of *The Forbin Project* or some other depiction of mainframe madness. You can almost hear H.A.L.'s unnervingly even voice in the background, "What are you doing in the pod, Dave?"

Actually, the concepts behind DBMS personal computer software *are* taken directly from the mainframe domain. In many ways, they represent quintessential "computerness." But that's part of the excitement of having these programs available on a micro. There is probably no other type of software that so firmly places mainframe-like power in your hands.

What kind of power? Power to store, sort, locate, print out, and otherwise manipulate *information.* A database, whether it exists on a remote computer that you access with a telephone, on a floppy disk inside your own computer, or between the covers of the latest phone book is nothing more than a collection of information. A database management program, and its less powerful "personal filing" program relatives, is simply the software that lets you *manage* that information.

*What Are They Good For?*

Database management and personal filing software is useful any time you have a sizable number of things to keep track of. In business, it can be used to keep track of parts in inventory, to ride herd on accounts receivable, to manage personnel files, to record expenses, to generate sophisticated mailing lists and labels, to prepare contract bids, and for many other applications.

In the home, it can be used as a check register and check writer, or to keep track of tax deductions and expenses. It can be used to index and retrieve letters and correspondence, recipes, record collections, books, magazine articles, stocks, bonds, stamp collections, and software reviews and other information you capture from such electronic databases as The Knowledge Index, The Source, or CompuServe. (see Appendix C.) You could even use this type of software as a calendar or as a "tickler" file to remind you of what you are supposed to do and where you are supposed to be on a given date.

Students can use these programs to quickly prepare bibliographies for term papers. Researchers and writers can use them to organize their notes for instant retrieval. And this type of software can make the job of a professional indexer a snap.

In short, any time you have perhaps 50 or more items to keep track of, some kind of information management software can probably be a big help. You might envision a pile of papers, newspaper clippings, letters, and magazine articles on your desk—each containing any number of facts, figures, and quotations on various topics of interest to you. A database management system, in effect, lets you hold out your hand, wave a wand and say, "I want all of the information relevant to Labrador Retrievers and rescue missions in my hand, and I want it now."

## Three Types of Programs

There are three main types of DBMS and DBMS-like programs for personal computers: free-form filing or "indexing" systems, file managers, and full-featured database management systems. They range in price from around $80 to $700, and, of course, with more money comes more features, capacity, and power. The type of program and the price you pay will depend not only on how *many* things you want to keep track of, but also upon how you want to file them and find them again once they have been recorded.

We'll look at each of these categories in a moment. Before we do, however, it's important to point out that there is no widely agreed-upon definition for the term "database management system" or the features a program must include to qualify. Software producers apply it freely, and it is thus used to describe a wide range of dissimilar programs. All electronic spreadsheets, for example, present you with a screen of rows and columns. This is something you can count on. But database management systems and programs that use the DBMS designation do not have a similar uniformity. Some of them are designed to index paragraphs of text that you have already typed, and some involve filling in onscreen forms the way you might complete a loan application.

Fortunately, there's a way to bring a degree of order to an otherwise confusing range of programs, because all of them have certain basic ideas in common. In fact, by asking four main questions, you can determine where any given product fits in the general information framework and have a better idea of whether it will suit your particular needs. When considering any information management program, ask yourself:

- Where does the information come from?
- How can you find it again?
- What *else* can you do with the information?
- What kinds of output and printed formats can you generate?

In the next section we will use this framework to look at the three major types of information management programs available for your personal computer. We'll start with the free-form filing type and use it as a basis for presenting some important concepts that apply to all information management programs.

---

**SoftTip:** The terms "file," "record," and "field" are the bread and butter of information management systems. They are explained in Chapter 4, and if their definitions aren't clear to you, you might want to go back and look at that chapter now. While you're there, you might also want to read about the ISAM filing technique. Almost all file management and DBMS programs use some variation of this method to allow you to sort and locate your information more quickly.

---

### Free-Form Indexing and Filing Programs

These do not all have the power and flexibility of a file manager or a full-featured DBMS, but they have many applications and are certainly the easiest to use. (Examples include VisiDex from VisiCorp and SUPERFILE from F.Y.I.) Basically, these types of programs allow you to attach a list of key words to a file that consists of paragraphs or pages or any other block of text. The text could be a letter you wrote with your word processor, some randomly typed notes, reports of a salesperson's sales calls, a memo, information downloaded from The Source or another online electronic database, or any other type of text.

In Figure 16.1, we have used a recipe and F.Y.I.'s SUPERFILE program as an example. After the recipe has been typed and recorded with your word processing program, you would load SUPERFILE and bring in the recipe. Then you would add the *C marker to indicate the beginning of a new record and *K marker to indicate the beginning of the keywords you will ultimately want to use to find the recipe again. The *E indicates the end of the record.

——— **Figure 16.1** ———

## A Free-Form Style Information Record

Here's a recipe as it would appear on your screen after you had indexed it with F.Y.I.'s SUPERFILE program. You would type the recipe with your word processing program, record it, and then bring it into the Superfile program to add the asterisks markers and keywords.

*C

Grandma Stroup's Lemon Bars

| 1 Cup flour | 1 Cup sugar |
|---|---|
| ½ Cup butter | 3-4 T. lemon juice |
| ¼ Cup powdered sugar | Rind of one lemon |
| 2 Eggs | 2 T. flour |
|  | ½ teaspoon baking powder |

Step 1: Combine butter and flour and powdered sugar. Cut with pastry blender. Pat firmly into an 8-inch pan. Bake at 350° for 15 minutes.

Step 2: While other stuff is baking, mix remaining ingredients. Pour over baked crust while still warm.

Step 3: Bake for 25 minutes at 350°. Let cool. Sprinkle with powdered sugar and cut into 2-inch squares.

*K
GRANDMA STROUP/LEMON BARS/DESSERT/DAVID LIKES *E

---

Now, assume that you've recorded your entire 3 × 5 card recipe collection as well as all the recipes you've clipped from magazines and Sunday newspaper supplements and stuffed into the cardbox. As required by the program, you have assigned one or more keywords to each recipe. The question now is, What's for dessert?

If you felt like something sweet, but you didn't know what, you could "query the database" by entering a command that would say, "Give me a printout or an onscreen listing of all my DESSERT recipes." Notice that DESSERT is the keyword. In information management words, DESSERT is also called the "search key" since it is the key that the search is based on. If Grandma Stroup had a reputation for making especially luscious desserts, you might enter a command that would search for: "All recipes with GRANDMA STROUP *and* DESSERT listed as keywords." If your son David were coming over for dinner, but you would be going out for dessert, you could search for "All recipes with DAVID LIKES but *not* DESSERT listed as keywords."

**SoftTip:** When you look for information on the basis of "AND, OR, NOT," you are using what is called a Boolean search or Boolean search logic. In the hands of a professional researcher, or with a little experience, it can be a powerful tool for locating the precise information you want. This is because Boolean functions can be linked together to search for things such as "All recipes with the keywords GRANDMA STROUP *and* DAVID LIKES *or* NANCY LIKES but *not* SIDE DISH."

Boolean searches can be even more elaborate, but ultimately they can be no more precise than the keywords used to "tag" a piece of information. The more keywords you have and the more precisely each describes what is in the information record, the more precise the search can be. This has little application for a file of recipes, but the selection of keywords can obviously be an important factor in a more business-related database.

---

**SoftTip:** Another technique used by free-form programs is to have you move the cursor over the text until you come to a word that you want to designate as a keyword. You then hit a function key or a control key combination to make the designation. This can be handy because it saves you having to retype information that is already in the file in a separate keyword area. However, when considering a program like this, be sure that it also allows you to enter keywords that are *not* part of the record itself, like DESSERTS or DAVID LIKES in Figure 16.1.

---

*"Key" Concepts*

As simple as it is, this example makes it easy to visualize one of the major techniques that even the most sophisticated database management systems use to locate the information records you seek. Although a specific program may not support the feature, we know that a computer *could* read through each recipe in your collection looking for the words GRANDMA STROUP or LEMON BARS or anything else. But that can take a very long time, even by human standards. Usually it makes much more sense for the program, with your help, to create a special file containing nothing but keywords and the locations of the records that contain them. (See the explanation of the ISAM file structure in Chapter 4.)

This means that finding a record is a two-step process for the computer. First, it searches its keyword file for the word you want. Then, when it finds the target word, it checks to see where the record associated with it is located and displays it. People do exactly the same thing when they look up a word in a book's index and then turn to the indicated page. Indeed, a file of keywords is often called an "index file" and the process of creating it is called "indexing the record." The file may also be called a "key file," and keywords may be simply called "keys."

*What Else Can You Do?*
Virtually instant information retrieval is one of the main advantages of all database-related programs. But once you have the information on disk, there is usually no reason why you can't do other things with it as well. The best example is undoubtedly a feature that allows you to *sort* your information.

You personally might not need to sort your recipes, but suppose the local chapter of the Junior League was contemplating yet another cookbook. The recipes could be collected and typed into your computer in any order. As long as you included the appropriate keyword (MAIN DISH, SALAD, CANAPES, etc.), you could tell the machine to sort the recipes on that basis and print all MAIN DISH recipes, followed by all SIDE DISHES, followed by SALADS, and so on.

Whether you are sorting recipes, parts in inventory, or addresses, a database program will probably use a key file to do the job. This is because a sort of complete records is an even more time-consuming process than a search, since when a computer performs a sort, it *physically rearranges* information.

There are many ways to accomplish this. But you'll have the general idea if you imagine the computer reading a complete record off disk and into its memory, then recording that record in a different spot on the disk, then getting the next record and recording it, and so on until a new file has been created. The file will contain exactly the same recipes or records as the original, but they will be arranged in a "sorted" order.

Because this can be such a long process—with large files it can literally take *hours*—it usually makes more sense to sort the key or index file instead. The contents of the index file also are physically rearranged by the sorting process. But, since there are far fewer words to read and write, it doesn't take nearly as long. The important thing is that once a key file has been sorted, you can access and print out your information just as if the complete records had been sorted and physically rearranged.

*What Kinds of Output and Printed Formats?*
The two points to concentrate on here are whether the program can copy selected records into a new file on disk, and the flexibility of the

printout options. The ability to create disk files containing only certain records can be important for a number of reasons. For example, if you have a very large database with lots of records, it may make sense to divide it into two or more sections, each of which would contain only those records pertaining to a particular subject. Each section would exist as a separate file and each could be treated as a database in its own right. This way neither you nor the program will have to deal with all of your information at the same time. The key files will be smaller, and searches and sorts will take place much faster.

You might also want to use the information in your database in a word processing program, perhaps to put a recipe into a letter or to incorporate a sales report in a business document. Similarly, you might want to put certain records contained in your database into a spreadsheet program. In both cases, it will probably be necessary to remove certain codes or to reformat the file before it can be used by the other program. But there are usually "utility" programs to do this. Whether reformatting is necessary or not, the option to have the computer make a duplicate copy of the information would save you the trouble of retyping it.

With a free-form filing system, "What you see is what you get" when you create a separate disk file. In other words, the record will appear the same way in a word processing program as it does in the filing system itself. If you were to put the recipe shown in Figure 16.1 into a word processing program, it would look exactly the way you see it there, though the asterisk and letter markers might have been removed.

Similarly, when you want to print a record with a program of this sort, it will almost certainly appear just as it does in your file. Using Figure 16.1 as an example, you might be able to call for a printout of part of the record, if you had set the record up to permit this beforehand. But you could not say, "I'm going shopping, so give me a printout of just the names of the recipes I've chosen and the ingredients they require." Since the ingredients and the preparation instructions are *all one block of information* as far as the computer is concerned, you would have to print out the complete recipe. Some programs offer a special mailing list option that will let your program generate labels, but again, the records must be created with a mailing list in mind.

### The Fundamental Difference

This may or may not be important to your application, but it illustrates the fundamental difference between a free-form filing system and a file manager or a complete DBMS. The reason a free-form system is so easy to use is that there are no limitations on the format of individual records in the database. One record can be a single sentence. Another can be a complete page. And all records can be a part of the same file. This means, however, that a free-form program cannot offer the same flexibility found in a more structured system. In many cases, particuarly for home use, this makes little difference. Even many business people and professionals will find that a free-form system is exactly what they need, though this lack can make such programs unsuitable for large-scale, sophisticated applications. The drawback is that in order to obtain greater flexibility, you must learn to use a more complicated program, obey certain rules, and often enter most of your data by hand.

## File Management Programs

File management programs are the second major category of information management software. Examples include T.I.M. III, Easy Filer, PFS:File, VisiFile, and DB Master. While markedly different from the free-form filing systems, these programs are very similar to complete database management systems and can usually be spoken of together. (We'll look at the features that set DBMS programs apart in a later section.) All file management and DBMS programs have at least one thing in common: They require you to create a "data entry" form and type in your information before you can do anything. For an example of a blank entry form as it might appear just after you finished designing it, see Figure 16.2. We will use that example (a file of college alumni) in the following discussion.

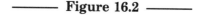

——— **Figure 16.2** ———

**A File Manager Data Entry Form at the Moment of Creation**

### ALUMNI CONTRIBUTIONS

```
FNAME:AAAAAAAAAAAAAAAAAAAA
LNAME:AAAAAAAAAAAAAAAAAAAAAAAAA
STREET:AAAAAAAAAAAAAAAAAAAAAAAAAA
CITY: AAAAAAAAAAA,
STATE:AA
ZIP: NNNNN-NNNN
AREACODE: (NNN)
PHONE: NNN-NNNN
GRADYR:NNNN
LASTYRCONTRIB:$NNNN.NN
THISYR:$NNNN.NN
PERCENTDIFF:CCC%
```

The *A*'s in the first and last name fields, as well as those for the city and state, perform two functions. They set aside a certain number of characters of space and they indicate that only alphanumeric (letters or numbers) characters are to go there. The *N*'s do the same thing for numerical data. And the *C*'s indicate that the percentage difference between last year's contribution and this year's will be automatically calculated and entered by the program.

These "field designators" would appear only at this stage. When you begin actually to enter names and addresses, you would be presented with a screen that had none of the variable designators, but included some kind of marker (*) to indicate the maximum length you have specified for the field:

## ALUMNI CONTRIBUTIONS

```
FNAME:_____*
LNAME:_____*
STREET:_____*
CITY: _____*
STATE: _____*
ZIP: _____-_____*
AREACODE: (_____)*
PHONE:_____-_____*
GRADYR:_____*
LASTYRCONTRIB: $_____.____*
THISYR: $_____.____*
PERCENTDIFF:_____%*
```

*The Structure of the Beast*

When you create a data entry form with a file management program, you are actually doing two things. First, you are laying out a form that will appear on your screen each time you want to add a new record to the file. Second, and more importantly, you are determining how the database will be structured and how you will be able to use the information you eventually enter. The central point to keep in mind is that, in contrast to a free-form program, there must be "field" for every piece of information in the record. (Unstructured comment lines similar to free-form paragraphs can usually be added, but we will pass over them for the sake of simplicity.)

This requirement is the source of both the power and the complexity of file managers and DBMS programs. At the simplest level, it means that you've got to think ahead. If you forget to put in a field for the telephone number, for example, you will not be able to generate a report that includes it. If you don't use a separate field for both the first and last names, you may not be able to sort your file alphabetically.

On the other hand, the fact that each piece of information has its own field can give you a great deal of flexibility. Using the format shown in Figure 16.2, for example, you could print out a list containing just the names, phone numbers, and amount of money each individual contributed last year. Or you could get a list of alumni sorted by year of graduation. You could find out how many people in the class were named "Biff." Or you could generate a list of everyone who increased his contribution by between 50% and 100% and send them a personalized thank-you letter. Once you break your information up into individually labelled fields, the number of ways you can search, sort, and print out reports is virtually unlimited.

Unfortunately, making sure to include all the fields you are going to need is only one of the things you have to think about when laying out a data entry form and setting up your database. You've also got to anticipate how many characters of space you are likely to need in each field. What is the longest last name you are likely to have to enter? What about the city, state, and address fields? How many spaces should you allot for the dollar contributions?

The reason for this lies in the way database programs usually structure their files. Without going into the technical details, you might think of a database file as a bookshelf that you yourself have cut to a certain length when laying out your data entry form. The shelf (record) is designed to hold just so many books. Each book (field) may occupy a different amount of space on the shelf, but the entire collection fits perfectly. If you were to remove one book and substitute a fatter volume, you would knock one of the books on the end off the shelf.

Thus, once you create the database file structure by laying out your form, the program will not let you add any more characters to a field than you have specified. If it didn't prevent you from doing this, adding more than the allotted number of characters would push the characters in the fields that follow out of position within the database file. This would make it impossible for the system to locate and display that information accurately.

*What If You Must Make a Change?*

If you discover that you've left something out of a form or failed to allocate all the characters you will need for a field, you can usually correct the problem easily—if you have not yet entered any information into the file. You simply edit the form you have created and record it again. Many programs have editing features to allow you to do this with varying degrees of ease. Programs that don't have these features may force you to retype the form completely.

But that is a minor irritation compared to the tragedy that can befall you if your program forces you to *reenter all of your data* whenever you want to change the form. This may be the single most important pitfall to watch out for when considering either a file manager or a DBMS. No one—particularly individuals who have never used one of these programs before—can anticipate every field and every field length that will eventually be needed in a database file. You must be able to add fields or expand them to accommodate more characters at any time.

Fortunately, many programs provide a way to do this. It may involve transferring the entire database into a new file with more and larger fields. And the process may take a while to complete. But it will take place automatically. Anything is better than having to retype all of your data.

### Variable Types of Field Designators

As you can see from Figure 16.2, when you lay out a form with a file manager, you not only specify the number of characters each field will contain, but you also usually specify the type of information as well. This is partially an error-prevention feature and partially a matter of structuring the file. For example, either letters or numbers can be typed into an alphanumeric field, designated with *A*'s in the illustration. But if someone mistakenly tried to type a letter in a numeric field *(N)*, the program won't accept it. On some machines, it will let out a loud beep of protest.

A calculated field *(C)*, such as the percentage shown in the example, is not filled in by you at all. Instead, you attach a formula or an equation to the field in much the same way that you would with VisiCalc or another electronic spreadsheet (see Chapter 15). The equation may be entered in another part of the screen and, to keep things simple, we have not shown it. As when using an electronic spreadsheet, the program will automatically figure out what should appear in a calculated field as soon as all of the numbers it needs have been typed in. The calculating abilities offered will vary with the program. Some file manager programs may have only simple arithmetical functions. Some full-featured DBMS programs will let you use sophisticated "IF. . .THEN. . .ELSE" and other functions: "IF a customer's total purchases are greater than $100, THEN subtract a discount of 10%. Otherwise (ELSE) put the full amount in the TOTAL field."

### How Can You Find the Information Again?

Once you have recorded the form and set up the file, the next step is to enter your information. Usually, you simply tell the program that you want to add records to a particular database file. The program then presents you with a blank data entry form for the first record. When you have filled it in and hit <ENTER>, the program records the form, clears the screen, and presents you with another blank form. Most programs will automatically assign a record number (*001*, *002*, *003*, etc) to each form.

The payoff for all of your hard work comes when you have entered your information and then want to find it again. File managers and DBMS programs offer exceptionally powerful search features. The reason they can do this is that every piece of information in a record is in its own unique field, which means that any field can be used as the basis of your search.

In a free-form system, you must think up and enter the keywords for each record. In addition to the descriptive words of the sort used for the lemon bar recipe in Figure 16.1, you could enter a part number or a ZIP code or some other fact appropriate to your record and use *that* as a keyword. But whether you moved the cursor over the file and designated keywords with a function or control key, or whether you typed up a separate list of keywords, you would still have to spend time going over the file again. With a file manager or DBMS, there is no need to do anything like this, since every field can automatically be used as a search key.

The computer will always know exactly where to look to find the ZIP code, the state, the inventory part number, the part number's verbal description, the balance due on an account, etc. In addition, with more fields to choose from than is usually practical in a free-form system, your search can be more precise.

Equally important, most programs in this category allow you to be very specific about the information you are looking for. For example, a free-form system may let you use greater-than (>) or less-than (<) symbols as well as the AND, OR, NOT functions mentioned earlier. But it probably will not include the "wildcard" search functions many file managers and DBMS programs offer.

To search on the basis of a wildcard, you might use asterisks or question marks in place of characters when telling the system what to look for in the target field. If you wanted to find all addresses with ZIP codes that began with *447*, at the appropriate time you might type in: *ZIP = 447\*\**. To the program, the wildcard designation says, "Any character can be in this space."

You might also be able to tell the program to look at a particular target field, but make its selection based on only a certain number of characters within the field. For example, if you had entered telephone numbers like this: *(123) 456-7890*, you might say, "Look at the PHONE field and select all records that have *456* in the sixth through the eighth positions."

You might also be able to tell the program to select records that have a certain word or number *anywhere* in the target field. Suppose you had a database consisting of book titles and you wanted to find a list of books written by former Washington political figures. In that case, you would ask the program to look for the word "power" in the book TITLE field since it is a rule that all books by former Washington political figures must include this word in their titles. "The word "power" could be the first word (*Power and Responsibility*—a rare title) or it could be the fourth word (*The Joys of Power and Perquisites*). Wherever it was, the program would find the record.

### The Other Questions

Because the records in a file manager or DBMS can be quite large, the ability to create an index or keyword file can be crucial. Usually, it is a simple matter of telling the program what fields you want to put into the index file. The program will then read through your records, make a copy of the information in each field you have specified, and put the information in a key file that it creates for that purpose. This file can be used to find records more rapidly and to execute sorts, just as it is with a free-form system. Usually, however, the sorts can be more detailed and powerful. You might tell the system, "First I want you to sort all the addresses by ZIP code, and when you've finished with that, I want all the names within each ZIP code group in alphabetical order."

This is called a "multi-key" sort, and it can be even more complex, with more keys than described here. You might be able eventually to accomplish the same thing with a less powerful system, but it would require much more work on your part. You would have to enter each sort command individually and wait for the machine to finish before entering another. Entering all of your sort keys at the same time saves both you and the computer a lot of time and work.

You will also be able to output the contents of a record to disk or to the printer. And here again, the operation is similar to that of a free-form system. The main difference lies in the greater flexibility provided by having all of your information in individual fields. With a file manager, you can produce a printed report that includes only a person's first and last names and phone number. You could produce another list that included his or her name and address but none of the other information in the record. In short, you can create a disk file or call for a printout that includes only the information in the fields you have selected.

**SoftTip:** If you own or are thinking of buying DB Master from StoneWare, Inc., you'll be interested in the firm's newsletter "StoneWare Age." Issued periodically, this publication is designed to provide end users with ideas, answers, and suggested applications for the firm's products. The cost is $6 a year, with the first year free to registered users of DB Master. Contact:

"StoneWare Age"
StoneWare, Inc.
50 Belvedere Street
San Rafael, CA 94901

**SoftTip:** The "Freeware" concept that has made the communications program PC-Talk such a success has been extended to file management programs by Jim Button with his PC-File. This is a powerful, user-friendly program for the IBM/PC with all the features of a file management program costing $150 or more. At a suggested contribution of $35, it is an incredible value.

You may be able to obtain a copy of it from a friend, but since Mr. Button keeps improving the program and adding additional features, you would be best off sending for your own. (Updates are announced regularly and are available for $6 if you send a blank, formatted disk. Be sure to specify single- or double-sided.) Contact:

Mr. Jim Button
P.O. Box 5786
Bellevue, WA 98006
Suggested contribution: $35

### Full-Featured Database Management Systems

DBMS programs look and appear to act almost exactly the way file managers do. But DBMS software is generally much more powerful and flexible. Because of this, a DBMS can more easily be used as an "engine" to drive a wide range of applications (inventory, accounting, payroll, check writing, mailing list) often handled by single-purpose programs. DBMS examples include Condor Series 20, Profile Plus, DataMaster, FMS-80, MAG/base3, PowerBase, and dBASE II.

To use any of these or other DBMS programs, you lay out a data entry form, enter data, search, sort, call for printouts, and so on. But, at almost every step, a DBMS will offer you more features and options than a file manager. Generally, you pay two prices for these extras. The first price is monetary: DBMS software usually lists for two to three hundred dollars more than file management programs, and even at a discount it will be more expensive.

The second price is in ease of use and in the time required to master the software. DBMS programs can do some amazing things with your data, but each task involves a separate command or command sequence, and there are many tasks such a program can perform. Because many file manager programs have fewer commands and options, they can provide you with a menu listing all your available choices at a particular point. With a DBMS, there are so many possible choices that menus may not be used. Instead, many of them are command driven. As when using DOS, unless you know the commands and what each is designed to accomplish, you will have difficulty using the program.

### A Programming Language All Its Own

The difference between the ease with which you can use a free-form indexing program or a menu-driven file manager and the ease with which you can use a full-featured DBMS can be so great that it can be a major factor in your purchase decision. The fact that a DBMS is complex and quite expensive does not mean that the software house will have taken the extra care you would expect in producing an instruction manual. Ashton-Tate, the creators of dBASE II, has proved this conclusively. The firm's program is by far the best-selling database management system. Yet nowhere will you find a single, comprehensive, and *comprehendable* explanation of how to use it. dBASE II is not alone in this. With few exceptions, clear manuals are not a frequently cited strong point of most DBMS software.

**SoftTip:** Ashton-Tate's dBASE II lists for $700 and is among the most powerful DBMS programs available for personal computers. The instruction manual, however, is so bad as to make the list price seem unreasonable. Since the program sells so well, it may be that Ashton-Tate sees no need to go to the trouble of producing a manual of equal merit. As it is, the company has tried to get by with the disappointing expedient of including in its documentation package both the original and a second manual of equal length written by a private user. Both manuals are densely packed with typewritten text and neither is up to par. For this reason, the only alternative for many people who want to learn how to use their $700 investment is to spend another $175 to $525 taking a one- to three-day course on the subject.

**SoftTip:** If you own or are thinking of buying dBASE II, there are two books you should know about. The first is *The dBASE II User's Guide* by Adam B. Green, president of a software distributor called SoftwareBanc. This 150-page, typewritten manual should be read *before* you tackle the dBASE II documentation. Far from complete, it nonetheless provides a reasonably easy to understand explanation of the program and how to use its major features.

The second book is *Everyman's Database Primer: Featuring dBASE II* by Robert A. Byers. Published by Ashton-Tate itself, it runs 295 pages and covers both the general concepts of database management systems and specific examples of using dBASE II.

*dBASE II User's Guide*
by Adam B. Green
$30 from:
SoftwareBanc
661 Massachusetts Ave.
Arlington, MA 02174

*Everyman's Database Primer:
Featuring dBASE II*
by Robert A. Byers
$15 from:
Ashton-Tate
9929 W. Jefferson Blvd.
Culver City, CA 90230

The commands used to run a DBMS program can be so extensive that they actually constitute a separate programming language. Using dBASE II as an example, if you wanted to print a list of all the names and addresses in your local college alumni association you would have to enter the following commands:

```
SET TALK OFF
USE ALUMNI
SET PRINT ON
DO WHILE .NOT. EOF
    ? TRIM (FIRSTNAME), LASTNAME
    ? ADDRESS
```

```
? TRIM(CITY) - ',', STATE, ZIP
?
?
?
SKIP
ENDDO
SET PRINT OFF
```

In lieu of a long explanation, let us just say that this series of commands tells the system to use your ALUMNI file and to print out every name and address in a certain format until it reaches the end of the file (EOF). The fact that you can use a variety of commands gives you a tremendous amount of flexibility in determining how information will appear on the page. The same idea applies when you want to sort or otherwise manipulate the information in the database.

Now, here comes one of the key reasons why you might want to buy dBASE II or a similarly complex program despite the difficulty in learning how to use it. When you want to produce a list of addresses, you have two choices. Either you can sit at the machine and type in all of the commands each time, or you can *record* the entire series in a "command" file. This way, the next time you want to run a list, you have only to tell the program to take its commands from that particular file.

Since some "programs" can be quite long and involved, this feature is a real lifesaver when using the system. But there's more. Just as there are "templates" available for VisiCalc and other spreadsheet programs that include the complete "setups" you need to perform a break-even analysis or to evaluate your investment portfolio, so also are there command files available for dBASE II that contain all of the commands you need to use the software for a particular application.

The best-known example of such a product is Quickcode ($295) from Fox and Geller Associates. Among other things, Quickcode will present a menu that includes the following options: add data, edit data, look at data, index data, convert data to WordStar/MailMerge, print labels, and print reports. When you select an item from the menu, the Quickcode program automatically issues the necessary commands to dBASE II. SBT Corporation offers a number of preprogrammed command files as well. One, .dINVOICE II ($195), contains the commands needed to produce invoices and maintain information for accounts receivable and sales analysis. Similar products are available from other firms.

**SoftTip:** For more information on the programs mentioned above and other dBASE II "add-ons" contact:

Fox and Geller Associates
604 Market Street
Elmwood Park, NJ 07407
(201) 794-8883

SBT Corporation
1140 Mountain View-Alviso Road
Sunnyvale, CA 94086
(408) 980-8880

**SoftTip:** If you would like a list of over 100 commercially available prepared command files for dBASE II, ask Ashton-Tate for the latest issue of "Applications Junction." This mini-newsletter will tell you what companies to contact to buy command files to use your dBASE II for accounting, medical billing, hotel management, farm management, and a lot more. The programs are "neither tested nor recommended by Ashton-Tate." Contact:

"Applications Junction"
Ashton-Tate
10150 West Jefferson Blvd.
Culver City, CA 90230
(213) 204-5570

*What Can You Do with the Information?*

A full-featured DBMS may offer you increased flexibility in laying out your data entry form. It may be possible, for example, to make the form look exactly like the paper you are now using, complete with subject titles, blank lines for each of the fields, etc., with all of the information in the same place as on the paper version. This is in contrast to the other rather rigid data entry form shown in Figure 16.2.

You may also be able to include more fields and more records in a given file, a subject we'll consider as it relates to all three types of information managing software in a moment. And, as indicated earlier, you will be able to conduct some very precise searches and some elaborate sorts of the database. But these are not the primary features that distinguish a DBMS from a file manager.

## The DBMS Difference

There is one minor and one major characteristic that set a "real" database management system apart from a file manager. The minor feature is the ability to work with more than one file at the same time. With a file manager you can look at or print out information in one file, close it, open a second file, and do the same thing. But you will probably not be able to use both your inventory and your customer files at the same time. With many DBMS programs, however, you can open two or more files and move back and forth among them. For obvious reasons, this is called a "multifile" capability.

---

**SoftTip:** To appreciate the advantages of a multifile capability, you must know a little bit about what happens when a file is opened and closed. Suppose you had a file with 100 records and were working with record number 88. If you were to close that file and open another, you would lose your place. To return to record number 88 you would have to close the second file, bring in the original file, open it, and specify record 88. A multifile capability lets you hold your place at record 88, look at another file, and return to your original position. It also makes it easy to transfer information between files.

---

The major feature that distinguishes a true DBMS from a file manager can be found in the words *relational database*. This is one of the most misunderstood and misexplained terms in the entire microworld. And the irony is that while the mechanics are complex, the concept is not difficult to understand. The whole idea behind a relational database is the conviction that there should be one and only one physical recording of any piece of information—regardless of the number of files that appear to contain that same information.

The words "conviction" and "appear" are important. While there *are* other ways to organize a database, program authors who choose the relational method usually are convinced that this is the best way to do it. In a relational database, a piece of information like a person's name can appear to be recorded in a number of different files (a customer list, an invoice file, a file of accounts receivable) and you can use the files as if this really were the case. But, in reality, the customer's name exists in only one place.

It doesn't work exactly this way, but here's a good way to visualize it. Imagine that you had a single master file containing every piece of information in your database. There are names, street addresses, states, and ZIP codes, telephone numbers, part numbers, prices, a record of each item purchased, invoice numbers—you name it. Now imagine that you want to create a file that contains some, but not all, of this information. With a relational database, you can tell the program what to go get to "put in" this new file. The program then acts like a fat lady selecting fruit at the supermarket. It goes to the master file and says, "Let's see, I'll take a name, but pass on the address and ZIP code. The part numbers don't look good today either. But I will take a telephone number and an amount due."

Creating *another* file is like sending *another* fat lady into the market with a grocery list. Only this time the complete name and address may be selected, along with the part number and description, and the amount due. The important thing is that both files are using the identical collection of information.

In actuality, no fat lady or fat man could work for a relational database, or if they did, they would have to run back and forth so fast that they wouldn't stay fat for very long. This is because when you order a record onto your screen, the program must go and find all of the information the record contains and display it. When you want to look at another record, it must repeat the process. In every case, it is returning to the master file to get its data.

As you stare into the green luminescence of your display screen, it looks as though a person's name and address or other information are recorded in two or more completely different files. But with a relational database, this is really an illusion. What is actually recorded in each file are instructions to the program telling it where it can find the name or address or other information that is supposed to be displayed there. This is the basis of the "relation" between the file you are presently looking at and the master file.

---

**SoftTip:** It is at this point that the mechanics become almost unbearably complex. Because in reality there may be no single master file. Instead, the information such a file would contain may be scattered over any number of files. If you were to list out all of the fields in your database files in separate columns and put them all on one large page, you could drive yourself crazy drawing all of the lines and pointers illustrating the relationships that exist in the database. In the interests of mutual mental health, the subject can safely be left at this point.

---

*What Does "Relational" Mean to You?*

Relational databases offer both convenience and power. On the convenience side of things, they make it easy to update the information in your files in one fell swoop. Since all the files in your database are drawing their information from the same "master" source, if you update the master source you effectively update all of your files.

For example, suppose that you're a business person who wants to cut the price on a particular item before mailing out invoices to the firm's customers. And suppose that there were 50 invoices listing a Widget II at $200 and you wanted to reduce the price to $160. Since the invoices all take their information about the Widget II from the same inventory, all you would have to do would be to change the price in that file. If you were not using a relational database, you would have to go through all 50 invoices and change the price on each one. For this reason some businesses find that a relational database is well suited to accounting and similar applications where the same information must often be entered in two or more ledgers or files.

Relational databases also give you more power over your information by allowing you to create a whole range of files containing different fields. For example, your master personnel file would naturally include everything your company needs to know about an employee, including his or her salary, health problems, supervisor comments, and so on. Clearly, this kind of information should be kept confidential.

So how do you have a clerk update a personnel file and still preserve the privacy of your employees? A relational database makes it easy. Instead of giving the clerk access to the entire personnel file, you create a separate file containing just the fields that the clerk must have in order to perform the updates. As long as this is the only file the clerk has access to, there is no way for that individual to view any information other than the fields the file contains. You could not create a new file like this if the database were not relational.

You might use the same technique to create a file containing just your customer's names and addresses, to build an index keyword file of the sort described earlier, and sort on the basis of ZIP code. You could do the same thing for another file, but sort *it* alaphabetically. When you wanted to generate mailing labels, you would use the ZIP code file. When you wanted a printed list of your customers for easy reference, you would use the alphabetical file.

Similarly, you could tell the program to "take the name and address out of this file, and the total purchase figure out of that one, and create a new file to hold this information." Or you could say, "I want you to merge this file with that one to create a single large file containing all the information in both of them." Essentially, then, a relational database lets you run rings around your data. You can do virtually anything you want with it.

*What Kind of Output?*

DBMS output options are the same as those found with file managers.

You can create a file on disk containing data that you might want to incorporate in a spreadsheet or a document created on your word processor. And you can print reports.

There may be a feature that will automatically remove the special codes used by the DBMS to make the file suitable for use with a word processing program. This can be convenient because it saves you removing the codes and reformatting the file yourself. There may also be a feature that automatically formats the output for use with VisiCalc or another spreadsheet that uses the DIF file structure. (See Chapter 15.)

As with some file managers, some DBMS programs may include a sophisticated "report generator." While all programs will let you print out information, their capabilities vary in how elaborately you can arrange that information. You may only be able to tell the program which fields to print, for example. In that case, everything is likely to begin at the far left margin and there will be only one piece of information, or one field, per line.

With a good report generator, you will be able to tell the computer to print information all over the page. You may be able to include vertical and horizontal lines, main titles in expanded print, column headings, underlined words, bold print, and other "presentation quality" features. You might be able to print your checks.

If the program says it has a "forms" feature, it may mean that you can load your printer with preprinted forms and instruct the software to put all the information in the proper blanks. In some cases, you may be able to eliminate the need for the special forms themselves by having the program print the complete form while it is filling in the blanks. Some report writers also include mathematical capabilities that automatically generate totals, averages, percentages, etc.

**SoftTip:** If you are interested in producing anything more elaborate than a quick, rough-and-ready printout with either a DBMS or a file manager, a report generator can be quite important. They are something to watch out for, though, since many programs do not include them as part of the main package but sell them as add-ons. The file manager PFS:File, for example, lists at around $125 for the Apple II and $140 for the IBM. But if you want to produce more elaborate printouts, you must buy PFS:Report, $95 for the Apple and $125 for the IBM. The DBMS MAG/base2 ($495) from Micro Applications Group in Canoga Park, California includes a report writer. But for truly sophisticated printouts, you must buy the MAG/base Advanced Report Writer ($295). MAG/base3 ($795) includes both "2" and the Report Writer, however.

## Limitations: How Many and How Long?

The "How Many?/How Long?" test recommended as one of the Twelve Rules for Software Success is never more important or applicable than when evaluating one of the three types of information management programs we have discussed. Almost all programs place some kind of limit on the number of records you can have in a single file, the number of fields you can have in each of those records, and the number of characters you can allot for each field.

These limits can vary widely. The number of records permitted can range from 100 to 65,535 to a number limited only by available disk space. There might be a maximum of 15 fields per record, or 32, several hundred, or tens of thousands. The total number of characters you can allot for each field could be limited to 25, to 250, or again, to tens of thousands. In some cases, the limits may be based on the total number of characters used: Specifying more fields might reduce the maximum number of characters you can put into each one, while fewer fields would increase it.

In a free-form indexing system, the size of the block of text you use in each record may be limited to a single screenful, or it may include several screens. The number of keywords you specify may be limited to 40 or fewer, or there may be no limit. Other limitations in other types of programs may include the number of keys you can sort on at any one time, the number of index files that can be associated with any one file, and on and on and on.

### What's a Software Buyer to Do?

While it is important to be aware of the limitations of individual packages, it is possible to get so caught up in the numbers that you can't tell whether you're coming or going.

The fundamental question for most people is, How many records, fields, or characters do I *need?* The pat answer is that it will depend upon the application you have in mind. But that isn't a lot of help.

It's usually better to take an entirely different approach that leaves the numbers until last. If you're thinking of buying an information management package for home use, the first thing to ask yourself is whether you are primarily interested in retrieving (finding) information or whether you want both to find information and to use the program for generating mailing lists, keeping track of your expenses or possessions, or performing any other jobs that often require single-purpose programs to accomplish.

If you just want to find information ("How many bottles of Chateau Neuf de Pape are in my wine cellar?" "Where's that article I downloaded from The Source on how to buy a hard disk drive?"), you probably can't beat a free-form indexing program. You'll have to have a word processing program if you want to enter data, but no information management program is simpler or easier to use.

If you need a more powerful program capable of serving as an "engine" to drive a number of applications, or if you want to be able to manipulate your data in a variety of ways, the choice is more difficult. A file management program or a DBMS will force you to create structured records, but you will be able to create many different disk files and printouts. Either type of software will take some time and effort to learn, set up, and use. Of the two, it is more likely that you will find an easy-to-use file management program than an easy DBMS. File management programs tend to be menu-driven, and DBMS programs tend to be command driven.

Ultimately, for a home user, it may be a simple matter of cost. There is no point in paying hundreds of dollars extra to get a powerful relational database if you will never be merging various files, frequently updating fields, or using the more advanced features it offers. Even if you can afford a DBMS, you may still be better off buying a file manager. Both types of software can accomplish the same things, but you will have to spend more time and effort learning to do them with a DBMS.

Things are different for business users. A business person might use a free-form package to keep track of memos, notes, summaries of phone conversations, and the like. And a secretary might use it as an aid in finding information in a paper filing system. (Each record could consist of a paragraph describing a particular paper file and include the name of the filing cabinet and drawer that holds it.) But for *real* information management, you should probably go straight to a full-featured DBMS package.

In the first place, a business has access to tax benefits that a private individual does not, so the effective total cost of the DBMS package will be less. Equally important, a business is more likely to have a use for the advanced features such a program provides. And because a firm's needs are likely to change much more rapidly than those of an individual, it is more probable that a company will "grow into" any DBMS features that it does not currently use.

### The Numbers Game

Once you have decided on the type of information management software you need, it will be easier to make sense of the numerical limitations described earlier. It will be even easier if you are buying the program for business use, since you will already know how many customers you have, how many invoices you produce, or how many part numbers you have in inventory. If you use those figures as a base and then try to project how many you are likely to have five years from now, you can come up with a pretty fair estimate of what you need.

The same general approach can be used when buying software for home use. How many bottles of wine are in your cellar already? How many names are on the membership list of your church group? What information do you think you'll want to keep track of: name, address, phone, and what else? And how many characters are required for the longest item? If you come up with a rough figure for these things and increase it by 25% as a safety margin, you'll have a pretty good idea of what you need today. Obviously, if you think there's a chance that the categories of things you have to keep track of will multiply in the near future, you must factor that in as well.

## Conclusion

Electronic spreadsheets "crunch" numbers. Word processing programs "crunch" words. And data management programs "crunch" information. As such, they can help you to deal effectively with "information explosion," for what good is having a wealth of information if you can never find it when you need it? There is an important caveat, however, that is often overlooked. And that is the data entry part of the process.

A program can't deal with information unless someone first types it in. For businesses this is usually not much of a problem—just bring on the hired help. But if you are a home user, you owe it to yourself to give some thought to the time and effort that will be required to build your database. It can be a time-consuming chore. On the other hand, once you have entered the bulk of the information, adding a few additional records every now and then is easy. If you're willing to do the initial work, you will find that you have created a powerful tool that you may not want to live without.

## Software Buyer's Quick Reference Checklist

*—Personal Filing and Database Management Systems—*

### Preliminaries

As mentioned at the end of the chapter, the first thing to do is to consider the kind of information you want to keep track of and which type of program is likely to do the best job for you. You should also consider how much money you can afford to spend and how much time you are willing to devote to mastering the program.

The amount of RAM you have can also be a consideration. The minimum required for information management programs of all types is usually 48K, but many programs run better and faster if you give them more room.

Since the more powerful programs are usually too large to fit into even 64K all at once, many of them go out to disk frequently to bring in overlays when you call for certain features. This can slow you down considerably and is a good reason for checking to see if the program can be copied into a RAM-based electronic disk or a hard disk.

## Free-Form Indexing Programs

☐ Where does the text or information come from? Can you use the output of *any* word processing program? More importantly, can you use the word processing software you already own or are thinking of buying?

☐ How much text can you have in any single record? A single page? Several pages? If you have downloaded a multi-page article from an information service you may not want to have to split it into two or more records.

☐ What is the process for entering your keywords? Do you have to type them in separately or move the cursor to them and hit a special key?

☐ How many keywords may you have for each record? The more complex and detailed the information you want to file, the more keys you will need.

☐ Will the program give you a "dictionary" listing of all the keywords you have entered for a particular file? This is essential since you can easily forget what words you have used.

☐ Can you use more than one keyword to search for a record? A program that lets you look for records filed under both BASEBALL *and* OAKLAND A'S will be more useful than one that limits you to BASEBALL.

☐ How sophisticated is the search function? Can you string together a chain of keywords linked by AND, OR, and NOT?

☐ Is it possible to tell the program to look for records containing a word that you have *not* previously designated as a keyword? This will take some time, but it is a handy feature.

☐ Is there any way to sort your records? If you have set your records up in a particular way, you may be able to do a limited sort.

☐ Is there a feature to strip a record automatically of the codes the program uses so you can use a record in a report or letter without removing the codes yourself?

☐ How flexible are the printing and display options? Must you print out the entire record every time, or can you specify just a part of it?

☐ Can the program be used to generate labels and mailing lists?

## File Managers and DBMS Programs

☐ If you will be dealing with a large number of records (200 or more), the speed with which the program does its job can be very important. Consequently, it can be important to find out what language it is written in. If it is written in UCSD Pascal or some other interpreted language, it may be too slow for you. The fastest programs are written in machine or assembly language.

☐ Is the program menu driven? Command driven? Or do you have an option of using either approach? A program that is command driven should allow you to record a series of commands as a "program" to save time when you next want to execute a particular function.

☐ It is worth noting that, while more difficult to master, a command driven program may be so flexible that you can in effect *create your own menus* using recorded command files. A computer-skilled manager could thus build more user-friendly "front end" to enable clerks to use the program without mastering its commands.

☐ How many records, fields, and characters may you have?

☐ Does the program limit you to one file *per disk?* If it does, and you have a lot of short files, it will cause you to buy more disks than you might want to.

*Laying Out the Data Entry Form*

Programs vary in how easily you can use them to create the form that establishes your database structure and allows you to enter data. The best approach is one that is as visually oriented as possible. Instead of telling the system how many characters you want in each field by typing in a number, you move the cursor or enter letters in the field itself so that you can *see* how long each field will be.

The more closely you can make the computer's form look like any paper form you are now using, the easier it will be for someone to enter data.

*For Business Users:* If you want to include information from your firm's mainframe in your own database, be certain that you find out whether the program will permit this and, if so, exactly what steps you must follow.

☐ How are the fields specified and how long a name can you use? Can you use a real name or must you call everything "Field 1, Field 2, Field 3," etc?

☐ Can you put dollar signs, dashes, decimal points, and other symbols in the fields? If you can make these part of your form, you will not have to enter them when you are actually typing in data.

☐ Can you specify different "variable" types, i.e., alphanumeric, numeric, calculated, etc.?

☐ Can you enter an equation to have the program automatically calculate the number that should go into a particular field? If so, what arithmetical or other operators can you use?

☐ How easy is it to *edit* the form before you record it? How easy is it to edit *after* you record it?

☐ VERY IMPORTANT: What happens if you set up a form, enter data, and want to add a variable to the form or change it in some other way? Will you lose all of the data you have entered? Or does the program offer a way around this potential disaster? You should not buy any program that does not let you change your data entry form without preserving your data.

### Data Entry

☐ How easily can you enter your data? Does the cursor automatically jump down to the next field after you have typed the last character in the field above it?

☐ Can you use your arrow keys or some other technique to go back to a field and edit or correct mistakes? The program should wait until you have made all of your changes and have the record exactly the way you want it before recording it.

☐ How easy is it to add a record or delete a record?

☐ How easy is it to go back and make changes in a record you have already recorded?

### Searching

☐ Can you locate a record by simply telling the program to look for a particular piece of information in a particular field?

☐ Can you create a ISAM index or keyword file for your database? This is sometimes called "indexing" a file.

☐ How many fields can you include in such an index? Is there any limit on the length of fields chosen for indexing versus those that are not indexed?

☐ What is the indexing process? How easily can it be done?

☐ Can you have multiple indexes for each file, each of which might contain a different selection of keywords? How many indexes?

☐ How sophisticated a search can you conduct? How many keywords can you specify and how can they be linked?

☐ Can you use Boolean functions AND, OR, and NOT? Can you use the logical operators TRUE and FALSE?

☐ Can you use "greater-than," "less-than," "not-equal-to," and other "relational" operators?

☐ What about IF . . . THEN . . . ELSE?

☐ Can you use BASIC string functions or those of some other language (ASC, CHR$, INT, VAL, etc.)?

☐ Is there a "wildcard" search function?

☐ Can the program find a specified string of characters or numbers *anywhere* within a given field?

☐ Can you zero in on just the first *N* characters of a field or the last *N* characters?

## Sorting

☐ Do you have the option of sorting both the physical records and the index or key files?

☐ How many keys can you sort on? A primary key and a secondary? Can you specify both keys at once or must you sort on one and then sort on the other? A multi-key sort will usually take less time.

☐ Can you sort alphabetically in both ascending (*A* to *Z*) and descending (*Z* to *A*) order?

☐ Can you sort numerically in ascending and descending order?

## Output

☐ Can you tell the program to record the data in a number of records in a disk file? Can you specify print parameters but "print to disk" instead of to the printer? (This should create a file in which the information appears just as it would have on paper had you actually printed it.)

☐ Can the program create files for use with your word processing program? Can it automatically strip the file of the codes used by the information management system so you don't have to do it manually?

☐ Will it create the kind of file needed if you want to load your database information in your spreadsheet? Does it create DIF files?

☐ Can the output be used as input for a graphics program?

☐ How flexible are your hard-copy print options? Does the program include a report generator to produce really snazzy documents, complete with titles, columns, labels, etc.? Or must everything be printed flush left, a single piece of information per line?

☐ Can you use the program to fill in preprinted forms? Will the program actually create forms to your specifications?

☐ If a report or forms generator is not included in the original package, what are your options? Can you buy an add-on module? How much?


*A Relational Database System*

☐ Can you open and use more than a single file at a time?

☐ Can you update information in one fell swoop? Will changing a field in one record automatically change the information in any other file that uses that same field?

☐ Can you break a large file into several subfiles, each of which contains some but not all of the fields found in the main one?

☐ Can you merge files containing different fields into one large file?


**Other Considerations for File Managers and DBMS**

☐ Is there a way to "password-protect" your files to preserve security?

☐ Will the program automatically tell you if you try to enter the wrong kind of data in a field?

☐ What, if any, onscreen "Help" functions are available? And how helpful are they likely to be?

☐ What happens if you get a "DISK FULL" error? Does the manual tell you what to do to avoid losing all the data you've entered? Trying to find error messages and instructions in the manual is a good way to test the documentation for usability.

☐ How are other errors handled? Will the program warn you before you make them, when possible?

☐ What kinds of support resources are available for the program? Do companies other than the manufacturer offer preprogrammed command files? Are there books on how to use the program? Courses? Is there a users group? A newsletter?

# ...17...

## How to Buy Communications Programs

A communicating computer is your passport to a vast and expanding electronic universe of information and communication. Want a summary of all the articles that have been published comparing various brands of imported beer and where to find the publications? Or maybe a market study comparing sales of St. Pauli Girl to Becks? Would you like to know whether baseball-hitting coach Charley Lau has ever published a book explaining his system? Or if anything has ever been published comparing the batting prowess of Honus Wagner, Ty Cobb, Rogers Hornsby, and Rod Carew?

Would you like to exchange recipes and household hints with the editors of *Better Homes and Garden?* Send a letter to Paris or Melbourne, Australia—instantly—for about 9¢? Access your company's mainframe from your home or hotel room? Or maybe you'd like to send and receive Telex and TWX messages, as well as international cables, without ever leaving your home and without renting a Telex terminal.

If any of this sounds interesting to you, then you should know that:

**With communications software, you can do all of these things today.**

Actually, what we've described so far is the merest hint of the scope and full range of power you will find in the electronic universe. For many people, online electronic communications and the world-expanding possibilities it holds is *the* best reason to buy a personal computer in the first place.

*Preliminaries and Background*

If you've read Chapter 8, you already know how a communicating personal computer can be used to search for the names of programs for whatever application you have in mind. And you know how it can be used to look for software reviews in the major computer publications via DIALOG's Knowledge Index. You've also read about the Special Interest Groups (SIGs) open to you on The Source and CompuServe. If

418

you've read Chapter 22 about how to buy investment software, you are aware of the corporate and stock market information available online from the Dow Jones News/Retrieval Service and other sources. And if you've read Chapter 12, you know that a communicating personal computer can be used to tap huge resources of free software available on the nation's computer bulletin board systems (BBS's), the phone numbers of which can be found in Appendix D.

But, like the examples given earlier, this is only the beginning. You can also order televisions, stereos, Waterford crystal, Cross pen sets, and over 50,000 other brand name products with your computer, and save as much as 40% off the list price. You can join the PARTI on The Source and PARTICIPATE in ongoing electronic conferences with experts and people who share your interests. You can check restaurant reviews and make complete travel arrangements at any hour of the day or night.

If you are a writer, you can help out with the new *Whole Earth Software Catalogue* and its associated newsletter—conferring with your editor, exchanging copy with your co-authors, and submitting the final draft—via the EIES ("eyes") system. If you have some poetry, a short story, an essay, or some other creative effort you'd like to share, you can publish it electronically on The Source, and possibly even earn a small royalty. If you're into CB radio—and even if you're not—you'll be happy to know that there is an online equivalent on CompuServe. (Things get started every night at 6:00 and continue long into the wee hours.)

---

**SoftTip:** You can think of CompuServe's CB section as a gigantic, ongoing telephone conference call involving a hundred or more participants all over the continent. The difference is that instead of speaking your comments, you type them and read those made by others who are online at the same time. At least two couples who met on the system later got married—on the system. The minister was in one state, the parents and the happy couple were in several other states, and the wedding guests were scattered all over the North American contintent. When it was over, all of the guests threw rice—by hitting the hyphen keys on their computers.

---

You will find a comprehensive description of the major databases available to you, the features they offer and how to use them, as well as information on how to send and receive Telex and TWX messages, how to become a "telecommuter" and work from home via your personal computer, and much more in *The Complete Handbook of Personal Computer Communications: Everything You Need to Go Online with the World* (St. Martin's Press, $14.95). However, if you need more information immediately, ask your local computer dealer or contact the following organizations:

| **Database** | **Description** |
| --- | --- |
| The Source<br>1616 Anderson Road<br>McLean, VA 22102<br>(800) 336-3366<br>(703) 734-7540 | Initial subscription: $100 hourly rate: Varies with speed and time of day. Lowest is: $7.75/hour; Telenet, Tymnet, and Uninet charges, included. |
| CompuServe<br>5000 Arlington Centre Blvd.<br>P.O. Box 20212<br>Columbus, OH 43220<br>(800) 848-8990<br>(614) 457-8600 | Initial subscription: $20 to $50. Includes several hours of free connect time. Hourly rate: Varies with speed and time of day. Lowest is $6.00/hour; Telenet and Tymnet charges, extra. |
| Dow Jones News/Retrieval Service<br>P. O. Box 300<br>Princeton, NJ 08540<br>(800) 257-5114<br>(609) 452-1511 | Initial subscription: $50. Available 9:00 AM, EST to 11:00 PM, EST, weekdays. Nine to five, weekends. Lowest rate: $9.00/hour. |

These are the "Big Three" general interest databases, and most individuals eventually subscribe to one or more of them. All offer a wide variety of information, and all of them can be used to send and receive electronic mail. You should know, however, that there are over 1,600 *other* databases accessible to you and your communicating computer. Some of these are highly specialized, single-subject databases not likely to be of interest to most computer owners. But others offer information drawn from many sources on a broad variety of subjects and are ideal for anyone needing more depth than either of the "Big Three" can provide.

*A Word about Cost*

These other general interest databases are also covered in *The Complete Handbook* mentioned above, as are numerous tips and tricks for saving money when you go online. Though it's a rare situation, there *are* individuals who have racked up hundreds of dollars in database charges in a single month. In some cases, this happens as a result of inattention to the clock. In others, it is the result of literal "database addition." But the point is that none of the online services is free—they are all designed as profit-making ventures.

Consequently, the most economical way to use CompuServe, The Source, Dow Jones, or any other service is to get in and get out as quickly as possible. A well-designed communications software package will make this much easier. You'll understand more about this after you read the rest of this chapter, but with the right program (and modem), you can sign on at 1200 baud (the fastest speed most databases support), download (capture) the information you want or the electronic letters you have received in a memory buffer or directly to disk (instead of waiting for your printer to print them), and sign off to "stop the meter." Once you have signed off, you can edit the information, print it out, or merely look at it on your screen—at leisure.

In some cases, the programs that offer these features cost more than those that do not include them. But if you use a database two or three times a week, the more expensive program can be well worth the extra cost. In the long run, they can save you more in database charges than they cost in the first place.

## Communications Software and Going Online

You may be relieved to know that telecommunications is one of the few reasonably standardized areas of computerdom. It has to be. Otherwise, one computer could never talk to another computer made by a different manufacturer. For this reason, all personal computer communications programs do exactly the same thing—they enable your computer to talk to the telephone. Where they differ, and where they compete, is in the nature and number of convenience features they offer. There is probably no other type of software in which the features that make the program easier or faster to use receive such emphasis.

Of course, any time you're confronted with a feature-packed program, it can be difficult to tell what's likely to be really useful to you and which features should be given less weight in your consideration of which program to buy. Consequently, before discussing the kinds of features you will find in communications software, it's important to have a general idea of what's involved when you go online. This way, you'll be able to tell where each feature "fits" in the overall scheme of things.

### *"Comm" Cards and Modems*

In addition to your telephone and your computer, you need a "communications card" and a device called a "modem." It is the job of the "comm" card to rearrange the electric impulses that whiz around inside your computer. Normally, for example, when you hit a key on your keyboard, electric impulses travel along eight parallel wires leading into the heart of your machine. You might think of them as cars travelling eight abreast down a superhighway. The comm card acts like a traffic-directing policeman at the entrance to a single-lane tunnel. It says, "Hold it, guys. You can't all go through here at once. We'll start with the car on the left. Okay, next car . . . now the next . . ." and so on. Thus the comm card converts the computer's natural "parallel" arrangement into a "serial" arrangement, in which each electric impulse passes one at a time. For this reason, it is often called a "serial interface."

In most cases, the comm card plugs into one of the expansion slots inside a computer. The card includes a place to plug in a cable leading to the outside world. This is called an "RS-232C" interface, and normally the cable you plug into it leads directly to the modem. (Apple owners can use a Hayes Micromodem card that includes the communications circuitry *and* the modem all on one plug-in card.)

---

**SoftTip:** A communications card alone usually costs around $100 to $125, depending on your computer. Often, however, all the circuitry and the RS-232 plug needed for communications can be found on the plug-in memory boards you buy when you want to add more RAM to your machine. This is such a common feature that you should not buy a memory board that does not include it. In fact, you might want to think about buying a memory expansion board with the minimum amount of RAM (64K) even if you are not ready for the extra memory at this time. You could use the board for communications and add memory as you needed it over time. This may be the least expensive way to go, and even if it isn't, having memory and communications on the same card does preserve one of your computer's card slots for other uses.

*Note:* If you have a Commodore VIC-20 or 64 computer, you already have a card that can serve for communications (IEEE-448 interface). You must use a special Commodore modem, however. See your dealer.

---

The word "modem" is short for "*mo*dulator/*dem*odulator," and its job is to convert the electric impulses it receives in serial fashion from the comm card into sound. This is necessary because it is generally impossible to send and receive the electric impulses your computer uses internally over ordinary telephone lines. The modem usually has a cable that plugs directly into a modular jack just the way your phone does. For obvious reasons, this is called a "direct-connect" modem. Many of the more expensive direct-connect modems have the ability to dial the telephone automatically. That means you can either type in the number from your keyboard or "send the modem a file" containing a phone number you have previously entered and recorded. Some modems can also automatically answer the phone to connect the caller's computer with your own (assuming your machine is on, and loaded with the necessary software).

---

**SoftTip:** There are also devices called "acoustic modems" that are equipped with foam rubber cups designed to accept a telephone handset and send and receive sound that way. But unless you are in an office or a hotel room that does not have modular telephone jacks, there is no reason to use them. Because of the increased possibility of interference from outside noise, they are generally not as reliable as a direct-connect modem, and since there is no direct connection, they cannot automatically dial the phone.

---

**SoftTip:** Space does not permit a complete discussion of modems. However, you should know about "baud" rates. "Baud" is basically a measure of the speed of communications—how fast you can send and receive information. Some modems, for example, can communicate at only 300 baud, while others can handle 150 to 1200 baud.

When shopping for a modem, give strong consideration to getting one with 1200-baud capabilities—even if it means putting off your purchase until you can afford it. Since modem prices are coming down, that may not be very long. Only a short time ago, a 1200-baud modem could easily cost $535, at a discount off the list price of $700. Now you may be able to buy the Anchor Automation Mark 12 1200-baud modem for about $270 (list price is about $400).

Anchor has been a leader in breaking the modem price barrier. At a list price of $70, the firm's 300-baud Volksmodem was the first low-cost direct connect modem on the market, for example. Other modem manufacturers can be expected to follow suit. For information, contact:

> Anchor Automation
> 6913 Valjean Avenue
> Van Nuys, CA 91406

## The Steps to Going Online

*Communications Settings*

It's easy to describe what it's like to be online with a remote database or a computer bulletin board. When the connection is made, a message from the remote system will appear on your screen. You type in an answer from your keyboard. More messages and information requests appear, calling for more keyboard input. This message and response sequence is exactly the way things would appear if the computer you were talking to were in the next room, connected to your machine by a cable.

The problem is that it's not. A remote computer could be only 10 miles away, or it could be several thousand miles away. Wherever it happens to be, however, the fact that your machine must talk to it over the telephone makes the process more involved than if it were in the next room. In addition to needing the physical connections provided by the comm card and modem, you also need to be able to tell your computer how you want it to communicate. How fast should it send and receive information? Should it add any error-checking impulses to what it sends out and look for such impulses in the information it receives? How many bits will be used to represent a character and should it add something called a "stop bit" after each one?

These instructions are called "communications settings" or "parameters," and this is where the software comes in. In the terminology of the field, these settings are known as "baud rate" (speed), "parity checking" (a technique for improving accuracy), "character length" (the number of bits used to represent a letter or character), and "stop bits" (a bit notifying the remote computer that one character has been sent). There is also a setting for "duplex" (full or half).

You don't have to know what *any* of this means. All you have to do is make sure that all of the settings on your computer match those used by the remote computer. Your communications software is what makes this possible. And as we'll see, this is one area where programs differ. Some will let you enter your settings once and forget about them; others force you to enter the settings each time you want to go online.

*Dialing the Phone*

Once the communications settings have been entered, the next step is to dial the phone and wait until you hear the high-pitched tone of the modem on the other end of the line. You may have to dial by hand, wait for the tone, and switch on your own modem. But if you have a modem that can dial by itself and *if your software supports it*, you will be able to turn on your modem and type in the phone number from your keyboard. When you hit your <ENTER> key, the modem will begin dialing.

You may even be able to record frequently called numbers on floppy disk and dial them by pressing a single key. Again, the software must offer this capability. The feature that makes this possible is usually called a "dialing directory." It consists of a "menu" of frequently called numbers that you have previously typed in and recorded. When you want to dial a number, you hit a single key corresponding to the "menu selection" on your listing.

### Database Addresses, Accounts, and Passwords

When accessing The Source, CompuServe, Dow Jones, or most other commercial databases, you usually dial a local telephone number to make the connection. The local telephone number is supplied by what's called a "packet switching" service, and all you need know about it is that it's cheaper than calling long distance. When you connect with Telenet, Tymnet, Uninet, or some other packet switching service, you will be asked for the "address" of the database you want to talk to. If you wanted to talk to The Source, you might enter "C 30128" on the Telenet system. For CompuServe, you would type "C 202202." This causes the packet switcher to plug you into the remote computer.

When the connection has been made, the remote database will ask you for your account number and your password. On The Source, you must type in something like this: ID TCA123 SECRET. CompuServe first asks for your account number (e.g., "70012,345") and then prompts you for your password (e.g., "MY*SIN"). Other databases require similar sequences, but once you enter them, you're "online" and free to roam around at will.

### Signing on Automatically

We've gone into some detail here for a couple of reasons. First, it's important to realize how much typing can be involved from the time you connect with the packet switcher until you get into the target system. And second, you should know that different databases prompt you for your account number and password in different ways.

Fortunately, most of these things can be handled by your communications program, if it has the right features. Programs generally take one of two approaches. They may let you type in and record all of your address, account number, and password information once and record it. From then on you can respond to each prompt from the remote database by hitting a single key. This causes your computer to send the required "string" (sequence) of characters automatically to the database.

The second approach is more complex for the program and more convenient for you. With some software, for example, you can press a single key to select The Source or CompuServe, and the complete sign-on procedure will take place automatically. Because these two databases prompt you for account and password information differently, the software must "know" what to expect and how to respond in each case.

### Bringing Information In

Much of the time, you will be happy to let the dialogue between you and the remote computer quietly scroll up and off the screen into oblivion. It has served its purpose and can safely be disposed of. However, there will be many times when you want to "capture" the information the database sends you. It could be a letter sent from an electronic correspondent. It could be a file listing magazines with the software reviews you need. Whatever it may be, a communications program that doesn't let you keep a record of the information you are sent is next to worthless.

Fortunately, the majority of communications programs offer one or more ways to accomplish this. In some cases, you may simply want to turn on your printer to generate a hard copy of whatever is appearing on the screen. The software should make it easy for you to do this, usually with a "toggle" function: Hit a key combination once to toggle the printer on; hit the same combination again to toggle it off.

Usually, you will also be able to capture or "download" information into a "buffer" as well. Comm programs that offer a buffer set aside a certain amount of your computer's memory to serve as a "holding tank" for whatever you allow to flow into it while you are online. Ideally, you will be able to toggle the buffer open and shut at will, capturing some things, and allowing others to pass on by. When you have finished using the database and hung up the phone, you will normally be able to record the contents of the buffer on a floppy disk. If the program has an "auto buffer dump" feature, it may automatically make the recording each time the buffer fills up. One way or another, once you have the information recorded, you can look at it and "massage" it with your word processor, print it out, or do anything else you might do with a text file.

### Information Going Out

All programs will let you send information to the remote computer by typing it in at your keyboard. But often it is important to be able to prepare a letter or a report "offline," that is, when you are *not* connected to a database and the connect time meter is *not* running.

Again, there are two major ways to do this. One way is to type up a letter or report with your word processor and record it as a file on disk. Then boot your comm program and load the file into the buffer the program has set aside for transmitting information. At the appropriate time, as when you see the words "Enter Text" appear to let you know that the remote system is ready to take a letter, you hit a key or two to "upload" the contents of the buffer.

This saves you money in at least two ways. It saves you paying for connect time while you are composing a letter. And, since a file sent from a buffer will be transmitted much faster than would be possible for even the fastest production typist, the time required to send the letter will be much less.

An even more convenient feature offered by some programs does away with the need to load the buffer at all. With these programs, you simply say "Send TEST.TXT from the disk in Drive B when I give the signal." The program will then automatically locate the file and transmit it to the remote system.

### Features that Fill in the Framework

These, then are the basic steps you must follow to go online and the basic things you'll be doing once you are connected to a remote system:

- Set communications parameters.
- Dial the phone.
- Enter address, account number, and password.
- Capture incoming information.
- Transmit information from your computer.

Virtually, all of the many features you will find in communications programs fit within this general framework. There are a number of "extras" that are not directly related to communications, like being able to get a directory of your data disk while using the comm program instead of going into DOS, or being able to "preview" the contents of a buffer before you send it. But these really are just extras. Unless they're really important to you, you shouldn't let them confuse the issue.

In the following section, we will use this framework to describe the various features you are likely to find in communications software. Then, we'll present a list summarizing what might be considered the "essential" features most people should look for in a communications package.

## Communications Parameters and Other Settings

*The Basic Settings*

All programs will let you set baud rate, parity, character or "word" length (to a computer, a single letter constitutes a "word"), and the number of stop bits. Again, it isn't necessary to understand what these terms mean, but your software must allow you to match the settings used by the remote database or "host" system.

Those are the basic settings, but the range over which you can adjust them may vary. You must be able to set the baud rate to 300 to communicate with a host system. And the software should allow you to select 1200 baud, even if you do not presently own a 1200-baud modem. But there's something else to consider. If you will ever be connecting two computers together, side by side without a modem, you will no longer be constrained by the speed limits of the telephone lines. (See Chapter 12 of *The Complete Handbook of Personal Computer Communications* for more information on the "cross over" or "null modem" cables needed to connect two computers.)

---

**SoftTip:** Very important. Even though they may allow you to specify 1200 baud, some programs on some computers have difficulty sending and receiving large blocks of text at this speed without dropping (losing) characters. One cause of this problem is the amount of time required for the computer to get an incoming character from the communications port and display it on the screen before the next character arrives. One solution is to toggle off the video display and thus free the machine to concentrate on capturing incoming characters. Another is to use an "interrupt-driven" program that takes advantage of certain features of the CPU to handle the get-a-character/display-a-character sequence a different way.

One of the main benefits of 1200-baud communications is the ability to send and receive blocks of text four times faster than at 300 baud. Consequently, the accuracy with which the program and the computer can communicate at 1200 baud is a key point to check when investigating and testing a comm program.

---

You might want to write something on a portable or transportable computer, for example, and "dump" it into your main personal computer. In that case, it can be convenient to be able to dump the information at 2400 or 9600 baud, four to eight times faster than would be possible using a modem and a telephone. All communications cards can handle these speeds, but not all communications packages will permit you to use them.

You should be able to set "parity" to odd, even, or none. One of these will be fine with virtually all commercially available databases. However, there are two other possible settings, "mark" and "mask." If the system with which you will be communicating requires these, then the software had better permit you to set them.

Similarly, most host systems require a word length of seven or eight bits. But on rare occasions, you may need a setting of five. Usually, only one stop bit is used. But, again, on rare occasions you may need to specify two.

### Full- and Half-Duplex

Most packages will also let you specify "full-" or "half-duplex" as a setting. This setting has nothing to do with your ability actually to communicate with a host system, but it has a profound effect on what you see on your computer's screen. When you are communicating in full-duplex, the words and letters you see on your screen don't come from your keyboard.

What actually happens is that they leave your keyboard, go to the host computer, and the host computer "echos" them back to your system, which then proceeds to display them on your screen. In half-duplex mode, the host system does not echo back. Consequently, if you want to see what you're typing, your own software must make sure that it is displayed on your screen.

Everything depends on the host system. If it is capable of echoing characters, then you would select full-duplex. If it isn't, then you must be able to select half-duplex. Most commercial databases and computer bulletin board systems (BBS's) work at full-duplex. But many business mainframe computers do not. Consequently, if you will be using your computer to access your company's mainframe, you should make sure that your software will let you select either duplex setting.

### Default Settings

Communications programs differ in how easily they allow you to deal with the above settings. At the lowest level of convenience are programs that force you to set your parameters each and every time you want to go online. This is a nuisance and is really unacceptable. Only slightly more convenient are programs that have built-in "default" settings. With these, you may be fine if all you ever want to do is to access a remote database at 300 baud. But if you want to change the baud rate or other settings—as when accessing your corporate mainframe or cabling your portable computer to your desktop system—you are no further ahead.

The most convenient feature in this area is the option to create your own defaults. If you spend most of your time talking to a company mainframe, for example, it can be convenient to get the program set up once, record the settings, and have it boot up and be ready to go every time.

### To Feed or Not to Feed

The final main setting to consider is whether or not you can have your software automatically add a "line feed" to incoming or outgoing information. "Line feed" is a term from the days when teletype machines were the only form of online communication. A line feed is an actual, nonvisible character that causes a printer to space up one line. It works the same way on your display screen. When you are communicating with a host system, one of you has got to send a line feed character at the end of each line. This is usually called sending a "line feed on carriage return." For "carriage return," read "Hitting your <ENTER> key."

Without a line feed, each succeeding line would overwrite the previously received line on your screen. There would be no scroll. And, as with duplex settings, the question of whether you must add line feeds depends on the host computer. If the host computer does not add them, then your software must automatically insert them each time it receives a "carriage return" character from the other system. Similarly, if the host system "needs to see" a line feed after each line, your software must supply it.

### Ease of Setting and "On the Fly"

A good comm package should make it very easy for you to enter your settings. Ideally, it will present you with a menu of choices and ask you to make your selection by moving the cursor and then hitting <ENTER>. With this approach you are less likely to make errors than with a program that simply prompts you for "Baud rate:" and forces you to remember the possible settings and type them in by hand.

It can also be important to be able to change your settings "on the fly," that is, while you are actually communicating with a host system. The line feeds mentioned above offer a good example. If you sign onto a system and find that there are too many blank lines between lines of text, it is because both you and the other system are adding line feeds. In that case, you will want to be able to tell your software to cut it out. And you will want to be able to do so without signing off, entering the new settings, and redialing the number.

**SoftTip:** If your software cannot match the settings of the host system, then you cannot communicate with it. If you will be talking to The Source, CompuServe, Dow Jones or some other commercial database, you will find that you can do so with almost every communications package. But if you will also be using your system to access a corporate mainframe, then extra caution is in order. One of the best things you can do in that case is to contact your firm's data processing experts to find out what the mainframe requires—*before* you buy a package for your computer.

## Dialing the Phone

If you have an acoustic modem or a modem that does not offer an auto-dial feature, please skip to the next section. But if you have a Hayes Smartmodem® or a comparable unit, you should definitely try to buy software that will take full advantage of the capabilities you have paid for. At the very least, the software should allow you to dial the phone by typing in the correct number from your keyboard, but a "dialing directory" is just about as important from the standpoint of convenience.

As mentioned earlier, a dialing directory consists of a "menu" of recorded phone numbers, any one of which can be dialed by pressing a single selection key. The directory is a file, and as you may have found, whenever you are dealing with computer files, the key questions are "How many?" and "How long?" Thus, a program's dialing directory may offer slots for five phone numbers or 25 or 100.

**SoftTip:** Why would you ever want a dialing directory with 25 or more phone number slots? If you routinely access only four or five databases, you probably wouldn't. But if you want to access a number of bulletin board systems, 25 or more slots can be very handy. Since BBS's can only accommodate one person at a time, they are often busy when you call. With a large dialing directory, you could tap a key to dial one, and then another, and another until you found one that answered.

For maximum convenience, a dialing directory should also allow you to attach communications settings to the phone number. This way, selecting a phone number from the directory will not only cause the modem to dial it, it will also make sure that your system is set to the parameters the host system needs. Perhaps most important of all, however, is the maximum length each phone number can be. Most dialing directories will allow you to enter *1* and an area code, but you should check to see if you will also be able to enter digits for Sprint, MCI, or some other discount long distance phone service.

---

**SoftTip:** If you will be using your computer to dial out of an office with a PBX or similar system, you will want to be especially careful in looking at a program's dialing directory. For not only must you be able to dial a number to get an outside line, but you must also be able to have your modem or software pause while the connection is made before trying to dial the next number in the sequence.

---

Among the "extras" when it comes to dialing the phone are features that allow you to make the system redial the last number by touching a single key. It is even possible to find a package, like PC Talk II, AS-COM, or PCMODEM that will *continue* dialing a number until it makes a connection. Typically, the software will signal you that a connection has been made. This can be useful for contacting BBS's. Since it is also possible to use your communications equipment to dial the number of someone you want to speak to, this feature can be handy whether you are trying to place an urgent call or merely calling department stores at Christmastime.

---

**SoftTip:** Whenever you are considering a package that includes any auto-dial feature, it is vital to make sure that the software fully supports the modem you will be using. The leader in auto-dial modems, the one that almost every software package supports, is the Hayes Smartmodem. The product literature and advertising should indicate whether the program supports Hayes modems, as well as whatever other modems one can use with the program. If no indication is given, be especially careful when considering this aspect of the package.

---

### Entering Addresses, Account Numbers, and Passwords

A feature that allows you to type database addresses and similar information once, record it, and transmit it as called for by hitting a single key in each case might be considered an essential "nonessential." If the electronic universe is ever to be accessible to large numbers of people, users must be freed of the need to type in long strings of characters and numbers every time they want to use a database. Ideally, a person should be able to turn on his or her computer and select The Source, CompuServe, or some other database at the touch of a button. The software would then take care of the entire log-on procedure, responding correctly to each of the host system's prompts. Among the few packages that offer this "completely automatic" log-on feature are Smartcom II from Hayes and the E-Z Term communications programs supplied with all Dow Jones software intended to access the firm's News/Retrieval Service. In the future, there will be many more.

A next-best alternative is a feature that allows you to load database addresses, account numbers, and passwords into one or more keys. Some packages, for example, load an entire sequence into a single key. As each prompt appears, you press that key and your computer sends the required information. Other programs have you load different keys with different information. This is better than the "single-key" approach because it keeps you from being locked into a particular sequence. If your account number is not transmitted correctly, for example, you can hit the proper key again. With a single key, the next string to be sent would be your password and the remote system would not accept that as your account number.

The ability to store a string of characters in a single key can also be convenient when you are sending electronic mail. Typically, when you are sending an electronic letter, the remote system will prompt you for a subject line that briefly describes the letter. This is the first thing your correspondent will see when scanning his or her electronic mailbox. Because the information is entered in response to a "Subject:" prompt, it usually cannot be prepared beforehand the way you would prepare a complete letter. However, if your software will allow you to load one or more keys with strings that are long enough (have enough characters), you can type up the subject lines and load them in before you go online. When the prompt appears, you can then just hit the appropriate "loaded" key (or sequence of keys). A program that includes this feature should also allow you to look at what you have stored in each key without actually sending it to the remote system.

## Capturing Incoming Information

*Printer Toggles and Capture Buffer*

As mentioned earlier, it is important to be able to toggle the printer on and off at will. (Your printer is switched on at all times, but only prints when you have "enabled" it by entering a command from the keyboard.) This is really an essential feature because you will find that you depend upon the information a database has sent you to decide what to do next. If that information has scrolled off the screen, it is not convenient (or cost-effective) to have the remote system send it to you again.

An excellent example might be someone using a BBS that requires unfamiliar commands. Instead of constantly calling for the "Help" file that contains a summary of the board's commands, you could call for it once, toggle your printer on, produce a hard copy for easy reference, and toggle your printer off so you don't waste paper. The same procedure has many applications when dealing with a commercial database.

As mentioned earlier, a second alternative is to open and close a buffer inside the machine to capture the information you want to save and later record on disk. With some packages, like Intelliterm for the IBM/PC from Philadelphia's Microcorp, you can set the capture buffer to any size permitted by your machine's available memory. With some other software, the size of the buffer is permanently fixed by the program.

A buffer should be easy to toggle open and closed. And if it fills up, you should be able to send a signal to the database to "Hold it!" and then record the buffer's contents on disk before resuming. Some packages will let you specify a filename and drive number before opening the buffer. As mentioned previously, this way, whenever the buffer fills, the system will automatically send the host computer a signal to stop transmitting for a moment and dump the buffer's contents to disk. This can be an important feature if you will be receiving large files, either from a commercial database or some other system.

Somewhat less important are features that allow you either to look at the text in the buffer before you record it or to manipulate and edit it the way you would with a word processing program. For some people, these features may be convenient, but others may find it just as easy to record a buffer and then bring the full power of a word processing program to bear on the material instead of using the limited editing capabilities of the communications program's text editor.

## Transmitting Information from Your Computer

The most bare-bones programs will not permit you to prepare a letter or other file and "upload" it to a remote system. Better programs will let you copy a file from disk into a "send" buffer either before you sign on to a remote system or at any time. Then, as mentioned earlier, you hit the correct keys to cause the system to transmit the buffer's contents.

The best programs, however, will let you type in a filename and send directly from disk. When one file has been transmitted, and you want to transmit another, you have only to type in the name of the second file, instead of clearing out and reloading the buffer each time. Obviously, a feature like this will be most important to a business person or someone else who plans to do a large amount of uploading and file transmission. It is nice, but not essential for most people who use the databases for pleasure or research.

### X-ON/X-OFF and Fine Tuning Features

As you read about communications programs, you are sure to encounter the terms X-ON and X-OFF. These are nonvisible characters that one computer sends another to tell it either to stop transmitting (X-OFF) or resume sending (X-ON). Usually, you will be able to send these characters from the keyboard. An X-ON is sent as a <CON-TROL><Q> and an X-OFF is a <CONTROL><S>. You might send these signals to tell Dow Jones to stop sending you the latest *Wall Street Journal* headlines while you tried to locate an empty disk. Or you might want to stop and look at something more closely instead of letting it scroll off your screen. Your software should also be able to send these signals automatically when your computer needs time to perform certain tasks, like recording the contents of a buffer or displaying a directory of one of your disks.

The X-ON/X-OFF protocol helps reduce the chance that you will lose several lines of information coming in from the host system when your system is busy with other things. Similarly, when the host sends an X-OFF to your computer, it reduces the chance that you will transmit information that will not be recorded by the host. This protocol, however, is only one of the ways that have been devised to meet the considerable challenge of synchronizing two distant computers so that information is not lost. The program you buy should definitely support the X-ON/X-OFF protocol. (All major databases do, and you will need it.)

Another feature found in some programs attacks the problem in a different way. Known as "upload throttling," this feature (or features) lets you automatically add a delay or a pause at the end of each line you transmit. This can be important because a mainframe that is busy servicing hundreds of callers can usually not accept line after line of text from your computer all at once.

It will capture a line from you and then a line from someone else, and someone else, then back to you, and so on. If you continue to send while the mainframe is off handling someone else, the mainframe is quite likely to miss some of your data. By adding a line pause of five or more tenths of a second, you can reduce the chance that this will happen. This is a good feature to have if you will be doing a lot of uploading of prepared letters and reports. But for many typical users, it is not essential.

---

**SoftTip:** If your software has upload throttling, you will have to experiment to find the correct setting for the databases or other mainframes you access most frequently. Since the precise delay required will vary with how many other people are using the service, you will probably want to set the delay for somewhat longer than the minimum. This way, you will not have to reset it every time you sign on.

---

Unless you're a business user, you won't have to worry about the other, less common, forms of upload throttling. Some programs, for example, can be set to wait for the mainframe to send a special series of characters before sending each line of text. Others may let you specify how many characters you must receive from the mainframe before sending the next line. When communicating with corporate mainframes these features can be important, if they are programmed to send that special series of characters or if they routinely send a certain number of characters after receiving each line. But you won't need these features with The Source, CompuServe, Dow Jones, or most other commercial databases.

*Machine Language Files and Special Protocols*

All programs can send and receive text files in which each letter or other character is represented by an ASCII (American Standard Code for Information Interchange) code number. These appear as regular words and phrases or as BASIC or other statements. However, some programs do not have the ability to deal with machine language files produced by assembling or compiling a program.

This might be a problem for a business user. But since most free software available from computer bulletin boards and other electronic sources consist of uncompiled text files of source code, you may not need this feature. (You can download the program and compile or assemble it on your own if you own the necessary software.) It all depends on what you will be using your communications capabilities for.

As we've said, there are many ways to improve the accuracy of file uploads and downloads through some form of synchronization of your computer and the host. The ultimate form of synchronization is a "file transfer protocol," and it can be used for any type of data, be it machine language or text or just numbers.

Space does not permit an extensive explanation, but essentially a file transfer protocol is a set of rules and error checking techniques that both computers use to make sure they are receiving accurate information. When the receiving computer detects an error, for example, it gives the sender a signal that says, "Wait a minute, I didn't get that last block of text. Send it again."

There are many different protocols (different rules and different signals), so it is essential that both you and the system you are communicating with use the same one. Often, if it is a friend's or an associate's personal computer, that means you must be running the same program. One of the main exceptions is Ward Christensen's XMODEM protocol. This is a public domain protocol that more and more comm programs are coming to support. It may one day become the standard file transfer protocol in the microworld.

If the program you buy includes this feature, you will be able to send and receive files from yours to any other computer that uses it with an accuracy rate as high as 99%. That can be important if the files you are sending consist of source code computer programming. But it is even more important if the files are undecipherable machine language. The XMODEM protocol is especially important because so many CP/M bulletin boards use it to transmit public domain programs to their callers.

## Other Features: A Brief Summary

*Translation Tables*

A translation table is a table of numbers that lets you convert either incoming or outgoing characters into other characters. For instance, if you wanted the host system to receive a *Z* every time you hit the *A* key, you could use a translation table to make the conversion. Since not all characters have a standard ASCII number, different systems use different numbers to represent them. What appears as a registered trademark (®) in the other system's files might appear as a paragraph symbol (¶) in your files. But with a translation table you can make the conversion so that the trademark shows up as it should.

SoftTip: Translation tables will also let you send characters for which there are no keys on your keyboard. If you do not have a key for a left square bracket ([), for example, you might use the table so that whenever you hit an ampersand (&) your computer

*SoftTip continued*

actually sends the ASCII code for a left square bracket. You would not be able to see it as such on your screen, but it would appear correctly to anyone with a computer that has a square brackets key or to a mainframe that needs to see that particular code number for one reason or another.

**SoftTip:** Many mainframe computers do not use the ASCII code to represent characters. Instead, they use an IBM code called EBCDIC (Extended Binary Coded Decimal Interchange Code). If your corporate computer cannot communicate in ASCII, you will not be able to use your personal computer to access it unless your software can handle EBCDIC. Often, a translation table is the answer. If it is large enough, it can be used to convert ASCII to EBCDIC and visa versa.

*A True BREAK Signal*

What do you do when you want a remote mainframe computer to stop whatever program it is running for you and accept a new command? If you are using The Source, you can hold down your <CONTROL> key and press <P>. For CompuServe, sending a <CONTROL><C> will do the same thing. The software that runs The Source, CompuServe, and other commercial databases is programmed to accept these control characters as a signal to stop. But many corporate mainframes require a "true" BREAK signal. This is not an ASCII character. It is a sustained signal that can usually be set to last anywhere from 200 to 600 milliseconds. (You can also send a true BREAK to most commercial databases.) If your corporate mainframe requires a true BREAK, make sure that the personal computer software you buy can generate it.

*Batch Files and Master/Slave Mode*

A batch file capability allows you to prepare a complete set of commands, settings, and instructions for automatic execution by your computer. When you run such a file, for example, the program might automatically dial the phone, log you onto a database, issue whatever commands are needed to retrieve the information you want, download the information and write it to disk, and then sign you off the system.

If your computer has a clock on a plug-in board or if you use a peripheral timer, you could get everything set up and go about your business. At the time you have set, the batch file would load in and begin to run. This capability can also be used to transfer files between two unattended personal computers.

In that case, however, there must also be a master/slave or "remote operation" feature to allow you to run the distant computer (enter commands, check disk files, etc.) as if you were sitting at *its* keyboard instead of your own. When using a batch file, the file issues the commands to the remote system. For the remote feature to work, both computers must be running the same software.

Neither of these features is likely to be of great interest to most people who will be accessing commercial databases. But business users may find them worthwhile. You should also know that batch files are not easy to create. One of the relatively few programs to offer this feature is ASCOM (Dynamic Microprocessor Associates, 212-687-7115), and it is probably one of the most technical and hard-to-master programs in the communications field.

## The Most Important Features

If you search the magazines, you will undoubtedly find one or more BASIC program listings that you can type in and use as a communications program. In some cases, there may be no more than 80 to 100 lines of code. These will work, of course. They will let you communicate. But they make you work too, since they contain none of the convenience features described above.

Excellent communications programs are available for most major brands of computers for about $100. There are more expensive programs, but you probably should not have to pay much more than that to get all you need. In some cases you may pay considerably less ($50 to $60).

If you will be using your personal computer to access a corporate mainframe or minicomputer, you must obviously consider the larger machine's requirements and buy a package that can meet them. However, if you will be using your computer to enter the electronic universe, the main consideration should be convenience. With that in mind, here are the "essential" features to look for:

• **Flexibility in setting communication parameters.** Should be able to communicate at 300 or 1200 baud.

• **User-set defaults.** Should be able to set communication parameters once, record them, and have the system default to them from then on.

• **Keyboard dialing.** If you have an auto-dial modem, the program should let you dial from the keyboard. A dialing directory is not essential, but it is very close. Check to see if the program "fully supports" your modem.

* **Prerecord strings.** You should be able to record database addresses, account numbers, and passwords and issue them at the touch of a single key.

* **Printer toggle feature.** Should let you easily toggle the printer on and off at will by hitting one or two keys.

* **Capture buffer.** You must be able to capture the information the host computer sends you and record it to disk.

* **File upload.** Whether from an upload buffer or directly from disk, you should easily be able to upload a file you have prepared offline.

* **XMODEM file transfer protocol.** This is not essential or even usable with The Source, CompuServe, or most other databases. But it is essential to anyone who wants to download free software from most computer bulletin boards without errors.

Most of the other features discussed in this chapter fall into the "nonessential but nice to have" category. If the program you are interested in has one or more of them, well and good. But if you make sure that you get the above features, you will have everything you need to use your computer easily and effectively to go online with the world.

---

**SoftTip:** Though mentioned elsewhere in this book, PC-TALK III for the IBM/PC is one of those rare and genuine values you can spend your life looking for. At a cost of $35 for a full-featured IBM/PC communications program, it is difficult to see how you can go far wrong. The program is available in both interpreted BASIC and compiled BASIC. The interpreted version requires 64K, but cannot handle 1200 baud if the system you're talking to does not use the X-ON/X-OFF protocol. The compiled version occupies 96K and will operate at 1200 baud without this protocol. Should you later buy a BASIC compiler, the interpreted version can be compiled "as is." Contact:

The Headlands Press, Inc.
P.O. Box 862
Tiburon, CA 94920

## Software Buyer's Quick Reference Checklist

*—Communications Programs—*

*Capabilities*

☐ How many different baud rates can you use? A setting of 300 or 1200 is the minimum acceptable; 2400 and 9600 baud are important when making a direct connection between two computers.

☐ Can the program communicate at 1200 baud without dropping characters?

☐ Can you specify odd, even, or no "parity"? Can you select the numbers of bits in a "word"? The ability to select either seven or eight is essential.

☐ Can you select full- or half-duplex?

☐ Does the program fully support your modem?

☐ When dialing, can your modem generate either tones or dialing pulses? If a modem cannot generate tones, you will not be able to use it with a discount long distance service that requires them.

*Setting the Parameters*

☐ Can you set your own defaults?

☐ Is it possible to verify your communications settings easily without disconnecting from the database or bringing in a separate file?

☐ Can you change your settings "on the fly"?

☐ How does the program handle line feeds? Can you add them to the information you send and to the information you receive? This can be especially important if you will be communicating with a corporate mainframe.

*Dialing the Phone*

☐ If you do not have an auto-dial modem, do you think you might buy one in the future? If you do, you might want to get a software package that offers an auto-dial feature.

☐ Can you dial directly from the keyboard?

☐ Is there a dialing directory listing frequently called databases and other numbers? How easy is it to add or delete items? Can you specify communications parameters for each entry?

☐ How many entries will the dialing directory permit and is the number large enough to suit your needs? Will you be accessing a large number of BBS's? Will you be using the program to dial the phone for voice calls?

☐ Does the program allow you to specify all the necessary numbers to use MCI, Sprint, or some other service? Can you call through a PBX system and, if so, exactly how will this be done? Can the program be made to pause while an outside line is connected?

☐ Is there an auto-redial feature to keep dialing until you get an answer? How does this work?

*Entering Account Numbers, Passwords, and Strings*
☐ Can you type in all of this information and record it so that it can be sent automatically at the touch of a key? How does this feature work? Is there any limit to the number of files you can create?

☐ The major databases do not require you to enter control characters as part of your password, but there are some that do (NewsNet, for example). Can you record and transmit control characters this way?

☐ What about a prewritten string function for filling in the "Subject line:" prompt when using electronic mail? The number of possible strings may be 10, 16, 40, or more, each one accessible by hitting a few keys.

☐ How many characters can be in each string?

*Capturing Incoming Information*
☐ How easily can you toggle the printer on and off?

☐ Does the program create a separate printer buffer? Printers can be slow and thus slow down the speed of communications since many programs have to wait on the printer. A portion of your computer's memory set aside as a separate printer buffer can eliminate or ease this problem.

☐ Does the program provide for a buffer to capture incoming data? How large is it? Some may be 18K to 28K, others will be limited only by the amount of memory available. (A single double-spaced typewritten page is equivalent to about 2K.)

☐ How easily can you toggle the buffer open or closed?

☐ Can you look at the contents of a buffer at any time? Can you tell the system to print out whatever the buffer contains? Can you edit the buffer with a word-processing-like feature?

☐ What will happen when the buffer gets full? Will the program notify you or simply stop capturing data?

☐ What is the procedure for dumping the buffer to a file on disk?

☐ Does the program have an auto-buffer dump feature? How does it work?

*Transmitting Information*
☐ Can you prepare a letter or report offline and then sign on to a system and upload it?

☐ Can you transmit a file by simply telling the system the filename? Is it possible to send file after file without disconnecting? Some programs can, others must make a separate phone call for each file.

☐ Does the program support the X-ON/X-OFF protocol? This is a virtual necessity.

☐ Can you add line pauses to prevent the host from losing the data you send? Are there any other "upload throttling" controls?

☐ Can the program transmit machine language files? Or is it limited to text files?

☐ Does the program offer a file transfer protocol of some sort for error-free transmission and reception of files? Does it offer Christensen's XMODEM protocol?

*Other Features*
☐ Translation tables? If so, what is the capacity? How many characters can be translated via a single table? It could be 10, or 100, or 256.

☐ Can you cause a key to generate an ASCII character that is not represented on your keyboard?

☐ What will you do if you must communicate in EBCDIC instead of ASCII?

☐ Can the program generate a true BREAK signal?

☐ Can batch files be used for automatic operation? If so, how difficult are they to prepare?

☐ Is there a master/slave or remote control option?

☐ Are there any DOS-like commands to let you check the contents of a disk without leaving the comm program?

☐ Is there a word-processing-like feature for editing? Is it a full screen editor or a simple line editor?

☐ Is there a "Help" file to give you a quick summary of available commands? Is the program menu driven, command driven, or both? Menus can slow you down after you know a program.

☐ What about error handling? What would happen, for instance, if you had information in the buffer and tried to leave the program and go into DOS? Would the program warn you? Or would you lose all of the information?

☐ Will the program report problems such as "parity error" or other messages?

# ...18...

# How to Buy Integrated Software:
## *(Lotus 1-2-3 and Context MBA)*

As rosy-fingered Dawn cracks the eastern sky sending forth shafts of user-friendly light, it is clear that a new day is about to begin in the world of personal computers. We are entering the age of "integrated" software, those magical packages that promise to forever eliminate the "Floppy Disk Shuffle" now being performed daily by countless computer-using business people and managers across the land.

Either today or in the not-too-distant future, managers will load in a single program containing everything they need to perform spreadsheet analysis, manage their databases, generate graphics, write memos, and communicate with corporate mainframes. No longer will it be necessary to load a separate disk for each of these chores. And most important of all, no longer will it be necessary to deal with the bothersome conversion procedures often needed to plug your database information into your spreadsheet and spreadsheet information into a graphics program and *everything* into a word processing program to produce a report you can take to the board or your boss.

According to a report prepared by Creative Strategies, Inc., a San Jose-based research firm, starting from nothing in 1982, the market for integrated software is expected to top $3.8 billion by 1987. Daniel Flystra, chairman of VisiCorp, producers of VisiCalc and the VisiON "operating environment" (see Chapter 7), predicts that "integrated software will take over from stand-alone programs" by 1985 or sooner. Clearly, something important is afoot.

*What's All the Shouting About?*

As with many other things in the microworld, it's impossible to appreciate the significance of a new development if you're not aware of the alternative. If you're not an executive, imagine for a moment that you are and that you want to look at some budget figures with a spreadsheet program. You flip through the grey, smoked plastic disk box that sits

445

next to your IBM/PC, fish out your VisiCalc disk, and load the program. Total load time: five seconds.

Not bad. But now you want to load your worksheet into the program. Maybe it's a simple worksheet stretching only 26 columns left to right and 56 rows top to bottom, not large at all by business standards. Total load time: one minute, 15 seconds. As you watch the blinking asterisk that the program displays on the screen to indicate that it's doing its job and as you listen to the whirring disk drive as the spreadsheet loads, that brilliant idea you had about a new way to analyze the figures slips your mind.

You work with your spreadsheet until your secretary buzzes you to remind you that you've got a speech to deliver that afternoon. Time to go over your notes. You close the worksheet file and shut down VisiCalc, pull the disks out of the drives, and return them to your file box. Then you get out your WordStar disk and boot it. Total load time: 10 seconds. You call for NOTES.TXT and wait for WordStar to bring it in. Total load time: 35 seconds.

Your day continues like this as you load and reload VisiCalc and WordStar, as well as your communications program to pull figures out of the company's mainframe computer, your graphics program, and your database management program. If you were to add up the minutes you spend over the course of a week waiting for one program or another to load, you'd probably be amazed at the total. To say nothing of the time spent looking for program and data disks.

And that's not the worst part. The worst part is that the files produced by the various programs in your software collection are probably not 100% compatible. You may be able to incorporate a VisiCalc spreadsheet in a text file produced by WordStar. But you might not be able to develop figures with your spreadsheet and automatically use them with a graphics program. In some cases, if you want to see what your figures look like as a pie chart, you or someone else will have to type them into a file that the graphics program can read. And when you produce the graphs, you might not be able to incorporate them in a report you have to produce.

The new integrated software packages solve both of these problems. You load them into your machine at the beginning of the day and leave them there until you power down to go home at night. As you use them throughout the day, moving from the spreadsheet program to the word processing program and back is as easy as changing channels on your television. You just enter a simple multi-keystroke command.

Even more important, the output of all of the programs is completely compatible. You can develop figures on your spreadsheet and almost instantly see what they will look like as a graph. Better still, if you leave the graph file open and return to your spreadsheet to make some changes, when you return you will find that the graph has automatically changed to reflect the new figures. Similarly, you can use the communications module to obtain figures from a mainframe computer, put the figures into the spreadsheet for analysis, transfer the new figures into the graphics program, and transfer the graph into a report produced by the word processing program. If need be, you could record the figures in a database management program as well.

That's what all the shouting is about, and it's the reason managers all over the continent are saying, *"Now, you're talking!"* Many managers who have begun using integrated packages estimate that the software has easily doubled their productivity when using their computers. As an additional benefit, it may have made them better managers as well.

When VisiCalc was introduced in 1979, for example, executives were quick to grasp the fact that it allowed them to do "What if?" projections and to analyze problems in ways that never were possible before. The ease with which integrated software allows a person to create pie charts and bar, line, and other graphs may have a similar impact. Everyone knows that it's much easier to see a relationship if it is presented graphically instead of as several columns of numbers. In the past, graphs have taken so long to create that they've been used primarily in presentations, annual reports, and advertising. But thanks to integrated software, graphs are likely to become what they have never been before: a flexible, easily available management tool.

## Why Now?

Integrated software may seem to have appeared on the scene quite suddenly, but it is actually the result of several trends that happen to have converged at the right time. For example, integrated software as it is and as it will be could not exist were it not for the vastly expanded memory addressing capabilities of the new 16-bit computers. You can't load powerful word processing, spreadsheet, graphics, and other programs into 64K of memory, the effective limit for eight-bit computers. But with 192K or 256K—out of a possible maximum of 1000K—of memory at your disposal, there is plenty of room.

Greater memory addressing capabilities, however, would be considerably less appealing were it not for the precipitous drop in the cost of 64K RAM chips that has taken place in recent years. Thanks largely to the price-cutting activities of Japanese chip makers, equipping a large number of personal computers with large memories is now both practical and affordable.

The reduction in both the size and the price of hard disk drives is also an important factor. Many business applications require the massive storage and quick retrieval only a hard disk can provide, and fiddling with a clutch of data disks is no more fun than constantly handling program disks. In addition, now that managers have been using computers for several years, software producers have been able to develop a clearer idea of what programs and features are most important to business people. Finally, there are large numbers of computer-experienced executives who can appreciate what the integrated packages have to offer. There are even larger numbers of executives who would be unwilling to use a computer any other, less convenient way.

*Lotus 1-2-3 and Context MBA: Leaders without the Pack*
    The field of integrated software is so new that there are really only two leading programs. These are Context MBA from Context Management Systems ($695) and Lotus 1-2-3 ($495) from Lotus Development Corporation. "The MBA," as its developers refer to it, includes programs for a spreadsheet, graphics, database management, communications, and word processing. When "Lotus" was issued in January 1983, it offered spreadsheet, graphics, and database features. However, shortly after its introduction, plans to add word processing and communications programs at no additional cost were announced by the firm.
    Context MBA is written in UCSD Pascal runs under the p-System. It was originally issued to run on the IBM/PC and compatibles (256K, required) as well as the Hewlett-Packard HP-9816 (512K, required), but since transportability is the central advantage of the p-System, it will undoubtedly be available for many other machines as well.
    Lotus 1-2-3 is written in 8088 machine language, and in addition to being available for the IBM/PC, PC-XT and compatibles (Compaq, Hyperion, Columbia, etc.) will also run on the Compass Computer from Grid Systems. In addition, computers from the following companies either are or soon will be supported: Texas Instruments, Wang Laboratories, Victor Technologies, Zenith Data Systems, Digital Equipment Corporation, and the Dynalogic Division of Bytec.
    Since these two programs are available on so many machines and since they are the acknowledged leaders in the field, they are probably going to be your two major alternatives. Thus, a look at the various capabilities of these two packages is likely to provide the most helpful information. Lotus has yet to announce its communications module. And the MBA module is so stripped down that once you've noted that and pointed out that it tends to drop (lose) characters at 1200 baud, there is not much else to say. Consequently, we'll look briefly at the spreadsheet, database management, graphics, and word processing or text editing components of MBA and Lotus.

**SoftTip:** If you have an Apple, you should know about what may be the only integrated program for any eight-bit computer. It's called The Incredible Jack and includes a personal filing system, a calculating program, as well as word processing and mailing label capabilities. "Jack" runs on an Apple II and requires 64K of memory. The list price is $79. For more information, contact:

Business Solutions, Inc.
60 East Main Street
Kings Park, NY   11754
(516) 269-1120

**SoftTip:** If you're one of the hundreds of thousands of people who own and use VisiCorp's VisiCalc and you think you may want some features similar to those offered by Lotus 1-2-3, you may be in luck, thanks to a program called StretchCalc from Multisoft Corporation. You'll need an IBM/PC with 128K and a graphics board and either an extended memory version of VisiCalc from VisiCorp or a version marketed by IBM (V 1.1 or higher).

StretchCalc makes full use of the IBM function keys and lets you produce eight types of graphs (bar, dot, line, pie, scatter, etc.). It also offers macros through a feature called Keysaver, as well as some 23 financial, mathematical, and other formula functions not found in VisiCalc. The program will also let you sort information on a single key. There are other features and enhancements as well.

You can purchase StretchCalc separately from Multisoft ($99 for the complete program, $49 if purchased without the graphic module) or you can buy VisiCalc IV from VisiCorp ($350) if you do not already own a copy of VisiCalc. Contact:

StretchCalc
MultiSoft Corporation
14025 S.W. Farmington Road
Beaverton, OR   97005
(800) 322-4110
(503) 626-4727, in Oregon

VisiCalc IV
VisiCorp
2895 Zanker Road
San Jose, CA   95134
(408) 946-9000

## Spreadsheet Capabilities

The spreadsheet (Chapter 15) is the heart of both Lotus and the MBA packages. The column and row format is used for virtually everything. MBA offers nearly 100,000 cells: 96 columns and 999 rows. The standard version of VisiCalc, in contrast, provides 63 columns and 254 rows (16,000 cells). Obviously, this means that you can create much larger worksheets with MBA. But there's more.

The column widths are both individually variable and the cells can be quite large. MBA, for example, allows you to put as many as 8,000 characters (the equivalent of about four double-spaced typewritten pages) into a single cell. Thus, when you are using the communications module, you open a cell and allow the information you are capturing to flow into it. As mentioned, almost everything takes place in a spreadsheet format.

There is an extensive range of commands and built-in functions for use when entering the formulas you want to attach to a particular cell. (See Chapter 15 for more background on this.) These include logical operators (TRUE/FALSE, AND, OR, NOT, etc.), internal rate of return and net present value, as well as most trigonometric functions. (The formulas you enter and their locations on the sheet can also be displayed on command.) The "replicate" function is especially powerful, allowing you to replicate complete blocks of the spreadsheet the way you might use a block-move feature in a word processing program, as opposed to just replicating a range of cells.

In addition, as with Microsoft's Multiplan spreadsheet, you can specify cell addresses with words (TOTAL, DISCOUNT, SALES, etc.) instead of using letters and numbers (*A1*, *P38*, *F14*, etc.). Two or more worksheets can be consolidated as well, though there is no linking feature similar to the one found in Multiplan.

With MBA it's also possible to "fold" your worksheet so that you can look at the columns headed by cell *A1* and *Z1* at the same time. But this is only part of the capability. The screen can also be split into as many as four windows, one of which might display a portion of your spreadsheet, while the others display graphs, text, or database information.

*Lotus 1-2-3*

The Lotus spreadsheet measures 256 columns by 2,048 rows—a total of 524,4288 cells—making it one of the largest spreadsheets available anywhere. The columns may be of variable widths. Like VisiCalc, you access a menu of options by entering a slash (/). But where VisiCalc displays a long row of letters, each of which represents a command, Lotus offers complete words ("Global" instead of "G"). You may either use the cursor to point at the selection you want, or type in its first letter. Lotus offers some 41 spreadsheet functions, compared to MBA's 32 and VisiCalc's 28. There is also a full complement of logical and relational operators (>,<, =, etc.).

The screen can be divided into two windows. And there is a "macro" feature that allows you to enter a series of commands or other keystrokes by pressing a single key. Lotus has another user-conscious touch for IBM/PC owners. There is no way to tell from the standard IBM/PC keyboard whether you have engaged the CapsLock, NumLock, or ScrollLock keys. But Lotus automatically displays that information in the lower right corner of the screen.

## Database Management

Both programs use a spreadsheet format for their database management systems as well. However, instead of having a record occupy several lines on the screen, as is the case in a dedicated DBMS or file manager, records are stretched out lengthwise so that each occupies a single line or row. The fieldnames are entered in at the heads of the columns.

With Lotus you may have as many records in a file as there are rows on the spreadsheet format (2,048) and as many fields as there are columns (256). With MBA, the maximum number of records in a file is limited only by available disk space. The number of fields, however, is limited to the 95 columns available on the worksheet.

Although the worksheet format seems a strange way to organize a database, it has some definite advantages over the more traditional DBMS approach. First, in both programs, there is no need to specify how long you want each field to be before you begin entering data. There is no need to lay out a form. You just begin typing. With MBA, you can type in as many as 8,000 characters per field, though all of the text will not be displayed at the same time. With Lotus, all text is displayed, so you may have to expand the width of the particular column if you find yourself running out of room.

The ability to manipulate columns and rows as you would with a spreadsheet "replicate" command or a word processing "block move" command is one of the best features of handling a database this way. Unlike a conventional information management program where the data entry form is rigidly fixed, you can pull fields (spreadsheet-like cells) from one location and insert them someplace else. Similarly, since all fields exist at the intersection of a row and column, you can move the position of a single field in all records by simply moving the whole column.

Searching and sorting is also column based. For example, since each field in a record is identified by a name at the head of a column, you move to the column that identifies the field you want to use as a search (or sort) key. Then you enter the target information. If you moved the cursor into a column headed "Purchases," you would then type something like ">$100" to find all records that had an amount greater than $100 in that field. In a conventional database system, you would have to type in both the fieldname and the search criteria.

Both programs let you use Boolean logic (AND, OR, NOT, etc.) and relational operators like "greater than" or "not equal to." And both offer a "wildcard" search function to let you specify only part of a word or a number as your search key and in effect tell the program that you don't care what the remaining characters are.

---

**SoftTip:** Both programs offer a forms-creation function that, among many other things, can be useful when entering data in your database. You can create a data entry form that resembles the paper form you may now be using and display it on the screen. When you enter the data, the program actually stores it in the row and column format described above, but you don't have to be concerned with that.

The forms-creation feature can also be used to format reports and generate invoices and other business forms for your data printouts. Because MBA lets you move the cursor all over the screen as you design your form and because of the other features it offers in this module, it will probably be easier to use than the less developed forms function offered by Lotus.

---

### Graphs

Both programs can create line graphs, bar graphs, pie charts, and scatter plots, but while both require a color/graphics card (a card with a special graphics microchip) on the IBM/PC, MBA does not produce a color output. On the other hand, MBA offers at least four additional types of graphs and it has an "overlay" feature that allows you to put one graph on top of another. You might combine a line graph with a bar graph, for example, and display them both together. In addition, Lotus permits only six variables (bars on a graph, slices of a pie chart, etc.), but MBA will allow as many as will fit on your screen.

As mentioned earlier, MBA also lets you divide the screen into four windows, making it easy to merge the graph in one window with the text in another. In a breakdown of true integration, Lotus will not permit this. Graphs must be printed separately.

The advantage that Lotus offers in this area—and it is a major one—is that it is incredibly fast. Graphs appear instantly. Thus, Lotus can accomplish in about two seconds what MBA requires nearly 15 seconds to do. Since you can quickly switch from spreadsheet to graph and back again to alternately change and view your data, this speed makes the Lotus graphics capability more suitable as a true management tool.

## Word Processing and Text Editing

Neither program offers anything like a full-featured word processing program. But, of the two, Context MBA's is better developed. Text is entered into a cell that you expand to accommodate it. You can move the cursor up and down (full-screen editing) to correct mistakes or insert text. And you can jump to the top or bottom of the document. The search and replace feature is effective if not sophisticated. You cannot easily tell by looking at the screen where one page will end and another begin when the text is printed.

Lotus doesn't really offer anything that can be properly called a word processor. It is a simple text editor at best—a module for entering, recording, and printing out text but nothing else. Text is typed on the spreadsheet form by specifying the range of cells you think it will occupy. When you are finished, you can justify the text and print it, but that's it.

## What's Up?

Because each package is unique, and because the impending flood of integrated packages is still in the offing, a checklist for integrated software does not seem appropriate. Instead we'll conclude with some general considerations you might want to keep in mind as you shop for these and similar packages.

Of all the software you might buy, this is the type you really must see demonstrated, because you are actually buying three or more programs and capabilities when you buy an integrated package. There is much to explore—too much to be adequately communicated in a software review. Equally important, if this type of software fulfills the role its designers intend for it, you will be living and working with it every day of the week. It is not too difficult to tolerate small inadequacies of design in a program that you use only occasionally. But it's a different story with a program that you use constantly.

Naturally, you've got to think about how you work and what you would use the program for. As a business person, a package's spreadsheet capabilities are likely to be most important to you. And MBA and Lotus have the features and capacity equivalent to almost any dedicated spreadsheet program. However, none of the other modules even comes close to the capabilities found in the best word processing, database, graphics, and communications packages.

Another crucial question to ask is whether your main goal is to use the program for "decision support," or is it more important to be able to completely integrate graphics and other files? If your goal is decision support, the speed with which the package operates can be vital. And here there is no comparison. Because it is written in machine language instead of interpreted Pascal, Lotus is several orders of magnitude faster at every point. A search of a 100-record database with MBA can take more than four minutes. Lotus can accomplish the same task in less than a tenth of the time. We have already mentioned the speed with which Lotus produces graphs.

This speed comparison may have changed somewhat since Context announced a new and improved version (V. 2.3) that may be as much as four times faster. An interpreted program can never completely match the speed of machine language software, but this may be fast enough for your needs. Be sure to compare both programs and be sure that the version of Context MBA you examine is either Version 2.3 or later. (If it is even newer, the version number will be higher.)

*A Final Suggestion . . .*

Before making up your mind in favor of either of these programs, be sure to read about Apple's Lisa, VisiCorp's VisiON, and Quarterdeck's DesQ in Chapter 7. These products may not provide all that you need, but knowing about them will give you a more complete view of what might be called the "paths to integration."

Second, unless you need an integrated package right away—wait. Mitch Kapoor, president and founder of Lotus Development Corporation, has called integrated packages "second generation" software. But, as they now stand, both Context MBA and Lotus 1-2-3 can best be thought of as "first generation, second generation" programs. Both are impressive in themselves, and even more so when compared to the inconveniences of using several programs, but neither is quite "there" yet. Both will be improved as time goes on. And new packages from Ashton-Tate (Culver City, CA), Gilchrist Software (Irvine, CA), Ovation Technologies (Canton, MA), Taurus Software (Lafayette, CA), and Softrend, Inc. (Windham, NH)—as well as 25 to 30 other firms—is on the way.

**SoftTip:** If you own an IBM/PC with 64K and a color graphics card, and you would like to try Context MBA free of charge, Context Management Systems has an offer you can't refuse: a free demo disk that will let you see what it's like to use the program. Contact:

Context Management Sytems
23868 Hawthorne Blvd.
Torrance, CA   90505
(213) 378-8277

To order your disk:

(800) 437-1513
(800) 592-2527, in California

# ...19...
## How to Buy Business Graphics Programs

The first graphics program for a microcomputer was called "Tiny Troll." Adapted for micros from a much larger mainframe program ("Troll") by Mitch Kapor, author of the best-selling Lotus 1-2-3, it was issued in 1979. This fact is more than a matter of historic interest. What it means is that many of the graphics programs on the market today haven't been around very long. Although the term is rather vague, most are still "first generation."

Thus, as a software buyer, you may find that your choice is somewhat limited compared to other computer applications. You may find that the programs, though impressive, are not quite as powerful as you might like. And, most important of all, you may find some of them extremely difficult to use. All of this is rapidly changing, however, since graphics is considered to be one of the hottest new areas in the software field.

There are two major categories of graphics programs. There are programs that are meant to turn your keyboard into a paint brush and your monitor into an easel. This kind of software will let you express your creative instincts. The second category is business graphics—programs designed to create pie charts and bar graphs from numerical data—and it is by far the larger of the two. According to *Software Merchandising* magazine, for example, more than 25% of the firms that buy personal computers eventually buy a business graphics package. As more software is introduced and as it becomes easier to use, that percentage will undoubtedly grow. This is the kind of software we will focus on in the following section.

### Basics: Business Graphics

It is not difficult to see why so many businesses are interested in graphics packages. In fact, "seeing" is what it is all about. A well-drawn chart or graph can make it much easier for a business person to spot trends or communicate ideas and information than can a stack of computer printouts containing nothing but columns and rows of numbers. Balance sheets, cash flow, financial modeling, forecasts, labor and cost

456

distribution, sales presentations and project proposals—there is hardly an area of business where graphics cannot improve the effectiveness of management, decision making, and communication. In fact, wherever there is a need to show relationships among numbers and quantities, or changes over time, a business graphics package can be an important asset.

## A Three-Stage Process

All graphics programs can be seen as having three major stages: putting in the numbers, turning the numbers into a graph, and generating a hard copy of the drawing. That sounds elementary, but it is a useful framework to bear in mind when considering this kind of software because programs vary considerably in how they handle these three stages. It is also important to be aware that of all the various types of software, graphics programs are the most "hardware intensive."

Prior to 1979, graphics on a microcomputer meant *character* graphics. Programs were and are available that take the numbers you give them and produce bar graphs or lines composed of small $x$'s or some other character. As far as the computer is concerned, displaying and printing character graphics is no different from displaying and printing text. There is nothing special about it.

The "real" graphics packages available today are much more complex. For example, with a line chart generated by a character graphics package, you would probably have to play "connect the dots" after the chart had been printed if you wanted some semblance of a continuous line. You would have to manually connect all of the little $x$'s on the page.

Today's business graphics packages don't generate $x$'s (unless you want them to). Instead, they produce continuous lines, circular pie charts, and different kinds of shading. To produce these elaborate effects, the programs must rely on certain microchips in your computer and in your printer, on the quality of the display monitor, and on the type of output device you use. As you know from previous chapters, any time a program gets that close to the hardware, it is going to be highly machine specific. Or, to put it another way, the power and capability of the graphics programs you can run is closely related to the computer equipment you are using. Before considering any graphics program, it is necessary first to consider the hardware that is required to run it.

## Pixels and 5 × 7 Blocks

Everything that appears on your screen is made up of tiny dots of light called *pixels*, a term that is short for "picture elements." Pixels are often thought of as being grouped in *blocks* measuring five across and seven down. If you picture each pixel in one of these blocks as a light bulb, it's easy to see how the different letters can be formed by turning some of them on and leaving some of them off. Though it is not completely accurate to do so, in computer terms you might say that pixels are like bits, and blocks are like bytes.

There are two ways for a computer to put information on the screen. Either it deals with things one pixel at a time, or it handles pixels in 5 × 7-block chunks. The approach used makes a difference because, along with the size of the pixels themselves, the method of handling them determines how sharp the picture will be. All of these factors are determined by two pieces of internal hardware: the video controller card and the character generator ROM

*Video Controller Card and Character Generator*

Every computer has a video controller card or equivalent circuitry and a ROM-based character generator. The controller card will normally contain a master chip that acts like a small computer. Together with the other chips on the card, it determines how large each pixel dot will be and thus how many of them will fit on the screen. It may be the largest number the monitor is capable of displaying, or it may be some smaller number.

With lots of little dots to work with, the pictures the computer draws can be much sharper and more highly detailed than would be possible with a lesser number of fatter dots. Consequently, the total number of pixels the video controller can make the screen display is used to measure its resolution. Should a computer salesman tell you that a machine has a resolution of 640 by 200, he would mean that the number of pixels on the screen totals 640 times 200, or 128,000.

The first number is always the number of pixels measured horizontally across the screen. The second number is the number of pixels measured top to bottom. The reason why the horizontal measurement is usually the larger of the two is that the width of most computer screens is greater than their height. This is called the "aspect ratio" of the screen and it is usually four units wide by three units high, or "four to three."

*"High" Resolution?*

Ads for computers and graphics software will invariably use the term "high resolution" in describing the product's display capabilities. But what constitutes high resolution, or "high rez"? The answer is that no one knows. Everybody says they've got it—no one ever owns up to having "low resolution" capabilities—but there is no widely accepted standard detailing the number of pixels or the exact width to height ratio of pixels required.

The IBM Personal Computer, for example, defines low resolution as 160 × 100, medium resolution as 320 × 200, and high resolution as 640 × 200. These are the specifications for the IBM Color/Graphics Monitor Adaptor card. Once again: *Resolution is determined by your hardware (video controller), not by the software you buy.* The software must work within the limits imposed by whatever in your machine is driving the video display.

The second piece of display-related hardware is the character generator chip. This is a ROM chip that contains what amounts to a hard-wired translation table. When you send a bit pattern coursing through your machine by hitting a key on the keyboard, it is the character generator that determines what character the pattern represents, and that displays the corresponding figure on the screen. Characters may be the standard letters and numbers within the ASCII code set, or they may be symbols or other shapes unique to your brand of computer. The key thing about characters is that they all consist of pixel blocks (usually 5 × 7 blocks). Some graphics programs build their onscreen images by combining partial blocks and symbols the way people form complete words by combining different letters.

> **SoftTip:** These are not the same as the "character graphics" mentioned earlier. The terminology can be confusing, but can be partially cleared up if you think of the graphs made up of *x*'s as "alphanumeric characters" and the partially formed blocks mentioned above as "graphics characters." A graphics character might look like an upside down *L* or a partially completed cinderblock wall. An alphanumeric character will always be a recognizable letter or number.

Business graphs produced this way may be quite adequate for your purposes. But because pixels are being handled in chunk fashion, this technique tends to produce somewhat fuzzy or ragged images. It simply doesn't permit the kind of precision control that is possible when you handle each individual pixel separately. Computers that have this capability are said to offer a *bit-mapped* screen. Again, this is a hardware matter. The software has no control over whether the screen is bit-mapped.

To understand bit-mapping, it can be helpful to first know about another term: *memory mapping.* Today virtually all computers "build the screen" in memory, which means they set aside a portion of RAM and label it "screen display." The computer assumes that the entire screen is divided into 5 × 7 blocks of pixels and that each block has a specific location. Naturally, each location has an address.

If this is beginning to sound like the wall of post office boxes cited in Chapter 1, you are absolutely on target. Each pixel block on the screen corresponds to a block containing a certain number of bits—each with its own memory address—in RAM. Thus, when the computer wants to change something on the screen, it locates the RAM address of the bits that control a particular pixel block and fiddles with the flip-flops to change or erase whatever was displayed in that block.

The computer's list of which RAM blocks control which pixel blocks is called a memory map. Now here's the payoff: A computer using a memory map can only control pixels in block-sized chunks, each of which represents a graphics character. As mentioned earlier, that tends to produce graphs and charts that are rough and ragged. With a bit-mapped display, however, each individual pixel on the screen—all 12,288 or 128,000 or 1,048,576 of them—is represented by a bit with its own address in RAM. Thus, each can be individually turned on or off or made to display some color.

*Bit-Mapping and You*

To a software buyer, this is important for at least two reasons. First, a bit-mapped screen will produce sharper images and graphs that are much more impressive than might otherwise be the case. And second, although many computers can support a bit-mapped screen, bit-mapping may not be part of the standard package, which means you may have to buy a special plug-in video controller board to give your machine this capability. Since some boards can cost $300 to $500, depending upon the computer, if you are a manager this may be beyond the limit of what you can claim as a simple expense item for your department, propelling you into the realm of capital expenditures and elaborate justification. If you are considering it for your home system, only you can be the judge of what will fit your budget.

*Printers and Output Devices*

Unfortunately, the extra cost of the hardware needed to take advantage of computer graphics does not end with video controller cards. The most expensive item may well be the device you use to produce a hard copy of what your graphics program draws on the screen. Indeed, at least one authority has estimated that the only thing standing in the way of a veritable explosion in business graphics is the cost of output hardware.

At the low end of the scale are the standard dot matrix line printers sold with most computer systems. Since these printers normally contain a character generator chip similar to the ROM in your computer, they may need an extra plug-in board or chip to allow them to "address" the paper in a bit-mapped fashion. At the high end of the scale, there are ink-jet printers capable of spraying virtually any shape you want onto a sheet of paper in any of a number of colors. Average cost: $10,000.

Somewhere in between are the pen plotters that use a mechanical arm to hold a Magic Marker-type pen and draw graphs on paper or overhead transparency foils. The Hewlett-Packard HP 7470A is probably the best-known machine of this type. Typical price: $1,800. Bausch & Lomb's Houston Instrument division sells its DMP-29 "desktop plotter" for about $2,300. There are also dot matrix type printers with four colored ribbons like the Radio Shack CGP-115 for about $250. The price is impressively low, but the machine will only work with a four-and-a-half inch roll of paper.

---

**SoftTip:** Most plotters can handle four to eight different colors. But while some can change pens themselves whenever a different color is called for, others depend upon you to put the pens in their hands. From a software standpoint, this is very important because if the software does not pause and prompt you to change pens with such a plotter, you will not get the kind of hard copy you were expecting.

You should also be aware that graphics plotters and printers capable of producing graphics are *slow*. Depending on the device, five or six minutes might be required to produce a four-column bar graph that is five inches high. That's not necessarily bad, but it can come as a surprise if you are accustomed to generating a printed page in less than a minute when producing text.

---

**SoftTip:** At $795, the Sweet-P™ Personal Plotter from Enter Computer, Inc. is probably the lowest-priced machine in the pen plotter class. The unit offers eight colored pens, each of which must be changed manually, and true plotter capabilities. It does not include all of the features of the more expensive plotters, but then you may not need that kind of sophistication. For more information contact:

> Enter Computer, Inc.
> 6867 Nancy Ridge Drive
> San Diego, CA   92121
> (619) 450-0601

## Critical Points

*Command- or Menu- Driven?*
The most important way in which the various business graphics packages differ is not so much in the types of graphs and charts they are capable of producing, but in the way they interface with the user. Some are "command driven" and some are "menu driven." Command-driven packages require you to tell the system exactly what you want it to do using a special command language.

When you boot a command-driven package, for example, you might see nothing but a blinking arrow on your screen. At that point, you would have to enter commands to tell the system what kind of monitor you want to use, the level of resolution, the foreground color and background colors, and a range of other parameters. The commands you enter might look like this: SE DE CON RGB 101. Translated, this means, "Set device console RGB 101." Translated again, this means, "Send the bloomin' output to the RGB color monitor. Thank you!" Similarly, when wanting the system to produce a graph, you might type in: "DR B," for "Draw Bar graph."

All in all, there may be a hundred commands to learn and enter in order to use the program. (Fortunately, you may not have to enter all the commands all the time.) Programs of this sort will usually let you record your setup commands as a separate file. Once you have created the file, you have only to load it into the program at the proper time instead of retyping each command.

When you boot a menu-driven program, in contrast, you will be presented with a menu listing option like "Define Chart," and "Define Graph." Select one of these options and you will be presented with a blank table into which you can enter your numerical data, the labels you want to use, and other information. When you finish, you can tell the program to use the data to draw a pie chart, a bar graph, a line, or some other graph. If you don't like the way the pie chart looks, for example, and feel that a bar graph might be more effective, it is a simple matter to switch from one to the other.

*Which Type Is Best for You?*
Proponents of command-driven programs argue that while the software may be more difficult to learn and use, it offers you a wide flexibility and a high level of precise control over the graphics it creates. Proponents of menu-driven programs maintain that ease of use is paramount and that the user gives up very little flexibility to get it. Both

have valid points, of course, and your choice will be based on how you plan to use the program.

It is difficult, however, to visualize a busy executive memorizing a command language when all he or she wants is to see what the numbers look like when presented in one or more graphic formats. Ideally, a business graphics package should turn your desktop computer into a quick-response graphics machine capable of producing a variety of graphic presentations at the push of a button. In such circumstances, any increased power and flexibility offered by a command-driven program would seem to be overkill and not worth the extra effort that may be required.

*Entering the Data*

The second most critical point regarding a business graphics package concerns the number of ways that data may be passed into the program. All of the packages will accept keyboard input, of course. But many will let you tell the program to take its data from a VisiCalc-like spreadsheet or other file. You merely type in the filename when prompted to do so. As long as the file is online (on a disk in a disk drive) and in a format that the program can read, everything should go smoothly.

The question to ask is how many different types of data files the graphics program can handle. Most will read DIF files (Data Interchange Format, see Chapters 4 and 15), but some have a broader range. Clearly, if you are using MultiPlan, Perfect Calc, SuperCalc, 1-2-3, or some other software, it is important to make certain that the graphics program can use the files created by these packages. Revised editions of a particular program may have expanded file-reading capabilities—yet another reason to make certain that you get the latest version when you buy.

**SoftTip:** To add to the complexity, the version of the spreadsheet program you will be using can also be important. For example, to use VisiCalc files with VisiPlot, your version of VisiCalc must be Version 1.37 or higher. If you have an earlier version, you must contact the firm or your dealer about obtaining an update.

*Generating the Graphs*

As you might expect, programs also differ in the number and variety of graphic formats they can produce. Most include pie charts, bar graphs, and line graphs. Some also include scattergrams for use when you want to put a large number of data-points on a screen to demonstrate a relationship or lack thereof. Since graphs are the heart of the product, the nature, range, and flexibility of the graphs the software can produce are obviously things you will want to consider carefully. Other features to look for include:

- **The ability to overlay several types of graphs to display several sets of data.** You might put a line graph on a bar chart, for example, and position it so that it is above the bars.

- **"Floating titles."** This feature lets you specify exactly where one or more of the identifying labels on the graph will appear. For example, after you have typed in a label, you may be able to specify a "floating title" option that will cause a rectangle to appear at the center of your screen. The rectangle will occupy the same space as the words in your label. You move the rectangle around until you have positioned it in the desired spot, then you enter a command to lock it in. If you do not opt to use the floating title feature, the program will automatically decide where to place the labels.

- **The ability to change the scale of the graph easily.** This lets you make it smaller or larger while still displaying the same relationships.

- **Statistical features.** Some packages include options for graphing multiple linear regressions, moving averages, and logarithmic, sine, and parabolic curves, among others. With other packages, you may be able to purchase statistical features as an add-on. The best example of this is VisiTrend, a statistical program designed to be used with VisiPlot.

- **"Slide show" option.** Designed for use in a live presentation, this feature will let you prepare several graphs and "stack" them up in the machinelike slides. You then tell the machine the order in which you would like to have the graphs appear on the screen and the timing it should use. A slide show feature may be incorporated as part of a complete package, or it may be available as an add-on.

*Output: Pen Plotter, Printer, or Both?*

As you know from the previous discussion of hardware, the output device is something of a lynchpin as far as graphics programs are concerned. Both the device itself and its compatibility with the program are crucial. Some programs can be used only with plotters, some are limited to printers, and some can drive either, though you may need special connecting cables and hardware.

Naturally, hardware interfaces vary as well. Like regular dot matrix printers, some plotters may require a parallel connection while others require an RS-232 serial port. And as with printers, the software will undoubtedly have to be installed for your particular machine. If the software house has not provided a device driver for your brand, you may not be able to use the program.

Ideally, you should not have to get involved with these technicalities. That's what dealers are for. Nevertheless, it's important to be aware that there may be compatibility problems and to use an extra measure of caution.

## Software Buyer's Quick Reference Checklist

*—Business Graphics Programs—*

Perhaps the first question to ask yourself is what kind and quality of graphics you need. Do you need "presentation quality" graphics suitable for inclusion in a report or proposal? Or will the hard copy output be mainly for your personal use? Your answer will determine whether you need a high-quality pen plotter or a dot matrix line printer with graphics capabilities. And that in turn will influence your choice of software.

---

**SoftTip:** If presentation quality graphics are normally created by your firm's art department or an outside agency, a graphics program may still be useful. Regardless of its quality, if you can give an artist a computer-produced graph to work with, you may find that he or she can offer a faster turnaround. Virtually anything is better than the rough sketches and scrawled notes many managers are forced to resort to when setting down their specifications for a graph.

---

*Entering the Data*

☐ Is the program command driven or menu driven?

☐ How are data entered from the keyboard? Will the program permit you to change, delete, or add information easily? Can you insert additional datapoints after the first version of the graph has been completed, and will the program automatically adjust for the insertion?

☐ How are the labels and titles that will appear on the graph handled? Is there any limit on the number of characters you may use for each? Can you use different styles and sizes of type?

☐ Is there a "floating label" option? Can all labels be positioned in this way? Can the program print labels sideways?

☐ Can you use data files from your spreadsheet, database management, or other program as the program's source of data?

*Types of Graphs and Specifications*

☐ How many different types of graphs (pie chart, bar, line, etc.) can the program produce? Can it generate the style of graph you or your firm normally use?

☐ Can you instantly switch from one style to another using the same set of data?

☐ Will the program allow you to create several graphs and then overlay them in a single chart?

☐ Can the program put two or more graphs on the screen at the same time?

☐ Can you easily change the scale of a graph? Are there perhaps six or fewer scaling options, or is this feature unlimited?

☐ What are the limitations of the graphs themselves? What is the maximum number of:
—bars on a bar graph (6? 100? 600?)
—slices in a pie chart (8? or unlimited?)
—columns and rows in a line graph (100 × 10? or more?)
—lines on a line graph (1? 4? unlimited?)
—datapoints on a scattergram?

☐ Can the pie chart be drawn with missing slices?

☐ *Very important:* Can the program plot against time? If you have data for January, March, and June, will the program spread the graph out by inserting spaces to represent the months for which you have no data?

☐ Almost every program will let you record your graph as a file on disk. But can the program's files be transmitted over the telephone or over a cable to another computer?

☐ Can you incorporate graphs with text files and have them print out together? Or must the graph be generated separately?

*Output*

☐ How easy is it to look at or "preview"the graph before you print it?

☐ Can you list the data on the printer before telling the program to go ahead? Since graphs take a long time to print, this may be helpful in spotting data mistakes and save you going through the printing process again.

☐ Is there an option to produce a "quick" bar or other graph on the plotter? Because these "rough draft" graphs contain just the outlines of the bars, they can be produced faster than the final draft in which the bars will be filled in.

☐ Will the graph print or plot in *color*. Some packages may produce colorful graphs on the screen but be limited to black-and-white output.

☐ How many different colors does the program support?

☐ If your plotter is not capable of changing pens when another color is called for, will the program stop and prompt you to make the switch before it continues?

☐ Is there an economical way to connect a plotter to your computer without having to unplug your printer every time you want to use it?

*Error Recovery*

☐ What happens if you make a mistake? Are there any safeguards to keep you from accidentally losing all of the data you have entered?

*Extra Features*

☐ Statistical graphing capabilities. Either built-in or available as an add-on.

☐ Slide show option. Again, built-in or add-on.

---

**SoftTip:** Affordable three-dimensional graphics packages have recently begun to appear. Some are so impressive that it may be worth waiting for them to be issued for your machine before deciding to buy one of the more conventional packages on the market. One such product is Energraphics™. Originally available for the IBM/PC (64K, color graphics adaptor board, one drive, dot matrix printer) and for the TI Professional, the program can produce an extensive range of 3-D graphs and graphic designs. The graphs can be rotated on the screen and it is possible to "zoom in" on

*SoftTip continued*

portions of them. Two-dimensional graphs and 3-D graphs can be displayed on the same multi-windowed screen.

The original list price of the package is $250. A demonstration disk is available for $50. Other machines will undoubtedly be supported in the future. For more information, contact:

Enertronics Research Inc.
150 North Meramec—Suite 207
St. Louis, MO   63105
(314) 725-5566

# ...20...

# How to Buy The Business "Big Four": *General Ledger, Accounts Receivable, Accounts Payable, and Payroll Software*

I n the opinion of many users, business software leaves much to be desired. To others, the current offerings are little short of disgraceful. Joseph Larson, president of Great Plains Software, is even more articulate: "There must be 200 packages available, and only about ten of them are top contenders. The reason they got to be top contenders is simply because they work. You load them in and something comes up on the screen. We're in such a young industry that a software package can rise to the top ten simply by virtue of the fact that it works."

Mr. Larson's company, it should be added, has recently introduced a line of business software. Yet, leaving aside the fact that his is not a totally disinterested comment, the experiences reported by various users of general ledger and other packages tend to bear him out. The situation is changing, but generally the business software available today rarely approaches the quality of the products available for other applications.

The problem is that both accounting and computer software are intricate subjects, and it is rare to find expertise in both fields centered in one individual. Consequently, business packages tend to be written by accounting specialists—in which case they run like an elephant with five legs—or they are written by computer specialists—in which case they demonstrate a lack of understanding of accepted accounting practices and procedures.

The situation is exacerbated by the fact that, although few applications require more intensive dealer support, most dealers treat accounting packages like customers proffering expired credit cards—as something to be avoided at all costs. One can hardly blame them. If the dealer sells you a game that fails to perform to your expectations, you might make a few pointed comments. But if he or she sells you an accounting package that manages to wipe out a whole month's receivables, you are likely to go shopping for a hit man.

Certainly, better quality packages are in the pipeline. The potential market is simply too large to ignore. After all, what business person can resist the possibility of generating a payroll in 10 minutes when the job is currently taking 10 hours? If your need is not pressing, you may want to wait for some of these newer packages to appear. Yet, whether you wait or not, you will want to be very, very careful when making your decision. Some authorities suggest spending as much as 12 hours or more testing each package with sample data before making your choice.

## The "Big Four"

This section looks at programs for the following accounting functions: general ledger, accounts receivable, accounts payable, and payroll. Together, these four applications constitute what is frequently referred to as the business "Big Four." Since accounting is such a detailed subject, a complete treatment of the steps to follow in choosing each package could easily occupy a book in itself. Unfortunately, an adequate volume has yet to appear. Until it does, it will help to be aware of the benefits and potential pitfalls associated with these packages.

Following some general guidelines for choosing any of the Big Four, we will present a Software Buyer's Checklist for each. The lists assume general familiarity with standard accounting practices and terms.

## Business Software Buyer's General Guidelines

*Bring in your accountant from the start.* If an accountant, bookkeeper, C.P.A., or someone else normally handles your books for you, it can be vital to enlist their aid at the earliest possible point—not just on the general advisability of converting to a computer system, but as a consultant who can help you evaluate the features and details of the packages you are considering. If you do the books yourself, it can still be worthwhile to get professional advice. In what may be a growing trend, computer stores willing to handle business software have begun to team up with CPAs and other qualified people to offer just this kind of service.

*Plan on a thorough hands-on testing.* Accounting programs, like accounting functions, are highly detailed. It is impossible to acquire even a cursory familiarity with most packages through a standard computer store demonstration. And, in contrast to spreadsheets, databases, and other business-oriented software, you may find that there are not many reviews of accounting software to guide you. Some authorities recommend taking a batch of real data with you and settling in behind the computer for several hours as you put the program through its paces.

---

**SoftTip:** If giving a program a thorough workout in a computer store proves to be difficult to manage, you might consider asking the dealer for the name of another business that has installed the same package. Ideally, you will be able to arrange to enter your data and run your tests at the other firm's site.

---

*Do you need a complete system or a stand-alone package?* Of the Big Four, a general ledger (G/L) program will be the most useful to the largest number of businesses. As the master repository of all of your firm's accounts and transactions, the general ledger is at the core of any accounting system. For many, a G/L package will be all the accounting software they need. Others, with large numbers of customers, vendors, or employees will need one or more of the other packages as well.

This is really the first point to weigh when considering business accounting software. General ledger programs fall into two broad categories. There are programs that are designed to handle the G/L function exclusively, and there are programs that offer features found in the other types of business software as well.

There is no clear division line between the categories, but the "G/L-only" programs are usually part of a series of packages available from the same manufacturer, each of which is meant to interface and work with the others. The latter type are usually meant to be used alone and rarely have all of the power and features of a multi-program configuration. They may nevertheless offer everything you need. Individual packages, whether modular or self-contained, range in price from $200 to $1,200. Though usually there is a discount if you buy a completely integrated system.

---

**SoftTip:** If you opt for a completely integrated Big Four system, or even if you buy only two or three modules, one of the most important points to focus on is account automation. One of the most attractive features of a computerized accounting system is multi-journal posting. If you make an entry in one journal, therefore, the system *should* be able to make the appropriate entry or entries automatically in any related journals.

---

*How Many? and How Long?* If you will train yourself to ask "How many?" and "How long?" when considering any accounting package feature, you can prevent many future frustrations and disappointments. It may not always seem appropriate, but following this rule can help uncover such unsuspected limits as the largest decimal number a package can handle or the number and length of departmental or cost center codes you may use. Since accounting deals with numbers over time, you might also want to add "How often?" and "For what periods?" to your inquisitorial catechism. How often can you run a payroll? Can you get a trial balance on demand? Can you call for one on a monthly basis?

*The program should let you do everything you do now, and more.* According to at least one software producer, "If 5% of your business doesn't fit the software, then you should change your business." That is, of course, the kind of advertising challenge you certainly don't want ever to accept. Considering the disruption even a small change can cause, reshaping your entire accounting procedure to fit the requirements of the software is not an appealing prospect. You will undoubtedly have to make some changes, however, and it is important to identify and be prepared for them. If nothing else, a computer system will force you to become more disciplined about your finances. And that may not be such a bad thing.

In evaluating any package, you will find it very helpful first to sit down and make a list of all the steps currently followed in the accounting cycle. If you already own a computer and have a word processing program, you might prepare the list by category of activity and then rearrange things chronologically to reflect a typical month, quarter, and year. For each appropriate step, you might include the How many?s and the How long?s of your present system. (How many deductions does the average employee pay stub include? How long are your General Ledger account numbers?) These kinds of lists will be very helpful in determining how closely the software you are considering matches your current system.

*Avoid the temptations of "information overload."* Information analysis is endemic to computerdom. Invariably, as soon as someone gets a collection of information entered and recorded, the first thing they want to do is see how many different ways they can analyze it. A computer makes this easy. Perhaps too easy, judging from the value and usefulness of many of the printed reports generated by this activity.

It is quite true that a computerized accounting system will give you a firmer grasp on your business than ever before. With the right software, properly installed, you will be able to see exactly where your money is going, what products or services are carrying their own weight as profit-producers, and where overhead and expenses can be trimmed, as never before. But it is important to avoid being distracted by all the extra reports, summaries, and analyses business packages offer.

The value of these "extra" reports will vary with the business and the individual, but you may not need or want to deal with all the reports the software can produce. After all, a report is useful only if there is someone to read and digest it. Consequently, you may find that it is best to deliberately focus on how the software handles the reports, journal entries, and written material you are using now.

*Security and G.A.A.P.* Any time money is involved, security must be a major concern. You will want to look carefully at the security schemes of the various packages you consider. Some may have no provisions for security. With others, entering a single password will give an individual complete access to the system. Still others will offer a hierarchy of passwords. This may include a master password for complete access and subsidiary passwords that permit the operator to enter but not view data, or to view but not enter.

In a related matter, one of the most troubling aspects of many business software packages is their failure to conform to the Generally Accepted Accounting Principles (G.A.A.P.) published by the Accounting Standards Board. These are the guidelines that professional accountants, IRS auditors, and other members of the profession use in determining the proper way to handle accounting functions.

For example, once an entry has been made in a ledger or journal, it cannot be removed. If it is in error, the only way to eliminate its effect on the bottom line is to write in a compensating entry to add or subtract the erroneous amount. Following this rule is vital to creating an audit trail of the exact activity in the account. Unfortunately, a number of business software packages allow users to add and delete entries as if they were dealing with a word processor. At best, this is not an approved procedure. At worst, it makes it possible for someone to write himself or herself a check and then erase all traces of it in the records.

*Pay special attention to the printing options.* Possibly because they were converted from mainframe and minicomputer packages instead of being specially written for a personal computer environment, many packages fail to offer even the most rudimentary printing features. Some will produce only capital letters. Others will produce both upper and lower case but prevent you from printing with compressed or expanded type. There may be other restrictions on the format and number of lines a report can or cannot have as well.

In a few cases, you may find that if you don't have your printer connected and turned on—even if you don't plan to do any printing—the software will refuse to run. With other packages, the program will crash if you tell it to print something and forget to turn the printer on. That could mean a loss of data. The "net net," as an accountant might say, is to investigate a program's printing capabilities thoroughly before you buy.

### A Final Word

A Big Four business package will not eliminate the need for an accountant or a CPA. But by preparing and presenting all of your records in a neat and orderly way, it can make it possible for an accountant to work faster and accomplish more. At an average hourly rate of between $50 and $75 for professional services, even a relatively expensive package can pay for itself in a short time.

It is also important to acknowledge at the outset that regardless of the package you choose, converting from your present system to a computer is going to be a major chore. Short of starting fresh in an entirely new business, there is simply no way to get around this fact. Things will go most smoothly if you plan for it and develop a methodical conversion procedure.

Although it will mean extra work, you may want to continue with your current paper-based system for several months, duplicating each activity on the computer. This will give you and your staff a chance to become accustomed to the new system without leaving you vulnerable to disastrous errors.

## Software Buyer's Quick Reference Checklist
### —General Ledger Programs—

#### Automation
☐ How many tasks will the software perform automatically? Will it automatically post entries to and from several subsidiary journals?

This will probably be the most important feature of a computer-based accounting package. To test it, make a list of the multiple journal entries you must now do by hand and carefully look to see how the package handles (or fails to handle) each one.

#### Account Setup and Capacity
☐ What is the maximum number of accounts the system can handle? It could be 500, 2,000, 65,000, or be limited only by the available disk space.

☐ How can the accounts be identified? How does the program's scheme compare to the system you are now using? Can you use both numbers and letters? What is the maximum character length of an account number? Three characters may be too restrictive for your business.

☐ When initially installing the system, can you input account names and opening balance at the same time, or must you first enter account numbers and then enter both account numbers and opening balances?

☐ How easy is it to add new accounts after the initial setup?

☐ What is the *largest decimal number* the program can deal with? And is it large enough to accommodate all current and future entries for your business?

☐ Can you set the system to operate on a fiscal year of your own choosing or must you use a calendar year?

☐ Does the software allow you to designate entries and allocate items to different departments or divisions? If it does, it should also be able to produce consolidated as well as by-division reports.

## Data Entry

☐ How does the system handle the double entry nature of accounting? Will it automatically add a credit or a debit in the proper place, or must you key in the same numbers twice?

☐ Can you use both upper and lower case when entering data? Or is the program limited to upper case? Does it automatically add decimal points?

☐ Does the system continuously display cumulative totals for both sides of the transaction?

☐ Does the system include a password feature to prevent unauthorized changes in accounting records? Surprisingly, many packages fail to prevent the deletion of posted transactions, a practice forbidden by all accepted accounting standards. Other packages offer various levels of password protection.

☐ How easy is it to leave one task and return to the main menu? Some systems will force you to wait for a printout of the transactions you have just entered before allowing you to return to the menu. This is time consuming and annoying.

☐ *Error trapping.* Some systems will not let you type an entry that is out of balance, for example. Since accuracy is one of the main benefits of accounting software, it is worthwhile to pay special attention to the features it includes to prevent typographic and other errors.

☐ *Error recovery.* What happens when you boot the program with the printer turned off or disconnected? Or with the wrong data disk in the drive? Does it lock up or stop and prompt you to correct the situation?

☐ *Disk-full errors.* What happens if you inadvertently allow the data disk to fill up? Are you likely to lose any of the transactions you have just entered?

### Key Reports

☐ *Summary trial balance.* To show just the balance on each account.

☐ *Detailed trial balance.* For a complete listing of all account entries.

☐ Can you obtain trial balances at any time? Can you obtain them for different time periods for use in preparing income statement information? Will the system provide trial balances on a monthly, quarterly, or annual basis?

☐ How does the system make sure that all accounts have been properly posted before it produces a trial balance?

☐ *Balance sheets.* For a snapshot of your current financial position at any given moment.

☐ *Income statement.* For a summary of your business's profit and loss over a time.

☐ *Chart of accounts.* How easily can the software produce a comprehensive report showing all accounts?

☐ How does it handle monthly and year-end closings?

☐ What type of *audit trail* will the system provide? Is every entry to the system assigned a transaction number, for example? Can the effect of a mistaken entry be corrected *only* by adding an entry to offset it, as required by generally accepted accounting procedures? Are there provisions to prevent the deletion of an account that has been zeroed out?

### Management and Analysis

☐ *Cash flow statements.* Can the package identify and combine all entries that affect your cash flow and produce a summary of where your money is coming from and where it is going?

☐ *Depreciation statements.* Can the software produce a summary of the depreciation deductions for each asset, produce a total, and identify the method of depreciation used in each case?

☐ *Customized reports and schedules.* Is it possible to focus on a selection of general ledger accounts and analyze the entries made to them as a group? How many entries can be analyzed this way? How many accounts?

## Other Features

☐ Is there a *general journal* or some other means of handling miscellaneous entries?

☐ Is there a *year-end journal?*

☐ What other special or customized reports can the software generate? And do you need them or are they likely to inundate you with information?

### Software Buyer's Quick Reference Checklist
### —*Accounts Receivable*—

## Initial Points

☐ Is the program designed to interface with a General Ledger program?

☐ Can the software issue invoices? Some packages will only keep track of your receivables; others include an invoicing feature.

☐ Is the system an "open item" or "detail" system or a "balance forwarded" system? Or both? The open item approach allows crediting of a payment against a specific invoice (the "open item"). A balance forwarded approach will only permit credits against the customer's total current balance.

☐ Is there a provision for credit card transactions?

☐ Can it produce a bank deposit form for use with cash receipts?

☐ Can the system incorporate a finance charge on overdue bills?

## Account Setup and Capacity

☐ What is the maximum number of customers you can include? 200? 500? 6,000? or limited only by disk space?

☐ What is the maximum number of individual transactions the program can handle? This is not the same as the number of customers.

☐ How are account numbers and customer identification codes assigned? How many characters in an account number? How many additional codes?

☐ How many addresses will the customer account form allow? One for billing and one for shipping? How many lines per address? Is there room to include a contact person and phone number?

☐ Can you specify a credit limit for each customer?

### Applying Payments and Adjustments

☐ How can payments be applied? By oldest invoice? By single invoice? By line item on an invoice? Or other?

☐ What does the program do about items returned for credit? How are other billing adjustments handled?

☐ Will the system automatically post income received to different departments or profit centers?

☐ How does it handle accounts that have been written off as bad debts? Can it generate a summary?

### Key Reports

☐ Can you get a report telling you how long a particular customer takes to pay a bill?

☐ *Cash receipts journal.* How often can it be run? Daily, weekly, monthly, yearly?

☐ *Aged trial balance.* Can this report show each customer's balance as well as a breakdown of money owed by 30-, 60-, 90-, or 120-day division? How many different formats can you use? One line per customer or show each invoice?

### Other Reports

☐ Can you look at a report on the screen? Or is printing it out the only way to view it?

☐ Can you obtain an historic report on each customer showing payment record, items or services purchased, etc.?

☐ What options are available for listing customers? By name, account, total purchases, payment record, etc.?

☐ Is there a report for separately listing finance charges applied or are finance charges lumped in with other income?

☐ Can the system generate a sorted list of your customers and their addresses? What sort options are available?

☐ Can the invoice file be sorted by product to give you an idea of what is selling best?

☐ Can you determine which customers are buying the largest amounts of particular items and thus suggest complementary products?

*Invoicing Features*
☐ Will the program allow you to specify discounts to be given to particularly good customers? How flexible can the discounts be? Will they be calculated automatically?

☐ Will the system automatically avoid sending statements to customers who don't owe you anything?

☐ Can the system search for past due accounts and send statements only to them?

☐ Is there a feature to let you print sales messages or other textual material on the statements the program sends out? How many characters? How easy is it to do?

☐ Will the system automatically print a description of the item on the invoice in addition to the part or other identifying number?

☐ Is there a mailing list/label-generating feature to automatically print address labels for statements and invoices?

## Software Buyer's Quick Reference Checklist

*—Accounts Payable—*

*Initial Points*
☐ Will the package interface with General Ledger, a purchase order system, and an inventory control system?

☐ Does the package include a purchase order system? Or must it be purchased separately?

☐ Is the package an "open item" or "balance forwarded" system? An open item approach will let you select the precise invoice you want to pay, possibly to take advantage of early payment discounts. The other approach applies payments to the total balance you owe a vendor.

### Account Setup and Capacity

☐ How many vendors can it handle?

☐ How many separate invoices can it handle?

☐ What provisions are there for taking automatic discounts? Can you specify the discounts? How many can be used? Can you take an early payment discount at the time the check is issued?

☐ How many lines can you put on a single purchase order?

☐ How many purchase orders can be accommodated? Will the system automatically multiply quantity by unit price and add in any applicable tax?

### Issuing Checks and Applying Costs

☐ Can the computer issue the checks or must you do it by hand? Can the system offer both options?

☐ Can checks be issued at any time?

☐ Can costs be distributed over a number of cost centers?

☐ Will the system automatically print labels or envelopes to mail the checks?

### Key Reports

☐ *Check register.* Can the system give you a summary of checks written, their individual numbers, amounts, payee, etc.?

☐ Can invoices be sorted and printed by invoice number, transaction date, vendor, etc.?

☐ *Purchase order journal.* If you have a purchase order system, can you ask it to give you a report on the basis of order number, product, vendor, etc.?

☐ Can you use the system to tell it to compare items ordered with items actually received?

☐ *Expense distribution report.* Will the system show you how the cost of various purchases was allocated among different General Ledger accounts?

## Other Reports

☐ *Vendor report.* Can you obtain a summary of purchases from and payments to each vendor?

☐ *Aged trial balance.* Can you find out how much you owe and have owed to each vendor on a 30-, 60-, 90-, or 120-day basis?

☐ *Cash requirements report.* Can the computer project how much income you will need in the coming month if you keep spending the way you did last month?

☐ *Prepayment report.* Will the system advise you as to the most pressing invoices or those that are eligible for prepayment discounts?

## Software Buyer's Quick Reference Checklist

*—Payroll—*

### Initial Points
☐ Will the package tie in with the General Ledger?

☐ How many different forms of compensation does your firm use? Salary, hourly, piece rate, sales commission, overtime, etc., and will the software accommodate all of them?

☐ What does the system do about repayments of an employee's draw against commission?

### Setup and Capacity
☐ What is the maximum number of employees the system can handle? 200? 1,000? or unlimited?

☐ How long can each employee number be? Is there room for a department code or designation?

### Capabilities
☐ How easily can employee data be entered and changed?

☐ Are there any limitations on pay periods? Can you issue checks weekly, bimonthly, or on a monthly basis? Can you use all three options, depending upon the employee?

☐ Can the system keep track of vacation days, sick days, and personal days and holidays?

☐ What provisions does it have for union dues, miscellaneous deductions, profit sharing, pension plans, stock options, health insurance, state and local taxes, etc.?

☐ How easily can the tax tables be changed? Do you have to contact the software house for an update or can you do it yourself?

☐ Can the program calculate different taxes for employees in different states?

☐ Does the program allocate payroll expenses to different departments or cost centers? How many departments may there be?

☐ Does the program keep track of F.I.C.A. and W-2 information?

☐ Can the system generate the forms needed for tax filing purposes?

☐ Can the system generate documents for a direct payroll deposit option?

### Reports

☐ Can you obtain a report before closing out for the month?

☐ *Payroll register.* Including totals paid and deducted for each payroll run.

☐ *Check register.* Can the program give you a listing of all checks issued, their numbers, amounts, employee payee, and date?

☐ *Cost allocation.* Will the program tell you how it has allocated labor costs over different General Ledger accounts?

☐ *Accumulated earnings to date.* By employee? Grand total? Can it produce subtotals on a monthly, quarterly, or year to date basis?

☐ *Tax payment summary.* Can you get a total of taxes paid broken out by municipal, state, and federal taxes?

☐ Is there an option to print out a list of employees with their addresses and phone numbers? Can the list be sorted?

*Security*

☐ What provisions are there to prevent checks from being issued to employees who have been fired or quit? Can their records be flagged so that no check can be issued without special clearance?

☐ Can you specify an upper limit on the size of the checks to prevent the system from giving someone a million dollars?

☐ What are the password provisions?

☐ What are the audit trail provisions?

# ...21...

# How to Buy Personal Finance Software: *Checkbook Balancers, Home Budgeting, and Personal Accounting*

Each evening from December to December,
Before he falls asleep upon his cot,
Wide-eyed, he tries to remember:
"Did I record that check—or not?"
—Anonymous

We've all seen the software ads: "Balance your checkbook! Do your home budget by computer! Make filing your income tax a breeze! Don't delay—put your financial house in order and BUY OUR PROGRAM TODAY!" If you think about it, these ads sound a lot like ads for the latest diet craze, with their promises to slim you down, shape you up, and turn you into a walking, jogging picture of fitness and health.

In both cases the program—whether diet or computer—will produce the desired results. But only if you follow it religiously. The hard work this kind of devotion involves is something that the advertising often neglects to mention. But the fact is that personal finance software can't give you a monthly summary of how much you blew on wine, women, and song—or martinis, men, and mariachi bands—unless *you* sit down and type in the exact figures. Similarly, it cannot balance your checkbook if you don't tell it each time you write a check, notify it of each cancelled check that comes back with your bank statement, and inform it of this month's service charges.

One probably shouldn't be too hard on the advertisers. After all, no ad for a lawn care product is going to show the backbreaking work and constant attention required to produce the thick carpet of weed-free grass it portrays. And no ad for this kind of software is going to show people booting the program and typing checks and expenses every time they come back from a movie or the grocery store.

484

The central truth about diet plans, lawn care products, and software of this kind is that they work—but not without work on your part. Thus, in many cases, the best answer to the question, How should I buy personal finance programs? is DON'T! Instead of sinking $150 or $75 or even $19.95 into a personal finance program, save your money and spend it on a word processing program and an electronic spreadsheet. A word processing program can be used to write your monthly checks automatically, and an electronic spreadsheet can be used to balance your checkbook, to display your budget, and to provide home accounting functions. In short, with these two programs you can accomplish everything that is of any real value in personal finance software, and a great deal more besides. In a special section at the end of this chapter, we'll show you how to do it.

*A "VisiCalc of the Home"*

It is important to point out that the personal finance programs on the market today are not *bad* programs. Some of them are well done and quite powerful. It's just that they are built on a faulty premise, namely, that the families of America want—and are willing to work for—the same kind of detailed financial accounting systems used by businesses. Time after time, however, the marketplace has proved that this simply isn't true. By mid-1983, for example, with over five million personal computers in the hands of users across the country, the best-selling program in this category was The Home Accountant from Continental Software (16724 Hawthorne Blvd., Lawndale, CA 90260; $75; for the Apple II-Plus and the IBM/PC). Total sales: 20,000. This particular program is intended for families, self-employed people, and small businesses, and as one review puts it, because it requires "a lengthy and rigorous setup, this program is not for the slightly interested."

To put those sales figures in perspective, consider the fact that VisiCalc and its clones have sold over one million copies, making this kind of program the single most popular type of software. The reason is simple: Electronic spreadsheets filled a definite need. In fact, the power to change assumptions and instantly see the effect on your projections was so desirable that hundreds of thousands of computers have been bought primarily because of their ability to run VisiCalc-like programs.

This fact, more than anything else, explains why there are so many home accounting, checkbook-balancing, personal finance programs on the market. The whole microcomputer industry lusts after another VisiCalc. Only this time they have their sights on a "VisiCalc of the home," hoping that somewhere, sometime, somebody will come up with a program or an idea so good that American families will buy computers and software just to take advantage of it.

*"That Ain't It, Kid. That Ain't It."*

So far, it hasn't happened. Although, as *The New York Times* recently noted, many Wall Street stock market analysts and others believe that communications, electronic mail, and online databases will eventually fill this role, personal finance software clearly is not the answer. Consequently, the software houses that produce these programs are very much in the position of Cinderella's older sisters, desperately trying to jam their feet into a glass slipper that simply does not fit.

Unfortunately, you can't always rely on the computer magazines to alert you to all the drawbacks of this kind of program. No magazine can afford to be totally insensitive to the needs of its advertisers. And besides, many of them are good programs that deliver everything they promise. The problem is that this is the first non-game type of program most new computer owners gravitate toward, and it's precisely the type of program they should not buy.

*Three Main Categories*

Personal finance software is designed to perform one or more of three main jobs:

• Balancing your checkbook.

• Presenting you with your budget and notifying you of whether your current expenditures place you over or under your budgeted amount for each category and by what percentage.

• Providing you with a General Ledger-like accounting system similar to that used in businesses (see Chapter 20).

Although checkbook balancers and budget programs are available individually, at prices ranging from $15 to about $50 each, accounting packages usually incorporate these two functions as well as offering accounting functions. Typically, they cost between $75 and $200.

We'll look at each type of program in turn and point out some of the important things to be aware of when considering this type of software. However, for a fuller understanding of how the programs work and the limitations they can impose, you may want to consult the Software Buyer's Quick Reference Checklist at the end of the chapter after reading each section. This will also give you a better appreciation of the reasons for using spreadsheets and word processing programs instead of personal finance software.

*Balancing Your Checkbook.* A checkbook program is essentially a computerized check register. Like the stubs or lines you fill in when using a traditional checkbook, it offers a means of recording check numbers, dates, payees, and amounts. It will also automatically perform the arithmetic to deduct checks or add deposits to your account, once you tell it what you have done.

If you have faithfully entered each transaction, including notifying the program when a check has cleared your bank, it will be able to tell you your current balance at any time. It will also be able to give you an update report on all checks and deposits you have made during the current month. Unfortunately, the bottom line produced by this report may not agree with your monthly bank statement. The reason is that most programs in this category have a monthly orientation. Which is fine if your bank looks at things the same way. But it is not so fine if the bank closes your account on the ninth or tenth of each month instead of on the last day of the previous month. If it does, your bank statement and your computer printout are destined to be forever out of sync.

In addition to keeping track of your checks, many programs in this category include a search function. The power of this feature varies with the program; however, you may be able to get a list of the checks you have written on the basis of the date they were written and/or the person or company to whom they were written. It is as if you had a manila file folder for each of your regular monthly bills. If you wanted to see how much you had spent on telephone calls in the past six months, for example, you might pull out the folder and your pocket calculator and add up the amounts. The computer does the same thing. It just takes a lot longer.

*The Computerized Budget.* Different programs work in different ways, of course, but with most home budgeting programs the first step is to type in your annual net income. The program will probably include a number of pre-identified categories ("Food," "Rent," "Electricity," "Telephone," etc.), but it may also contain a number of category slots for you to name as you feel appropriate ("Dog Food," "Tennis Lessons," "Herbal Substances," etc.).

As when using pencil and paper, you then type in the amount of money you want to budget for each category. In some cases, you may be able to specify a percent of your net income and let the program calculate the dollar amounts. In others, you may specify the dollar amount for the year and the program will automatically divide by 12 for the monthly figure. In still other cases, you may be able to budget a different amount for each month (less for heat during the summer, more for partying during the holiday season, etc.).

To keep your budget up to date, each time you write a check you must boot the program and go through the menus to get to the spot where you can type in the amount in the proper category. Or categories, since if the check is to pay for a number of items in different budget categories, you must apportion it correctly.

A good example would be your monthly MasterCard or Visa statement. Or any other credit card, for that matter. You might have charges for videotape rentals, restaurant meals, clothing, tires for the car . . . whatever. Naturally, you will want to go through each statement and apportion the amounts properly for your budget. You'll also want to pay the amount in full, since most budget programs have no way to deal with minimum monthly payments.

When you want to look at your budget to see how you're doing, you can tell the system to print out a report indicating the budgeted amount and the amount actually spent for each category. Many programs include a "budget analysis" feature that basically gives you both the dollar amount and the appropriate percentages. In some cases, you will be able to generate an up-to-the-minute report. In others, you may have to wait until the end of the month. In almost every case, you will be able to get a year-end summary of the same sort.

*Home Accounting.* If you are unfamiliar with traditional business accounting procedures but are interested in applying them to your personal life, you might want to look at Chapter 20 before reading further. The concepts of General Ledger, Chart of Accounts, posting debits and credits, etc., used for business packages are very similar to those used in home accounting packages.

The first step in setting up a home accounting program is to define your accounts. This is similar to defining expense categories in a budgeting program. The program may provide as many as 200 or more "slots" for you to identify and designate as either expense or income accounts.

However, once the accounts have been defined and the ledger has been created, it may not be possible to go back and add another account or two at a later date, at least not without starting from scratch and reentering all of the data in your ledger. Consequently, if you can identify perhaps 50 accounts, it is wise to include a number of extra, undefined accounts in the initial setup. As long as the account has been included, it can usually be given a name at a later date should you decide that you need it.

The overall goal of a home accounting system is to let you keep track of where and how you spend your money. In this sense, it is similar to a budgeting program. Where it differs is in the refinement of focus. A budgeting program may offer you a total of 15 or 20 expense categories, but an accounting program will offer many more. In addition, a budgeting program usually has no way to account for income, but income accounting is an important part of accounting packages. As mentioned earlier, many accounting packages include modules capable of calculating expenses as a percentage of income, and many include checkbook register modules as well.

To enter an expense using this kind of software, you must decide which account the expense belongs in. As with budgeting packages, if a single check covers expenses for several accounts, you must apportion the amounts accordingly. In many packages, the usual procedure is to record a check in the check register portion and then move to the accounting portion to post the amount(s).

If all income and expenditures have been faithfully entered, the program will be able to give you a printout of your total income and expenses for a particular month, or possibly a series of months. It will also be able to generate a subsidiary report listing the total expenses for each account, or possibly several—but not all—accounts. That can be helpful if you want to see how much you are spending on just food and shelter, for example.

In addition, depending upon the program, you may be able to get a budget report comparing actual with projected expenditures, a personal balance sheet that shows the month's actual balances for each category. In addition to the current month's totals, such a report might also include the previous month's actual and budgeted figures for easy comparison. You may also be able to get a statement of your net worth at any given time, though that may require a considerable amount of initial preparation. (You would have to tell the program what value you place on your home, your car, your investments, and your other possessions.)

---

**SoftTip:** With all three of these classes of programs, the reports they make possible are one of their most useful features. However, for an annual or year-to-date report of checks written or expenses and income to be truly worthwhile, it obviously must include all relevant information from the beginning of the year up to the present. Thus, if you buy any of these programs in June, for example, you will have to enter six months' worth of checks and expense records to bring it up to date.

---

**SoftTip:** The Internal Revenue Service has ruled that computerized records of expenses are not acceptable in an audit. Therefore, if you use one of these programs, be sure to save your actual receipts and cancelled checks.

*The Two Most Valuable Features*

In addition to the basic features outlined above, some personal finance packages have the ability to *write* your checks for you automatically. And some offer an interface to VisiCalc that lets you transfer all of the information you have entered in the program's ledger or budget module onto a spreadsheet, without having to retype the data. For many software buyers, these will be the two most important and useful features of any personal finance software. Usually, they are found only in the more expensive accounting-type packages, as opposed to the checkbook balancers and budget planners. The VisiCalc interface may be included, or it may be sold separately as an add-on for about $20.

The benefits of a program that will automatically write your checks for you are obvious to anyone who pays monthly bills. The benefits of a spreadsheet interface are less obvious, but only somewhat less important. However, if these are the features you are most interested in, you will be much better off buying a word processing program and a spreadsheet program instead of personal finance software. The total cost might be a bit more than a single finance program, or it might be about the same. It all depends on the specific programs you are comparing. In either case, however, the word processing/spreadsheet combination will give you more power, flexibility, and value for your money.

## The Software Buyer's Money-saving Plan for Handling Money

If you own a word processing program, you already have all the software you need to produce your checks automatically each month (see Chapter 12). If automatic check production is your main interest at this time, you might want to jump ahead to "The Computerized Check Writer's Survival Kit" further along in this section. However, if you would like to get more control over your money and make better-informed decisions about your financial life, stick around and take a look at what an electronic spreadsheet can do for you.

*How Spreadsheets Can Put You in Control*

Why would you want to put your budget and expenses on an electronic spreadsheet? The answer is, to ask the same kind of "What if . . .?" questions that business people ask when considering whether to build a new plant or take some other action (see Chapter 15). For example, imagine a spreadsheet listing each of your budget categories ("Food," "Entertainment," "Savings," etc.) and imagine that on each line next to the name of the category there is a dollar figure. On the surface, it will look just like an ordinary budget.

What's different about a spreadsheet is where those dollar figures came from. There are many ways to do it, but let's assume that you have simply told the spreadsheet program that you want to spend *X%* of your net income on Food, *Y%* on Clothing, and *Z%* on Entertainment. If you set things up this way, the only number you would have to type in would be your net income. Based on your instructions, the program would automatically calculate the actual dollar amounts for each budget category.

*Waving the Wand*

That's convenient, but not too impressive. Where the magic really takes place is when your boss begins to make rumblings about giving you a raise. You rush home, fire up your computer, and say, "Oh, CRT get on the ball. What would happen if I spent it all?" Again, the only number you would have to give the program would be your new projected net income. The spreadsheet would recalculate all of your budget items in a twinkling and tell you how many more dollars you would have to spend in each category.

Similarly, you could use a spreadsheet to ask, "Can I afford to go to Club Med this year? Where would I have to cut back, by how much, and for how long? What if I reduced my entertainment expenses by 50%? No, that's no good. Okay, how about a 30% reduction in entertainment, a 10% reduction in clothing, and a 5% reduction in gasoline? I'll walk or ride my bike and take one less trip to mother's each month . . . "

This is the kind of flexibility and power that most personal finance programs by themselves rarely provide. There is no need to enter your expenses each month, though if you wanted to create a budgeting program with a spreadsheet, you could easily do so. You turn to your spreadsheet only when you need it—to help you make decisions or to project the effect of a change in income or expenses.

*Good News/Bad News*

Depending upon your computer, you may be able to buy a spreadsheet that will do all of this for as little as $50. Heath and Zenith users, for example, might consider ZenCalc from The Software Toolworks (14478 Glorietta Drive, Sherman Oaks, CA 91423; 52 columns, 254 rows, $49.95). TRS-80 Model I and III users might look at EasyCalc (Instant Software, Peterborough, NH 03458; 99 columns, 99 rows, $50). CalcStar from MicroPro (33 San Pablo Avenue, San Rafael, CA 94903; 127 columns, 255 rows) is available for Apple, IBM, and other computers for as little as $120. SuperCalc (Sorcim Corporation, 2310 Lundy Avenue, San Jose, CA 95131; 63 columns, 254 rows) is available for many CP/M computers for $129. PlannerCalc, a program said to offer 90% of what VisiCalc offers, sells for $50 (Comshare, 1935 Cliff Valley

Way, Atlanta, GA 30329). If you own a Commodore 64, there is an indication that you may soon be able to run Microsoft's Multiplan. These are discounted, mail order prices. If they have changed, they have probably dropped lower still. The point is that for either less than or about the same amount of money as a full-featured home personal finance program, you can have an electronic spreadsheet that will better serve your needs. To say nothing of the other things you can use a spreadsheet for.

The main disadvantage of an electronic spreadsheet is that you may have to set it up yourself. Although the setup procedures for many home accounting programs may require a similar amount of time, they may be primarily a matter of following instructions. With a spreadsheet, you could be on your own.

*Templates, Models, and Enter-it-Yourself Listings*

Then again, you may not. As mentioned in Chapter 15, a growing number of companies have begun to sell spreadsheet "templates" or "models" that include all of the equations and all of the labels you need to accomplish different tasks with your main spreadsheet program. Most can be customized to your particular situation. Using them is as easy as loading in a regular program.

---

**SoftTip:** Here are at least three places you might contact to inquire about the models you need:

Spreadsoft™
P.O. Box 192
Clinton, MD 20735
(301) 856-1180

Twelve VisiCalc templates (six for personal finance, six for business) selected from the firm's library of over 150. For Apple III: $34; for Apple II: $24. Postage and handling: $1.50. Visa/Master-Card.

Software Models
P.O. Box 1029
Crestline, CA  92325
(714) 338-5075

For Apple II, TRS-80 I-III, IBM/PC, Atari 400, 800, Commodore, and Osborne computer owners using VisiCalc, SuperCalc, or Multiplan. Package: Personal budget, Shopping list, Mortgage & loan,

Individual Retirement Account, IRS Schedule A. Cost: $29.95, plus $3.00 shipping and handling. Cashier's checks or money orders. No credit cards.

ITM Software Division
936 Dewing Avenue
Lafayette, CA 94549-4292
"Spreadsheet Hotline": (800) 334-3404
In California: (415) 284-7540

"Choose from over 4,500 programs. Largest selection of spreadsheet application templates. Call for free catalogue."

*Look in the Book*
If you cannot find the template you need on disk or if you would rather not spend the money, there is another less expensive alternative: Buy a book containing listings of spreadsheet templates and type them in yourself. This may prove no more difficult or time consuming than setting up a personal finance program.

For example, Osborne/McGraw-Hill publishes *VisiCalc: Home and Office Companion* by Castlewitz, Chisausky, and Kronberg. The book sells for about $16 and contains the listings of 50 VisiCalc models. Among others, the book contains everything you need to create the following:

• Personal Finance and Budget Plan
• Personal Check Register
• Home Inventory and Personal Possessions Evaluation
• Net Worth Statement
• Personal Insurance Requirements
• Vacation Tour Planner

The listing for the Personal Finance and Budget Plan begins like this:

```
>B 7: "M O N T H
 B 8: / - =
>B 9: "SOURCE
>B10: /—
>B11: "WAGES & S
>B12: "HUSBAND
>B13: "WIFE
>B14: "PROFIT FR
>B15: "BUSINESS,
```

It continues for some 800 lines of similar length. Clearly, it will take you some time to enter all of the lines. But once you've done it, you will never have to do it again.

---

**SoftTip:** There are similar books for SuperCalc, MultiPlan, and other spreadsheet programs. If you can't find the book you need on the shelves of book or computer stores, don't despair. Firms like McGraw-Hill, John Wiley, Howard Sams, Prentice-Hall, Sybex, dilithium PRESS, and other publishers with an extensive computer book line send illustrated catalogues to their retail outlets. Ask a salesperson if the store has such publications behind the counter and if you might look at them. This will be much easier than trying to find titles in the various editions of the *Subject Guide to Books in Print.*

---

**SoftTip:** You will also find "enter-it-yourself" spreadsheet templates and models in the more technically oriented computer magazines like *Creative Computing, Interface Age, Micro,* and others. Sometimes the author will make the models available for a nominal fee. And sometimes the magazine will offer a number of these templates and other programs on disk. If you are looking for a particular template, see Chapter 8 for information on locating articles in back issues of the magazines.

---

### The Computerized Check Writer's Survival Kit

For many people, the main advantage of a personal finance program is that it helps them get organized. None of the programs will work unless you pull together all of your information and arrange it in a logical fashion. You don't need special software, however, to accomplish this goal. All you need is the will, your computer and word processing program, and about $62.00 to create a check-writing, bill-paying system that will last a lifetime. At the very least, it will make it easy for you to get organized and stay that way. And conceivably, it could cut the time you now spend paying bills each month by half or more.

Consider, for example, the steps you must take from the time you open the envelope containing the bill until you place the envelope containing your check in the mailbox:

* • Write the date on the check.
* • Write the name of the payee.

\* • Fill in the amount in numbers.

\* • Write the amount out in words.

\* • Write your charge card account number on the check so they don't lose it.

\* • Write the date in the check register or "stub" portion of your checkbook.

\* • Write the name of the payee.

\* • Write the amount in numbers.

• Sign the check.

• Subtract the amount from your current balance.

† • Mark the bill "Paid" and note the date.

• File the bill.

\* • Put the check in the supplied envelope, or address one of your own envelopes, and seal it.

† • Put a postage stamp on the envelope.

† • Write your name and address in the upper left corner.

All of the steps marked with an asterisk (\*) can be handled by your computer and your word processing program. The steps marked with a dagger (†) can be handled with inexpensive rubber stamps or a postage stamp device. The only steps that cannot be at least partially automated are signing the check, subtracting the amount, and filing the paid bill.

*The $25 Lifetime Filing System*

To create an easy-to-use, easy-to-access filing system, all you really need is a collection of manila folders and an accordian style "expanding portfolio." You can purchase the folders individually or in a box of 100 for about $10. The portfolio will cost about $3.00 (You'll want one made of heavy paper since you will be using it a lot.) Alternatively, you could buy a letter-sized cardboard filing box and several Pendaflex file hangers and metal frame for about $15. All of these items will be available at any good stationery or office supply store.

With this system, setting up your "Chart of Accounts" is as easy as writing "MasterCard," "Sears," "Exxon," and other companies on the tabs of the folders. Filed alphabetically, these folders will make it easy for you to "retrieve" information about your account and payments faster than any computer program.

You will also be able to get all of the rubber stamps you need at the same store. A stamp to mark bills with the date they were paid might cost $4.54. A customized name and address stamp to put your return address on the envelope might cost about $12.79. A San Diego based firm called Data-Link Corporation manufactures a device for applying postage stamps. It will hold one roll of stamps and it has its own water supply. You merely place it on the correct location on the letter and push down to dispense a stamp. The device is widely available and sells for about $16. The only additional item you might need is a roll of continuous-form pressure-sensitive labels for use in addressing envelopes when preaddressed envelopes are not included with your bill. Avery International sells a roll of 200 labels for about $5.25.

There is no reason why you would have to buy all of these items or buy them in the quantities listed here. But if you did, your total cost so far would be about $64.

### Where Can You Get Continuous-form Checks?

If you have a friction-fed printer and a checkbook that contains three checks per page, you may be able to simply tear out a page and twirl it into the printer. However, for maximum efficiency and speed, you will need continuous-form checks with the detachable sprocket hole strips on either side.

Businesses have used checks like these for many years. But until very recently they were not available in "homeowner" quantities. The minimum order was typically 2,500, and you had to do some digging to locate the firms that could supply them. Today, all that has changed. Increasingly, business forms companies are advertising in computer magazines and gearing their offerings to the small business or private individual.

Deluxe Computer Forms, for example, one of the largest producers of any kind of checks in the country has taken two-page, four-color ads in many magazines to make computer owners aware of their continuous-form checks. The typical minimum order is now 500. And interestingly, the cost is only about a penny a check more than the conventional checks you order from your bank. In both cases, printing your name and address is included in the price.

### How to Order Continuous-form Checks

You may be able to order the checks you need directly from your bank, though, since many banks are not up to speed on this area, you may find it easier to order directly from the company. You'll find a wide variety of styles to choose from, including both carbonless and carbon-based two-part checks. Color selection may be limited, but there is no problem having your name imprinted on each check. If you are a business person, you should be able to have your logo or other special graphic design imprinted on the checks for a small additional charge.

Typically, you will have to send a voided copy of one of your current checks so the firm can include the proper bank and account numbers. The total turnaround time from the moment the firm receives your order until you receive your checks is usually less than two weeks. Prices for 500 checks range from about $39 to $43, and as with conventional checks, the second 500 is only about $15 more.

Most firms will send you a catalogue and samples to help you decide. Here are three companies you may want to contact for more information:

Deluxe Computer Forms
530 North Wheeler
P.O. Box 43046
St. Paul, MN   55164-0046
(800) 328-0304
(612) 483-7300, in Minnesota

Nebs Computer Forms
12 South Street
Townsend, MA   01469
(800) 225-9550
(800) 922-8565, Massachusetts

Checks To-Go
8384 Hercules Street
La Mesa, CA   92041
(800) 854-2750
(800) 552-8817, in California

*Keeping Track: A Slight Change*

You can order continuous-form checks from these and other companies in just about any format you like. But the format most people use, and the one that the companies consider their standard, consists of both a check and a "voucher." The whole unit measures 9½ inches wide by 7 inches tall, with the check in the top portion and the removable voucher attached beneath. When the sprocket strips have been removed, both voucher and check measure 8½ inches wide by 3½ inches tall.

When businesses issue checks, the voucher portion is usually printed with payroll deduction information or the name of the project or product the check is to be applied against. Usually it is mailed with the check, while the business keeps a carbon of both the check and the voucher. In a home-based system, the voucher can be used as your check register. You can include the date, the payee, and the amount just as you would on a check stub.

When your printer prints out a check and voucher, you would tear the check off, sign it, and put it in an envelope with the bill you are paying. You would then tear the voucher off and put it in a file. The file of check-sized vouchers would become your check register. This is a different way of keeping track of checks than the spiral-bound stubs or wallet-sized booklet, and it may take some getting used to. But you may find that it offers you much more flexibility, and certainly much more room to make notes to yourself about the checks you write than conventional methods.

*How to Set Things Up with Your Word Processor*

You will have to take the time to work out the spacing, but basically, you can use your word processor to create a check/voucher "page" for each creditor. You can type in the date, the payee, the numerical amount, the amount in words, and your account number in such a way that each item will print out in the proper location on the check. And you can do the same thing with the voucher.

Once you know where everything should go on the "page," you can use your word processor's features to quickly produce a page for each bill you pay each month. For example, let's suppose that you have a number of creditors to whom you pay the same amount each month. Your rent or mortgage, a budget plan for gas, oil, or electricity, a car loan, etc., are all good examples. You issued your checks last month and are now ready to begin the process again.

The only item that needs to be changed on these checks is the date. Consequently, all you have to do is use the search and replace feature of your word processor to substitute last month's date with today's date. If all of these checks are part of the same file, that can be accomplished in a matter of seconds. You record the file with the new date, turn on your printer, and away you go. Clearly, this makes much more sense than writing the same information over and over again by hand each month.

Checks with variable amounts are only slightly more trouble. Again, you would use the search and replace feature to take care of the date. Then you would use the program's navigational commands to go to each check. Once there, the only things you would have to change would be the numerical amount and the amount written out in words. The payee and your credit card or other account number would remain unchanged. Again, you would record the revised page and print the checks and vouchers.

**SoftTip:** Since the voucher sections are going to be used as a check register, you might want to make them look more like the traditional type of register. You could include spaces labelled "Balance

Forwarded," "Deposits," "Total," "Amount This Check," and "Balance." You could even include a little box for "Tax Deduction." Since all of these items would be part of your standard form, you would only have to type them once.

---

**SoftTip:** Even today, some firms do not supply preaddressed return envelopes. But you can eliminate the inconvenience of writing out the same address each month as well. Using the continuous-form pressure-sensitive labels mentioned earlier, you can run off a year's worth of addresses for these firms at one time. Type the address once on your word processor and tell the system to print up 12 labels. Then stick the labels onto envelopes and put them into your file for that creditor. Presto! Instant (or almost instant) pre-addressed envelopes.

---

*Conclusion*

If you already own a word processing program and you want to produce your checks automatically each month, the only additional item you will need is a supply of continuous-form checks. A word processing program will not automatically deduct withdrawals and add deposits, the way a checkbook balancing program will. But many check balancers cannot print checks. With a pocket calculator, performing the arithmetic is so easy that it hardly seems worth worrying about—or paying for in a special program. If you have not yet bought your word processor, be sure to see Chapter 13, and be sure to get one with flexible printing parameters and a search-and-replace feature.

If you own a spreadsheet program, you should seriously consider putting your budget on it. If you don't own one, you may be able to get one for between $50 and $120. You will find that even the most stripped-down spreadsheet will give you precisely the kind of financial overview, control, and decision support that you need—none of which is offered by most home budgeting and accounting programs.

In addition, spreadsheet programs do not require an often tedious monthly maintenance process. You turn to them when you need them. Period. If you want a program to tell you how much over budget you are in each category, you can use a low-cost spreadsheet template (or a pocket calculator).

Finally, if you are interested in software of the personal finance persuasion, please be certain to check the following list before you buy.

## Software Buyer's Quick Reference Checklist
*—Personal Finance Programs—*

## Checkbook Balancing Programs

*Capacity and Capabilities*

☐ How many checks will the program handle? How many deposits? How many records can a single disk hold?

☐ How does the program handle withdrawals made from a cash machine? The money is coming out of your checking account but there is no check. What does the program do? How does it handle bank service and per-check charges?

☐ Is there a provision to designate a check as tax deductible?

☐ Is there a check-writing feature? (If so, see Check Writing, under Personal Accounting Programs, below.)

☐ Is there any room to include the kind of additional notes you may now write in your paper check register?

☐ On what basis can you search for records of checks or deposits? Check number? Date? Payee? Tax deductibility?

☐ Can the program show you a report on your screen, or can it only give you a report via the printer?

*Ease of Use*

☐ What does the data entry process involve? What must you type in for each check?

☐ How quickly can you get to the data entry point once you know the program? Do you always have to work your way through a series of menus or can you "go direct"? The easier it is to enter a check, the more likely it is that you will use the program faithfully.

☐ Will the program automatically increment the check number when you are ready to enter a check? If you have just finished check 101, will "102" automatically appear, or do you have to type it in yourself?

☐ Will the program automatically enter the decimal and two zeroes for you when you are entering whole numbers? It's a minor point, but convenient.

☐ What happens if you mistakenly enter an incorrect digit when recording a check? Can you edit the digit and replace it with the correct number? Or must you retype all of the information for the check?

Inadequate error handling is the mark of a poorly written program. Anything that makes the program more difficult to use is going to make it less likely that you will use it faithfully.

## Home Budget Programs

*Capacity and Capabilities*
☐ How many budget categories does the program permit when setting up your budget? Some may offer 14. Some may offer 26 or more.

☐ Are the categories preset for items like "Entertainment," "Food," "Shelter," etc.? If so, can the names of the categories be changed?

☐ Are there any unlabelled categories for you to use in customizing the program to your own needs?

☐ Are there enough categories and is there enough flexibility for the types of expenses you have and the specific information you want the program to provide? If you had only a few categories, for example, you might have to lump all fun things under "Entertainment." With more categories, you could specify "theater," "movies," "rock concerts," "record albums," etc.

☐ What is the largest decimal number the program will handle? The program may only be able to go up to 9,999.00 making it useless if you have a net income of $10,000 or more.

*Ease of Use*
☐ Will the program keep a running total of expenses throughout the month, allowing you to enter information at any time? Or must you enter expenses only once during the month?

This is one of the most crucial weaknesses to watch out for. Some programs are not capable of adding the expense you enter today to the expense you typed in last week in the same category. They simply replace last week's figure with the current figure. That doesn't make the program unworkable, but it makes it less than convenient to use since you must remember to perform the addition yourself.

☐ What happens if you make a mistake when typing in an entry? How easily can the mistake be corrected?

☐ If you want to look at the current expenses entered in a specific category, how easily can you obtain that information? Can you go right to it or must you page through all the categories?

☐ Can you generate a report of all budget categories on a monthly basis? Can you get a report of what you have spent in a single category over a period of months? Can you select the number of months, or are you locked into 12?

☐ What other reports does the program generate?

## Personal Accounting Programs

*Preliminaries*

☐ Before you do anything, look at the documentation and ask yourself how much knowledge of accounting you will need to use the program? As a test, see if the documentation clearly explains how and why the amount you issue a check for is entered as a "credit."

If accounting knowledge is required, does the program contain a good tutorial? Does it recommend any textbooks? Are there sample data on the enclosed disk?

*Capacity and Capabilities*

☐ How many accounts can you set up? Are there enough to let you include some undefined accounts for use later should the need arise? How difficult is the setup process likely to be?

☐ How many *transactions* (individual data entries) will the program handle? It could be 2,500. It could be 4,000 or more.

☐ How many accounts will a single disk hold?

☐ Does it include an interface to let you transfer your budgeting data to VisiCalc or some other spreadsheet? Is an interface available at extra cost?

☐ Can the program write your checks for you? If so, does it come with a supply of checks? Is there a provision for putting your name, address, and bank number on the check? Are the checks acceptable to your bank? What provisions are there for reordering when you use up all of the checks?

☐ Does the program include a "net worth" feature to give you a report on this fact of your financial life? What must you go through to set it up? Does the documentation give you any suggestions for determining the current depreciated value of your car, boat, or other major possessions? Does it give you any guidance in estimating the value of your house?

☐ Do you want a program that includes a scratchpad and offers pocket calculator-like features?

*Ease of Use*
☐ What kinds of information must be entered and how easy is it to do so?

☐ Can you change the account structure you have set up without having to reenter all the data?

☐ If the account categories are designated by two-letter or similar codes, are the codes easy to remember and use?

☐ What does the documentation say about handling your credit card expenses? How easy is it to allocate your individual credit card purchases to different accounts? How long will this take you each month?

*Check Writing*
☐ Can you print a given check more than once if the first printing contains a mistake? Or must you destroy it, go back into the program and mark it destroyed, then start again to write a new check?

☐ Can you print a single check? Or must you print all of the checks at the same time?

☐ Does the program require that you use continuous-form checks or could you use a friction-fed printer and the checks you are now using?

☐ Do you need a program capable of putting the payee's address on the check for use with envelopes having see-through address windows?

*Reporting Functions*
☐ Can you get a report of the current expenditures in just one of your accounts? Can you get a report of, say, five of them? Over what period of time?

☐ What other reports can the program generate? Check register, account totals and subtotals, year-to-date summaries, month-to-date?

☐ Will the program print in either the 40-column or the 80-column mode? How flexible is it?

☐ Can you get a report on your display screen, or can the program only produce reports on the printer?

☐ Does the program include bar charts or line graphs or any other graphic analysis features?

☐ Will the program allow you to use compressed print? If it doesn't, you may need either a 132-column printer or resign yourself to having reports divided into two or more letter-sized pages. You may have to tape them together to be able to use them.

# ...22...

# How to Buy Investment and Portfolio Management Software

If Lorne Greene were doing television commercials for personal computers instead of Alpo dog food, he might say, "Feed them stocks, bonds, warrants, and options, for investments are their natural food." There is no evidence that your PC will live longer if you give it a steady diet of stock quotes, but your investments probably will, and your portfolio will probably be healthier for it.

Computers are ideally suited for taking the drudgery out of many of the chores investors must perform each day. The computer can remember the formulas and instantly perform most of the calculations that formerly required a pencil, lots of paper, and a pocket calculator. With the right programming, you can feed a computer a bond quote and it can instantly give you its yield to maturity. Load in a different program and feed it the day's closing stock prices, and in seconds it will calculate 50-day and 200-day moving averages. Ask it, What will be the effect on my portfolio if I unload everything but IBM and fly to Tahiti? and it will tell you in an instant. Using the communications module supplied with some investment software, the machine may even be able to make the plane reservations for you.

If the "What if . . . ?" and automatic calculation features of this kind of software sound vaguely familiar, if it sounds as though it might perhaps be a "VisiClone" or other electronic spreadsheet in disguise—you are absolutely right. Spreadsheets and many investment programs share the ability to remember formulas and execute calculations based on the numbers you give them. Indeed, many people forego investment software altogether since they find that their spreadsheet programs are more than adequate for their needs.

This is an alternative you may want to consider yourself. The fact is, much of the investment software on the market in recent years has been "challenging," to say the least. If "volume liquidity ratios," "beta coefficients," and "exponential moving averages" appear only infrequently in your dinner table conversation, you may have a problem working with these specialized programs.

Most software designed to analyze investments assumes at least a basic knowledge of the particular market the program is to deal with. And many assume more than that. By and large, the analytical, "number-crunching" programs available today are at least as complex as the markets they track and, as such, are not suitable for novice investors. But fortunately, analytical programs are not the only type available.

---

**SoftTip:** If you are interested in investing and own a copy of Visi-Calc or SuperCalc, a gentleman named Andrew Williams just may be able to save you some money. In an article published in *PC World* (Vol. 1, No. 4), Mr. Williams presents all of the information you need to transform your spreadsheet into a pretty nifty portfolio program. With his worksheets and programming you can use your software to determine gross and net profit based on the latest stock quotes, brokerage commissions, percentage change on an annualized basis, and other important information.

The article is adapted from *WHAT IF . . . A Guide to Using Electronic Spreadsheets on the IBM Personal Computer* (Wiley), and if you would rather not take the trouble to construct the worksheets yourself, Mr. Williams will send them to you on disk for $10. (Be sure to specify whether you want the VisiCalc or the SuperCalc version.) Contact:

> Mr. Andrew T. Williams
> Keeping Track of Your Stocks
> P.O. Box 9563
> Berkeley, CA   94707

---

### Basics: Investment and Portfolio Management Software

*Two Major Categories*

Programs in this area differ considerably in the types of investments they are designed to deal with, the features they offer, the kinds of output they generate, etc. But overall, there are two main functions you can expect investment software to perform: analysis and portfolio management. The analytical programs are the number crunchers. They manipulate data, plug it into either preset formulas or equations of your own design, and generate results that can make relationships clearer, help you spot trends, and make any number of comparisons. These programs are designed for serious investors and experts, and they can cost $500 to $700 or more.

Portfolio management programs, in contrast, are available for as little as $75 and require virtually no expertise. Most are easy to use, and even for an occasional investor they can be a real boon. A portfolio program will help you keep track of the number of shares, bonds, or other securities you own, what you paid for them and when, the total value of your holdings based on today's closings, all of your buy/sell transactions, and more. The only catch is that, as with any computer program, the results will only be as good as the data you enter. Thus, if you use a portfolio manager, it is important to develop the habit of updating it religiously after each transaction.

To obtain all the features you want, you may have to buy both an analytical program and a management program. Or you may find elements of both in a single product. Whichever option is best for you, there are three main questions to ask when considering any investment program:

- Where does the information the program needs come from and how does it get into the machine?
- What does the program do with the information?
- What kind of output can the program generate?

*Dow Jones Calling*

With most other software, the answer to the first question is easy. Information is simply typed in from the keyboard. But with investment software, there is usually another alternative. Thanks to a growing number of online financial databases, it is often possible to have the latest market quotes and other information pumped directly into your computer over the telephone.

According to the Datapro *Directory of On-Line Services*, there are at least 40 different firms offering financial and security pricing information to corporations and individuals equipped with communicating personal computers. Of these, however, the Dow Jones News/Retrieval Service (DJNS) is undoubtedly the best known. With a subscription base of more than 100,000 and a growth rate of over 4,500 new subscribers per month, it is also one of the largest and the fastest growing services in the entire information industry.

**SoftTip:** For information on the Dow Jones News/Retrieval database, as well as other easily available sources online of investment information (Commodity News Service, Standard & Poor's, Value Line, etc.), see:
*The Complete Handbook of Personal Computer Communications*
by Alfred Glossbrenner, St. Martin's Press, $14.95

Many analytical and portfolio management programs rely upon DJNS as their primary source of data. In fact, in some cases, you may not be able to get data into the program any other way. To use a program of this sort, you will need a communications card and a modem. If you don't already own this equipment, you may have to spend anywhere from $300 to $600 in addition to the cost of the program.

The good news is that programs offering this feature may include a free subscription to DJNS and one or more hours of free connect time. That can be worth anywhere from $60 to $75. Since the software house may have contracted for a limited number of subscriptions, however, the actual copy of the program offered may not include one. It may be worth checking with several dealers to see if a copy with a free subscription is available.

The initial subscription may be free, but once your free time has expired, you will be billed for using the service to update your portfolio or to collect financial data. The actual monthly cost will depend upon how often you use the service and which DJNS features you access. The firm offers a number of special arrangements that can save you money if you use it frequently. In any case, the fees you pay, and possibly even the software you buy, may be tax deductible. As in all tax matters, be sure to check with your accountant.

*At the Touch of a Button*
With most programs, obtaining information online from DJNS requires an initial setup process in which you enter the stock exchange and other codes used to identify the information you seek. If you are using a portfolio management program, for example, you will have to spend some time entering all the information the program needs (company name and exchange code, number of shares owned, etc.). You will also have to enter the phone number you want the computer to dial and your DJNS account number and password.

Once you've done this, updating your portfolio on a daily basis can be as easy as pressing a single key on your keyboard. Most programs can be used with an acoustic modem (a modem with rubber cups for the phone handset), and if you have one, you should make sure that you can use it with the program. But most work best with an auto-dial direct-connect unit like the Hayes Smartmodem. In fact, in some cases the program will be written specifically for use with Hayes equipment.

With a properly connected auto-dial modem, you have only to boot the program and select an item from an onscreen menu to begin the updating process. The program will dial the correct number, sign you onto the system, issue the commands DJNS needs to see to retrieve the stock quote and other information you seek, and sign you off— all automatically. Once the information has been received, the program will store it on disk and you will be able to use the other modules of the program to work with it, print it out, or analyze it in some way.

Clearly, an automatic DJNS access feature can be very convenient. But it can also be quite cost effective. Since the two computers (Dow Jones's and yours) can usually accomplish things much faster when allowed to converse without your intervention, an automatic update process will usually cost you less than if you had to do it all yourself.

You should also know that between 6:00. PM and 4:00 AM, EST, the rates for using DJNS drop by as much as 80%. If you have a clock on one of your memory expansion boards or if you have some other timing device, you may be able to have your computer come on automatically, update your portfolio when the rates are low, and shut off. Ask your dealer for details.

*Information Manipulation and Output*

What a program *does* with the information after obtaining it will naturally vary widely. A program designed for bond investments will automatically calculate the standard collection of yields, equivalent taxable return, basis price, etc. A program designed to analyze options may put the data through the Black/Scholes or some other model. Mutual funds, puts and calls, commodities—there are programs designed to be used with all of these types of investments and more, not to mention programs that can analyze and compare equities in virtually every conceivable way.

*Output: Tables, Charts, and Graphs*

Virtually all investment programs have the ability to present relevant data in the form of tables, but some can create charts or graphs as well. Portfolio management programs, for example, typically can produce a number of tables:

- *Holdings by Portfolio.* For use when you maintain several groupings of stocks and bonds (a "high tech" portfolio, a "blue chip" portfolio, an "aggressive investing" portfolio, etc.); provides security code, purchase date, quantity purchased, unit price and total cost, current value based on the latest price quotes, unrealized gains or losses, etc.
- *Holdings by Symbol.* For use when you want a program to tell you how many shares of a particular stock you own, when you made each purchase and at what price, how much your holdings are worth on paper today.
- *Realized Gains or Losses.* For use when you want a summary of all of the securities you have sold to date, when and at what price, and whether the transaction generated a gain or a loss.
- *Year-to-Date Transactions.* For a complete summary of what you've bought, what you've sold, when and for how much, etc., at any time.

Analytical programs can usually produce their share of tables as well. But since programs in this category tend to be designed for technical analysts, they may include some graphing features as well. In contrast to "fundamentalist" investors who usually form opinions on the basis of a company's management, balance sheet, price/earnings ratio, and other fundamental points, technical analysts usually make their decisions by comparing current and historical trends. This is much easier to do when you can look at a graph or a chart in addition to a table of figures.

The graphing and charting capabilities of different programs vary widely, so this is obviously something to check carefully before buying the program. You may find that the information you display graphically is strictly limited, or you may find that you can use virtually any kind of data. From the standpoint of visual quality, you may also find that investment programs rely on character graphics where datapoints are represented by asterisks, hyphens, periods, or other characters, instead of using the more sophisticated techniques of a true business graphics program (see Chapter 19).

---

**SoftTip:** If the program you are interested in does not have the ability to generate graphs, you might see if it is possible to use the data files it produces with a free-standing business graphics program of the sort described in Chapter 19. If you already have a graphics program, this approach could save you money since investment software with graphics capabilities can cost several hundred dollars more than similar programs.

The key points to consider are whether the types of graphs generated by a free-standing program will fill your needs and whether
the programs can use each other's files. If both products store information in the DIF format, there's a good chance that this will
be possible. Be sure to check before you buy.

## Critical Points

*The Communications Module*

You may be able to save yourself the expense of buying a separate
communications program if the communications module many investment programs use to access DJNS can also be used by itself. Check to
see if the menu normally used to dial Dow Jones automatically includes
a "manual" option. If it does, you may be able to select this option and
dial some other database. Needless to say, the program will not have all
of the capabilities of a full-featured communications package (see Chapter 17), but it may be adequate, particularly if it is possible to generate
periodically a hard copy of whatever appears on the screen. If this is of
interest, be sure to ask the salesperson to show you how to do it.

*Recording Historical Prices*

When most programs automatically access DJNS and download stock
information, they usually replace whatever information is currently in
your files with fresh data. If you are interested primarily in determining
the value of your portfolio on the basis of the most recent prices, this
will be of no consequence to you. However, if your main interest is
portfolio management, but you would also like to compare a stock's current price with its historical prices or look at how the price has fluctu-
ated over the past month, the lack of a daily price record could be a
problem.

You may find that some portfolio management programs will allow
you to save historical price quotes. But more than likely, you will have
to buy analytical software to obtain this feature. In many cases, this is
less than an ideal solution since an analytical program may not be able
to manage your portfolio and may include expensive features that you
will never use. There are other alternatives, however, and you should
be aware of them before deciding to buy both a portfolio management
program and an analytical program.

The simplest course is to take advantage of the historical pricing information maintained by DJNS itself and other databases. The "Historical Quotes" section of DJNS, for example, provides past prices for

common and preferred stocks and warrants traded on the New York, American, Midwest, and Pacific Exchanges, as well as the OTC market. It offers daily quotes for the past year, quarterly summaries beginning with 1978, and monthly summaries from 1979 to the present. All of this information is accessible to you using either the communications module included with your portfolio management program or separate communications software.

CompuServe's MicroQuote includes current and historical information on more than 40,000 stocks, bonds, and options. The firm also offers Standard & Poor's General Information File and Arnold Bernhard & Company's Value Line II. The Source offers STOCKVUE, a service provided by Media General Financial Services and including some 58 statistics on nearly 4,000 stocks. A more extensive version of the same service is also available on the Dow Jones.

Some of the online services mentioned will provide you with historical analysis and thus may eliminate the need for you to do anything but sign on and request the information on the stock you are interested in. Depending upon the software, you may also be able to download (capture) the information in a disk file and feed it to a business graphics program for visual display. Since this can be a bit more complicated, however, you will definitely want to investigate the process and possibilities thoroughly.

As another alternative, you could print out your entire portfolio after each day's update. But since that is likely to be cumbersome and generate a lot of paper, it might be easier to go into DOS and copy the portfolio data files to a separate disk before updating them each day. You could rename the files in the process to reflect the day's date ("6-2-84.STOX"). Since most portfolio programs require a program disk and a data disk, looking at any record in your file could be as simple as inserting a different data disk.

Then again, it might not be that simple. It depends upon the program. For example, the IBM/PC version of the Dow Jones Market Manager, a portfolio management program, is written in UCSD Pascal and is equipped with a run time p-System interpreter. It works quite well by itself, but unless you have purchased a copy of the p-System, you will not be able to use the files it creates for any other purpose.

*Secret Formulas*

Since the manipulations and calculations a program performs are its most crucial features, you will obviously want to focus intensely on this area. It goes without saying that if you have a certain technique or investment strategy, you will want a program that enables you to employ it to best advantage. However, regardless of your preferred area of investment, if you use a unique formula or equation or any other special form of analysis, make sure that the program you buy will allow you to incorporate it in the analysis. Some programs are considerably less flexible here than others.

### Buffer Boxes and Spoolers

Because charts and graphs of any sort usually take a while to print out, you may want to consider buying a buffer box. Without one, you may not be able to use your computer until the graphic printout is finished. A software print spooler may also work, but here you should proceed with caution.

Depending upon the program, the amount of memory it requires, and where it loads into that memory, you may not be able to use a software spooler and the program at the same time. The communications and other modules of many investment programs are quite extensive, and they may require the memory normally used by the spooler. Be sure to check this point carefully in a live demonstration before you buy.

### Software Buyer's Quick Reference Checklist

*—Investment and Portfolio Management Programs—*

### Preliminaries

☐ Do you want a portfolio management program or an analytical program, or one that provides both features?

☐ What hardware is required? How much memory? Single- or double-sided disk drives? Will you need a communications card, a modem, and a video graphics adaptor?

☐ Can you use a keypad attachment for rapid data entry?

☐ Does the program include a free subscription to the Dow Jones News/Retrieval Service? Does it include any free time?

☐ Can the communications module be used by itself to access other databases?

☐ Can the program's data files be used with any business graphics package you may own?

☐ Will the program run without the printer being turned on or not? Many will not.

### Capacity and Capabilities

☐ How many stocks or other individual investments can the program handle? Is there a numerical limit or is it limited only by available disk space?

☐ How many stocks and transactions can the program store on a single disk?

☐ Are multiple purchases of the same stock tracked separately, or are they placed in the same portfolio?

☐ How many separate portfolios may you have?

☐ Can stock prices be entered manually and can they be entered as a whole number and a fraction? Or must you convert to decimal first?

☐ Does the program have an auto-dial, auto-update feature to access DJNS or some other service at the press of a key?

☐ Can the program retrieve and deal with information on all of the types of investments in your portfolio (common and preferred stocks, mutual funds, bonds, warrants, options, Treasury bills, etc.). Some programs may be limited to just equities.

☐ Is there any type of investment information that *must* be entered manually? A program may be able automatically to retrieve common and preferred stocks and warrants but require manual entry of historical quotes for corporate or foreign bonds, options, or mutual funds.

☐ Can the program handle Over-the-Counter (OTC) investments, including asked and bid prices, spread calculations, and volume?

☐ Will the program retrieve and store the following information:
—trading volume
—high/low and last prices
—closing prices
—opening prices
—net change at close

☐ Will the program:
—keep track of purchases and sales
—"date stamp" each transaction
—allow you to enter brokerage commissions and automatically deduct them with figuring net profit
—automatically calculate gains and losses
—provide a tax report of the sales transactions (including dividend yield as well as profit and loss)

☐ Does the program include a field for the ex-dividend date? Does it flag options by expiration date? And will it automatically remind you of those dates?

☐ Will the program allow you to enter buy or sell points and automatically notify you when the investments reach those points, according to the latest update?

☐ How are stock splits handled?

☐ What does the program do when you sell a stock? Does it automatically remove it from your portfolio? And if it does, what happens to the information?

☐ Will the program account for short sales of stocks or options?

☐ Does the program store ticker symbols, purchase date, share cost, number of shares purchased, current price, quarterly dividend, and ex-dividend date in a DIF file format?

This is essential should you want to transfer the data to your Visi-Calc or other spreadsheet program. If it doesn't use the DIF format, you will have to reenter all of the information on your spreadsheet.

*Reports and Output*
☐ What kinds of reports can the program generate? Do they provide everything you need?

☐ What do the reports look like? Are they easy to read? Is the information arranged logically? Are the headers clear or cryptic, "user-friendly" or "un-"? You should be able to find examples and explanations of all of them in the documentation. If you can't, proceed with caution.

☐ Will the program automatically sort your investments alphabetically? Or does it list them in the order in which they were bought? With a large list of stocks, an alphabetical sort feature is a must.

*Analytical Programs*
☐ How do the program's features and capabilities compare on a one-to-one basis with the procedures you are using now?

☐ Can the program compute simple moving averages, weighted moving averages, exponential moving averages, volume indicators, etc.?

☐ Will the program allow you to enter your own personal analytical equations and formulas?

☐ How many different trends can be compared on the same chart or graph?

☐ Are the labels and legends on the graphs and charts clear and easily understood?

# ...23...

# How to Buy Programs for Consultants and Professionals: *Medical, Dental, and Legal*

P hysicians, attorneys, and dentists may practice completely different professions, but like all professionals and consultants, they have one thing in common: a need to keep track of the time they spend, to allocate it properly to their clients and patients, and to issue bills for their services. Essential as it is, for many professionals this process represents a major headache.

Since time is all a professional or consultant has to sell, it is extremely wasteful for him or her to spend it doing the books each month. Yet for many young doctors, lawyers, and dentists, there may be no alternative. More established practitioners inevitably hire a bookkeeper, an accountant, an office manager, or contract with an outside billing service. But even with this kind of assistance, there is no way to escape the cumbersome folders, file cards, and appointment books most professionals use to conduct their business. Nor is there a way to get an instant update of the office's current financial standing, or any easy way to determine whether certain procedures are worth the malpractice premiums a doctor or dentist must pay, or how much each partner is contributing to a law firm.

Clearly, many professionals could benefit from some type of personal computer-based accounting system. Yet, unlike the accounting software described in Chapter 20, it clearly can't be oriented toward discrete products or "units." It must be flexible enough to account for time, and at the very least it should have a built-in feature to allow the practitioner to bill at different rates for time spent performing different services.

Not surprisingly, the first "time accounting" software packages on the market were little more than regular business accounting programs that had been adapted for professional use. Sometimes they weren't modified enough. There is at least one example of a program designed for legal office use that printed reports with a column labelled "Products Sold.' Increasingly, however, programs have begun to appear that take into account the unique requirements of a professional. In this chapter, we will be focusing on software for the legal, dental, and medical professions. As yet, there is not much software available for professional consultants. But since many of the time accounting, billing, and office management problems are the same, you may want to use the information presented here as a guide when more generic "consultant-oriented" software does appear.

### At Least Three Options

The programs are different for each profession, of course. But they have many basic similarities stemming from their common goal of accounting for a professional's time. Generally, there are three ways to purchase this kind of software. You can buy a generalized time accounting package that basically keeps track of the time you spend and generates the appropriate bills. One such package, the Time Accountant from Image Software (3678 Nicole, Las Vegas, NV 89120), runs on the Commodore CBM 8032, accommodates 800 clients, and costs about $425.

Alternatively, you can buy a package that is designed for your profession and offers many more features. Medical professionals, for example, will find a number of packages capable of automatically filling out insurance forms. A package for lawyers may include a calendaring feature to take the place of a "tickler" file. And packages for all three professions may include database management features to enable the computer to search for and locate clients or patients on the basis of criteria. (All patients who have been prescribed a particular drug; all *pro bono* cases; all patients who have had extractions in the past month; etc.)

Naturally, these features cost extra. And being professionals, you will probably be charged more for them than might otherwise be the case. Software with these and other capabilities typically starts at about $1,400 and can cost $5,000 or more, with an option to receive quarterly updates for about $700 a year.

A third alternative is to purchase a complete "turnkey" system that includes the computer, the printer, the software, and dealer support in a single package. This can be an attractive option for many professionals since choosing the right computer hardware is not something that can be done quickly. Provided you can find a knowledgeable dealer, you may feel that your time would be better spent pursuing your profession than learning all you need to know to choose the right system. If you opt for this alternative, you should plan to spend a minimum of $10,000 to $12,000, though the actual total may be closer to $15,000 by the time you've got everything you need.

**SoftTip:** If you buy ten to twelve thousand dollars worth of equipment and software from the same dealer at the same time, the dealer may be willing either to give you a discount or to throw in some additional software (like a word processing package) at no cost. Much depends on the amount of effort the dealer puts into the sale and the amount of support he offers afterward. Certainly, if the dealer merely fills out an order form, takes your money, and hands you a stack of boxes to take back to the office you are justified in indicating that some sort of discount would be appropriate.

Since your time is money, however, it might be much better to find a dealer who will visit your office, analyze your needs, recommend a package, and take responsibility for installing it and making sure that it runs properly. In that case, it would be well worth paying full price and possibly a small consulting fee as well.

*The Question of Cost*

Is professional software overpriced? Yes, it probably is. Admittedly a software house cannot expect to spread its development cost over as many purchasers as it might with a program designed for the general business or mass market. And in many cases, the price includes the direct support of the software house should you run into problems. That can be crucial since, unlike a regular business, a professional office usually has no one on staff to handle data processing problems. In addition, a local dealer who does a wonderful job of supporting VisiCalc users may not be much help when it comes to the type of software you are using.

Nevertheless, it is important to be aware that most of these packages use standard techniques found in accounting and other business programs that may sell for half the price. Although they had to be customized for a professional's needs, little if any new conceptual ground had to be broken to create most professional time accounting packages. Conceivably, some of them may even incorporate the same programming modules used for standard accounting packages.

Unfortunately, there is probably not much you can do about the price of the program itself. But there may be room for negotiation elsewhere. Some software producers, for example, sell user support and program maintenance as a separate item, and you may be able to persuade them to write the contract to extend the coverage for a longer period without charging you accordingly. If there are features in the program that can be customized to better suit your needs, that may be an item for negotiation as well.

## Basics: Professional Software

The heart of every time accounting system is the list of patients or clients it contains. When a new client is added to the system, a blank client record form will appear on the screen. Among other things, the form will have blanks (fields) for name, address, phone number, and client code or record number. Each doctor, lawyer, or dentist will also have an identifying code. And there will be codes to represent the specific services the professional performs. In a legal package, there would be a code for court appearances and one for telephone consultation. In a medical or dental practice there would be a code for each procedure.

These codes are the way the program identifies the client, the practitioner, and the service performed. But one other piece of information is needed—the billing rate for each service or hour of time. All packages allow the user to set the rates to be charged for each professional service. But they will handle it in different ways.

A medical program, for example, may allow you to set the charge for each procedure or service code. That way, a bill can be calculated on the basis of just that code. A legal package may include a separate set of billing codes to allow an attorney to designate different hourly rates. This would allow the individual to charge a standard rate and one or more special rates for the same amount of time or service, depending on the client.

When using the system, a secretary or office manager would call up a client's record on the screen and enter the appropriate codes to identify the practitioner, the service, and possibly the billing rate. The system might automatically calculate the correct dollar amount and display it in the correct location. Or it might do nothing until the client's bill is generated. Either way, the new information is recorded on the client's record.

As long as the client records have been kept up to date, at the end of the month generating bills or statements is a simple matter of pressing a few keys. The system will perform all of the calculations and print out the names, addresses, and billable charges for each patient or client. Most systems will print the necessary labels or envelopes as well, in some cases drawing the information directly from the correct fields on the client record. Of course the system also keeps track of how much has been billed to each client.

When payments are received, the client's record is again called to the screen and the amount of the payment is entered and recorded, and at some point the ledger listing amounts billed is updated to reflect the payment. The details will differ with the software, but in essence this is the way the time accounting/billing section of such a program works.

## Billing Is Only the Beginning

In addition to taking the chore and much of the expense of billing off your hands, most of these programs also provide something you may never have had before—easy access to precise information on the financial health of your practice, lists of past due accounts divided in "aged billing" fashion by 30, 60, 90, and 120 days or more, and a variety of other reports that can help you gain a firmer grasp on your business.

For example, you may be able to find out how much you've earned in a given day. You may be able to easily discover how many injections you have administered in a month and use the information to determine whether you should order more supplies. And you may be able to ascertain whether it makes good financial sense to continue to offer certain services. Many other "management reports" like these may be possible, depending on the program.

## Additional Features

Programs vary in the detail and flexibility of the management reports they can produce, and they also differ in the number and nature of the extra features they offer. Some may offer a word processing module, for example, for writing referral letters and other correspondence. Some may include a module designed to handle appointments and scheduling. In addition to being able to fill out a variety of insurance forms automatically, a medical package may be able to print prescription labels.

The more sophisticated programs may offer a feature that can be of particular importance to doctors and dentists. Some will allow you to make free-form, unrestricted notes on the patient's billing record so that the record can serve many of the functions of a patient folder. You may not want to phase out folders completely, but keeping some information in electronic form has a number of advantages.

For one thing, it may be easier to enter using a computer than a typewriter. But the biggest plus is ease of retrieval. This benefit will depend upon how many patients you have, but more than likely it will be much easier to call a patient's record up on a screen than to search for a folder in a file. Perhaps even more important, the most advanced packages will allow you to search for patients on the basis of the comments you have entered on their records. Conceivably, if you have entered the phrase "Contact in June" on a number of records, you could ask the system to give you a list of every record containing that phrase in its comment section.

You may find that it is worthwhile to create a patient record and print out a hard copy of it for your file, but leave the record in your system. This would produce neither an increase nor a decrease in the time a secretary or assistant is now spending typing and filing patient records. But it would give you the benefits of both a manual system and an electronic system. If you plan to use your system in this way, make sure that it is capable of printing complete patient records on an individual basis.

## Critical Points

*Consider a Hard Disk*

Most professional time accounting packages can run on a floppy-disk-based system. The program disk may reside in one drive, and the data disks containing client records and other information would reside in one or more additional drives. However, if you are new to computers, you should be aware that swapping floppy disks in and out of the machine can be quite awkward.

For example, if the program itself is contained on several disks, it will be necessary to locate the disk with the desired module and put it into the machine before you or your assistant can use that program feature. In addition, if you or your office has several hundred clients, you will need any number of data disks. And they too will have to be located and inserted in the machine before you can access the information they contain.

For many professionals, the answer is to purchase a hard disk system (see Chapter 5) of sufficient capacity to store all of present client information and to provide room for future expansion. You should probably figure on about 2K of storage per client, more if you will be adding comment lines to each record as described above. Thus a 10-megabyte hard disk could accommodate as many as 5,000 patients or clients, making all of their records instantly accessible at any time.

You should also check to see whether it will be possible to put the software on hard disk as well. This way all program modules will be as accessible as patient records. If the program is issued in copy-protected form, it will not be possible to put it on hard disk, but you may be able to arrange with the software supplier to have it installed.

It is also important to be aware of the need to constantly back up your data by making frequent copies of the information. This is a good procedure in any business, but it is particularly important in a professional practice. The order forms, shipping receipts, and other "paper trail" items associated with a manufacturing concern make it easier to reconstruct erased billing data than is usually the case in a professional office.

Hard disks can be backed up to floppies, though your dealer will be able to show you any number of devices designed to make this process more convenient. And, of course, floppies can be copied. Regardless of the system you use, however, it is absolutely crucial to establish a definite, daily backup procedure.

*Support*

You should also pay close attention to the quality and extent of support you can expect to receive. Ideally, this would be the province of the local dealer and ideally he or she would be able to visit your office to sort out any serious problems you may encounter. The dealer should be able to solve any hardware problems, but for answers on using the program, you will probably have to look to the software house itself. Be sure to ask if there is a customer "hotline" to call and, if so, whether it will be available throughout the working day as measured by your local time.

You should also be prepared to pay an additional fee for support beyond the initial installation stage. Most firms can be expected to help you get your system up and running, but they are understandably reluctant to provide unlimited consultation throughout the year. Consequently, you may be offered a contract for customer support. Prices vary, but $500 to $700 a year is about average, and you should probably agree to take it at least for the first year. Once you and your staff have learned the program's ins and outs, continuing support may not be necessary.

*Getting More Information*

Since the market for professional programs is relatively small compared to most other software, you may have difficulty locating ads and reviews of the products in which you are interested in the popular computer magazines. These publications are worth checking, but your best source of information and advertising will be the various journals published for your profession. Interest among professionals is rising, and you can expect to see an increasing number of articles and ads.

If you are interested in computerizing your dental practice, you may want to subscribe to a newsletter edited and published by Dr. E. J. Neiburger, D.D.S. For more information write to:

"Dental Computer Newsletter"
1000 North Avenue
Waukegan, IL 60085
(Cost: about $15/year)

Physicians and other medical professionals may be interested in a newsletter published by one of the largest suppliers of professional software, Charles Mann & Associates. For information write to:

"Micro Medical Newsletter"
Charles Mann & Associates
7594 San Remo Trail
Yucca Valley, CA 92284
(Cost: about $65 a year)

Regardless of your profession, you should also look into NewsNet, an electronic information service that will give you access to over 150 different newsletters via a personal computer. In addition to the "Altman & Weil Report to Legal Management," NewsNet offers many newsletters that cover the personal computer and software field. Among them are "Advanced Office Systems," "The Seybold Report on Office Systems," and "The Computer Market Observer." All of these newsletters can be electronically scanned for reports on medical, dental, or legal software.

You'll need a computer equipped for telecommunications (talking on the phone), a telephone interface box called a "modem," and a subscription to NewsNet. You will also need communications software (see Chapter 17). (If you are an attorney and are currently accessing LEXIS or WESTLAW, you *may* be able to use the same equipment to access NewsNet.) For more information, contact:

NewsNet
945 Haverford Road
Bryn Mawr, PA 19010
(800) 345-1301
(215) 527-8030, in Pennsylvania

**Software Buyer's Quick Reference Checklist**

*Programs for Professionals*

*Preliminaries*

☐ Do you need a package for a single-person office or for a practice involving two or more professionals?

☐ What information is there on the background of the person or people who *wrote* the software (as opposed to just distributing it)? Do they have a background in your profession?

☐ Do you need a software package or a "turnkey" system? If you need a complete system, give serious consideration to buying one built around one of the newer 16-bit machines since it will offer more memory and be able to accommodate a more powerful program.

☐ Do you need the appointment and scheduling features often sold as an extra-cost module? (See below.)

☐ If yours is a large firm, you may want to consider a package that is designed to interface with a General Ledger program (see Chapter 20).

## Capacity

☐ How many professionals is the system designed to accommodate?

☐ Is there a provision to keep track of the time spent by paralegals, nurse practitioners, and other personnel? This would be over and above the provisions made for professionals.

☐ How many clients or patients will the system handle? It could be 200, 800, 2,000, or unlimited, depending on the program.

## Client Records

☐ In addition to the name, address, and phone number, what other kinds of information can be placed on each client or patient record? How many fields?

☐ How many characters long is each field and is it sufficient? Can the telephone field accommodate an extension number? Is there a place to put the responsible party if bills are not to be sent to the patient?

☐ Are there any user-defined fields for you to customize? Is there provision for a free-form comment area on each record, and if so, are there any limitations on the amount of space you can use?

☐ How many billing codes for services and procedures are available? And how easy is it to assign dollar figures to them? There might be seven. There might be 250 or more.

☐ Will the software house customize the billing codes for you if you want them to and what will they charge?

## Ease of Use

☐ How easy is it to add a new client to the system? How easily can out-of-date client information be edited or changed? (Does the package include passwords or other security provisions to prevent unauthorized changes?)

☐ When you want to look at records or bills do you have to use the printer or can the program show them to you on the display screen?

*Billing*

☐ Can you adjust your rate at will for different patients or clients? Will the system allow you to set up a customized payment schedule for different clients?

☐ Is there a provision for work performed by paralegals and nurses to be billed at a separate, lower rate?

☐ Will the system allow you to print out one or more bills at any time, or must you wait until accounts are closed at the end of each month?

☐ Does the bill generation module interface with the client record file, enabling the system to pick up the names and addresses automatically? Or must you create a separate billing address file, reentering each patient's name and address?

☐ Can you tell the system not to print a bill for one or more clients but still to maintain the billing information?

☐ Will the software issue a receipt on the spot for clients or patients who pay before leaving the office? Can it handle partial as well as full payment?

☐ Is the billing system an "open item" system or a "balance forwarded" system or are both options available? (See Chapter 20.)

☐ If a detail or open item system is used, how specific can the listed items be? Can you print bills that include phrases like "Time spent in connection with the matter of ———.""?

☐ Do you have the option of itemizing or billing a flat fee for different clients or must they all be one or the other?

☐ Can the program add finance charges to second notices? And will it track those monies separately?

☐ What provisions are there for billing for expenses and materials?

☐ Can the system send out reminders indicating that payment is overdue? Can you include a message of some sort on the notice? How long can the message be?

☐ How are write-offs and bad debts handled?

*Management Summaries and Reports*

☐ Will the system give you a daily cash journal report as well as a monthly summary?

☐ Can you get a cumulative ledger listing the year's income to date and including overdue balances broken out on an aged basis?

☐ Can you get a report at any time that will include: number of accounts, total services billed, expenses billed, total accounts receivable, total overdue accounts, and total hours spent per account?

☐ Can you say to the system, "Give me a list of all accounts that are 180 days overdue," or specify some other time period?

☐ How flexible is the account balance reporting feature? Can it give you up-to-the-minute balances at any time reflecting all payments received to date, or are balances accurate only to the close of the previous month?

☐ Can you order a printout of an individual's billing and payment history at any time?

☐ Can you ask the system to tell you how much time you have spent on a particular case or client as of this moment? Or must you wait until the end of the month?

*Appointment and Scheduling*
☐ Is there a calendaring feature to remind you of important form filing and other dates?

☐ How does the appointment and scheduling module work? Is it easy to make and change patient appointments? Will it generate a log of the next day's appointments, complete with patient phone numbers, to be used for telephone confirmation?

☐ How many ways can the appointment file be searched? By patient name? By day and date? Can you say, "Who is scheduled for 10:00 AM a month from next Thursday?

☐ Does the system let *you* decide how many hours constitute a working day? Or does it force you to use an eight-hour day? Can you determine how much time will constitute an appointment and how long an interval there will be between appointments?

☐ Can the software automatically generate appointment reminder cards and any necessary address labels? Can it produce a card on the spot, as the appointment is made?

*Extras and Special Features*
☐ Are there database management features to let you retrieve client records by searching on the basis of different criteria? What criteria are possible? Can the system search for words in a comment area?

☐ Does the package include any word processing features and, if so, are they adequate to your needs? (See Chapter 12.)

☐ Will the software house customize the program to produce personalized letterheads for your bills and statements? This might cost as little as $30. The customized headers would print out at the top of each bill. This feature could save you the expense of buying special forms, though you would want to verify the quality and appearance of headers produced in this way.

☐ Can the program generate a label for a client file folder at the time the client is entered into the system?

☐ Can the program print out bank deposit slips for each day's transactions?

## Special Considerations: Attorneys

☐ Can you track time spent on *pro bono* work without issuing a bill?

☐ Does the package enable you to use NEXIS or WESTLAW or some other online service?

☐ Can the system automatically identify potential conflicts of interest?

## Special Considerations: Physicians and Dentists

☐ Have you thoroughly explored the software's insurance form generation capabilities? Can it handle all of the forms your office currently uses? How easy is it to update the program should an insurance form change? You may be able to do it in house, or you may have to contact the software supplier for an update to the program.

☐ How does the program deal with patients who have multiple insurance coverage?

☐ Are account balances maintained on an up-to-the-minute basis, making it possible to generate an insurance form at any time, or must you wait until the end of the month?

☐ What does the record maintained for each insurance company look like? Are there fields for the name and phone number of a contact person? Will the system keep track of the current balance owed in from each firm?

☐ Will the system handle the standard AMA form for third-party billing?

☐ Will it handle the five-digit Current Procedural Terminology codes recommended by the AMA?

☐ Can you enter the International Codes of Diagnoses (ICD) required by many insurance companies? How easy is it to update patient records should any of those codes change: Will the system automatically change all patient records or must each record be changed separately?

☐ What does the system do about billing when, in the absence of the primary physician, another doctor treats a patient?

# ...24...
## How to Buy Educational Software

There is a problem with educational software. A problem, and a promise. The problem can best be illustrated by the initial results of a study begun in 1983 by the Education Products Information Exchange, a nonprofit organization based in Watermill, New York, and Consumers Union. The project enlisted the aid of some 300 teachers to evaluate educational programs. As reported in the *Wall Street Journal*, "Of the initial 50 programs reviewed, only a fourth got a grade of 60% or better." Other professional educators are less precise but more to the point. "The quality of educational software today," says one, "ranges from poor to horrendous."

That's the problem. The promise is best illustrated by projections contained in *Personal Computer Educational Software Market Report*, a study produced by the highly respected Future Computing company based in Richardson, Texas. Future Computing projects that the educational software market will grow by 71% a year, from a 1982 market of $70 million to a 1987 market of $1 billion. Those figures don't mean much until you realize that in 1982, approximately 2.4 million educational software packages were sold. By 1987—the year of the billion dollar market—the number of packages is expected to top 34 million, 24 million of which will be bought for use at home.

What all this means is that, while the quantity, availability, and overall quality of educational software have been poor in the past, it is slated for a vast improvement in the future. Belatedly perhaps, software developers have begun to realize the enormous potential of the personal computer as a teaching machine. And while it will take some time for new and better programs to appear, it is fair to say that every major software house and every computer firm that also supplies software currently has one or more "second generation" programs in the pipeline.

*The Computer as Tutor*

The industry buzzword for software that teaches and the field of which it is a part is "Computer Assisted Instruction" or "CAI." Educational software, however good, will never replace a human teacher, but

CAI has a number of things to recommend it. For example, according to a study done under the aegis of the U.S. Office of Technology Assessment in 1978, CAI was shown to be superior to or equal to conventional teaching methods. "Some students showed improvement of up to 50%. . . . The net effect proved, beyond a doubt, that computers are effective teachers."

Of course, in 1978 the personal computer was barely three years old, and all of the CAI studies cited by the report were conducted with mainframes or minicomputers. Thus, at the time, the price of the necessary equipment was a major consideration, and questions were raised as to whether CAI could ever be cost effective. Today all that has changed. Indeed, a 1983 study by the same governmental office estimated that personal computer-based CAI may cost as little as 30¢ an hour—compared to an average of $2 per student hour of conventional instruction in a typical school system.

The cost figures are attractive, to say the least, but do computers really make good teachers? The answer is yes, given the right software. There is a further qualification as well, and that is that on the whole computers are better at teaching some subjects than others. They are absolute demons when it comes to "drill and practice" routines like teaching someone to type or helping a child learn fractions and multiplication. They are somewhat less suited to teaching higher level analytical skills where it is necessary for the machine (the programmer) to anticipate a wide range of student responses and requests for information. Nevertheless, again given the right program, they have the potential to show impressive results in this area as well.

### Nobody Does It Better?

The easiest way to appreciate what a personal computer has to offer as an educational tool is to look first at conventional teaching. A teacher in a classroom has a certain amount of knowledge to be communicated to the students. The realities of the situation dictate that knowledge be delivered in relatively large chunks. Students are then tested on their comprehension. A score is set to symbolize a minimum acceptable level of mastery. Students whose performance falls below that score are, hopefully, given the personal attention they need. And the cycle starts again as the teacher presents the next large chunk.

With few variations, this is the way subjects have been taught for centuries. And, by and large, the technique has been very effective in achieving its goal of educating large numbers of children to a minimum acceptable level of competence. A small percentage excel. A small percentage "under achieve." But the vast majority can be found within the bell of a classic distribution curve.

Since this is the system most of us passed through on our way to bigger and better things, we take it for granted and often fail to see it for the relatively crude scattershot approach that it really is. But in years past, there has been no choice. Now, however, it is possible to hand a computer a chunk of knowledge and program it to present it to students in small pieces. The computer presents a parcel of information, helps the student work with it, and then quizzes the student to test for comprehension. If the student demonstrates mastery, the computer moves on to present the next parcel of knowledge. If not, the computer will present the original parcel again, possibly in a different way.

Ideally, CAI enables the machine to act very much like a personal, human tutor. It thus has at least two qualities to recommend it from a teaching standpoint. First, it allows each student to learn at the pace best suited to his or her needs. If the student is having difficulty grasping certain concepts, as demonstrated by the results of the quizzes the computer administers, the machine can re-present the material. In those areas where the student learns quickly, the machine can move on immediately to introduce new material. In a conventional classroom, the overall pace of instruction cannot be slowed down or speeded up on an individual basis; consequently, the same student may be alternately frustrated or bored.

The second characteristic of CAI is the interaction it demands on the part of the student. There is a tendency to think of "interaction" as merely sitting at the computer and punching keys. Citing the popularity of video games as an example, CAI proponents often maintain that children are going to be more motivated to learn something with a computer than to learn the same thing reading a book. They are probably right, but punching keys is only the most superficial aspect.

What interaction really means is that the program encourages students to wrap their minds around a subject and to play an active role in the education process. So often in a conventional classroom students are forced to sit like rocks in a stream of information flowing from the teacher. Hopefully, they pick up something as it courses past them.

With a computer, in contrast, they are not only in control of the flow, but they must also take action to turn on the spigot. At its best, CAI can involve a student in seeking information, thinking about alternatives, and learning from mistakes made in the process of solving a problem. It's the difference between being lectured on how the pieces of a puzzle fit together and being handed the pieces and given a chance to assemble them yourself.

### The Most Important Quality

By their very nature, computers are ideally suited to subtly demand student interaction. As we all know, the machines will just sit there unless they are told what to do. In many ways this is a double-edged sword, for in addition to the positive aspects of demanding interaction, it also means that the student must *want* to make the thing work. If a CAI program doesn't motivate a student by presenting information in an interesting or intriguing way, it might as well not exist at all.

Clearly, there are many other factors to consider when buying educational software for your children—or for yourself—but the question of how well the program motivates a student must be at the top of the list. The difficulty is in determining whether a program is likely to provide the necessary motivation before you buy.

This is ultimately a subjective judgment since an approach that motivates one person may be of little interest to another. However, as a rule of thumb, it is a good idea to look at how extensively and imaginatively a program uses a computer's resources. For example, how does the program use color, graphics, and sound to make the experience of using it interesting? This is an admittedly superficial criterion, but since writing a program that takes full advantage of the computer's hardware requires more time, effort, and care than one that does not, it can serve as an indication that these virtues will be reflected in other aspects of the software as well.

*Content, Educational Theory, and Other Aspects*

The programs that make the most extensive and imaginative use of computer hardware to create excitement and provide rewards are video games. And whatever educational value their producers may claim, video games are not what most parents have in mind when shopping for educational software. A program may have overtones of a video game, but as with all educational software, the information it offers and the way that information is presented is crucial.

Unfortunately, this is the most difficult characteristic to judge. It requires expertise in education and a thorough exploration of the program. Since most software buyers are likely to have neither the training nor the time required to form an opinion on this basis, the only alternative is to rely first on the good name and reputation of the software producer and second, on the reviews of the program published in computer magazines.

It is by no means a foolproof criterion, but if a program has been produced by a firm with an extensive background in educational and textbook publishing, it is reasonable to assume that the software will present appropriate information using sound educational techniques. For example, software from these firms would probably not respond to an incorrect answer by flashing a big red $X$ on the screen and sounding a loud buzzer. Many educators would agree that such a response is tantamount to saying, "You dummy! That's the wrong answer. Now wake up!" A sounder, more productive response might politely indicate that the answer was incorrect and ask the child if he or she would like to try again.

As mentioned in Chapter 9, the key to software quality is money. The large educational publishers have the money to hire consultants and to submit their products to review boards and committees made up of professional educators before releasing them to the public. They also have a reputation and a standing in the industry to uphold.

Smaller firms have neither the money nor the reputation. But it would be a mistake not to consider their products as well since imagination and creativity tend to flourish more readily in a small company than in a large corporation. Here it is important to check the ads and company literature for indications of a professional background in education. And it is important to read the published reviews of the product, preferably reviews written by educators.

### Waiting for the "Seal"

There is a great need today for some kind of authoritative "seal of approval" that parents can use to guide them in their purchase of educational software. In the future, with more and more programs on the market, the need will be even more pressing. Consequently, it seems likely that one or more organizations will eventually establish a reliable, independent review process to judge the quality of individual programs.

Until that happens, however, you may want to consult with your children's teachers before buying software for your home computer. This will probably be possible only if your school system already uses personal computers. But since more and more systems are purchasing them, it may not be too difficult.

---

**SoftTip:** It may or may not be practical in your system, but educational software, the guidelines for buying it, and reviews of specific products could form the basis for a P.T.A. or other meeting. If enough people were interested, it might be worthwhile to ask a consultant, a qualified computer store manager, or some other outside authority to address the group and answer your questions.

---

### What Types of Programs?

The terminology of CAI software is still evolving. Thus, it is possible to encounter statements that "three broad categories can be distinguished: drill and practice, tutorial, and simulation." And it is possible to read that CAI "software divides generally into drill-and-practice/tutorials, simulations, and productivity tools." The terminology picture is further clouded by the refusal of most programs to fit neatly into any one category. How should a program designed to help students improve their S.A.T. scores be classified, for example? Is it a drill, a tutorial, a simulation, or all three?

Actually, thinking of CAI software in categories is not terribly helpful in any case. Far more important are the subjects the programs are designed to teach and the general approach each program uses to teach them. Arithmetic, fractions, geometry, vocabulary building for both English and foreign languages, speed reading, S.A.T. preparation, and chemistry are just some of the subjects available.

Depending upon the age group, many of these programs will be built around some kind of game: A child has to answer a certain number of questions correctly to get a rocket ship to blast off, a Mother Goose-like figure guides the child through puzzle-solving exercises, or the child has to guess the contents of a missing square or other figure. Even touch-typing programs, one of the most popular of all types of CAI software, use games and graphics to liven up the learning process.

More complex programs are designed to teach reasoning, analytical, and general learning skills and techniques. For example, the student might find that the program has set him or her up in the business of selling lemonade. As the program progresses, the student might purchase raw materials, spend money on advertising, face competition, and deal with business concepts while learning analytical and rational skills.

One of the most popular programs, "Snooper Troops" from Spinnaker Software (215 First Street, Cambridge, MA; $45), challenges players to discover "Who stole the dolphin?" Students must collect clues, make notes, place "telephone calls," and ask questions at various points in the program in an effort to solve the mystery. Many students find the program so captivating that they hardly realize that it is teaching them skills in organization, note taking, and deductive reasoning as they play.

*Logo and Turtle Graphics*

Other types of programs are designed to teach logic and reasoning through elementary computer programming. The most popular of these are undoubtedly the ones that use some version of a computer language called Logo. Developed at the Massachusetts consulting firm Bolt, Beranek and Newman some 15 years ago, the language bears the stamp of Seymour Papert, a highly respected educator and theoretician. As a programming language, Logo combines Papert's work with the ideas of Swiss psychologist Jean Piaget and artificial intelligence techniques developed with LISP, another computer language.

Educational programs can be written in Logo, but it is not the programs so much as the writing of them that is the main focus of software in this area. Logo is a simple, flexible language that is ideally suited to introducing children to computer programming and to teaching logical and rational skills.

As mentioned in Chapter 3, Logo is most often applied in "turtle graphics" or "turtle geometry." Using simple Logo program commands, children can cause a triangular "turtle" to draw the lines they specify on the screen. Designs can be saved and used to build up quite complex pictures, again with simple Logo commands. The turtle is central to the Logo concept of helping children understand computers because it provides an instant "effect" to the "cause" of a student's typed-in command. A Logo command to move the turtle "RIGHT 90" and the immediate results it produces are far more concrete and easy to understand than a BASIC statement like "$X = X + 1$."

---

**SoftTip:** For more information on Seymour Papert's seminal educational concepts, see:

*Mindstorms: Children, Computers, and Powerful Ideas*
by
Seymour Papert
Basic Books, 1980
$6.95

For more information on Logo, what it can do, and how you and your children can use it, see Dan Watt's excellent book:

*Learning with Logo*
by
Dan Watt
BYTE Books/McGraw-Hill, 1983
$14.95 (spiral bound)

---

*Caution: Different Versions are NOT the Same*
Programs that implement the Logo language ranging in price from $90 to about $200 are available for many major brands of computers. However, because of differences in hardware and other factors, there may be important differences among them. Graphic resolution, color, animation, music, and the other capabilities offered by a full implementation of Logo may be limited or nonexistent.

Logo, for example, includes powerful list processing features that may not be present in a version that provides only turtle graphics. Even the versions of Logo available for the same computer can differ in the features they offer. If you already own a computer, you may or may not have a choice. If you are buying a computer principally for Logo applications, the Apple II Plus and Apple IIe are considered to have the most complete implementations among eight-bit computers, while DR Logo from Digital Research for the IBM/PC may offer the fullest version in the 16-bit world.

## Locating and Buying Educational Software

Educational software can range in price from about $20 to about $70, and from a marketing standpoint there are two main categories. There is software for the home user and there is software for use in the schools. The latter is sometimes referred to as "courseware," though the distinction is often blurred. About the only feature that clearly distinguishes the two is that courseware sometimes has teacher lesson planning and record keeping features that the use-at-home software does not.

Educational software will eventually be sold in bookstores and mass merchandising outlets like Sears and K-Mart, but until that happens, it may be difficult to locate a copy of the program you are interested in. Computer stores typically stock more word processing, spreadsheet, and business-related programs than they do educational software. Consequently, you may find that the only educational programs available are the popular typing-tutor programs and one or two of the best sellers in the educational field.

Until this changes, you will have to rely on the reviews published in the various computer magazines instead of a hands-on demonstration, and you will probably have to order either directly from the software firm or from a mail order house. See the tips in Chapter 8 on using CompuServe and DIALOG's Knowledge Index to run down published software reviews and the suggestions on buying through the mail. If an ad in a computer magazine features a program that looks interesting, fill out the reader's service card or contact the firm directly and ask for a catalogue and more information.

## Final Words

Before "implementing" educational software in your household, there are at least two points to bear in mind. The first is the possible need for "rules" about using it. Like many adults, your child may be nearly addicted to *Zaxxon* or *Frogger*. If that's the case, the most thoughtfully designed CAI software in the world may not prevail. Thus, you may want to think about or at least be prepared for the need to institute a rule or two: "One hour of *Galaxy Math* before any *Cosmic Crusader.*" This is probably a plan you should hold in reserve since it has the unavoidable effect of drawing a distinction between the CAI program and "fun" programs. It is naturally preferable to give the child access to the educational program and hope he or she finds it interesting enough to "play with" on its own.

Second, while it is certainly a good idea to initially work with a child in using a program, it can be important to guard against spoiling the fun and the thrill of discovery. We are all children at heart, and some CAI software can tap that inner curiosity in an adult as well as in a youngster. It is definitely a good idea to run through a program yourself, since it can give you a clear idea of what your child is learning and help you help the child should difficulties arise. But it is far better to wait until the kids have gone to bed and so avoid spoiling their excitement.

Lastly, CAI software can teach both knowledge and skills, but of all the skills it is possible to teach, touch-typing may ultimately prove to be the most valuable. Naturally, you will have to wait until the child's hands and motor skills have grown sufficiently to make typing practical. But there is probably no other physical skill that so qualifies a child for life in the computer age.

Typing has always been a useful skill to have, but the advent of word processing software alone has increased its value by several orders of magnitude. Typing is no longer a matter of merely operating a mechanical device to produce term papers or earn extra money while in college. Thanks to word processing, today it is a means of expression, like the physical ability to form words when speaking a language. In the future, people who can't type, whether when creating text with word processing software or when "talking" to a computer from a keyboard, are likely to suffer from the same disadvantages that chronic stutterers suffer from when attempting human speech. Fortunately, there are many entertaining and effective CAI typing programs available, and there will certainly be more in the future.

## Software Buyer's Quick Reference Checklist

*Educational Software*

*Use of the Computer's Resources*

☐ In your opinion, how imaginatively and completely does the program use the computer's resources?

☐ Does it use a range of colors in its visual display?

☐ Do the graphics and screen displays strike you as both imaginative and easy to read or comprehend? Or are they flat and mundane?

☐ Does the program make use of sound, and if so, how many different sounds does it use? A "trumpet blast" and a variety of short musical pieces are likely to hold a child's interest more effectively than a simple beep.

☐ Does it use a voice synthesizer, if one is available for your system, and if so, how effectively?

☐ Does the program use a printer to let the child print out results and, if so, how easy is it for the child to use?

### Documentation and Instruction Manual

☐ Does the manual clearly specify the intended age group?

☐ How does the documentation "feel" to you? Is it well done or inadequate? Keeping in mind that the documentation will probably be addressed to you as a parent or to a teacher, does it tell you what you want to know about the software?

☐ Does the documentation clearly spell out the educational goals of the program: What will be taught, how it will be taught, how progress will be measured, etc.?

☐ Does it include examples? Does it inform you of what equipment you need? Does it include the credentials of the author of the software? Is there a trouble-shooting section to help you should your child run into problems?

☐ Does the manual include suggestions for the most effective way you as a parent can work with the child and help him or her benefit from the program?

☐ Does the manual address the topic of "Where do we go from here?" For example, does it suggest books or other materials for you and your child to use in exploring the topic further? Is the program part of a series of programmed instruction materials? Will other programs be issued to pick up where the current one leaves off?

### Ease of Use

☐ Once the disk has been booted or the cartridge has been inserted, can the child use the program immediately, without any instruction?

☐ Can you participate in a demonstration, shut the machine off, and have the child do it all alone?

☐ What happens if you or the child hit a wrong key? How does the program respond? It probably should not respond at all since the programmer should have deactivated all but the selected keys.

*Effectiveness*

☐ One way to test how effective a program is likely to be is to deliberately enter the incorrect answer several times in a row. Generally, the less sophisticated programs will slavishly respond the same way, constantly displaying and redisplaying the same screen.

More effective programs have a "branching" feature built into them. After a certain number of incorrect responses to the same question on the same screen, they will respond by branching out and presenting a new approach to the same material, like a tutor taking another tack.

*Flexibility*

☐ Does the program offer different levels of difficulty? And as a parent, can you set those levels as most appropriate to your child's needs?

☐ Can you determine the order in which information will be presented? You may find this feature helpful in matching the order in which the subject is being taught in the child's school.

☐ Is there a provision for the program to record the child's progress and save it as a report to be printed out and gone over by you at a later time?

# ...25...

# How to Buy Computer Game Programs

According to a recent Gallup poll, game playing is by far the most popular home computer "application." With more than 50% of all home computer owners reporting that they use their machines in this way, it's clear that entertainment software has been a driving force in introducing the personal computer to the American family. Game-playing software has also been used by savvy businesses as a means of introducing the machines to their employees and aiding them in overcoming "computerphobia."

The most important characteristic about any game, however, is that the decision of whether it is worth the $20 to $50 you will probably have to pay is largely subjective. Either you like it (or think you might like it) or you don't. Thus, there is really only one rule to follow when buying entertainment software: *Make sure you see a live demonstration before you buy.*

At the risk of overstating the obvious, this is important for a number of reasons, the first of which is the enticing four-color artwork that graces the magazine ads and the product packaging. It's wonderful to see an X-wing fighter or some similar craft soaring through outer space, all guns ablaze. The lavishly and lovingly painted dragons, wizards, and lethally armed robots that stalk you through the pages of a computer magazine can cast a spell of anticipation. But the spell can be quickly broken when, upon first booting the program, you find nothing but a very earthbound grid and some colored blotches on your screen.

In addition, many computer games are derived from games that first became popular in the video arcades and purport to provide "arcade action." A recent edition of the "Hot List" published by Softsel, the nation's largest software distributor, listed *Zaxxon* and *Frogger* as the two most popular computer games. The Apple, Atari, Commodore, and IBM versions were introduced only after each game had garnered an important share of the $5 billion worth of quarters the nation's "arcadians" spend each year.

Unfortunately, what you see at the arcade may not be what you get on your home computer. Few home computers have the graphics capabilities or the often prodigious quantities of internal memory found in arcade machines. And, in most cases, the clock speed that determines how fast a microchip can handle information is usually slower for a computer's CPU than for the CPU used by an arcade machine.

All of which means that if you are seeking an "arcade quality experience" from your personal computer, you may be in for a disappointment. Then again, you may not. Some computers do an admirable job of duplicating the graphics, speed, sound, and other characteristics of a quarter-a-pop arcade game. That's why the only way to tell is to actually see what the game looks like and how it plays in a live demo.

## Basics: Computer Games

It is probably fair to say that if you have not yet used your computer to play a game of some sort, you're in for an enjoyable experience. It depends upon what you're interested in, but if you are among the *other* 50% of home computer owners who do not use their machines for fun, you should know that computer games are not limited to the hand-eye coordination activities of an arcade game.

Some display nothing but text on the screen: "A crystal bridge now spans the fissure . . . There are diamonds here." Yet these can be so engrossing that you can completely forget about time for an hour . . . or two . . . or five. Others combine both text and graphic pictures or maps to show you your location and surroundings. And still others present you with graphic figures that move according to your typed instructions.

Since it is impossible to tell from the name of the game what type it is, you will have to rely on the ads and reviews in deciding which games you may be interested in. It may be helpful, however, to have an idea of the general categories of computer games that are available. The emphasis should be on the word "general," since in many cases a game could qualify for more than one classification.

*Arcade Style Games*

These are either home computer versions of trademarked arcade games or frank imitations. (At least one game producer advertises its products as being "Like *Centipede* . . ." or "Like *Pac-Man* . . ."). There are also arcade-style games that have no arcade equivalent. In most cases, games in this category either require or play better with a joystick.

Since joysticks and any plug-in cards required to interface them with your computer represent an additional expense, you may want to consider carefully before you commit yourself to this kind of software. Where joysticks are not used, the figures on the screen can be controlled by pressing keys on your keyboard. Some programs will let you decide which keys will do what. Others do not give you this option. In addition, since sound is such an important part of the arcade game experience, the game will definitely be less enjoyable if your computer does not have built-in speakers. If you use a television set as your display, the game may generate sound the way an *Atari* or *Coleco* unit does.

### Computer Versions of Traditional Games

Chess was one of the first games ever played with/on a computer, and many personal computer versions are available. There are also computer versions of bridge, blackjack, craps, solitaire, cribbage, gin rummy, and even pool, as well as football, golf, baseball, shuffleboard, and *Monopoly*. The game field is vast, but if you have a favorite conventional game, you can probably find a computer version of it without too much trouble. With the possible exception of chess, the experience of playing any game in this category is considerably enhanced when you use either a color television or a color monitor.

### Simulations

The most popular experience to simulate via a computer is that of sitting in the cockpit of an airplane. Although they vary in sophistication, some programs can divide the lower portion of your screen into an airplane instrument panel, complete with independently turning altimeters, air speed indicators, and other gauges. The top half of your screen may be transformed into two or more windows showing the scenery as it passes.

All of the readings and scenery react to your commands just as they would in a real plane. A number of challenges are presented by such programs. You may have to land your plane at a particular airport. You may have to fly the plane using the instruments alone. Or you may find yourself flying a Spitfire in pursuit of a Messerschmidt 109 during World War II.

## Strategy Games

Games in this general category reward the player for problem solving, thought, and imagination. These games are usually played by typing in verbal commands or responses from the keyboard, though the visual elements may differ. Some display only text. Some display text and static graphic pictures. And some constantly display a scrolling map or other illustration with a graphic character to represent your current position and surroundings. They are divided here by general subject matter.

### Fantasy and Adventure Games

*Adventure* was probably the first game in this category, and it has sold so many copies over the years that it has become a genuine classic. Originally developed at M.I.T. in the days before the personal computer revolution, it was passed around via an *Adventure* underground for several years before the commercial version appeared. As in all such games, you as the player are presented with a challenge or a quest to be pursued in a fantasy realm. In the case of *Adventure*, your goal is to explore the Colossal Cave, discover all of the treasure there, and successfully bring it to the surface.

Many challenges face you, including dealing with dwarves, greedy trolls, dragons, and even a sneaky pirate who seems to appear to beset you whenever you've collected a goodly portion of diamonds, gold coin, and other riches. Perhaps the greatest challenge of all is that, in an instance where deliberately vague documentation is part of the plan, the manual gives you only the scantiest notion of what commands the program will accept. It is up to you to figure things out for yourself.

---

**SoftTip:** Many *Adventure* players keep elaborate maps of the portions of the Colossal Cave they have discovered. However, unless you're a real fanatic, you might find that a commercially produced map makes the game more fun to play. A map is available from CompuServe Information Service. It provides an excellent guide without revealing any of the secrets of the Cave. The map is black and white, measures 17 × 25 inches, and sells for $2.95, plus shipping. Contact:

          CompuServe Information Service
          5000 Arlington Centre Boulevard
          Columbus, OH 43220

---

Most games in this category play this way. The thrill of discovery is an important part of the fun. Some can go on for months. And some, like *Zork*, have three successive levels, each purchased separately. Fortunately, virtually all such games allow you to record your current position so that you can get some sleep and take up the quest again at another time.

*Historical and "Real Life"*

Similar games will put you at the head of a multinational corporation and present you with a competitive challenge to your market share or some other business. With others, you can become a commodities trader and pit your skills against a computer-created market.

In a somewhat different area are historical or possible future strategy games. You might be placed in the middle of a Soviet-NATO confrontation in the North Atlantic. You might have an opportunity to fight Napoleon's campaigns of 1813 and 1815. Or you might be in charge of the pursuit of the *Bismark's* sister ship, the *Graf Spee*.

## Critical Points

As mentioned, for arcade style games the critical factor for most people is how closely their graphics and speed resemble a real arcade game. For simulations, the more elaborate and authentic the simulation, the better. With a strategy game, much will depend on the adventure, situation, or role the game places you in and whether you find it appealing.

Perhaps the most critical point regarding strategy games is the option of saving your current position before you end a game-playing session. It doesn't make much sense to freeze an airplane in mid-air in a simulation game, but strategy games tend to be linear. If you have labored for two hours to escape from Castle Wolfenstein without being gunned down by the Nazi guards, you don't want to have to retrace your steps the next time you play. Virtually every game of this type offers a "save" feature, but it may not hurt to check. You might also want to ask your retailer whether there is a club dedicated to playing a particular game in your area, or whether there is a national association, complete with regular conventions and newsletters.

Just as individuals who use their machines for nothing but game playing may be cheating themselves out of many other interesting and useful computer-based applications, people who use their machines for nothing but "worthwhile" tasks may be losing out on much of the fun a personal computer can provide. If you are one of the folks in the latter class, you owe it to yourself at least to look into what's available. The variety is so great and the field is so rich, that you are virtually certain to find something you'll enjoy.

## Software Buyer's Quick Reference Checklist

☐ Will the game require you to buy any additional hardware? Will adding more RAM improve the quality of play?

☐ If planning to use your computer primarily to play games, you may find that a home video game unit will be cheaper than buying additional hardware. Since such units are designed for game playing, they may also perform better.

☐ You might also think about where you want to have your computer in the house and whether the same location is equally well suited for family game playing and other computer activities.

☐ What do the reviewers say? Games are like novels and movies, and a review is often a matter of personal opinion. Consequently, you may want to try to read at least two different reviews of the game.

☐ Can two or more people play the game? Can you save your scores? Are there several user-selectable levels of difficulty?

☐ *For an arcade style game, a live demonstration is an absolute must.*

☐ How elaborate and authentic is the simulation game? Is it highly detailed, or superficial?

☐ Does the strategy game sound challenging? Does it produce a different game each time you play, or is it predictable? Predictability may not be a bad point, particularly if you've spent a considerable amount of time mapping a maze on some other part of the game.

☐ Can you save your position in the game? Does the game offer an option to let you print out your commands and the computer's responses?

# Appendix A
## Software Guides and Sources

Sometimes it seems as though there are almost as many guides and catalogues as there are personal computer programs. And you can bet there will be several times as many tomorrow. The following list contains information on some of the guides and source books you might want to consider in developing the list of "possibles" suggested in Chapter 8 as a first step to buying any personal computer program.

Some of them are quite affordable, but others are clearly aimed at and priced for the corporate or reference library market. You may find these at your local library, in your corporate library, or in your firm's data processing department. Increasingly, you will find catalogues and guides in the magazine section of your bookstore, though some may still be available only through the mail. You might also check with members of your users group to see if anyone has a catalogue you could borrow. Also, don't forget to check the computer section of your bookseller's shelves for volumes like *The Addison-Wesley Book of Apple Software* (annual; $19.95. Also available in IBM and Atari editions.) Since more computer stores are now carrying books and magazines, you might check there as well.

*What to Expect*

Some catalogues include reviews of a few selected programs, but many offer little more than the name of the program, the hardware and operating system required, and the address of the software house. If there is any descriptive information, it is not uncommon for it to have been written by the marketing or public relations department of the software company itself. In other words, many catalogue listings are only a hair's breadth away from advertising. There is nothing wrong with that. Indeed, with so many programs to consider, reviewing and evaluating each one individually would be a monumental task. It's just important to remember that what you are reading may have come straight from the software house and thus will not be an objective evaluation of the product.

Keeping a catalogue current and making it comprehensive is an equally difficult task. So difficult that even the most expensive catalogues do not contain information on all the programs available for a certain application. Sometimes even programs issued by major software houses are left out. This is not necessarily the fault of the publisher. Many catalogues solicit information from software houses, and if the firms do not respond or respond too late, their products cannot be included.

In addition, no catalogue can be 100% up to date. Programs are simply being issued too fast for that to be possible. This is especially important to remember when looking at a listing that is in a catalogue. The program it refers to may have been updated or improved since the publication went to press and those improvements may be just the features you are looking for.

*How to Choose a Catalogue*

If you decide to buy a catalogue through the mail, there will probably be no way to examine it beforehand. But if you buy one at a book or computer store, the first criterion should be how easily you can locate the information you seek. How good is the index? Is the publication laid out so that you can tell where one category ends and the next one begins? A publication that contains several thousand program listings will be very difficult to use without an excellent index.

In fact, the most useful catalogues have several indices. You may be able to locate a program by its name, the name of the software house, by the operating system it requires, by the brand of computer(s) it runs on, and, of course, by the particular application you are interested in.

Next, check the number of programs listed for your computer and your target application. How many word processing programs are listed for the TRS-80 Model 4? How many accounting packages for DEC computers? How many games or educational programs for your Texas Instruments machine?

*How to Use a Catalogue*

Finally, look at the listings themselves. The main question should be, Do the listings give me enough information to decide whether I should pursue the product further or cross it off my list? You need to know what computer and operating system a program requires and whether you will have to buy any additional equipment (like a graphics card, a color monitor, a plotter, a modem, etc.). You also need some indication of price. Naturally, some description of the program's features would also be helpful—though it may not be essential because you will probably not want to buy a program solely on the basis of what you read in a catalogue. In many cases, you will need more information than even the most complete catalogues can give you. Consequently, the best way to use a catalogue is as a source of places to contact for more information and as an aid in locating reviews of particular products.

To get the most complete and up-to-date information on a given program, you will probably want to contact the software house directly. If a toll-free number is given, give them a call and ask for the latest information on the program you are interested in. If there is no free phone number, or if you have a number of places to contact, consider typing up a form letter and sending out customized photocopies. (Dear Sir: Please send me the latest information on the program called ———. I have a Commodore 64 and feel that your product may be just what I need.)

---

**SoftTip:** Sending a letter as suggested above is one way to identify promising companies (even if you have never heard of them before) while winnowing out the software houses you may not want to deal with. If you get no response, or if the response is uninformative and poorly done, it may be an indication that the firm's products also fit that description.

---

## Software Guides and Sources

*Commodore Software Encyclopedia*
Howard W. Sams & Company, Inc.
4300 West 62nd Street
Indianapolis, IN 46268
(317) 298-5400

Price: $9.95.

This book is also available at your book store, from Commodore Business Machines (681 Moor Road, King of Prussia, PA 19406), or directly from the publisher. If you are a CompuServe subscriber, you may also order the book online by accessing the computer book section Howard Sams & Company offers through the system.

The encyclopedia contains 406 pages and includes 13 categories of software for PET, CBM, VIC-20, and SuperPET computers. Firmware and hardware listings are also included, as are programs originating in Europe and Canada (Commodore has extensive overseas and non-U.S. operations.) More than 1,000 entries in all, including name, description, required hardware, vendor's address, retail price, etc.

*Datapro Directory of Microcomputer Software*
Datapro Research Corporation
1805 Underwood Blvd.
Delran, NJ 08075
(800) 257-9406
(609) 764-0100, in New Jersey

Price: $420 for annual subscription; extensive updates issued monthly.

This is one of the most extensive—and expensive—directories available. Though clearly not suited for individuals, it is an ideal publication for a library or a corporate data processing department. There are over 52 tabbed software categories (accounting, legal, transportation, sales and distribution, plus all of the categories you would expect), and each begins with a "contents" section that includes many subcategories.

The Word Processing contents page, for example, tells you where to look for programs for "automated letter preparation," "compositional typesetting," "direct mail systems," and other applications, as well as straight word processing. Product listings include the required computer and operating system, hardware requirements, and other key points, as well as 200 to 300 word descriptions supplied by the software house.

There are also master indices organized by product name, by application, and by the name of the software house (vendor). Although prices are given in each program entry, there is also a master price list guide that includes the product name and price. There is a "Vendor Profile" section that includes the names of the software companies, the names of the president and marketing director, number of employees, and a paragraph citing the firm's major products.

There is a User Rating section that summarizes the results of Datapro surveys on major software products. There is a Feature Reports section containing in-depth articles (e.g., "Software Concepts: Programs and Languages").

Each month, subscribers receive packets containing 50 to 100 or more pages of updated information designed to supplement or replace pages already in the two manuals. There is also a monthly newsletter that reports on new product announcements and industry trends.

Finally, if you cannot find the information you seek in the publication, Datapro includes "Inquiry Service" privileges with each subscription. You may contact the firm by phone, mail, or Telex to ask for more technical information on a product, for information on a product that has not yet been included in the directory, and to seek advice on "your specific microcomputer software-related problems that may go beyond our published software analysis."

*The Infopro Directory*
Infopro, Inc.
P.O. Box 22
Bensalem, PA 19020
(215) 750-1023

"The Directory of Independent IBM Personal Computer Hardware and Software." This three-ring notebook measures 8½″ × 5½″ and contains 145 pages of information on hardware and software for the IBM/PC. In addition to information on required operating system and hardware, the question, "Can backup copies be made?" is included in every software product listing. Many of the entries include "review/comment" sections written by Infopro staff to give you an idea of what the program is, does, and is like to use.

If you need more information on a particular program or if you need information on something not found in the directory, you may call the above number. Infopro will do its best to locate the information you seek. Telephone consultation is generally free, though there may be a slight charge for photocopying and mailing of additional materials.

*InfoWorld Report Card*
375 Cochituate Road
Box 837
Framingham, MA 01701-9987
(800) 343-5730
(617) 879-0700, in Mass., call collect

Price: On newsstands at $3.95; subscribers to *InfoWorld* magazine receive as part of their subscription. One year subscription is $31 (52 issues).

This publication consists of reprints of hardware and software reviews that originally appeared in the weekly *InfoWorld* magazine.

*LIST*
Redgate Publishing Company
3407 Ocean Drive
Vero Beach, FL 32960
(305) 231-6904

Price: $23.10 for 12 issue subscription; includes two "locator" publications (see below). $3.50 for single copy of *LIST* magazine. $4.50 for each semiannual "locator."

Redgate Publishing is an affiliate of E.F. Hutton. First issued in the spring of 1983, *LIST* was originally to be published quarterly; however, it very quickly went to a monthly schedule. Two publications are available. Each issue of the monthly magazine contains articles on particular software applications and a version of the firm's trademarked "LIST Software Locator" that has been focused on the programs dealing with those applications. *LIST* accepts advertising.

The second publication is a comprehensive LIST Software Locator containing 4,500 or more listings for programs of all types. It is issued in January and July and costs $4.50 if you buy it on the newsstands. Subscribers to *LIST* magazine automatically receive both "Locators" as part of their subscription.

*1983 Microcomputer Market Place*
Dekotek, Inc.
2248 Broadway
New York, NY 10024
(212) 799-6602

Price: $75, plus $3.25 for postage and handling; 15-day money-back guarantee. Quantity discounts are available.

This is intended to be a "super sourcebook" to the microcomputer industry. Consequently, it covers both hardware and software. There are entries for software vendors, distributors, magazines and newsletters, consultants, associations, computer manufacturers, peripheral equipment manufacturers, etc. There are "13 separate easy-to-use index sections, which allow you to locate software for specific hardware needs and by application area, and a separate index for microcomputer supplies."

*Online Micro-Software Guide and Directory*
Dept. S/D
Online, Inc.
11 Tannery Lane
Weston, CT 06883
(203) 227-8466

Price: $40; send check or call and charge to major credit card. A 25% discount is given for orders of four or more copies.

Created by the publishers of *Online* magazine, a periodical dealing with online information retrieval, this spiral-bound directory contains listings of some 736 personal computer programs. Each entry includes the name, address, phone number, and person to contact at the software house; the name of the product and its current version; the list price; the application; the "operating environment" (required hardware, operating system, hard and soft disk support, etc.); a two-to-three-sentence summary of the documentation provided; a description of the program; and "other software used with system." There is a final category called "where purchased" to indicate whether you are likely to find the program at a computer store or whether you should contact the vendor directly.

There are indices by program name, by vendor, and by application. There is also a bibliography of articles and books likely to be of interest to software buyers, a glossary, and a collection of helpful essays by various authorities.

Regular annual updates are planned.


*The PC Clearinghouse Software Directory*
PC Clearinghouse, Inc.
11781 Lee-Jackson Highway
Fairfax, VA 22033
(800) 368-4422
(800) 552-4422, in Virginia

Price: $29.95 (plus $2.50 postage and handling if ordered through the mail). Major credit cards; 15-day money-back guarantee. Also available in book and computer stores.

This is a publication of PC Telemart, and it was first issued in 1980 as the *Software Vendor Directory*. It contains over 21,000 software product listings, including 488 word processing packages, 382 database management programs, 45 foreign language programs, and 7,143 general business programs.

Listings are cross-referenced by hardware, operating systems, application, price, and microprocessor. Entries include system name and compatible hardware, as well as the name, address, and phone number of the vendor. Billed by the firm as "the yellow pages to the world of microcomputers," this publication is meant to be used exactly that way: as a directory of whom to contact for more information.

*Personal Software Magazine*
P.O. Box 2919
Boulder, CO 80321

Price: $17.97/year (charter subscription rate) for 12 monthly issues; $2.50, single copy newsstand price.

This is a collection of software reviews culled from the pages of *Personal Computing* magazine. Each issue will include 25 of "the best software packages of all the new personal software releases." Advertising for this publication indicates that programs will be reviewed in depth including sample on screen displays, samples of the documentation, and "what the software is like to use."

*Smartware® Personal Computer Catalogue*
121 Second Street
San Francisco, CA 94105
(800) 762-7892
(415) 974-5297

Price: Free.

This is an exceptionally fine catalogue from a firm that specializes in mail order sales to businesses. It has a great deal to offer individual users as well. Smartware has been in business since 1978, and unlike many mail order firms, its publications do not overwhelm you with scads of programs for every application. Instead, Smartware is selective. To be included in its catalogue each program must meet the firm's standards for flexibility and reliability. It must have a good track record in the field, and user reports and evaluations are carefully considered. Many of the products are tested by Smartware staff before being included in the catalogue.

Product descriptions are informative and generally longer than those found in most other catalogues. They appear to have been written by the company and not by the software vendor. The catalogue layout is attractive and easy to use.

Perhaps the only drawback is that the prices are not heavily discounted, but there are a number of points to sweeten the deal. First, there is a technical support hot line. Second, there is a volume purchase plan. The more you buy, the lower your price on future purchases. Smartware even suggests that firms use this plan to benefit both themselves and employees interested in acquiring software for their personal systems.

And most unusual of all: "Every one of our products is fully guaranteed to meet your expectations as superior performers. If you are not totally satisfied with our product within 15 days, contact us for a proper authorization to return all or part of your order." In other words, "send the software back in new condition . . . and we'll issue a credit or refund."

*The Software Catalogue*
Elsevier Science Publishing Co.
52 Vanderbilt Avenue
New York, NY 10017
(800) 223-2115, 9 AM-9PM, EST
(212) 867-9040, in New York, 9 AM-5PM, EST

Price: Two editions yearly, $69 each; updates to each edition available for $15.

This publication supersedes *The International Software Directory* formerly published by Imprint Software, Ltd. It's available in two versions, one for microcomputers ($69; about 800 pages) and one for minicomputers ($95; about 560 pages). If you have a personal computer, you will naturally want to specify the "microcomputer" version.

The book is published twice a year (spring and fall), and updates are issued between publication dates. The updates for the microcomputer edition are available for $15. If you or your organization were to buy the spring and fall editions and both updates, the total cost would come to $168, but the firm offers a 15% discount bringing the total down to $142.50 if you place a standing order.

Each edition of *The Software Catalogue* includes more than 10,000 software packages, cross-referenced by type of computer, application, operating system, keywords, vendor, type of microprocessor chip (6502, 8088, etc.), programming language, name of software product, and general subject. The new International Standard Program Numbers (ISPN) designations similar to those long used for books (ISBN) are also used.

If your computer is equipped for telephone communications, you can search this publication electronically via DIALOG or The Knowledge Index. See Chapter 8 for samples and details.

*Software in Print*
Technique Learning
40 Cedar Street
Dobbs Ferry, NY 10522
(914) 693-8100

This publication is intended to be the software equivalent of R. R. Bowker's *Books in Print* series. Technique Learning hopes to introduce a new industry-wide software registration and identification system under which each program would be assigned a Universal Software Market Identifier (USMI) number. Like the universal product codes you see on most grocery products, a USMI number would identify the software vendor, the application, the hardware required, and other points regarding each program.

If it succeeds, this system could make it much easier both to catalogue and to find individual programs. If the firm is successful in establishing this code, it hopes to publish a *USMI Market Directory* in addition to *Software in Print*.

*The Software Source*
Software Source, Inc.
2701 CW 15th Street–Suite 109
Plano, TX 75075
(800) 621-5199
(800) 972-5855, in Illinois

Price: $26.95. Updates included; major credit cards accepted.

*The Software Source* offers what may be characterized as a "major league Datapro-like" approach at a price the individual user can afford. (See the Datapro listing in this appendix.) Consumers receive a three-ring notebook containing over 400 pages divided into 16 or more tabbed sections for such categories as "agriculture," "professional," "database," "educational," "games," "graphics," etc. Updates and additional information are issued periodically and are intended to be placed in the notebook.

Each page consists of three columns. On the left is the name of the product; in the middle are several paragraphs of description; and on the right are the names of the computers the program will run on. Although undoubtedly derived from product literature, the descriptive information for each program appears to have been written by *The Software Source* and not by the software vendors. Though not evaluative, this gives the listings more focus and uniformity than might otherwise be the case.

There is an index by program name and one by software house listing those of its products included in the directory. Each program is given a *Software Source* number, and the number is used to locate the price in a separate section.

The price section provides both the suggested list price and the discounted *Software Source* price. You can order any product in the catalogue by mail or by phone. The firm will also do its best to obtain any program not found in the catalogue at a discount for you.

*Software Supermarket*
2 Disc Drive
P.O. Box 4004
Sidney, OH 45365
(513) 498-2111

Published by Amos Press, Inc., a firm that also produces *Coin World*, *Stamp World*, and other magazines, *Software Supermarket* is designed to provide the average software consumer with expert reviews and advice written in a distinctly user friendly style. Software reviews present the manufacturer's claims first ("what the program is supposed to do"), followed by the reviewer's evaluation of how closely the product's performance matches those claims. In addition to approximately a dozen software reviews, each monthly issue includes feature articles on topics like computers and education, self-improvement, sports, fitness, hobbies, etc.

As the publisher points out, *Software Supermarket* is aimed at people with a moderate level of experience but "who have little interest in writing their own programs and are more interested in knowing about the practical applications they can expect from their computers than in the RAMS and ROMS of their hardware or the PEEKS and POKES of their software.

*The Whole Earth Software Catalog*
Doubleday & Company, Inc.
245 Park Avenue
New York, NY 10167
(212) 953-4561

Conceived by Stewart Brand, the creator of the acclaimed *Whole Earth Catalog*, edited by Art Kleiner, and written by many of the country's leading computer writers and software reviewers, this publication promises to become a milestone of computer books. As David Bunnell, publisher of *PC World*, has said: "It's tremendously good for the industry. *The Whole Earth Catalog* was *the* tool book of the sixties. [Stewart Brand] can make the personal computer *the* tool of the eighties."

Reviews are informal, direct, and personal. They are written from the perspective of what a particular program can do for you, how it can change your life. Also of interest, according to Mr. Kleiner, is how the programs will change "the way you work, the way you think, the way you spend time, the way you create, and the way you perceive and affect reality."

The catalog will be issued each year, but there will also be a *Whole Earth Software Review*. This will be published quarterly and will carry no advertising.

# Appendix B
# Magazines and Newsletters You May Not Have Heard Of

Without good magazines to publish software reviews and other important information, the task of picking the program would be considerably more difficult. Most major computer magazines will be available on newsstands and at your book or computer store. But there are small magazines that do not receive wide distribution, and many newsletters that you're likely to hear about only if you are on the right mailing list.

These too contain a wealth of product reviews, tips for using your computer and software, names and addresses to contact, and other hard-to-find information. The following list contains many of them, but there are undoubtedly many more. If you have found any to be particularly useful or if you know of any new publications that seem promising, please feel free to contact the author at the address given at the back of this book.

Many of the publications listed below welcome subscribers from Canada, Mexico, Europe, and other countries. However, rates are naturally higher, and most publishers stipulate payment in U.S. dollars. Some offer discounts for subscriptions of more than a single year, regardless of where you live. And most will sell you a sample issue to give you a better idea of whether you want to subscribe or not. Small publications do come and go, and as always, subscription prices are subject to change.

### General Computing Magazines and Newsletters

"AdaData"
International Resource Development, Inc.
30 High Street
Norwalk, CT 06851
(203) 866-6914

559

Annual subscription: $185 (12 issues).

A newsletter. Carries no advertising. Designed to provide programmers and firms interested in the Ada language with up-to-date information on developments concerning Ada, the Department of Defense, software products, etc.


"Baron's MicroComputing Reports"
P.O. Box 695
New York, NY 10956

Annual subscription (12 issues): $40.


A newsletter. Carries no advertising. Emphasizes techniques for using software effectively. Issues are customized to your brand of computer. (No connection with Dow Jones & Company, publisher of *Barron's*.)


"Classroom Computer News"
Box 266
Cambridge, MA 02138

Frequency: Bimonthly. Computers in education.


"Computer Consultant"
Battery Lane Publications
P.O. Box 30214
Bethesda, MD 20814
CompuServe: 70001,655


Annual subscription: $48 (10 issues).

For the independent computer professional: consultants, contract programmers, freelance software authors, etc.


"Computer Farming Newsletter"
P.O. Box 22642
Memphis, TN 38122
CompuServe: 71535,1522

Annual subscription: $33 (12 issues).

For farmers who use personal computers; sponsors users group. (It is also available electronically via the NewsNet system. See Appendix C.)

*Computer Gaming World*
1919 E. Sycamore #203
Anaheim, CA 92805

Annual subscription: $11 (six issues)

Features software reviews, articles, ads for computer games.

*Computer Graphics World*
A PennWell Publication
P.O. Box 122
Tulsa, OK 74101

Annual subscription (12 issues): $28.

Hardware, software, articles, etc., of interest to personal computer-produced business graphics.

*Computer Shopper*
P.O. Box F
Titusville, FL 32780
(305) 269-3211

Six-month subscription: $6; annual subscription (12 issues): $10.

Articles, reviews, and classified ads for personal computer hardware and software. A rich source of information, tips, used hardware, etc.

*DP Directory*
P.O. Box 562
Bloomfield, CT 06002

Annual subscription: $48 (12 issues).

Publishes the tables of contents of more than 100 computer-related periodicals each month.

*Dr. Dobbs Journal of Computer Calisthenics & Orthodontia*
People's Computer Company
Box E
Menlo Park, CA 94025

Annual subscription: $21 (12 issues).

Programming and technical tips for the advanced user.

"Lifelines"
Lifeboat Associates
1651 Third Avenue
New York, NY 10028
(212) 722-1700

Mainly information on CP/M and related software.

"Microcomputer Software Letter"
610 Fifth Avenue, Suite 706
New York, NY 10020
(212) 581-7389
(800) 526-0359, ext. 123
(800) 932-0878, ext. 123, in New Jersey

Annual subscription: $166 (12 issues).

Quick and to-the-point summaries of new-product announcements and other items of interest to the micro-owning business person. Each issue includes five or more reviews and summaries of major applications programs. The newsletter carries advertising and pulls no punches. If the editor (Robert L. Perry) and staff do not feel a program measures up, they will tell you and tell you why.

"Micro Moonlighter Newsletter"
2115 Bernard Avenue
Nashville, TN 37212

Annual subscription: $25 (12 issues).

Tips, advice, experiences, etc., for programmers interested in turning a profit on their skills. (Also available electronically via the NewsNet system. See Appendix C.)

*Microsystems*
CN 1897
Morristown, NJ 07960

Annual subscription: $25 (12 issues).

"*Not* for beginners or game players . . . the only advanced journal written for sophisticated programmers and operating system users."

"Pascal Market News"
P.O. Box 5314
Mt. Carmel, CT 06518

Annual subscription: $24 (six issues).

*PC News Watch*
Hyatt Research Corporation
P.O. Box 662
Andover, MA 10810

Annual subscription: $185 (12 issues).

"Emphasis is placed on . . . professional use of personal computers." Provides headlines and paragraph summaries of articles appearing in major computer magazines, classified by topic. Includes facts and enough information to let you know whether you want to locate and read the whole article.

*Recreational Computing*
People's Computer Company
P.O. Box E
Menlo Park, CA 94025

Annual subscription: $12 (six issues).

Home learning and entertainment with computers, from the publishers of "Dr. Dobbs."

*SoftSide*
6 South Street
Milford, NH 03055
(603) 673-0585

Annual subscription: $30 (12 issues).

Heavy emphasis on software reviews and "how-to's" for IBM/PC, TRS-80, Atari, and Apple. (Monthly collections of disk or cassette programs for various computers also available.)

"Software Arts Technical Notes" (SATN)
Software Arts
P.O. Box 100
Newton, MA 02162

Annual subscription: $30 (six issues).

Newsletter from the creators of VisiCalc for users of that program. Tips, applications, problem-solving, etc.


TK! SATN
Software Arts
P.O. Box 100
Newton, MA 02162

Same kind of newsletter as SATN, but devoted to users of the firm's TK! Solver program.


## Apple, Atari, Commodore, and Other 6502-Based Systems

"Ad Astar"
c/o Jack McKirgan II
4749 State Route 207 NE
Washington CH, OH 43160

"The Journal of the Atari Microcomputer Net." Amateur radio operators users' groups tap into the on-air Atari users' groups; questions, tips, conferences, etc.

Jack McKirgan's call sign: WD8BNG. For information on local Atari nets, frequencies, times, etc., contact him at the address given above, or call (614) 869-3597.


"Apple Orchard"
P.O. Box 2227
Seattle, WA 94017


"Applesauce"
20013 Princeton Avenue
Carson, CA 90746
(213) 637-8917

"The Apple Shoppe"
P.O. Box 701
Placentia, CA 92670

## Radio Shack Computers (TRS-80, Color Computer, etc.)

*The Alternate Source*
704 North Pennsylvania Avenue
Lansing, MI 48906

*Basic Computing*
The TRS-80 User Journal
5615 West Cermak Road
Cicero, IL 60650

Annual subscription: $19.97 (13 issues).

Founded in 1978 as "80-U.S. Journal," this publication changed its name in 1983. "An international magazine covering all models and aspects of the TRS-80 microcomputers."

"CHICATRUG News"
EBG Associates
203 North Wabash
Chicago, IL 60601

Annual subscription: $12.

This is the newsletter of the Chicago TRS-80 users' group.

"Color Computer News"
REMarkable Software
P.O. Box 1192
Muskegon, MI 49443

Annual subscription: $9 (six issues).

Programs, articles, tips, software exchange, etc., for the Radio Shack Color Computer and the users who own it.

"Computronics"
50 North Pascack Road
Spring Valley, NY 10977
(800) 431-2818

Annual subscription: $24.


"The Rainbow"
5803 Timber Ridge Drive
Prospect, KY 40059

Annual subscription: $12 (12 issues).

For the Radio Shack Color Computer.


TCUG Newsletter
P.O. Box 2826
Fairfax, VA 22031
(703) 978-8393
BBS Number: (703) 960-2056

This is the newsletter of the Washington, D.C. TRS-80 users' group. Articles of general interest to TRS-80 owners.

## IBM Personal Computer

IBM/PC
REFERENCE Magazine
P.O. Box 100
Milford, NH 03055

Annual subscription: $18 (6 issues).

"The business journal for IBM Personal Computing."


"IPCO INFO"
IPCO, Inc.
P.O. Box 10426
Pittsburgh, PA 15234
CompuServe: 71545,467

Annual subscription: $25 (six issues).

IPCO stands for the "International PC Owners," and this 40+ page newsletter is for owners of the IBM/PC. An invaluable source of tips and tricks, contributed by PC owners around the world, on free or inexpensive software, software reviews, etc. Edited by Jim and Cindy Cookinham.

*PC Data*
Autumn Revolution
P.O. Box 55329
Tulsa, OK 74155
(918) 438-4582

Annual "membership": $30 (no frequency indicated).

A publication of what is probably the best organized national IBM/PC users' group. "Revolution" newsletter, published monthly. Detailed software reviews and articles on using software effectively. These folks are serious.

*Softalk for the IBM/PC*
P.O. Box 60
North Hollywood, CA 91603

Annual subscription: $24 (12 issues).

*Special note:* Although this magazine is available at book and computer stores, we have included it here because of a special offer the magazine has traditionally run for new IBM/PC owners. If that's you, you may be able to get your first year *free* by sending in your machine's serial number. Contact publisher or pick up a copy for details.

## Other Computer-Specific Publications

*Personal and Professional*
Box 114
Springhouse, PA 19477
(215) 542-7008

Annual subscription: $42 (12 issues).

"The Independent Magazine for Digital Personal Computer Users." Rainbow, DECMate, VT180, etc.

"Os/TECH"
P.O. Box 517
Clearwater, FL 33517
(813) 446-7239

Annual subscription: $9.00 (six issues); sample copy: $1.50.

"A How-to, What-to, Where-to newsletter for the beginning and experienced owners of the Osborne I computer."

"Foghorn"
Box 3474
Daly City, CA 94015

Annual subscription: $24 (12 issues).

Publication of an especially large and active First Osborne Group. Particular emphasis on free software guides and sources (see Chapter 12).

*68 Micro Journal*
3018 Hamill Road
Hixson, TX 37343

Annual subscription: $18.50.

For users of 6800 and 6809 microprocessors.

*System 68*
P.O. Box 310
Conyers, GA 30207
(404) 929-0606

Annual subscription: $24 (12 issues).

For users of 6800, 6809, and 68000 chips and machines.

"SYNC"
39 E Hanover Avenue
Morris Plains, NJ 07950
(800) 631-8112

For users of Timex and Sinclair computers.

"Syntax Newsletter"
RD 2 Box 456
Harvard, MA 01451
(617) 456-3661

Annual subscription: $29 (12 issues).

"News, tips, programs, and projects" for owners of Timex Sinclair 1000, 1500, and ZX81 computers. (Back issues are available.)

"Keyboard"
TAS BAM Users Group
P.O. Box 644
Safe Harbour, FL 33572

For users of Timex/Sinclair and Sinclair computers.

"Superletter"
Abrams Creative Services
369 South Crescent Drive
Beverly Hills, CA 90212
(213) 277-1588

Newsletter for users of Superbrain computers.

"Sextant"
716 East Street, SE
Washington, DC 20003
(202) 544-0900

Newsletter for Heath/Zenith users.

## Publications for Business People and Professionals

"Legal Systems Letter"
The Medford Press, Inc.
270 Madison Avenue, Suite 1505
New York, NY 10016
(212) 889-5666

Annual subscription (12 issues): $140. Contact publisher for international rates.

News, advice, tips, software reviews, etc., relevant to using a personal computer in a law office.

"Lawyer's Microcomputer"
R.P.W. Publishing
P.O. Box 1046
Lexington, SC 29072

Annual subscription: $28 (12 issues).

Emphasis is on TRS-80-using attorneys.

"Software Protection"
Law & Technology Press
P.O. Box 4658 T.A.
Los Angeles, CA 90051
(213) 748-9418

Annual subscription: $48 (eight issues); sample copy: $5.00.

"The only publication written for both lawyers and nonlawyers focusing solely on legal and technical aspects of protecting computer software."

"Computertalk For Physicians"
1750 Walton Road
Blue Bell, PA 19422

Annual subscription: $39.

"Dental Computer Newsletter"
1000 North Avenue
Waukegan, IL 60085
(312) 244-0292

Annual subscription: $15.

Written by Dr. E. J. Neiburger, D.D.S., for dentists and physicians interested in computerized office management (see Chapter 23).

"Laboratory Computer Letter"
Information Research
10367 Paw Paw Lake Drive
Mattawan, MI 49071

Annual subscription: $68.

Software reviews and tips for using micros in a laboratory environment.


"Microcomputer Investor"
902 Anderson Drive
Fredericksburg, VA 22405

Using personal computers to help with investment decisions and recordkeeping.


"Financial Systems Report"
Syntax Corporation
P.O. Box 8137
Prairie Village, KS 66208

Annual subscription: $60.

"A monthly review of new computer programs, products and services for financial and tax specialists."


*Design Compudata Exchange*
45 Van Brunt Avenue
Dedham, MA 02026

Annual subscription: $60.

For computer-using architects.


"Digital Design"
1050 Commonwealth Avenue
Boston, MA 02215

Annual subscription: $35. (Free to research, development, and design engineers.)


"Engineering Computer Applications Newsletter"
5 Denver Tech Center
P.O. Box 3109
Englewood, CO 80111

Annual subscription: $48.

Software and other product reviews for the computer-using engineer.

"Construction Computer Applications Newsletter"
1105-F Spring Street
Silver Spring, MD 20910

Annual subscription: $48.

Software and product reviews for computer-using contractors.

## Publications for Educators

"The Computer Teacher"
Computing Center
Eastern Oregon State College
La Grande, OR 97850

"Hands On!"
Technical Education Research Centers
8 Eliot Street
Cambridge, MA 02138
(617) 547-3890

Annual subscription: Free (3 issues).

Forum for teachers of science and technology.

*Journal of Courseware Review*
Apple Educational Foundation
20863 Stevens Creek Blvd.
Cupertino, CA 95014

Issued quarterly, $5.95 per copy.

Reviews of commercially available educational programs for the Apple.

"Apple Educators' Newsletter"
9525 Lucerne Street
Ventura, CA 93004
(805) 647-1063

Annual subscription: $15 (six issues).

For teachers using Apples.

## Trade Magazines for Retailers

*Computer Merchandising*
Eastman Publishing Company
15720 Ventura Blvd. Suite 222
Encino, CA 91436

Annual subscription: $18 (12 issues).

"The Magazine for High Technology Retailers." Includes hardware and software reviews from a merchant's viewpoint. If you want to know what your dealer knows . . .

*Computer Retailing*
1760 Peachtree Road
Atlanta, GA 30357
(404) 874-4462

*Computer + Software News*
Lebhar-Friedman, Inc.
425 Park Avenue
New York, NY 10022
(212) 371-9400

A trade magazine for software retailers.

*Computer Systems News*
560 Northern Blvd.
Great Neck, NY 11021

*Software Merchandising*
Eastman Publishing, Inc.
15720 Ventura Blvd. Suite 222
Encino, CA 91436
(213) 995-0436

Annual subscription: $24 (12 issues).

Aimed at the owner/manager of a computer and/or "software only" store. Particular emphasis on products for the home market. (Soon to be available on NewsNet.)

*Software Retailing*
Gordon Publications, Inc.
Box 1952
Dover, NJ 07801-0952

Annual subscription: $24 (12 issues).

Aimed at the owner/manager of a computer and/or "software only" store.

# Appendix C
## Online Databases Offering Software Reviews

Here is the subscription and cost information for the databases discussed in Chapter 8. In addition to The Source, CompuServe, Newsnet, and The Knowledge Index (KI), we have also included information on DIALOG, KI's parent. *The International Software Directory* and the *Microcomputer Index* are available on both systems, but DIALOG is accessible 22 hours a day, compared to KI's 6:00 PM to 5:00 AM schedule. It also costs considerably more to search these files on DIALOG (as much as $60 an hour, compared to KI's hourly rate of $24).

NOTE: The hourly charges for "connect time" are typically calculated to the nearest minute or fraction thereof. The hours and rates quoted below are for weekdays. CompuServe and The Knowledge Index are accessible for longer periods of time on major holidays and over the weekend. Telenet, Tymnet, and Uninet are the services that make it possible for you to dial a local phone number to access one of these systems.

CompuServe
5000 Arlington Centre Blvd.
P.O. Box 20212
Columbus, OH
(800) 848-8990
(614) 457-8600

*Initial subscription:* $20 to $50 (see "Comments").

*Availability:* Computer stores and bookstores.

*Hours of operation:* 21 hours a day, your local time.

*Costs: Prime Service (8:00 AM–6:00 PM):* $12.50/hour for 300-baud service; $15.00 per hour for 1200-baud service.

*Standard Service (6:00 PM–5:00 AM):* $6.00/hour for 300-baud service; $12.50/hour for 1200-baud service.

Telenet and Tymnet charges are $2.00 per hour extra. But CompuServe has its own network that you can use free of charge, provided it is available in your locale.

There is a minimum charge of one minute's worth of connect time (10¢ to 25¢) each time you sign on.

*Monthly minimum fee:* None.

*Comments:* To obtain a subscription to CompuServe, you purchase a "CompuServe Starter Kit" that includes everything you need (account number and password) to go online immediately. The kit sells for about $50 and entitles you to five free hours on the system. Subscription packages may also be available from Radio Shack computer stores for $20. In the past these have included a free subscription to the Dow Jones News/Retrieval Service as well. These packages usually include one free hour on each system.

After your free time has expired, the CompuServe system will automatically ask you if you wish to continue your account. If you do, follow the prompts for your name, address, phone and credit card number. A new password will be mailed to you within 10 days.

The Source
1616 Anderson Road
McLean, VA 22102
(800) 336-3366
(703) 734-7540

*Initial subscription:* $100.

*Availability:* Computer stores and bookstores.

*Hours of operation:* 24 hours a day.

*Costs: Prime Time (7:00 AM–6:00 PM):* $20.75/hour for 300-baud service; $25.75 per hour for 1200-baud service.

*Non-Prime Time (6:00 PM–7:00 AM):* $7.75/hour for 300-baud service; $10.75/hour for 1200-baud service.

Telenet, Tymnet, or Uninet charges are included in the above rates.

\

The Source is in the process of establishing its own network as well. There is also a charge of 25¢ each time you sign on.

*Monthly minimum fee:* $10. Of this, $9 is a credit against usage.

*Comments:* When you purchase a subscription to The Source, your dealer must phone the company to obtain your password and to provide your credit card and address information. This can usually be done while you wait, though sometimes it can take an hour or so if the lines are busy. If that happens, you can leave and call your dealer back later to get your password.

The Knowledge Index
DIALOG Information Services, Inc.
3460 Hillview Avenue
Palo Alto, CA 94304
(415) 858-3777

Ask for extension 415 when dialing the following numbers:

(800) 528-6050
(800) 528-0470, in Alaska and Hawaii
(800) 352-0458, in Arizona

*Initial subscription:* $35.

*Availability:* Direct from DIALOG and at a growing number of computer stores and bookstores.

*Hours of operation:* 6:00 PM–5:00 AM, your local time.

*Costs:* $24 per hour, regardless of baud rate. Telenet, Tymnet, and Uninet charges are included in this figure.

*Monthly minimum fee:* None.

*Comments:* The initial subscription includes a three-ring notebook of documentation and two free hours of connect time.
   The Knowledge Index is a subset of DIALOG, one of the largest collections of publicly available online information on the planet (more than 150 individual collections of information). DIALOG is available 22 hours a day and there is no initial sign-up fee, though you should plan to spend about $50 or so buying the manuals you will need to make full use of the

system. It is considerably more expensive than The Knowledge Index. Each information collection is priced separately, but the average cost is about $75 per hour, with an additional $6.00 an hour for Telenet or Tymnet access. You can subscribe over the phone. For more information on DIALOG, call (800) 227-1927, or (800) 982-5838 in California.

NewsNet
945 Haverford Road
Bryn Mawr, PA 19010
(800) 527-8030
(215) 345-1301, in Pennsylvania

*Initial subscription:* No charge.

*Availability:* Direct from NewsNet.

*Hours of operation:* 24 hours a day.

*Costs: Prime Time (8:00 AM–8:00 PM):* $24/hour for 300-baud service; $48/hour for 1200-baud service.
  *Non-Prime Time (8:00 PM–8:00 AM):* $18/hour for 300-baud service; $36/hour for 1200-baud service.
  Telenet, Tymnet, or Uninet charges are included in the above rates, except from Alaska and Hawaii.
  Rates for reading newsletters vary with the publication itself. Cost can vary from about $24 an hour to $120 an hour, depending on the newsletter. Individuals who already subscribe to the printed version are charged less than nonsubscribers.

*Monthly minimum fee:* $15. This is applied as a credit against usage.

*Comments:* NewsNet offers over 150 industry and professional newsletters. Among those of interest to software seekers are:

"The Computer Cookbook"
"Advanced Office Concepts"
"Viewtext"
"Personal Computers Today"
"The Seybold Report on Office
  Systems"

"The S. Klein Newsletter on Com-
  puter Graphics"
"The Computer Consultant"
"Computer Market Observer"
"Consumer Electronics"
"Office Automation Update"

# Appendix D
## The OLCTD List of Free Computer Bulletin Board Phone Numbers

The following list of computer bulletin board systems was supplied by James A. Cambron, editor and publisher of *The On-Line Computer Telephone Directory*. Issued quarterly, the OLCTD contains the most accurate list of BBS phone numbers available, thanks to proprietary software developed by Mr. Cambron. Before each issue goes to press, Mr. Cambron has his TRS-80 Model III computer automatically dial every number. The machine sits there dialing on into the night. Bulletin board systems that are still up and running are automatically placed in a "save" file, while those that have been disconnected are flagged for editing.

**SoftTip:** Jim Cambron has his newsletter typeset by computer, too. He transmits the copy to a typesetting house over the phone and receives the stats by express mail soon thereafter. Since the list exists on magnetic media anyway, it was a simple matter to upload it to CompuServe for downloading into the author's word processor. The entire file was received in less than 20 minutes. No one had to retype anything.

**SoftTip:** Accurate as the list was at the time of this writing, it is important to remember that BBS's are owned and operated as hobbies by private individuals and they do have a tendency to come and go. For a subscription to "The On-Line Computer Telephone Directory," write to:

OLCTD
P.O. Box 10005
Kansas City, MO 64111-9990
CompuServe ID: 70040,414

*SoftTip continued*
One year (4 issues): $9.95
Two years (8 issues): $15.95
Overseas (U.S. funds only): Add $6.00 above rates.

*Note:* Please send any updates or phone numbers for any new boards you discover to the above address. Any additional information (type of equipment, type of bulletin board software used, hours of operation, etc.) you may have about the system will also be appreciated.

## Tips for Using Computer Bulletin Boards

1. *Communication settings:* Set your modem to "originate" and your software to 300 baud, 8 data bits, 1 stop bit, and no parity. If that does not work, try 300 baud, 7 data bits, 1 stop bit, and even parity. (Note that boards marked with a plus sign ( + ) on the list below will support both 300 and 1,200 baud.)

2. *Ring-back:* The ring-back system lets the computer share the telephone with human beings. When accessing a ring-back system, dial the number, let it ring once, hang up, then dial again to make the computer connection. A single ring alerts the SYSOP that the next call will be for the computer and gives him or her a chance to switch on the auto-answer modem.

   Ring-back systems are designated by "rb" in the Use Code column.

3. *Hours of operation:* Boards that operate around the clock are marked with an asterisk (*), though they may be down for maintenance. Boards that do not operate around the clock usually go on the air in the evening. In such cases, you probably should not call any earlier than 6:00 PM in the board's local time zone; 8:00 PM would be even safer.

4. *Off the air:* If a board of any sort doesn't answer after two or three rings, it is out of commission, either permanently or for maintenance. Save yourself the long distance charges by hanging up after two or three rings.

5. *Any computer can:* If your computer can communicate, you can talk to any of the boards on this list. They have been divided by the

brand or "family" of bulletin board software they use to make it easy for you to know what commands you will have to enter.

If you download the instructions offered when you first sign on and print them out, you can have them by your side when you use a particular type of system. This can save you constantly calling for the help file and command summary when you are online and the long distance telephone meter is running.

**6.** *If it's busy:* Since virtually all BBS's operate with a single phone line, you are bound to encounter your share of busy signals. Consequently, it's a good idea to have several phone numbers lined up and ready to go before you start.

This is one excellent reason to buy a communications package with a built-in dialing directory. The feature requires an auto-dial modem, but once you type in the phone numbers of your favorite boards, you will be able to dial each by pressing a single key.

**7.** *Be considerate:* Most SYSOPs want you to use and enjoy their systems. And certainly when you're just starting, you have to spend some time learning your way around. But try to remember that other people may want to use the system too. And don't forget that the longer you are connected, the more your long distance phone charges will be.

## The Legend for the List

*Use Codes*

rb = Signifies a ring-back system; let it ring once, hang up, and dial again to connect your computer.

so = Sexually oriented topics, meet-and-mate, find a date, etc. Also may contain topics of interest to the gay community.

\* = Twenty-four hour operation; down only for system maintenance.

+ = Supports both 1,200 and 300 baud communication under the Bell 212A and 103 standards. (Don't worry. Unless you've got a Vadic modem, you've got them.)

$ = System uses Vadic standards at 1,200 baud.

*System Information*

This column may contain the name of the SYSOP, the type of bulletin board software that is being used, or the name the SYSOP has given the board ("Warlock's Castle," "Software Exchange," "Asylum," etc.). It may also contain any password that may be necessary at sign-on.

If you see "#1" in this column, it means that the board is owned and operated by the person who wrote the BBS software used in the main classification. For example, Nick Naimo is the creator of the Net-Works BBS package, listed with a #1 in this column.

Some systems may require you to type in a password. Where the passwords are known, they have been included. If a listing has "PW = " or a similar designation in this column, sign onto the system and wait until you are prompted to enter the password. The SYSOP can change the password at any time, so you cannot always be certain that the word given will work. Normally before the password request is presented there will be some information on how to contact the SYSOP by mail or voice line, so you might do this if you want to obtain any new password.

## Apple-Based Bulletin Board Systems

The following section contains numbers of boards using various BBS software packages (ABBS, Net-Works, etc.) that run on Apple computers. Also included are systems that may be running on Franklin and other Apple II-compatible hardware. They are not necessarily exclusively devoted to Apple information, but if you are interested in free Apple software, these are the places to look.

*ABBS (Apple Bulletin Board System)*

| Telephone Number | Use Code | Location (City, State) | System Information (Operator, etc.) |
|---|---|---|---|
| 201 864 5345 | | Union City, NJ | APPLEMATE Bob Strauss |
| 201 994 9620 | * | Livingston, NJ | |
| 206 525 5410 | | Seattle, WA | Apple Crate |
| 206 935 9119 | | Renton, WA | Apple Crate |
| 213 829 1140 | | Santa Monica, CA | Computer Conspiracy |
| 214 530 0858 | * | Dallas, TX | Teledunjon II |
| 214 960 7654 | | Dallas, TX | Teledunjon III |

| | | | |
|---|---|---|---|
| 216 644 1965 | * | Akron, OH | |
| 216 745 7855 | * | Akron, OH | Digital Group |
| 216 779 1338 | | Cleveland, OH | |
| 303 759 2625 | | Denver, CO | |
| 305 261 3639 | | Miami, FL | Byte Shop |
| 305 486 2983 | | Ft. Lauderdale, FL | ABBS Byte Shop |
| 305 848 3802 | | W. Palm Beach, FL | |
| 312 420 7995 | | Naperville, IL | Illinois Microcomputer |
| 312 475 4884 | * | Chicago, IL | Gamemaster |
| 312 537 7063 | * | Glen Ellyn, IL | CODE |
| 312 789 0499 | * | Hinsdale, IL | AIMS |
| 312 973 2227 | | Rogers Park, IL | |
| 319 353 6528 | | Iowa City, IA | Apple Med |
| 402 339 7809 | | Omaha, NE | |
| 404 733 3461 | * | Atlanta, GA | AGS |
| 405 353 2556 | | Lawton, OK | |
| 414 637 9990 | * | Unknown, WI | Colortron Computer |
| 415 469 8111 | so | San Francisco, CA | South of Market |
| 415 881 5662 | * | Hayward, CA | |
| 417 862 7852 | * | Springfield, MO | |
| 604 437 7001 | | Vancouver, Canada | |
| 609 228 1149 | | Turnersville, NJ | ABBIES |
| 612 377 7747 | * | Minneapolis, MN | Captain Video's Log |
| 612 472 3985 | * | Navarre, MN | Calvary Mission Church |
| 612 571 5965 | * | Minneapolis, MN | Loki's Net |
| 612 645 0826 | * | Minneapolis, MN | Mario's Hideout |
| 612 724 7066 | * | Minneapolis, MN | The Safehouse |
| 612 920 3975 | * | Minneapolis, MN | Erik's Net |
| 613 725 2243 | | Ottawa, Canada | Compumart |
| 703 471 0610 | | Herndon, VA | Software Sorcery #1 |
| 704 364 5245 | | Charlotte, NC | |
| 713 455 9502 | | Houston, TX | Madam Bokeatha Society |
| 713 693 3462 | * | College Station, TX | Youngs Elect. Service |

| Telephone Number | Use Code | Location (City, State) | System Information (Operator, etc.) |
|---|---|---|---|
| 816 358 6222 | * | Kansas City, MO | NBC DTCLO BBS role-playing games |
| 904 743 7050 | | Jacksonville, FL | |
| 915 533 7039 | | El Paso, TX | |

*ACCESS (BBS Software)*

| Telephone Number | Use Code | Location (City, State) | System Information (Operator, etc.) |
|---|---|---|---|
| 301 267 7666 | * | Annapolis, MD | Bogart Brociner |
| 517 353 5269 | | Lansing, MI | |
| 602 275 6644 | | Phoenix, AZ | Call-A-Lawyer |
| 602 275 6644 | | Phoenix, AZ | |
| 602 957 4428 | *+ | Phoenix, AZ | Desert Technology |
| 602 996 9709 | * | Phoenix, AZ | I.I.I. #1 |
| 602 998 9411 | * | Scotsdale, AZ | Cactus Net |

*Conference Tree*

| Telephone Number | Use Code | Location (City, State) | System Information (Operator, etc.) |
|---|---|---|---|
| 201 627 5151 | | Unknown, NJ | |
| 201 627 5151 | * | Rockaway, NJ | |
| 404 892 9627 | * | Atlanta, GA | |
| 408 475 7101 | | Berkeley, CA | |
| 415 538 3580 | | Hayward, CA | |
| 415 861 6489 | | San Francisco, CA | |

*Dial-Your-Match*

Dial-Your-Match is an interesting combination of bulletin board and computer dating service. Some may charge a fee, but many systems operate at no cost to the user.

| Telephone Number | Use Code | Location (City, State) | System Information (Operator, etc.) |
|---|---|---|---|
| 201 272 3686 | so | Cranford, NJ | #14 |
| 201 462 0435 | so | Freehold, NJ | #21 |
| 206 256 6624 | so | Vancouver, WA | #16 |
| 209 298 1328 | so | Clovis, CA | #26 |
| 213 345 1047 | so | Tarzana, CA | #9 |
| 213 390 3239 | so | MarVista, CA | #19 |
| 213 764 8000 | so | N. Hollywood, CA | #28 |
| 213 783 2305 | so | Sherman Oaks, CA | #4 |
| 213 840 8252 | so | Burbank, CA | #7 |
| 213 842 3322 | so | Burbank, CA | #1 |
| 213 842 9452 | so | Burbank, CA | #25 |
| 216 932 9845 | so | Cleveland, OH | #34 |
| 219 845 4200 | so | Hammond, IN DYM | #35 |
| 312 243 1046 | so | Chicago, IL DYM | #38 |
| 313 736 1398 | so | Flint, MI | #37 |
| 402 571 8942 | so | Omaha, NE | #23 |
| 415 467 2588 | so | San Francisco, CA | #10 |
| 415 991 4911 | so | Daly City, CA | #17 |
| 617 334 6369 | so | Lynfield, MA | #18 |
| 619 434 4600 | so | San Diego, CA | #11 |
| 713 556 1531 | so | Houston, TX | #12 |
| 714 220 0239 | so | La Palma, CA | #31 |
| 714 671 2927 | so | Brea, CA | #29 |
| 804 838 3973 | so | Newport News, VA | #32 |
| 904 795 8850 | so | Crystal River, FL | #30 |
| 907 479 0315 | so | Fairbanks, AK | #6 |
| 912 233 0863 | so | Savannah, GA | #2 |
| 912 233 0863 | so | Savannah, GA | #3 |
| 919 362 0676 | so | Cary, NC | #20 |

*Net-Works*

| Telephone Number | Use Code | Location (City, State) | System Information (Operator, etc.) |
|---|---|---|---|
| 212 410 0949 | * | Brooklyn, NY | II |
| 213 336 5535 | | Los Angeles, CA | Coin Games |
| 213 346 1849 | * | Woodland Hills, CA | PMS O A C |
| 213 388 5198 | * | Los Angeles, CA | Magnetic Fantasies |
| 213 473 2754 | | W. Los Angeles, CA | Softworx |
| 214 340 5689 | | Dallas, TX | Fantasy role-playing games |
| 214 239 5842 | | Dallas, TX | Eclectic Comptuter |
| 214 644 5197 | | Dallas, TX | Apple Grove |
| 214 680 9322 | | Richardson, TX | Fantasy role-playing games |
| 214 824 7160 | | Dallas, TX | Hacker Net |
| 217 429 4738 | | Decatur, IL | C A M S |
| 303 343 8401 | * | Aurora, CO | |
| 304 345 8280 | | Charleston, WV | |
| 305 948 8000 | | Miami, FL | Big Apple |
| 309 342 7178 | | Galesburg, IL | MAGIE |
| 404 733 3461 | * | Augusta, GA | AGS |
| 614 475 9791 | * | Columbus, OH | Apple Crackers |
| 618 345 6638 | | E. St. Louis, IL | Warlock's Castle |
| 618 466 9497 | | Unknown, IL | N A G S |
| 618 692 0742 | | Unknown, IL | Asylum |
| 713 492 8700 | | Houston, TX | Weekender |
| 808 521 7312 | | Unknown, HI | |
| 812 858 5405 | | Newburgh, IN | #1 Nick Naimo |
| 816 232 3153 | * | St. Joseph, MO | The Silver Tongue |
| 816 483 2526 | | Kansas City, MO | ABC |
| 904 932 8271 | | Pensacola, FL | Beach BBS |
| 914 725 4060 | | Unknown, NY | |

*Online*

| Telephone Number | Use Code | Location (City, State) | System Information (Operator, etc.) |
| --- | --- | --- | --- |
| 514 931 0458 | * | Montreal, Canada | Computerland |
| 619 561 7271 | * | Lakeside | "PMS" ID = GUEST pw = PASS |
| 619 692 1961 | * | San Diego, CA | Saba |

*PMS (Peoples Message System)*

| Telephone Number | Use Code | Location (City, State) | System Information (Operator, etc.) |
| --- | --- | --- | --- |
| 201 932 3887 | | Piscataway, NJ | Rutgers University Microlab |
| 206 486 2368 | * | Kenmore, WA | Software Unlimited |
| 212 997 2488 | | Manhattan, NY | McGraw Hill Books |
| 213 334 7614 | * | Los Angeles, CA | |
| 213 346 1849 | * | Woodland Hills, CA | O.A.C. |
| 216 832 8392 | * | Massillon, OH | |
| 216 867 7463 | * | Akron, OH | RAUG |
| 301 465 3176 | | Ellicott City, MD | |
| 301 653 3413 | | Pikesville, MD | |
| 312 295 6926 | * | Lake Forest, IL | NIAUG |
| 312 373 8057 | * | Chicago, IL | |
| 312 964 6513 | | Downers Grove, IL | Downers Grove/SRT |
| 317 787 5486 | * | Indianapolis, IN | |
| 408 370 0873 | * | Campbell, CA | |
| 408 688 9629 | * | Santa Cruz, CA | |
| 415 462 7419 | * | Pleasanton, CA | |
| 501 646 0197 | | Ft. Smith, AR | Ft. Smith Computer Club |
| 503 245 2536 | | Portland, OR | |
| 503 689 2655 | * | Eugene, OR | Computer Solutions |
| 513 671 2753 | | Cincinnati, OH | |
| 606 299 1998 | | Lexington, KY | |

| Telephone Number | Use Code | Location (City, State) | System Information (Operator, etc.) |
|---|---|---|---|
| 612 929 6699 | * | Minneapolis, MN | |
| 612 929 8966 | * | Twin Cities, MN | Pete the Hermit |
| 619 265 3428 | | San Diego, CA | Ed. Technology San Diego State University |
| 619 271 8613 | * | San Diego, CA | Datel Systems |
| 619 561 7271 | * | Santee, CA | (Type "PMS" to activate) |
| 619 561 7277 | * | Santee, CA | Bill Blue #1 |
| 619 582 9557 | | San Diego, CA | Computer Merchant |
| 619 746 0667 | * | Escondido, CA | |
| 702 878 9106 | * | Las Vegas, NV | Century 23 |
| 713 444 7098 | | Houston, TX | DTCLO CNN BBS |
| 714 772 8868 | * | Anaheim, CA | "IF" Video systems |
| 913 341 3502 | * | Overland Park, KS | Apple Bits UG |
| 913 677 1299 | * | Leawood, KS | Your Computer Connection |

## Atari-Based Bulletin Board Systems

| Telephone Number | Use Code | Location (City, State) | System Information (Operator, etc.) |
|---|---|---|---|
| 305 238 1231 | rb | Miami, FL | AMIS APOGEE |
| 312 789 3610 | * | Chicago, IL | AMIS |
| 313 978 8087 | * | Sterling Hghts, MI | AMIS A R C A D E |
| 405 722 5056 | * | Oklahoma City, OK | GREKELCOM ARMUDUC ATARI |
| 408 253 5216 | | Cupertino, CA | AMIS GRAFEX Inc. H.Q. System |
| 408 298 6930 | | San Jose, CA | AMIS IBBBS |
| 503 245 9405 | * | Portland, OR | PACBBS Portland Atari Club BBS |
| 503 343 4352 | * | Eugene, OR | A.C.E. (Atari Mike Dunn) |

| 509 582 5217 | * | Kenniwick, WA | A2 D2 BBS (Atari Ted Meier) |
| 616 241 1971 | * | Grand Rapids, MI | AMIS G R A S S |

## Commodore-Based Bulletin Board Systems

| Telephone Number | Use Code | Location (City, State) | System Information (Operator, etc.) |
| --- | --- | --- | --- |
| 307 637 6045 | * | Unknown, WY | PET BBS SE Wyoming PUG |
| 312 397 0871 | * | Chicago, IL | PET BBS (Commodore) |
| 314 625 4576 | * | St. Louis, MO | PET BBS |
| 317 255 5435 | * | Indianapolis, IN | PET BBS AVC Comline |
| 414 554 9520 | | Racine, WI | PET BBS S E W P U G |
| 512 285 5028 | * | Unknown, TX | Color Connection VIC-20 |
| 816 257 2502 | * | Kansas City, MO | Commodore UG BBS |

## CP/M™-Based Bulletin Boards and Remote CP/M Systems

*Note:* CBBS™ is a trademark of Ward Christensen and Randy Suess, the creators of the CBBS software package and the originators of the BBS concept.

| Telephone Number | Use Code | Location (City, State) | System Information (Operator, etc.) |
| --- | --- | --- | --- |
| 206 458 3086 | *rb | Yelm, WA | Dave Stanhope |
| 301 948 5717 | * | Gaithersburg, MD | CPEUG & NBS/ICST |
| 312 545 8086 | * | Chicago, IL | |
| 312 852 1305 | * | Downers Grove, IL | |
| 313 288 0335 | | Detroit, MI | |
| 313 674 3881 | | Pontiac, MI | |
| 319 364 0811 | * | Cedar Rapids, IA | |
| 404 394 4220 | * | Atlanta, GA | |

| Telephone Number | Use Code | Location (City, State) | System Information (Operator, etc.) |
|---|---|---|---|
| 412 822 7176 | * | Pittsburgh, PA | PACC |
| 414 241 8364 | * | Milwaukee, WI | MAUDE |
| 415 357 1130 | * | San Leandro, CA | Proxima |
| 415 658 2919 | so | Berkeley, CA | LAMBDA Koala Bear |
| 503 284 5260 | *+ | Beaverton, OR | CBBS N.W. Altair S-100 |
| 503 646 5510 | *+ | Beaverton, OR | CBBS N.W. 512K Semidisk Emulator |
| 516 561 6590 | * | Unknown, NY | Long Island Computer Assoc. |
| 602 746 3956 | * | Tucson, AZ | TSG |
| 612 423 5016 | * | Richfield, MN | Doug Poole/Kevin Uhlir |
| 617 646 3610 | * | Cambridge, MA | |
| 617 646 3610 | * | Boston, MA | |
| 617 683 2119 | * | Boston, MA | Lawrence General Hospital |
| 617 752 7284 | | Worcester, MA | MicroStar |
| 703 734 1387 | * | Unknown, VA | AMRAD |
| 716 244 9531 | | Rochester, NY | RAMS |
| 808 944 0562 | | Honolulu, HI | Strictly Software |
| 812 334 2522 | | Bloomington, IN | |

## Heath/Zenith-Based Bulletin Board Systems

| Telephone Number | Use Code | Location (City, State) | System Information (Operator, etc.) |
|---|---|---|---|
| 201 363 3122 | | Howell, NJ | |
| 214 742 1380 | * | Dallas, TX | DFW HUG (Heath) |
| 215 288 0262 | | Philadelphia, PA | |
| 301 768 1499 | | Glen Burnie, MD | Al McClure |
| 303 343 8401 | * | Denver, CO | |
| 303 423 3224 | * | Denver, CO | DENHUG (Heath) |

| | | | |
|---|---|---|---|
| 303 634 1158 | * | Colorado Springs, CO | CSHUG (Heath Arvada Electronics) |
| 314 291 1854 | | St. Louis, MO | SLUG (Heath) |
| 404 252 4342 | * | Atlanta, GA | ATHUG (Heath) |
| 419 537 1888 | + | Toledo, OH | RBBS Heath |
| 612 778 1213 | | St. Paul, MN | Heath |
| 617 237 1511 | | Wellesley, MA | |
| 617 531 9332 | * | Peabody, MA | HUG North Shore (Heath) |
| 716 835 3091 | | Amhurst, NY | |
| 904 725 4995 | * | Jacksonville, FL | JUG (Heath) |
| 919 299 5390 | | Greensboro, NC | Heathkit Center |

## Remote CP/M Systems

(Remember: "You are the console.")

| Telephone Number | Use Code | Location (City, State) | System Information (Operator, etc.) |
|---|---|---|---|
| 201 584 9227 | * | Flanders, NJ | MCBBS Ken Stritzel |
| 201 775 8705 | *+ | Ocean, NJ | RBBS S Jersey Heath |
| 201 932 3879 | * | New Brunswick, NJ | RBBS Rutgers |
| 206 458 3086 | rb | Yelm, WA | RBBS |
| 206 525 3412 | * | Tacoma, WA | Dave |
| 213 296 5927 | * | Los Angeles, CA | RBBS Sofwaire Store |
| 213 360 5053 | | Los Angeles, CA | RBBS Granada Engineering |
| 213 541 2503 | *+$ | Palos Verdes, CA | RBBS GFRN Data Exchange |
| 213 655 8894 | | Hollywood, CA | Entertainment Industry |
| 214 931 8274 | | Dallas, TX | |
| 215 398 3937 | * | Allentown, PA | RBBS |
| 215 836 5116 | | Cheltenham, PA | |
| 301 229 3196 | | Bethesda, MD | RBBS |

| Telephone Number | Use Code | Location (City, State) | System Information (Operator, etc.) |
|---|---|---|---|
| 301 661 4447 | | Baltimore, MD | Heath |
| 301 953 3753 | * | Laurel, MD | RBBS |
| 303 499 9169 | | Boulder, CO | RBBS |
| 303 781 4937 | * | Denver, CO | CUG NODE |
| 305 791 7302 | | Plantation, FL | (Heath) |
| 312 252 2136 | | Chicago, IL | Logan Square |
| 312 359 8080 | *+ | Palatine, IL | |
| 312 647 7636 | *+ | Niles, IL | A.B. Dick Co. |
| 312 789 0499 | | Hinsdale, IL | AIMS |
| 313 559 5326 | | Southfield, MI | |
| 313 584 1044 | rb | Detroit, MI | |
| 313 588 7054 | rb | Royal Oak, MI | |
| 313 729 1905 | rb | Westland, MI | |
| 313 846 6127 | | Detroit, MI | |
| 313 535 9186 | *rb | Detroit, MI | MCBBS PW = SORCERER |
| 313 559 5326 | * | Southfield, MI | RBBS |
| 313 846 6127 | * | Dearborn, MI | MCBBS TCBBS |
| 408 263 2588 | | San Jose, CA | Collossal Oxgate |
| 408 732 2433 | | Sunnyvale, CA | RBBS DataTech 004 |
| 408 732 9190 | | Sunnyvale, CA | Silicon Valley CP/M |
| 414 342 4599 | | Milwaukee, WI | OZZY |
| 414 563 9932 | | Ft. Atkinson, WI | RCPM |
| 414 647 0903 | | Milwaukee, WI | RBBS Mike's |
| 415 383 0473 | * | Mill Valley, CA | RBBS Marin County |
| 415 595 0541 | *+ | San Carlos, CA | RBBS DataTech 001 |
| 415 965 4097 | * | Unknown, CA | RBBS PICONET |
| 503 621 3193 | | Roseburg, OR | |
| 503 641 7276 | | Beaverton, OR | |
| 604 584 2543 | | Vancouver, Canada | Terry O'Brien |
| 607 797 6416 | | Johnson City, NY | SJBBS |
| 614 272 2227 | * | Columbus, OH | |

| | | | |
|---|---|---|---|
| 617 862 0781 | *+ | Lexington, MA | MCBBS/Superbrain |
| 619 273 4354 | *+ | San Diego, CA | |
| 703 524 2549 | * | McLean, VA | CBBS RLP |
| 703 536 3769 | | Arlington, VA | |
| 713 497 5433 | | Houston, TX | RBBS Amateur Radio |
| 714 534 1547 | *+ | Garden Grove, CA | RBBS GFRN Data Exch |
| 714 774 7860 | * | Anaheim, CA | RBBS ANAHUG |
| 716 223 1100 | * | Fairport, NY | RBBS |
| 803 548 0900 | * | Fort Mill, SC | RBBS Bill Taylor |
| 804 898 7493 | | Grafton, VA | RBBS |
| 805 527 2219 | | Simi Valley, CA | Pete Mack |
| 805 527 9321 | | Simi Valley, CA | CP/M-Net Kelly Smith |
| 813 988 7400 | * | Tampa, FL | RBBS Computerized Services |
| 814 238 4857 | * | Unknown, PA | CUG NODE Penn. State Univ. |
| 914 679 6559 | rb | Bearsville, NY | SJBBS |
| 914 679 8734 | | Woodstock, NY | |
| 915 533 2202 | * | El Paso, TX | Comp Tech Associates |
| 915 598 1668 | | El Paso, TX | RBBS |

## Remote North Star Systems

| Telephone Number | Use Code | Location (City, State) | System Information (Operator, etc.) |
|---|---|---|---|
| 303 444 7231 | | Boulder, CO | |
| 503 760 7609 | | Portland, OR | L. Dixon |
| 804 340 5246 | * | Virginia Beach, VA | |
| 804 898 7493 | * | Grafton, VA | |
| 805 682 7876 | | Santa Barbara, CA | |
| 805 964 4115 | * | Santa Barbara, CA | |

## IBM Personal Computer-Based Bulletin Board Systems

| Telephone Number | Use Code | Location (City, State) | System Information (Operator, etc.) |
|---|---|---|---|
| 213 649 1489 | | Culver City, CA | IBM BBS George Peck H.Q. System |
| 301 251 6293 | * | Gaithersburg, MD | IBM PC |
| 301 460 0538 | * | Bethesda, MD | IBM PC |
| 301 949 8848 | * | Rockville, MD | IBM PC |
| 312 259 8086 | *+ | Mount Prospect, IL | IBM PC RBBS Gene Plantz |
| 404 252 4146 | | Atlanta, GA | BBS IBM HOSTCOMM H.Q. System; evenings only |
| 404 252 9438 | * | Atlanta, GA | IBM PC |
| 415 845 9462 | * | Oakland, CA | BLUE BOSS IBM PC |
| 608 262 4939 | * | Madison, WI | IBM PC |
| 703 425 7229 | * | Springfield, VA | BBS IBM HOSTCOMM |
| 703 425 9452 | * | Fairfax, VA | BBS IBM HOSTCOMM |
| 703 560 0979 | * | Annandale, VA | IBM PCUG |
| 703 560 7803 | * | Vienna, VA | IBM PC |
| 703 680 5220 | * | Dale City, VA | IBM PC |
| 703 978 9592 | * | Fairfax, VA | BBS IBM HOSTCOMM |
| 704 365 4311 | * | Charlotte, NC | PC BBS (IBM & Apple) |
| 713 890 0310 | | Houston, TX | IBM PC HOSTCOMM |
| 714 624 1767 | * | Claremont, CA | IBM PC File Transfer System |
| 913 842 5749 | | Lawrence, KS | IBM PC-BBS |

*Note:* Be sure to see "BBS Watch" by Gene Plantz in each issue of *PC World* Magazine.

## Tandy Radio Shack-Based Bulletin Board Systems

Includes systems that run on the Color Computer (COCO), Model I and Model III. Software written for the Model I also runs on the Model III in most cases.

*Radio Shack Color Computer Systems*

| Telephone Number | Use Code | Location (City, State) | System Information (Operator, etc.) |
|---|---|---|---|
| 212 423 4623 | * | Unknown, NY | COCO's Nest |
| 212 441 3755 | * | Woodhaven, NY | Bob Rosen COCO (Mod 3) |
| 212 441 3766 | | New York, NY | Bob Rosen COCO |
| 212 441 5719 | * | Woodhaven, NY | RAINBOW CONNECTION III |
| 213 563 7727 | | Los Angeles, CA | Don Brown COCO |
| 305 683 6044 | * | W. Palm Beach, FL | R.S. Computer Center |
| 312 260 0640 | | Wheaton, IL | Terry Haas COCO/ Model III |
| 313 548 7278 | | Dnld Dearborn, MI | |
| 313 728 5484 | | Dnld Westland, MI | |
| 404 378 4410 | | Atlanta, GA | Lee Blitch |
| 408 733 6809 | | Sunnyvale, CA | Shawn Jipp H.Q. Sys |
| 512 285 5028 | | Elgin, TX | Peter Banz COCO/Mod 1 |
| 612 533 1957 | | Minneapolis, MN | Bob Shaw |
| 707 257 1485 | | Napa, CA | Phil Rusin COCO |
| 816 358 6222 | * | Kansas City, MO | Steve Odneal OCCCS H.Q. System |

*TRS-80 Model I/III Systems*
*Bullet-80*

| Telephone Number | Use Code | Location (City, State) | System Information (Operator, etc.) |
|---|---|---|---|
| 203 629 4375 | * | Greenwich, CT | |
| 203 744 4644 | * | Danbury, CT | #1 |

| Telephone Number | Use Code | Location (City, State) | System Information (Operator, etc.) |
|---|---|---|---|
| 212 740 5680 | * | Hollis, NY | Period Computer |
| 214 769 3036 | * | Hawkins, TX | |
| 216 729 2769 | | Chesterland, OH | |
| 313 335 8456 | | Pontiac, MI | |
| 313 398 5293 | | Hazel Park, MI | |
| 313 669 4952 | | Walled Lake, MI | |
| 313 683 5076 | * | Waterford, MI | |
| 617 266 7789 | *+ | Boston, MA | |
| 703 978 5656 | | Fairfax, VA | |
| 713 331 2599 | * | Houston, TX | |
| 714 770 5052 | | Laguna Hills, CA | |
| 714 952 2110 | | Anaheim, CA | Orange County |
| 914 297 0665 | * | Poughkeepsie, NY | |
| 918 749 0059 | * | Tulsa, OK | |

*COMNET 80*

| Telephone Number | Use Code | Location (City, State) | System Information (Operator, etc.) |
|---|---|---|---|
| 215 855 3809 | | North Wales, PA | DRUCOM, Dru Simon |
| 216 645 0827 | *+ | Akron, OH | |
| 313 465 9531 | | Mt. Clemens, MI | |
| 702 870 9986 | + | Las Vegas, NV | |
| 714 359 3189 | + | Riverside, CA | |
| 714 877 2253 | + | Riverside, CA | |
| 817 767 5847 | * | Wichita Falls, TX | |

*Connection 80*

| Telephone Number | Use Code | Location (City, State) | System Information (Operator, etc.) |
|---|---|---|---|
| 201 667 2504 | *+ | Nutley, NJ | C. Amlung |
| 201 790 6795 | * | Haledon, NJ | Photo 80 |

| | | | |
|---|---|---|---|
| 212 277 5851 | | Brooklyn, NY | |
| 212 441 3755 | * | Woodhaven, NY | |
| 212 991 1664 | * | Bronx, NY | Scanners |
| 217 787 5552 | * | Springfield, IL | |
| 303 690 4566 | * | Denver, CO | |
| 305 644 8327 | * | Orlando, FL | |
| 305 894 1886 | * | Winter Garden, FL | |
| 313 823 4775 | * | Detroit, MI | |
| 414 271 7580 | * | Milwaukee, WI | Vanmil |
| 415 651 4147 | * | Fremont, CA | |
| 501 372 0576 | | Little Rock, AR | |
| 514 622 1274 | * | Laval, Canada | Laval BELE |
| 516 293 5519 | | Massapequa, NY | |
| 516 482 8491 | * | Great Neck, NY | |
| 516 536 3510 | | South Shore, NY | |
| 516 588 5836 | * | Centereach, NY | |
| 517 339 3367 | * | Lansing, MI | |
| 603 924 7920 | * | Peterborough, NH | |

*Forum 80*

| Telephone Number | Use Code | Location (City, State) | System Information (Operator, etc.) |
|---|---|---|---|
| 201 528 6623 | * | Brielle, NJ | Monmouth |
| 205 272 5069 | * | Montgomery, AL | |
| 205 343 1933 | + | Mobile, AL | |
| 206 723 3282 | * | Seattle, WA | Bruce |
| 216 486 4176 | + | Cleveland, OH | |
| 302 762 3170 | * | Wilmington, DE | Tim Ihde |
| 305 772 4444 | * | Ft. Lauderdale, FL | |
| 316 665 3985 | * | Hutchinson, KS | |
| 316 682 2113 | *+ | Wichita, KS | |
| 415 348 2139 | * | San Francisco, CA | Steve Filice |
| 503 535 6883 | * | Medford, OR | Jackson Computer Society |

| Telephone Number | Use Code | Location (City, State) | System Information (Operator, etc.) |
|---|---|---|---|
| 512 655 8143 | | San Antonio, TX | |
| 518 355 1826 | * | Albany, NY | |
| 602 458 3850 | * | Sierra Vista, AZ | |
| 615 847 2930 | | Nashville, TN | |
| 617 692 3973 | * | Westford, MA | |
| 617 899 6524 | | Waltham, MA | |
| 703 670 5881 | * | Woodbridge, VA | |
| 714 730 1206 | | Orange County, CA | John McGorety |
| 714 771 0883 | | Orange, CA | |
| 803 279 5392 | * | North Augusta, SC | |
| 813 988 7400 | | Tampa, FL | Wild Goose Board |
| 816 931 9316 | + | Kansas City, MO | (Commodities) |
| 901 276 8196 | * | Memphis, TN | Medical |
| 913 829 3282 | *+ | Olathe, KS | R.S. Comp. Marketing |
| 915 755 1000 | * | El Paso, TX | |
| 919 977 9089 | | Rocky Mount, NC | Southern Software |

*Greene Machine*

| Telephone Number | Use Code | Location (City, State) | System Information (Operator, etc.) |
|---|---|---|---|
| 213 445 3591 | * | Arcadia, CA | Fricaseed Chicken |
| 305 965 4388 | so | Winter Park, FL | |
| 305 968 8653 | | Winter Park, FL | Corsair |
| 315 337 7720 | | Rome, NY | |
| 714 354 8004 | | Riverside, CA | |
| 714 551 4336 | | Irvine, CA | Irvine Line |

## MCMS

| Telephone Number | Use Code | Location (City, State) | System Information (Operator, etc.) |
|---|---|---|---|
| 312 462 7560 | *+ | Wheaton, IL | P.C.M.S. |
| 312 622 4442 | * | Chicago, IL | Message 82 |
| 312 740 9128 | | Round Lake, IL | L.A.M.S. |
| 312 927 1020 | *+ | Chicago, IL | CAMS |
| 612 533 1957 | * | Minneapolis, MN | NC Software |
| 815 838 1020 | * | Lockport, IL | J.A.M.S. |

## RATS (Radio Amateur Telecommunications Society)

| Telephone Number | Use Code | Location (City, State) | System Information (Operator, etc.) |
|---|---|---|---|
| 201 794 9563 | * | Elmwood Park, NJ | RATS NEST Mike Friedman #1 |
| 609 468 3844 | | Wenonah, NJ | |
| 609 468 5293 | | Wenonah, NJ | |

## ST-80

| Telephone Number | Use Code | Location (City, State) | System Information (Operator, etc.) |
|---|---|---|---|
| 305 277 0473 | * | Orlando, FL | MOUSE NET |
| 802 862 7023 | * | Burlington, VT | ST80 CC Lance Micklus, Inc. #1 |
| 813 885 6187 | * | Tampa, FL | ST80 CC Buddy's Super BB |
| 914 782 7605 | | Monroe, NY | ST80 PBB Monroe Camera Shop |

| Telephone Number | Use Code | Location (City, State) | System Information (Operator, etc.) |
|---|---|---|---|
| 305 426 8080 | * | Pompano Beach, FL | |
| 305 525 1192 | | Ft. Lauderdale, FL | H.Q. System |
| 305 947 7930 | | Miami, FL | |
| 814 898 2952 | * | Erie, PA | |
| 912 439 7440 | * | Albany, GA | Richie Dervan |
| 915 942 8035 | * | San Angelo, TX | Ted Hackler |

# Glossary:
## *The Computerese and Jargon Interpreter*

This Glossary is designed to be used as a quick reference when you are reading a computer magazine article, ad, or software product brochure. Here you will find definitions for much of the jargon you'll encounter in these publications.

The terms that are most vital to a software buyer are explained in the main text, so if you don't find them here, please consult the Index for the appropriate page number. That leaves some words of computerese, however, that may not be vital to picking the right program but can still be mildly perplexing if you don't have some idea of what they mean. They are the main targets of the following section.

acoustic coupler—A type of modem designed to transmit and receive data through a telephone handset. The handset is placed in a cradle consisting of two rubber cups, one for the earpiece and one for the mouthpiece. Sometimes called a "data set." Used when it is not possible to plug a direct-connect modem into a telephone jack, as in some offices and most hotel rooms.

ANSI—American National Standards Institute, an organization of computer professionals responsible for setting standards for everything from floppy disk quality to computer languages.

ASCII—Acronym for American Standard Code for Information Interchange. Pronounced "az-key." Used in virtually all personal computer data communications, the standard ASCII code set consists of 128 numbers ranging from 0 to 127, each of which has been assigned a particular meaning. Standard ASCII is a seven-bit code (seven binary bits are required to represent each number). But an eighth bit is added for parity checking in many instances.

Standard ASCII is used to represent all of the upper-and-lowercase letters and all of the numbers and punctuation marks, and all computers and communications software agree on the meaning of each code number. However, if the eighth bit is not used for parity

601

checking, then it can be used to increase the possible code numbers to 255. It is in the 128 code numbers between 127 and 255 that the standardization breaks down. These are the code numbers computer manufacturers use to represent graphics and other characters, and every company uses its own scheme. (See *The Complete Handbook of Personal Computer Communications* for more information.)

asynchronous communication—Data communication of the start-stop variety. Each character is transmitted as a discrete unit with its own start bit and one or more stop bits. This is what most personal computers use whether talking on the telephone or talking to one other computer. "Synchronous" communication is also possible, but it is most often used when a personal computer is talking to a corporate mainframe or a local network of computers linked together within a group of offices.

auto-dial/auto-answer—A feature offered by more expensive modems. The auto-dial feature allows you to dial your telephone by typing the numbers from the keyboard. This feature also lets you use communications software to record phone numbers on disk and dial each by pressing a single button. Auto-answer refers to a modem's ability to answer the phone and connect the calling computer to your system as with a computer bulletin board (see Chapter 12).

baud—A unit for measuring the speed of data transmission. Technically, baud rates refer to the number of times the communications line changes states each second. Strictly speaking, baud and bits-per-second are not identical measurements, but most nontechnical people use the terms interchangeably. Because 10 bits are required to transmit a single character, as a rule of thumb you can divide the stated baud rate by 10 to discover how many characters are being sent per second. Thus 300 baud translates to 30 characters per second and 1,200 baud translates to 120.

Bell-compatible—A term used to describe modems. The term means that the audio tones issued by the modem meet Bell Telephone standards. Variants of the term include Bell 103-compatible (standard for 300-baud modems) and Bell 212A-compatible (standard for full-duplex, 1,200-baud modems).

benchmark—A test or the testing process used to determine the capabilities of a computer or a program. The tests are often ones of speed. (How long does it take to sort a certain amount of data? How much time is required to perform a given set of calculations?) Magazines will frequently "benchmark" several machines or programs by feeding them identical sets of data and reporting the results. Hardware manufacturers will also report benchmark results of their equipment. But here you have to be careful, because companies tend to choose tests that show their products in the best possible light. Without a detailed knowledge of the conditions of the test, it is difficult to form a judgment on the basis of advertised benchmarks.

beta test—When a software house wants to issue a new product, it will usually test it in-house (alpha test), make corrections and improvements, and then release it for "beta testing" by a number of selected users. The users serve as test-consumers, reporting any bugs they may have encountered and making suggestions for improvement. After the product has been improved again, it is ready to be shipped. Not all software houses follow this procedure, though they should.

bit—Acronym for "*binary digit*." The smallest unit of information in the computer world. Eight bits together are called a "byte," and four bits are called a "nibble." (See Chapter 1.)

bubble memory—A chip-based memory system that fulfills the same role as RAM but has an important difference. Data in a bubble memory are stored as tiny "bubbles" of magnetism, and once it is stored it remains, even after the power is shut off. Thus bubble memories are suitable for portable computers. Bubble memories are slower than RAM, more complex to make, and more expensive. That will probably change in the future.

buffer—Any portion of your computer's internal RAM that is set aside by a program as a temporary "holding tank." In a word processing program, the software may create a "type-ahead" or "keyboard buffer" to allow you to type faster than the computer can display characters on the screen. It may also create a buffer to hold the blocks of text you want to move from one page to another. A communications program may set aside a "capture buffer" into which you can pour incoming data instead of waiting for the printer to print it. The technique of "print spooling" described in Chapter 4 sets up a buffer to temporarily hold text before it is sent to the printer.

bug—Broadly speaking, any kind of malfunction, whether of hardware or software. One explanation for the origin of this term involves the doorbell-like relay circuits that were used to create the first computers (see Chapter 1). This type of switch works by causing a bar of metal to move physically toward an electromagnet. It is thought that a moth or some other insect at one time managed to get in the way of the contact and caused the computer to malfunction. Whether true or not, the logbook for one of the early computers built under the aegis of the Department of the Navy has a dessicated moth pasted into it with a notation in the computer operator's handwriting that he had found a bug in the system.

byte—Eight binary digits. Because it takes eight bits to represent a single letter or other character using the ASCII code set, the word *byte* is often used synonymously with *character*.

CBBS—Computer Bulletin Board System. The name of what is generally acknowledged to be the first bulletin board program (written by Ward Christensen and Randy Suess). (See Chapter 12.)

character length—A communications setting referring to the number of data bits in each character transmitted. Since seven data bits (not including parity, start, or stop bits) are required to transmit each character in the standard ASCII code set, the character length under these circumstances is seven. To transmit characters represented by numbers above 127, eight binary bits are required. In such cases, the character length is said to be eight. Sometimes called "word length," using "word" in a special computer sense of the term to represent a single character.

checksum—One of several techniques computers and programs may use to verify accuracy whenever data is transmitted from one place to another. When two personal computers are linked by telephone, for example, one may send a file and then say to the other, "I sent you 1,000 characters. How many did you receive?" The other machine will have been counting the characters as they came in and if it says, "Yup, I got 1,000 characters," it is an indication that the file was received accurately. If the other machine says, "Uh-oh, I only got 981 characters," the sending machine will say, "Hmm. Must be a problem. Hang on, I'll send the same file again." A checksum is used to count characters (or bytes). Parity checking (q.v.) counts the number of bits in each character.

clock speed—All microprocessors in personal computers have a built-in clock that "ticks" with a frequency of anywhere from one million times a second to ten million times or more. The speed is measured in "megahertz" (MHz). The significance of the clock speed is that nothing can happen inside a computer until the clock "ticks" or pulses. No data can be transferred. No instructions can be executed. The faster the clock, the faster the computer can work. In Chapter 25 we noted that one of the reasons why computers usually don't quite match the responsiveness of the games you play at an arcade is that the chip in a computer usually has a slower clock speed than the chip in the arcade game.

The standard Intel 8080 chip found in many eight-bit computers has a clock speed of 2 MHz, though other versions are faster. The Zilog Z80 chip runs at 3 MHz. The Z80A used in TRS-80 Model III computers runs at 4 MHz. The Intel 8088 that is the heart of the IBM/PC runs at 4.77 MHz. All of which is interesting, but largely irrelevant.

Some people get caught up in clock speeds, but it is not a good way to pick a computer. Concentrate on the software that is available for the computer instead, and have faith that no major company is going to offer a machine with a clock speed so slow that you would notice it in most applications.

CMOS—Any time you see the acronym MOS (pronounced "moss"), you know you are reading about the "*M*etal-*O*xide-Semiconductor" technology used to make different kinds of memory chips. Though fast-moving, the computer industry is no rolling stone, for it has gathered a lot of MOSes over the years. There's PMOS and NMOS and DMOS and VMOS and more. CMOS ("sea-moss") is a lichenous plant found in great abundance among the rocks of the Irish coast. It is also "*C*omplementary MOS" technology, a technique for building memory chips that requires very little electric power to retain what has been stored in them. Developed for use in outer space, CMOS is now being applied to create truly portable battery-powered computers that retain what you have typed into them even when you shut them off. Examples include the Gavilan (about $4,000) and the Radio Shack Model 100 (about $800).

combo board—A plug-in circuit board whose main function is to let you add memory chips to your system. However, many "combination boards" also include a battery-powered clock/calendar circuit (to save you from setting the date and time each time you turn your computer on), a serial communications port, a parallel printer port, and a place to plug in a joystick. In addition to being cheaper than buying a separate board for each of these functions, combo boards only occupy one plug-in slot in your computer, preserving your other empty slots for other boards.

command-driven—When a program is command-driven, you as the user must remember what commands to type to get the software to perform a particular task. (Your computer's DOS is a good example.) Though more difficult to master than menu-driven (q.v.) programs, by eliminating the need to wait for and interact with on-screen menus, command-driven software offers the advantage of speed to experienced users.

communications board—The plug-in circuit board that enables your machine to communicate on the telephone. Also called a serial communications board.

connect time—The time you spend online with a database. Connect time, measured in fractions of a minute, is the usual basis of database billing.

coprocessor—A microprocessor CPU chip that is plugged into the computer's circuit board to assist the main CPU. When you run CP/M on an Apple, for example, the Z80 chip on the board you have plugged into your machine takes control and the 6502 chip that the Apple came with serves as a coprocessor to handle the keyboard, disk drives, and other chores. The IBM/PC is designed to accept an Intel 8087 chip to complement its main 8088. The 8087 is meant to help out the 8088 by handling heavy-duty math applications faster than the 8088 alone could manage.

cross-over cable—Cable designed to connect the serial ports of two computers. See "null modem cable."

cursor addressable CRT—A video display that allows you to use your arrow keys to move the cursor all over the screen. (See Chapter 4.)

CUSIP—Commission on Uniform Securities Identification Procedures. A stock's CUSIP symbol is the abbreviation used to refer to it on the stock exchange. Relevant for stock quote information retrieved from various databases by portfolio management and investment software packages.

database—Any collection of information, though usually *computerized* information. A database can be your address list, your personnel files, your inventory, or anything else. (See Chapter 16.) The term is also used to refer to the collections of information available over the telephone and to the organizations that provide it (The Source, Dow Jones News/Retrieval, CompuServe, NewsNet, etc.).

DDD—Direct Distance Dialing. The technique most personal computer owners use to access databases, computer bulletin boards, and other online services. The term is most significant in the data communications industry where DDD is but one form of computer access.

default—See Chapter 4.

DIF files—Data Interchange Format. A technique for storing information designed by Software Arts, Inc. (creators of VisiCalc). The goal is to make it possible for different programs from different software houses to share the same data files. (See Chapters 4 and 15.)

documentation—Computerese for "instruction manual." (See Chapter 4.)

download—To capture the information sent to your computer by another computer, as opposed to letting it disappear as it scrolls off the screen. (See Chapter 17.)

EPROM—Erasable Programmable ROM. This is a PROM (q.v.) chip that can be erased and reprogrammed an indefinite number of times. The chip has a little window in its casing and when high-intensity ultraviolet light is shown through it for 15 to 20 minutes, all of the bit patterns are erased. The chip can then be reprogrammed with a special machine. EPROMS are useful to software houses or other firms wishing to develop programming that will eventually be hard-wired into a ROM chip.

field—The computer equivalent of the blanks you fill in with your name, address, and other information when completing a sweepstakes entry, driver's license, or other form. (See Chapter 4.)

file—The computer equivalent of all of your cancelled checks for the month, the year, or some other period. Each check is a record. Each blank on the check is a field. The whole collection is the file. (See Chapter 4.)

flippy disk—This is a regular 5¼-inch floppy disk that has information recorded on both sides. To use it, you insert it in a single-sided disk drive and read the first side into your machine, then pull it out, flip it over, and repeat the process with the other side. This is possible for two reasons. First, the magnetic material is the same on both sides of a regular floppy disk. (Though if you buy a single-sided disk, usually only one side will have been tested for quality by the manufacturer.) Second, with most regular floppy disks there is a notch on the left side of the cardboard envelope that holds the disk itself. If the disk drive does not encounter this notch when you insert the disk, it will not accept it. Flippy disks have notches punched on *both* sides of the casing.

If you want to convert any standard floppy into a flippy, send for the Nibble Notch, a device that enables you to punch a second notch in a disk's casing at exactly the right spot. If you decide to do this, however, be extra careful to keep your disks clean and free of dust. There is a dust collecting fabric inside floppy disk casings that works quite well as long as the disk always spins the same way. When you use a flippy, however, you will be spinning the disk in both directions, depending on which side you are using. Here's the address for the Nibble Notch:

Nibble Notch
4211 N.W. 75th Terrace
Lauderhill, FL 33319

(Check or money order; $14.85 plus $1.50, postage and handling)

floating point arithmetic—See Chapter 4.

flow control—Controlling the on-screen scroll of text when you are online with a database by using the X-ON/X-OFF commands (q.v.) [<CONTROL><R>] and [<CONTROL><S>], respectively.

footprint—The amount of space on your desk or table occupied by any piece of computer equipment.

full duplex—See Chapter 17.

handshaking—The little ritual of signals exchanged between two computers or a computer and a printer or any other two pieces of equipment before communications can begin. Signals are sent back and forth so that each machine is prepared for the other's input or output.

hex or hexidecimal—This is the base 16 numbering system. In the decimal system there are 10 digits *(0* through *9)* to use in expressing a number. In "hex" there are those 10 digits plus six letters *(A, B, C, D, E, F)*. The main advantage of the hexidecimal system is that it is easier to read and deal with than the *1*'s and *0*'s of the binary system. It also lets you express the same number in less space. For example, the decimal number *14* can be expressed in binary as *1110* or in hex as *D*. Similarly, a number that would require sixteen *1*'s and *0*'s to express in binary form can be written in hex as "89AD."

high codes—ASCII code numbers above 127. High codes are nonstandard and are used to represent a wide variety of characters. See ASCII.

hires or hi-rez—It's confusing, considering the root beer, but "hires" and "hi-rez" are short for "high resolution." The abbreviation is pronounced "hi-rez," even if it isn't always spelled that way. (See Chapter 19.)

I/O—The first moon of Jupiter. Also known as "I." One of the first bodies in the solar system discovered with a telescope (Galileo, 1610). Followed by Europa (II), Ganymede (III), Callisto (IV), and a lot of other unnamed flotsam.

IEEE-448 interface—A standard created by the Institute of Electrical and Electronics Engineers to define the signals used for a parallel interface. One might say that this is the parallel equivalent of the RS-232-C (q.v.). Commodore VIC, 64, PET, and CBM computers use this interface instead of an RS-232 serial card. The firm sells adaptors to convert the IEEE-448 to an RS-232, but as long as you buy a Commodore modem, this will not be necessary.

ISAM—Indexed Sequential Access Method. Pronounced "eye-sam." (See Chapter 4.)

kilobyte—A unit of 1,000 bytes, or more precisely, a unit of 1,024 bytes. But no one worries about the 24 bytes. One kilobyte or "K" of memory can hold 1,000 characters, or about half a double-spaced, typewritten page. (See Chapter 1.)

letter-quality—Typewriter-like printing, in contrast to printing with a dot matrix printer. A letter-quality printer uses a printing element containing fully formed letters, whereas a dot matrix printer creates each letter as necessary by pushing forward the correct combination of wires in its printing element.

listing—A printout of a computer program. Many of the more technically oriented magazines publish listings of programs created by their readers and contributors. If you have the time and patience, you can type these into your machine, record them, and use them like a program that you might buy at a store.

macro—Short for "macro-expansion" or "macro-instruction." A technique a programmer can use to save work when writing a program. But can also be used in applications software. For example, whenever hitting a single key or issuing a single command causes the software automatically to issue a whole string of commands, you are using a macro-expansion feature. You might "load" today's date into a key with some word processing programs, for example, then hit a single key to insert the date at the beginning of a letter.

megabyte or "meg"—A unit of 1,000,000 bytes (actually, 1,000 kilobytes, or 1,024,000 bytes). Abbreviated Mb or Mg.

menu-driven—Refers to the technique of letting you choose options from an onscreen menu to accomplish what you want with a program, instead of having to remember and enter individual commands. A key element in the user friendliness of a program. (See Chapter 4.)

MIS—Management Information System. Usually, a corporate division responsible for supplying all levels of management with the information they need to make decisions. The information typically comes from the firm's computers and databases.

mnemonic—An abbreviation that is designed to be easy to remember, such as "LD" for "load," "ADI," for "add," or "STA" for "store." These are commands used by assembly language programmers and are much easier to remember than the *1*'s and *0*'s used in machine language programming. In applications software, a program that has you enter *P* for *print* or *Q* for *quit* is said to use mnemonic commands.

modem—An acronym for "*mo*dulator/*dem*odulator." This is the device that translates the signals coming from your computer into a form that can be transmitted over standard telephone lines. A modem also translates incoming signals into a form that your computer can understand. Two modems, one for each computer, are needed for any data communications over telephone lines.

MODEM7—A public domain CP/M communications program designed to send and receive computer programming over the telephone without errors. (See Chapter 12.)

mouse—A hand-held device attached to your computer with a cord.

Used to move the cursor around the screen and to enter menu or other choices by pressing a button once the cursor is on the target. (See Chapter 4.)

nibble—Half a byte, or four bits.

null modem cable—A cable designed to connect two computers via their serial ports that are ordinarily connected to a modem. A null modem cable "fools" each system into thinking that it is actually talking to a modem instead of another computer.

OEM—Original equipment manufacturer. This term can be confusing, but an OEM is a computer equipment *assembler*. For example, when Company A sells a disk drive or a monitor or some other component to Company B, and Company B uses it as part of a product that it will then sell to the public, Company B, the firm doing the assembling, is called an OEM. OEMs usually pay wholesale prices for the components they buy.

online—In computer communications, "online" means "connected to a remote database." But the term also means "when you are using a program." Thus an "online help function" is help that is available while you are actually using your spreadsheet or word processor or some other program. The help information exists on the program disk, which usually must be "online" (inserted in a disk drive) for you to take advantage of it.

originate/answer—The two modes of operation for a modem. In any communications arrangement, one modem must be set to "originate" and the other must be set to "answer." (See Chapter 17.)

overhead—The amount of memory occupied by a program of any sort. If you have 128K of memory in your machine, and the program you want to use occupies 32K when it loads in, 32K is its overhead. Overhead is significant because the more memory occupied by a program, the less "room" there is for you to use when working with the program. If a word processing program loads in all at once and has a high overhead, you will not be able to keep as many pages in memory at the same time as with a lower overhead program. That can slow things down when you want to move from one page to another one that is several pages away.

overlay—A piece of an applications program that is brought into the machine from disk on an "as needed" basis. (See Chapter 4.)

parity checking—Whenever data is sent from one spot to another, there is always the chance that electrical interference or some other problem will alter the bits along the way. Parity checking is one of the most widely used techniques for verifying that the data received are identical to what was sent. It is most frequently used when computers talk on the telephone, but it may also be used when data are moved about within a computer itself.

Parity comes in three flavors: odd, even, and none. And the sender and receiver must agree beforehand which type of parity they will use. Since each character consists of bits represented as *1*'s and *0*'s, it is possible for the sending computer to add up all the *1*'s used to represent a character before sending it. If even parity has been agreed upon, and the bits add up to an even number, the sender will add an extra *0* bit to the character before sending it. A *0* will not have any effect on the evenness of the total. But if the number of *1*'s adds up to an odd number, the sender will add an extra *1* bit to make the total even. Since the receiving machine is expecting each total in each character to be even, it will know that something has happened to one or more of the bits should it receive an odd character.

patch—A piece of programming added to your main applications program to give it additional features or to make it work with your printer or other hardware. (See Chapter 4.)

pixel—Short for "picture element." The smallest dot of light your video display is capable of displaying. (See Chapter 19.)

populate—To fill in. When you buy an add-on memory board, it will usually contain 64K of memory chips and a lot of empty sockets. When you buy more chips and plug them into the board, you are "populating" it. A fully populated board contains all of the memory chips it can hold.

power down—To turn off your computer.

power up—To turn on your computer.

PROM—A *Pro*gramable *ROM* chip. Programming can be placed in a PROM by using a special device to blow certain fuses within the chip itself, as opposed to designing the programming into the circuitry when the chip was made. A PROM chip can only be programmed once. An EPROM (q.v.) can be programmed and reprogrammed an indefinite number of times.

RCPM—Remote CP/M system. Accessible by telephone, such systems serve as repositories for a vast array of public domain CP/M software. Anyone with a CP/M system running MODEM7 (q.v.) software can dial up an RCPM system and download software at no charge. (See Chapter 12.)

record—One part of a file. If the file consists of all of your cancelled checks, each individual check is a record.

ring-back—Technique used by the operators of some computer bulletin board systems to avoid installing a separate telephone line for their computer. To use a BBS with a ring-back specification, dial the number, let it ring once, hang up, then redial with your computer ready to communicate. (See Appendix D.)

RS-232-C—A standard developed by The Electronics Industry Association (EIA) specifying what signals and voltages will be used to transmit data from a computer to a modem. The full standard covers some 25 pins on the RS-232-C plug interface found on a communications card, but most personal computers make use of only a handful of these. The *C* is often dropped when using this term. (See *The Complete Handbook of Personal Computer Communications* for more information.)

S-100 bus or system—A computer using a certain type of main circuit board. (See Chapter 4.)

serial interface or serial card—A circuit board installed in a computer or word processor designed to convert the machine's internal parallel (eight-bits-at-a-time) communications into serial communications (one-bit-at-a-time). The card includes an RS-232-C interface plug to accept the cable that connects your machine with your modem. Also called a communications or comm card. (See Chapter 17.)

spooling—A software-based technique to let you print out information while simultaneously using your computer for other things. (See Chapter 4.)

string—A word or sentence or any other continuous "string of characters." In a computer program, a string is information that the computer is supposed to treat as text and is thus usually set off from regular program instructions by single or double quotation marks. For example, if you were to boot a program and see the sentence, "Welcome to Tommy's Holiday Camp," you would know these words exist within the program as a character string, preceded by a programming instruction that tells the computer to "display the following text on the screen."

synchronous communication—Data communications technique in which bits are transmitted and received at a fixed rate. Used to transmit large blocks of data over special communications lines. Much more complex than asynchronous communication.

SYSOP—Pronounced "sis-op." The system operator. The individual who operates and maintains a computer bulletin board system. (See Chapter 12.)

system call—An instruction in a computer program that calls on the operating system to do something like put a character on the screen, or read or write a record to disk. In Chapter 2 we said that applications programs are written to "talk" to the operating system instead of talking directly to the hardware, thus eliminating the need for the program itself to include all of the instructions necessary to get characters displayed or printed. A system call within the program is the mechanism that makes this possible.

terminal mode—When communicating with a large computer, your machine must appear to the mainframe as merely one of its own terminals. Communications software creates this illusion, or "emulation." Any time you are communicating, you are in terminal mode.

terminal program—Communications software.

tutorial—A series of planned lessons in how to use a program. (See Chapter 4.)

UART—Acronym for "*U*niversal *A*synchronous *R*eceiver/*T*ransmitter." Pronounced "You-art." This is the microchip responsible for converting parallel signals into serial signals and vice versa. It is the heart of a serial interface card.

upload—To send information over the telephone lines to another computer directly from your floppy disk, cassette tape, or buffer, as opposed to typing at your keyboard.

user friendly—A superlative like "new" and "improved" that software and hardware producers routinely stamp on their product labels, ads, and brochures. (See Chapter 4.)

variable—The actual information that gets put into a field (q.v.). Examples include name, address, Social Security number, etc. Because this information can be different for each record (q.v.), it is called a "variable."

winchester—A hard disk system. So called because "Winchester" was the code word IBM used when it developed the first hard disk drive. (See Chapter 5.)

X-ON/X-OFF—These are start/stop signals issued by two communicating computers to make sure that each is ready to send or receive at the proper time. This protocol is usually built into the communications software, and in most cases you won't be aware that the signals are being sent and received. However, you can generate each signal yourself to stop or start an onscreen scroll when accessing most databases. X-ON is generated by entering a Control-Q, and X-OFF by entering a Control-S. (See Chapter 17.)

# Index

## About the Author

Alfred Glossbrenner is president of FireCrystal Communications, a worldwide producer of computer documentation, films, and corporate communications for industry and science. Based in Bucks County, Pennsylvania, FireCrystal and Mr. Glossbrenner make extensive use of personal computers, word processors, and a wide range of online electronic databases to pursue their goal of making today's high technology accessible, understandable, and above all, useful to everyone. *How to Buy Software* is Mr. Glossbrenner's ninth book.

## Also by Alfred Glossbrenner

At all bookstores. 325 pages, Appendices, Glossary, Index. $14.95 paperback.

A Main Selection of the Small Computer Book Club.

A Book-of-the-Month Club/Science Alternate Selection.

Here's what expert readers had to say after buying *The Complete Handbook of Personal Computer Communications:*

"An enjoyable book. Invaluable."
> —Bert I. Helfinstein,
> president and C.E.O.,
> Source Telecomputing Corporation (The Source)

"Alfred Glossbrenner is a master explainer. He really does deliver 'Everything You Need to Go Online with the World.'"
> —Ardell Taylor Fleeson,
> Graphnet, Inc.

"Informative and easy to understand."
> —Barbara Isgur,
> industry analyst,
> Paine Webber Mitchell Hutchins, Inc.

"Fills an enormous void. Personal computer users are really hungry for this kind of information."
—Thomas B. Cross,
director,
Cross Information Company

"Clear, well-written, packed with useful information—it's an absolute must for computer owners everywhere."
—Gary G. Reibsamen,
vice-president and general manager,
NewsNet, Inc.

"Not only is Glossbrenner's the best book to use with a personal computer, it may be the best reason to *buy* one."
—David Elias, Inc.,
newsletter to investors

"Unequivocally the most informative and best-written I have ever seen."
—Norman Burnell,
president,
Electronic Safety Products, Inc.

"An outstanding effort. I looked hard and couldn't find anything missing."
—Michael North,
Matrix Learning Systems

"Thanks for collecting a lot of good information in one place. We will be recommending your books to our customers."
—Larry Hughes,
Mycroft Labs

"The tips were worth the price of the book alone."
—Roger Harmon,
Microcomputer Assistance Center

"I'm thrilled about it. A very valuable book."
—Steven K. Moyer,
president,
Space Research Enterprises

"Your book gave several of us a quick education. It deserves to be a great success."
—Pat O'Neil,
chairman,
Exec Software

648 . . .

The author welcomes comments and suggestions about this book. They should be mailed to Alfred Glossbrenner, c/o St. Martin's Press, 175 Fifth Avenue, New York, NY 10010. Reader comments can also be sent to the author, via communicating computer, at the following electronic addresses:

Source: TCS772
CIS: 70065,745

For a forthcoming book answering questions about computerized tele-communications, the author is interested in hearing from readers with questions, problems, or tips—and regrets that he will not be able to respond individually to these.

To order additional individual copies of this book, please send your name, address and zip code with a check or money order to St. Martin's Press, Attention: Cash Sales, 175 Fifth Avenue, New York, NY 10010. Enclose $14.95 for each copy ordered, plus $1.50 postage and handling for the first book and 50¢ for each additional copy. New York State residents please add applicable sales tax.

Books are available in quantity for promotional or premium use. Write to Director of Special Sales, Marcella Smith, St. Martin's Press, 175 Fifth Avenue, New York, NY 10010 for information on discounts and terms, or call toll-free (800) 221-7945. In New York, call (212) 674-5151.